Behavior in Infancy and Early Childhood

infancy

A Book of Readings

behavior in

and early

childhood

Edited by

Y V O N N E   B R A C K B I L L

Professor of Psychology, University of Denver

GEORGE G. THOMPSON

Professor of Psychology, The Ohio State University

THE FREE PRESS, *New York*

COLLIER-MACMILLAN LIMITED, *London*

Collier-Macmillan Canada, Ltd., Toronto, Ontario

Library of Congress Catalog Card Number: 67–15056

Third printing February 1969

To Gail

Preface

In these days of very large classes in almost all of our colleges and universities it is unrealistic for instructors to assign specific readings in professional journals. Conscientious students become extremely frustrated by their inability to obtain the journals during their available study periods. The assigned papers become worn, torn, and eventually unusable through excessive handling. Books of readings that students can buy and study at their leisure appear to offer the only satisfactory solution to these problems at the present time. Such volumes provide a desirable step-between the summary surveys of integrated textbooks and the admittedly broader perspectives potentially available from a well-stocked library of professional journals and monographs.

The editors of the present collection of scholarly reports hope that this book may serve as a useful teaching aid. We believe that it can be used to advantage as a basic, or supporting, textbook in collegiate and university courses designed to survey the most reliable and interesting information on behavioral development during infancy and early childhood. We have attempted to stimulate student interest and to provide guidance for an integration of knowledge through our introductions which describe the broad social and psychological significance of each report. Even the quotations from philosophers and scientists of other centuries, which serve as convenient chapter dividers, were carefully selected to remind the reader of the deep roots of man's inquiry into the biological and social antecedents of human development and behavior. The more serious and ambitious students are encouraged to delve deeper into areas of special interest by the supplementary references presented at the end of each paper.

Our professional colleagues in psychology and pediatrics constitute another potential audience whose interest and approval we have deliberately sought in our selections and editorial contributions. This volume offers a generous sampling of the most influential writings on behavioral development during the early stages of acculturation. The papers especially translated for this book from German and Russian journals of psychology and neurophysiology may well present new information to professional colleagues who have never taken the time, or who may possess only rusty facilities, to read these important scientific reports in their original form. It also seems probable that some of our colleagues in psychology may have missed in their regular program of reading some of the interesting reports that have appeared in the pediatric and psychiatric journals. It seems equally likely, of course, that scholars in the biological and medical sciences will find some previously overlooked papers in the selections made from psychological journals. We share a conviction with many of our co-workers in the life sciences that a multidisciplinary approach to child development, with a maximum of communication across the disciplines, is mutually advantageous. According to our interpretation, this does not mean that we must work as one big, happy family in the same vineyard; but rather that everyone can profit from being familiar with the contributions that each discipline finds most impressive.

Although other editors would undoubtedly have selected a somewhat different collection of papers as a representative sampling of the "best" of present knowledge about the behavioral development of infants and young children, we sincerely believe that there would be a substantial nucleus of common reports in the majority of such collections. Some papers almost demand inclusion because they are classic "firsts," because they represent the apogee of a well-designed and sustained program of scientific study, because they describe what have proven to be fruitful conceptual and experimental methods of inquiry, or because they represent the zenith of prior contributions to some currently neglected area or investigation.

We would like to express our appreciation to the many people whose contributions made the publication of this volume possible. First and foremost, we are grateful to the authors and publishers who granted us permission to reproduce their scientific reports in a form that would serve the purposes of this source book. Without exception they seemed to share our view that books of readings are useful adjuncts to the process of communication, a convenient means for dispersing knowledge to a broader audience. This volume is dedicated to Gail Adams who served as a faithful and indispensable expediter-assistant in securing permissions, art copy, and the like. She truly served as our girl Friday in almost every phase of our editorial work. She was ably assisted by Dale Weese to whom we also express our appreciation. We were fortunate in having the following offer advice and criticism on the selection of papers to appear in the book: Darrell Adams, Charlotte Loring, Raymond Starr, Jr., and William Spears. To them, to Kenrick S. Thompson who helped with proofreading, and to Alexandra Hendee who assisted with the translations we express our appreciation.

Y. B.

G. G. T.

Contents

ii. motor development and physical growth

iii. sensory and perceptual development

iv.   conditioning and learning

v.   from vocalization to functional language

vi.   intellectual growth

vii.   socialization and the development of social behavior

viii. emotional responses and the developing personality

To the Students

When compared with the physical sciences, psychology in its scientific phase has a very brief history. It still has a decade to go before celebrating the centennial of its first experimental laboratory. Specialized psychological interest in developmental processes has an even shorter history, certainly not more than half a century of scientific inquiry to its credit when evaluated by current standards of acceptable research. The scholarly papers presented in this volume provide a good yardstick for assessing the substantial progress made by developmentally oriented psychologists during the twentieth century.

Why was psychological research with infants and young children neglected for so many years? Although there is obviously no simple answer to this question, some possibly relevant precursors can be cited. Scientific methods of empirical inquiry were not regarded as appropriate for describing and explaining behavioral change until late in the nineteenth century. Although philosophers like Plato, Aristotle, Locke, and Rousseau freely offered advice on the best ways to rear children, they looked for supporting arguments within their general philosophical systems and ignored potentially available empirical evidence. Even during the beginnings of scientific psychology the adult was favored as an experimental subject, and psychological problems related to infant care and child rearing were largely left for mothers and teachers to solve as best they could.

What forces tilted the balance in favor of research and theory related to a better understanding of developmental processes and behavioral change during early childhood? Whatever these forces may have been, it is convenient to associate them with the contributions of several outstanding personalities whose theories and research methodologies undergird most of the reports in this volume.

At the turn of the twentieth century, psychological research with human infants and young children was given a tremendous boost by the writings of Pavlov who found a way through his conditioning procedures to study the modification of behavior in nonverbal organisms. It soon became obvious that these procedures could be used to advantage in research with infants and very young children. Two of the translated papers in the present volume stemmed directly from Pavlov's influence; and conditioning procedures, both classical and instrumental, continue to be used widely and successfully in expanding our knowledge about the psychological development of the young child.

Pavlov's influence became pervasive in America through the writings of John B. Watson who chose a human infant as his experimental subject to illustrate the conditioning principles on which he believed a new philosophy of child rearing could, and *should,* be based. The conditioning model has been further extended and elaborated by such noteworthy American psychologists as Edward L. Thorndike, Clark L. Hull, Kenneth W. Spence, and B. F. Skinner. It would be difficult to overestimate the influence of the conditioning paradigm in stimulating psychological research with infants and young children. The reader will have no difficulty in verifying the fruitfulness of Pavlov's methodology as represented in many of the scientific papers of this volume.

Another equally strong influence on developmental psychology was provided by the truly revolutionary writings of Freud, who attributed the mental ills of adult man to psychologically adverse experiences during early childhood. His persuasive theory proposed that an understanding of rational man is impossible without a simultaneous knowledge of "the child who is father to the man." The tenets and extrapolations of Freud's psychoanalytic theory and methodology have so permeated Western culture that it is impossible to delineate their boundaries. It is clearly safe to conclude, however, that the majority of psychological studies related to young children's personality development and their socialization stem either directly or indirectly from Freud's contributions. The influence of the psychoanalytic model is patently visible in several of the reports included in the present book.

The psychological study of young children's intellectual development was given a significant forward thrust by Alfred Binet. The research of this seemingly tireless investigator opened up a previously unexplored dimension of cognitive functioning among young children. Psychometric assessment, before Binet's contribution was mainly physical and psycho-physical according to the practices made so popular by Francis Galton—the measurement of height, weight, grip strength, reaction time, and so on. Binet broke with this well-established tradition and proposed new ways of measuring young children's mental competencies, new ways that were distinctly *psychological* in design and scope and which, as it turned out, provided information significantly related to the child's future performance in school and in later adult life. Many psychologists helped to capitalize on this psychometric innovation, including such noteworthy investigators as Lewis M. Terman, John Anderson, Nancy Bayley, and others—some of whose contributions were selected for this book.

The most recent, and still contributing, psychologist whose research and theorizing promise to have profound impact on developmental psychology is Jean Piaget. In contrast to Binet who viewed intellectual development as largely a process of gradual acquisition and accretion, Piaget proposes the existence of developmental stages during which intellectual, or cognitive, processes are drastically reorganized. According to his views, the growing child is not only assimilating information from his environment, he is also continuously accommodating to this information by changes in his cognitive functioning. Several times during the ontogenetic span these continuous accommodations produce significant restructurings, quantal shifts that can be identified and used to predict the child's use of substantially different ways of adapting to and operating on his environmental surroundings. Piaget's perspective is mirrored in several papers in this volume; however, it appears that his influence may be dramatically more pervasive within the next decade, especially in bringing about pedagogical reforms.

The foregoing provides only a fleeting glimpse of some of the more salient precursors of current interest and the burgeoning research activity related to the behavior and development of the young child. It is presented to whet the reader's appetite for knowing more about the grand scope of child development, a relatively small part of which is represented by the papers in this book. As editors, we have tried to provide the means by which an interested reader can go further in his understanding of infant behavior and psychological development during early childhood. Carefully selected supplementary references are provided at the end of each paper for the reader wishing to pursue a specialized interest. In addition the following selection of books is offered as a convenient guide for the reader who may wish to increase his knowledge of any, or all, of the many fascinating dimensions of behavior during infancy and early childhood.

RECOMMENDED READING

Baldwin, A. L. *Behavior and development in childhood.* (New York: Dryden Press, 1955.)
"A textbook presenting a systematic neo-Gestalt position. Part I describes children's characteristic behavior and abilities; Part II is devoted to the developmental processes underlying change in the child."*

Barker, R. G., J. S. Kounin, and H. F. Wright (editors). *Child behavior and development: a course of representative studies.* (New York: McGraw-Hill, 1943.)
"An introductory chapter on the history and prospects of research in child psychology and thirty-four research reports condensed by their original authors span most of the areas of research in this field. Classics difficult to find elsewhere are included."

Brackbill, Yvonne (editor). *Research in infant behavior: a cross-indexed bibliography.* (Baltimore: Williams & Wilkins Co., 1964.)
A bibliography of 1733 titles on infancy and early childhood. Cross-indexed references on the following topics: sensation and perception, motor behavior, learning and conditioning, language, cognitive development, social behavoir, and personality development.

Carmichael, Leonard (editor). *Manual of child psychology.* (2nd ed.) (New York: Wiley, 1954.)
"Twenty chapters by twenty-two authors, dealing with topics peculiar to childhood, such as physical and mental development, acquisition of language, and adolescence, and with general topics bearing on child psychology, such as learning, cultural influences, mental abilities, and sex differences."

Erikson, E. H. *Childhood and society.* (New York: Norton, 1950.)
"A psychoanalytically oriented examination by a distinguished child analyst of the child's personality, and of the influences of social factors on its development. Extensive reference is made to the author's researches on American Indian children."

Flavell, J. H. *The developmental psychology of Jean Piaget.* (Princeton: Van Nostrand, 1963.)
"Summarizes the essential themes in all of Piaget's major writings, traces the chronological development of his theorizing about children's thinking and impartially evaluates Piaget's ideas, methodology, and contributions."

Kessen, William. *The child.* (New York: Wiley & Sons, 1965.)
An interpreted review and presentation of selected papers from such philosophers as Locke, Rousseau, and Darwin; also selected writings of such influential developmental psychologists as Binet, Gesell, Watson, Freud, and Piaget.

Martin, W. E., and Celia B. Stendler. *Child behavior and development.* (Rev. ed.) (New York: Harcourt, Brace, 1959.)
"A readable text focused on psychoanalytic and learning theory approaches to socialization. The revised edition retains a cross-cultural flavor while adding a chapter on effects of early experiences and a section on the course of normal development (physical, cognitive, and motivational)."

Mussen, P. H. (editor). *Handbook of research methods in child development.* (New York: Wiley, 1960.)

* The annotations in quotes are taken from *The Harvard List of Books in Psychology.* (Cambridge, Mass.: Harvard University Press, 1964. With permission of Publisher.)

"Methodology of developmental study and the use of observational and experimental methods in studying biological growth, cognitive processes, personality, social behavior, and environment. Research findings are often cited in illustrating methods. Authors differ in their success at separating method from problem."

Mussen, P. H., J. J. Conger, and Jerome Kagan. *Child development and personality.* (2nd ed.) (New York: Harper & Row, 1963.)
"This behavior-theory oriented, chronologically organized text discusses psychological processes during five basic periods: first year, second year, preschool years, early school years, and adolescence. Topics emphasized are motives, conflicts, intellectual development, and their interrelations."

National Society for the Study of Education. Committee on Child Psychology. *Child psychology: the sixty-second yearbook of the Society, Part I.* Edited by H. W. Stevenson, with the assistance of Jerome Kagan and Charles Spiker. (Chicago: National Society for the Study of Education, 1963 [distributed by the University of Chicago Press]).
"Syntheses of findings of recent research in selected areas of child psychology. Eleven active and representative areas are covered by fourteen authors, with excellent up-to-date bibliographies. A final chapter is concerned with developmental theory in transition."

Peiper, A. *Cerebral function in infancy and childhood* (translated by B. and H. Nagler). (New York: Consultants Bureau, 1963.)
A comprehensive review of the literature on the infant's physiological and psychological responses. Good coverage of the infant's neurological organization and sensory functioning.

Piaget, Jean. *The origins of intelligence in children.* (New York: International Universities Press, 1952.)
"Describes sequences in growth of intelligence: use of reflexes, first-acquired adaptations and primary circular reactions, secondary circular reactions, and invention of new means through mental combinations. Implications for theories of intelligence are discussed. Translated from the French."

Sears, R. R., Eleanor E. Maccoby, and Harry Levin. *Patterns of child rearing.* (Evanston, Ill.: Row, Peterson, 1957.)
"A description of the practices of 379 New England families in rearing their preschool children. Discussion of the outcomes of some of these practices; for example, parental training methods are analyzed in relation to the amount of dependency, aggression, and 'conscience' displayed by the child."

The psychoanalytic study of the child. (New York: International Universities Press, 1945–65, Vols. I–XX.)
"A yearbook of original papers on problems of developmental theory and clinical technique. Written chiefly by clinical psychoanalysts."

Thompson, G. G. *Child psychology.* (2nd ed.) (Boston: Houghton Mifflin, 1962 [1952]).
"Thorough coverage of the research and theoretical literature. Major sections describe theories and research methods, maturation and learning, the development of major psychological functions (e.g., emotional growth, language acquisition, social attitudes, personal values), and emotional antecedents of child behavior."

i

Psychophysiological Dimensions of Early Development

ales and females would be formed, so far as possible, in the following manner. Females, inclining more to water, grow from foods, drinks and pursuits that are cold, moist and gentle. Males, inclining to fire, grow from foods and regimen that are dry and warm. So if a man would beget a girl, he must use a regimen inclining to water. If he wants a boy, he must live according to a regimen inclining to fire. And not only the man must do this, but also the woman.

HIPPOCRATES, *Regimen.* 5th Century B.C.

studies on the
psychophysiology
of infancy*

EARLE L. LIPTON and ALFRED STEINSCHNEIDER

[Even very superficial observations lead one to believe that there are marked individual differences among newborn infants in visceral and somatic behavior. Different infants appear to be highly sensitive to some types of stimulation and not to others. Some infants are highly labile in visceral responsiveness (e.g., tachycardia and rapid, shallow breathing), but may be slow to return to a basal level. Other infants are slower to respond with autonomic activity but return to a basal state much more quickly. Only in recent years has electronic instrumentation been available to study these types of responsiveness with precision. In the present paper, Dr. Lipton and Dr. Steinschneider, of the State University of New York, summarize their solutions to some of the technical problems involved in such investigations. They also present longitudinal data on infants during the first five months of life which promise much for increasing our understanding of psychophysiological processes during infancy. Although they find stable individual differences among infants during the first weeks of life, it appears that these differences do not become intra-individually stable until about two months of age. It is the hope of these investigators that their techniques for studying psychophysiological processes during infancy may encourage further longitudinal studies in which ontogenetic sequences can be identified. Because of their medical orientation they are especially interested in possible demonstrations of organic predisposition to psychosomatic disease.]

Understanding the labile and seemingly disordered behavior of the infant's autonomic nervous system has been one of our major tasks for many years. This prolonged and concentrated study has resulted in an experimental model which we feel may lead to a better understanding of early infant behavior and its relationship to personality and disease in later life. The

* From E. L. Lipton & A. Steinschneider. Studies on the psychophysiology of infancy. *Merrill-Palmer Quarterly*, 1964, 10, 102–117. (With permission.)

following discussion relates primarily to the methodologic approaches in three problem areas: individuality of neurophysiologic behavior in early life, stability and maturational trends, and autonomic end organ and skeletomuscular responsivity to various exteroceptive stimuli.

How, one might ask, did a group of research-oriented pediatricians come to investigate problems which have, almost exclusively in past years occupied the attention of psychologists and child development specialists? The answer rests in the curiosity which accrued from years of attending to clinical medical problems for which there were no simple or direct answers. Whenever a so-called psychosomatic problem was investigated whether it was a case of peptic ulcer, eneuresis or rumination, there always remained the question of constitutional predisposition within the affected organ system (Mohr, Richmond, Garner, & Eddy, 1955). Psychologic factors alone did not seem adequate to explain the course of events, since many individuals with comparable problems and personalities either did not manifest psychosomatic disease or demonstrated pathology involving other organ systems. It was the search for possible predisposing factors that initiated our studies of the autonomic nervous system in early life (Lipton, Richmond, & Lustman, 1955; Richmond & Lipton, 1959).

The first task was to demonstrate that infants shortly after birth manifested individual traits with respect to autonomic end organ function (Lipton, Steinschneider, & Richmond, 1961b, 1961c). If this were also demonstrated in premature infants and even in fetuses, one would accept the likelihood that such characteristics are congenital and possibly hereditary. Some of the evidence concerning individual differences in early life will be described later in this paper.

We next investigated whether such subject-specific visceral control mechanisms continued to characterize the individual infant as he matured, and/or whether there were developmental trends.

Once some of the techniques for data collection and analysis were established, it was possible to explore other pertinent questions. One that has preoccupied us has been the description of the neonate's capacity to sense stimuli in the world about him. Our initial explorations confirmed previous studies which demonstrated that he does not react in an "all or none" fashion to all forms of stimulation (Richmond & Lipton, 1959). It has been even more fascinating to discover the relatively sophisticated nature of the infants' sensory-response systems: an example is the study of sound discrimination which will be described briefly herein (Lipton, Steinschneider, & Richmond, 1963). The possible applications of these techniques in problem areas such as conditioning and adaptation will hopefully become evident to the reader.

TECHNIQUES: PAST AND PRESENT

Pratt's (1954) comprehensive chapter on the neonate describes the attempts, which date back many decades, to study visceral and somatic responsivity in early life. Much fascinating and productive work resulted from those attempts to record objectively cardiac, respiratory, and muscular responses to varied stimuli. Pulse waves from the anterior fontanel sometimes provided the only means for recording cardiac rate. Tambours and smoked drums captured much of this information. The most objective and accurate measures of responsivity involved motor reaction times derived from various stabilimeters (Pratt, 1954). Movement, an inescapable "enemy" of the neonatal investigator, often precluded studies of visceral activity during varied behavioral states.

Later, in the thirties, electronic devices offered some relief but, as with adult studies, the extraction of data even from electrocardiographic (ECG) tracings was so time consuming that simple averaging techniques were generally used. This allowed a limited vantage point for interpreting complex changes. However, a few of these studies included laborious measurements of cardiac cycle lengths to allow descriptions of responses in greater detail (Sontag & Wallace, 1936).

When we first began these studies our major tool was the ECG. However, it was soon apparent that other devices would facilitate an understanding of the data. The cardiotachometer became available (Lacey, Bateman, & Van Lehn, 1953) and has been responsible for the elaboration of cardiac responses in detail. Such a device electronically transforms cardiac cycle durations ("interbeat" intervals) into cardiac rate, allowing for a readily interpretable visual display of the successive changes in rate (Fig. 1). One can easily understand the problems inherent in trying to analyze just the accompanying ECG tracing.

Upon our becoming proficient at obtaining artifact-free tracings of moving neonates, it was then possible to study cardiac rate control under even the most adverse conditions. Furthermore, extremely subtle changes which would have remained hidden within the maze of the ECG tracings could readily be detected. The detailed aspects of this technique are described elsewhere (Lipton *et al.*, 1961b).

Respiration has been recorded in these studies (Lipton, Steinschneider, & Richmond, 1960a) by means of a tiny thermistor bead placed beneath the nares (Fig. 2). The thin wire leads are taped to the skin and lead to a' circuit including a battery which, in turn, supplies the changing signal recorded via an A.C. coupled electroencephalographic preamplifier, amplifier, and oscillographic recorder. Modifications of the nose lead have been detailed elsewhere (Lipton, Walsh, Mueller, & Salamy, 1964).

A more recent development by our Bioelectronic Laboratory is a device we have facetiously labeled the "peak-picker." This instrument detects the precise moment at which inspiration and/or expiration begin, and allows a recording of respiratory cycles in a fashion analogous to the recording of heart rate by the cardiotachometer. Unlike previous devices, it precisely measures each and every cycle and should markedly facilitate our current laborious data reduction of respiratory responses.

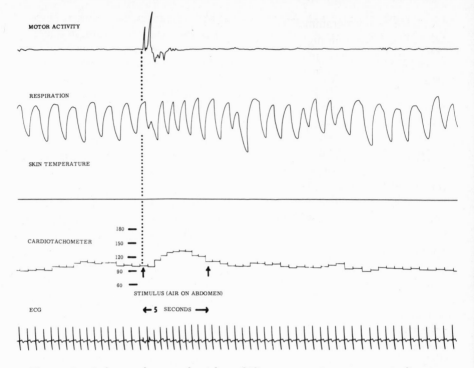

Figure 1—Polygraph record with stabilimeter tracing on top, indicating rapid startle response.

During stimulation, the respiration rate increased and amplitude decreased. The heart rate, shown rising in the cardiotachometer record within less than one second, achieved a peak of 135 beats per minute, returning then to pre-stimulus levels. Changes were not so readily discernible in the EEG tracing at the bottom.

CURRENT ANALYTIC METHODS

A detailed description of the techniques underlying our analyses would be far beyond the scope of this paper. It has, in fact, been the major content of a series of recent papers (Lipton *et al.,* 1961b, 1961c; Richmond *et al.,* 1962a; Steinschneider, Lipton, & Richmond, in press) to which the reader is referred. Nevertheless, a brief description is necessary for an understanding of what is to follow.

The cardiac rate of an infant or child generally increases within a second or more after the onset of a supra-threshold external stimulus. Typically the rate accelerates and then gradually peaks to form an ogive. The peak is usually followed by a response curve of a similar nature, but in the opposite direction, which attains a reasonably stable rate termed the return level. The various parameters are shown in Figure 3.

Occasionally responses are flat (relatively unchanging rate), in a downward direction, or sometimes are erratic and not analyzable. (These parameters have been programmed for a 7070 IBM computer, so that the measures can be extracted from digital information recorded on magnetic tape during the experiment. These machine definitions of the parameters were used in the extraction of data in the "white noise" study described later.)

The flat or downward responses (decreases in heart rate) are usually associated with high heart rates prior to stimulation. In fact, the magnitude measures of these responses (primary slope, peak, secondary slope, and return magnitudes) are all negatively correlated with their respective prestimulus rates. Thus the largest changes in rate are associated with low cardiac rate levels before stimulation (Lipton *et al.*, 1960a, 1961b, 1961c; Richmond & Lipton, 1959). As a consequence, we have utilized a regression model which takes into account all the response measures of a given parameter. It allows estimates of average responses obtained at various points on the best fit line. The lowest prestimulus rate is associated with the average *maximal* response, while the mean prestimulus heart rate predicts the most stable point on the line—the *mean* responses. These statistical estimates, among others, can be used to compare conditions either within a subject or between infant subjects.

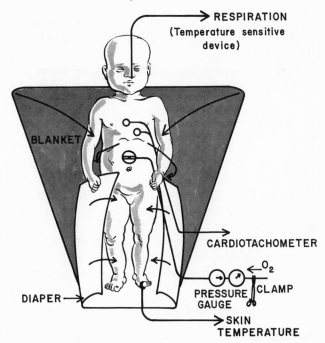

Figure 2—The drawing shows an infant subject with electrodes attached, and a plastic cone attached above the umbilicus for delivery of an airstream stimulus.

The diaper holds the legs in extension. The light receiving blanket restricts movements of the other body parts as desired.

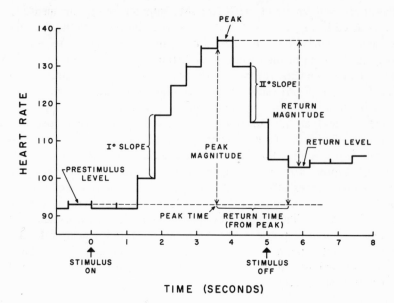

Figure 3—Simulated cardiotachometer record, illustrating the "physiological" parameters employed in the studies described by the authors.

Fortunately, not all the analyses are so complicated. Each of the parameters can be measured with respect to its timing and, since these values are largely unrelated to the prestimulus level of activity, means and variances, can be directly obtained for comparisons. As with much biological data, however, both prestimulus heart rate and these time measures assume a log normal distribution and must be so transformed before analysis.

The primary slope parameter represents simply the greatest change between two adjacent cardiac cycles. With few exceptions it is readily identifiable on the polygraphic record. Despite its seeming simplicity and its representation of but a microscopic piece of the cardiac response, it potentially affords important information.

Excluding the slope parameters, the remaining magnitude and time measures are extracted from the respiratory tracings. They are analyzed in a similar fashion (Lipton, Steinschneider, & Richmond, MS).

EXPERIMENTAL VARIABLES

Many elements must be considered in designing and later interpreting any studies involving nervous system activity. When stimulating the infant it is important to eliminate, insofar as possible, concurrent external stimulation or stimulation resulting from physiologic change within the organism. Some dramatic cardiac changes often occur during such activities as hiccoughs, yawning, and defecation (Lipton *et al.,* 1964). Our laboratories are made relatively sound proof, with temperature and humidity controlled and with constant illumination to minimize external stimulation. Most experiments are conducted with the infant isolated in the laboratory, and observed through a window.

Included in a previous discussion of this problem (Richmond *et al.,* 1962b) were such other variables as habituation to the stimulus, changes in state of consciousness, and interactions between musculo-skeletal and autonomic end organ activity. These can, to some extent, be controlled in the analysis and experimental design. The latter interaction was the target of several studies which utilized swaddling to restrict motor activity.

SWADDLING

In two separate studies we confirmed the impressions of experienced nursery nurses that tight "bundling" of newborns decreases motor activity and crying, and promotes sleep (Lipton *et al.,* 1960a; MS). When the subjects were completely or partially (arms-free) swaddled, there were fewer stimulus trials during which a motor response was detected to the 5-second abdominal air stream stimulus.

In the later analysis of autonomic responsivity in these 18 neonates, only the motor change trials were included (Lipton *et al.,* MS). This provided an independent estimate that the infant had sensed and responded to the stimulus. These studies demonstrated that the cardiac and respiratory responses, both with respect to magnitude and timing, were generally comparable under all conditions of motor restraint. Since the *degree* of motor activity was attenuated by the restraints, this indicated that autonomic responses are not wholly dependent upon motor activity. These relationships will be explored further in future studies.

The restraint technique enhanced the collection of data. The infant subjects were more "cooperative"; thus it was possible to maintain them at lower heart rate levels and obtain a larger number of maximal responses to stimulation. As a result of this experience, the subjects in our subsequent studies have always been at least partially, if not completely, swaddled.

These data are discussed elsewhere in detail within the framework of swaddling as an infant care practice (Lipton *et al.,* MS). Also included in that monograph are some neurophysiologic interpretations of these findings and a review of the history of swaddling in various cultures.

INDIVIDUAL DIFFERENCES IN NEONATES

In attempting to demonstrate consistent differences in autonomic function between subjects, 16 neonates were studied between the second and fifth days of life. The stimulus in these early experiments was a stream of air on the abdomen of 5 seconds duration administered under standard pressure (Fig. 2). The resultant cardiac responses were studied by means of the techniques previously alluded to, and the results confirmed the

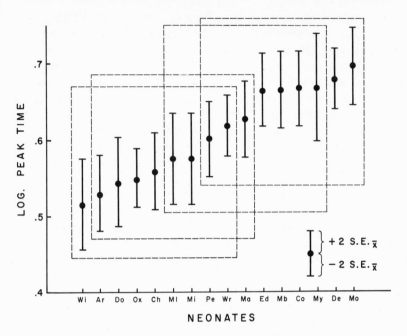

Figure 4—Means and the respective standard errors for log peak time for individual subjects.

Each box encloses a group of infants whose means *cannot* be differentiated (e.g., *Wi* is significantly different from *Ma* and all other infants with greater mean log peak time).

hypothesis that even neonates manifest individualistic patterns of autonomic behavior (Lipton *et al.,* 1961c). Figures 4 and 5 present two examples of the results: peak magnitude and time. It is clear that certain infants (e.g., *Ox*) may be exceedingly labile in their responses, yet they may manifest rapid reactivity. Others (e.g., *Wi*) may show relatively small, yet rapid, responses. The correlation in the 16 infants between these two parameters was close to zero, indicating that time and magnitude probably provide different information. Furthermore, the various other magnitude and time parameters also were, in large measure, independent.

The capacity of these infants to return to prestimulus levels was also explored and significant differences were found (Richmond *et al.,* 1962a). This was also the case with respect to variability of response (Stein-schneider *et al.,* in press). These latter measures have particular pertinence to the question of the homeostatic capacity of an individual's visceral response system. They relate to a subject's capacity to maintain a reasonably steady state despite stimulation and whether he registers a stereotyped or a varied response to presumably identical stimulations. It seems clear from these studies that Lacey's concepts of "labile" and "stabile" adult reactors apply equally well to younger subjects (Lacey & Lacey, 1958).

DEVELOPMENTAL TRENDS

Fifteen infants who were studied as neonates returned to the laboratory at approximately two and five months of age. The same experimental techniques were used at all ages. The infants when older were sometimes uncooperative during the procedure, and swaddling was unsuccessful in pacifying most of them.

Two findings appear to be of primary importance. First, whether asleep or awake, the cardiac rate response curves, in most older infants, are modified as compared to the newborn responses. Characteristically the peak occurs more rapidly and is attenuated in magnitude at two and five months. Furthermore, the return phase begins very early in the response and the heart rate not infrequently drops below prestimulus levels even during the 5 seconds of stimulation (Lipton *et al.*, 1960b; MS). These responses at two and five months are often less variable than the neonate measures. Between the second and fifth months there were no consistent trends toward further modification of the response curve.

A classical example of this phenomenon is found in Fig. 6. The data were obtained during the first four months of life in a premature infant weighing 2½ pounds at birth. These are the maximum response curves, reconstructed from estimates derived at the respective lowest prestimulus cardiac rates. On the left, one can see the *increase* in the heart rate *level* several weeks after birth and the subsequent decrease in later months. These changes in level are also found as term infants mature. On the right, the same response curves are presented as starting from a comparable baseline of zero. This more clearly demonstrates the changing response curve with age. This premature infant showed the more typical "mature" response pattern at four months, whereas term infants often manifest this change within the first two months of life. Some premature and term infants show no such trend.

Second, in the study of 15 full-term infants, correlations were generally non-significant between measures in the newborn and the later

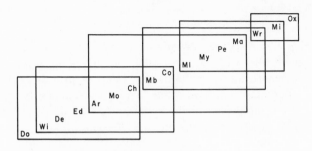

PEAK MAGNITUDE

Figure 5—Rank order of infant subjects in terms of peak magnitude.

The boxes have the same meaning as in Fig. 4.

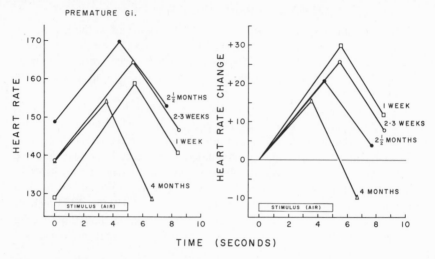

Figure 6—Reconstructed maximal cardiac responses of a small pre-mature infant to an abdominal air-stream during early months of life.

months. However, significant correlations were demonstrated between the two- and five-month values. Thus evidence was provided to indicate that the responses of individuals maintain their relative ranking within a group of infants *after* the newborn period.

The first finding is significant in that it demonstrates that basic changes in autonomic control mechanisms do occur in humans during the early months of life. Such evidence is consistent with other studies of man and animals. The demonstration of some stability after two months suggests that many of these findings are stable, and that they may have predictive value for later behavior both in and out of the laboratory. This is not to deny, however, that even the early newborn findings may allow predictions and prove to be of heuristic value.

SENSORY CAPACITY

Describing the responses of infants at one or more age periods to essentially the same stimulus represents a step toward understanding individual characteristics. Of potentially greater importance is the description of the differential sensitivities and response capacities of infants to a wide variety of stimuli. One might hypothesize that infants, for example, vary in their sensitivities to *different stimuli*—some being relatively more responsive to sound as compared to tactile stimulation, and vice versa. Furthermore, it is likely that the capacity to discriminate between *qualities within a given sensory modality,* such as intensities of sound, is a congenital characteristic. Bergman and Escalona (1949) provided clinical descriptions of behaviorally disturbed children who appeared to be hypersensitive to certain stimuli—such as sound—and hypothesized distorted perceptivity as a precursor or concomitant feature of childhood psychoses.

An exploratory study involved 10 neonates exposed to repetitive sound (85-decibel buzzer), tactile (abdominal air stream), and light (flashing 1/second 100-watt bulb at 2 feet) stimulation. Each stimulus was of 5 seconds duration (Lipton *et al.,* 1961a).

The intensities of these stimuli were chosen arbitrarily, except for some previous observations which suggested that they were all well above threshold. Each of the stimuli resulted in cardiac response curves having the same general characteristics.

We were somewhat surprised to find that the 10 infants manifested essentially no differences in the magnitude and timing aspects of the cardiac response curves when stimulated with either the sound or the air stream. In contrast, the response to the light was attenuated in all but one of the eight infants so tested. (Two subjects were identical twins and stimulated only with sound and the air stream.) The motor responses to the light often consisted only of eye blinks—although one very light, red-haired infant could not be included in the study because he startled and became hyperirritable with almost every exposure to the light!

Of considerable interest was the finding that the latencies of the motor responses, as recorded by a strain-gauge stabilimeter, demonstrated significant differences between the sound and air-stream responses in 6 of the 10 infants. Two reacted significantly faster, on the average, to the air-stream stimulus and the other four to the 85-decibel sound. Again, as in all our experiments thus far, there were consistent differences between infants with respect to both cardiac and motor responsivity.

It is apparent, then, that human infant behavior cannot be *arbitrarily* assessed with any measuring device that happens to be available. The choice of the instrument is often fortuitous and the resultant measures cannot be considered as representative of the overall reactivity. There are complex interrelationships between autonomic end organs, as well as between these and skeletal-motor and biochemical systems. It is essential ultimately to tap into many systems simultaneously, but this might best be accomplished only after probing at some depth into each, so as to avoid accepting arbitrary and superficial relationships.

One of our more recent studies was designed to measure the capacity of neonates to discriminate between graduated intensities of "white noise." Would certain infants manifest "better" discrimination than others and could thresholds be established by this technique? We were interested in determining whether infants who were relatively more responsive to the high-intensity sound (100 decibels) would likewise respond more when exposed to the lower intensities (85, 70, and 55 decibels). These four sounds of 5 seconds duration were presented in random fashion, along with non-stimulated control periods, during three separate sessions. This totalled 180 stimulus trials for each of nine subjects.

The results are most stimulating but, unfortunately, too complex for detailed presentation here (Lipton *et al.,* 1963). Essentially, it was found that the percentages of startle and "motor change" responses tended to differentiate the stimulus levels in all subjects. Motor latency decreased with increasing stimulation even when startle trials were eliminated from the analysis.

Autonomic "reaction time" (primary slope time) also decreased progressively with increasing stimulus intensity. Conversely, the durations of the primary (peak) and secondary (return) phases of the response increased with intensity.

Analysis of the magnitude responses predicted from the *mean* prestimulus heart rate in most infants revealed that there was a progressive increase in all of the parameters (primary slope, peak, and return magnitudes) as the stimulus intensity increased. We were intrigued to find that the use of the *maximal* response capacity (response predicted at the subjects' lowest prestimulus heart rate) resulted in fewer such trends. There was less tendency for differences to be found even between higher intensity levels. Thus, at mean heart rate levels when the infant tends to be more active and aroused, discrimination was more discernible in the cardiac responses.

However, the maximal response estimates were extremely stable, as demonstrated by high correlation coefficients across intensity conditions. This again supports the hypothesis of individual differences in responsivity. Furthermore, the capacity to discriminate (as measured by autonomic and musculo-skeletal responses) between the four intensity levels appeared to vary between infants.

These data showed no evidence of adaptation during a given session when the measures were transformed to standard scores. We have, however, witnessed the waning of a cardiac response even to 100-decibel white noise when the stimulus was presented at lessened intervals. In this experiment, as in the others, the trials were never less than 40 seconds apart.

We are currently studying responses of infants during the first two months of life to smaller gradations of intensities. This is an attempt to describe the discrimination curves in more detail and to delineate possible trends or stability over time. Concomitantly, higher and lower frequencies are being presented as a first approximation to the problem of pitch discrimination.

Besides the theoretical importance of such studies we recognize, as pediatricians, the limited skills now available for evaluating hearing in early life. This experimental model appears to have clinical implications. Recently this was demonstrated in a case tested in the laboratory. It was predicted with reasonable confidence that this severely jaundiced newborn infant had profound, if not total, hearing loss, presumably due to brain damage from the bilirubin pigment. This was confirmed clinically and on testing some eight months later.

CONCLUDING REMARKS

The experiments outlined in this paper have focused largely upon individual infants and small groups. Nevertheless, the amount of data and information obtained has been at times overwhelming and, but for the use of large computers, would have precluded the analytic approach which has been described. The problems, in a sense, necessitate an understanding of *individual* subjects, for the characteristics of visceral and somatic behavior in the human species are extremely varied and interactive.

Initially it would seem propitious, then, to study human infants in some depth and over long periods of time. The experiments thus far attest to the individuality of response capacity in early life and to some degree of stability of these measures. Simultaneous investigations of psychological characteristics and life experiences would seem rewarding (Darrow & Heath, 1932). At this point in time, we can only evaluate the visceral responsivity of a group of children who have been subjects in a longitudinal study of personality over the past five years.

It is planned to study a new group of children who will be followed both physiologically and psychologically from early infancy. If there are specific physiologic responses attending certain emotional states as suggested in adult studies, the earlier counterparts of these might be discovered during childhood. It might also be possible to demonstrate an association between autonomic behavior and overt emotional characteristics such as impulsivity, hyperactivity, emotional lability, and so on.

A somewhat more remote possibility would be the demonstration of organ predisposition to psychosomatic disease, since this would probably require a larger population to obtain enough cases. A recent, apparently successful, study along these lines demonstrated that a certain number of children from a sizeable population developed hypertension as adults (Barnett, Hines, Schirger, & Gage, 1963). This disease was statistically related to their hyperreactivity to the cold pressor test during early adolescence.

The studies described in this paper indicate a detailed approach for "tapping" into the world of the infant. They seem to contain the ingredients for developing other techniques to allow even deeper future probing into the intricate behavior of the young child. Where else these studies may lead —in the arbitrary divisions of our knowledge termed physiological, medical, psychological, and the like—is a question which only the future can resolve.

SUPPLEMENTARY READINGS

Richmond, J. B., & Lipton, E. L. Some aspects of the neurophysiology of the newborn and their implication for child development. In L. Jessner & E. Pavenstedt (Eds.), *Dynamic Psychopathology in Childhood*. New York: Grune & Stratton, 1959.
Richmond, J. B., Lipton, E. L., & Steinschneider, A. Autonomic function in the

neonate: V. Individual homeostatic capacity in cardiac response. *Psychosom. Med.*, 1962, 24, 66–74.

Richmond, J. B., Lipton, E. L., & Steinschneider, A. Observations on differences in autonomic nervous system function between and within individuals during early infancy. *J. Amer. Acad. Child Psychiat.*, 1962, 1, 83.

Richter, D. Metabolism and maturation in the developing brain. In F. Linneweh (Ed.), *Die Physiologische Entwicklung des Kindes* (The physiological development of children). Berlin: Springer-Verlag, 1959.

cortical electrical responses
to visual stimulation
in the human infant*

Robert J. Ellingson

[One cannot help being impressed by the slowness with which the newborn infant responds to external stimulation. For example, in response to a loud noise the newborn may display the Moro reflex some three to four seconds after the stimulus is presented. This is in sharp contrast to the 300–400 millisecond latency for the startle pattern in older children in response to a similar acoustic stimulus. The electroencephalogram (EEG) provides a procedure whereby the scientist can measure the amount of time required for peripheral receptors to transmit neural information to the central nervous system. Dr. Ellingson, of the Nebraska Psychiatric Institute, has collected extensive data on the effects of various types of visual stimulation on electroencephalographic recordings for almost 700 infants. Longitudinal studies have been carried out on more than 100 of these infants who have been returned to the laboratory one or more times for repeated electroencephalographic examinations. Responses recorded from the occipital cortex demonstrate much longer latencies and greater "fatigability" in newborn infants than in older subjects. The longitudinal data show that with increasing age there is a systematic decrease in response latency and an increasing ability to respond to more and more rapidly repeated stimuli. The author of this report presents an interesting discussion of the relationship between physiological and anatomical evidence on developmental changes in neural functioning. He notes, for example, that myelination is a poor criterion of neuronal development, because data from infrahuman subjects show reasonably good functioning of completely unmyelinated neurons.]

Studies of cortical evoked responses in the primary sensory areas of infant animals (Ellingson & Wilcott, 1960; Grossman, 1955; Hunt & Goldring, 1951; Marty, Contamin, & Scherrer, 1958; Rose, Adrian, & Santibanez,

* From R. J. Ellingson. Cortical electrical responses to visual stimulation in the human infant. *EEG in clinical Neurophysiology,* 1960, 12, 663–677. (With permission.)

1957) have revealed that such responses differ from those in mature animals of the same species in several respects, and that they show developmental changes which are reasonably similar among the modalities studied (visual, auditory, and somesthetic) and between the species studied (cat and rabbit). Several investigators have also emphasized that, while the sequence of developmental changes is generally uniform, there are considerable individual differences in rate of development.

We have stimulated a number of human infants with flashes of light and clicks while recording cerebral electrical activity from a number of electrodes fixed to the scalp. Thus far we have been able to record only certain generalized brain electrical responses to auditory stimuli (to be described elsewhere), but never specific evoked responses from the temporal area. On the other hand we *have* been able to record specific evoked responses to visual stimuli from the occiput, as well as more generalized responses ("driving" and "blocking"). Preliminary results have been reported previously (Ellingson, 1957, 1958a, 1958b). This paper is a complete, detailed report of our data on visually elicited responses during the immediate postnatal period, and a preliminary report of longitudinal follow-up data.

METHOD

Visual stimulation was carried out on 693 subjects of whom 622 were full-term babies and 71 were prematures. Although a few of these babies have since died, all are believed to have been normal at the time of recording. Babies on whom there was evidence of abnormality at the time of recording or who have since displayed disorders which could be of a congenital or developmental nature have been excluded from the series reported here. Of course, since we have not been able to keep track of all the babies studied, we may have retained some in the series who should have been excluded by these criteria.

All but a few of the subjects were born in the University of Nebraska Hospital, and complete birth histories and more or less complete prenatal histories are available. The few exceptions were prematures delivered elsewhere and admitted to the hospital for care.

Before discharge from the hospital, one or more EEGs were recorded in a special laboratory in the Newborn Nursery. For full-term babies this was usually on the first postnatal day. In the case of prematures the first recording was made as soon as permitted by the attending pediatrician, and an attempt was made to repeat the recording at one-week intervals until discharge. Following discharge from the hospital, 107 babies have returned one or more times to a similarly equipped laboratory for repeat examinations. A total of 1142 recordings have been obtained, 944 from full-term babies and 198 from prematures.

Flashes of light were provided by a Grass PS-1 Photic Stimulator. The stroboscope unit was positioned about 10 inches in front of the baby's eyes with its axis corresponding as nearly as possible to the line of vision. There was some variation in angular position and distance from subject to subject depending upon the position in which the baby's head was lying. Various intensities of stimulation were employed both through the closed eyelids and with eyes open. Best results were obtained through closed lids (baby apparently asleep) with intensity setting "8" on the PS-1 Photic Stimulator, and most of the results to be reported were obtained under those conditions. In some instances the baby was awake during recording, and in some passed from sleep to wakefulness or vice versa. Single and, in most cases, repetitive flashes were presented. Low rates of repetitive flashes (1 f/sec to 4-5 f/sec) were almost always used; often rates up to 50 f/sec were also used.

Bipolar recording technique was used with 12 solder disk electrodes fixed to the scalp with Bentonite paste. These were positioned on the bilateral, frontal, precentral, parietal, occipital, and anterior- and posterior-temporal areas. In the early records of all the premature babies—and in a few full-term babies—an 8-electrode arrangement was used: bilateral frontal, central, occipital, and mid-temporal electrodes. During photic stimulation a midline occipital electrode, just superior to the inion (external occipital protuberance of the skull), was also used. In later recordings a vertex lead was added. In a number of cases responses from the inion or the right or left occipital leads were recorded by cathode-ray photography simultaneously with the ink-writer.

Evoked responses have also been recorded from 14 normal adults with the same equipment and under the same conditions to provide control data.

RESULTS

OCCIPITAL RESPONSES EVOKED BY SINGLE FLASHES IN THE FULL-TERM NEWBORN

Single flashes were presented to 622 infants on one or more occasions during the first 120 hours of life. Evoked potentials were recorded from one or more of the occipital electrodes paired with one electrode more anteriorly placed on the head in 350 *S*s (56%). Most often only the mid-occipital (inion) electrode yielded the evoked potentials, but in some cases the right and/or left occipital electrodes (placed 2-3 cm on either side of the midline) also yielded the response (Figs. 1 and 5). Rarely, one of the lateral occipital electrodes yielded responses while the midoccipital electrode did not. We have never been able to record responses from more anteriorly placed leads, although in every case tracings from anteriorly placed electrodes were recorded, as in Fig. 1.

While there is considerable *inter*subject variability in waveform, amplitude, and latency of responses, *intra*subject responses are highly consistent (see also Ellingson, 1958a, Fig. 8). In some subjects, however, amplitude variation is observed: in some no responses may be elicited at first, but as stimulation is continued responses may appear, and may even become prominent (Fig. 2); in others the opposite trend is observed, responses being seen in the beginning but diminishing in magnitude as the recording session continues and even disappearing altogether.

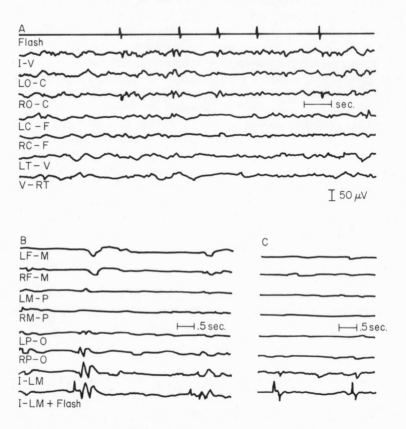

Figure 1—Evoked responses elicited by single flashes.

All full-term babies. Labeling of tracings in this figure is according to the following code: I = left, R = right, F = frontal, M = motor (precentral), C = central (rolandic), P = parietal, O = occipital, T = mid-temporal, I = inion, V = vertex. A. 16 hours postpartum, asleep. Paper speed = 3 cm/sec. Responses are seen recorded from the I, LO, and RO electrodes. B. 63 hours postpartum, awake. Paper speed = 6 cm/sec. Stimulus artifact superimposed on the bottom channel, marked I-LM + Flash. Latencies were measured on this type of recording. Responses are seen recorded from the I and RO electrodes. C. 60 hours postpartum, awake. Same type of recording as in B. Responses are seen recorded from the I electrode only. Note differences in wave-form among the responses of the 3 subjects, and also failure to record responses from non-occipital electrodes.

The vast majority of responses shows an initial, brief, positive phase (Fig. 3). Some subjects show only this positive wave, but in many it is followed by a negative wave of longer duration which may in turn in some cases be followed by a second positive phase. Five subjects (1.4%) yielded double positive responses, and 7 others (2.3%) yielded only responses which were initially negative.

The amplitude of responses varies from a few microvolts to at least $50\mu v$ for the initial positive phase and as high as 100 μv for the negative wave.

Quite accurate latency measurements can be made from tracings like those shown in Figs. 1B and 1C. The mean of 10 measurements of latency from the peak of the stimulus artifact to the peak of the positive wave was taken as the measure of response latency. Latencies measured from ink-writer tracings correlated highly with latencies of the same responses recorded by cathode-ray photography ($r = 0.99$, $P < 0.001$, N = 20). Test-retest reliability for two sets of responses during the same recording session was also highly significant ($r = 0.73$, $P < 0.01$, N = 14), but distinctly lower than the correlation of 0.95 obtained for recordings within the same session, probably due in large part to variability in time lapse between test and retest for the various subjects.

For full-term newborns 0–30 hours old the mean latency is 189 msec. or about twice that for the adult. For full-term infants 90–120 hours old

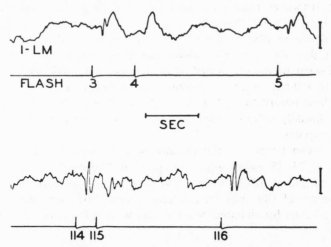

Figure 2—Long-term fluctuation of response amplitude, and "fatigability."

Both strips are from the same recording session. After 20 min. of stimulation responses to flashes 114 and 116 are of higher voltage than responses to flashes 3 and 5 at the beginning of the session. At both times responses to flashes coming less than 1 sec after a previous flash (flashes 4 and 115) are suppressed; this phenomenon has been called "fatigability." Vertical calibration lines indicate 50 μv.

the mean latency has decreased to 178 msec. The range of individual latencies is considerable. Although it is somewhat leptokurtic, the distribution approximates well to a normal distribution by the χ^2 test of goodness of fit ($\chi^2 = 7.075$; $P > 0.10$).

OCCIPITAL RESPONSES EVOKED BY SINGLE FLASHES IN THE PREMATURE NEWBORN

Single flashes were presented to 71 prematures on one or more occasions before discharge from the hospital. Prematures are defined as infants weighing less than 5 lb, 8 oz (2500 gm) at birth, regardless of estimated duration of gestation. Recording was often done on the first postnatal day, but some were not tested until as long as 2–3 weeks had elapsed.

The responses of prematures differ from those of full-term newborns in only two notable respects: (a) more prematures exhibit responses which are initially negative, and (b) the latencies of the responses of prematures are on the average greater than those of full-term babies.

Six prematures (11.1%) exhibited initially negative evoked responses on either the first, or first and second, testing. Only 7 full-term babies (2.0%) did so. The difference is statistically significant (X^2 corrected for continuity $= 9.654$; $P < .01$). Babies exhibiting such initially negative responses, yielded the more typical initially positive responses at later testings (Fig. 3). In no case did a baby, premature or full-term, yield initially negative responses after once exhibiting initially positive responses. The earliest baby to exhibit initially negative responses was a 2 lb, 12 oz premature delivered after a 28-week gestation period* and tested on the first postnatal day. The earliest to exhibit initially positive responses was a 4 lb, 6 oz, 32-week premature, tested on the first postnatal day. The oldest baby to exhibit initially negative responses was a full-term at 110 hours after birth. These observations, together with data from animal studies, suggest that the initially negative response is a primitive form of primary cortical evoked response.

The mean latency of the initially positive evoked responses of prematures at 34–35 weeks after conception is 219 msec, at 36–37 weeks, 209 msec, and at 38–39 weeks, 200 msec. Compare these values with a mean latency of 189 msec for full-term babies 1–30 hours after birth, and one of 183 msec for all babies tested 40–41 weeks after conception (Fig. 4).

DEVELOPMENTAL CHANGES IN RESPONSES EVOKED BY SINGLE FLASHES

Our material provides longitudinal data on a number of subjects, prematures and full-term, seen on several occasions over periods up to 6

---

* The durations of gestation given are those cited on the mothers' hospital charts by the Department of Obstetrics and Gynecology as the best estimates on the basis of evidence available at the time of birth, and based on a term of 40 weeks.

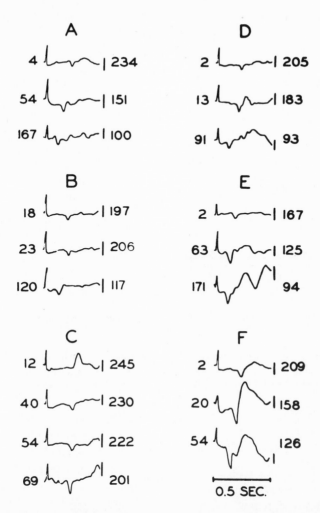

Figure 3—Typical evoked responses of 3 premature (A-C) and 3 full-term (D-F) subjects recorded at different times during the first 6 months of life, showing developmental changes.

The number at the left of each tracing is the age of the subject in days at the time of recording; the number at the right is the latency of the response shown in msec. All latencies are to the peak of the positive wave, except for the first (initially negative) response of subject C, which was measured to the beginning of the negative wave. A. 5 lb, 5 oz at birth; estimated gestation 39 weeks. B. 3 lb, 5 oz at birth; estimated gestation 34 weeks. C. 2 lb, 6 oz at birth; estimated gestation 28 weeks. D. 6 lb, 6 oz at birth. E. 7 lb, 0 oz at birth. F. 8 lb, 4 oz at birth. Vertical calibration lines indicate 50 μv.

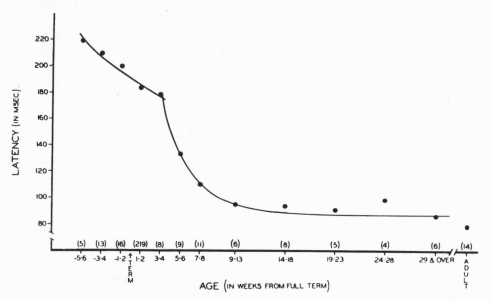

Figure 4—Plot of mean evoked response latencies of all subjects against age.

The dots represent the mean latencies of biweekly age groups up to 7–8 weeks post-term and 5-week groups beyond that point. The mean latency of adult controls is shown at the far right for comparison. The numbers in parentheses just above the abscissa represent the numbers of subjects upon whom the dots above are based.

months or more, and also upon cross-sectional data on a much larger number of subjects.

Figure 3 shows typical responses recorded at various ages in 3 premature and 3 full-term babies. No *consistent* changes in wave-form or amplitude are apparent, except for the change from an initially negative response at 12 days to an initially positive response at 40 days in one subject (C), a change which was observed in all other subjects who showed initially negative responses at first.

The principal change occurring with increasing age is a decrease in latency. The pertinent data are summarized in Fig. 4 which shows a consistent decrease in latency with increase in age to 7–9 weeks post-term, at which point the curve apparently becomes asymptotic. Bearing in mind that some of the points in Fig. 4 are determined by only a few cases, it appears as if the curve is two-legged.

These data, however, should not be taken to indicate that no further developmental changes take place beyond the first few months post-term. The latency of the occipital evoked responses of 14 adults, recorded under the same conditions as those under which the babies' responses were recorded, was 76 msec, $\sigma = 10.2$ msec.* Further, the amplitudes of the responses of adults are in general much lower than those of infants, the initial positive response rarely exceeding 10 μv.

The plot of visual evoked response latency against body weight is highly similar to the plot of latency against age. The product-moment coefficient of correlation between weight and evoked response latency is $-.80$ (SE $= 0.025$). Since the curve is somewhat non-linear, this coefficient may be a slight underestimate.

RESPONSES TO REPETITIVE PHOTIC STIMULATION

Two types of responses to repetitive flashes of light have been recorded: (a) specific evoked responses like those evoked by single flashes of light (Fig. 5A) and (b) rhythmic waves occurring at or about the frequency of the stimulus, so-called "driving." Figure 5B shows both of these responses occurring to the same train of stimuli.

The specific evoked responses, like those evoked by single stimuli, are recorded only from the occipital area. If the frequency of stimulation is low enough, responses may be evoked at every flash (Ellingson, 1958a, Fig. 7C). If the frequency of stimulation is more rapid, a response may be elicited only at the onset of stimulation (ON response) and more rarely at the cessation of stimulation (OFF response) (Fig. 5A; also see Ellingson, 1958a, Fig. 7B and 8). ON and OFF responses were observed to the extent of 29% and 14%, respectively, in the 625 records of full-term babies tested during the first 120 hours after birth; in 28% of the 169 records of prematures recorded before discharge from the nursery; and in 42% and 17% of the 106 records of babies returned for follow-up testing. Most of the follow-up cases were between two weeks and three months of age, although a few were older.

ON responses are generally indistinguishable from responses to single flashes occurring in the same subject. Data leading to this conclusion have been presented in a previous paper (Ellingson, 1958a).

OFF responses, however, appear to differ significantly from ON responses and responses to single flashes in the following three respects. First, OFF responses occur much less regularly and frequently than ON responses; they are best elicited by long trains (5-sec or more) of high-frequency flashes (15 f/sec and up). Second, OFF responses are often not of the same wave-form as the ON responses in the same subject; most notably, a greater proportion of OFF responses than ON responses are initially negative in the less mature groups (50% vs. 15% among prematures before discharge and 31% vs. 5% among full-term babies before

---

* Others have reported the latencies of visual evoked potentials of adults as 95–115 msec (Brazier, 1951) and 48–62 ± 5 msec (Monnier, 1952), but since latency varies with stimulation conditions (e.g., intensity of the light flash) the only valid comparison is that with our own control data. Monnier also reported the amplitude of the initial positive wave in the adult as 6.5 ± 4 μv., which is in agreement with our observations.

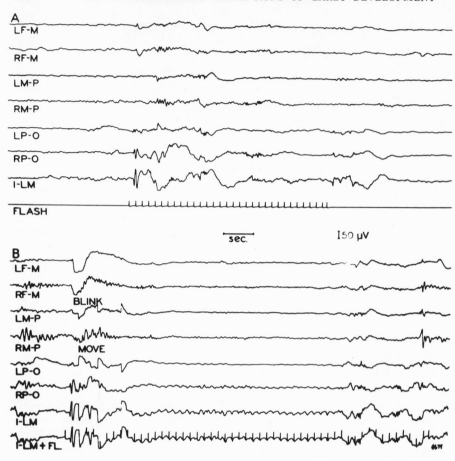

Figure 5—ON and OFF and "driving" responses.

A. Full-term, 7 lb, 12 oz, 63 hours postpartum. Prominent triphasic ON
response at onset of train of flashes; smaller, monophasic OFF response after
cessation of flashes; both most prominent in the inion tracing, but also seen in the
lateral occipital tracings. B. Same subject. Same stimulus elicits an identical
ON response, but also a clear, rhythmic "driving" response at the same frequency
as the flashes (5 f/sec). Note the flattening of background activity during the
period of optimal driving.

discharge), but like initially negative responses to single flashes, they are
not observed in babies older than 5 days post-term. OFF responses are of
longer latency than ON responses, mean latencies being 197 msec for ON
responses and 269 msec for OFF responses among those full-term subjects
for whom both types of responses could be measured at first testing. These
data would seem to indicate that OFF responses are probably different from
ON responses and from responses to single flashes and that they are likely
subserved by at least partially different neural elements (Jung, 1953).

Table 1—Percentage of Subjects Responding to Each Flash at Stimulation Frequencies of 1/sec. to 5/sec

AGE	N	FLASHES/SECOND							
		1	1.5	2	2.5	3	3.5	4	5
Less than 40 weeks	54	5.5	—	—	—	—	—	—	—
41st week	176	10.8	0.6	0.6	—	—	—	—	—
41 weeks and over	79	35	32	23	16.5	10	5	2.5	1.3

Developmental changes have also been observed with respect to responses to repetitive stimulation. The pertinent data are summarized in Table 1.

It is clear that with increasing age the frequency with which the visual system will respond increases. This tendency can also be demonstrated by examination of the "photic driving" data. Driving is rare in the newborn immediately after birth, having been observed in only 5% of the 484 full-term babies and 4% of the 67 prematures tested. Driving is more commonly elicited with increase in age, having been observed in 39% of 105 EEGs recorded on full-term babies 2 weeks of age and up (only a few over 3 months). The driving response is more widely distributed over the posterior half of the head than are specific evoked responses, but was never seen over the anterior half of the head in our young infants.

Driving, when observed, is usually obtained only over a narrow frequency range, and often occurs to one frequency of stimulation only. The "driven" rhythm is either identical with, or very close to, the frequency of stimulation. Harmonic responses are rare, having been observed in only 2 cases, in which 5/sec responses were observed to 2.5 f/sec stimulation. Driving has not been seen at frequencies below 1.5/sec nor above 5/sec among our infants (premature and full-term) up to 6 months of age post-term. Nor is there any significant change in optimal driving frequency up to 6 months of age: mean optimal driving frequency for prematures delivered in the 8th month of gestation or earlier was 3.6/sec $(N = 9)$; for prematures delivered in the 9th month of gestation, 4.0/sec $(N = 9)$; for all babies during the first week post-term, 3.7/sec $(N = 86)$; during the 2nd to 13th weeks post-term, 3.3/sec $(N = 23)$; during month 4–6, inclusive, 4.3/sec $(N = 19)$; and over 6 months, 4.5/sec $(N = 6)$. The data for the older groups are still fragmentary, but a developmental trend toward higher optimal driving frequencies is suggested. Optimal driving frequency is here defined as: (a) the frequency at which driving occurs, if it occurs at only one frequency; (b) if driving occurs at more than one frequency, the frequency at which the "driven" waves are of highest voltage and most persistent; *or* (c) if they are of equal voltage and persistence at 2 or more frequencies, the mean of those frequencies.

FLATTENING ("AROUSAL") RESPONSE
TO PHOTIC STIMULATION

Photic stimuli, even very intense flashes, are not very effective arousal stimuli in the young infant. Auditory stimuli are more effective (Ellingson, 1958a) and somesthetic more effective still. However, if photic stimuli (especially repetitive) are presented during sleep when diffuse irregular slow waves (5/sec and slower) are the dominant feature of the EEG, a transient, generalized flattening of the tracings is occasionally observed. This may occur together with a driving response, the "driven" waves appearing against the flattened background (Fig. 5; see also Ellingson, 1958a, Fig. 11).

DISCUSSION

Various investigators have studied the development of evoked responses in the auditory system of cats (Ellingson & Wilcott, 1960; Grossman, 1955; Rose *et al.,* 1957), the somesthetic system of cats (Grossman, 1955; Scherrer & Oeconomos, 1954), the visual system of cats (Ellingson & Wilcott, 1960; Marty *et al.,* 1958), and in the visual cortex of rabbits (Hunt & Goldring, 1951). The results of those studies show developmental changes which are in many respects very similar to our results, but in some respects different. The various points of comparison, and their implications, will be discussed.

COMPARATIVE DEVELOPMENT IN EVOKED
RESPONSES OF WAVE-FORM AND DIFFERENCES
IN TIME OF APPEARANCE

The following tentative generalizations would appear to be justified on the basis of the animal data presently available. The earliest response to appear is a surface-negative wave (an exception would seem to be the auditory evoked response of the cat, which has been reported always to show an initial positive phase even in the youngest animals yielding responses [Ellingson & Wilcott, 1960; Grossman, 1955; Rose *et al.,* 1957]); sometimes a double negative wave is seen, the first component being usually, but not always, of higher amplitude than the second. Occasionally a train of waves of diminishing amplitude is seen. Later in development a small brief surface-positive wave appears, preceding the negative wave. As more time passes, the positive wave increases in amplitude relative to the negative wave. Eventually the positive wave may be seen alone at least part of the time.

Our human data are in accord with the conception of the initially negative response as a primitive evoked response. The fact that it is seen as infrequently in the human as it is, suggests that the human visual system is of relatively more advanced development at birth than that of the cat and rabbit. Another line of evidence leading to the same conclusion concerns time of appearance of cortical evoked potentials. Only in the somesthetic system of the cat have evoked potentials been recorded on the first day after birth (Scherrer & Oeconomos, 1954). All other animal studies report failure to record evoked potentials until the 3rd to 11th days, the results varying with species, modality, and individuals. In the human, on the other hand, we have recorded visual evoked responses as early as the 28th week after conception.

Changes in the wave-form of cortical evoked potentials may be due either to developmental changes in the nature of the volley of impulses approaching, and arriving in, the cortex, and/or to changes in the responses of cortical cells to the arriving stimuli. Such anatomical information as is available partially supports both of these possibilities (Hunt & Goldring, 1951).

COMPARATIVE DEVELOPMENT IN AMPLITUDE OF EVOKED RESPONSES

While our results from human infants show generally higher voltage responses than in adults, the results of animal studies are quite clear in showing increasing amplitude with increasing age. This is one of the major discrepancies between our findings on infants and findings on animals. The most reasonable explanation of this discrepancy appears to be in terms of the buried position of the primary visual cortex in the human, because of which we are probably often not obtaining optimal responses, but are rather recording from the periphery of a field of evoked potential change much of the time. Marty *et al.* (1958) have reported that in the early stages of development of visual evoked responses in the cat, they may be recorded over approximately the posterior half of the lateral hemispheric surface. Then the zone of the recorded potentials seems to narrow down. If a similar developmental sequence occurs in the human, it could account for our results. We have seen that evoked potentials can often be recorded from electrodes 2–3 cm lateral to the midline in infants, but not from similarly placed electrodes in adults.

COMPARATIVE DEVELOPMENT OF LATENCY OF EVOKED RESPONSES

There can be no question that the latencies of evoked responses in the primary sensory cortices of the immature animals studied are significantly longer than in adult animals, and that they decrease progressively with increasing age. However, several questions arise in connection with these observations.

What parts of the afferent systems are responsible for the long latencies observed? The data of Rose *et al.* (1957), who recorded auditory responses simultaneously from the round window, medial geniculate, and cortex, and that of Scherrer and Oeconomos (1954), who recorded somesthetic responses simultaneously from the cervical cord and cortex, indicate that all segments of afferent systems transmit slowly in immature animals, but that most of the delay is attributable to structures between the receptor and the cortex rather than to either of the two latter.

Zetterström's observations (1951, 1952, 1955) on the infantile ERG, previously reviewed (Ellingson, 1958a), suggest that retinal processes account for no more than 1/5 of the difference between newborn and adult visual evoked response latencies. Beyond this we can only infer from the animal studies cited that the remaining structures of the afferent visual system all contribute to the remaining difference. In this connection, several studies have demonstrated increasing velocity of peripheral and central neuronal conduction with increasing age in different species (del Castillo & Vizoso, 1953; Hursh, 1939a, 1939b; Thomas & Lambert, 1958; Ulett et al., 1944). The magnitudes of such changes as observed, strongly suggest that the major factor in decreasing evoked response latencies is probably the increase in conduction velocity of afferent fibers.

How is anatomical development of the visual system related to the latency data? The only histological observations which have been made in connection with the animal studies cited are those of Hunt and Goldring (1951) who concluded that "myelination is not the chief factor determining latency in the central visual pathway" in the rabbit, although the deposition of myelin is of course a feature of anatomical development.

Data bearing upon the histological development of the subcortex of the human brain, which might be directly correlated with our latency data, are not plentiful (Flechsig, 1876, 1920; Langworthy, 1932; Mann, 1950). Collectively these data appear to indicate a period of rapid development of the afferent visual system between birth and 2–3 months of age, agreeing generally with our latency data. These data, however, deal with maturation only in terms of myelination, which cannot be taken as the sole criterion of neuronal or fiber development (Conel, 1952). Animal data clearly show reasonably good, although not mature, functioning of completely unmyelinated neurons (Bishop, 1950; Hunt & Goldring, 1951; Langworthy, 1932; Ulett et al., 1944).

What is the significance of our two-legged curves? Our developmental curve of response latency (Fig. 4) appears to be two-legged rather than a monotonic curve like that of Rose et al. (1957). Rejecting, for the sake of argument, the hypothesis that it is an artifact of our data, two possible explanations suggest themselves: (a) a growth spurt occurs somewhere in the visual system between the 4th and 8th weeks post-term, and (b) the curve is a composite developmental curve of two systems, or two different segments of one system, one of which does not begin to show significant physiological development until about the 5th week post-term. There is, unfortunately, no direct anatomical support for either of these hypotheses, but neither are there any contrary data.

The growth spurt hypothesis is quite tenable. Various observations have shown that rate of growth can vary from time to time and from system to system within the nervous system. However, a more closely ranked temporal sequence of infant brains would have to be examined histologically to provide data bearing directly upon the hypothesis that a specific growth spurt occurs within the visual system, or a part of it, following the 4th week post-term.

The dual system hypothesis is of course in accord with the duplexity theory of vision, but the literature provides only two fragments of data bearing upon this question, one anatomical and one physiological. (a) The only part of the retina not completely differentiated histologically at birth is the macula (all cones), which continues to develop until at least 16 weeks post-term (Mann, 1950). However, extramacular cones are not reported to show a similar lag in development; (b) Zetterström (1955a) observed that the flicker ERG of the newborn infant is of the so-called scotopic type, and concluded that the reaction of the newborn retina is that of a rod-bearing retina only. At 4 weeks of age flicker fusion frequency curves begin to assume a two-legged shape. This is about the time that our latency curve breaks. At 2 months of age "a distinct change can be recorded with the flicker ERG," consisting of a rising fusion frequency, and at high light intensities, a transition to a photopic type of flicker. During the following weeks a distinctly photopic flicker ERG appears, and the flicker fusion frequency curve becomes indistinguishable from that of an adult. These events correspond in time with the final complete histological development of the macula, and with the period during which our latency curve becomes asymptotic. It is during the same period that effective ocular fixation develops.

These data are hardly conclusive, but they suggest that the first leg of our developmental curve of evoked response latency may be attributable to the scotopic, and the second to the photopic, system.

COMPARATIVE DEVELOPMENT OF RESPONSES TO REPETITIVE STIMULATION

All investigators who have studied response to repetitive stimulation in infant animals (Ellingson & Wilcott, 1960; Grossman, 1955; Hunt & Goldring, 1951; Scherrer & Oeconomos, 1954) have observed that the younger the animal the more time must be allowed between stimuli in order that stimuli after the first will evoke responses of equal magnitude to that evoked by the first stimulus. In the case of very young animals when the initially negative response first appears, many seconds often must elapse between stimuli to obtain equal responses. This phenomenon has been called "fatigability." Again our baby data are in accord with findings on cats and rabbits. There are no data indicating which elements of the visual system are responsible for this phenomenon.

INDIVIDUAL DIFFERENCES

Most investigators have remarked on individual differences in all features of evoked responses among animals of presumably the same age (Ellingson & Wilcott, 1960; Hunt & Goldring, 1951; Rose *et al.*, 1957; Scherrer & Oeconomos, 1954). Anatomical workers have also remarked upon the considerable individual differences among specimens of the same apparent age (Conel, 1939, 1941, 1947, 1951, 1952; Flechsig, 1876; Langworthy, 1932).

These differences can be explained partly, but not entirely, by errors in estimating actual age since conception. For example, the responses of a premature weighing 4 lbs may be of shorter latency than those of a full-term baby of 8 lbs; a full-term baby of 7 lbs may show initially negative responses while a 5 lb premature shows initially positive responses. It is not possible that errors in estimation of conceptual age can be great enough to account for these differences. Genetic factors, and possibly other factors, must be operative.

SUMMARY

Full-term and premature babies have been stimulated on one or more occasions by single and repetitive flashes of light. The responses recorded from the occipital cortex (scalp) differ from those of adults in being of (a) more variable wave-form, (b) more variable (and often higher) amplitude, (c) longer latency, and (d) greater "fatigability." Developmental changes with increasing age have been demonstrated; the most notable of these are (a) change from a response with initial negative phase in the earliest records of some subjects to the classical response with initial positive phase, (b) decreasing response latency, and (c) increasing ability to respond to more and more rapidly repeated stimuli. Response latency is also inversely correlated with body weight up to about 12 lbs ($r = -0.80$). Curves of response latency versus age and of response latency versus body weight are two-legged rather than monotonic, the breaks in the curves occurring at 4 weeks post-term and 9 lbs, respectively. This phenomenon may reflect either a growth spurt in the visual system or different developmental rates in the two parts (scotopic and photopic) of the visual system. The physiological evidence appears to be related to anatomical evidence of immaturity and developmental change, but available anatomical data are not detailed enough for close correlation. The human data described are in most respects similar to those reported for cats and rabbits. The visual system of the human infant appears to be physiologically more mature at birth than that of the cat and the rabbit, but the latter develop more rapidly postnatally. Individual differences are as striking in the human as they are in the other two species.

SUPPLEMENTARY READINGS

Ellingson, R. J. EEG's of normal, full-term newborns immediately after birth with observations on arousal and visual evoked response. *EEG clin. Neurophysiol.*, 1958, 10, 31–50.

Ellingson, R. J. Studies of the electrical activity of the developing human brain. In W. A. Himmwich & H. E. Himmwich (Eds.), *Progress in brain research. Vol. 9. The developing brain.* New York: Elsevier, 1964.

Harris, R., & Tizard, J. P. M. The electroencephalogram in neonatal convulsions. *J. Pediatr.*, 1960, 57, 501–520.

Kellaway, P., & Fox, B. J. EEG diagnosis of cerebral pathology in infants during sleep. I. Rationale, technique and the characteristics of normal sleep in infants. *J. Pediatr.*, 1952, 41, 262–287.

Marcus, R., Gibbs, F. A., & Gibbs E. L. EEG in the diagnosis of hearing loss in the very young child. *Dis. nerv. Syst.*, 1949, 10, 170–176.

Mills, P., Derbyshire, A., & Carter, R. Changes evoked by auditory stimulation in the EEG in sleep. *EEG clin. Neurophysiol.*, 1961, 13, 79.

pupillary activity

in the infant*

ALBRECHT PEIPER

[Poets have called the human eyes "the windows to the soul." Do the infant's eyes provide an avenue to better understanding of his mental processes? It has been known for more than 60 years that infants respond to skin stimulation by a dilation of the pupils. Scientists have also known for some time that the iris of the adult eye is in a state of constant unrest (30 to 120 slight oscillations per minute), and that these tiny changes in dilation–constriction are concomitant with psychological functions of attention and exertion of mental effort. Under normal conditions "pupillary unrest" is not under conscious control. Since there is a correlation between pupillary unrest and psychological activities in adults, there has existed a possibility of finding similar relationships during infancy. Dr. Peiper, Professor Emeritus of Leipzig University, addressed himself to this exciting possibility in the following study. He made the disappointing discovery that "pupillary unrest is completely absent in premature, as well as in newborn, children." Even with the magnification provided by the Hess differential-pupilloscope, Dr. Peiper found it difficult to identify precisely the age at which pupillary unrest first appears. This activity becomes first clearly discernible in infants of 4–5 months; however, the types of oscillation involved are substantially different from those found in older subjects. The oscillations observed during this time in infancy occur very slowly and irregularly in response to external stimulation. Dr. Peiper hypothesizes that "pupillary unrest" is activated by cerebral functioning which he believes, along with the majority of psychologists and neurologists, is poorly developed in the newborn infant.]

Our means for exploring brain activity in the infant are limited because at this age level we can only examine the physical concomitants which more or less clearly reflect brain activity. It is now known that the pupil of the adult represents a sensitive indicator for external and internal stimulation of all kinds, so that Schiff, in his time, actually designated it an esthesiometer.

* From A. Peiper. Über das Pupillenspiel des Säuglings. (Pupillary activity in the infant.) *Annales Paediatrici,* 1926, 112, 179–183.

Observation of pupillary activity in infancy is therefore of special importance; yet few findings are available in this area. Pfister (1899) found that pupillary dilation to skin stimulation occurred toward the end of the second month of life. In the second quarter of the first year this was present in 87%, later only in 40% of the children examined. Only after the tenth week of life did pupillary dilation occur to auditory stimulation: from seven to nine months it was present in 64% of all cases. In contrast, Bartel (1904) found pupillary dilation to intense skin stimulation present in all neonates tested for this reaction.

It appears that both scientists always examined the pupils without magnification; therefore, no findings exist on the so-called pupillary unrest [*Unruhe*] which is not visible to the naked eye. But pupillary unrest especially could yield conclusions as to brain activity. When the pupil of a healthy adult is examined with the help of magnification it can be seen that the edge of the iris is in constant unrest, and this is quite independent of any bodily movement. These changes occur 30 to 120 times per minute. They are related to the psychic events which are inseparably connected with the waking condition of adults. Every external stimulus increases pupillary unrest; but this also occurs as a function of affect, of attention, and of mental effort generally (Bumke, 1904). It is not possible to suppress it deliberately.

The conditions under which pupillary unrest occurs in the infant seem not to have been investigated up to now. Bach (1908) only states that it is more active in "youthful age" than later. My own tests were designed to clarify the question of pupillary unrest in the infant. At the same time I undertook to resolve the contradictory findings of Pfister and Bartels. The tests were undertaken with the Hess differential-pupilloscope. Here, one eye of the subject is illuminated and observed under magnification. Of course, the infant is not as easy to examine as the adult. Nevertheless, it was usually possible to obtain results in the following manner. The head of the subject is turned to one side in such a way that the beam of the pupilloscope hits one of his eyes. He is carefully held in this position. If the child does move anyway, he is returned to the previous position. When necessary, the eyelids of the child must be opened by hand. Of course it is necessary to keep the child in a good mood, because when crying he moves and closes his eyes. A test is likewise impossible as long as the child himself moves his eyeballs, because the changing lighting in itself alters the pupillary dilation. In particular the nystagmus-like, jolting eye movements that sometimes appear in neonates or prematurely born children are extremely disturbing. In general, however, even very young children keep their eyes still long enough; slightly older infants even stare at the light for a period of time.

The test showed without exception that pupillary unrest is completely absent in premature, as well as in newborn, children. Nothing even remotely resembling pupillary unrest could be seen in any of the infants. Even though no great difference exists between the pupillary dilation of the neonate and that of the adult, I nevertheless tested this by using an increased magnification. In all cases the result remained unchanged; reaction to light was, of course, always present. In general, pupillary movements in the young infant are slower and stronger than in later life. Consequently, all activities taking place in the infant's pupil are recognizable with the naked eye although, of course, they can be better observed when magnified. Completely absent, however, are the minute oscillations of the pupillary edge which are always found in the adult, magnified eye.

It is impossible to state precisely the age at which pupillary unrest appears for the first time; it begins so gradually that the change appears to be altogether fluid. In this it is similar to all such new acquisitions in infancy. The pupil of a somewhat older infant can at times remain entirely quiet. However, as soon as the child is excited for some reason, the pupil suddenly begins to oscillate. Likewise, external stimulation is not infrequently followed by prolonged oscillation. Generally, a clearly discernible pupillary unrest is constantly present in infants of four to five months; it differs, however, from that of the adult in that oscillations occur more slowly and quite concentrically, while in later life the pupillary edge moves fast and irregularly.

We not infrequently found the so-called hippus in our subjects. This term designates a rhythmical, concentric movement of the entire pupillary edge, independent of external stimulation. Pfister found it in only 3 cases out of 300 children. I believe I have observed it more frequently. The hippus, however, was not found regularly, but rather only occasionally. It differs from pupillary unrest through its slowness and the strength of its pulsation, so that the hippus is visible without magnification. The significance that should be ascribed to the hippus has not yet been determined; it has been explained both as a chronic convulsion and as a tremor of the *sphincter iridis*. The youngest child in which the hippus occurred was a prematurely born child of eight days weighing 1,500 grams. Whether the hippus constitutes a precursor of pupillary unrest or whether it has an entirely different genetic origin has not yet been determined.

We tried to elicit pupillary dilation to external stimulation—the sound of a whistle and needle pricks. As in all such reactions at this age, dilation occurred very irregularly, i.e., it was sometimes present and sometimes absent in the same child. If one tested several times in succession with the same stimulus, pupillary dilation might suddenly appear or disappear. Thus the predisposition to react changed constantly. The older the examined infants were, the more certainly one could count on the presence of pupillary reactions. But even in prematurely born infants it was on occasion reliably elicited as early as the first days of life. I have already mentioned in other papers the fact that these children reacted to stimuli with changes in breathing rhythm and general movements. Compared with these reactions, pupillary movement is more difficult to elicit, but because it occurs so irregularly, it is of no help to express the frequency of its occurrence in figures.

It should be especially emphasized that in many children pupillary dilation to external stimulation is present consistently while pupillary unrest is absent. This fact seems to throw some light on the question of the origin of pupillary unrest. Behr has given the following explanation for this fact: sensory stimuli constantly flow into consciousness so that it is continuously changing. Consequently, in the waking state, the pupil constantly receives impulses for dilation from the cortex and these are constantly in conflict with those for contraction. As my tests show, the external stimuli alone are unable to produce permanent pupillary unrest, even though pupillary size may oscillate for a time in connection with external stimuli. Since the stimuli are relegated to the vegetative centers in the *thalamus opticus,* the pupil can dilate on external stimulation without excitation of the higher centers. Elsewhere I have shown that, in the neonate, the brain works only up to the striate body, while an activity of the higher parts of the brain, and particularly that of the cortex, cannot be confirmed yet. The activity of these higher parts of the brain is probably accompanied by pupillary unrest, and the external stimuli initiate or strengthen them only when the excitation proceeds to the cortex. Brain activity in the infant is certainly considerably more limited than in the adult, and the absence of pupillary unrest is regarded as evidence for this.

Translated by Alexandra Hendee

SUPPLEMENTARY READINGS

Gorman, J., Cogan, D. G., & Gellis, S. S. An apparatus for grading the visual acuity of infants on the basis of opticokinetic nystagmus. *Pediatrics,* 1957, 19, 1088–1092.

Paine, R. S. Neurological examination of infants and children. *Ped. Clin. N. Amer.,* 1960, 7, 471.

Paine, R. S. Neurologic conditions in the neonatal period. *Ped. Clin. N. Amer.,* 1961, 8, 577–610.

Peiper, A. *Cerebral function in infancy and childhood.* New York: Consultants Bureau, 1963.

Pendleton, M. E., & Paine, R. S. A visual, photographic and electroencephalographic study of eye movements in the newborn. *Neurology,* in press.

neurologic development

of the infant.

the contributions

of andré thomas*

S. SAINT-ANNE DARGASSIES

[There are many recorded instances in the history of science where systematic observation of abnormalities in nature have eventually led to a better understanding of what is "normal." The following paper is a tribute to that great clinical neurologist André Thomas, whose detailed observations and descriptions of deviant developmental trends in the neurological growth of the infant have provided a better understanding of the behavior and responsiveness of normal infants. Dr. Saint-Anne Dargassies, an admiring student of André Thomas, also contributes from her own experience to our knowledge about neurological deficiencies during infancy. Dr. Saint-Anne Dargassies, of the Clinique Obstétricale Baudelocque, Paris, favors giving primary attention to such response variables as degree of wakefulness, general tonus, quality of the Moro reflex, and abnormal movements. She notes, as have other investigators, that such common reflexes as the grasp, stepping, and lateral curvature of the body are not differentially diagnostic signs because they are well developed even in the microcephalic or anencephalic infant. Perhaps of greatest interest to psychologists is the emphasis given by these skilled diagnosticians to longitudinal data: "In this work, we cannot make exact diagnoses on the basis of neurologic lesions; rather, we must emulate André Thomas' approach by studying the development of the neurologic deficit over a period of time."]

My purpose at this time is not to examine the methods adopted by pediatricians, neurologists, or psychologists to elucidate and observe the neurologic maturation of the newborn child but simply to outline the contribution made by André Thomas to this question, to bring out the originality

* From S. Saint-Anne Dargassies. Neurologic development of the infant: The contributions of André Thomas. *World Neurology*, 1960, 1, 71–77. (With permission.)

of his clinical researches, and to explain the principles that are fundamental to the study of the signs he has bequeathed to us. In order to realize the profundity of his knowledge of newborn and suckling children, the way in which the dominant ideas that form the basis of his work have been built into his precise study of the neurologic growth of the infant must be understood.

Only after a long career devoted to the study of adult neurology did André Thomas turn to the study of newborn infants. After his anatomo-pathologic and clinical training, he became well known for his study of the cerebellum in 1897, and of diseases of the spinal cord in 1910. Step by step, he clarified those neurophysiologic mechanisms which could lead to a deeper explanation of functional disturbance, and his great work, *Équilibre et Équilibration,* appeared in 1940. In 1948 appeared his magnum opus, in collaboration with J. de Ajuriaguerra. In 1946, he described neonatal automatic movements, and, in 1949, almost fifty years after the beginning of his scientific work, he began to elaborate on the neurologic examination of newborn babies. Finally, in 1952, he published, in collaboration with me, *Études Neurologiques du Nouveau-né et du Nourrisson.*

These facts seem to indicate that André Thomas was led to his study of symptomatology in the infant by his knowledge of pathologic processes in the adult. He was struck by the peculiar tonic and reflex manifestations in the baby and attempted to correlate these with the clinical picture in the adult affected by specific lesions. He considered the possibility that lesions of the cortex might free subcortical centers from all control and inhibition and that diffuse cortical lesions might allow free play to medullary physiologic function. Little by little, he evolved the fundamental idea that the newborn child is essentially a medullary, subcortical being in whom the cortex is not yet functioning. In his view, the cortex at birth is backward in anatomic, physiologic, and biologic growth, as compared with subcortical centers. At this stage, therefore, the infant has a normal neuromotor activity which is specific but transitory and which must be recognized. Moreover, his growth is rapid and reflects cerebral maturation, so that new functions are acquired in the transition of the newborn infant to the suckling child and then to the young adult.

ANDRÉ THOMAS' STUDY OF SIGNS

The very young baby, who is at this subcortical stage of nervous functioning and is maturing rapidly, cannot be studied by the classic methods of neurology that are suited to the adult. Therefore, André Thomas adopted a three-step method for his work: observation of spontaneous activity, elicitation of reflex capacities, and estimation of the extent to which latent reactions might be present. In this way, he hoped to uncover systematically the whole extent of motor activity in the newborn infant, who exhibits poverty of movement at first sight.

André Thomas stressed the differences between trunk and limb motility.

The trunk develops earlier than the limbs, for the limb buds do not appear until almost the fifth week of life. The trunk is absolutely essential to life, and any pathologic manifestation in it is likely to be associated with some central damage. On the other hand, neurologic disturbances limited to the limbs may often be associated with a spinal or even a peripheral lesion. Motility in the newborn child is greatest in the trunk and head, as manifested by facial expression; active rotational movements of the head; early orientational movements; and torsion movements of the trunk, which accompany lateral displacement of the head. Movements of the limbs are, by contrast, much less marked and, above all, more stereotyped, though they are asymmetric.

André Thomas did not limit his study to the differences between the motility of the trunk and the limbs but showed that tonus had a definite distribution at different levels. Thus, in neck and trunk, tonus of the extensors is particularly well marked, resulting in the characteristic attitude of the newborn child and the remarkable reactions of orientation elicited from his head and trunk. The limbs, on the other hand, show dominant tonicity in the flexors, and the extensors are hypotonic.

So far as the Magnus-de Kleijn reflex is concerned, whereby position of the head influences tonus of the arms and the attitude they take up, André Thomas believed that the phenomenon is not always present in the newborn baby. He thought, rather, that it occurs more commonly in the abnormal infant.

That the membranous labyrinth is fully formed by the first few weeks of life and that the vestibular nerve myelinates very early are well-known facts. Nevertheless, André Thomas maintained that only minimal labyrinthine reflexes are present at birth. In his opinion, indeed, those reactions which take place when equilibrium is upset are only seen when displacements or swaying movements are slow. Thus, they represent something other than simple labyrinthine reactions.

In the same way, contrary to the opinion of certain authors, Thomas held that the Moro, or crossed arm, reflex results from rapid displacement of the head in space. He looked upon this reflex as a deep neck reflex independent of the labyrinth. Similarly, the doll's eyes reaction, a transitory eye movement to the opposite side when the head is rotated passively, present from birth, does not occur when the head is merely displaced in space without altering its relation to the body, and it is therefore difficult to accept it as a labyrinthine reaction. André Thomas regarded it as a simple synergistic reaction of the eyeballs to passive head movement, and he emphasized again the importance of interplay between agonists and antagonists in every provoked reaction.

In his evaluation of neural phenomena in newborn children, André Thomas laid great stress on righting reflexes—spontaneous righting of the head when the infant is supported in a sitting position, righting of the trunk from the flexed position in response to movements of the ankle joints, and reaction of the infant as a whole when given solid support against the soles of his feet. He maintained that these were complete reactions rather than simple reflexes. Thus, they exhibit a certain progression in their course and slowness in onset demanding maintained stimulation. These reactions appear to be proprioceptive in origin in that they originate in muscles or tendons, excite medullary reflexes, are set off by the weight of the head or of the whole body, and are made up of a chain of tonic extensor responses —first of the legs, then of the trunk, and, finally, of the neck. This theory is associated with the idea of the myotatic stretch reflex.

Some authors, bearing in mind the labyrinthine reflexes that originate in the otoconium mechanism, see these changes as consequent upon movement of the head in space. Although it is true that displacement of an animal's head downward and forward increases the supporting tonus in the hind limbs, precise observation, as André Thomas correctly pointed out, shows that, when orientation of legs and trunk takes place, extensor tonus sets in from below, moving upward, and readjustment of the head is the last to occur.

While Thomas stressed the importance of examining body reactions thoroughly, he did not neglect an equally meticulous examination of the tonus and primitive reflexes of the limbs. He distinguished two features in the assessment of hypertonicity: (1) extensibility, or passive increase to the maximum extent of the distance between the points of attachment of the muscles under consideration, and (2) flaccidity, or swinging limb. He regarded the former as a useful sign of pyramidal involvement and the latter as an indication of faulty coordination of the antagonist muscles, suggesting cerebellar pathology. From evaluation of these two factors, an exact estimate of the tonic state of the muscles can be made. The two halves of the body can then be compared region by region so that the presence of a hemisyndrome of central origin can be determined.

André Thomas was unimpressed by deep reflexes, since it is known that the patellar reflexes are active, while ankle and triceps jerks are limited because of normal flexor tonus. More important, in his view, was the systematic study of primary reflex activity amounting to automatic coordinated movements. He thought it necessary to know how to elicit these movements in the newborn child. Note the descriptions, long since classic, of stepping reflex, crossed extensor reflex, grasp reflexes of the hands, and lateral curvature of the trunk.

Even more noteworthy are those orientational reflexes in the newborn baby in which emergence of sensation can be distinguished. The sucking reflex, in which movements of tongue and head result from lip stimulations —that is, orientational changes are brought about by a very primitive anatomic reflex—is a case in point. Of similar type is the avoidance reaction, shown by active rotation of the head in response to a painful stimulus, such as pinching the lobe of the ear.

This neonatal motor nervous activity evolves parallel to maturation of the nervous system and depends on fade-out of primitive reactions, development of tonus, and acquisition of new functions, more specialized and increasingly adapted to needs.

During the first two to three months after birth, archaic automatic movements gradually disappear. Some movements undergo change before finally disappearing, which may confuse an observer who is not aware of this fact; others make only a transitory appearance, for example, the Landau reflex—passive flexion or extension of the head governing the posture of the legs. In this way, the newborn infant becomes a full-fledged suckling child, both emotionally and functionally. This rapid growth is so continuous and well integrated that it is misleading to speak of stages. However, for the sake of order, it is feasible to mark off development during the first year of life according to the acquisition of major functional activity of a more mature type. From this arises the idea of the functional age of a child—an idea conforming closely to the spirit of André Thomas.

Thomas, however, was not content with merely observing the process of acquiring progressively greater cortical control. As a neurologist, he looked carefully for expected signs at a given age and fitted them into their proper setting, which he then investigated fully. In this way, fundamental facts of neurologic growth in the young infant were established against a broad background of knowledge of the evolution of tonus, reaction, and emotional response.

In the infant, stable tonus evolves rapidly. Thus, flexor tonus, which at birth primarily affects the limbs, diminishes progressively and the child passes into a phase of generalized hypotonia by 3 months. Support reactions no longer occur. This stage of astasia-abasia continues until about the seventh month. The child then gradually acquires static reflexes once again, until, by the age of 10 months, he becomes able to support his body weight unaided. At the same time, tonus in the trunk undergoes modification. Thus, the previous dominance of extensor tonus in the neck muscles becomes counterbalanced by the flexors so that head stability is achieved. Later, the flexors of the trunk mature so that the child is able to sit up without support.

By following the development of motor activity in light of the evolution of tonus, André Thomas sought to clarify the mechanism of general or partial retardation and abnormalities or absence of certain acquired functions. These transformations of tonus, evidences of cerebral maturation, come about simultaneously with the appearance of major functional activity as the infant becomes more mobile and is daily enriched by new experiences. They are, in fact, closely bound to both external and internal conditions of the child. Long capable of registering sensory changes, the infant becomes progressively a sensitive creature, with volition and free choice of movements, gestures, and attitudes. Any functional retardation may result from an isolated motor deficiency, some delay in the development of new functions, or a combination of both.

These changes take place over several months. Among them, visual maturation is of the greatest importance. Gaining ability to fix his hand visually, together with grasping and finer manipulations which appear later, opens up for the child various play activities and possibilities of orientation in space. After the infant is 6 months old, equilibration begins to appear; at the same time, adaptational movements of the hands in breaking a fall appear, followed by quick swaying movements of the trunk.

The parachutist reflex, extension of the arms when the infant is suddenly lowered, is another example of the firm establishment of equilibrational reflexes. The infant is now able to react to sudden movements and loss of balance and is no longer the prisoner of his body position. In the opinion of André Thomas, this is a true equilibration faculty, which begins to appear in the child from the age of 7 to 8 months and which is much more elaborate than a simple labyrinthine reflex. It is to be noted that this faculty finally allows independent walking.

However, it would be a misrepresentation of the spirit of André Thomas' work to imply that he thought of the maturation of the child as regulated solely by the evolution of tonus and the acquisition of function in correlation with myelination of the neuraxis and increasing cortical activity. André Thomas stressed the importance of affect, which stimulates, influences, and even directs the harmonious growth of the infant as his field of experience enlarges, from the earliest weeks of life.

Each of the components—motor evolution, acquisition of functional activity, and quality of affect—is equally important in studying the normal as well as the abnormal child. With André Thomas, I would emphasize the difficulty of diagnosis and prognosis, especially before the truly cortical phase of cerebral maturation has been reached. This difficulty is caused on the one hand by the fact that the time scale of growth is variable to a certain extent and on the other by the fact that substitutions may later be supplied in the damaged infant by other intact parts of the nervous system. Later still, when the child enters upon the more intellectual period of his development, his own individual make-up and capacity for adaptation must be taken into account, as well as his ability to accept and integrate his perceptual experience. These capacities will help form his intelligence and personality.

APPLICATION TO STUDY OF
ABNORMAL NEWBORN CHILD

Since I have worked under the guidance of André Thomas and have made his methods my own, I have taken a special interest in the problems of the newborn infant after abnormal gestation, difficult birth, and marked prematurity. In this article dedicated to the work of André Thomas, I can only sketch the salient features of this contribution to pathologic neurology. I have had to adapt the usual clinical methods of examination because of the fragility of the injured, shocked, malformed, or premature child. Accordingly, I have foregone all manipulations and have considered it enough to observe the infant closely, to touch him only with gentle, stroking movements, and to examine him slowly region by region, keeping him always on his back. In this way, I seek to arrive at a neurologic assessment of the infant's condition without running the risk of aggravating his struggle for survival. This broad study of signs gives perhaps an even better view of the general manifestations of neurologic disorder. As a result, all signs of abnormality are very important.

In addition to the states of tonus and the primary reflexes investigated by the methods of André Thomas, I have noted other signs which may yield information about the child: disturbance of respiratory rhythm, cardiovascular abnormality, type of crying, pathologic eye signs, temperature regulation, vasomotor irregularities, and, above all, character of spontaneous or evoked movement. However, I do not intend to catalogue all pathologic signs but rather to give an over-all impression of them. To do this, a relative importance must be allotted to each sign. My purpose is not to find out if a stepping reflex is present or if the infant can grasp but to determine which signs are of minor and which of essential value, to get a better idea of the real condition of the infant.

After more than ten years' experience, I am now able to list some abnormal signs in the order of their importance: degree of wakefulness, disorders of provoked movement, abnormal attitude, general tonus, quality of Moro reflex, existence of abnormal eye signs, type of cry, and occurrence of convulsive or abnormal movements. I regard as less important other signs and automatic reactions which may, for example, be well developed even in the microcephalic or anencephalic infant: the grasp reflex, the stepping reflex, the crossed extensor reaction, and the lateral curvature of the body.

My true intention is not to extend knowledge of pathologic signs and tonic and motor phenomena in the newborn child but to determine the basis of the child's difficulties. For example, it may happen that a respiratory or circulatory disorder will aggravate a cerebral lesion; but in some cases, a cerebral lesion may not be the basis of the clinical condition of the infant, for not all neurologic signs necessarily result from an organic neurologic lesion.

Every day, examples of the difficulty of determining the primary cause in a chain of events in neonatal disease are seen. The study of clinical signs helps to clarify this difficult problem, making it possible to determine whether the basic neurologic condition of the child is normal apart from some predominant sign of disease. In this way, such study may give valuable aid in foretelling if the child will improve or fail as the outstanding symptom becomes accentuated or recedes. Thus, the relationship between cause and effect may sometimes be seen.

However, pursuing this course, repeated neurologic examinations must be made in order to assess fundamental disturbances. In observing abnormal signs from an infant's earliest days or weeks, I have often noticed that a misleading impression may be gained when full recognition is not given to the course of his motor and mental growth right up to the time when the cortex comes into play and even later. With this in view, I have sought to study methodically and in continuity those signs which have been present from birth, endeavoring to learn the ways in which they evolve, their inter-relationship, and their altered manifestations during the course of the long period of cerebral maturation.

The same approach has been made to the study of early prematurity of the child born in the sixth month of gestation. At birth, the character of movement of such a child—slow and generalized, as in the still younger fetus—with its primitive reflexes still imperfect, particularly in the legs, shows him to be more similar to the fetus than to the normal child born at term. Background tonus diminishes after three days, but active tone enables quite varied and prolonged movements to be carried out. Develop-ment takes place gradually but continuously, and changes in the tonic state reflect cerebral maturation. Thus, increased tone of the flexor muscles, which is characteristic of the normal child at term, begins to appear after a few weeks, becomes particularly well marked in the proximal parts of the legs, and explains the characteristic resting attitude of the 7½-month pre-mature infant, that is, flexion of the legs with abduction of the thighs in a froglike attitude. Supporting reactions that are notably absent at 6 months gradually appear as transient, jerky extension movements of the knees, like myotatic reflexes. Not, however, until after 7½ months do true righting reflexes appear.

Eight months from the time of conception, tonus increases in the flexor muscles, automatic movements are perfected, and, from the neuro-logic point of view, the premature infant comes to resemble the infant of normal gestation. Thus it would seem that, so far as tone and reflexes are concerned, maturation in utero and in the incubator proceeds in very much the same way.

To conclude this analysis of the work of André Thomas, I should like to summarize what I have gained from his teaching: the ability to evaluate the pathologic newborn child, whatever the basis of his condition; an under-standing of the special features of the 6-month premature infant, who stands close to the fetus in his behavior; and the ability to conjecture about the future growth of infants who are abnormal at birth.

The comparative study of early and late signs in progress at the Clinique Baudelocque should become quantitative rather than simply qualitative and so broaden still further the scope of this work, which is based on that of André Thomas. His study of the signs of disease remains fundamental for any deep understanding of the young infant, either normal or abnormal. Certain points must, however, be emphasized. In this work, we cannot make exact diagnoses on the basis of neurologic lesions; rather, we must emulate André Thomas' approach by studying the development of the neurologic deficit over a period of time. A study of the various lines of evolution which the child shows will allow an assessment of his handicaps and his permanent disabilities, as well as the adjustments he is able to make because of the plasticity of his growing brain.

SUPPLEMENTARY READINGS

Saint-Anne Dargassies, S. La maturation neurologique de prématurés. *Et. néo-natales,* 1955, 4, 71–123.

Dekaban, A. *Neurology of infancy.* Baltimore: Williams & Wilkins, 1959.

Humphrey, T. Some correlations between the appearance of human fetal reflexes and the development of the nervous system. In D. P. Purpura (Ed.), *Progress in brain research.* Vol. 4. *The developing brain.* New York: Elsevier, 1964.

McGraw, M. B. *The neuromuscular maturation of the human infant.* New York: Columbia Univer. Press, 1943.

Paine, R. S., *et al.* The evolution of postural reflexes in normal infants. *Neurology,* 1964, 14, 1036–1048.

Paine, R. S. The contribution of developmental neurology to child psychiatry. *J. Amer. Acad. Child Psychiat.,* 1965, 41, 353.

Chapter Five

preliminary observations
of the sleep-dream pattern
in neonates, infants,
children and adults*

HOWARD P. ROFFWARG, WILLIAM C. DEMENT,
and CHARLES FISHER

[Dreaming has always had a peculiarly strong fascination for man. It has been a central theme in saga, poetry, and song from the very beginning of recorded history. Its influence on individual personalities has extended across the whole spectrum of human emotions; from supreme bliss to abject terror. The functions of dreaming have been variously interpreted as being prophetic, wish fulfilling, sleep protecting, and spiritually renewing. The first significant progress toward a scientific understanding of dreaming was made by Freud who found a way to relate the content and symbols of dreaming to personality functioning during the waking state. The profound insights of this magnificent contribution should not be underestimated; however, scientists by their very nature always want to know more. After the publication of Freud's *The Interpretation of Dreams,* the next notable advance in methodology was the discovery that adult dreaming is accompanied by rapid eye movements (REM's) which can be electronically sensed and recorded. REM's, in conjunction with EEG's (electroencephalographic recordings or "brain waves"), show great promise for advancing our knowledge of the antecedents, concomitants, and consequents of dreaming. As suggested in the following developmental study by Dr. Roffwarg, of Columbia University, and Drs. Dement and Fisher, analysis of concurrently recorded REM's, EEG's, and body-movements may lead us to a better understanding of the maturation of the central nervous system. The authors' speculations about possible interpretations of their developmental findings suggest numerous hypotheses, e.g., the possibility that the pronounced reduction in REM time around 3–4 years of age may be related to the emergence of repression as an important defense mechanism.]

* From E. Harms (Ed.) Problems of sleep and dream in children. *Monographs on child Psychiatry, No. II.* New York: Pergamon Press, 1964. (With permission.)

Although much information has been accumulated in recent years pertaining to the psychophysiology of dreaming sleep, nearly all the studies have made exclusive use of young adult subjects. In this age group, it has been shown that dreaming occurs concurrently with discrete periods of rapid, conjugate, eye movements (Aserinsky & Kleitman, 1955a; Dement & Kleitman, 1957a). These eye movements bear an intimate relationship to the hallucinatory events of the dream that is functionally analogous to the relationship between the purposeful fixation shifts and scanning movements carried out in relation to the external visual field in the waking state (Dement & Kleitman, 1957a; Dement & Wolpert, 1958; Roffwarg, Dement, Muzio, & Fisher, 1962). Brain wave recordings indicate that the rapid eye movement (REM) periods are uniquely associated with the low voltage, non-spindling phase of a strikingly regular EEG sleep cycle (Dement & Kleitman, 1957b). Since the pattern and frequency of the individual REM's are more or less determined by the specific content of the dream and may vary from virtually none to many, depending upon what the dreamer is doing and at what he is looking, the actual presence of dreaming (its duration, onset and termination) can be most easily measured by the EEG. It is now felt that the simultaneous recording of these two variables, EEG and REM's, gives a highly reliable picture of the pattern of dreaming during a night of sleep.

It will be the purpose of this preliminary communication to report on the particular characteristics of the dream pattern in other age groups as determined by all-night EEG and REM recordings. Data have been accumulated by sampling small numbers of subjects at various intervals from birth to old age. There need be no apology for the preliminary nature of the study since the acquiring of comprehensive data for all age levels comparable to that available for young adults will be a tremendous undertaking requiring many years of effort. In our studies to date we have focused mainly on two questions: do REM periods associated with a characteristic EEG stage occur, and, what is the pattern of their occurrence throughout the night? It is obvious that as more subjects are studied in the future, some of the figures reported herein may require revision. However, it is not anticipated that the overall trend will be significantly affected.

It is possible to give a detailed description of the typical adult sleep cycle with great confidence owing to the many observations made by different groups of investigators including a recent analysis of several hundred recordings in our laboratory (Dement & Fisher, in preparation) among which there were 180 all-night records from 23 subjects between the ages of 20 and 30. It is against the yardstick of this description that we will measure the sleep cycle of other age groups.

The sleeping EEG patterns may be conveniently divided into 4 stages: *Stage 1*—a low voltage, relatively fast, non-spindling pattern. *Stage 2*— sleep spindles and "K" complexes with a low voltage background. *Stage 4* —predominancy of high voltage, slow activity in the ½ to 2 cycle per second range. *Stage 3*—intermediate between stage 2 and stage 4.

Upon falling asleep, the young adult passes through Stage 1 transiently without exhibiting REM's (refer to Fig. 3—Young Adult). Within 10–15 min. his sleep record assumes a regular, high voltage, slow appearance (Stage 4). After about 40 min., the motionless regularity of this sleep stage is broken by some gross body movement and a progression ensues in the sleep EEG to a lower voltage (Stage 2) pattern. After about 60–80 min. from the sleep onset, a brief period of Stage 1 EEG with REM's emerges. Following its termination, the EEG again progresses through Stage 2 to Stage 3 or 4. A second, longer, period of Stage 1 EEG with REM's appears at about 160 min after the sleep onset. Successive Stage 1-REM periods are generally separated by 60–80 min. intervals. Usually, 5 REM periods are seen in a typical night of sleep lasting 7½–8 hours. They show a trend toward successively longer durations with the last or next to the last period generally the longest. Their length may vary from a few minutes to more than an hour, but most frequently is between 10 and 30 min.

In addition to the Stage 1 EEG, REM's are associated with a more or less unique behavior of other variables. Heart rate and respiratory rate are elevated and irregular (Aserinsky & Kleitman, 1955a; Dement, in press; Kamiya, 1961). The incidence of gross body movement is lower during the REM period than during adjacent periods of sleep, and about the same as the overall nightly average. In other words, there are peaks of body movement activity preceding and following REM periods, but at other times, for example during Stage 4, there is almost no body movement (Dement & Kleitman, 1957b). Recent work, however, indicates that there is no diminution of either gross or fine body movement for Stage 1 as a whole when compared to Stage 2.

In many hundreds of nights of normal sleep recordings, we have not seen a single exception to the general picture described above. In addition, the *dream* (REM) *time per cent* (fraction of the total sleep time occupied by REM periods) is remarkably constant from night to night and the average figure for a series of several nights may be used to characterize an individual. In young adults, the dream time per cents are usually between 20 and 25. There is a definite tendency for the higher per cents to occur in those subjects nearer 20 years of age.

NEONATES (1–15 DAYS)

Aserinsky and Kleitman (1955b) observed a dual-phase motility cycle during sleep in this age group that had an average periodicity of 50–60 min. They reported that for about 20–25 min. of the cycle (the *quiescent* phase), the infant lies virtually motionless. During the remainder of the cycle (the *active* phase), the newborn manifests considerable fine muscle movement, gross limb movement, fluttering of the eyelids, and movement of the eyeballs. (The criteria of sleep at the time were closed eyelids and absence of crying.) These authors maintained that infants do not have bilaterally synchronous REM's as do adults, but repeated observations by us in nurseries at the

University of Chicago Lying In Hospital, and at Columbia-Presbyterian Hospital indicate that the eyeball deflections during sleep are indeed rapid, and have many of the same characteristics as the REM's of sleeping adults. They are observed to occur only during the active phase. Accordingly, there is a regular cyclic alternation of REM and non-REM periods, the former marked by muscular activity and the latter by almost motionless sleep punctuated by occasional gross body twitches resembling Moro reflexes. REM sleep accounts for from 40–60 per cent (average 50 per cent of each 50–60 minute sleep cycle).

The EEG patterns of the *active* and *quiescent* phases of sleep are distinct and characteristic even in the first day of life. The non-REM EEG contains a moderate number of high voltage slow waves and 13–15 cps rhythms resembling the sleep spindles of adult Stage 2 sleep. These forms are superimposed against a low amplitude background. The REM EEG consists of low voltage, relatively fast wave forms and is very similar to the waking EEG. It contains some 1–3 cps "sawtooth" activity in the EEG record in conjunction with the bursts of ocular activity. The REM EEG is usually devoid of high voltage and spindle-like activity, though the tracing of the very first REM period after sleep onset is generally a mixed non-REM and REM EEG pattern (see Fig. 1).

One major difference between the sleep of newborns and that of older children and adults is the way in which it commences. Newborns characteristically enter REM sleep directly from the waking state. This is not seen in adults (see above) except in narcolepsy (Rechtschaffen, Wolpert, Dement, Mitchell, and Fisher, 1963) or after prolonged REM sleep deprivation (Dement, 1964). Because of the similarity of the waking and REM EEG, a specific designation of sleep onset would not be possible were it not for the assistance provided by the measurement of EMG from the face and neck musculature. As in adults, there is a complete suppression of resting muscle tone in REM sleep. Accordingly the start of REM sleep is signalled by a sharp drop in the amplitude of resting muscle potentials.

Respiratory and heart rates show differences between the REM and non-REM states in newborns similar to those seen in older individuals. There is an overall increase in rate and an accentuation of variability in the two parameters as REM sleep succeeds non-REM intervals. In REM sleep, muscle contraction of one kind or another is almost continual. There are grimaces, smiles, sucking, frequent fine twitches of the extremities, intermittent gross athetoid excursions of the limbs and stretching of the torso. These movements usually begin 5 to 10 minutes in advance of the REM period, announcing the eventual flattening of the EEG tracing and the development of REM's. The sucking and large body movements are most frequent during the transition from non-REM to REM phases. Considerable body movement also heralds the onset of an REM period in adults but it tapers off soon after the period begins. In the neonate, muscle activity ebbs off towards the end of an REM period, only to increase again briefly with transition to a non-REM stage. Not yet observable when the new-

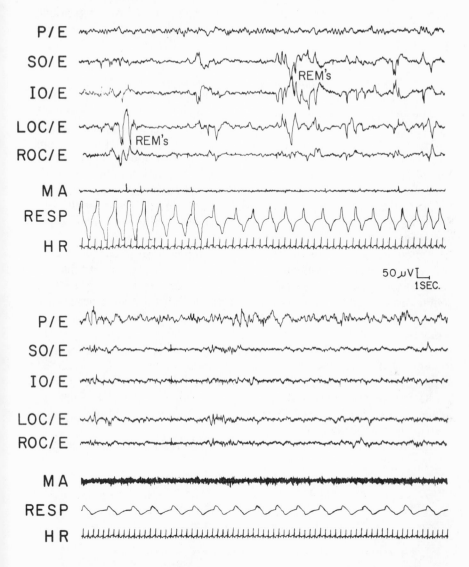

Figure 1—Recordings of 30-second intervals from the two stages of sleep in a newborn.

Top, REM sleep; bottom, NREM sleep. EEG lead: *P/E,* parietal referred to both ears. Eye-movement leads: (vertical) *SO/E,* supraorbital ridge to ears; *IO/E,* infraorbital ridge to ears; (horizontal) *LOC/E,* left outer canthus to ears; *ROC/E,* right outer canthus to ears; *MA,* resting muscle activity (recorded submentally); *RESP,* respirations; *HR,* pulse. The electroencephalogram is low-voltage and fast in REM sleep and higher-voltage, with frequent 1- to 2-cycle-per-second waves, in NREM sleep. There are short trains of saw-tooth waves in upper EEG tracing just preceding sharp vertical and horizontal REM's. Note the absence of muscle activity, the rapid respiratory rate, and the changing respiratory amplitude in REM stage.

born is awake, facial contractions are manifested in REM sleep which would, in adults, be interpreted as expressive of delicate affective shades.

INFANTS (14 WEEKS–2 YEARS)

Very young infants continue to show a sleep pattern similar to that of neonates. Accordingly, the alternation of REM (*active*) and non-REM (*quiescent*) periods begins as soon as sleep supervenes. The cycles, for the most part, remain uniform in duration with considerable muscular activity during the REM periods. A small group of infants who ranged in age from 14–20 weeks showed an REM Stage 1 time that occupied about 40 per cent of the total sleep time. In using the phrase, "Stage 1," we do not mean to imply that the Stage 1 tracings in children and adults are similar in every detail. Rather, the EEG tracings during REM periods are distinctly different from other phases of sleep, and, allowing for age differences, are analogous in all age groups. In infants, as in adults, the lower voltages and faster frequencies accompany REM's while at other times sleep spindles are very prominent along with an increase in the overall amplitude and an appearance of slower frequencies. Figure 2 is an illustration of a single continuous sleep period in a 20-week-old infant. Note the regular occurrence of REM periods accompanied by the Stage 6 tracings. We have not found it practical to subdivide the non-REM EEG at this age. Sleep spindles are prominent throughout, and although there are distinguishable differences in terms of the frequency and amplitude, these are not nearly so marked as in older children and adults. Body movement is very prominent during the REM periods and hence the phrase, "active phase," may still be applied to this portion of the sleep cycle. However, the body movement is not nearly as frequent as in the neonate.

During the latter half of the first year of life, the REM periods average

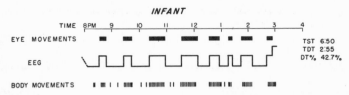

Figure 2—Graph of an all night sleep record—infant, age 20 weeks.

TST—Total sleep time; TDT—total REM time; DT%—per cent of TST spent in REM sleep. The elevated portions of the EEG graph represent a moderately low voltage, fast wave tracing (Stage 1 sleep); the lower portions denote the presence of sleep spindles and higher voltage, slow waves (Stages 2–4). Note that bursts of rapid eye movements (REM's) appear during each Stage 1 period and extend throughout its entire duration. Note, too, the preponderance of body movement during REM Stage 1 periods. Of importance, is the emergence of the REM phase soon after sleep onset, and its staccato-like re-emergence all during the night's sleep. This same pattern is true of younger infants as well, except that in earlier infancy the DT% is higher.

about 30 per cent of the total sleep time. There is also less muscle movement accompanying REM periods. By this age, of course, the infant is enjoying longer periods of wakefulness and augmented muscular activity during the waking portions of his day.

It is of interest at this point to mention the experimental finding, in adult humans and cats, of a distinct diminution in general muscular tone during REM sleep (Berger, 1961; Dement; in press; M. Jouvet, 1961; M. Jouvet, Dechaume, & Michel, 1960). Many small isolated muscle contractions do occur during REM sleep in adults (Dement & Kleitman, 1957b; Wolpert, 1960; Antrobus, 1962). It would be interesting to know whether or not the resting muscle tone of infants is reduced as it is in adults during REM periods. But muscle tone notwithstanding, there is, in infancy, a higher frequency of both small and large body movement associated with REM's. Jouvet has reported similar findings in newborn kittens (D. Jouvet, Valatx, & M. Jouvet, 1961).

Three infants, ages 9, 16, and 24 months, were studied. The youngest took 2 naps a day. The latter two took only 1 daytime nap and usually slept through the entire night. They still tended, however, to show Stage 1-REM periods of approximately uniform length throughout the night. Four EEG stages could be distinguished. The relative incidence of the various stages was about the same in any portion of the night.

CHILDREN (2–5 YEARS)

As the child matures and the amount of time spent awake increases, a gradual change is observed in the uniformity of duration of the REM periods. The first REM period of the night may be quite short while succeeding periods tend to become longer toward morning. There is also a slight lengthening of the overall cycle (from the beginning of one REM period to the beginning of the next). The REM per cent averages about 30. Muscular movement during Stage 1 is still considerable, but much less frequent than in younger infants. Awakenings in 3- to 4-year-old children during REM periods elicited clear narratives of visual dreams although the overall incidence of recall was lower than found in adults. No attempt has been made to interrogate younger subjects.

There seems to be one important difference between the sleep pattern of 4- to 5-year-olds in contrast to 2- to 3-year-olds. The latter still show their first REM period within one hour after sleep onset (as in Fig. 2), but the first REM period often does not appear until about *three* hours after sleep onset in the older children (Fig. 3—Children). After about 60–90 min. of sleep have elapsed, there is a "lightening" of their EEG tracing, just as there is in adults, who at this point have the emergence of their first Stage1-REM period (Fig. 3—Adult). But in the children the EEG does not go beyond Stage 2. Thus, in the older children the first period is usually "missed" and the tracing again slows in frequency and increases in voltage without REM's having appeared. It is only after another 60–90 minutes,

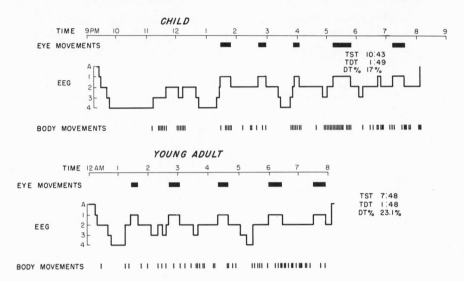

Figure 3—Graphs of all night sleep records of a child, age 5 years, and a young adult, age 27 years.

TST—Total sleep time; TDT—Total REM time; DT%—per cent of TST spent in REM sleep; A—awake; 1, 2, 3, 4—EEG stages of sleep (1—low voltage, fast, non-spindling record; 2—presence of spindles and K complexes; 3 and 4—spindles plus high voltage slow waves). Note the long non-REM period before the first appearance of REM-Stage 1 in the child. Where the sleep level turns up (at 11:30), a REM period would be seen in adults. This child has probably missed 2 REM periods whereas only 1 is missed usually. Of importance, is the diurnal pattern of the adult, specifically the tendency of the REM periods to progressively increase in length toward morning. The lack of this uniform diurnal progression in the child is more similar to the infant than to the adult. When the first REM periods are no longer missed in the child, the diurnal pattern in REM duration emerges. As the graphs indicate, gross body movements during Stage 1 tend to occur less with advancing age. Although the TDT's are the same, DT% is less in the child because of the extended period of nightly sleep.

when the tracing again "lightens," that the first REM period actually appears. Sometimes, two such "misses" occur before the onset of the first Stage 1-REM period.

The reason for this delay is probably in some way related to the fact that these children have reached the stage of a highly developed waking-sleeping diurnal pattern. They rarely nap during the day. Moreover, theirs is a very active age when full mobility has been achieved and curiosity is high. It is reasonable to suppose that in the course of the day, they endure considerable muscular fatigue which dramatically affects their nocturnal sleep pattern. It is noteworthy that this same age group spends as much as 2 hours in Stage 4 sleep immediately following the sleep onset, as compared to the 45–60 minutes seen in adults. Also, the bulk of the Stage 4 sleep in these children is seen in the first half of the night. Thus, extreme fatigue may play a role in determining the pattern of occurrence of Stage 4 sleep and may also, in some way, antagonize the physiological mechanisms responsible for REM sleep. Children who have just assumed a diurnal waking pattern may be particularly sensitive to these effects of fatigue. (Adults, too, often show more Stage 4 and a delayed or "missed" first REM period when they are greatly fatigued or when sleep deprived.) Largely because of this factor, one also sees at about 3 years of age the commencement of a striking reduction in REM per cent from 30 or above to around 20 or below.

Accordingly, the gradual changes in the sleep pattern with age, the increase in Stage 4 time and its preponderance early in the night, the delay in the appearance of the first REM period, and the progressive increment in length of the REM periods, perhaps as sleep overcomes the fatigue deficit in the latter part of the night, all apparently bear a close relationship to the augmenting periods of wakefulness during the day. This progression continues until about 3–4½ when daytime napping has terminated. By this age distinct differences between early and late portions of the night have emerged. It is undoubtedly representative of the well established overall diurnal rhythm in sleep and wakefulness described by Kleitman (1939). The dream (REM) periods, thus, occur in the general setting of sleep and are related in their time of appearance and duration to the overall sleep behavior of the developing organism.

OLDER CHILDREN (5–13 YEARS)

Seven subjects were studied in this age group. Each was studied for 2 or 3 consecutive nights. The first REM period did not appear until 2–3 hours of sleep had elapsed in 15 of 17 nights. As a rule, in this group REM periods became longer as the night progressed. However, in some cases, after the prolonged initial non-REM sleep, the REM periods tended to be of similar duration and quite regularly spaced. Thus, there seems to be some evidence of a transition stage in this age group between (a) the infant pattern of regularly spaced REM periods of equal length commencing within less than 1 hour after the sleep onset (Fig. 2), and (b) the pattern seen in young adolescents of sequentially lengthening REM periods following an extended non-REM sleep.

In this group, the REM per cent is about half that of infants. Although there is substantial night-to-night and subject-to-subject variability, the group as a whole averages 18.5 per cent of the sleep time occupied by REM periods. This represents a considerable diminution in the total number of minutes spent in the REM phase.

Body movements during Stage 1 in the 5- to 13-year-old group, though less than in younger children, are generally more frequent than in the post-puberty population and certainly more than in adults. The child's vulnerability to the fatigue accruing from waking activity may be reflected in the difference between the Stage 4 time of 110–120 min. in the 4½- to 7-year-old children and 75–80 minutes in the 11- to 14-year group.

In the few instances when vocalization was noted in our child subjects, it occurred in association with non-REM sleep. This has also been found to be the general pattern in adults (Rechtschaffen, 1964). Similarly, enuresis occurs usually during non-REM sleep in children (Pierce, Whitman, Maas, & Gay, 1961).

ADOLESCENTS (14–18 YEARS)

The post-puberty subjects begin to show an almost adult sleep-dream pattern, but certain elements of the earlier patterns may be observed at times. The amount of body movement in late adolescence assumes the adult levels but may remain as high as in younger children. REM periods are now clearly longer in length the later in the night they occur. Stage 4 time is around 45–60 min., as in adults. However, the younger adolescents still frequently "miss" the first REM period, thus belatedly manifesting the sensitivity to fatigue characteristic of younger children. Of 21 nights of adolescent sleep studied, there was a delayed first REM period in 8.

This age group, like the 5- to 13-year-olds, showed an average REM time per cent of approximately 18.5. However, values as low as 14 per cent and as high as 25 per cent were seen on individual nights.

It is of interest that the post-puberty group showed the same average REM time per cent as the pre-puberty group. However, it should be noted that the REM time per cent is a function of both REM time and total sleep time. Thus, although the post-puberty group showed no difference in REM time per cent, they actually dreamed 17 min. less per night on the average which was accounted for by the fact that they averaged about 8 hr. of sleep per night as compared with about 10 hr. in the pre-puberty group. Our expectation that there would be an increase in the per cent of dreaming at puberty, along with the general upsurge in sexual drive at this time, was not borne out.

YOUNG ADULTS (18–30 YEARS)

This group averages about 22 per cent REM time and shows a characteristic, well documented pattern which has already been described in detail. There seems to be a significant rise in REM per cent from age eighteen to the early twenties. This is a result of both a lengthening of REM periods and the cessation of the tendency seen in younger individuals to "miss" the first period.

MIDDLE TO OLD AGE (50–70 YEARS)

Only 5 subjects in this age range have been observed to date. They show the typical adult pattern with a few differences. For example, total sleep time is lower but so is total REM time. Consequently, the REM time per cent of 13–18 represents an appreciable lessening of total REM time in comparison to younger adults. This is true even if REM per cent is comparable to young adult values.

The EEG pattern of high voltage, slow waves (Stage 4) is less prominent. The periods of Stage 4 are shorter and contain a considerable admixture of faster frequencies. It is difficult to know whether this represents an alteration in CNS function for this age group, or whether the diminution of Stage 4 is because of reduced exertion and exercise and less muscle fatigue. The REM periods are more nearly equal in duration with less prominence of the characteristic adult diurnal pattern of progressively lengthening periods.

DISCUSSION

After pointing out that REM's during sleep are known to be intimately associated with dreaming in adults, we have reported that discrete periods of REM's associated with a characteristic EEG pattern were seen without exception in all subjects from birth to 70 years. Does this mean that dreaming is present at birth? It depends, of course, on what one means by dreaming. There is no way of disproving the possibility that the REM period, even on day one, may be a time during which the neonate re-experiences in some rudimentary form what little experience he has accumulated. The question of whether memory traces are established at such an early age and whether they are highly transient or permanent is not accessible to investigation. It is known, however, that learning of the conditioned response variety is found at birth and even before (Munn, 1946).

If by dreaming is meant the occurrence of hallucinatory visual imagery which is correlated with the specific spatial patterns of the REM's, as in adults, then the possibility of dreaming in the newborn infant must be negated. Even if the immaturity of the visual cortex and oculomotor system were ignored, it would be necessary to invoke some factor such as inherited racial memories in order to postulate that REM patterns represent hallucinated imagery in newborns. However, the presence of REM's in neonates is not entirely incongruous. They seem to be an attribute of a unique physiological sleep state which later becomes associated with patterned dreaming. M. Jouvet (1961) has shown that REM's in sleeping cats depend on the integrity of a center in the pontine reticular formation. The presence of REM's during sleep has also been reported by this group in decorticate cats as well as in a decorticate human (M. Jouvet, Dechaume, & Michel, 1960). Hence, REM periods are dependent for their periodic manifestation neither upon the availability of the cerebral cortex nor upon the presence of visual imagery in dreams.

It is likely that what goes on in the infant's mind during the REM period of sleep is fairly closely related to what goes on in his mind while awake, about which, of course, nothing is known. However, what is known about the physiological behavior of the brain during the REM phase of sleep suggests that it is in many ways behaving as if the individual were awake (Dement & Fisher, in preparation). Thus, it is possible that as perception and memory functions develop in the growing infant, dreaming develops in a parallel fashion and takes place as a more or less obligatory concomitant of the quasi-awake neurophysiology of the REM period. Probably sometime during or after vision has been gained by the infant, a correspondence develops between the spatial pattern of the REM's and the visual imagery of the dream. This correlation is probably effected by the cortex. The occurrence of REM's in newborns, therefore, may be analogous to their presence in decorticates. That is, in both instances, the phenomenon of REM periods is most likely a *pure* brainstem function. Prior to the acquisition of visual perception and visual memory, it seems possible that dreaming may be expressed in other modalities (olfactory, gustatory, tactile, kinesthetic, etc.). Those who prefer to reserve judgment as to whether infants dream at a very early age or even up until the time that they are able to give a verbal report, may at least accept the fact that infants spend a considerable amount of time in the physiological stage of sleep during which dreams are known to occur in adults.

The basic sleep pattern, and the amount of time spent in the physiological phase of sleep during which dreams occur, changes with maturation. REM periods occupy about 50 per cent of the relative cycle of activity and quiescence in newborns, only the active phase being associated with the presence of REM's. Older infants show a similar sleep pattern configuration, but the REM periods comprise a smaller proportion of the cycle. Newborn kittens, too, have a much higher proportion of REM sleep than do older kittens (Jouvet, Valatx, & Jouvet, 1961). With inchoate diurnal activity and longer periods of wakefulness, the quantity of Stage 1-REM sleep diminishes sharply and REM periods become associated with progressive inhibition of gross muscle activity as compared to the extreme muscular activity in the neonatal and early infancy period. In addition, the REM period emergence begins after an extended non-REM sleep onset of up to 3 hours and the REM periods begin to exhibit a distinct lengthening as the night progresses.

Children between the ages 5 and 18 show a lower REM time per cent than adults, but their actual average nightly REM time still exceeds adult levels because they sleep much longer. From the average of 18.5 per cent REM time in adolescence, there appears to be an increase in the proportion at the beginning of the third decade to around 25 per cent and from this point on, it gradually diminishes to the range of 13–18 per cent in old age.

It is assumed that these changes are part of the normal growth of the human organism, the development of a diurnal cycle and changes in level of daily activity playing a major role. It is also possible that basic personality development is a factor. For example, the rather sharp reduction in REM time around 3–4 years of age may be related to the emergence of repression as an important defense mechanism. Although there is as yet no evidence to support this speculation in children, preliminary work with adults points in the direction of a relationship between characteristic defense type and the proportion of sleep time in which dreaming occurs. It was found that subjects who characteristically rely on repression and denial to bind anxiety show significantly less (though the differences are small) dream (REM) time per cent than those who, for instance, utilize fantasy and intellectualization (Antrobus, 1962; Orlinsky, 1962). It has been shown in adults that other factors may modify an individual's basic sleep-dream pattern at least transiently, including drugs (Rechtschaffen, 1962), anxiety (Dement & Fisher, in preparation), hypnotic suggestion (Stoyva, unpublished), dream deprivation (Dement, 1960), and acute psychosis (Fisher & Dement, 1961).

Evidence now being gathered indicates that most adult subjects show a significant reduction in dream (REM) time per cent during their first night in the laboratory in comparison with their average on subsequent nights (Dement & Fisher, in preparation). It is possible that this "first night effect" may have influenced the dream-sleep pattern of the children in our study who were old enough to appreciate a change in their usual environment. However, an attempt was made to make the children comfortable by familiarizing them thoroughly with the experimenters. The younger subjects had their parents with them. It is not probable that this factor significantly altered the general findings concerning the sleep-dream pattern in these age groups, but it should be nevertheless considered.

The REM period constitutes a phase of sleep when considerable somatic and CNS activity occurs. It may be that in infants, whose waking life is limited in time and scope and offers little occasion for activity, the REM period allows for a substantial discharge of activity during sleep. Perhaps as waking activity increases, the need for its discharge during sleep decreases. Thus the REM periods may become shorter and associated with less muscular activity at about the time that a diurnal waking-sleeping pattern is being established.

It may be speculated that the prime function of REM sleep is executed during fetal and early postnatal development. The substantial increments in neuronal activity and vascular flow in the brain during REM sleep (which is abundant at this time) may be essential for normal growth of central nervous tissue (Roffwarg, Muzio, & Dement, in press). Hence, the REM mechanism may be particularly crucial during early ontogenesis when initially the uterine sac and later long periods of sleep serve to screen out a substantial portion of environmental stimuli. REM sleep may constitute a built-in stimulating system serving to "prepare" the CNS for the later influx of sensory input from the external world.

SUMMARY

REM periods are present during sleep from birth to old age. They appear at regular intervals during the night and account for a major share of the total sleep time in neonates (50 per cent) and young infants (40 per cent). Some time around the third or fourth year there is a fairly distinct change in the sleep pattern in which the REM per cent drops to 20 or below, and a great discrepancy between the early and late portions of the night develops. Early in the night, there is a preponderance of Stage 4 sleep while the REM periods are delayed and shortened.

Although the total nightly sleep time gradually diminishes, the per cent of REM time remains about the same (18.5) until after 18 years of age when it increases to about 25 per cent and then slowly falls off to old age.

There can be no certainty as to whether infants have actual sensory hallucinations ("dreams") during REM sleep. But there is no doubt that they exhibit from birth the characteristic sleep stage during which dreaming is experienced by older individuals.

SUPPLEMENTARY READINGS

Bartoshuk, A. K., & Tennant, J. M. Human neonatal EEG correlates of sleep-wakefulness and neural maturation. *J. Psychiatr. Res.*, 1964, 2, 73–83.

Luce, G. G. *Current research on sleep and dreams*. Wash. D.C.: National Institute of Mental Health, 1965. Public Health Service publication no. 1389.

Metcalf, D. R. EEG development in infancy. *Current research on sleep and dreams*. Wash. D.C.: National Institute of Mental Health, 1965. Public Health Service publication no. 1389.

Parmelee, A., Akiyama, Y., Wenner, W., & Flescher, I. Activated sleep in premature infants. Paper read at Assoc. for Psychophysiol. Study Sleep, Palo Alto, Calif., 1964.

Samson-Dollfus, D., Forthomme, J., & Capron, E. EEG of the human infant during sleep and wakefulness during the first year of life; normal patterns and their maturational changes; abnormal patterns and their prognostic significance. In P. Kellaway & I. Petersen (Eds.), *Neurological and EEG correlative studies in infancy*. New York: Grune & Stratton, 1964.

Trillin, C. A reporter at large: A third state of existence. *The New Yorker*, Sept. 18, 1965, 58–125.

arousal level in neonates
and older infants
under continuous auditory
stimulation*

YVONNE BRACKBILL, GAIL ADAMS,
DAVID H. CROWELL, and M. LIBBIE GRAY

[An infant's typical response to the onset of stimulation or to change in the quality or intensity of stimulation is one of increased level of arousal. Depending on the intensity of stimulation, this response may be shown as an orienting reflex—Pavlov sometimes called this the what-is-it? reaction—or as a full-blown startle reflex. (The articles by Bronshtein and Petrova, p. 163, and by Hunt *et al.*, p. 134, describe the orienting and startle reflexes more fully.)

Nevertheless, if the stimulation is continued without changing its intensity level the infant's response to it changes drastically, for *continuous* stimulation has a marked quieting effect on the child's behavior. For example, babies cry more and sleep less in a quiet environment than they do in a noisy environment, e.g., when a radio is played nearby. This quieting can be seen both in terms of behavioral changes, e.g., less crying, and physiological changes, e.g., lower and more regular heart rate. Furthermore, within the limits studied to date, the noisier the environment the greater the quieting effect. Perhaps the most interesting aspect of this phenomenon is that it is not limited to any one sensory modality: infants are also quieter in the light than in the dark, when they are rocked rather than when they are lying still, when they are clothed rather than unclothed.

In the following report Dr. Brackbill and her colleagues, at the University of Denver and the University of Hawaii, inquire whether this quieting phenomenon is differentially affected by the quality or type of auditory stimulation. Their results are consistent with the earlier findings of Irwin and his associates in indicating that quieting is principally a function of intensity rather than quality of stimulation.]

* From Y. Brackbill, G. Adams, D. H. Crowell, & M. L. Gray. Arousal level in neonates and preschool children under continuous auditory stimulation. *J. exp. child Psychol.*, 1966, 4, No. 2, 178–188. (With permission.)

Quite a few years ago, Warner (1883, 1887), in trying out his new invention for the objective measurement of movement in man, reported that infants move about less when they are "listening" to something. Somewhat later, in 1913, Canestrini noted that infants' pulse and respiration rates become more regular when they hear continuously presented sounds that they "enjoy" (Canestrini, 1913).

In 1934, the first systematic study of the effects of continuously presented sound on infant behavior was carried out by Weiss, under the direction of Irwin. This was part of a series of studies carried out by Irwin and his students that was concerned with the quieting effect on neonates of relatively high intensities of stimulation from various sensory modalities (Irwin, 1941; Irwin & Weiss, 1934a, 1934b, 1934c; Redfield, 1937, 1939; & Weiss, 1934). As stimuli Weiss used pure tones generated by an oscillator. In an own-control design, she measured gross motor activity in neonates under a 50 db tone of 5 minutes' duration and under a 75 db tone of 5 minutes' duration. Either tone produced a quieter infant than did a corresponding period of silence, and the louder tone had a significantly greater pacifying effect than the softer one. These results have been confirmed without substantial extension by Bartoshuk (1962b), Stubbs (1934), and Birns, Blank, Bridger, and Escalona (1965).

Recently, Salk (1960, 1961, 1962) presented a paired heartbeat at 72 beats per minute and at 85 db to 102 newborn infants in a newborn nursery continuously for four days. These Ss were compared to 112 Ss in a control group on weight gain, amount of crying, and food intake. Seventy per cent of the experimental group had gained weight by the end of the four-day period, as compared with thirty-three per cent of the control group, although food intake for the two groups did not differ. There was approximately 60 per cent more crying in the nursery during the no sound condition than during the heartbeat condition.

Since Irwin, Weiss and others had already demonstrated that level of activity in infants decreases under continuous auditory stimulation, Salk's results are hardly surprising, and it seems unnecessary to postulate, as he does, that the infant's response is due to intrauterine imprinting. However, Salk also presents data from an additional experiment with 26 two-year-old institutionalized infants in which three types of sound and a no sound control were compared for their relative effectiveness in putting the children to sleep at bedtime. The three types of sound used were those of a normal heart beating at 72 beats per minute, a metronome ticking at 72 beats per minute, and lullabies. In this case the results he reports are quite surprising: an average of 23 minutes was required for children to fall asleep when the heartbeat tape was being played, but twice that many minutes under any of the other conditions. Furthermore, there was no difference between the no sound condition and either the lullaby or metronome condition.

A more recent study (Tulloch, Brown, Jacobs, Prugh, & Greene, 1964) repeated the essential features of Salk's experiment with neonates with but one exception: the intensity level of heartbeat was only 45 db. Their failure to replicate Salk's results is probably attributable to the choice of a stimulus intensity level that is not clearly audible to neonates.

As noted earlier, several studies have shown that level of activity in infants is affected by stimulus intensity. We also know it to be affected by such parameters as stimulus complexity. and the more gross temporal characteristics of stimulation (Spears, 1964), e.g., stimuli of brief duration are differently responded to than are intermittent or continuous stimuli. Nevertheless, no one has previously considered that level of arousal, particularly in a neonate, might also be a function of the more subtle aspects of stimulus quality, e.g., the difference between 72 heartbeats and 72 metronome beats per minute. The purpose of the present study was to see whether the empirical data Salk reported were replicable.

METHOD

E X P E R I M E N T   I

Subjects. The Ss were 41 normal infants with a mean age of 34 months (S.D. = 3.89) who attended one of four Honolulu nursery schools run by a single administration. In all cases, the children attended school for a full day, five days a week. Twenty-four of the 41 Ss formed an own-control nucleus within the total group, i.e., their attendance at nursery school was regular enough throughout the five weeks of experimentation so that at least one day's data were obtained from them under every experimental condition.

Design and procedure. The Latin square design of the experiment is shown in Table 1. The stimulus conditions consisted of one-hour presentations at nap time. The dependent variable was the number of minutes until each infant fell asleep.

Table 1—Sequence of Stimulus Presentation for Four Nursery Schools Used in Exp. I

Nursery school	Preliminary equalization period (1 week)	First	EXPERIMENTAL WEEKS Second	Third	Fourth
1	No sound	Heartbeat	No sound	Metronome	Lullaby
2	No sound	No sound	Metronome	Lullaby	Heartbeat
3	No sound	Metronome	Lullaby	Heartbeat	No sound
4	No sound	Lullaby	Heartbeat	No sound	Metronome

Experimental sessions were held on Mondays, Wednesdays, Thursdays, and Fridays. Each experimental session lasted for one hour, beginning immediately after lunch when all children had been bedded down for a nap. The children's cots were arranged in same-age clusters, and a tape recorder was placed in the center of the cot area. As soon as the last child lay down, the tape recorder was turned on, and the first observation was made. Once every minute for one hour each S was judged to be awake, asleep, or in an indeterminate state if sleep or wakefulness could not be determined. The infant was judged to be awake when his eyes were open, and to be asleep when his eyes were shut and he showed no voluntary muscular movement. Five judges showed an interjudge agreement of 97% when this rating procedure was tested in pilot work. Because the four nursery schools reported differences in the extent to which they ordinarily used recorded lullabies at nap time, a preliminary equalization period of one week of a no sound condition preceded actual experimental work. At the beginning of each week of experimentation, a new auditory stimulus was presented, and this same stimulus condition continued to be presented on all four experimental days of that week. The stimulus conditions were (1) no sound, (2) paired heartbeats at 72 beats per minute, (3) the beating of a metronome at 72 beats per minute, and (4) unfamiliar lullabies sung in a foreign language. The last three of these were recorded on tape and played at approximately 20 db above ambient noise level, as measured by a db meter. Ambient noise level varied among schools and also within schools from the beginning to the end of each session.

EXPERIMENT II

Subjects. The Ss were 24 full term, normal neonates born at one of two Honolulu hospitals. Their average age was 48 hours. Fourteen Ss were females, and 10, males; no male infant was run within 24 hours of circumcision. Subjects were run approximately 1½ hours after feeding.

Design and procedure. The design of Exp. II is shown in Table 2. The stimulus conditions consisted of four consecutive, 15-minute presentations of the auditory stimuli. The dependent variables were amount of crying, general motor activity, heart rate, regularity of heart rate, and regularity of respiration.

Experimental sessions were held in private laboratories in the two participating hospitals. For one laboratory the average room temperature was 83° F. and the relative humidity, 50%; for the other laboratory, the same

Table 2—Sequences of Stimulus Presentation Used in Exp. II. No Sound Appears in Each Position Twice; Position Within Sequence Was Randomly Determined for the Remaining Stimulus Conditions. N = 3/sequence

Sequence of stimulus presentation	POSITION WITHIN SEQUENCE			
	First 15 min.	Second 15 min.	Third 15 min.	Fourth 15 min.
Tape #1	No sound	Heartbeat	Metronome	Lullaby
Tape #2	No sound	Lullaby	Metronome	Heartbeat
Tape #3	Heartbeat	No sound	Metronome	Lullaby
Tape #4	Heartbeat	No sound	Lullaby	Metronome
Tape #5	Lullaby	Heartbeat	No sound	Metronome
Tape #6	Heartbeat	Metronome	No sound	Lullaby
Tape #7	Metronome	Lullaby	Heartbeat	No sound
Tape #8	Heartbeat	Metronome	Lullaby	No sound

readings averaged 76° F. and 62%. The illumination was 2.1 ft.−c. The infant was brought to the laboratory 1½ hours after his last feeding; with few exceptions, this was approximately 3:30 P.M. The child's arms were swaddled; the lower part of his body was not swaddled but was covered with a lightweight blanket.

The infant's heart rate, respiration, and gross motor activity were simultaneously recorded on either a Grass Model 5-D Polygraph or an Offner Type R Dynograph, with paper speed of 5 mm per sec. Heart rate was recorded by means of two precordial EKG electrodes attached 0.5 inch above the xiphoid process and 0.5 inch below the manubrium. A ground electrode was attached to the lateral surface of the left calf. Respiration was measured with a probe thermistor (Yellow Springs Instrument Co., Model 421F) taped below the left nostril. Gross motor activity was transmitted by a stabilimeter designed by Crowell, Yasaka, and Crowell (1964). An observer recorded amount of crying in seconds. Prior to actual experimental work, three observers had shown 99% agreement in recording this measure.

The stimulus conditions, the sequences of which are shown in Table 2, were presented by tape recorder; loudness was 85 db at the source (approximately five feet from the infant).

The differences in methodology between Salk's study and this one stemmed from the fact that Salk ran his Ss as a group, while ours was an individual procedure. Salk played a recorded heartbeat continuously, day and night, within the hospital nursery he used. Such group experimentation limits the number of measures available and in fact Salk used only three: amount of crying, food intake, and weight change. The present investigators were not able to run all infants as a group; at one hospital the nursery was not soundproofed sufficiently to contain a sound played continuously at 85 db, and at the other hospital the use of a lying-in arrangement meant that infants remained in the nursery for only 24 hours after birth. Running Ss on an individual basis for a brief period of time meant that although it was not possible to use weight change as a measure, it was possible to use such physiological measures as respiration and heart rate.

RESULTS AND DISCUSSION

Analysis of the data from both experiments involved three statistical tests for each dependent variable. The tests and the rationale for their use are as follows: (1) A *t*-test of the mean differences between the level of any variable obtained under the heartbeat condition vs. the average level for that variable found under the three other experimental conditions combined. This sort of test is the only fair one from Salk's point of view, i.e., on the basis of the data he has reported, he would predict a significant mean difference in arousal level as a function of heartbeat vs. any other experimental condition, but no difference among the other three experimental conditions. (2) A *t*-test of the mean differences between the level of any variable obtained under the no sound condition vs. the average level for that variable found under the other three experimental conditions combined. This test is the only fair one from Irwin's point of view, i.e., on the basis of the data he and his students reported, he would predict a significant mean difference in arousal level as a function of no sound vs. any sound, but no difference in arousal among three continuous sounds of the same intensity. (3) Analysis of variance of the means obtained under the four experimental conditions for any variable. From neither Salk's nor Irwin's points of view is this a particularly appropriate test. On the other hand, it is not statistically inappropriate, and was therefore used for the sake of readers who might feel disinclined toward the other two statistical tests.

In *Exp. I,* the dependent measure was simply the number of minutes taken for S to fall asleep under each of the four experimental conditions. For the 24 infants for whom data were obtained under every condition at the four cooperating nursery schools, the mean number of minutes awake was 20.04 under the no sound condition, 17.96 under the lullaby condition, 17.95 under the metronome condition, and 14.64 under the heartbeat condition. (There was not, by the way, any sequence by condition effect for the four schools combined.) There is a significant mean difference in time taken to fall asleep under the no sound condition vs. the average time for all sound conditions ($t = 2.09$, $df = 23$, $P = 0.05$). There is no difference in time to fall asleep when the heartbeat condition is compared to all others ($t = 1.27$). The analysis of variance was not significant ($F = 1.44$, $df = 3,69$). Although the authors have not chosen to use one-tailed tests, it should be noted that one-tailed tests would be altogether appropriate for all t tests reported in this article.

For *Exp. II,* the 24 hour-long polygraph records were divided into 30-sec periods. All data contained within the odd-numbered periods were tabulated by two people working independently.

The first behavioral measure in Exp. II was the total number of seconds during which Ss cried under each of the four experimental conditions. The rate per minute for this measure for all Ss is shown in Table 3. The data on crying for the group as a whole contained an excessive number of zero scores, since 10 Ss did not cry at all under any condition. Therefore, t tests were carried out on the scores of those 14 Ss who cried under at least one condition. (There was no correlation between age and disposition to cry.) The mean crying scores under all four conditions for these Ss are also shown in Table 3. Amount of crying under the no sound condition is significantly greater than it is during auditory stimulation, but for this measure, as for all the other measures, there is no difference as a function of the heartbeat condition vs. all other conditions (Table 4).

The second behavioral measure in Exp. II was the number of seconds during which the infant's motor activity was sufficient to cause a 3-mm deflection of the polygraph pen. Motor activity is greater under a no sound condition, but not significantly so.

Table 3—Exp. II: Rate Per Minute Scores on Four Measures Taken Under Four Conditions

Measure	No sound	EXPERIMENTAL CONDITION Lullaby	Metronome	Heartbeat
Crying rate for all Ss. N = 24	6.43	4.41	4.50	3.16
Crying rate for those Ss who cried at least once during experimental hour. N = 14	11.02	7.56	7.71	5.42
General motor activity: Oscillation rate. N = 24	8.65	6.24	6.89	6.46
Heart rate. N = 24	131.50	126.08	124.53	124.41

The first physiological measure for Exp. II was heart rate, in beats per minute, under the four experimental conditions. The second physiological measure was regularity or stability of heart rate. For this, the number of heartbeats in 45 ten-second periods was tabulated, and degree of regularity defined as the dispersal of these 45 frequencies about their mean. As indicated in Tables 3 and 4, heart rate was significantly higher and less regular in the absence of sound.

The third physiological measure was regularity of respiration. The number of inspirations per 10-sec period was tabulated by counting as an inspiration any pen deflection of 2 mm or more in the appropriate direction. Again, there were 45 such 10-sec periods of data collected under each condition, and regularity was defined as the dispersal of these 45 frequencies about their mean. Tables 3 and 4 show that respiration was more variable in the absence of sound than during sound stimulation.

None of the analyses of variance proved to be significant. As discussed earlier, it was not to be expected that any should be significant. Finally, there was no correlation between any of the dependent variables and Ss' age, sex, or hospital of birth.

Table 4—Exp. II: Results of Statistical Analyses

Measure	RESULTS OF t TESTS No sound condition vs. average of all sound conditions: "Irwin's test"	Heartbeat condition vs. average of all other conditions: "Salk's test"	Results of simple analysis of variance
Crying	13.57, $df = 13$, P < .001*	1.02, NS**	.56, $df = 3, 92$, NS
General motor activity	1.33, $df = 23$, NS*	.63, NS	.38, $df = 3, 92$, NS
Heart rate	2.70, $df = 23$, P < .02*	1.43, NS	.98, $df = 3, 92$, NS
Heart rate regularity	2.32, $df = 23$, P < .05*	.02, NS	1.85, $df = 3, 92$, NS
Respiration regularity	2.04, $df = 23$, P = .05*	1.79, NS	1.27, $df = 3, 92$, NS

* In each case arousal was higher under no sound than during auditory stimulation.
** The degrees of freedom are the same as those shown for "Irwin's test."

Table 5—Rank Order Correlations Indicating the Extent of Intra-individual Score Consistency Among the Five Dependent Variables of Exp. II. The Correlations in Which Crying Is One Variable Are Based on Ns of 14; The Other Correlations Are Based on Ns of 24

	Heart regularity	Respiration regularity	General motor activity	Crying
Heart rate	− .54	− .31	.76	.84
Heart regularity		.49	− .42	− .37
Respiration regularity			− .09	− .18
General motor activity				.92

There is one question that is not answered by the statistical tests we have just reported relating the four independent variables to arousal level. This question concerns the extent to which a common element is being measured by the five dependent variables or the extent to which the dependent variables reflect intra-individual consistency. For example, are the infants whose heart rate decreases under sound the same infants who cry less under sound? Table 5 contains the rank order intercorrelations among the five dependent measures that indicate the extent of intra-individual consistency across those measures. The intercorrelations are based on the difference, for each individual, between his score under the no sound condition and his average score for the three sound conditions. Thus, the first entry in Table 5 indicates that infants whose heart rate decreased under sound stimulation as compared to the no sound condition also had more stable heart rates under sound stimulation, to some extent ($\rho = 0.54$). A comparison of the size of the correlations shown in Table 5 suggests that there may be an interaction between consistency and the nature of the dependent variable. In particular, for this set of data, correlations involving respiration regularity are noticeably lower than are the correlations involving only the remaining dependent variables.

The phenomenon of a decreased level of arousal under continuous stimulation is not specific to the auditory modality. Quite the same phenomenon appears in infants under continuous light stimulation (Irwin, 1941; Irwin & Weiss, 1934a; Redfield, 1937, 1939; Weiss, 1934), under continuous tactile and kinesthetic stimulation (Irwin & Weiss, 1934b; Lipton, Steinschneider, & Richmond, 1960a, 1965), and probably under continuous stimulation in other modalities, e.g., proprioceptive, although these have yet to be studied systematically. Furthermore, long before any of these studies was done on infants, Pavlov had repeatedly observed the same phenomenon in his dogs. As he remarked in 1922, "*Every monotonous and continuous stimulation leads to drowsiness and sleep*" (1928, p. 307). Pavlov had concluded by that time that somnolence, sleep, and inhibition were all manifestations of the same process, i.e., that lowered states of arousal were simply extreme states of inhibition—specifically, inhibition that was no longer confined by excitation within localized areas of the cortex, but that had both irradiated throughout the cortex and spread downward to subcortical levels.

Pavlov's description of how it happens that continuous stimulation affects arousal does not begin to answer the question of *why* the phenomenon occurs. Evidence from several sources (for example, Hebb, 1955) strongly suggests that living organisms, particularly human organisms, need a fairly constant and generous supply of sensory stimulation in order to function normally. The results of such studies suggest that the phenomenon of change in arousal level in infants as a function of the nature of sensory stimulation may well be the earliest demonstration, developmentally speaking, of the organism's need for sensory input and the consequent increase in excitability or arousal when sensory input is lacking.

SUPPLEMENTARY READINGS

Bridger, W. H. Sensory habituation and discrimination in the human neonate. *Amer. J. Psychiat.*, 1961, 117, 991–996.

Irwin, O. C. Motility in young infants: I. Relation to body temperature. *Amer. J. Dis. Child.*, 1933, 45, 531–533.

Irwin, O. C., & Weiss, A. P. A note on mass activity in newborn infants. *Ped. Sem.*, 1930, 38, 20–30.

Lipton, E. L., Steinschneider, A., & Richmond, J. B. Swaddling, a child care practice: Historical, cultural and experimental observations. *Pediatrics Suppl.*, 1965, 35, No. 3, Part II.

Richards, T. W. The relationship between bodily and gastric activity of newborn infants. II. Simultaneous variations in the bodily and gastric activity of newborn infants under long-continued light stimulation. *Hum. Biol.*, 1936, 8, 381–386.

sequelae of

premature birth*

Lula O. Lubchenco, Frederick A. Horner, Linda H. Reed,
Ivan E. Hix, Jr., David Metcalf, Ruth Cohig,
Helen C. Elliott, and Margaret Bourg

[Anyone who has studied living organisms is deeply impressed with the "wisdom" of nature. There is a delicate timing of many interacting growth processes that is infinitely more complex than the scientist has as yet been able to conceptualize. When nature goes awry, the scientist's efforts to redirect the course of the relevant variables appear clumsy and inept, even under the best conditions of present knowledge. A good example of this is the physician's attempts to keep prematurely born babies alive. As hindsight now shows us, providing the prematurely born infant with too high a concentration of oxygen —a substance on which his life depends—very frequently leads to retrolental fibroplasia (a bursting of the tiny capillaries in the retina) and subsequent blindness. This scientific finding makes one wonder how many other types of blunders we may be committing in our "crude" attempts to help the prematurely born human infant survive. The present report by Dr. Lubchenco and her colleagues, at the University of Colorado Medical Center, presents a bleak picture of the future for prematurely born infants who survive for ten years after birth. These scientists made follow-up examinations of 63 of 94 surviving children who weighed 1500 grams (3 lbs 4 oz) or less at birth. The children have consistently evidenced a large variety of physical and psychological problems. Furthermore, the incidence in severity of handicap among these children is inversely related to degree of prematurity—typically indexed by birth weight. This report also includes an excellent discussion of the counseling problems involved in working with parents of the prematurely born infant who later develops physical and psychological handicaps.]

Until recently, it was considered that premature infants might have an increased possibility of being handicapped but that the total number of such involved children was likely to be small and the severity of handicaps

* From L. O. Lubchenco, F. A. Horner, L. H. Reed, I. E. Hix, Jr., D. Metcalf, R. Cohig, H. C. Elliott, and M. Bourg. Sequelae of premature birth. *American Journal of Diseases of Children,* 1963, 106, 101–115. (With permission.)

relatively mild or of limited duration (Hess, 1953; Gesell, 1933; Shirley, 1938). Recent reports (Drillien, 1959; Dann, Levine & New, 1958; Knobloch, Rider, Harper & Pasamanick, 1956; Harper, Fischer & Reder, 1959; Douglas, 1956) dealing with the growth and development of prematurely born children give an unfavorable prognosis for central nervous system growth.

Since the mid-1950's, reports on the incidence of handicaps found in premature infants show an increased number of children to be abnormal. The predominant type of defect described appears to vary with the experience of the authors. For example, Dann *et al.* (1958) found a lowering of the intelligence quotient in 44% of the children that they were able to follow, a high incidence of ophthalmologic defects, but very few physical defects except delay in attaining normal stature. Drillien (1959) noted intellectual, behavioral, and physical defects in more than 60% of her group of infants.

This paper presents a detailed survey of abnormalities in premature infants of low birth weights studied approximately ten years after their birth and confirms the discouraging reports of a high incidence of physical and mental defects.

SUBJECTS AND METHODS OF STUDY

All surviving infants with birth weights of 1500 gm (3 lb 4 oz) or less, born between July 1, 1947 and July 1, 1950 (the first three years of the Premature Infant Center's operation) and admitted to Colorado General Hospital Premature Infant Center, were included for study. Admissions included infants born in Colorado General Hospital, as well as those born elsewhere and transferred to the Premature Infant Center. During this time, a total of 187 infants were admitted of whom 87 died in the neonatal period while 6 succumbed in the subsequent 11 months. The 94 who survived the first year of life constituted the sample to be followed.

The examination included medical and neurological examinations, psychological testing, electroencephalography, ophthalmological examination, and evaluation of the social situation of the families of the patients. The children returned to the Out Patient Department of the Colorado General Hospital for these examinations.

Of the 94 children who constituted the group to be re-evaluated at approximately ten years of age, 63 were available for follow-up examinations. Twelve children had been placed in adoptive homes, ten could not be located but pertinent information on them was present in the medical records, and nine children were lost to the study.

Children who had recently been examined in the Out Patient Department at Colorado General Hospital were included in the study without necessarily returning for re-examination. Ten children who were not available at ten years of age had been examined previously in the various clinics

Table 1—Physical, Neurological, and Mental Handicaps: Individual Premature Infants

Pt	B Wt, Gm (Lb)	Race, * Sex	Birth-place	Socioecon. level	Maternal complications	Neonatal course
1	789 (1¹¹⁄₁₆)	AA, F	Outborn	Private	Placenta abruptio	Respiratory difficulty, sepsis mongolism, congenital heart disease
2	851 (1⅞)	AA, M	Inborn	Part pay	Premature rupture of membranes	Ecchymoses, respiratory difficulty
3	920 (2)	AA, F	Inborn	Part pay	Vaginal bleeding	Uneventful
4	992 (2³⁄₁₆)	AA, M	Outborn	Part pay	None	Apnea, pneumonia
5	999 (2³⁄₁₆)	SA, F	Outborn	Part pay	Prolonged labor	Cyanosis
6	1,000 (2³⁄₁₆)	AA, F	Inborn	Part pay	Fetal distress	Uneventful, URI
7	1,000 (2³⁄₁₆)	SA, F	Outborn	Indigent	None	Aspiration pneumonia, diarrhea, poor Moro
8	1,006 (2¼)	AA, M	Outborn	Private	Membranes & fetus delivered intact	Uneventful
9	1,034 (2¼)	SA, M	Outborn	Indigent	None	Respiratory difficulty, scierema, apnea, ecchymoses
10	1,049 (2⁵⁄₁₆)	N, F	Outborn	Private	None	Gastrointestinal tract bleeding, diarrhea, URI, skin infection
11	1,050 (2⁵⁄₁₆)	AA, M	Inborn	Part pay	Vaginal bleeding, prolonged labor	Uneventful
12	1,063 (2⁵⁄₁₆)	AA, F	Outborn	Private	None	Prolonged edema
13	1,077 (2⅜)	SA, F	Outborn	Private	Vaginal bleeding	Aspiration pneumonia, apnea, omphalitis
14	1,091 (2⅜)	AA, M	Outborn	Private	Triplet gestation (one died); breech delivery, prolonged labor	Bronchopneumonia
15	1,106 (2⁷⁄₁₆)	AA, M	Outborn	Private	Vaginal bleeding	Respiratory difficulty, apnea, URI
16	1,148 (2½)	AA, F	Outborn	Private	Vaginal bleeding	Hydrocephalus, skin infection
17	1,148 (2½)	AA, M	Outborn	Private	None	Hemangioma, excised; inguinal hernia
18	1,162 (2⁹⁄₁₆)	AA, F	Outborn	Private	None	Uneventful, URI
19	1,162 (2⁹⁄₁₆)	SA, M	Inborn	Part pay	Placenta abruptio; genitourinary tract infection	Respiratory difficulty, apnea
20	1,162 (2⁹⁄₁₆)	AA, M	Outborn	Private	Assisted breech delivery	Aspiration pneumonia
21	1,170 (2⁹⁄₁₆)	AA, F	Outborn	Part pay	Premature rupture of membranes	Diarrhea, URI
22	1,184 (2⁹⁄₁₆)	AA, M	Outborn	Private	Triplet gestation (one died); prolonged labor	Difficult resuscitation, diarrhea
23	1,191 (2⅝)	AA, M	Outborn	Private	None	Bronchiolitis, apnea, sepsis, pylorospasm
24	1,240 (2¾)	AA, M	Inborn	Part pay	Mitral valve disease, fetal distress, premature rupture of membranes	Bronchopneumonia, diarrhea
25	1,240 (2¾)	AA, F	Outborn	Part pay	Premature rupture of membranes, prolonged labor	Uneventful
26	1,247 (2¾)	AA, F	Outborn	Private	Twin gestation (one died)	Apnea, URI
27	1,247 (2¾)	N, M	Outborn	Private	Twin gestation (one died)	Sepsis
28	1,267 (2¹³⁄₁₆)	SA, F	Outborn	Part pay	None	Uneventful, URI
29	1,270 (2¹³⁄₁₆)	AA, M	Outborn	Private	Prolonged 2nd stage of labor	Respiratory difficulty, apnea
30	1,276 (2¹³⁄₁₆)	AA, M	Outborn	Private	None	Bronchopneumonia

* Race: AA indicates Anglo-American; SA, Spanish-American; N, Negro; Or, Oriental.

| IQ, Full Scale † | NEUROLOGICAL FINDINGS | | EYE FINDINGS | | |
	Spastic Diplegia, 0–3+	Other	Residual RLF, Stage IV	Strabismus	Other
10 approx	0	Petit mal	0		Myopia
20 approx	0	Microcephaly convulsions	V		
NR**	0	Temporal lobe seizures	0		Traumat retinal detach
96 (85–108)	1+		I		Nystagmus
70 (75–69)	0		0	Bilateral alternating	
— (115–?)	1+		V		Cataracts
56 (61–60)	Exam unsatisfact		IV	R. internal	
65	Incomplete		V		
72 (74–75)	1+	Generalized hyperreflexia	0		
67 (74–65)	1+		I	L. internal	Myopia
83 (81–59)	1+	Microcephaly, mild	0	L. internal	Myopia
— (58-?)	0	Microcephaly, mild	V		
98 (100–96)	0		0		
80 (87–76)	3+		0		Poor vision
102 (85–121)	1+		0		
77 (84–75)	2+	Arrested hydrocephalus	II		
— (95–?)	1+	Convulsions, onset age 12 yr	V		
91 (99–85)	1+		0		
83 (91–76)	0		0	L. internal	
122 (121–118)	0	Mild cerebellar dysfunction	0		
NR	0	Convulsions	0	Present	Myopia
99 (97–100)	1+		0	R. internal	Myopia, R; amblyopia. mild
117 (110–121)	1+		0		Myopia
20 approx	3+	Subdural hematoma at 1 yr; convulsions	V		
— (121-?)	0		IV		
100 (91–104)	0		0	Alternating internal	
100 (111–101)	1+		0		
88 (94–83)	1+		I	Bilateral divergent	
99 (96–101)	0		0		
121 (111–128)	0		0		Macular degeneration R. eye

** NR indicates no record.

† Full scale IQ as determined from the Wechsler Intelligence Scale for Children. Parenthetical figures give score obtained on verbal items, followed by score obtained on performance items. ? Indicates performance test not given due to blindness.

Pt	B Wt, Gm (Lb)	Race, * Sex	Birth- place	Socioecon. level	Maternal complications	Neonatal course
31	1,276 (2¹³⁄₁₆)	SA, F	Outborn	Part pay	None	Uneventful
32	1,290 (2¹³⁄₁₆)	AA, F	Outborn	Private	None	Bronchiolitis, pneumothorax, sepsis
33	1,300 (2⅞)	SA, F	Inborn	Part pay	Vaginal bleeding	URI
34	1,301 (2⅞)	AA, M	Outborn	Private	None	Uneventful
35	1,304 (2⅞)	AA, F	Outborn	Part pay	None	Abscess, buttocks
36	1,346 (2¹⁵⁄₁₆)	AA, M	Outborn	Private	Cesarean section for fetal distress	Apnea, URI
37	1,361 (3)	AA, F	Outborn	Private	Twin gestation (one died); assisted breech delivery	Uneventful
38	1,361 (3)	AA, F	Outborn	Private	None	Respiratory difficulty
39	1,361 (3)	AA, M	Outborn	Private	None	Diarrhea, inguinal hernia
40	1,368 (3)	AA, F	Outborn	Private	None	Suspected meningitis
41	1,370 (3)	AA, M	Outborn	Private	Premature rupture of membranes	Uneventful
42	1,375 (3)	AA, F	Outborn	Private	None	Uneventful
43	1,389 (3¹⁄₁₆)	AA, M	Outborn	Private	Twin aborted at 3 mo gestation	Uneventful
44	1,389 (3¹⁄₁₆)	AA, M	Outborn	Private	Twin gestation (other twin + 1,500 gm survived)	Uneventful
45	1,403 (3¹⁄₁₆)	AA, F	Outborn	Private	None	Respiratory difficulty, abscess, URI
46	1,410 (3⅛)	AA, F	Outborn	Private	Placenta praevia	Respiratory difficulty, URI
47	1,417 (3⅛)	AA, M	Outborn	Private	Premature rupture of membranes	URI
48	1,417 (3⅛)	AA, M	Outborn	Private	Precipitous delivery	URI
49	1,424 (3⅛)	AA, F	Outborn	Private	Premature rupture of membranes; induction of labor	Bronchopneumonia
50	1,439 (3⅛)	SA, F	Outborn	Indigent	Assisted breech delivery	URI
51	1,453 (3³⁄₁₆)	SA, M	Outborn	Part pay	None	URI
52	1,460 (3³⁄₁₆)	AA, F	Outborn	Private	Vaginal bleeding	URI
53	1,466 (3¼)	AA, M	Outborn	Private	None	Uneventful
54	1,467 (3¼)	AA, M	Outborn	Private	Full breech delivery	Diarrhea, URI
55	1,474 (3¼)		Outborn	Private	None	Suspected sepsis, cleft lip & palate
56	1,474 (3¼)		Outborn	Private	Twin gestation (other twin + 1,500 gm survived)	URI
57	1,480 (3¼)	SA, F	Outborn	Part pay	None	URI
58	1,482 (3¼)	SA, F	Inborn	Part pay	None	Respiratory difficulty, ecchymoses, diarrhea
59	1,485 (3¼)	SA, M	Outborn	Private	Prolonged 2nd stage of labor	URI
60	1,488 (3¼)	AA, F	Outborn	Private	Triplet gestation (other 2 died)	Respiratory difficulty
61	1,488 (3¼)	AA, F	Outborn	Private	Twin gestation (one died)	Uneventful
62	1,496 (3⁵⁄₁₆)	Or, F	Outborn	Private	Placenta abruptio	Uneventful
63	1,500 (3⁵⁄₁₆)	SA, F	Inborn	Part pay	Vaginal bleeding	Diarrhea

| IQ, Full Scale † | NEUROLOGICAL FINDINGS | | EYE FINDINGS | | |
	Spastic Diplegia, 0–3+	Other	Residual RLF, Stage IV‡	Strabismus	Other
70	3+	Convulsions	0		Poor vision
108 (105–110)	1+	Premature closure, sagittal sutures	0		Myopia
91 (87–96)	0		0		
99 (100–97)	0		0		Myopia
96 (96–96)	0		0		Myopia; astigmatism
113 (116–107)	0		0		
85 (79–94)	0		0		
82 (81–86)	0		0		Traumat retinal detach
— (101-?)	1+		V		
— (109-?)	0		0		
107 (101–111)	0		II	R. internal	
104 (114–93)	0		0		Myopia
NR	0	Microcephaly, mild	0		
70 (72–74)	0	Eyelid tic	0		
103 (101–104)	0		0		
108 (123–90)	0		0		Myopia
96 (91–103)	1+		I	R. internal	Myopia
97 (92–103)	0		0		
104 (110–97)	0		0		
54 (60–55)	1+		0		
37	0	Convulsions	0		
99 (97–100)	0		0	R. external	Astigmatism
104 (104–104)	0		0		
— (114-?)			II & III	L. external	
10 approx	2+		0		
104 (104–103)	0		0	Surgically corrected	Nystagmus; myopia
85 (87–86)	0		0		Refractive error
78 (77–83)	1+		0	Bilateral external	Myopia
85 (84–89)	0		0		
96 (90–103)	0		0		
95 (101–90)	0		0		
97 (89–107)	0		0		
89 (97–82)	0		0		

in the Out Patient Department, and adequate data for study were available in their medical records. Eight were mentally retarded, had convulsions and/or residual retrolental fibroplasia. Two children were well at the time of their last evaluation. No attempts were made to locate the 12 children placed in adoptive homes. There was hesitation on the part of the investigators and the social agencies to identify these children and concern about the agencies' role ten years later in providing special services to these families if handicaps were disclosed.

Table 1 details the findings of the examinations in individual infants and evaluates clinically the severity of the findings. The data in Table 1 may be summarized by noting that of the 63 children examined, 20 had no handicap, 31 showed a central nervous system disorder, 25 were slow learners or retarded, having IQs of 89 or less, and 20 had serious eye defects. Of the 20 children classified as normal, some had relatively minor physical findings, such as myopia, strabismus, or behavior problems of minor degree. One child, though "normal" in all respects, was considerably below the intellectual level of parents and siblings.

The major positive findings were related to the central nervous system and the eyes—43 of the 63 children (68%) available for follow-up examination exhibited such handicaps. Multiple handicaps were present in 26 of the 43 children. In the main, the central nervous system lesions consisted of spastic diplegia and intellectual retardation.

Other characteristics peculiar to this group of children were smallness of stature (Table 2), plus a variety of social and emotional problems related to the rearing of a handicapped child. Perinatal difficulties were frequent in the histories of these children.

Intellectual status. The full scale IQ was determined from administration of the Weschler Intelligence Scale for Children (WISC). The IQ of children blind from retrolental fibroplasia was obtained from the verbal items only. Twenty-five of the 60 children tested (42%) had IQs below 90 (and 16 of these IQs below 49). There were indications that many of the children who had intelligence quotients above 90 also had some handicap in their intellectual functioning. Twenty of the 35 children with normal intelligence were found to have experienced difficulties in their schooling. Reading difficulties, problems with numbers, or difficulty in learning were voluntarily cited by the parents of these children. Eleven children repeated one or more of the first three grades. Four others were not enrolled in kindergarten until they were six years old. Three had received speech therapy, and three others were considered emotionally disturbed (Table 1).

Visual problems. Permanent visual impairment due to retrolental fibroplasia was found in 16 children. Seven of these 16 children were blind (cicatricial stage V, Reese, King, & Owens, 1953) and two were in sight-saving classes (cicatricial stage IV).

The use of liberal amounts of oxygen in the incubators of premature infants, termed "unscrutinized high oxygen" (Gordon, Lubchenco, & Hix,

ELECTROENCEPHALOGRAMS

Pt	Degree of Abnormality, 0–4+	EEG Diagnosis	Other abnormalities	School performance	Severity of handicaps 0–3+§
1	NR		Mongolism; died at 9 yr	In institution for mentally retarded	3+
2	4+	Seizure discharge		Referred to institution for mentally retarded	3+
3	NR	Has seizures		Reading difficulty; average student	2+
4	3+	Moderate slowing, generalized; disorganized		Repeated 1st & 4th grades; reading difficulty	1+
5	0	Normal		Special education classes; stutters	3+
6	0	Normal, poor organization of record		In school for blind; no problems; A's mostly	3+
7	0	Normal (awake)		Special education classes	3+
8	4+	Dysrhythmia, generalized, occipital; slow & spikes		In institution for mentally retarded	3+
9	2+	Disorganized; anterior fast activity; no alpha waves	History of hydrocephalus subdural hematomas at 8 mo	Repeated 1st grade; special education planned	3+
10	2+	Poor organization; moderate slowing, with hyperventilation, focal		Repeated 3rd grade; average work	3+
11	3+	Not well organized; spikes random 14/sec		Repeated 1st & 2nd grades	2+
12	2+	One seizure discharge during sleep		School for blind, 1 yr; ineligible for special education classes	3+
13	NR			B's	0
14	0	Normal, sharp & fast waves, anterior area, focal		Poor school record, Cs'; in sight-saving class	2+
15	0	Normal		Repeated 1st grade & part of 2nd grade; in slow section, 3rd grade; speech therapy	1+
16	1+	Not well organized; sharp & fast activity, asleep		Satisfactory	3+
17	3+	Seizure discharge	Emotion problem	Repeated 2nd grade; failing 5th grade	3+
18	2+	14/sec spikes		Average student	1+
19	1+	Poor organization; slow & dysrhythmia		Average student	2+
20	3+	6 & 14/sec spikes; seizure discharges with photic stimulation		Trouble with multiplication; some D's	0
21	3+	Slow & spikes, temporal	Nervous	Special education classes	2+
22	0	Normal; R. slow & sharp waves with photic stimulation		No problems	1+

| | ELECTROENCEPHALOGRAMS | | | | |
Pt	Degree of abnormality, 0–4+	EEG Diagnosis	Other abnormalities	School peformance	Severity of handicaps 0–3+§
23	3+	6 & 14/sec spikes	Asthma	Repeated 1st grade; C's & D's	1+
24	4+	Severe disorganization; generally slow waves, occipital slow & spikes	Deaf	In institution for mentally retarded	3+
25	2+	Slow waves in R. posterior area		Sight-saving classes; about 1 yr behind	2+
26	2+	Moderate slowing, generalized		B's & C's	0
27	0	Normal		A's & B's	1+
28	1+	Moderate slowing		B's	2+
29	0	Normal		Repeated 1st grade; immature	0
30	3+	Spikes, R. posterior temporal area; disorganization		A's & B's	1+
31	NR	Has convulsions		Special education	3+
32	3+	Focal slowing & spikes parietal & occipital; disorganization with photic stimulation	Numerous febrile illnesses; heart murmur, nervousness, enuresis	A's & B's	1+
33	3+	14/sec spikes; normal, awake		Entered kindergarten at 6 yr; repeated 1st grade; speech problem with treatment	0
34	1+	Normal; poor organization; almost no alpha activity		Has had speech therapy; upper half of class	0
35	0	Normal, poor organization		Average student	0
36	0	Normal		Entered kindergarten at 6 yr; near A student	0
37	0	Normal; no alpha activity on L; L. slow & dysrhythmic		Repeated 3rd grade; now special education classes; stutters	2+
38	3+	6 & 14/sec spikes	Severe hearing loss; emotional problem	Special education classes for deaf; speech therapy	2+
39	1+	No alpha activity; fast activity, anterior	Emotional problem	Repeated 1st grade; B's & C's	3+
40	0	Normal; anterior fast & sharp activity, asleep		No problems	0
41	0	Normal; poor organization; poor alpha activity		B's & C's; reading difficulty	1+
42	0	Normal		Entered kindergarten at 6 yr; A's & B's	0
43	NR			Special education classes	2+
44	4+	Seizure discharges; 14/sec spikes; disorganization	Pes cavus	Regular classes, but only accomplishes ⅓ of work; C's; speech therapy	3+
45	0	Normal		A's, B's, C's	0
46	2+	14/sec spikes		Mostly A's	0

47	0	Normal; occipital spikes with photic stimulation	Behavior problem	Entered kindergarten at 6 yr; having difficulty in school	1+
48	NR			Repeating 3rd grade; reading difficulty	0
49	0	Normal	Pes cavus, mild	Entered 1st grade at 6½ yr; C's reading problem	0
50	NR			In orphanage; slow reader	3+
51	0	Normal		In institution for mentally retarded	3+
52	0	Normal		Repeated 1st grade; reading problem; speech therapy	0
53	3+	6 & 14/sec spikes; slow and spikes, L. with hyperventilation		B's, C's	0
54	2+	Mild generalized slowing with dysrhythmia; no alpha activity	Emotional problem; nervousness	Repeated 1st grade; arithmetic problem; sight-saving classes	1+
55	NR		Cleft lip & palate	In institution for mentally retarded	3+
56	4+	Seizure discharges; R. Parietal-occipital slowing		Repeated 2nd grade; average student	0
57	3+	14/sec spikes		C student; arithmetic problem	2+
58	3+	Seizure discharges; slowing, mild, generalized		Repeated 2nd grade; C's & D's	3+
59	0	Normal		B's & C's	2+
60	4+	6 & 14/sec spikes; isolated parietal-temporal spikes		No problems	0
61	3+	6 & 14/ sec spikes; slow & spikes, parietal-temporal areas; dysrhythmia; moderate slowing, generalized		Poor performance; C's; learning difficulty	0
62	0	Normal		B's	0
63	0	Normal		B's, C's reading difficulty	2+

§ Severity of handicap: 0 indicates none (includes refractive errors, mild reading, arithmetic, learning or speech difficulties): 1, mild spastic diplegia, RLF stages I and II; 2, slow learner (IQ 80–89), moderately severe spastic diplegia, RFL stages III and IV; 3, IQ below 80, blindness, severe spastic diplegia.

Table 2—Physical Growth of Premature Infants With Birth Weight of 1500 Grams or Less Admitted Between July 1, 1947 and July 1, 1950

SUBJECTS WHO WERE BELOW THE TENTH PERCENTILE ON WEIGHT AT APPROXIMATELY 10 YEARS OF AGE			SUBJECTS WHO WERE BELOW THE TENTH PERCENTILE ON HEIGHT AT APPROXIMATELY 10 YEARS OF AGE		
Sex	N	%	Sex	N	%
boys	13/24	54	boys	14/22	64
girls	9/29	31	girls	9/26	35

1954), was a routine practice during the years when these children were hospitalized. The flow meters were set routinely at five liters of oxygen per minute in order to produce a concentration of approximately 60% in the Gordon Armstrong type incubators. Oxygen administration was continued for a minimum of three weeks. Only seven infants received less than 21 days of oxygen, and there were three in whom the duration of oxygen administration was unknown.* The use of high concentrations of oxygen in the environment of premature infants and the subsequent development of retrolental fibroplasia has been documented (Patz, Hoeck, & De La Cruz, 1952; Kinsey, Jacobus, & Hemphill, 1956).

Eye disorders, other than retrolental fibroplasia, were found in three children. Two had traumatic retinal detachments not due to retrolental fibroplasia, and one had evidence of macular degeneration. There was an unusual incidence of myopia and strabismus in the remainder of the 44 children—19 of these children were so affected. In summary, 19 of the 63 children had severe visual defects and 19 others had minor problems— an over-all visual morbidity of 60%.

Neurological deficits. Spastic diplegia was the most frequently encountered central nervous system disturbance and was present in 22 of the 30 children with central nervous system lesions. A variety of other conditions was noted including mongolism, premature closure of the sagittal sutures, arrested hydrocephaly, and microcephaly.

The developmental histories in the children with spastic diplegia showed striking similarities. There was usually a delay in sitting, standing, and walking. After walking was established, it was poorly coordinated; the children were noted to be clumsy and had a tendency to walk on the toes. Muscle tone and coordination improved to near normalcy at school age.

Examination in all cases revealed bilateral symmetrical increase in muscle tone, which was only slightly more than normal in the upper extremities but much greater in the lower extremities. This increased tone frequently produced heel-cord shortening and pes cavus. There was very little, if any, weakness in the upper extremities, while weakness in the lower extremities in an elective distribution was readily demonstrable. The deep tendon reflexes of the upper extremities were normal or minimally increased, while those of the lower extremities were markedly hyperactive at both knee and ankle with sustained and unsustained ankle clonus frequently being present. Athetosis was not present, and no instance of clinical kernicterus was discovered.

Electroencephalograms. The incidence of abnormal electroencephalographic findings in these children was high—60% of the records were abnormal (33/55). This is in contrast to the incidence of abnormal electroencephalograms (6%) found in full-term infants followed in the Child Re-

* Patients in Table 1: No. 30 and 60, no oxygen; No. 17, less than 8 days of oxygen; No. 40 and 42, 8–14 days of oxygen; No. 59, 11 days; No. 62, 18 days; No. 37, 15–21 days; No. 20, 44, and 63, duration of oxygen unknown.

search Council (Metcalf, unpublished). In 13 children, the electroencephalograms revealed only mild aberrations.

The most frequently observed disturbances were seizure discharges, disorganization of the record and 6 and 14 per second spikes. There were eight children with seizure discharges. Two of the eight (patients 55 and 59, Table 1) were considered to be entirely normal except for electroencephalographic abnormalities. Evidence of neurologic disease was noted in the other six children; only one of these had convulsions. Disorganization of the record was present most frequently in the children with severe intellectual retardation and usually was accompanied by other abnormalities such as focal or generalized slow waves and spikes.

There were 12 children who showed 6 and 14 per second spikes during sleep. The records of six contained no abnormality other than the 6 and 14 per second spikes. However, only half of the children with normal electroencephalograms (11/22) slept during the examination. The presence of 6 and 14 per second spikes was found predominantly in children with normal intelligence. There was no significant correlation between 6 and 14 per second spikes and emotional or behavioral problems in the children.

Occipital abnormalities of the electroencephalograms in blind children have been reported (Metcalf, 1959). Two of the seven blind children in this series showed occipital spikes, but two children with normal vision and one with partial sight also had occipital spikes in their electroencephalographic records. Disruption of alpha activity was noted in three additional blind children. Only one blind child had a normal electroencephalogram. Four of the sighted children with retrolental fibroplasia (stages I–IV) had disorganization of their records, but acceptable alpha activity was present in all but one. One child with normal vision showed no alpha rhythm.

MATERNAL FACTORS AND NEONATAL COURSE

A review of perinatal events in the maternal and infant records revealed considerable pathology both in the mother prior to delivery and in the infant following birth.

Sixty-two per cent of the deliveries were complicated (Table 1). Vaginal bleeding and premature rupture of the membranes were the most frequent obstetrical problems encountered. Multiple pregnancies, breech delivery, and prolonged labor were next in frequency and often were associated with the above complications. There was no correlation between obstetrical problems and the weight of the infant.

Illnesses in the infants were primarily respiratory difficulties and infection. Unlike obstetrical complications, their distribution was closely related to birth weight. The smaller the baby, the more frequent was illness present and the more severe was the disease process. Only five out of 23 infants with birth weights less than 1200 gm (2 lb 10 oz) had uneventful nursery courses, while one-half (20/40) of those with birth weights over 1200 gm were free of illness. Infants having a description of apneic periods in their records were reviewed for handicaps of intelligence or neurological disease. Of the nine infants having apnea, only two were seriously handicapped, four had normal intelligence but repeated a grade in school, and three were normal.

Severity of handicaps. To determine whether there was a relationship between the birth weight and the occurrence of handicaps later in life the following correlation was made: The severity of handicaps was defined and classified arbitrarily into four categories and then plotted according to birth weight. The severity of the handicaps at ten years of age in those children whose birth weights were below 1200 gm was significantly greater than in those with birth weights above 1200 gm. Only two of the 23 infants with birth weights of 1200 gm or less were considered normal, while 18 of the 40 with birth weights over 1200 gm were normal.

It may be argued that mild handicaps are not incapacitating to the child and should be disregarded. If these children are considered normal, half of the children in this study are still unquestionably handicapped. Rather than minimize the findings or continue to excuse the premature infant for subnormal functioning, all abnormalities, whether or not they were serious handicaps, were reported.

Physical growth. The physical growth of the children was evaluated by plotting their heights and weights on the growth charts adapted from the Harvard School of Public Health and the Iowa Child Welfare Research Station Data (Jackson & Kelly, 1945). The results are summarized in Table 2. There were significantly smaller children among this group of premature children than in the general population. Forty-one percent of the prematures were below the tenth percentile for weight, and 47% were below the tenth percentile for height.

Social situation. During the time when the children were admitted to the Premature Infant Center, all of the families were interviewed by a social service worker in order to evaluate social problems and to offer practical assistance when needed.

In the present study, approximately ten years later, the interviews were aimed toward finding out the effect on the families of having a premature infant. It was apparent that the rearing of a handicapped child, especially one with retrolental fibroplasia, added a strain to the adjustment of these families. Fourteen of the 63 sets of parents continued case work services after the children were discharged from the hospital. A few required intensive medical and social work counseling to make an adequate adjustment to the serious defects present in their children.

In general, by the time the premature infants reached ten years of age, most of the problems encountered by parents in rearing a seriously handicapped child were resolved or accepted. However, where the premature infants' handicaps were mild or unsuspected, many unresolved problems and anxieties persisted. This was particularly true of parents whose children had difficulty in learning. These children were considered normal through-out early childhood and only at school age were the intellectual deficits evident. It was necessary in several of these families to offer case work services as part of the follow-up study.

A few dramatic marital situations occurred in which the premature infants were purported to be the factors leading to divorce of the parents. However, the divorce rate for the entire group of premature infants' families was no greater than that in the general population.

COMMENT

The foregoing data leave little doubt about the high incidence of residual handicaps in small premature infants born between 1947 and 1950 and cared for in the Premature Infant Center in Colorado. These handicaps include visual defects primarily due to retrolental fibroplasia, brain damage, retarded growth, and social and emotional problems.

It has become clear that there is a significant correlation between birth weight and the presence of handicapping conditions later in life. The rela-tionship is found for total or individual handicaps. For instance, there is also a greater incidence of individual problems such as retrolental fibro-plasia, and most of the blind children were in the weight group below 1200 gm. The incidence of retarded children was greater, and there were more children with spastic diplegia and other neurological lesions in the smaller weight group. The incidence of difficulties in the neonatal period are more frequent and severe in infants weighing less than 1200 gm than in infants weighing more than 1200 gm at birth. Whatever the basic problem is in the premature infant which enhances the development of central nervous system damage, it is associated with the degree of immaturity as determined by birth weight. The poor outcome of the small premature infants is in general a depressing revelation, but the study did reveal some positive values.

One of the benefits of this study was the realization that infants diag-nosed as having spastic diplegia improve in their physical abilities during the succeeding years and that many are nearly asymptomatic by school age. This knowledge was helpful in predicting the course of the disease and in interpreting the outcome of new cases to the parents. Another benefit of this study was the observation that parents with severely handicapped chil-dren responded well to social service and medical counseling. The early recognition of the severe defect was thought to be an important factor in the acceptance of counseling by the parents. If this is true, there is an in-creased need to discover less severe defects at an early age.

There was a troublesome lack of correlation between intelligence quotients and school performance, particularly in children with normal intelligence. It is not clear why many of these children are unable to com-plete the early school grades satisfactorily. Among factors suspected of playing a role in the poor performance are subtle brain damage, specific reading problems, and hearing losses. Immaturity of behavior was mentioned by the mothers of some of these children, and evidence of delay in social adaptation was noted by the psychologist in others. It is not clear whether or not these findings are related to overprotection in rearing of a premature infant.

Two-thirds of the children gave discrepant scores of ten points or more between verbal and performance items on the WISC. However, they are equally divided between those excelling in performance items and those excelling in verbal items, and there is no relation between discrepant scores and school failure. Specific reading problems are not necessarily detected by the tests administered. Partial hearing losses were not investigated in this study but could account for speech and learning difficulties.

The finding of 6 and 14 per second spikes in the electroencephalograms of 12 children and the possibility that other records may have shown this finding, had the children slept, is of interest because of the association of the presence of these discharges with behavior disturbances (Metcalf, 1959). In that study, the children were 12 to 16 years of age—slightly older than the children in our study. It will be of interest to follow these children through adolescence to determine whether behavior problems occur later.

Retardation in physical growth of premature infants has been described (Dann, Levine, & New, 1958; Alm, 1953; Drillien, 1961). Premature infants were found to be smaller than the general population during the childhood years and also as adults. The cause for physical retardation has not been determined. The children in this study were smaller at birth than the weight expected for their gestational ages. They remained relatively small throughout their childhood years (Lubchenco, 1962). Insufficient food intake in suckling animals has been shown to influence later growth (Wallace, Weil, & Taylor, 1958). Undernutrition, so common in the first few weeks of the premature infant's life, is appealing as an explanation for growth retardation.

The high incidence of defects noted in the children in this study causes concern about the 12 children who did not return for the examinations because they were placed in adoptive homes. The adjustment of adoptive parents to unsuspected neurologic handicaps must have been difficult and accompanied by feelings uncomplimentary to the adoptive agencies. On the basis of the findings presented in this review, one would suggest that adoptive parents be fully informed of the possible later sequelae of premature birth. Knobloch (1959) has shown that one can be reasonably sure of neurological damage by 40 weeks of age. The adverse effects on emotional growth of the child and the difficulties in adoptive home adjustment when placement is delayed until 10 or 12 months must also be considered.

One of the questions raised, in part by this survey and in part by the results reported by others, is whether there has been an actual increase in the incidence of handicapped premature infants in recent years and whether there are different types of defects noted in premature infants cared for in different centers. If such questions are answered in the affirmative, investigation of postnatal influences will become even more important than they have been in the past.

SUPPLEMENTARY READINGS

Alm, I. The long term prognosis for prematurely born children. *Acta Paediat.,* 1953, 42, Suppl. 94.

Dann, M., Levine, S. Z., & New, D. The development of prematurely born children with birth weights or minimal postnatal weight of 1000 grams or less. *Pediatrics,* 1958, 22, 1037–1053.

Dreyfus-Brisac, C. The EEG of the premature infant. *World Neurol.,* 1962, 3, 5–15.

Drillien, C. M. The incidence of mental and physical handicaps in school-age children of very low birth weight. *Pediatrics,* 1961, 27, 452–464.

Dunham, E. C. *Premature infants.* New York: Hoebner, 1961.

Knobloch, H., Rider, R., Harper, P., & Pasamanick, B. Neuropsychiatric sequelae of prematurity. *J. Amer. Med. Ass.,* 1956, 161, 581–585.

a study of an infant
with a gastric fistula*

GEORGE L. ENGEL, FRANZ REICHSMAN, and HARRY L. SEGAL

[The following report is truly a unique document in the annals of science. For the first time a description is available of the behavior and psychophysiological responses of an infant (15–20 months of age) who was *never* able to secure her nutrition through the regular oral channel. When it was noted two days after her birth that she regurgitated all fluids, she was referred for diagnosis and found to have a congenital atresia (complete blockage) of the esophagus. A gastric fistula was surgically provided at that time. Because of parental apathy, neglect, and financial distress this little girl was not returned to the hospital for the surgery necessary to permit normal swallowing until she was 15 months of age. (This type of operation is normally provided when the child is 4–5 months of age.) Because of her debilitated condition when she was returned to the hospital, surgery was not attempted for 5½ months, at which time the esophagus and stomach were surgically joined. In order to allay the reader's anxiety it should be noted that during the next six months the little girl learned to feed herself, to stand, and to walk with help. During the 5½ months that Monica was hospitalized prior to surgery, Drs. Engel, Reichsman, and Segal, of the Departments of Psychiatry and Medicine of the University of Rochester School of Medicine, made extensive observations of the gastric contents of her stomach under different conditions of emotionality. Among the many interesting findings detailed in this report, psychologists may be especially interested in the following observation: "Monica . . . would become quite excited during meal time and sitting on parent's lap would attempt to grab and devour any food she could reach. Swallowed food, of course, ran out through the esophageal fistula." She also loved to suck on lollipops. These activities are interpreted by the authors as giving strong support to the "primacy" of orality during infancy. The degree to which psychologists may be impressed with the authors' interpretation of the obtained relationships between gastric activity and emotional state in this young subject will depend on their persuasion toward psychoanalytic theory. Regardless of one's persuasion, however, the parallels that these scientists draw between reduced gastric secretion, the

* From G. L. Engel, F. Reichsman, & H. L. Segal. A study of an infant with a gastric fistula. *Psychosomatic Medicine,* 1956, 18, 374–398. (With permission.)

depressed-withdrawal state of the subject, and the psychoanalytically conceived anaclitic depression are most provocative.]

Since the classic investigations of Beaumont on Alexis St. Martin, a number of individuals with gastric fistula have been studied, mainly from a physiological point of view. Wolf and Wolff's (1943) classic study of Tom was the first systematic effort to relate manifest behavior, emotions, and gastric function in such a patient. Margolin (1951) subsequently psychoanalyzed such a patient and attempted to relate gastric activity and unconscious mental processes. Although a few observations of children (Wolf and Wolff, 1943) have been made, to our knowledge no detailed psychophysiologic investigation of an infant with a gastric fistula has been reported. This is a study of an infant girl with a congenital esophageal atresia, (i.e., absence of a channel between esophagus and stomach), on whom a gastric fistula was established in the fourth day of life. We began our research when the child was 15 months old and made detailed observations of behavior and gastric secretion until she reached the age of 22 months, when an operation was performed to join her esophagus and colon at a point below the sternum. During these six months we observed the child in 59 experiments and collected more than 600 specimens of gastric juice. This paper is a report on those data that have been analyzed to date.

HISTORY OF THE INFANT

The infant girl, Monica, was born during July, 1952, in a small hospital about 90 miles from Rochester, New York. When it was discovered two days after her birth that she regurgitated all fluids, she was referred to the Pediatric Service of the Strong Memorial Hospital, where a diagnosis of congenital atresia of the esophagus was made. The next day a cervical esophageal fistula was established, and the day thereafter a gastric fistula. After a smooth postoperative course Monica was discharged, having been hospitalized for ten days. The mother was instructed to feed the baby through the gastrotomy on a four-hourly schedule. The parents were also told that when she was four to five months old, the child should receive an operation that would allow her to swallow normally.

At the time of Monica's birth her parents and her 20-month-old brother lived in the maternal grandmother's home. Our knowledge of this setting, particularly of the emotions and attitudes of the figures around Monica, is somewhat limited because of the guardedness of the parents in their communication with us and with others interested in the child. The mother was 19 years old when Monica was born. She appeared a child-like, timid woman, obviously dominated by her husband. She usually allowed him to do the talking and when faced directly with a question, often answered in a questioning tone through her husband. The father, 13 years older than the mother, was employed as a long distance truck driver. He spoke volubly and glibly and presented himself as a forthright, solid citizen. We know from other sources that he is considered unreliable and irresponsible. Both parents were brought up on farms, with restricted social background and limited education, but they seemed to have average intelligence.

Both parents were "frightened" when the malformation was discovered, and particularly by the baby being taken to Rochester. When Monica came home from the hospital, the mother was squeamish and anxious about the gastrotomy and the gastric tube. She could not reinsert the tube without "feeling faint" and at times could not bring herself to do it at all. Furthermore, she was afraid to fondle and hug the child for fear of disturbing the gastric tube, which she regarded, with some justification, as the baby's lifeline.

For the first five months of her life, while she lived at the grandparents' house, Monica gained weight and to all observers seemed to be developing adequately. During this time the grandmother helped materially with the care of the malformed infant, picking her up when she cried and holding her on her lap for long periods. Toward the end of 1952 the relationship between the father and his in-laws, which apparently had been strained for some time, worsened. An open conflict erupted, particularly over the grandparents' handling of the children, and the parents decided to move. At about the same time, in December, two other events took place. The operation that Monica was to undergo about that time did not take place because, for some administrative reasons, the state aid to cover hospitalization costs did not materialize. Furthermore, the mother discovered that she was pregnant again. Throughout this unplanned and unwanted pregnancy she was afraid that this infant also might be defective.

In December, 1952, the family moved to an isolated farmhouse. During this winter they were snowed-in repeatedly for days at a time, on some occasions when the father was away on one of his trips. It was at this time that Monica started to go downhill. The mother said, "She acted tired out, like a person who is discouraged." Because the parents were quite reticent, we can only conjecture about the relationship between mother and child. We know the mother was a very dependent, immature woman who, in this situation, thrown on her own resources, was afraid to get too close to the child.

Monica's downhill course continued through the spring of 1953, while the parents made several moves in rapid succession (allegedly to avoid payment of rent). Her condition was further aggravated when she contracted chicken pox in May. She was described by the parents as "cranky and irritable" and as "crying all the time." She began to refuse the sugar nipple that the mother had given her to suck before and during gastric feedings, in accordance with the doctor's instructions. The parents began, instead, to give her lollipops. Monica also would become quite excited during meal time and if sitting on a parent's lap would attempt to grab and devour any food she could reach. Swallowed food, of course, ran out through the esophageal fistula. She had failed to gain weight for some time and now began to lose weight. After a brief admission to a local hospital she was again referred to the Strong Memorial Hospital in June, 1953, where she arrived looking marasmic. The nurse described her as "very neglected" and "lethargic." She was not studied by us on this admission.

During a hospitalization of one month Monica improved considerably, both physically and emotionally. She maintained this improvement at home for about one month, until the mother gave birth to a baby girl at the end of August. Following this event Monica's condition again declined sharply. She became very irritable and fretful and seemed particularly disturbed when the baby sister was held or fed. When the baby was held near her, Monica would push her away or claw at her. During this period she was particularly avid for food by mouth. When she heard her mother setting the table she cried to be fed by mouth, and when given juices by spoon, "she couldn't get enough." Within a few weeks she lost the weight she had gained during her hospitalization, and because of her increasing marasmus she was readmitted to the Pediatric Service on October 12, 1953; she was 15 months old and weighed 4500 grams. She was in a state of malnutrition and very poor health, and the pediatric house officer described her as "very depressed." She was unable to sit up or even to turn over in bed.

During the first 2½ months in the hospital she gained only one kilogram. By the end of 5½ months she showed considerable improvement in strength and her weight had reached 7500 grams. During this time she became quite attached to one of the nurses and to one of the investigators, both of whom became quite attached to her.

During her nine months in the hospital, Monica's parents visited only seven or eight times, three of these visits around the time of the operation. At times the social worker and public health nurse had to make extensive efforts to contact the parents. Because their visits were infrequent and unpredictable, we unfortunately have no direct observations of Monica's response to her parents. The nurses, however, reported that Monica always recognized them and responded with signs of pleasure. We do not know whether this response was immediate or delayed. The father was more active with her and she was reported to be more responsive in general to him than to the mother. The parents' visits were brief and they occasionally left her a small gift.

The nurses and doctors openly expressed their feeling that the parents were not sufficiently interested in Monica and that particularly the father seemed insincere in his display of affection and expression of interest. Some of them looked upon Monica as a deserted waif and were especially attentive to her for this reason. Throughout the prolonged period of hospitalization Monica became something of a celebrity and there was great interest in the outcome of her case. For some ward personnel she became "the darling of the ward"; a few resented the special attention she received. At the outset some of the hospital personnel identified the investigators with Monica's persecutors, but later most considered the interest of the investigators to exert a beneficial effect. At the end of 5½ months' hospitalization she was deemed physically fit for colonic substernal anastomosis between esophagus and stomach. After a somewhat stormy postoperative course, Monica regained her preoperative developmental level, and during the next 6 months she learned to feed herself, to stand, and to walk with help. She also developed some speech.

During the 5 months there were 59 observation periods during which gastric juice was examined, 44 fasting and 15 after eating. Only the 44 fasting observations are reported in this paper. In nearly all experiments one of us (F.R.) was the experimenter, but on 13 occasions the experimenter was a relative stranger to the baby. The observation periods occurred from two to four times per week and each lasted from one to five hours, making a total of 161 hours. Most of the studies took place in the laboratory, with the observers behind a one-way vision screen; some were in a cubicle on the infant ward with the observer behind a glass partition, visible to the baby. In the latter setting the usual activities of a busy infant ward were visible and audible to the baby, experimenter, and observer. Additional sources of psychological data included an interview with the parents, an interview with the public health nurse, a daily diary kept by the pediatric nurse, spot observations made by the pediatric resident staff, multiple daily visits by Dr. Reichsman, psychological testing, and observations from one to five hours in length with or without simultaneous gastric analysis.

Particular attention was paid to the development of object relationships between Monica and the various experimenters. F. R. quickly became the favored experimenter, and the relationship became highly invested on both sides. Within the framework of this relationship, Monica manifested her more advanced ego development. When new experimenters were introduced they were first experienced as strangers, from whom Monica withdrew, lapsing into a state that we have called the "depression-withdrawal reaction." (Engel and Reichsman, 1956, discuss this in greater detail.) With repeated contacts, this reaction became attenuated and Monica made efforts to establish contact with the new experimenter. The experimenter was not instructed specifically how he should respond to these overtures. The depression-withdrawal response was always alleviated promptly when the stranger left and F.R. returned. F.R.'s return invariably evoked unmistakable signs of pleasure. These characteristic responses to different experimenters offered a convenient method of studying the behavioral and gastric secretory responses to variations in object relationships. When pediatric care necessitated procedures such as catheterizations we obtained behavioral and secretory data characteristic of such periods of external stress.

In this paper we are reporting on 389 specimens of gastric juice in which the rates of total hydrochloric acid secretion in the fasting state were calculated. The rates of secretion were calculated only when the stomach had been emptied of gastric juice immediately before the sample was collected and the exact time of collection and the exact volume of the sample were available. In most instances the interval between specimens did not exceed three to four minutes, and usually was one minute. We arbitrarily excluded any specimen in which the preceding interval exceeded the duration of the specimen; in most instances the interval was much shorter.

In considering the psychological-behavioral observations, one should keep in mind that we were dealing with an infant with a chronological age of 15–21 months but who was much retarded physically and mentally. Monica was unable to sit up and she did not speak at all. Gesell rating at the age of 16 months was approximately 4–8 months; at 22 months it was 9–15 months. Behavioral observations were therefore limited to recumbent bodily positions and movements, facial expressions, and a variety of inarticulate, but quite expressive sounds.

Our observations were recorded without preconceived ideas of what behavioral categories should be studied; only at the completion of the study were the various categories established. After criteria had been established, the protocols of the observer and the experimenter were independently analyzed by two of us (G.E. and F.R.), without knowledge of or reference to the results of the gastric analyses. The independent judgments were then compared. With the rare exceptions noted below, there was agreement. The behavioral categories reported in this paper are the following: affects, object relations, non-nutritional oral behavior, sleep-walking status, and non-nutritional feeding experiences.

RESULTS

In Monica we could identify six affects, which we classify under two major headings: pleasure and unpleasure. We distinguish two degrees of pleasure, contentment and joy, and four kinds of unpleasure, depression, depression-unpleasure, irritation, and rage. The last two are different degrees of anger.

CONTENTMENT

This was a state of rather quiet relaxation. The posture was comfortable and uninhibited. It was appropriate for quiet play activity, self-stimulation, or repose. When she was flat on her back, her most usual position, her knees were usually flexed. Movements were generally slight and rather gentle, but occasionally more vigorous waving or reaching occurred. The facial expression during contentment was placid, with not infrequent smiles, narrowing of palpebral fissures, and mimicking. Vocalization consisted of occasional cooing or gurgling.

JOY

This was a very active pleasure response. Movement overshadowed posture and usually was vigorous and almost continuous. It included waving, reaching, kicking with stretched legs, arching and turning of trunk. Facial expression was very active and mobile with much smiling and laughing. Vocalization consisted of almost continuous cooing, gurgling, or baby talk. Joy was marked by striking responsivity of the infant to the experimenter.

IRRITATION

During this state Monica either had a relatively low tolerance to stimulation or was responding to disagreeable stimuli, as, for example, when intubation through the gastric stoma evoked pain or memory of pain. Under these conditions, stimuli that were ordinarily pleasurable often produced an unpleasurable effect. In this state her posture was relatively hypotonic; the legs often lay flat on the bed with the knees slightly bent. The facial expression was impassive, even to the usual pleasurable stimuli, or she responded wtih scowling or frowning. Vocalization consisted of whimpers, whines, or complaining grunts from time to time.

RAGE

This was a vigorous and sometimes violent response to an excessive stimulus, be it pain or a threat, real or anticipated. Posture was stiff and vigilant at the same time. Movements were those of vigorous resistance and evasion. She pushed, kicked, and hit with her extremities. The facial expression was contorted, eyes were wide open or squeezed tightly shut. At times she covered her face with her arms. Her mouth was wide open, she cried, and her face was often reddened and moistened by tears. Loud crying, high-pitched wailing, screaming, and sobbing comprised her vocalizing.

DEPRESSION

The most striking feature of this state was the lack of movement and of any kind of activity. At the point of transition into depression, which always occurred in the presence of a stranger, movement ceased and the limbs tended to fall gravitationally. Posture remained hypotonic and flaccid. The head was either turned away or straight ahead. With less severe degree of depression, there were slight and slow movements such as fingering inanimate objects. With severe degree of depression she closed her eyes and eventually fell asleep. When she was awake, her facial expression during this state was characteristic: the face sagged flabbily; the corners of the mouth were down; the inner parts of the eyebrows were elevated and the brow furrowed; all producing "the omega of melancholy." Although she was usually silent, there were occasional brief whimpers or wails.

DEPRESSION-UNPLEASURE

This reaction occurred during depression when the child could not entirely avoid external stimulation by withdrawing. Elements of the fight-flight pattern of the anxiety reaction were then superimposed upon the underlying depression. In contrast to depression, there was more tendency to turn away more actively from the experimenter. Bodily movements were evasive and resistive. Such movements, however, were less vigorous and less well-integrated than similar ones during the rage response. Facial expression and vocalization included crying, wailing, whimpering, and sobbing; the brow became deeply furrowed, the face puckered, and the mouth opened in a square fashion. Occasionally there was flow of tears.

COMMENTS

The identification from the protocols of the major affect categories—contentment and joy, irritation and rage, depression-unpleasure and depression—presented no difficulties. The investigators (G. E. and F. R.), who independently categorized affects, always agreed on these major categories. There were occasional disagreements between contentment and joy and between irritation and rage. These disagreements were resolved by mutual discussion of the detailed recorded data. Audiences viewing motion pictures illustrating the various affects also found the affects readily distinguishable.

OBJECT RELATIONS

Monica's interest in things or persons in the environment, as expressed behaviorally, was classified in different degrees of object relations. We first established five such degrees but later reduced these to three when it became clear that the finer subdivisions, although easily distinguishable, did not differ materially in correspondence to the secretory data.

OBJECT RELATION 1

For the most part the child was motionless and relatively unresponsive. She did not look at the experimenter. Her eyes were often closed, and at most she glanced occasionally toward the observer. No activity could·be interpreted as effort to contact the experimenter by either motor behavior or vocalization. Those activities that occurred were usually limited to small movements.

OBJECT RELATION 2

For the most part she was actively concerned with looking, examining, manipulating, dissecting, touching, or stroking such objects as a piece of gauze, a clamp, a piece of tubing, or parts of her body such as fingers, the stomal region, face, neck, feet. The motor patterns were appropriate for such activities, and her attention was largely occupied by them. Occasionally she might look toward, smile at, or even touch the experimenter, while continuing the previous activity. More often she appeared oblivious of the experimenter.

OBJECT RELATION 3

In this category the child's visual, vocal, and motor behavior all were directed predominantly toward attracting, contacting, or maintaining contact with the experimenter. These included looking, calling, smiling, reaching, touching, grasping, stroking, hitting, pushing, and kicking the experimenter. Although they were infrequent, we regarded placing her fingers in the experimenter's mouth or bringing the experimenter's fingers to her mouth as patterns indicative of high object relations.

NON-NUTRITIONAL ORAL BEHAVIOR

Mouth activities not related to actual ingestion of food were classified in three categories. In the first, there was no oral behavior (or only fleeting oral behavior) during the period of observation. In the third, at least half the period was occupied with vigorous oral activity, or there was some kind of oral activity during the entire period. Non-nutritive oral behavior exemplifying the second category fell between categories 1 and 3.

Those classified as "oral" were activities in which the mouth and adjacent structures alone were involved, such as smacking, sucking, licking, protruding tongue, swallowing, and biting at well as activities involving fingers or hands and mouth, or objects and mouth, such as touching of lips, teeth, tongue or buccal mucosa, sucking, chewing, biting, and licking.

SLEEP

We classified sleeping periods by (1) depth and (2) the setting. In the latter category we differentiated between fatigue sleep and withdrawal sleep on the basis of the following criteria. Fatigue sleep was preceded by yawning, stretching, scratching, seeking a comfortable position, and resisting any disturbance of this comfortable position. After the eyes had begun to close, they reopened only infrequently for an occasional glance. There was a gradual, fluctuating reduction of spontaneous activity preceding sleep, and the affects preceding it were those other than depression or depression-unpleasure.

A relative lack of yawning, stretching, and sleep positioning preceded withdrawal sleep. After the eyes had closed, they would reopen frequently to glance. During this period there was often a sustained, if quite low, level of activity. The preceding affect was depression or depression-unpleasure.

In classifying depth of sleep, we regarded arbitrarily as deep sleep all periods during which either no motor activity occurred or not more than one movement in five minutes. If there was any more activity the period was classified as light sleep. (The first specimen obtained after falling asleep was not included under sleep unless Monica had been asleep for 10 minutes or longer.)

NON-NUTRITIONAL FEEDING EXPERIENCES

Two procedures were followed in observing the responses to feeding situations in which food did not reach the stomach. By the first procedure lollipops and crackers were given by mouth, and the swallowed material was extruded through the esophageal fistula. Under the second, the baby was shown or permitted to handle a bottle of her formula that was tightly stoppered so that no contents entered the mouth. Monica was accustomed to seeing her formula before receiving it through the fistula.

The specimens following non-nutritional feeding experiences were not included in the analysis of the behavioral categories in the fasting state.

AFFECTS

Figure 1 illustrates the range of rates of total hydrochloric acid secretion in milli equivalents per minute (mEq./min.) during the six affects. In Fig. 1, higher mEq. rates indicate higher concentrations of acid. While there is considerable spread within each affect, the data reveal that the secretion was lowest during depression and highest during rage. Statistical

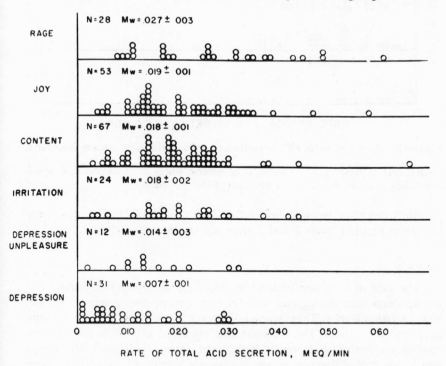

Figure 1—Rates of total hydrochloric acid secretion in mEq./min. during the various affects.

Each circle represents one specimen of gastric juice. N = number of specimens. Mw = mean weighted for duration of the specimen.

analysis by *t*-test shows that the mean rate during depression was significantly less than during all other affects. These differences are significant ($P < 0.02 > 0.001$). The mean rate during rage was significantly higher than the mean rates during all other affects. The significance again is between the 0.02 and 0.001 levels.

There were no statistically significant differences between rates of hydrochloric acid secretion during irritation, depression-unpleasure, contentment and joy.

OBJECT RELATIONS

These data, presented graphically in Fig. 2, revealed that the mean rate of total hydrochloric acid secretion during object relation level 1 was sig-

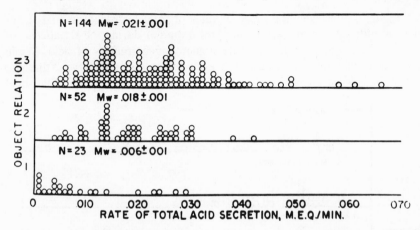

Figure 2—Rates of total HCl secretion in mEq./min. and object relations.

Each circle represents one specimen of gastric juice. N = numbers of specimens. Mw = mean weighted for duration of the specimen.

nificantly less than during either levels 2 or 3 ($P < 0.001$). The mean rates for object relation levels 2 and 3 were not significantly different.

SLEEP

The rate of secretion of total hydrochloric acid was significantly less during sleep than during any wakeful state except during depression and object relation level 1. There was no difference in secretion rates during light sleep and deep sleep. The secretion rate appeared to be less during sleep coming on during a depressed-withdrawal state (0.007 ± 0.001 mEq./min.), but this difference is not statistically significant ($P < 0.1$). Since much higher rates of secretion generally preceded sleep-fatigue, in comparison with sleep-withdrawal, this difference may merely reflect a lag.

When we classified sleep specimens according to the amount of non-nutritional oral behavior during the sleep, we found a highly significant difference ($P < 0.001$) between hydrochloric acid secretion rates during periods of active sucking in comparison with those with no sucking.

In two experiments we were able to secure a continuous record of intragastric pH by placing within the stomach a glass electrode and a salt bridge extension of the calomel electrode. The pH was recorded on a Photovolt pH meter. When the baby fell asleep there was a fairly rapid rise in pH, after a lag of 10–20 minutes, corresponding to the affect preceding sleep. Then with sucking and other activity during sleep there were rapid decreases in pH, such fluctuations occurring until the baby awakened.

HISTAMINE

Histamine diphosphate, in doses of 0.1 mg per 10 Kg body weight, was administered subcutaneously on nine different occasions. A striking correlation was found between the amount of acid secreted in response to this drug and the behavioral state of the infant. As illustrated in Fig. 3, when the baby was outgoing and relating actively to the experimenter, pleasurably or unpleasurably, the stomach secreted large amounts of hydrochloric acid in the 55 minutes after histamine administration, the total secretion ranging from 1.52–2.39 mEq. On the other hand, when she was depressed, withdrawn, or asleep, the same quantities of histamine were noted to have little or no effect. Total secretions were 0.16–0.68 mEq. in 55 minutes, values which did not differ from those obtained in comparable behavioral states without histamine. The high rates, on the other hand, were considerably greater than those observed during comparable behavioral situations without histamine.

RANGE OF TOTAL HYDROCHLORIC ACID SECRETION RATES

Table 1 illustrates the mean fasting secretion rates of hydrochloric acid under the conditions so far analyzed. The highest mean rates occurred during sham feeding and feeding with the bottle of formula that she did not taste.

It is noteworthy that individual specimens with higher secretion rates than those observed during sham feeding or feeding with the bottle occasionally occurred during rage, irritation, contentment, joy and object relation level 3. In these four affect categories there were 19 specimens out of 172 in which secretion rates ranged from 0.035 to 0.066 mEq./min. In object relation level 3 there were 18 specimens out of 144 in which secretion rates were in excess of 0.035 mEq./min. In other words, the rates of secretion were consistently high in response to sham feeding and the bottle; however, sustained, active, outgoing states were occasionally accompanied by secretion rates of a comparable order.

The lowest secretion rates occurred during the depressed, withdrawn state and during sleep. Rates of less than 0.001 mEq./min. occurred occa-

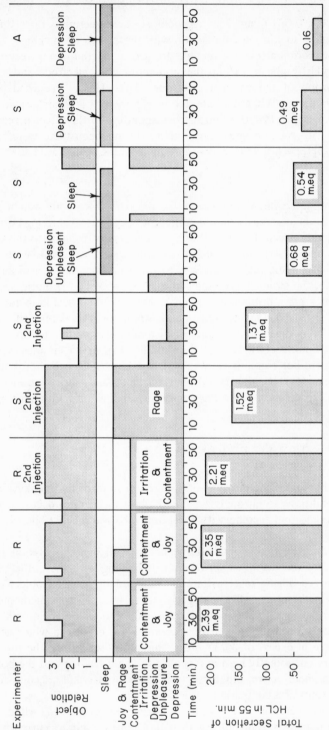

Figure 3—Effect of histamine.

Secretion is recorded as the output of total HCl in mEq. in the 55 minutes after the histamine administration. When arranged in order of decreasing amounts, secretion is greatest in the outgoing states and least in the withdrawn states.

98

Table 1—Total HCl—Rates of Secretion, mEq./min. (Gastric secretion rates are arranged in order of magnitude)

Bottle	.039 ± .003
Sham feeding	.035 ± .004
Rage	.027 ± .003
Object relation level 3	.021 ± .001
Joy	.019 ± .001
Contentment	.018 ± .001
Irritation	.018 ± .002
Object relation level 2	.018 ± .001
Cry	.017 ± .001
Sleep—non-nutritional oral behavior 3	.017 ± .001
Depression-unpleasure	.014 ± .003
Sleep-fatigue	.010 ± .001
Sleep—non-nutritional oral behavior 2	.009 ± .002
Sleep-light	.008 ± .001
Sleep-deep	.008 ± .001
Depression	.007 ± .001
Sleep-withdrawal	.007 ± .001
Awakening	.007 ± .002
Object relation level 1	.006 ± .001
Sleep—non-nutritional oral behavior 1	.006 ± .001
Depression-sleep	.003 ± .001

sionally during the sleep of the depression-withdrawal reaction, representing for all practical purposes a cessation of gastric secretion.

Table 1 clearly indicates that when rates of gastric secretion are listed from the highest to the lowest, the corresponding behavioral processes fall from the most active and outgoing to the most withdrawn and inactive.

DISCUSSION

We are aware that it is both tempting and hazardous to generalize from the study of a single infant. The detailed study of the single subject provides valuable information on the laws governing biological processes within that individual, but a different design is necessary to establish the range of variability of the same processes within a population. In this study we deal with a relatively unique individual, a baby born without continuity between mouth and stomach, who was fed for the first two years of her life through an opening in the abdominal wall. Food taken by mouth leaked out of an esophageal fistula in the neck. It is evident that this infant differs in a number of ways from infants without such a defect and that these differences in original endowment and in life experience resulting therefrom must be significant factors in her general development. In this sense she is a member of a population of infants who share the same defects and who may be studied as a group. On the other hand, she also shares many more qualities with infants not so afflicted and, therefore, can be viewed as part of the population of human infants. In discussing the findings of this investigation, the most reliable interpretations will be those that apply only to this one infant. Yet we will call attention to ways in which the data for this infant conform with, as well as differ from, data and concepts obtained from other sources, infant and adult. It remains for future study to establish their general validity.

Although many factors not investigated in this study undoubtedly influenced the rate of secretion of hydrochloric acid by the stomach in the fasting state (this is indicated by the wide spread among values in each behavioral category), it is nonetheless evident that gastric secretion was intimately integrated with the total behavioral activity of this infant. For example, when the child withdrew and her activity was low, as during the depression-withdrawal state and sleep, there was marked reduction, at times almost cessation, of hydrochloric acid production. The data that we have presented in this respect suggest that in this infant, at the level of development at which she was studied, the processes whereby relationships with objects in the external world are established include a general intaking, assimilative organization in which the stomach participates as if the intention is also to take objects into it. In other words, along with other behavioral activities, such as reaching, touching, grasping, looking, hitting, pushing, kicking, all of which take very active cognizance of the object in the environment, the stomach also behaves as though preparing for food, as if that which is in the external world is literally to be ingested and digested.

We also regard these findings as evidence that the oral phase of development in the infant, as postulated by Freud, is indeed accompanied by corresponding physiologic activity of the stomach. Further, it would seem that such an oral phase represents not a behavioral organization that is necessarily dependent on the continuity of the connection between mouth and stomach, but rather a total assimilative pattern that includes activities in the service of feeding and the organs associated therewith. From this it appears that the genesis of early object relations includes an assimilative process, largely orally organized. The processes concerned in establishing mental representations of objects and their libidinal and/or aggressive cathexes involve an essentially oral, intaking model. In Monica the secretion rates of hydrochloric acid paralleled in a highly significant way the other behavioral expressions of object cathexes, libidinal or aggressive. Such a finding was predicted from the discoveries of psychoanalysis; whether this is a general phenomenon remains to be established from the study of a series of infants within the first year of life. Theoretically we would predict that this close correlation between gastric secretion and behavioral processes would diminish with further development of the mental apparatus. Whether regression to the oral phase in later life would also involve the corresponding physiological regression, a suggestion by Alexander for the pathogenesis of peptic ulcer, remains to be demonstrated experimentally (1934).

Whether the increased gastric secretion may be merely part of a general increase in the physiological activity of the body and not have the specific meaning we have proposed cannot be settled from a consideration of the data of this study. There is evidence, however, that vigorous muscular activity is usually associated with a decrease rather than an increase in acid secretion (Hammar and Obrink, 1953). Further clarification may be obtained by studying gastric secretion at a later level of development and by studying other physiological systems not directly involved in intaking, assimilative processes.

The results indicate also that at the level of development of this infant, affect may be regarded as the behavioral expression of instinct. In the relatively undeveloped ego one is able to see undisguised the attempts at discharge, e.g., instinct gratification. Here one might distinguish between attempts at tension reduction related to external objects and their mental representations (contentment, joy, irritation and rage), which are accompanied by patterned motor activity and augmented gastric secretion; and attempts at tension reduction of a narcissistic type (the depression-withdrawal reaction and sleep), in which muscular hypotonia, inactivity, and reduction of gastric secretion predominate. Other physiologic systems were not studied, but it was certainly established that the stomach participated in a major way in instinct expression, a phenomenon also predicted by psychoanalytic theory.

No less interesting than the data indicating that the oral phase has its physiological counterpart, is the indication of the existence of a relatively objectless, narcissistic phase in which secretory activity of the stomach largely ceases. In the depression-withdrawal reaction, as described above, there is a profound withdrawal of interest and activity in relation to the external world. This invariably occurred when the baby was confronted with a stranger. A more detailed consideration of the genetic dynamic background of this reaction will be published elsewhere (Engel & Reichsman, 1956). Suffice it to say we believe that this reaction developed out of significant disturbances in the mother-child relationship in the first year of life, interfering seriously with the baby's capacity to tolerate object loss. As described in the history, she suffered two depressions in the first 15 months, variants of what Spitz has called "anaclitic depression" (1946). Both occurred in response to attenuations of the mother-child relationship and were alleviated by the establishment of more secure and satisfying object relationships in the hospital. Thereafter Monica responded, when confronted by a stranger, with the same mechanisms used in the earlier anaclitic depressions, withdrawing cathexes from the external world and from the systems concerned with it. The end result was a state of sleep, a narcissistic withdrawal with a reinstatement of the heightened stimulus barrier of the neonatal or fetal state. During this situation, as well as during natural sleep, secretion of acid by the stomach greatly diminished.

We interpret this to mean that when cathexes are withdrawn from the external world, when the child no longer seeks contact with persons in the environment and withdraws interest, not only does she abandon use of the motor system, as evidenced by the hypotonia and immobility, but also she behaves as if nothing is to be taken into the stomach. This is in contrast to the observation in the outgoing affective states described above. However, the last statement should not be interpreted to mean that the baby now decides nothing is to be taken into the stomach, an adultomorphic interpretation, but rather that a state of organismic organization exists, in which things are not taken into the stomach, a pre-oral organization. Such a state, of course, existed during fetal life, when nutrition was achieved passively through the umbilical circulation, and it perhaps is perpetuated to varying degrees in the biological withdrawals of sleep, even in the adult. Greene has suggested the term "umbilical stage" (1956). As one of us has developed elsewhere, biologic process and action precede the development of mental representations thereof, and therefore these data mainly point to the biologic anlage of processes that may later have psychologic expression (Engel, 1953).

Clinical and theoretical considerations have also led us to suggest that what we are calling the depression-withdrawal reaction represents an early developmental phase of depression, the anlage, so to speak, for depressive patterns of later life. Originating in a setting of helplessness unduly prolonged and accentuated by disturbances in the mother-child symbiosis, the reaction is reprovoked with exquisite regularity when the infant is threatened, through object loss, with a reactivation of the original shock state of helplessness. This fits well with the concepts of primal depression. The clinical manifestations are those concordant with the development of this child. Later libido and ego developments and the formation of superego add important features to adult depressions, not to be expected in infantile depressions (Engel & Reichsman, 1956).

Finally, we wish to call attention to the remarkable reduction in the response to histamine in the depression-withdrawal reaction and in sleep. This suggests an alteration in physiological mechanisms and may provide an opportunity to elucidate some physiological processes in narcissistic states. This matter is now under investigation in our laboratory.

SUPPLEMENTARY REFERENCES

Miller, N. E., & Kessen, M. L. Reward effects of food via stomach fistula compared with those of food via mouth. *J. comp. physiol. Psychol.,* 1952, 45, 555–564.
Wolf, S., & Wolff, H. G. Evidence on the genesis of peptic ulcer in man. *J. Amer. Med. Ass.,* 1942, 120, No. 9.

ii

Motor Development
and Physical Growth

nature provides for the child's growth in her own fashion, and this
should never be thwarted. Do not make him sit still when he wants to
run about, nor run when he wants to be quiet. If we did not spoil our
children's wills by our blunders their desires would be free from caprice.
Let them run, jump, and shout to their heart's content.
ROUSSEAU, *Emile ou De L'Education*, 1762.

sucking

in infancy*

T. BERRY BRAZELTON

[Precursors of the sucking reflex appear during intrauterine life, perhaps as early as the fifth lunar month after conception, according to Hooker's observations. The full constellation of swallowing and sucking movements makes its appearance by at least two months prior to the time of normal delivery, according to Gesell. The sucking reflex is well established in full-term healthy human infants and permits them to obtain food through their own motor activities. Some few weeks after birth the human infant sucks not only to obtain food but also to establish sensory contact with parts of his own body (fists and fingers) and with other objects in the external environment. This extranutritional sucking has attracted the interest of psychologists, and has been a source of anxiety to many inexperienced mothers. Some mothers still feel apprehensive about the later effects of extranutritional sucking, and are generally bewildered by the sometimes conflicting advice that they receive from their pediatricians and from reading various "baby books." In the present report, Dr. Brazelton, a pediatrician at Harvard University and Massachusetts General Hospital, shows that all infants engage in some extranutritional sucking during the first 3 months of life and that this behavior increases in intensity from 3 months to 7 months, at which time it begins to decline spontaneously. According to the observations of the cooperating mothers who were reporting to Dr. Brazelton only four of the 70 infants who were studied during the first two years of life would be termed "problem suckers." Two of these four infants showed little extranutritional sucking during early infancy, while the other two continued into the second year "despite gratification in earlier infancy." On the basis of the information provided by this study and other similar investigations, Dr. Brazelton offers what appears to be very reasonable advice to mothers: extranutritional sucking "is normal and its disappearance is spontaneous in most infants when not inhibited."]

The sucking reflex of the infant assumes a voluntary aspect as it increases in its importance to him. Extranutritional sucking which occurs in infancy is often a source of concern to parents and to physicians. The importance of

* From T. B. Brazelton. Sucking in infancy. *Pediatrics*, 1956, 17, 400–404. (With permission.)

this kind of sucking as a source of gratification has often been overlooked. A more complete understanding of what this activity means to the infant is important in providing gratification of his need for sucking, nutritional and nonnutritional.

The mechanism for sucking is normally instituted in fetal life. Hooker (1942) observed activity in the 17-week fetal infant which he felt was a precursor to sucking. Gesell placed the beginning of full swallowing and sucking at the 32- to 36-week fetal stage. Maturation of this ability occurs in the last 2 months of fetal life. From birth onward, sucking activity becomes an expression of the basic instinct of self-preservation. Gratification of this primary instinct constantly reinforces the oral drive to suck. Freud (1930) postulated that with oral gratification from nutritional sucking, the act itself assumed importance and became an associated goal. Non-nutritional sucking then evoked pleasure, eased tensions, and assumed an importance all its own. After the infant has experienced such gratification, interference with it may affect the feeding situation (Freud, 1946a), or may affect emotional development in other areas (Wolf, 1952).

A series of babies were cup fed from birth by Fredeen (1948) and no nutritional sucking was allowed. These infants discontinued sucking movements by the sixth week after birth and did little or no sucking thereafter through infancy or in the second year. This study was carried out in an attempt to prove that sucking was not an important source of gratification if the infant never experienced it as such. Sears and Wise (1950) pointed out that the frustration which an infant showed when the sucking process was interfered with was directly proportional to the duration and amount of gratification the infant had had in its feedings prior to the frustration. Hence, in the cup fed babies of Fredeen, lack of reinforcement of sucking activity simply deprived these infants of any gratification in that area, and no interest in it was developed.

Most babies are fed by sucking methods, and do learn to enjoy the process. Extranutritional sucking normally appears to increase in importance for the infant up to 7 months if he is allowed to enjoy it, and then spontaneously decreases in its significance. It seems to be common in the first year for babies to seek extra sucking, and to enjoy it. It does not necessarily appear to be a manifestation of unusual tension or frustration. Spock (1945) refers to this sucking as evidence of some unfulfilled need and urges mothers to examine their handling of the infant when this occurs. As a result, many conscientious young mothers feel guilty and bring their concerns to their physicians.

The present study was undertaken in an effort to allay this concern and substantiate the normality of extranutritional sucking.

PATIENT MATERIAL AND PROCEDURE

Seventy healthy, apparently contented infants were followed throughout their first year. Mothers were asked to make observations for 24-hour periods once a week. These babies were chosen from private practice; 20 were entirely formula fed while 50 were breast fed for 3 months or more and were weaned gradually. In an attempt to minimize the factor of environmental tension, they were selected with the following criteria: These were primiparas who seemed to enjoy their first babies, who had no overt problems with the babies or themselves, and who seemed permissive in their approach to the feeding situation and to sucking. The feeding situation in each instance was felt to be a gratifying one on the whole for both mother and infant. The type of feeding, i.e., breast or bottle, was not an influence in the decision to include them as a unit, as the above requirements were considered more important to this study. No attempt has been made in this study to correlate sucking with the type of feeding, as long as the feeding situation was a satisfactory one. The amount of sucking associated with each feeding varied from 15 to 40 minutes, and the mothers were urged to satisfy the babies' sucking requirements with each feeding. Each infant varied in his required sucking time, and the mother was assisted in her evaluation of this requirement.

RESULTS

Of these 70 babies, 61 manifested an appreciable amount of extra sucking which was not associated with feeding. This activity was present at times that could not be attributed to fatigue, hunger, or discomfort. It seemed to have purpose in itself. The mothers' spontaneous observations were "She seemed to be sucking for the pure pleasure of it," or "He got too full if he kept at the breast, so he seemed to know enough to stop and use his fist instead." In 2 babies the ability to find the fist was present from birth and sucking started as a repeated, patterned activity at 1 week. Nine other babies showed repeated voluntary sucking by three weeks, 50 babies by six weeks, and all but nine were sucking their fists or fingers by three months. Of the 9 babies in whom no extra sucking was noted in the first few months, 5 were quite placid and their mothers satisfied this need by consciously offering around 30 minutes of sucking with each feeding (Levy, 1928; Roberts, 1944). Two others began finger sucking at 9 months, have continued with increasing intensity beyond the first year and continue to be "problem suckers." (A "problem sucker" might be classified as one who sucks his fingers beyond infancy to such an extent that it becomes a problem to his environment, thence to himself.) In the other 2 in this group of nonsuckers, motor development was accelerated and the parents consciously stimulated the infants' attempts to motor performance (Wolf, 1952).

The extranutritional sucking increased in intensity from 3 months to 7 months when it began to lessen spontaneously, coincident with motor accomplishments such as creeping, crawling, sitting, and pulling up. In this period, the mothers observed that sucking was associated with investigation of their hands, with teething discomforts and with frustrations associated with developmental progress. One mother reported that her baby seemed to want to sit up and when he realized he couldn't accomplish it by himself, he looked around for her; not finding her, he resorted to his thumb.

By 9 months of age 45 babies and by 12 months 57 babies had ceased extra sucking except with they were tired, hungry or unhappy (Gesell and Ilg, 1943). Four have continued to suck their fingers rather intensively into the second year; 2 of these have lessened in intensity by the age of 2 years, 2 have not and are "problem suckers." Of the latter pair, 1 was breast fed, 1 was formula fed, and both have had unsatisfactory environmental situations in the second year. These 2 are comparable in intensity to the former 2 who were not suckers in the first year. All 4 of these "problem suckers" give up their thumbs in pleasurable situations but quickly fall back with relatively minor frustrations. These babies substantiate the relationship between prolonged sucking and unsatisfactory environmental relationships, pointed out by various workers (Bakwin, 1948; Kaplan, 1950; Klackenbush, 1949).

INTENSITY

Constitutional differences in an infant's muscular tone are apparent from birth. The intensity of basic drive which demands expression varies from then on and affects the infant's response to such an activity as sucking. M. Fries (1944) believes that the response to a sucking test in the immediate neonatal period is an indication of the inherent degree of this basic drive.

In babies who are constitutionally a driving and hypertonic type, extra sucking may serve as a gratifying outlet. Five of the babies studied were of this type and cried pitifully as if in pain except when their mouths were full. A pacifier at first, later their own fists, satisfied their urgent need for long periods and it seemed apparent that extra sucking was an activity which calmed them. They changed from unhappy, "gassy" babies to more contented ones with the introduction of a pacifier or the thumb (Levine and Bell, 1950). The 9 babies who did little or no extranutritional sucking were more placid types who were gratified in the oral area by the relatively short intervals of sucking that they got with meals. The other 56 babies fell into neither group and seemed to need varying amounts of nonnutritional mouthing and sucking. The effect of the environment on the intensity of this drive could not be fully evaluated in this study. The intensity of sucking varied from time to time in individual infants. Most often it could be correlated with tension in the infant from within or without.

COMMENT

Extranutritional sucking is common in healthy and contented babies in whom it is not inhibited. In babies whose feeding situations are satisfying ones, gratification strengthens the sucking. This source of gratification is carried over to extra periods apart from feeding. Thus the infant may learn to relive a pleasant, dependent situation independent of the parent figure by reproducing the sucking. A resourceful baby learns to alleviate his inner needs and frustrations by substituting this pleasurable act for situations where comfort depends upon the environment. Several authors have suggested that strengthening this activity in infancy serves to encourage the growth of independence in the infant (Kaplan, 1950; Klackenbush, 1949; Escalona, 1952).

In this series of 70, only 4 might be termed "problem suckers" in the second year. Two of these were not sucking at the earlier times in infancy and seem to have resorted to it later. Thus, early gratification of sucking was not a factor in this development. The other 2 have carried over their need for oral activity into the second year despite gratification in earlier infancy. In 59 infants, gratification of this oral drive did not lead to prolonged thumbsucking (Klackenbush, 1949; Mead, 1947; Sullivan, 1954).

Frustration of such sucking is reported to lead to difficulties in other areas, such as: (1) accelerated motor development, as reported by K. Wolf, which may not be healthy (Wolf, 1952); (2) infantile feeding disturbances (Freud, 1946); (3) sleep difficulties, nailbiting, anorexia, persistent thumbsucking, enuresis, tonguesucking, as reported by others (Bakwin, 1948; Kaplan, 1950; Klackenbush, 1949; Sullivan, 1954).

The air-swallowing which occurs coincident with such sucking in small infants can easily be counteracted by occasional offerings of fluid and "bubbling." Permanent dental arch deformity does not occur as a result of finger sucking in infancy, according to Lewis (1930) and others in the field of orthodontia, and only results if the sucking remains as a persistent habit until 5 or 6 years of age.

SUMMARY

Seventy healthy, apparently happy babies were studied in an attempt to evaluate the common occurrence of extranutritional sucking and its importance. Sixty-one manifested an appreciable amount of extra sucking which seemed to be gratifying in itself to the infant and which did not necessarily represent fatigue, hunger or discomfort. The onset of this varied from birth to 3 months of age. Its intensity increased until 7 months and then began to decrease spontaneously, coincident with other motor accomplishments. By 12 months all but 4 of these babies had ceased to suck their hands except under stress. Only 2 have continued beyond the age of 2 years. The importance of extranutritional sucking as a source of gratification in infancy is pointed out; its occurrence is normal and its disappearance is spontaneous in most infants when not inhibited.

SUPPLEMENTARY READINGS

Crump, E. P., Gore, P. M., & Horton, C. P. The sucking behavior in premature infants. *Hum. Biol.*, 1958, 30, 128–141.
Halverson, H. M. Mechanisms of early infant feeding. *J. genet. Psychol.*, 1944, 64, 185–223.

Papoushek, G. A method for the investigation of food-conditioned reflexes in infants up to the age of six months. *Pavlov J. high nerv. Act.*, 1959, 9, 124–129.

Peiper, A. Die Führung des Saugzentrums durch das Schluckzentrum. (Control of sucking center through the swallowing center.) *Pflüger Arch. gesam. Physiol.*, 1939, 242, 751–755.

Traisman, A. S., & Traisman, H. S. Thumb and finger-sucking: A study of 2,650 infants and children. *J. Pediatr.*, 1958, 52, 566–572.

level of sleep

and the rooting reflex*

ELIZABETH F. GENTRY and C. ANDERSON ALDRICH

[In 1667 Samuel Pepys wrote in his *Diary,* "They tell me what I did not know that a child (as this do) will hunt up and down with its mouth if you touch the cheek of it with your finger's end for a nipple, and fit its mouth for sucking." This is the rooting reflex in the newborn infant, another of those reflexes that we infer may have had survival value during the early phylogenetic history of man. Many observers have noted that the rooting reflex is often accompanied by sucking and swallowing movements. In the present report, Drs. Gentry and Aldrich, of the Rochester Child Health Institute, show the relationship between the wakeful state of the infant and the probability of his responding with the rooting reflex to tactual stimulation on the face. During their observations they were able to elicit the rooting reflex from a baby only one-half hour old. They found that when the newborn infant was deeply asleep, he did not exhibit the rooting reflex, open his mouth to receive a nipple, or suck on it. The common practice of some nurses to depress the chin of the infant who refuses to take the nipple for feeding probably grew out of the routinization of infant care in the hospital environment. The present findings would indicate that when the infant is fed by the clock he may frequently be placed in the feeding situation during such a deep state of sleep that he cannot be encouraged to hold the nipple in his mouth or produce sucking-swallowing movements. Since sucking stimulation is necessary for the mother to continue producing milk, some observers have blamed rigid hospital practices as a principal antecedent of the modern mother's frequent inability to produce sufficient milk for her infant. Therefore, "rooming-in" arrangements, which are provided in some modern hospitals, are viewed as a distinct advantage for mothers who may wish to breast feed their infants on a self-demand schedule.]

The health of the newborn infant depends on an adequate intake of nourishment shortly after he becomes independent of his mother. Therefore, it is of importance to study the various activities which constitute suckling be-

* From E. F. Gentry & C. A. Aldrich. Rooting reflex in the newborn infant: Incidence and effect on it of sleep. *American Journal of Diseases of Children*, 1948, 75, 528–539. (With permission.)

havior. At the touch of the nipple the infant's lips open, his lower jaw drops so that the nipple can enter his mouth, his lips close about the nipple, and he begins to suck. If this results in the flow of milk or water, he swallows. In addition to the activities just described, there are other specific types of behavior which are said to be related to suckling. One of these types, which is called the "rooting reflex," has been selected for study in addition to the first two acts of suckling: (1) the behavior of the infant's lips when brought into contact with the nipple and (2) actual sucking.

Our purpose in this study was to find out whether every baby is born with the ability to perform the rooting reflex and, if not, to determine what factors influence its occurrence. The factors studied were age, hunger, satiety and wakefulness. The term "wakefulness" is used to include all gradations observed, from deep sleep to wide-awakeness.

METHOD

Subjects. The subjects were 71 healthy newborn infants, each of whom weighed 2,500 grams or more. They were observed every day during their neonatal stay of eight to ten days in the hospital.

General considerations. The time of day selected for observation of all subjects was from thirty to forty-five minutes before feeding time. In addition, approximately one-third of the infants were observed after they had been fed. Subjects remained in their cribs in the sleeping part of the nursery while being tested. This was a room separate from that in which examinations and other procedures were carried out.

The majority of the infants were fed on a four hour schedule, most of them at the breast. Those who were fed from a bottle were given it by the mother, as a rule.

Evaluation of sleep or wakefulness. At the first approach to the infant, notice was taken of his state of wakefulness. If he was crying, it was obvious that he was awake. If he was not crying, he was observed for one minute before judgment was made. In the last half of the study an attempt was made to distinguish depth of sleep also. With some revision of Wagner's (1937) gradations of depth of sleep, six classifications were made, ranging from deep sleep to full wakefulness:

1. "Deep sleep" meant closed eyelids, with no observable movement whatever, except respiration.

2. "Light sleep" denoted closed eyelids and one or two movements of body, eyelids or mouth.

3. "Dozing" indicated closed eyelids, with more general or more frequent body movements, often associated with movements of the eyelids and mouth.

4. "Sleepy" described a state in which the eyelids were opening and closing or were partly open and the eyes had a "sleepy" look.

5. "Awake and not crying" signified eyelids constantly open and eyes

with an alert expression, a state usually associated with active general body movement.

6. "Crying" referred to eyelids open or closed, usually the latter, always associated with active general body movement.

Test for the rooting reflex. When the cheek of an infant is stimulated by either constant or moving light pressure of a person's finger, the baby turns his head toward the finger and opens his mouth. This is the rooting reflex. The act of opening the mouth is an essential part of this activity, distinguishing it from three other side to side movements that may be confused with the rooting reflex. The three movements in question are the so-called random side to side movement of the head, often associated with other bodily activity seen during the waking state, the turning of the head toward the "preferred" side and the turning of the head either toward or away from the presenting finger without opening the mouth. The first two movements are not evoked in response to the finger, whereas the third is. The third movement, however, is not the rooting reflex, because it is not directed at securing the finger.

Inasmuch as a baby less than 2 months of age commonly lies on a preferred side of the head, the head of the child under observation was always placed so that he was "looking" straight forward, in order that both sides of his face could be tested. If the baby was crying, he was pacified prior to testing by patting him or sitting him up, so that he would close his mouth and stop all vigorous movements of the head.

With the tip of the tester's finger, light pressure was applied to the cheek of the infant approximately one-half inch lateral to the angle of the lips. If no reflex occurred within five seconds, this steady pressure was replaced with a to and fro movement of the same degree of pressure, care being taken not to touch the lips of the infant. The finger was moved to and fro seven times before contact was broken, unless the reflex occurred before the seven strokes had been completed. This was done to both cheeks.

Tactile stimulation of the lips. A dry rubber nipple was touched to the lips of the infant, and notice was taken of whether he opened his mouth or made labial movements.

Test for sucking behavior. The test for the rooting reflex always preceded the use of the nipple for the determination of sucking behavior. Sucking, or the absence of it, was observed after the nipple had been placed in the mouth of the infant. Sucking, or the absence of it, was rated according to the following scale: 0, failure of the infant to make any movements of the lips or mouth; 1, movements of the lips or tongue which could be described as "mouthing," consisting of opening and closing of the lips, or licking and pushing movements of the tongue; 2, actual sucking movements which were few in number with long pauses between them, usually necessitating disturbance of the infant by some kind of stimulation to obtain continued sucking; 3, a series of a few sucks at a time with short pauses, or continuous sucking without pauses, totaling at least twenty-five sucking movements. This was satisfactory sucking.

Awakening the infant. If the rooting reflex was not obtained and if the baby was not crying at the time testing was initiated, attempts were made to awaken the baby. After each attempt, the infant was tested for the reflex. A definite routine for awakening him was carried out, comprised of the following steps: (1) turning him over if he was lying prone, (2) vigorously rubbing him on the chest and abdomen, (3) sitting him up and rubbing him vigorously and (4) compressing his large toe between thumb and fore-finger in an effort to induce crying. This last-named maneuver consisted of firm pressure and was in no sense pinching. Maneuvers (3) and (4) were repeated twice, and testing followed each repetition. If the child was judged to be deeply asleep initially, usually all these maneuvers were necessary.

RESULTS

Except where otherwise specified, all the data reported in the present study were obtained from infants tested before they had been fed. All the titles, "asleep," "awake and not crying" and "crying" in the tables refer to the state of the infant when testing began. The state of wakefulness of the baby at the time the reflex was obtained was usually different from the original state, for testing followed a procedure of awakening.

ROOTING REFLEX

The rooting reflex was manifested by every one of the infants at one time or another. We observed it to be influenced by at least four factors: the state of wakefulness, sucking behavior, age and whether or not the infant had been fed.

State of wakefulness. Three different states of wakefulness could be distinguished on the basis of the incidence of the rooting reflex: (1) deep sleep, (2) light sleep or dozing and (3) awakeness, whether the infant was crying or not (Table 1). Inasmuch as all babies who were deeply asleep

Table 1—Effect of Sucking on a Nipple on the Incidence of the Rooting Reflex (Just before feeding)

State of wakefulness	Observations total number	BEFORE SUCKING Number	Per cent	AFTER SUCKING Number	Per cent
Deep sleep	16	2	12.5	9	56.2
Light sleep or dozing	69	40	58.0	50	72.4
Awake and not crying	83	53	63.8	72	86.7
Crying	85	70	82.3	76	89.4
Total	253	165	65.2	207	81.8
Awake and not crying and crying	168	123	73.2	148	88.1

or dozing did not manifest the rooting reflex and had to be awakened before it was seen, the factor actually being tested was the extent to which one can arouse sleeping infants. Even after they had been awakened, of the 16 infants initially deeply asleep, only 2, or 12.5 per cent, exhibited the rooting reflex, whereas 73.2 per cent of those initially wide awake, whether or not they were crying, exhibited the reflex (Table 1).

Sucking behavior. When the baby was retested for the rooting reflex after he had sucked on the dry rubber nipple, the percentage of reflexes elicited was decidedly increased. Table 1 shows the effects of sucking behavior on elicitation of the reflex. Among the infants who initially had been deeply asleep, the percentage occurrence of the reflex in question increased from 12.5 before sucking to 56.2 after sucking. The act of sucking also had a definite influence on occurrence of the reflex among lightly sleeping infants and infants awake and not crying, but it had little, if any, influence on occurrence of the reflex among crying babies.

Age. The third factor which influenced manifestation of the rooting reflex was age. This was strikingly apparent when observations made on the first day of life were compared with observations made on all succeeding days (Table 2). Again, these figures are most significant when the fact

Table 2—Per Cent of Subjects Showing Rooting Reflex Just Before Feeding. The Number of Observations on which Each Percentage Is Based Is Shown in Parentheses

	Asleep		Awake and not crying		Crying		Total		Awake and crying	
First day	34.6%	(26)	76.5%	(17)	50.0%	(4)	53.2%	(47)	71.4%	(21)
Second day	70.8%	(24)	73.3%	(15)	76.9%	(13)	73.1%	(52)	75.0%	(28)
Third day	71.4%	(21)	94.4%	(18)	81.2%	(16)	81.8%	(55)	88.2%	(34)
Fourth day	62.5%	(24)	93.3%	(15)	95.0%	(20)	81.3%	(59)	94.2%	(35)
Fifth day	69.2%	(26)	100%	(10)	92.0%	(25)	83.6%	(61)	94.2%	(35)
Sixth day	100%	(14)	100%	(12)	100%	(33)	100%	(59)	100%	(45)
Seventh day	81.8%	(22)	84.6%	(13)	100%	(24)	89.8%	(59)	89.1%	(37)
Eighth day	79.1%	(24)	100%	(11)	95.0%	(20)	89.1%	(55)	96.8%	(31)
Ninth day	83.3%	(18)	83.3%	(6)	100%	(7)	87.1%	(31)	92.3%	(13)
Tenth day	83.3%	(6)	75.0%	(4)	100%	(7)	88.2%	(17)	90.9%	(11)
Totals	67.9%	(215)	88.4%	(121)	92.9%	(169)	81.2%	(505)		

STATE OF WAKEFULNESS

of whether the infant was originally awake or asleep is considered. On the first day the percentage of infants initially asleep and then aroused who exhibited the reflex was only 34.6 (Table 2). During the next four days this percentage increased to a height which appeared to be fairly constant. This constancy was maintained at a somewhat higher figure during the last four days, if the figure for the sixth day is ignored.

When we examined the charts of individual infants to ascertain the day on which the rooting reflex was first manifested, regardless of the state of wakefulness, we observed that, of the 71 babies the reflex was exhibited in 31, or 43.7 per cent, on the first day; 55, or 77.4 per cent, within the first two days; 62, or 87.3 per cent, within the first three days; 65, or 91.5 per cent, within the first four days; 67, or 94.4 per cent, within the first five days; and 71, or 100 per cent, within the first six days.

Intake of food. The fourth factor which influenced the incidence of the rooting reflex was the intake of food. Of the 55 observations made on babies who had just eaten, 41.8 per cent resulted in elicitation of the reflex.

TACTILE STIMULATION OF THE LIPS

When the rubber nipple was touched to the lips of an infant who was wide awake, the lips opened and the nipple slipped into his mouth. In 87 observations there were 26 failures to open the lips, but all except 4 of these failures were noted in sleeping babies or in babies who initially had been asleep and were then wakened. The distribution of sleeping infants who did not open their mouths on tactile stimulation of the lips was the same throughout the period of hospitalization.

SUCKING

Sucking is influenced by wakefulness, age and intake of food, but to a somewhat lesser degree than the rooting reflex. Of 457 observations of sucking behavior, 403, or 88.1 per cent, were of satisfactory sucking. Two-thirds of the infants who did not suck satisfactorily were less than 2 days old. Three of the 4 infants who refused to make mouth or lip movements of any kind when the nipple was placed in their mouths were less than 1 day old. After the first two days, 100 per cent of those infants who were initially awake when they were tested sucked satisfactorily and 72 per cent of those who were initially asleep at the time they were tested also sucked satisfactorily.

RELATION OF THE ROOTING REFLEX TO SATISFACTORY SUCKING

Infants who sucked unsatisfactorily and who lacked the rooting reflex were more frequently less than 1 day of age than any other age. The rooting reflex was manifested in 86.5 per cent of 334 instances of satisfactory sucking on the test nipple. Satisfactory sucking on the test nipple was present in 96 per cent of 300 instances in which the rooting reflex was elicited. Infants who were awakened from sleep were more likely to suck satisfactorily than to exhibit the rooting reflex. Of infants initially deeply asleep at the time of testing and then awakened, 73.7 per cent sucked satisfactorily on the nipple and 56.2 per cent exhibited the rooting reflex.

COMMENT

ROOTING REFLEX

The behavior which has been called the "rooting reflex" was described by Blanton (1917), Jensen (1932), Dennis (1934), and Pratt, Nelson and Sun (1930), but none of these authors mentioned opening of the mouth as a part of the reflex. Pratt and associates (1930) attributed the first description of the reflex to Samuel Pepys, who, in 1667, wrote in his *Diary:* "They tell me what I did not know that a child (as this do) will hunt up and down with its mouth if you touch the cheek of it with your finger's end for a nipple, and fit its mouth for sucking." The significance of the rooting reflex lies in the fact that the touch of the mother's breast to the cheek of the child will cause him to turn his head and open his mouth to receive the nipple.

It is possible that the rooting reflex which occurs after sucking on the nipple is different from that which occurs before sucking. Bühler and Hetzer (1935) observed that if the feeding is interrupted after a few minutes the infant moves his head toward the breast or bottle and tries to grasp it again with the open mouth. (We saw this reaction, also, on eight or ten occasions when the nipple was removed from the baby's mouth.) We believe that the interpretation of anticipation for the rooting reflex behavior after sucking is justified because this reflex was usually obtained immediately after stimulation by the finger, whereas when an infant was tested before sucking the reflex was obtained in many instances only after delay or not at all.

Another possible explanation of the fact that the act of sucking induced a higher percentage of occurrence of the rooting reflex in our subjects is that sucking acts as a stimulant or a reinforcement in some way, perhaps also on a basis of anticipation. This is suggested by the fact that the stimulating effect was greater in the baby awakened from sleep than in the one awake and not crying and was absent in the one who was crying.

Pratt and associates and Dennis wrote that the rooting reflex was manifested by an infant a few hours old. We elicited it from a baby one-half hour old and from another 1 hour old. Of the 13 babies tested before they were 6 hours old, 8, or 61.5 per cent, manifested the rooting reflex.

TACTILE STIMULATION OF THE LIPS

Ford, Dennis, and Gesell and Ilg described the opening of the infant's lips on contact with the nipple. The response is a reflex which is important in the act of sucking, for it is necessary for the reception of the nipple.

Nurses who care for newborn infants frequently depress the chin of the infants who refuse to open their mouths when the nipple touches their lips. We wished to learn whether this maneuver is necessary only in the feeding of sleepy babies or whether it is needed because of developmental absence of the reflex. The fact that 22 of 26 failures to open the mouth were noted in babies who were awakened from sleep seems to suggest that drowsiness is the important factor. In fact, we observed time and again that when we aroused the infant he opened his lips to the touch of the nipple, whereas while he was asleep he did not do so.

The infant was less willing to open his mouth after he had been fed; hence, it was necessary to depress his chin oftener so that his mouth would receive the nipple. Jensen referred to this as being one of the reactions to satiety. (We must add, however, that we were not so thorough nor so vigorous in our attempt to awaken the child who had just been fed as we were in awakening the one who had not.)

SUCKING BEHAVIOR

When a method of rating sucking behavior was set up, it was observed that without some measure of effectiveness, such as the amount and rate of intake of milk or water or the degree of force involved in the act of sucking, further discrimination was impossible within the category we rated "sucking" (Blanton, 1917) or "satisfactory sucking." Jensen (1932) measured the pressure involved in the process of sucking and observed that the differences in pressure among infants were greater than the differences from one time to the next in the same infant. He described three different types of sucking reactions, all of which are included in our rating 3. He did not evaluate them in terms of effectiveness, but he did say that the most vigorous and long-continued sucking is done by hungry, awake babies.

We hoped that by using a rubber nipple as a standard stimulus to elicit sucking it would be possible to isolate infant factors which entered into either satisfactory or unsatisfactory sucking behavior. Inasmuch as only 11.8 per cent of the babies did not suck well on the nipple, it is obvious that most of them were born with this type of behavior fairly well coordinated. Of the 11.8 per cent who did not suck satisfactorily, 79 per cent had been aroused from sleep before they were tested. Therefore, drowsiness appears to be a definite factor in reducing the effectiveness of this activity. However, the fact that half of those who sucked satisfactorily were 1 or 2 days old suggests a lack of practice effect or some deleterious factor or factors associated with birth among those who did not suck satisfactorily. The latter problem will be considered later.

We observed some of the same types of behavior in sleepy infants both before and after feeding that Jensen said are reactions to satiety. He wrote that it was often necessary to depress the infant's chin to allow the nipple to enter his mouth, but that once the nipple was in place the infant often sucked well. Apparently, the act of sucking has a lower threshold for its elicitation than has opening of the infant's lips to the touch of the nipple. Jensen also described long pauses between sucks and disorganization of the sucking response necessitating stimulation. Because satiety usually is associated with falling asleep in the newborn infant, this behavior in both situations may be due to sleepiness and not to satiety.

When we analyzed our data in search of factors which might have some relation to the lower incidence of the rooting reflex and satisfactory sucking in the first few days after birth of the infant, we were unable to determine that size of the baby, duration of the mother's labor, anesthetic agent administered to the mother or type of delivery had anything to do with it.

WAKEFULNESS

Although our purpose was to study reflex and other behavior that might be related to the act of sucking or to the taking of nourishment, we found that we were studying various states of wakefulness as well. The extreme difficulty we experienced in trying to arouse or to awaken some of the infants, so that they would suck, was surprising. It was especially astonishing when it is remembered that the testing was done no more than forty-five minutes before the next feeding period, when presumably the infant should have been hungry. In several cases we carried out the entire routine of stimulation outlined previously, but even so, we did not succeed in awakening the infant. The extreme drowsiness of these infants is further confirmed by the fact that they fell asleep immediately when we ceased to stimulate them. This recalls to anyone who has worked with newborn infants the frequent complaint of mothers in the hospital that they are unable to awaken their babies so that they will nurse.

Is it possible that babies sleep more in the first day or two of life after birth? Gesell and Amatruda (1947) and Bühler (1930) studied sleep in newborn infants for twenty-four hours a day. Both their reports mentioned the fact that even when the newborn infant seems most awake the quality of the wakefulness is not the same sort of alertness he later attains. There is a developmental aspect to the quality, as well as to the quantity, of wakefulness behavior, just as there is in other types of behavior.

Inasmuch, then, as the newborn infant awake is less responsive than he will become later, it would seem to be indicated that those who care for him should take advantage of his best period for feeding. On the basis of our experience with these infants, this period would seem to be the time at which the infant awakens spontaneously. If the most effective suckling behavior is to be obtained, then the feeding of the infant must be achieved according to a self-regulating schedule. The infant must be permitted to determine his own time of feeding. This time is in part synchronous with his waking schedule. He always awakens when he needs to eat, but he does not always need to eat when he awakens.

SUPPLEMENTARY READINGS

Blauvelt, H. H. Capacity of a human neonate reflex to signal future response by present action. *Child Developm.*, 1962, 33, 21–28.

Denisova, M. P., & Figurin, N. L. K voprosu o pervykh sochetatelnykh pishchevykh refleksakh u grudnykh detei. (An investigation of the first combinative feeding reflexes in young infants.) *Voprosy geneticheskoi refleksologii i pedologii,* 1929, 1, 81–88.

Papoushek, G. A method for the investigation of food-conditioned reflexes in infants up to the age of six months. *Pavlov J. high. nerv. Act.,* 1959, 9, 124–129.

Prechtl, H. F. R. The directed head turning response and allied movements of the human baby. *Behaviour,* 1958, 13, 212–242.

precocious development

of newborn

african infants*

MARCELLE GEBER and R. F. A. DEAN

[Psychologists are loath, as a general practice, to postulate genetically determined differences in development and behavior among the identifiable human races. Such scientific caution is understandable when one reviews past reports on the alleged inferiority of certain racial groups, the evidence for which was simply prejudice and wishful thinking. It does seem probable, however, that, depending on the extent of genetic homogeneity within groups, there may be inborn differences between groups. It would appear that very early infancy would be an opportune time to look for such differences, if they exist, since one would not expect the fairly uniform intrauterine environment to have differential effects upon developing behavior patterns. The authors of the following report, scientists at Mulago Hospital in Kampala, Uganda, seem thoroughly convinced that newborn African infants are in a more advanced state of motor development than newborn European infants. Drs. Geber and Dean report that much of the motor activity of the newborn African infant corresponds to the responses of European infants as old as 4–6 weeks. They reject as unlikely the possibility that this developmental acceleration is due to local climatic or geographical conditions. European and Indian infants conceived and born in the same environment are comparable in their development. The young African infant shows his superior motor development in a number of ways: a lesser degree of flexion, a remarkable control of the head, and the frequent absence of certain of the more primitive reflex activities.]

In the course of work intended to define the psychological changes accompanying kwashiorkor it became necessary to obtain information about the psychomotor development of African children who were healthy and well nourished. The development was assessed by Gesell tests, as used in

* From M. Geber & R. F. A. Dean. The state of development of newborn African children. *Lancet,* 1957, 1, 1216–1219. (With permission.)

Paris (Roudinesco & Guiton, 1950). It was found that, up to the age of about 3 years, the development was usually in advance of European standards, and that the degree of advance was greatest in the youngest children. The tests, which are normally considered to be applicable only to children more than 1 month old, were extended to younger children, and it was established that, at the age of 2 or 3 weeks, the development was equal to that of European children twice or three times that age. The results were not altogether unexpected, because clinical observation of African children in the first year of life had already shown that the accepted "milestones" of development—raising the head, sitting, standing, walking, and so on—were passed at an earlier age than in European children. Some of the results have already been published (Geber, 1956). The present communication describes a recent extension of the work—the study of the African child at birth.

MATERIAL AND METHOD

The technique used was that of André Thomas and his collaborators (Thomas & Saint-Anne Dargassies, 1952; Saint-Anne Dargassies, 1954; Koupernik, 1954). Of 107 babies, 101 were seen in the maternity department of Mulago Hospital, Kampala, where they had been born; the others had been born at home and were seen there. They were all born in July or August, 1956. At birth none weighed less than 2.5 kg, and only 1 (who weighed 4.8 kg) more than 4.1 kg. All the babies and their mothers were without any known disease, and delivery had not been assisted with instruments or by operation. About 60 children were of the Ganda tribe, which is indigenous to the region round Kampala and belongs to the Bantu-speaking groups, and the rest were of other tribes, some of them Bantu, but others Nilotic or Hamitic. No difference associated with tribe could be distinguished. There was no selection of cases. The nurses were asked to bring for examination any children that were available in the maternity wards. Twins and children delivered either by caesarean section or by forceps were brought with the others and were examined but were excluded from the present series. For the examinations a bench or a table with a hard top was used, covered with a thick white cloth.

The children numbered 107. Their ages at the time of examination were as follows: less than 24 hours, 37; 25–48 hours, 45; 49–72 hours, 14; 73–96 hours, 6; 6 days, 1; 7 and 8 days, 2 of each. There were 52 boys and 55 girls.

TECHNIQUE

Since the technique of detailed examination of newborn children is not practiced widely in Britain, an account of some of the more important points may be helpful. It has been drawn largely from Koupernik (1954) and Thomas *et al.* (1955).

At birth the European child usually adopts an attitude that is a continuation of the intra-uterine position: the arms and legs are held tightly in flexion and the fingers clenched over the thumb; lying on his back, he has his head to one side, and the positions of his arms and legs are asymmetrical, flexion and asymmetry being characteristic of the earliest age.

The tone of the arm muscles can be judged by the resistance to extension and by pulling the hand across the thorax and over the opposite shoulder. The position is like that reached when a scarf is thrown over the shoulder, and "the scarf movement" is an appropriate name. The legs are not only flexed but also externally rotated. Their hypertonicity causes the angle at which the knees can be bent to be limited to 90°, and the angle between the legs in abduction to be only 60° (a child whose legs are continuously in extension, or whose hands are permanently open, is deemed to be pathologically hypotonic). If the child is placed on his belly he turns his head to the side, with his cheek laid flat. The head cannot be turned from this position, nor, if the chin is put to the table, can the head be raised to free it. The rest of the body is bunched up, with the arms bent and the elbows in to the sides, and the thighs flexed so that the buttocks are raised. Sometimes, in this position, the child makes a kind of creeping movement (reptation). If the child is put into the sitting position, his trunk tends to collapse, with a kyphosis extending from the neck to the sacrum. The head falls forwards, and falls back if the trunk is made to lean backwards. The falling back, or rather the "head-lag" is seen best when the child is drawn up by his hands into a sitting position.

Many details of reflex activity have been described. The most spectacular, and one of the most consistent in European children, is the Moro reflex. It is best seen when the child is on his back and can be elicited in many ways, including knocking sharply on the table on which the child is lying, and by almost any sudden movement of the limbs or trunk—for instance, by raising the body by pulling on the arms until the head is just clear of the table and letting go. The arms are thrown out in full extension (one name for the reflex is "the arms of the cross"), the back is extended or arched, the head is drawn back, the fingers are fanned out, and the legs are extended. After the extension there is a characteristic return of the arms across the trunk.

The grasping reflex is well known and is also very constant. It should be equal in left and right hands and has two components, one the closing of the hand when the palm is pressed, and the other the maintenance of tension in the flexors, which makes it possible to raise the whole child by a stick grasped in the two hands.

Two other important reflexes can be shown when the child is held standing with his feet on the table: one, which can be called the "straightening reflex," is a tendency of the whole body to be straightened from its usual flexion; the other is the "automatic march" which is a walking step made with the knee flexed and the toes raised, the heel being the first part of the foot to touch the ground.

Tendon-reflexes are usually easy to find but vary with the tone of the part of the body.

Of the cutaneous reflexes the easiest to examine is the plantar reflex. It can be elicited over a large area of the outer side of the legs, as far up as the thighs, but is complicated by the grasping reflex of the toes, which is much like that of the fingers.

Among many other reflexes may be mentioned the ciliary and the photomotor (the tight closing of the eyes when the eyelashes are stroked or a light is shone into them), the "doll's eye" (the movement of the eyes in the opposite direction to passive movement of the head), the auricular (the turning of the head away when the lobe of the ear is rubbed), and the masseteric (the raising of the jaw when the chin is tapped).

Most of the hypertonicity disappears in the normal European child after 6–8 weeks, and the general attitude of flexion is lost. The ability to control the head so that it no longer flops forwards or back, and to straighten the back in the sitting position, is not acquired until 8–12 weeks. The Moro reflex, the automatic march, and the straightening reflex do not persist after 6–8 weeks.

Children at about 2 weeks follow with their eyes near moving objects and at 3 or 4 weeks start to move the head to help the pursuit.

RESULTS

It was immediately obvious that the distribution of muscle tone in the African child differed from that in the European. When the African child was lying quietly at rest, his flexion was much less accentuated. Often the knees were only slightly flexed, and only one of the arms was flexed, with its hand half-open; the other arm might be fully extended, with its hand open completely.

When the child was put down on his back, his head was usually on one side but could be turned from side to side and held in the median position. The eyes were wide open, and had a lively look. In many children, even in the first days, moving objects could be followed with the eyes, and rotation of the head accompanied the pursuit. There was plenty of spontaneous activity, and it was not unusual for the child to turn half on his side. The activity of the arms and legs was bilateral and symmetrical but greater in the legs than in the arms. The legs were chiefly flexed and extended but were also crossed and uncrossed. The feet were usually rotated so that the soles faced each other. The arm movements were not so brisk as those of the legs. The flexion of one arm and extension of the other have already been mentioned; when the child had his head to one side, the arm of that side would often be abducted and lying beside the face. The hands, which were usually open, were moved in all directions and were carried frequently to the face, particularly to the mouth. One child, a day old, who had received at birth a slight scalp wound in the occipital region, continually fingered the bandage over the wound. The thumb was less active than the other fingers but was often in extension. The fingers were spread from time to time.

When he was placed on his belly the child immediately turned his head to one side or (even more remarkable) raised his head, propping himself on his forearms. Sometimes the head was only raised momentarily in the median position and was then lowered, resting on the chin, but most of the children raised the head for several seconds, with the lumbar lordosis and the flexion of the legs increased, and with the arms pressed firmly on the table, the elbows against the body, and the forearms straight ahead. The hands were open, and sometimes the fingers clawed and scratched. The knees were as often flexed as partly extended, but the thighs were almost always flexed on the abdomen so that their fronts were rarely in contact with the table. The legs were less active than when the child was on his back, but fairly often they made creeping movements.

By far the most remarkable feature of the prone position was the control of the head and neck; it seemed almost as though all efforts were concentrated on that control, which was evident again when the children, lying on their backs, were drawn up into a sitting position. Of the 107 children, 90 could prevent their heads from falling back. In these children the trunk remained straight.

When the child was sitting the head remained in the median position and was sometimes turned from side to side before finally falling forwards. When it had fallen, many children could immediately raise it again. The back was straight and upright, or inclined forwards, and a kyphosis was exceptional. The knees were moderately flexed, and the feet were rotated internally.

Some children, when being drawn into a sitting position, pressed on their heels as they were raised and straightened themselves until they were nearly standing. Held upright with the feet touching the table most of the children produced a straightening reflex, some pressing hard with both feet, and some with only one. A few children merely bent the legs. The automatic march reflex was found in only a few children, all aged 1–3 days.

The Moro reflex was by no means constant. In some children, mostly aged 1 or 2 days, the reflex was brisk and full, with extension and abduction of the arms and the usual slow return to the position held before, but in others, whatever means were used for trying to elicit the reflex, the amplitude of the response was poor. The reflex was found in no child aged more than 4 days. (Although the present communication is limited to the description of children who weighed 2.5 kg. or more, it is relevant that some smaller children, who might have been premature, produced a thorough-going reflex.) The grasping reflex was also inconstant, and if the child closed his hand on the object pressed into his palm he rarely continued to hold it firmly but soon relaxed his fingers and allowed the hand to resume its former attitude.

Further examination of tone showed that the extensibility of the flexors, in arms as well as legs, was much greater in African children than in European. The flexion was less hypertonic; it was easy to extend the forearms, and they did not return immediately into flexion but usually remained outstretched. On the contrary, the angle of flexion of the wrist was greater than 90°. The scarf movement, the test of adduction of the arm, could be made easily. Abduction and the carrying of the forearm behind the shoulder also met with little resistance. Similarly, in the legs the popliteal angle was more than 90° and the angle between the straightened abducted legs more than 60°.

On the whole, then, the tone of the flexors in the African children was less in the limbs but more in the head and neck. Other reflex activity— ciliary, photomotor, masseteric, the sucking reflex, and the turning of the head on stimulation of the corners of the mouth—was present. On the other hand, the "doll's-eye" and auricular reflexes could not be elicited. Of the tendon reflexes the patellar was very easy to elicit and the radials were almost as easy. Curiously, despite the relatively light tone of the arm flexors, the olecranon reflex could not be obtained. The cutaneous plantar reflex was nearly always extensor, and the grasping reflex of the toes was more constant than that of the fingers.

When the child was held horizontally face downwards on the open hand of the examiner, the back was straight, the head was kept from falling forwards, and the legs were usually extended in the line of the trunk. Held similarly, but face upwards, the child let the head fall back, and his back arched.

So far as could be determined in this series the results did not vary with the sex of the child, its birth-weight, or the parity of the mother. Unfortunately it was impossible to discover the length of the period of gestation, because the dates of the last menstruation were not accurately known.

DISCUSSION

There seemed to be no doubt that these African children had been born at a more advanced stage of development, judged by the method used, than the normal European child. The results of the examination were so consistent, and the degree of advance was so great, that there was little room for uncertainty. Much of the activity corresponded to an age of 4–6 weeks. Some was even more precocious: for example, the raising of the chin and the scratching of the fingers on the table, when the children were placed on their bellies, might be expected at 6–8 weeks, and so might the maintenance of the head in the mid-position when they were on their backs.

We do not intend, at this stage, to advance theories or facts in attempted explanation, but it is clear to us that the state at birth is consistent with some clinical observations: that the African child sucks vigorously at the breast almost from the first hour, and that he passes the milestones of development at a very early age. It is consistent also with the findings of psychomotor precocity in the earliest years to which we have already alluded. As we have said elsewhere (Geber, 1956) an extensive investigation of all facets of the development of the African child is imperative. A more detailed study of the newborn child is planned, and will include twins, children born by caesarean section, others whose birth has been associated with trauma, and others born before term. The last-named should be especially interesting; it is well recognized that African children whose weight at birth would by ordinary standards cause them to be classed as "premature," are often sturdy and active and can be reared without the special care that has to be lavished on European children of the same weight.

It is conceivable, even if it is in our opinion unlikely, that some of our findings could be explained by the existence of local conditions obtaining at Kampala, which is almost on the equator, and about 3500 ft above sea level. We are prepared to consider a number of possibilities, but we have one piece of evidence that may be helpful in making a judgment. At the same time as the African children, a group of 15 European children—all that were available in the European Hospital, Kampala—and another group of 60 Indian children in the Asian Hospital were studied by the same method. The European children gave exactly the results that have been found in Europe, and the Indian children gave almost similar results. Neither group showed any great degree of overlap with the African children. The work on the European and Indian children will be reported when it has been extended to greater numbers; at the moment it may perhaps be admitted as a confirmation, in part, of the validity of the findings in the Africans.

SUPPLEMENTARY READINGS

Geber, M. The psychomotor development of African children in the first year, and the influence of maternal behavior. *J. soc. Psychol.,* 1958, 47, 185–195.

Geber, M., & Dean, R. F. A. Gesell tests on African children. *Pediatrics,* 1957, 20, 1055–1065.

Knobloch, H., & Pasamanick, B. Further observations on the behavioral development of Negro children. *J. genet. Psychol.,* 1953, 83, 137–157.

Pasamanick, B. A comparative study of the behavioral development of Negro infants. *J. Amer. Med. Ass.,* 1947, 135, 340–342.

Scott, R. B., Ferguson, A. D., Jenkins, M. E., & Cutter, F. F. Growth and development of Negro infants. V. Neuromuscular patterns of behavior during the first year of life. *Pediatrics,* 1955, 16, 24–30.

Uklonskaya, R., Puri, B., Choudhuri, N., Dang, L., & Kumar, R. Development of static and psychomotor functions of infants in the first year of life in New Delhi. *Indian J. Child Hlth.,* 1960, 9, 596–601.

swimming behavior
of the human infant*

MYRTLE B. MCGRAW

[Darwin's theory of the gradual evolution of organisms, in a form modified and extended by later scientists, has now gained general acceptance. Although discoveries of fossil remains of early man tell us something about his anatomical evolution, they still leave us in the dark about possible precursors of his adaptive behavior. Some scientists, including Darwin, have been impressed with the reflexes of the newborn infant as possible evidence on the basis of which to infer something about man's earlier phylogenetic history. The most interesting feature of these early reflexes is that they largely disappear during the first year of the infant's life. In cases where there has been extensive structural damage to the cerebral hemispheres some of these reflexes may fail to disappear. In other cases where the cerebral hemispheres are damaged during later development, some of these reflexes may reappear and thereby become indicators of various types of neurological damage. The "neuropsychological" theory related to the gradual disappearance of certain of the infant's reflexes during the first year of life has been most adequately developed by Dr. Myrtle McGraw, of Briarcliff College. In the present study, Dr. McGraw provides a detailed description of the swimming behavior of the human infant during the first 2½ years of life. When the infant is placed in a prone position in the water during the first few weeks of life, he displays well-coordinated swimming movements. In addition, his breathing is inhibited while he is submerged. Dr. McGraw presents tracings of moving picture films which show clearly the three phases of aquatic behavior during infancy: initial reflex swimming movements, then disorganized or struggling activity, then deliberate or voluntary movements. Dr. McGraw's theory, presented in the volume *The neuromuscular maturation of the human infant,* is that the disorganized phase of aquatic behavior is due to the inhibitory influence of the developing cerebral structures.]

* From M. B. McGraw. Swimming behavior of the human infant. *Journal of Pediatrics,* 1939, 15, 485–490. (With permission.)

The swimming behavior of the human infant bears striking testimony to the phylogenesis of man. Literature on the subject is sparse, limited largely to comments on the random movements of the newborn infant having a swiminglike quality. The only instances of actual experimental evidence cited are those of Watson (1919) and the writer (McGraw, 1935). Watson's observations were on the behavior of three infants tested immediately after birth, as soon as breathing had been well established. His method was to support the baby's back with his hands and gradually lower him in a supine position into the water, maintained at body temperature, so that the body was immersed, but the face was above the water level, thereby preventing water from entering the respiratory passages. Watson reports, "Violent expression of fear—a cry, checking of breathing, followed by deeper inspiration and rapid, entirely uncoordinated, slashing of hands and feet were all that could be observed." On the basis of these observations Watson discounts any evidence of swimming movements in the newborn behavior repertoire.

The present report comprises a more intensive study of the data which formed the basis of the descriptive analysis reported in *Growth* (McGraw, 1935). Descriptive notes and cinema records were accumulated on 42 different infants, ranging in age from 11 days to 2½ years. Observations of the same infants were repeated at different intervals, the total number of observations on the 42 babies being 445. Of this total, 164 consisted of motion picture records, and 281 were in the nature of written notes. The number of repeated observations on the same child varied from 2 to 51, the median being 10. Although in several cases these repeated observations extended over a period of 18 or 20 months, the data were insufficient to justify longitudinal analysis. On the other hand the fact that the same children were tested at different intervals over a period of time indicates, more convincingly than purely cross-sectional observations would, that the changes in this behavior pattern have developmental import.

At each examination the baby was placed in three different positions: (1) With the hands of the experimenter placed under his chin and on the crown of his head, he was supported in the water in such a way that his body and extremities could move freely while his nose and mouth were protected above the water level; (2) he was submerged in a prone position without any support whatsoever; and (3) he was submerged without support in a supine position. The movements in each position were observed and described especially with respect to their organization, rhythmicity, and perseveration.

The movements of the infant only a few weeks old are striking when he is placed in water in a prone position. The baby usually remains in the prone position. Definite rhythmical associated flexor-extensor movements in upper and lower extremities together with a lateral flexion of the trunk corresponding to the flexor phase of the lower extremity are usually manifested. These movements are ordinarily sufficiently forceful to propel the baby a short distance through the water. The character of the movements is essentially the same whether the baby is supported under the chin or submerged in a prone position. Definite organization and rhythmicity of movements are, however, more pronounced when the infant is submerged. While similar to the reflex crawling and stepping movements which involve frictional hindrance, these swimming movements of the newborn infant are distinctly more synchronous and rhythmical. Even when the same infant is suspended in a prone position in air, and there is no friction with a hard underlying surface, his movements are not so rhythmical or organized as they are in water. Another outstanding feature of the infant's behavior during the newborn phase is breath control. Apparently a reflex inhibits his breathing while he is submerged, since he does not cough or show disturbances common among the older babies after they have been submerged. In fact, there seems to be a summation effect of the two reflex mechanisms since the neuromuscular activity is better integrated when respiration is inhibited, as indicated in the submerged situation. For the simple reason that the young baby remains in a prone position and engages in these rhythmical movements with sufficient force to propel his body forward through the water the term "reflex swimming movements" seems suitable to indicate this period. These rhythmical movements of the human infant are quite similar to those of other young quadrupeds in water.*

After the baby is 4 months of age or older, the rhythmicity and pattern of the early behavior become disorganized. Often the babies are quite inactive when supported under the chin, and when submerged prone they usually rotate into a dorsal position, and the movements of the extremities are of the struggling order. They clutch at the experimenter's hand, try to wipe the water from the face, or they may sink deeper into the water without marked manifestations of motor activity. Both the struggling activity and the comparative inertia are, for the sake of convenience, classed as representing the disorganized phase of development in this type of behavior. This phase, i.e., the struggling type of movement and the tendency to rotate from a prone to a dorsal position, continues as the most characteristic mode of behavior until about the time the baby is capable of independent erect locomotion. It was apparent during this phase that the baby had more noticeable difficulty with respiration, or controlling respiration, when he

* For comparison we have studied the swimming behavior of the following mammals: (1) pouch young opossum ranging in length from 10 to 165 millimeters, (2) newborn rat, (3) kitten, (4) rabbit, (5) guinea pig, (6) *macacus rhesus* monkeys ages 5, 6, 15, and 340 days, and (7) one 2-month-old chimpanzee. All maintained the prone position and engaged in rhythmical movements of upper and lower extremities with the exception of the 2-month-old chimpanzee which was immobile and sank to the bottom, and the 15-day-old monkey, which maintained a vertical position in the water and whose movements were less organized and rhythmical than those of the younger monkeys. These observations suggest that the primitive reflex was beginning to disintegrate in this monkey by the time he was 2 weeks old. Observations should be made on a newborn chimpanzee before inference can be drawn as to the developmental status represented by the animal observed. This occasion is taken to express gratitude to Dr. Margaret A. Kennard for the privilege of photographing the primate behavior.

Figure 1—Line drawings representing three phases in the development of aquatic behavior of the human infant.

A. Reflex swimming movements. B. Disorganized behavior. C. Voluntary or deliberate movements. These drawings were obtained by tracing successive frames of 16 mm. movie film illustrating the quality of consecutive movements at different chronological or developmental stages.

was submerged. Often the ingestion of fluid was considerable, and the infant would cough or otherwise show respiratory disturbance when he was taken out of the water.

Toward the beginning of the second year the child again shows a tendency to remain in the prone position, to engage in flexor-extensor movements of the extremities, especially the lower extremities, and to propel his body through the water. The quality of these movements is distinctly different from the rhythmical movements of the newborn; they are more deliberate and apparently of voluntary order. The child is not merely fighting; he is making purposeful movements, fairly well organized, but less automatic than the reflex movements, in order to gain the edge of the pool. At no time did any baby show himself capable of raising his head above the water level for the purpose of breathing.

In the dorsal position, with few exceptions, the disorganized or struggling movements were characteristic throughout the age range, and so the movements made when the child is submerged in the supine position do not show outstanding developmental changes. Although the baby engages in struggling movements, he does not rotate from a supine to a prone position. This observation on movements of the baby in a dorsal position probably explains why Watson (1919) found only "uncoordinated slashing of the hands and feet" in the aquatic behavior of the newborn.

The characteristic pattern of the newborn swimming movements is illustrated in the line drawings of Fig. 1A. These drawings were obtained by tracing sequential projections of moving picture film in order to illustrate synergic movements. Figure 1B shows similar tracings representing the disorganized phase of the behavior pattern. It will be noticed in these drawings that the baby tends to rotate into a dorsal position and that there is no definite consistency or pattern in the consecutive movements. Figure 1C illustrates the deliberate movements of the ambulatory child. The impression gained from our observations of the children around this age is that without sustained swimming experience these movements subsequently become disorganized and the older child must learn to maintain the prone position for swimming. Sometimes these children, after making a few strokes in the prone position, would tend to assume a vertical position. Most children of 5 or 6 years whom the writer has had occasion to observe when they were learning to swim have shown a tendency to maintain an upright rather than a prone position in the water. This vertical position is probably an adaptive response for the purpose of getting the head above the water level. Apparently the ability to maintain the prone position in water is a definite phase in the achievement of swimming, and it is a characteristic, together with the quality of limb movements, which critically differentiates developmental phases in the growing infant.

In order to show the general trend of development in aquatic behavior, the data on these 42 infants were tabulated on a plus-minus basis in chronological periods of 20 days. The results are indicated in the three curves (Fig. 2), showing (a) the decline of the reflex phase, (b) the period when

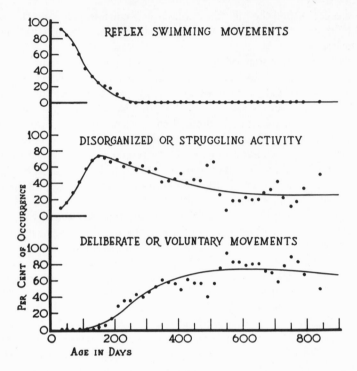

Figure 2—The incidence of three phases in the aquatic behavior of infants.

disorganized behavior is most prominent, and (c) finally the period when the more deliberate movements are manifested. Since these curves represent group data, the phases are not so well differentiated as is the case when successive examinations of individual children are similarly analyzed. The scatter is the resultant of the fact that individual children vary considerably as to the inception and decline of different phases in the development of any activity. However, despite the scatter, the decline of the reflex phase in this activity corresponds closely to the declining period of other atavistic reflexes, such as the Moro reflex, suspension grasp, crawling and stepping movements in the young infant.

INTERPRETATION

This study covers an analysis of the neuromuscular movements of infants when submerged in water. The manifestation in the newborn infant of a rhythmical, coordinated, reflex movement simulating the aquatic movements of other newborn mammals suggests functional evidence of the phylogenesis of man. The maturation of the central nervous system is reflected in the sequential changes of aquatic behavior as well as in other types of neuromuscular activity common to the human infant. It is interesting that developmental changes in swimming behavior correspond in chronological order to the major phases of other behavior patterns which also appear to be of phylogenetic origin.

SUPPLEMENTARY READINGS

Ames, L. B. Some relationships between stair climbing and prone progression. *J. genet. Psychol.,* 1939, 54, 313–325.

Gesell, A. Reciprocal interweaving in neuromotor development. A principle of spiral organization shown in the patterning of infant behavior. *J. comp. Neurol.,* 1939, 70, 161–180.

Mayerhofer, A. Schwimmbewegungen bei Saüglingen. (Swimming movements in infants.) Archiv für Kinderheilkunde, 1953, 146, 137–142.

McGraw, M. B. Development of neuromuscular mechanisms as reflected in the crawling and creeping behavior of the human infant. *J. genet. Psychol.,* 1941, 58, 83–111.

Peatman, J. G., & Higgons, R. A. Relation of infants' weight and body build to locomotor development. *Amer. J. Orthopsychiat.,* 1942, 12, 234–240.

from the moro reflex

to the mature

startle pattern*

WILLIAM A. HUNT, FRANCES M. CLARKE, and EDNA B. HUNT

[The Moro, or Umklammerungs reflex, can be observed in all young infants. It is a clasping movement in which the arms are extended in a curve and slowly brought over one another, while the legs are also brought up in a similar pattern. The Moro reflex gradually drops out of the movements of the infant during the first 4 or 5 months of age and is replaced by the startle pattern which continues to be present throughout the remainder of human life. As technically described by Strauss, the startle pattern in a mature human subject consists of closing of the eyes, head movement, raising and bringing forward of the shoulders, abduction of the upper arms, bending of the elbows, pronation of the lower arms, clenching of the fists, forward movement of the trunk, contraction of the abdomen, and bending at the knees. As may be seen, this is essentially a flexion complex, while the earlier Moro reflex consists first of extension movements and then later flexion movements. In the present report, Dr. Hunt, of Northwestern University, and his colleagues utilized a research technique with infants that had been widely used to study the startle pattern among older subjects. They took ultra-rapid moving pictures of 60 infants ranging in age from 8 days to 18 months under standard stimulus conditions. The stimulus selected to evoke the Moro reflex and startle pattern was the firing of a blank cartridge from an electrically controlled revolver placed about 3 feet to the side of the infant. These investigators conclude that around the age of 4 months the Moro reflex disappears and is followed by the regular startle pattern typical of adults. Their analysis clearly shows that the relationship between the disappearing Moro reflex and the emerging startle pattern is complex and open to several possible interpretations.]

The verification by Landis and Hunt (1939) of Strauss' (1929) claims for a definite bodily reaction pattern in startle (occurring in response to a revolver shot) raises some interesting questions as to the genetic develop-

* From W. A. Hunt, F. M. Clarke, & E. B. Hunt. Studies of the startle pattern: IV. Infants. *Journal of Psychology*, 1936, 2, 339–352. (With permission.)

ment of the pattern. In his original investigation Strauss claims that in very young infants the typical startle response is not present, and one finds instead the Moro reflex or "Umklammerungs reflex" (Moro, 1918), a clasping movement in which the arms are extended in a curve and slowly brought over one another, while the legs are also brought up in a similar pattern. In older infants the Moro reflex is not found and the reaction develops out of the same typical movements as in adults; namely, closing of the eyes, head movement, raising and bringing forward of the shoulders, abduction of the upper arms, bending of the elbows, pronation of the lower arms, clenching of the fists, forward movement of the trunk, contraction of the abdomen, and bending at the knees. Since Strauss' material was admittedly scanty, due to the fact that only a small number of children were available, it seemed advisable to repeat the experiment on a larger group, paying particular attention to that stage of development at which the Moro disappears and is succeeded by the startle response. Such a study would not only make clear the genetic development of the startle pattern but ought to help in understanding its relationship to the Moro reflex.

PROCEDURE

The subjects were a group of 60 infants ranging in age from 8 days to 18 months. Since some of the subjects were given second and third tests on subsequent occasions, a total of 97 observations were available for study. It was impossible to obtain a series of pictures at different age levels from all of the children as many of them left the home before the study was finished. The children were placed on their backs on a comfortable mat and ultra-rapid moving pictures were taken with a camera six feet directly above them. The camera was running at a rate of 64 frames per second, or four times normal speed. A few of the older infants were photographed standing, with the camera placed before them. The stimulus was the firing of a blank cartridge from an electrically controlled revolver placed about 3 feet to the side of the infant. Previous studies have shown that the response is independent of the direction of the shot. The gun was connected in series with an electric stimulus marker which registered in the picture. A 1/5 second clock, placed beside the infant, was also included in the camera field. The pictures were subjected to both slow-motion and static analysis by a committee of three persons and were scored for the presence or absence of the various elements of response. Since it was impossible to attach the lever system used in the previous study of adults, there is a higher proportion of doubtful or "?" judgments in this study. A few of the pictures could not be scored, due to the fact that the infants were in movement when the gun was fired.

RESULTS

The data show definitely the presence of the Moro reflex in response to the shot in the very young infants. Figure 1, *A* and *B,* illustrates typical

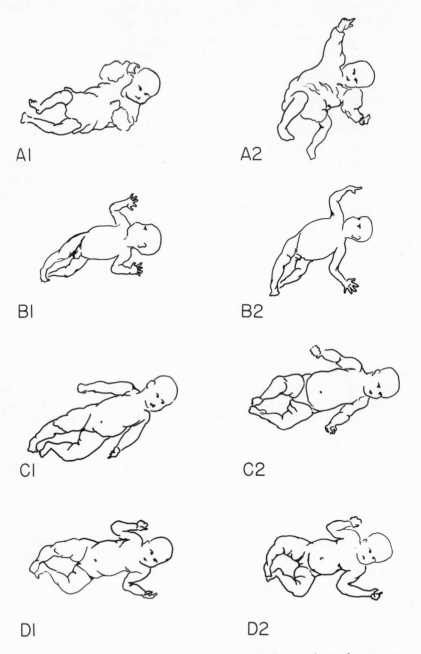

Figure 1—Moro reflexes in young infants (A and B) and startle responses in older infants (C and D).

Table 1—Presence of Moro Reflex*

Age group	Number of subjects	Excellent Moro	Fair Moro	Decayed Moro	No Moro
14 days	3	2	1		
28 days	3		1	2	
2nd month	6		2	3	1
3rd month	9		1	6	2
4th month	6		1	3	2
5th month	5				5

* This table treats all the observations, including second observations at a later date on the same individual, in one general group. Inspection of the genetic development shown by the 2 or 3 samples available on certain of our individual cases reveals nothing different from the general group picture as represented by our table.

response; pictures A_1 and B_1 show the infant before the shot, while pictures A_2 and B_2 show him after the shot. Table 1, in which the lunar month is used as a unit, shows the incidence of the Moro response through the fifth month, by which time it has disappeared in our group. This disappearance of the Moro reflex after the fourth month is in general agreement with the literature. Gordon (1929) sets it between the fourth and sixth months. In our work, excellent Moro responses appeared only during the first two weeks. From then on, as the table shows, decay is rapid. This matter of the rapid decay of the response is important, because in its most decayed form it resembles the Strauss startle response. Compare the description of the startle pattern given in the introduction with Gordon's description of his least intense Moro reflexes as involving tautening and shrugging of the shoulders with a slight forward movement of the arms and flexion at the elbows. Our group would seem to show the Moro disappearing more rapidly than in some studies. This might be due to the fact that other experimenters may have confused true startle responses with degenerate Moro responses and thus been led to believe in the persistence of the Moro beyond its true point of disappearance. This seems particularly plausible in the case of Gordon. The confusion becomes clearer if one compares A and B in Fig. 1, true Moro reflexes in very young infants, with C and D, startle responses in much older babies. In the case of two responses, one at 6 and the other at 11 months, the writers are in real doubt as to whether the movement present should be scored as startle response or very decayed Moro. Further investigation of the Moro reflex in the light of what is now known about the startle pattern should help to clear up the difficulty. We shall return to this similarity between Moro and startle response later.

We did not find the asymmetry in the Moro response that Strauss reports, and which he attributes to the influence of tonic neck reflexes since the head of the child was turned to one side out of its normal orientation to the trunk. Eight of our subjects were photographed in such a posture. Only two showed any asymmetry in the subsequent Moro responses. In both these cases, an apparent tonic neck response involving the customary turning of the head and movements of arm and leg appeared *immediately* after the shot and *before* the Moro, which was delayed. Both Moros, when they did appear, showed a symmetrical disposition of the arms, but asymmetry in the legs, inasmuch as one leg was drawn up while the other remained extended. The appearance of some sort of tonic neck reaction in response to a shot stimulus and its apparent temporal precedence over the Moro reflex are interesting, but two cases are not sufficient to warrant discussion. It may not be amiss, however, to point out the importance of our ultra-rapid photographic technique in separating the total response picture into its temporal components.

In those cases where the Moro reflex is not found, the startle response, as described by Strauss, appears. The general presence of the startle pattern is clear, and the various elements of the pattern have been scored for each subject.

Figure 1, C and D, shows typical startle responses; C_1 and D_1 being taken before the shot, C_2 and D_2 at the height of the response. As with adults, the blinking of the eyes is the most reliable element of the pattern, with head movement next. Two of the babies, one at 5 months and one at 15 months, failed to show the lid reflex, although both showed other elements of the response and both showed the presence of the lid reflex on other occasions, one at a previous testing, the other at a subsequent one. So far in our study, no adult has failed to show the lid reflex. Gross arm and leg movement is greater, both in incidence and quantity among the infants. There would also seem to be a slightly higher incidence of opposed movement in the babies. Much of this may be due to the less developed neuro-muscular coordination of the infants. Much of it is certainly due to the interference of various postural attitudes. The infant has little sense of his photographic responsibility in posing. Perhaps the inhibiting contact of the child's body with the mat affected the response. This last may be particularly true as regards the appearance of negative trunk movement (extension with arching instead of flexion with curling), which does not appear in the adult. Anyhow, this negative movement is definitely the exception and not the rule. Much of the absence of trunk and abdominal movement in the babies is due to the inability to observe because of the objection of some of the mothers to completely undressing the infants. There seems to be no difference in the relative amount of arm and leg movement as the child develops, both being equally active at all stages.

Now let us turn to the resemblance between the Moro reflex and the startle pattern and deal with their possible relationships. Strauss' conclusion that these are two separate patterns following one another in the development of the child is no doubt the safest conclusion. Our observations, however, indicate the possibility of two other interpretations: the startle pattern may be simply a decayed, degenerate form of the Moro; or both may be present from birth on with the startle pattern obscured by the grosser Moro reflex and only being observable when the larger response has disappeared. It would seem best to give some attention to these three possible interpretations.

1. The Moro and the startle pattern are two distinct responses, with the Moro appearing first and the startle pattern coming in when the Moro disappears around the fourth month of life. This is perhaps the most cautious conclusion, and involves the least interpretation. The Moro is clearly present in the very young infants. The startle pattern does not become evident until the Moro has degenerated and been dropped from the infant's behavioral repertoire. Furthermore, there is a distinct opposition of the hand movement in the two patterns (extension for the Moro, flexion for the startle pattern), and in much of the elbow movement in our infants (with elbows bent at an acute angle as in Fig. 1, *D*).

2. The Moro and the startle pattern are distinct responses, both present at birth, with the less noticeable startle pattern concealed at first by the grosser Moro reflex. The possibility of such concealment is evident. This view is supported by the fact that certain elements of the startle pattern, *i.e.,* blinking, head movement, contraction of the abdomen, are present in our youngest children who react with the Moro response although these are not usually considered part of the Moro reflex. The main support (revealed by our ultra-rapid photography) comes from two cases who seem to respond first with the startle pattern and then show the Moro reflex. In the youngest infants, however, the Moro reflex comes immediately, and the delayed Moro, which in both cases mentioned occurs in older infants, may simply be a phenomenon of the transition point where both patterns may overlap temporarily.

3. The startle pattern is simply the perseveration of the Moro reflex in a very degenerate and decayed form. This view is supported strongly by the general similarity of the two responses. It would necessitate expanding the description of the Moro to include the elements such as blinking, abdominal movement, *etc.,* mentioned above, but this may be necessary anyway. If we conclude that the very young infant responds to a shot with the Moro reflex, what can we say about the blinking, *etc.,* which were clearly present. These responses cannot be overlooked and must be included somewhere in the total response picture. The similarity of the two patterns is again shown by pointing out that in the adult standing erect with arms at his sides, a decayed Moro response would resemble the startle pattern, *i.e.,* hunching of the shoulders, abduction of the upper arms, bending at the elbow, pronation of the lower arms. The antagonism in the hand movement (extension versus flexion) still remains, but the behavior of some adults shows us a possible resolution of this antagonism by assuming a temporal sequence. Thus, as was pointed out in a previous study, some of the adults show a flexion of the fingers followed immediately by extension.

It should be remembered, too, that some changes (possibly involving a shift to an opposite type of movement) would arise due to continuing neuromotor development as the child becomes older. Let us illustrate this by an analogy from the development of the tonic neck reflex (*TNR*). The *TNR* is almost universal from 4 to 12 weeks, gradually disappearing at 16 weeks, and gone by 20 weeks. This disappearance of the *TNR* is correlated

with the free ranging mobility of the head at this age. This does not necessarily mean that the *TNR* has dropped out of the child's neurological constitution; it may well be that some latent form perseveres and may appear in
the course of his versatile activity, so transient and fleeting, however, as to
be lost in the multitude of other patterns and to escape observation. So, too,
the Moro may persist in the startle pattern, being changed through its
dependence on the neuromotor development of the infant. Thus the appearance in the Moro in the very young infant of a certain amount of elbow
movement which is antagonistic to the startle pattern may be due merely to
the neuromotor development of the child and the gradual liberation of the
elbow for independent movement.

A further connection between Moro and startle pattern is shown in an
element of the Moro reflex apparently previously unnoticed but clearly
evident in most of our subjects, namely, that as the legs are drawn up the
feet tend to rotate inward. In four adults, photographed in a prone position,
while no leg movement was apparent, three of the subjects did show the
inward rotation of the feet. This might be used as an argument for the
identity of the two responses.

At present, however, the authors see no way of eliminating all but one
of these alternatives. Among the necessary work preliminary to a decision
is a careful further investigation of the Moro reflex in all its forms in the
light of what is now known about the startle pattern. The authors propose
to initiate such a study, and reserve further discussion of the above points
until its results are known.

SUPPLEMENTARY READINGS

Clarke, F. M. A developmental study of the bodily reaction of infants to an
    auditory startle stimulus. *J. genet. Psychol.*, 1939, 55, 415–427.
Clarke, F. M., Hunt, W. A., & Hunt, E. B. Plantar responses in infants follow-
    ing a startle stimulus. *J. genet. Psychol.*, 1937, 50, 458–461.
Hunt, W. A., Clarke, F. M., & Hunt, E. B. The startle pattern in infants in
    response to nonauditory stimuli. *J. genet. Psychol.*, 1938, 52, 443–446.
Irwin, O. C. The latent time of the body startle in infants. *Child Develpm.*,
    1932, 3, 104–197.
McGraw, M. B. The Moro reflex. *Amer. J. Dis. Child.*, 1937, 54, 240–251.

conflict between
overlapping
learning functions*

CLARK L. HULL and BERTHA IUTZI HULL

[If a poll were taken among contemporary American psychologists as to which colleagues had been most influential during the short history of this science, it seems very probable that the name of Clark L. Hull would be near the top of the list of nominees. His seminal work on learning theory, while he was a professor of psychology at Yale University, established the hypothetitico-deductive method as a favored approach to psychological inquiry. Dr. Hull was a scientist of many interests and broad understanding. The following report, presenting the results of Dr. Hull's early excursion into developmental psychology, raised a number of questions to which later investigators have directed their attention. This report is also a fine tribute to the patient cooperation of Mrs. Hull, a trained nurse, who made the observations. One is also forced to the sentiment that this investigation is a testament to the tolerance of the young subject who sometimes spent as long as 20 minutes on the toilet—and not always with success! The most widely quoted finding of this study, that the early stages of learning to talk interfere for a while with further learning of voluntary control of the bladder, has yet to be tested by comparable, rigorous research. This type of interference between simultaneously developing psychological functions (e.g., learning to walk interfering with vocabulary growth) is now pretty much taken for granted, even though the domain of such interfering activities has yet to be specified.]

The present report is concerned chiefly with the progress of a young child in securing voluntary control of the bladder and in the acquisition of spoken vocabulary. There is already a considerable body of literature on vocabularies of early childhood but despite the peculiar insistence of the problems involved, the present writers have not been able to find any systematic

---

* From C. L. Hull & B. I. Hull. Parallel learning curves of an infant in vocabulary and in voluntary control of the bladder. *Pedagogical Seminary,* 1919, 26, 272–283. (With permission.)

studies of the learning processes concerned with urinary control. It is entirely possible that if this obscure chapter of child psychology were better understood the number of cases of enuresis and quasi enuresis might be considerably reduced.

The subject whose behavior is made the basis of the present study is a female child born of a primipara in the month of August after a normal and uneventful period of gestation. At birth her weight was six and three-fourths pounds. Grasping reflexes were vigorous though probably not strong enough to support her entire weight. Similar reflexes were observed in the feet. Despite great care in the matter of diet, appetite was rather indifferent during the second year and weight throughout was slightly less than Holt's norms for girls. Teething began early (sixth month) and proceeded rapidly with little suffering. None of the contagious diseases of childhood were encountered during the period reported here, though she occasionally had colds. She was very active and especially persevering in infantile projects. She crept at ten months and walked in the middle of the thirteenth month. Her first real words were spoken at seventeen months. She had a vocabulary of 129 words at two years and one of 500 words at 28 months. At the latter date she had a reading vocabulary of 20 words. At three years she had a reading vocabulary of 70 words.

We had been teaching her a few minutes per day for about six weeks at the time, by cutting the names of objects in which she was interested from a primer and pasting each on a 2 x 5 inch blank card. On the opposite side of the card would be pasted the picture of the object and after the word had been read, the card would be turned over at once to see if it had been read correctly, thereby strengthening the association. This technique proved extremely attractive, evidently appealing to her play instincts for she would gather up her cards several times a day and come to us saying "Reada carts!" Apparently a child may learn to read much earlier than is ordinarily supposed (Terman, 1918a).*

At the age of 28 months, she was also given the Binet-Simon tests (Stanford revision) by the first author under excellent experimental conditions. This testing yielded a mental age of three years and two months or an intelligence quotient of 135.

The mother before marriage was a trained nurse with some university work, especially in psychology. The father holds a Ph.D. degree and is an instructor at the University of Wisconsin.

There seems to be little difference of opinion among medical writers as to the best method of teaching children to control the bowel and bladder.

---

* It was noticed that she seemed to recognize the words almost as readily wrongside up as right. Accordingly when she had eleven words learned, we presented each word to her seven times wrong and seven times right side up, and measured with a fifth-second stop watch the time elapsing from the ocular fixation of the word to the spoken reaction. The same word never came twice in succession. The two ways were alternated irregularly to equalize the effect of practice. The seventy-seven reactions each of the inverted and correct positions averaged respectively 1.97 and 1.52 seconds. The inversion thus caused an increase of only 30% in reading time.

Dennet for example says (1912) that the child should be placed on the chamber every hour of the day beginning with the eighth month. Others would begin the practice somewhat earlier (Holt, 1912). It was begun with the present subject at about the eighth month, although records were not taken until early in the ninth (calendar) month. An examination of these records shows that we fell short of Dennet's strenuous program in the frequency of the trials. An ordinary closet bowl was provided with a supplementary seat suitable for a young child. This was used instead of a chamber. During the early months of the experiment, micturition would often not take place for half an hour or even longer. If it took place within 20 minutes or thereabouts, a plus was recorded on a score sheet placed conveniently for the purpose. If not, the trial was usually given up as a failure and a minus recorded. From these data taken by months the per cent of the total trials which resulted in successes were computed and the results taken as a convenient index of the level of control attained.

As a child becomes somewhat older however, it is also possible to record with certainty the number of micturitions taking place when not at the toilet. The number of these "accidents" in a month is added to the number of successful trials, giving the total number of micturitions in that period. The per cent of successes of this total clearly affords a second and possibly more satisfactory index of the level of control attained.

From a theoretical point of view these two indices might be expected to represent distinct processes: the first the power to relax the sphincters at will initiating micturition; the second the power to inhibit spontaneous tendency to such relaxation while in situations inappropriate for micturition. Whether this reasoning is incorrect or whether the two processes are so highly correlated that each serves as a measure of the other, the fact is that despite a certain amount of variation between the two, the average of the indices by each of the two methods for the six lunar months during which both were used, are almost identical. Consequently the first method was discontinued after the twenty-fifth month. The average of the percentages by the two methods is taken as the final index of control for the six months during which both were taken. The observations cover a period of twenty-two lunar months and include over forty-six hundred entries on the original charts. The progress in acquiring control from month to month is shown graphically by the upper or heavy curve of Fig. 1. The part of the curve extending over the first ten of the four-week periods is a straight broken line indicating that no records were taken during this time.

The general shape of the curve proves to be that of the familiar learning curves for skill and for the simpler mental processes (Ladd and Woodworth, 1911), rising more rapidly at the beginning of the learning process and continuing progressively slower as the score approaches the limit of perfection. Its most striking characteristic is the pronounced plateau beginning at the eighteenth four-week period and continuing without perceptible improvement through nine lunar months. Such an extended plateau could not result from chance and accordingly calls for explanation. Having

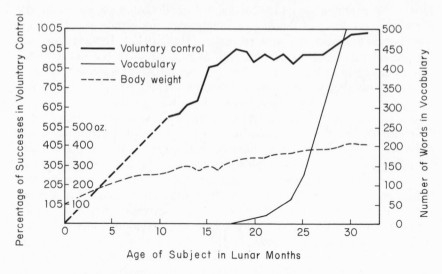

Figure 1—The development of voluntary bladder control, vocabulary, and body weight over the first 31 months of life.

noticed a certain tendency to lack of control associated with severe colds, the idea was suggested that the plateau might have been caused by a mild but continuous deterioration of the health during that period. Accordingly the body weights were plotted parallel to the curve of control for the entire thirty-one months. It appears as a light dotted line in Fig. 1. It was assumed that any such general disturbance of the health would be shown objectively by a corresponding plateau in the bodily growth. Inspection of the curve shows, however, that there is no suggestion of such a plateau. Indeed in this region as in other parts of the curve, it follows very uniformly the course determined by the authoritative norms of Holt (1912), though somewhat lower.

A more plausible explanation is suggested by the fact that the difficult early stages of talking (light curve, Fig. 1) coincide exactly with the beginning of this plateau. That walking interferes with talking has been observed repeatedly (Tracy and Stimpfl, 1909). It is possible that learning to talk has in this case interfered with the acquisition of voluntary control of the bladder. Unfortunately, owing to the lack of exact studies on this subject it is impossible to say whether such a plateau is an exception or the rule in such learning.

The curve of learning in acquisition of a spoken vocabulary (Fig. 1) has already been mentioned. All the new words used up to two years of age were carefully recorded by calendar months, and the vocabulary was again completely determined four months later. These vocabulary records thus cover nearly a year and permit us to get an excellent view of the learning process perhaps at its most interesting level. The form of this curve offers a sharp and striking contrast to the curve just considered. Instead of having its most rapid rate at the beginning and continuing progressively slower as is usual with the learning curves so far published, we find here the exact opposite taking place. It begins at an extremely slow rate and continues at progressively more *rapid* rates as far as investigated. Some of Terman's results (1918a), though obtained by a different method, indicate that by the seventh year the rate of increase has become stable and that this continues for eleven years almost without change, though ending at a slower rate. The type of curve thus presented seems so far to have been found only in analytical learning. Ruger (Thorndike, 1913) found it with puzzles and the writer (Hull, 1919) found it very uniformly in the evolution of concepts. It may be significant that the acquisition of the meaning of words is essentially a process of analytical learning, viz: the evolution of concepts. And while the mental processes involved here and particularly the method of constructing the curve is by no means identical with the two studies just mentioned, there is sufficient identity to make the striking similarity of the shape of the curves suggestive.

The curve shows that no real words were spoken until the seventeenth month. At two years, there were 129 words. Beginning was thus somewhat later than the average and at two years the number of words was still somewhat below the 200 set by Nice (1918) as the minimum. (In this connection it may be well to add that the subject showed at two years a slight tendency to be ambidextrous; at three years this had entirely disappeared.) The four months following however, show an average increase of nearly a hundred words per month, so that at the end of this time the score was about 10 per cent above the average of the six vocabularies for the twenty-eighth month assembled by Bateman (1916). The moral of this seems to be that delay at the beginning of the language learning process is consistent with excellent progress later on.

Previous to a careful examination of the records and the plotting of the curve, the writers were of the opinion that special environmental influences had played a great part in the process. During the slow period the subject played with other children almost not at all, whereas during the rapid period she played vigorously several hours every day with two older girls. But careful examination of the curve gives scant support for this view. During the twenty-fourth month while she was alone she gained 19 words while in the following month during which she had playmates she gained only 24 words. It will also be noted that the curve had already started on its rapid upward movement before she entered on her vigorous play relations.

An analysis of the 24 and 28 month vocabularies reveals a surprising similarity as to grammatical constitution when it is considered that the second is about four times as large as the first. This analysis is given in some detail by Table 1.

The proportions of the various parts of speech found at both age levels

Table 1—Analysis of Vocabulary at Two Age Levels

Parts of Speech	TWENTY-FOURTH MONTH		TWENTY-EIGHTH MONTH	
	Number of words	Per cent	Number of words	Per cent
Common nouns	74	57.4%	289	57.8%
Proper nouns	9	7.0%	34	6.8%
Verbs	24	18.5%	85	17.0%
Adjectives	8	6.2%	41	8.2%
Adverbs	6	4.6%	24	4.8%
Pronouns	2	1.5%	8	1.6%
Prepositions	2	1.5%	9	1.8%
Interjections	4	3.1%	10	2.0%
Conjunctions	0	0.0%	0	0.0%
Total	129	100.0%	500	100.0%

differ but little from those given by Tracy (1909). The combined nouns in each vocabulary exceed slightly the 60 per cent given by him while the verbs are in each case slightly less. Conjunctions are entirely lacking in both vocabularies.

SUPPLEMENTARY READINGS

Brazelton, T. B. A child-oriented approach to toilet training. *Pediatrics,* 1962, 29, 121–128.

Despert, J. L. Urinary control and enuresis. *Psychosom. Med.,* 1944, 6, 294–307.

Halverson, H. M. Genital and sphincter behavior of the male infant. *J. genet. Psychol.,* 1940, 56, 95–136.

Scoe, H. F. Bladder control in infancy and early childhood. *Univer. Iowa Stud. Child Welf.,* 1933, 5, No. 4.

bowel training

and bed wetting*

J. W. B. Douglas and J. M. Blomfield

[Many social scientists have charged that Western Man has made a fetish of cleanliness. And it cannot be denied that in our child-rearing practices we are often preoccupied with routines related to sanitation and hygiene. For example, toilet training is initiated during very early infancy, and the young child is frequently admonished to wash his hands, brush his teeth, or wipe his nose. We are prone to rationalize that these instructions are important in promoting the child's health, even though we recognize that other civilized countries manage to have equally healthy children without such vigorous scrubbing of toilets and washbasins and without the wrapping of all consumables in cellophane. From the extensive array of rituals related to cleanliness, psychologists have selected toilet training for intensive study. This interest derives from Sigmund Freud's writings in which he postulated an antecedent-consequent relationship between early toilet training and the development of anal character traits like cleanliness, miserliness, and orderliness. The following report by Dr. Douglas, of the Medical Research Unit at the London School of Economics, and Miss Blomfield is based on the results of a longitudinal survey of 5386 British children studied from birth. The survey found that 60% of English mothers start to "pot" their infants during the first two weeks of life—a time at which voluntary control of the anal sphincters is not yet possible. (Neurologists generally consider that six months is the earliest age at which myelination is sufficiently developed to support voluntary control.)

The significance of toilet training *per se* on personality remains a debated question. In contrast to Freud's inference of a cause-effect relationship, the majority of contemporary psychologists believe that the observed correlations may be a by-product of other child-rearing practices. Regardless of the stand one may take on this issue, the diversity of toilet training practices found among different cultures continues to attract the interest of many behavioral scientists.]

* From J. W. B. Douglas & J. M. Blomfield. *Children under five*. London: George Allen & Unwin, Ltd., 1958. Pp. 127–132. (With permission.)

The conflicts that may be aroused in a child during toilet training are widely thought to be related to the emergence in later life of such character traits as excessive orderliness, frugality, obstinacy and, in extreme instances, compulsion neuroses. Accordingly it is sometimes recommended that strictness in toilet training should be avoided and that the training itself be postponed until the child can understand what is required of him. If this is done, it is claimed, compulsive traits will be less likely to develop and subsequent bed wetting or soiling will be rare. These claims need to be confirmed by following the later progress of children who have been trained in different ways, and some information of this type is given in the present study.

The mothers were asked the age at which they started to 'pot' their children, the age when they were clean and whether there was any later soiling. These questions were asked when the survey child was six years old. Many of the mothers (60 per cent), started to 'pot' their children within two weeks of birth, 25 per cent did so between two weeks and six months and 15 per cent after six months. It is of interest that the practice

Table 1—Age at Which 'Potting' Was Started in Each Social Group
(Tabular entries are percentages)

| Age at starting | NON-MANUAL WORKERS | | | MANUAL WORKERS | | | | |
	Professional and salaried	Black-coated	Skilled	Semi-skilled	Un-skilled	Agri-cultural	Self-employed	*All groups
During first month	74.1	67.9	58.9	57.6	48.1	59.5	62.5	60.0
1–6 months	16.9	22.0	25.9	22.9	31.3	25.3	26.2	24.8
After 6 months	9.0	10.1	15.2	19.5	20.6	15.2	11.3	15.2
Total	100.0	100.0	100.0	100.0	100.0	100.0	100.0	100.0

* Corrected for sampling.

of early training was more marked in England and Wales than in Scotland, the proportions starting to 'pot' the child within the first two weeks being 64 and 55 per cent respectively.

There were no significant differences between first- and later-born children or between boys and girls in the date of starting training.

It will be seen in Table 1 that 'potting' was started earlier among the well-to-do than among the poor.

The younger mothers in most social groups started to train their children later than the older mothers, as will be seen in Table 2.

Table 2—The Proportion of Mothers of Different Ages in Each Social Group Starting to 'Pot' Their Children During the First Months of Life
(Tabular entries are percentages)

| Mother's age | NON-MANUAL WORKERS | | | MANUAL WORKERS | | | |
	Professional and salaried	Black-coated	Skilled	Semi-skilled and unskilled	Agri-cultural	Self-employed	*All groups
Under 25	72.7	61.1	55.4	49.7	51.7	55.2	55.1
25–35	75.6	69.9	60.1	57.1	61.7	66.0	62.4
Over 35	75.2	73.5	67.7	55.8	63.6	61.5	65.7

* Adjusted for sampling.

These differences were most marked and only statistically significant in the middle social groups—i.e., the black-coated and skilled manual workers —and were small in the professional and salaried and in the semi-skilled and unskilled.

By the age of one year, 47 per cent of children were clean, and by the age of 18 months, 83 per cent. Those who were potted in the first six months were at an advantage; for example, among the children of skilled workers 49 per cent were clean by a year and 83 per cent by 18 months, as compared with 29 per cent and 69 per cent of those whose training had been postponed. There was also a low incidence of later soiling among children who were potted early; 3.4 per cent of these became dirty later, as compared with 8.6 per cent of those whose training had been postponed. These figures also refer to the children of skilled manual workers. Similar differences were found in each social group.

Girls gained control of their bowels at an earlier age than boys and were rather less likely to have later trouble. In both sexes later soiling was slightly but not significantly more common when there was a younger brother or sister. At eighteen months 86 per cent of girls and 80 per cent of boys were clean; later breakdowns were found among 2.9 per cent of girls and 4.1 per cent of boys. When there were younger sibs the proportion of breakdowns was 4.8 per cent, and when there were none 4.0 per cent.

Another aspect of bowel function on which we have information is the use of laxatives. The position at six years old was that 51 per cent of children were never dosed, 31 per cent only occasionally and 18 per cent once each week, or more often. There were considerable differences in the use of laxatives between the social groups, as Table 3 shows. They were particularly marked among those giving laxatives for other reasons than hard stools; that is to say among mothers who believed in the weekly purge. The younger mothers, particularly in the professional and salaried group, refrained from giving laxatives in this way.

Table 3—The Proportion of Mothers in Each Social Group Giving Their Children Laxatives at Least Once a Week at 6 Years (tabular entries are percentages)

| | NON-MANUAL WORKERS | | | MANUAL WORKERS | | | |
Reason for giving laxative	Professional and salaried	Black-coated	Skilled	Semi-skilled and unskilled	Agri-cultural	Self-employed	*All groups
Hard stools	3.4	4.3	5.8	5.7	4.3	4.2	5.2
Others reasons	3.9	10.2	13.2	15.7	14.2	6.6	12.3
Total giving laxatives once a week or more often	7.3	14.5	19.0	21.4	18.5	10.8	17.5

* Adjusted for sampling.

Twelve per cent of the children wetted their beds at 4¼ years; 3.5 per cent were wet several nights a week and the remainder only occasionally. They included three mongoloid imbeciles and nine mental defectives. We describe here only the children who were wet several nights a week, since they must have given the most trouble to their parents and were also the most likely to be persistent bed wetters at later ages. Among the more prosperous families boys more often wetted their beds than girls; the percentages were 3.81 and 1.71 respectively. Among the manual workers bed wetting was equally common in the two sexes, being 3.57 per cent for the boys and 3.22 per cent for the girls.

A larger proportion of the manual workers' children than of the non-manual workers' wetted their beds. This was accounted for by the high incidence of bed wetting among girls in the former group which, it may be added, was found at later ages as well as at 4¼ years.

Jealousy of a younger child is generally thought to be an important cause of bed wetting, but our figures neither support nor disprove this view: 3.7 per cent of the children with younger sibs were regular bed wet-ters as compared with 2.9 per cent of the rest, a difference in the expected direction though not statistically significant. Nor did the mothers themselves often associate bed wetting with the birth of a younger child; out of 27 who suggested a cause for bed wetting only 5 gave this reason—the two most common ones advanced being illness and return to school.

We have already seen that the younger mothers postponed bowel train-ing and this appears to be related to the high incidence of bed wetting among their children: 5.6 per cent were wet, as compared with 2.9 per cent of the children of older mothers. Our reason for suggesting this is that bed wetting was more common when potting had been started after the age of six months. This relationship was more marked for girls than for boys. For girls who were six months or younger when potting was started, 2.8 per cent were regularly wet at six years; for girls over six months when started, 5.4 per cent were regularly wet at age six years. The corresponding figures for boys are 3.5 per cent and 4.4 per cent, respectively.

It is difficult to be certain of the importance of potting in relation to bed wetting since others factors, such as more conscientious care, may be as-sociated with a particular mother's preference for early training. In any case, not all the social differences in bed wetting can be explained in terms of different patterns of training, since among agricultural workers potting started late but the prevalence of bed wetting was low.

A low standard of maternal care is in fact associated with bed wetting; for example, in the manual workers only 13 per cent of the mothers of bed wetters were classed as giving the best maternal care as compared with 29 per cent of those mothers whose children were dry. Our maternal care code includes both an assessment of the management of the child and of its cleanliness (and that of the home), and it is of interest that the former appears to be the more important in this context.

In order to look at the characteristics of the regular bed wetters we matched them with children from similar families who were dry. We ex-cluded the three mongolian imbeciles and the nine mental defectives and this left 131 matched pairs. The results of the clinical examinations in 1952 showed no significant differences between the two groups, whether we considered individual abnormalities or gave a score for the whole examination. The doctors did, however, more often record bitten nails and speech defects among regular bed wetters, the former difference being highly significant and the latter not, and it is of interest that at the same time more of the mothers of the children reported nightmares or bad habits such as thumb sucking and nail biting. Bitten nails were reported by doctors among 17.6 per cent of the bed wetters and 6.1 per cent of their controls, and speech defects among 6.9 per cent of the former and 2.3 per cent of the latter. Nightmares were reported by mothers among 37 per cent of the bed wetters and 30 per cent of their controls, and bad habits among 40 per cent and 30 per cent, respectively.

Since some of the children who were wet at four years had become dry later, we looked at these separately to see whether the excess of nervous habits was found only among those who were still wet. According to the mothers this was so, but the doctors reported just as great an excess among earlier bed wetters who had become dry as among those who were still wet. Perhaps when mothers are worrying about a child who is bed wetting, they are more likely to notice other habits and worry about them too.

SUPPLEMENTARY READINGS

Bostock, J., & Shackleton, M. G. Enuresis and toilet training. *Med. J. Australia,* 1951, 2, 110–113.

Bott, E. A., Blatz, W. E., Chant, N., & Bott, H. Observation and training of the fundamental habits in young children. *Genet. Psychol. Monogr.* 1928, 4, 1–161.

McGraw, M. B. Neural maturation as exemplified in achievement of bladder control. *J. Pediatr.,* 1940, 16, 580–590.

the development
of handedness*

ARNOLD GESELL and LOUISE B. AMES

[Mature man is predominantly righthanded in all known societies, both primitive and civilized. Although the neurophysiological basis for righthandedness remains a mystery, it is well known that special psychological experiences during early childhood can modify this preference. It is also known that a small percentage of children develop a pronounced preference for the left hand. During several periods of recorded history the lefthanded individual has been regarded as having unusual mental powers, as being sinister (a word whose origin means *lefthanded*), and as having other special attributes. In many early schools the lefthanded child was often regarded as perverse and uncooperative, and was forced to write with his right hand. The psychological theory of cerebral dominance, extremely popular over the decade 1930–1940, attributed a variety of speech disturbances to a lack of cerebral dominance and associated laterality functions. One of the most thorough investigations of the development of handedness was conducted by Drs. Gesell and Ames at the Yale Clinic of Child Development. They took copious cinema and direct observational records of many children between 8 weeks and 10 years of age. The descriptive analysis of their data is presented in great detail. They very wisely note that the morphogenesis of handedness is extremely complex. The growing child moves through many phases of symmetrical and asymmetrical response tendencies in the use of his hands. Their conclusions that handedness is a product of maturation and that true ambidexterity would be largely maladaptive for the organism seem well established in this comprehensive paper.]

The problem of handedness has been somewhat oversimplified in literature. There has been a tendency to regard handedness as a specific trait comparable to eye color or skin pattern. It has been too freely assumed that a child is either right handed or left handed, once and for all.

The present study assumes that handedness is an extremely complex

* From A. Gesell & L. B. Ames. The development of handedness. *Journal of Genetic Psychology*, 1947, 70, 155–175. (With permission.)

trait which is intricately bound up with the total action system of the child. Accordingly, it becomes important to inquire into the various developmental expressions of laterality, and to approach the whole subject from the standpoint of ontogenetic patterning and organization.

A few investigators have already noted that the acquisition of lateral dominance does not take a straight line course. Giesecke (1936), in particular, found "evidence of transfers in dominance in the individual developmental history, apparently occurring at fairly definite age levels, noticeably during the seventh month of age and again at the ten-months age level." Lesne and Peycelon (1934) found that the normal infant goes through a short phase of "ambidexterity" between the fifth and ninth month, prior to the establishment of unidexterity by 10 or 11 months. Lederer (1939) likewise observed shifts with temporary periods of dominance of the left hand during the first year of life.

If such shifts occur, when do they take place; and what is the developmental rationale of the shifts? When do the manifestations of handedness become predictive? How do individual as well as maturity differences express themselves? A complete answer to such questions would entail a comprehensive study of laterality in all its aspects—postural asymmetry, eyedness and footedness as well as hand preferences. Much information, however, can be gained from an analysis of the hand posturings and the hand movements of children under the standardized conditions of a developmental examination of behavior. Extensive cinema and stenographic records of the Yale Clinic of Child Development supply the basic data of the present study.

SUBJECTS AND DATA

The subjects included normal infants, preschool children, and school children ranging from 8 weeks to 10 years of age. During the first five years of life these subjects were given the systematic Yale developmental examination as described elsewhere (Gesell, 1940 and Gesell & Amatruda, 1941). From 5 to 10 years of age, test situations were instituted to secure responses to cube, pencil and paper, and free construction situations. At all ages the responses were recorded both stenographically and by cinema. During the first 60 weeks of life, records were made at lunar-month intervals. Thereafter, the records were made at 80 weeks and annually from 2 through 10 years of age. Seven cases, to be designated as basic cases, were documented through the entire age period. In an additional case, daily cinema records were made throughout most of the first year. The total number of cases analyzed at any given age level varied from 12 to 45.

During the first 32 weeks, the subjects were photographed in the supine position as part of the routine examination. The subjects also reacted in the sitting position to the stimulus objects. Test objects were presented in accordance with a standardized procedure which afforded a high degree of experimental control. Objects were generally presented in the mid-line.

In the course of time, we found that the age of 2½ years was of special interest from the standpoint of laterality. Developmental examinations had not been given to the basic cinema cases at that age. This deficit was partly corrected by supplementary observations and stenographic records of the behavior of a group of guidance nursery children who were routinely examined at the age of 2½. All the photographic records were studied in detail by the method of cinemanalysis described elsewhere (Gesell, 1935 and Gesell, 1946). Two types of analysis were employed: (a) quantitative, (b) descriptive. Heavy reliance was placed on the descriptive narrative type of analysis. The quantitative analysis provided percentages for the following data: (a) Total time spent in right handed, left handed, and bilateral contact of stimulus object at each age level, both in supine and sitting positions. (b) The percentage of time in which the subject while supine maintained a left tonic neck reflex position, a right tonic neck reflex position, or bilateral postures.

The detailed descriptive analysis was concerned with the actual flow of the manual behavior, taking note of all of the shifts or changes of handedness which took place within a given test situation and within the examination as a whole. These descriptive protocols formed the basis of the data presented below.

DEVELOPMENTAL SHIFTS IN HANDEDNESS

Detailed cinemanalysis of the manual responses of children developmentally examined between 16 weeks and 10 years of age revealed that even in those children who eventually establish clearcut right handedness there occur marked shifts in handedness from age to age, particularly in the first year of life. Contact and manipulation of objects tend to be first with the non-dominant hand, then bilateral, then with the dominant hand alone, once again bilateral, then with one hand, usually and increasingly the dominant. At 1½ years in many children there comes a period of marked bilaterality, followed by definite use of dominant hand alone at two years. Considerable bilaterality is again manifested from 2½ to 3½ years. From four years on, the dominant hand is used mostly, but in some cases even at seven years there is a transient period of use of the non-dominant hand or of both hands together.

Table 1 presents in schematic chronology the characteristic age shifts in the handedness of subjects all of whom eventually showed definite, clearcut right handedness. Although Table 1 gives a fair indication of age sequences in the development of handedness patterns, it does not do justice to individual differences and to the fluctuations which occur in a single individual in the course of a behavior examination. Such fluctuations are more frequent at some ages than at others, and they also tend to occur with some consistency in relation to specific stimulus objects. This does not necessarily mean that the physical qualities of a given test object provoke a

Table 1—Schematic Sequence of Major Forms of Handedness

16–20 weeks: Contact unilateral and, in general, tends to be *with left hand.*

24 weeks: A definite shift to *bilaterality.*

28 weeks: Shift to unilateral and most often *right hand* is used.

32 weeks: Shift again to *bilateral.*

36 weeks: Bilaterality dropping out and unilaterality coming in.
Behavior usually characterized "right or left." *Left predominates in the majority.*

40–44 weeks: Same type of behavior, unilateral, "right or left," but now right *predominates in the majority.*

48 weeks: In some a *temporary, and in many a last shift, to* use of left hand—as well as use of right—either used unilaterally.

52–56 weeks: Shift to clear unilateral dominance of *right hand.*

80 weeks: Shift from rather clearcut unilateral behavior to *marked, inter-changeable confusion. Much bilateral, and use of non-dominant hand.*

2 years: Relatively clearcut unilateral use of *right hand.*

2½–3½ years: Marked shift to *bilaterality.*

4 years: Unilateral, *right-handed* behavior predominates.

change of pattern. Rather the test object simply reveals the strength of a given laterality trend at a given stage of maturity. If the trend is weak, it is readily affected by the test situation, including the shape and size of the object; if the trend is strong, it shows less fragility.

The following, more detailed, outline better indicates the extent of fluctuations in handedness and individual differences during the first three years of life.

Twelve weeks. Behavior rather variable. Postures are chiefly bilateral though nearly all subjects still show traces of the tonic neck reflex. On sight of stimulus object, both arms may be active somewhat alternately or one arm at a time may be active. No contact of object.

Sixteen weeks. Posture, activity and contact (when it occurs) are chiefly unilateral. For most children the left arm is the more likely to contact an object. Most children slump toward the side of the extended arm. The flexed arm may be active in a gross, crude manner. Body posture may bring this arm nearer the stimulus object and thus bring about contact of object with the right hand.

There occurs a shift of handedness apparently determined by the place in the developmental examination at which the response occurs. Some subjects show a marked change of laterality about halfway through an examination. This shift often occurs with the cup or the bell, and once it occurs it is usually maintained. The size and shape of the stimulus object seem also to influence the response. Very small objects, such as the pellet, do not cause arm activation even though they attract attention. Also, although behavior is mostly unilateral, large objects, such as cup and formboard or a tall object such as the bell, usually cause a shift from the initial handedness preference.

Twenty weeks. For the most part both activity and contact are unilateral. Even when both arms are active at once, one is the more active and contacts the object. There is no shift of handedness during the examination at this age.

Twenty-four weeks. This is a rather bilateral age. In about half the cases behavior is predominantly bilateral even to the exent of bilateral approach and contact of object, although often the dominant hand tends to reach the object a little sooner.

There is no marked shift during an examination although cup and formboard seem to attract more bilateral behavior than do other objects. Also, if an object is hard to reach or hard to grasp, behavior tends to become bilateral.

Twenty-eight weeks. Behavior at this age is highly complex and extremely variable. Nearly every child uses some right, some left and some bilateral approaches although there is more unilateral than bilateral behavior. There is in nearly every case a dominant hand; and there is usually a differential use of the two hands whether they are used independently or together. The dominant hand performs in a more advanced manner. When the dominant hand makes the initial approach it is used for some time alone. When the non-dominant hand is used, the dominant hand is held ready. Most children now use the right as the dominant hand.

In many cases there is a gradual shift in dominance as the examination goes on, the shift occurring about halfway through the examination and being maintained. At this age, behavior is much influenced by the size, shape, and placement of objects. Large objects such as cup and formboard are for the most part handled bilaterally.

Thirty-two weeks. This is one of the two strong bilateral ages. There occur several kinds of bilateral behavior: simultaneous approach and grasp of large objects; grasp of an object in one hand after which there is a transfer to the other hand or a bilateral grasp; and simultaneous manipulation of two objects, one in each hand.

In general at this age there is no shift in handedness during the developmental examination.

Thirty-six weeks. The behavior picture is quite similar to that seen at 32 weeks except that there is considerably less bilateral behavior. The trend toward 40 weeks' unilaterality is now starting. Bilateral behavior occurs for the most part when an object is at the mouth, in the handling of large objects, or when the child is holding a separate object in each hand. Bilateral approach, even to large objects, is dropping out. Nearly all initial approach and contact, and most manipulation of single objects, is unilateral.

Few infants show a definite shift of handedness as the examination progresses. Behavior is so complex that it is difficult to say that a particular stimulus object determines behavior.

Forty weeks. Nearly all initial approach and contact, and most manipulation is unilateral. Even quite complex manipulations, such as combining the cup and spoon, are carried out unilaterally.

This is an extremely patterned age; the same pattern occurs repeatedly in any one child, and also from child to child. Most common pattern, perhaps, is grasp in one hand, brief bilateral holding, transfer, and then waving or banging in the other hand. In keeping with general unilaterality of the age is the fact that, even though both hands are alternately active, when either one is used the other remains extremely passive.

Forty-eight weeks. Unilaterality continues to predominate over bilaterality. The two hands are for the most part readily available and interchangeable, but there is little bilateral behavior. When it occurs it is usually in response to multiple stimulus objects. Bilateral approach and contact, or bilateral manipulation of a single object is rare.

Sixty weeks. At this age there is extreme and clearcut unilaterality of one dominant hand, to the point that the non-dominant hand may remain completely passive on the table even in multiple stimulus situations. The behavior picture is now more straightforward in this respect than in any following age until 5 years.

Eighteen months. This is an age of considerable confusion and variability of behavior. The unilateral use of the one dominant hand does predominate while the passive hand is usually very passive, but there is nevertheless a good deal of bilateral behavior. Bilateral behavior is more like that seen in the adult: a simultaneous attack, but with one hand used in a definitely helping capacity. It is as though the two hands now were beginning to come back together but in something approximating an adult bilaterality.

The chief age characteristic seems to be confusion and variability of behavior even though there is little transfer, and the hand which starts manipulation usually keeps it up. But there is no detectable pattern within any one child's behavior, or from child to child. Some children actually reverse handedness at this age and use predominantly the hand which has been the passive hand hitherto.

There is no patterned shift of dominance during the examination.

Two years. Most children show well determined unilateral behavior. There is little transfer.

Two and one-half years. This is a strong age for bilateral behavior. In nearly every individual case bilaterality is strong. This is characteristically an age of "opposite extremes" and we see this plainly in handednes. Bilaterality occurs in three ways: (1) Simultaneous bilateral approach and manipulation; (2) Passive hand held ready to come in as a helping hand. In almost no case does passive hand remain down by the side. (3) Use of one hand in one part of examination and of the other at a later time in the examination.

Three years. Unilaterality of one sort or another predominates in all cases, but there is a good deal of bilateral behavior in at least half the cases. Behavior of the passive hand varies considerably from ready to help at any minute, to active abeyance, to passive on table top, to hanging down at side.

Three years appears to be the middle of a long cycle in which bilateral behavior is prominent, a cycle extending from 30 months through 42 months. Bilateral behavior is a little less strong at 3 years than at the six month nodes just preceding and just following. Bilateral behavior consists mostly in bringing in a second hand to help out, or simultaneous bilateral attack upon a large object. Behavior is not clearcut or well patterned at this age.

Four years. Unilateral behavior predominates in the great majority of children, and in nearly every instance it is unilaterality of one predominant hand even sometimes to the extent of the passive hand remaining completely passive beside the body. However, bilaterality occurs in some cases strongly at the beginning of the developmental examination, as at 60 weeks, this being soon replaced by unilaterality. This variability will gradually decrease until the age of 8 years when there is a clearcut unilaterality of the dominant hand.

THE TONIC NECK REFLEX AND HANDEDNESS

The earliest manifestations of human handedness are in some way bound up with the phenomenon of the tonic neck reflex. The tonic neck reflex is an attitudinal behavior pattern which figures fundamentally in the mechanics and the morphogenesis both of locomotor and prehensor movements. The head and neck very early exert a controlling influence upon the attitudes assumed by the limbs and the torso. In its classic form, the tonic neck reflex consists of: (a) the head turning to the right (or to the left); (b) the ipsilateral arm and leg extending, the arm at right angles; (c) the opposite leg and opposite arm flexing. A well defined tonic neck reflex may be observed even in the fetal infant as early as the 28th week after conception.

All infants do not assume an equally emphatic right or left tonic neck reflex, but normative studies of full term and of premature infants, indicate an unmistakable predilection toward rightward orientation (Gesell and Thompson, 1938).

A more specific question now arises. Does a right tonic neck reflex predict right handedness, and a left tonic neck reflex left handedness? The present study assembled 19 cases in which data were available as to the dominant tonic neck reflex, and as to the handedness evident at 1, 5, and 10 years. In 14 out of the total of 19 cases, the direction of the tonic neck reflex was definitely predictive. In five cases it was ambiguous or contradictive. There were four cases in which left handedness was correctly foretold by a predominant left tonic neck reflex in early infancy.

Handedness is not a simple trait, but must be regarded as a focal symptom of the current status of an ever changing action system,—which system, nevertheless, displays consistent symmetry and asymmetry trends over a long reach of growth. The morphogenesis of handedness, therefore, is complex. Like the tonic neck reflex in which it is rooted, it is subject to many variables.

SUPPLEMENTARY READINGS

Dennis, W. Laterality of function in early infancy under controlled developmental conditions. *Child Develpm.*, 1935, 6, 242–252.

Gesell, A., & Ames, L. B. Tonic-neck-reflex and symmetro-tonic behavior. *J. Pediatr.*, 1950, 36, 165–176.

Gesell, A., & Halverson, H. M. The development of thumb opposition in the human infant. *J. genet. Psychol.*, 1936, 48, 339–361.

Gordon, K. A study of hand and eye preference. *Child Develpm.*, 1931, 2, 321–324.

Updegraff, R. The correspondence between handedness and eyedness in young children. *J. genet. Psychol.*, 1933, 42, 490–492.

Sensory and Perceptual Development

Incidentally, it is very noticeable how much sooner little babies learn to recognize human forms and faces, and to follow them with their eyes, than they do in the case of other objects. Naturally forms of persons are more interesting and attractive than other things, and are distinctly different from the other objects in the field of view owing to the kind of motions they make. These motions have too a connected character; and the face, appearing as a pale reddish spot with its two brilliant eyes, is always a place in this image that can easily be recognized again, even by anybody who has only seen it a few times.
HELMHOLTZ, *Treatise on physiological optics*, 1886.

the auditory analyzer

in young infants*

A. I. Bronshtein and E. P. Petrova

[Most mothers have noticed that their young infants sometimes cease their ongoing behavior and become quiet when stimulated by novel sounds. The perception of an unusual sound has two effects on an organism: it causes him to orient physically toward the source of the sound (the *orienting reflex*), and it inhibits other ongoing activities (*external inhibition*). Since inhibition regularly accompanies orienting, it can be used as an index of orienting, especially with human neonates, because the organism has such poor muscular control of voluntary skeletal and eye movements that it is difficult or impossible to observe the overt orienting reflex. Drs. Bronshtein and Petrova, who carried out their research in the Leningrad Pediatric Medical Institute, have used as their index of orienting the extent to which an infant's regular and vigorous sucking movements cease when he hears various sounds. They found that upon its first presentation a novel sound typically inhibits sucking. After the same stimulus has been presented again and again, however, it ceases to be novel and fails to have any further effect on the infant's ongoing sucking activities. Under these conditions the orienting response may be said to have extinguished. (American psychologists call this "adaptation" or "habituation.") It can be reinstated immediately however, by changing either the pitch of the sound or some other acoustic property. From this finding, Bronshtein and Petrova inferred that the infant has *discriminated* the difference in pitch between the two sounds. They further inferred that the unconditioned orienting reflex can sometimes be more suitable than the conditioned reflex as a means for studying the functioning of the sensory analyzers. They have also concluded, with perhaps less basis for doing so, that ". . . the cerebral cortex functions to some degree from the first day of life." Soviet and American psychologists take markedly different positions on the functional state of the cortex during early infancy.]

* From A. I. Bronshtein & E. P. Petrova. Issledovanie zvukovogo analizatora novorozhdennykh i detei rannego grudnogo vozrasta. (An investigation of the auditory analyzer in neonates and young infants.) *Zh. vyssh. nerv. Deiatel.*, 1952, 2, 333–343.

The analyzing function of the nervous system of newborns and young infants has been insufficiently studied. Because of this, it is difficult even to begin to try to clarify the nature of the interaction between the child and his environment. The cause of such a position of things is concealed to a significant degree in difficulties of a methodological order.

As we know, I. P. Pavlov pointed out two objective methods for studying the work of an analyzer via overt reactions. One method is to use orienting reactions—the investigatory reflex. "This reflex can be used to ascertain in what degree the nervous system of a given animal can distinguish one thing from another. But, as an exclusive method for the study of the nervous system's analyzing activity, the investigatory reflex, not withstanding its great sensitivity in many situations, presents some drawbacks. Of these, the main difficulty is its instability" (1949).

The other method—the formation of conditioned reflexes on the basis of certain agents of the external world—answers the purpose very well in the study of analyzer activity. It is natural that the most reliable information about the work of analyzers in the maturing nervous system was gotten by means of conditioned reflex formation. Here it is important to recall the works of Krasnogorskii (1907, 1939, 1951), Kasatkin (1948), Figurin and Denisova (1949) and, in connection with children over five years of age, those of Ivanov-Smolenskii and his co-workers (1927, 1933, 1935).

Unfortunately, this method of research into the activity of analyzers is not suitable for neonates and young infants, since one cannot form strong conditioned reflexes at this early age. N. I. Krasnogorskii wrote in 1939 that the formation of conditioned connections in children is possible in the second half year of life. Later, he came to the conclusion that this is also possible in the first four weeks of life, although on an extremely limited scale.

According to Figurin and Denisova (1949) the formation of natural conditioned reflexes can be observed by the end of the first month, and artificial conditioned reflexes by the middle of the second month. Kasatkin indicates approximately the same time in his well-known monograph (1948).

Thus, all authors agree on the fact that the working out of an even moderately strong conditioned reflex, not to mention a stable differentiation, cannot be done in the first days of man's existence. Consequently, in order to study the analyzing activity of the child's nervous system, we are left only one way—the method of recording his behavior in response to some stimulus that evokes orienting. In doing this we must remember Pavlov's observation that the orienting reflex can be thus used either by itself or as an agent which influences, which inhibits, or which disinhibits other reflexes.

The sucking reflex has the advantage that it can be elicited even in neonates and that the motor component of the reaction, on introducing a nipple into the infant's mouth, is distinguished by being relatively stable and rhythmical. Thanks to this, any change in rhythm or amplitude of movements under the influence of one or another factor, is quite noticeable.

Sucking movements easily lend themselves to the graphic recording that is altogether necessary for our purposes.

It must be said that the use of the sucking reflex for the study of nervous activity in children is in itself not an innovation. In his early works, Krasnogorskii indicates that he initially observed sucking and swallowing movement (1907). Subsequently, however, he rejected this method and began to record the tonic, mouth-opening reflex. This was because of his interest in salivation in children. Kasatkin has also written about the recording of sucking movements, although he does not give any details, unfortunately (1948). A summary of data on the observation of these movements, unaccompanied by kymographic recordings, can be found in the book of Ivanov-Smolenskii (1933).

PROCEDURE

The following device was used for recording sucking movements. The type of nipple that is called a "pacifier" was put on a hollow, ebony plug and was attached to a plastic ring of the sort that prevents the nipple from being swallowed. To the other end of the plug was attached a rubber pipe that joined the cavity of the nipple with a small Marey capsule. The kymograph record was made in ink by means of a barographic pen. The moment of delivery of the stimulus was marked by another pen.

Organ pipes, a harmonica, and a whistle were used to produce the sound stimuli. In some cases the tap of a pencil on a table was also used. As a rule, the stimulus was of an intermittent character. Most frequently, every stimulus consisted of four identical sound impulses. The length of each impulse was approximately 0.5 seconds, and the intervals between them, 1 second. The intervals between separate stimuli ranged from one to two minutes.

The research was carried out in the Third Hospital Clinic and in the Leningrad Pediatric Medical Institute's Section for the Newborn, which is under the direction of Professor A. F. Tur.

Two groups of children were followed: one group of 10 children who ranged in age from one to five months, and a second group—in which we were principally interested—of 33 children who ranged in age from 2 hours to 8 days. Many of the children were observed repeatedly. For this reason, they appear in more than one age group in the following tabulation. In the younger group, 16 children were observed between the ages of birth and 12 hours, 5 between 12 and 24 hours, 6 between 24 and 48 hours, 10 between 2 and 4 days, and 11 between 4 and 8 days. In the older group, 5 children were observed between the ages of 1 and 2 months, 4 between 2 and 3 months, 8 between 3 and 4 months, and 5 between 4 and 5 months.

The graphic data show that in the typical case sucking consists in a series of separate rhythmic acts interrupted by short pauses. The number of separate sucking movements between pauses numbers from 5 or 6 to

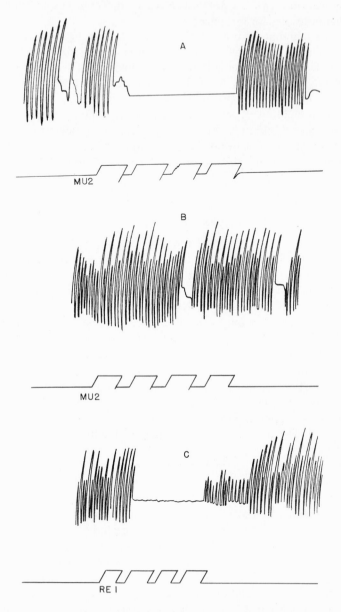

Figures 1A, B, C—The differentiation of musical tones by a child 4 hours and 25 minutes after birth.

A) Orienting reaction to tone Mu2 at the beginning of the session. B) Extinction of the orienting reaction to tone Mu2 after its ninth presentation. C) Orienting reaction to tone Re1 seconds after the last extinction reaction to Mu2. In each case the upper line shows the sucking movements and the lower line, the stimulus events. Speed of paper movement is 0.16 cm per second.

several tens; most often the series consists of 12 to 15 movements performed in a rhythm of some 70 to 110 sucks per minute.

Sucking is an inborn, unconditioned reflex appearing in the very youngest of children. We recorded sucking movements in infants shortly after birth, before the child was first put to the breast.

The rhythm and amplitude of sucking movements is subject to change by a variety of events. The advantage of the graphic method of recording lies in the fact that it is sufficiently precise and objective to allow us to note these changes.

Figure 1A presents a record of sucking movements and shows how they are influenced by a sound stimulus. One can see quite distinctly that the rhythmical sucking movements cease after the organ pipe has begun to sound and that they begin again sometime after the organ pipe has ceased to sound. This inhibition of the sucking reflex by means of a sound stimulus was observed by us with great regularity. In a few cases it was expressed not as a complete cessation, but as a temporary slowing of rhythm and a decrease of amplitude of these movements. In rare cases an increase of frequency and amplitude of the response was produced. We were able to record an orienting reaction to a tone in all ten of the older children (age, 1–5 months) and in 29 of the 33 younger children (age, birth to 8 days). In two children in whom an orienting response to a tone was not displayed, we noticed a distinct inhibition of sucking movements during the tapping of a pencil on a table (carried out at a considerable distance from the child's bed).

The basic stimuli in our research were musical tones, the loudness of which did not exceed 60 to 70 db. These tones were produced by an organ pipe which was located at some distance from the child. (This was to preclude the possibility that the stimulus could activate any other than the auditory receptor.)

Owing to these results we cannot agree with Koltsova's opinions that in the first days of life children do not respond to sound unless it is accompanied by an air current or movement of the child's body; that reactions to sound stimuli *per se* do not appear earlier than 8 to 10 days of age; and that only by the 20th or 22nd day do such reactions become more or less differentiated (1949). We are of the opinion that the reason for the divergence of our data from the data of Koltsova and also from the data of Bekhterev and Shchelovanov (1925), lies in a difference in methodology, and that up to the third week of life children respond only to the action of a sharp, abrupt sound and this response appears only in localized reflexes (the fluttering of eyelids and blinking) and is not expressed in other reactions. The interruption of sucking movements could easily remain unnoticed during a casual observation of the child, since gross motor movements in the neonate in response to sound are sometimes absent.

It is our firm belief, based on a large number of observations, that the characteristic reaction to sound stimuli in infants—even those who have just been born—consists precisely in a change of the course of other reflexive acts, among which is sucking. The sound stimulus plays in this case the role of external inhibitor.

The process of external (or unconditioned or passive or indirect) inhibition, as Pavlov called it, is best of all studied through inhibition of conditioned reflexes. But Pavlov noted that "External inhibition of conditioned reflexes corresponds fully and without the slightest difference to external inhibition of unconditioned reflexes" (1949).

Therefore, we must consider that in our case as well, external inhibition of the unconditioned sucking reflex by sound shows that the auditory analyzer of the neonate is already able to function and that its excitation leads in turn to the development of inhibition around the centers that control the act of sucking.

In the older children inhibition of sucking movements was accompanied by the distinct appearance of an orienting motor reflex. In the younger children inhibition was also expressed on those occasions when the motor component of the reaction to sound appeared so indistinctly that it was difficult to record it. Perhaps these occasions are related to those of which Pavlov spoke when he said that during them, " . . . there is no external indication of the orienting reflex, and an inhibitory state appears straightaway" (1949).

The possibility cannot be excluded that an inhibitory reaction is in any given case the manifestation of a response of biological caution or self-preservation. However, everyone who has written about this reflex (Pavlov, 1949; Maiorov, 1929; Maiorov & Byrzhikovskii, 1933; Zevald, 1938; Usievich, 1951) has noted its close tie with orienting reflexes. It is also a reaction to change in the surrounding situation, "a reflex to novelty".

Orienting reflexes and external inhibition can, as we know, come about by virtue of the activity of subcortical centers. Therefore, that part of the experiment described above does not give us a basis for drawing conclusions about the function of the cortex in neonates, nor, more particularly, about the function of the cortical areas of the auditory analyzer in neonates. Some material touching on this question does come from our further observations of reflexes to sound.

If individual sound stimuli are administered several times in a row, it will be noticed that the inhibitory effect which was seen initially gradually decreases and finally disappears. Figure 1B shows a section of kymographic record made under such conditions.

The extinction of the reaction to sound proceeds in an altogether regular fashion. Out of 40 Ss, we observed it in 37 cases. Experimentation with the remaining three Ss was interrupted for various reasons before the extinction process could be developed. In the older infants we observed extinction in all cases excluding one in which the child quickly fell asleep. The speed of development of extinction is shown in Table 1.

It should be noted that we quite frequently observed signs of extinction the second or third time the stimulus was applied: the inhibition of the sucking reflex by sound was shorter and less complete than it had been

Table 1—Speed of Extinction of an Orienting Reaction to Sound

	NUMBER OF STIMULUS PRESENTATIONS TO EXTINCTION			
No. Ss showing extinction	3	4–5	6–7	8 or more
Younger group	5	10	16	6
Older group	2	8	7	3

during the first stimulus presentation. On the other hand, after having been extinguished on the fifth or sixth stimulation, the reaction could, without the apparent influence of outside agents, spring up again. Extinction frequently appeared to have an "undulating character". However, "acute extinction" could pass over into "chronic extinction". Thus, as a rule, the children did not react to the sound of the engine whistles that are so clearly heard in the territory of the Leningrad Pediatric Institute. "Chronic" extinction was also reproduced by us in the experimental situation.

One can hardly doubt that extinction of orienting reactions is occasioned by the development of the process of internal inhibition. This was shown in their time by Zavadskii (1908), Chechulin (1923), and Rozental (1924). Dr. I. P. Pavlov noted that "The process underlying the disappearance of an orienting reflex corresponds in every detail to the "extinction" of conditioned reflexes; it is the expression of inhibition" (1949). Elsewhere he wrote, "The disappearance of the investigatory reflex is based on the development of inhibition and is quite similar in every detail to the extinction of conditioned reflexes" (1949).

As evidence of the correctness of this position, I. P. Pavlov had observed several facts. The first of these was that when the agent eliciting the orienting (investigatory) reflex is repeatedly applied over short intervals of time, it ceases to elicit the reaction, while after longer intervals of time the reaction reappears anew. Secondly, once having disappeared during any given session, the investigatory reflex can be revived by another investigatory reflex. Finally, inhibition of the investigatory reflex leads to drowsiness and sleep.

While carrying out our experiment, we more than once were met by facts suggesting that the extinction of an orienting reaction to sound is determined by the development of an inhibitory process. First, we noticed that when the reaction to sound had disappeared, an interruption in the running of Ss was followed by a recovery of the reaction. Aside from this, we observed that a new acoustical stimulus could disinhibit the "lost" orienting reaction. For example, to a boy who at the beginning of our tests was 4 hours and 25 minutes old, we administered the tone Mu2. Inhibition of the orienting reflex was apparent after the ninth presentation of the tone (Fig. 1B). Then, when the sound Re1 was substituted for Mu2, the cessation of sucking movements occurred again (Fig. 1C). This disinhibition indicates that the disappearance of the orienting reaction following the repetition of the same auditory stimulus was occasioned not by lack of excitation in the auditory analyzer, but by inhibition of this excitation.

From this we can see how unjustified is the widespread opinion that, since young infants sometimes display no visible reaction to sound, the acoustical analyzer must not be functioning and noise must not have any physiological effect on them.

There is another observation which suggests that internal inhibition develops during the repeated action of identical sound stimuli. This is that when the child is exposed to such repeated stimulation he drifts off into a sleepy state, a phenomenon fully in accord with Pavlov's observations.

I. P. Pavlov, in considering the question of the inertness of the sub-cortical centers and of the interacting influences of cortex and subcortex, wrote, "In a normal dog, the investigatory (orienting) reflex to weak stimuli and to those of medium strength is extinguished by means of in-hibition after three to five repetitions and sometimes more quickly. In a dog without the large hemispheres, extinction can never be attained during such repeated stimulation." And further—a conclusion from this and other ob-servations: "The large hemispheres somehow overcome the inertness of the subcortical centers, both in relation to stimulation and also in relation to inhibition, since in most cases the large hemispheres must excite the organism to activity—or to stopping its activity—through the agency of the subcortical centers" (1949).

The role of cortical influences in the process of extinction was not long ago demonstrated by Musiashchikova (1951), who showed that in cats, the vegetative components of a reaction to auditory stimuli do not extin-guish after the animal has been administered bulbocapnine, a substance which lowers cortical activity, according to the data of Deriabin (1951), Kotliarevskii (1951), and Dolin (1951). Musiashchikova created in cats an artificial catatonia while reproducing earlier observations on the stability of such reactions in sick people who were in a catatonic state (Bronshtein, 1928).

The clearly expressed process of extinction of the reaction to sound is occasioned, apparently, by the development of the process of internal (active) inhibition. Thus it appears that the cerebral cortex functions to some degree from the first day of life. Further, the above data suggest that the analyzers—in particular the auditory analyzer—also function from birth.

An extremely difficult question is that of the limits of ability of the analyzers during the first days of the child's life. Even in the youngest of children one can, as we have already noted, establish the existence of re-actions to novelty. The appearance of such reactions is always dependent upon the analyzing process, since the reaction to novelty is possible only when the analyzer reacts to some change in the environment. However, it is impossible to identify a simple distinction in quality or intensity of stimuli with a stable differentiation formed during the working out of conditioned reflexes. At the base of such a differentiation one always finds an active inhibitory reaction to the discriminative stimulus. The appearance of a response to novelty—an "on-the-spot-differentiation", as it were—does not presuppose a tense struggle between excitatory and inhibitory processes; nevertheless, the precision of analysis can be equal in both cases. Fursikov wrote, "It is interesting that the elementary analysis of stimuli during the orienting reflex is no less precise than the discriminative threshold in digestive reflexes" (1921).

I. P. Pavlov noted that the struggle between excitation and inhibition can in some cases hinder the full utilization by the organism of the results of its valid analysis of external agents (1949). In speaking of the analysis of sound by neonates it is necessary, of course, to keep in mind that it is only an elementary analysis expressed by a response to novelty. Nevertheless, the ability to distinguish one event from the rest in the external world suggests the possibility of shaping the development of the analyzing function. The study of thresholds of sound discrimination by neonates and young infants is a problem which we have only begun to investigate. For this aspect of the study we also use the method of recording changes in the nature of sucking movements under the influence of sound. Using a tone as stimulus we first observe inhibition of sucking. We then repeat the administration of that stimulus to the point that inhibition is no longer expressed. After that we change the pitch of the sound, or some other aspect of its character, to see whether the new stimulus will now elicit a lag in sucking.

During the analysis of the results of this phase of experimentation it was impossible not to notice the difference in performance between the younger and older groups of subjects. In the older group all eight subjects reacted to one or another change in frequency of the tone, and half of them discriminated either a change of tone within the limits of the same octave or two equivalent tones in adjacent octaves. Subjects in the younger group proved to be less able to differentiate. Out of 22 children, 10 distinguished tones of different octaves, 6 distinguished tones within the same octave, 1 infant distinguished Re1 from Re3 but did not distinguish Re3 from Re4 and another distinguished Mu1 from Mu2. In both groups all children reacted to the sound of the whistle, the harmonica, or the pencil tap, after the reaction to the musical tones was extinguished. Thus, one must conclude that even newborns are able to differentiate sounds.

These data are insufficient for describing fully the analytic function of the nervous system of neonates and young infants, but they do show that between infancy and childhood the difference in ability in the elementary analysis of sounds is not so great as was supposed.

Translated by Yvonne Brackbill

SUPPLEMENTARY READINGS

Bartoshuk, A. K. Human neonatal cardiac acceleration to sound: habituation and dishabituation. *Percept. mot. Skills,* 1962, 15, 15–27.
Chun, R. W. M., Pawsat, R., & Forster, F. M. Sound localization in infancy. *J. nerv. ment. Dis.* 1960, 130, 472–476.

Hardy, J. B., Dougherty, A., & Hardy, W. G. Hearing responses and audiologic screening in infants. *J. Pediatr.*, 1959, 55, 382–390.
Kasatkin, N. I., Mirzoiants, N. S., & Khokhitva, A. Ob orientirovochnykh uslovnykh refleksakh u detei pervogo goda zhizni. (Conditioned orienting responses in children in the first year of life.) *Zhurnal vysshei nervnoi Deiatelnosti,* 1953, 3, 192–202. (Reprinted in: *The central nervous system and behavior,* translations from the Russian medical literature collected for participants of the third Macy conference on the central nervous system and behavior, Princeton, N. J., Feb. 21–24, 1960, 343–358. Prepared and distributed by the Russian scientific translation program, National Institute of Health. Library of Congress Catalog Card Number: 5960785.)
Polikanina, R. I., & Probatova, L. E. Stanovlenie i razvitie pishchevogo dvigatelnogo uslovnogo refleksa na zvuk u nedonoshennykh detei. (The formation and development of the conditioned feeding movement reflex to sound in premature children.) *Zhurnal vysshei nervnoi Deiatelnosti,* 1955, 5, 234–245.

testing the
visual acuity
of infants*

JOHN J. GORMAN, DAVID G. COGEN, and SYDNEY S. GELLIS

[Physicians have long been frustrated by their relative inability to diagnose possible organic damage to the human infant's eyes during the first weeks of life. Early diagnosis of partial vision is of paramount importance in planning an optimal environment for the growing infant. Moreover, information about the infant's visual acuity is important in its own right. In the present report, three physicians, Dr. Gorman, late of Harvard University, and his colleagues, Dr. Cogen, of Harvard University Medical School, and Dr. Gellis, of Boston Floating Hospital, introduce an ingenious method of assessing infants' visual acuity during the first five days of life. This procedure also opens the door to scientists' obtaining expanded knowledge about visual development. The response under observation is optico-kinetic nystagmus, familiarly known as railway nystagmus ("in which the eyes of a passenger looking through a train window follow the passing telegraph poles in a rhythmic pattern"). The stimulus consists of a series of alternate stripes (black and white of equal width) moved at a speed of approximately 0.7 inch/sec across the infant's field of vision. At different sections of the long strip of paper on which the stripes are presented the width of the alternate stripes is varied from 0.02 inch (the equivalent of 20/200 vision) to 0.06 inch (equivalent to 20/600 vision). These investigators found that within their sample of 100 newborns all responded to patterns which would represent a visual acuity of approximately 20/450. Previous investigators had estimated the human infant's visual acuity to be in the neighborhood of only 20/2500, even at four months of age. The present findings correct this erroneous impression and show that infants have fairly good near vision.]

Physicians now use various instruments to discover the condition of the infant eye in terms of possible organic damage. But a thorough eye

* From J. J. Gorman, D. G. Cogen, & S. S. Gellis. A device for testing visual acuity in infants. *Sight-Saving Review,* 1959, 29, 80–84. Copyright 1959, National Association for the Prevention of Blindness. (With permission.)

examination is time-consuming, requires use of anesthesia and offers only inconclusive evidence as to visual acuity of a young baby.

The principal difference between an eye examination of a newborn and of an older child or adult is the degree of cooperation a physician may expect. The device we have developed is designed to test the infant's response to visual stimuli, through movement and fixation of the eyes. The test takes only a few minutes and does not require the baby's cooperation.

The device is intended to induce optico-kinetic nystagmus, known more familiarly as railway nystagmus in which the eyes of a passenger looking through a train window follow the passing telegraph poles in a rhythmic pattern. This movement is similar to vestibular nystagmus in that there is a slow and fast component.

EARLY DEVELOPMENTS

Our first tests were made with a simple striped drum, such as is used by ophthalmologists and neurologists when looking for alterations in the response pointing to varied intracranial pathology in adults. This was about the size of a kymograph, covered with vertical stripes, and was rotated at various distances in front of the baby's eyes. The occurrence of the response was so inconsistent in a number of infants from one to four months old that it was very difficult, if not impossible, to quantitate, and the drum was therefore abandoned.

Next, a cylinder adapted from the one used by McGinnis was constructed. This was two feet in diameter and two feet in depth, with lines on its inner surface. The child was placed in it, lying in a small hammock. The cylinder was rotated around the infant by means of a motor and the speed controlled with a rheostat. The subjects were 60 babies under the supervision of Dr. Alfred J. Vignec at the New York Foundling Hospital, varying in age from eight days to four months. They were tested at feeding time and were fed while in the apparatus, thus insuring their wakefulness and immobility. Of the 60 babies only 4 failed to respond. One of these was known to be blind, and another was suspected of being so.

With such a high percentage of positive responses we were encouraged to consider using the response as a basis for investigating the development of visual acuity in early infancy and childhood and, if possible, for establishing standards, since to date this has been done with only questionable accuracy. In addition we hoped to standardize the construction of a simple apparatus for use in the average office for determination of presence or absence of vision.

PORTABLE MODEL

An apparatus was then devised which simulates the effect of the rotating cylinder, but is of less bulk and awkwardness, so that it can be transported and used with greater convenience. It consists of a roll of white

Figure 1—The infant is placed under the arc of paper that is illuminated from behind his head.

paper, 9 inches wide and 42 feet long, on which black stripes are printed.

There are no available data on the visual acuity of newborns, and only roughly estimated and approximate data on young infants in general. Worth places it at "at least" 20/2500 at four months, and Schwating at 20/400 at six months. These estimates guided us to some extent in our choice of the width of lines and spaces. The finest pattern used consisted of lines and spaces of 0.02 inch which when viewed at six inches would be the equivalent of 20/200. The next size was 0.06 inch which is the equivalent of 20/600.

The stripes are equidistant and of the same thickness as the white spaces between. Every six feet the stripes and spaces become wider. The whole roll is reeled manually from one spool to another over two narrow one-inch-wide Plexiglas arcs with six-inch radii. The edges of the paper rest on these arcs; and the paper has enough thickness and rigidity to maintain its shape without buckling as it is reeled. The infant is placed under the arc of paper which is illuminated from behind his head by two small 25-watt floodlights.

SPEED FACTOR

In relation to speed two things had to be considered: the flicker fusion frequency phenomenon, and the effect on acuity of motion per se. As to the latter, Ludvigh found that motion had an adverse effect upon acuity, and he was able to correlate the percentage loss with the angular velocity of the object viewed. He found that at angular velocities of 20 degrees/sec acuity drops a little more than one per cent; and with increasing speeds the drop becomes more marked. The apparatus we have used has a gear ratio which moves the paper along at approximately 0.7 inch/sec when the handle of one spool is turned as slowly as possible, at the same time maintaining a smooth rotation. This amounts to angular velocity just under 7 degrees/sec. This speed, we felt, should have a minimal effect on acuity.

Although there are no standards for critical flicker fusion frequency in this age group the rate of flicker at which fusion occurs at the illumination we have used is approximately 50 light stimuli/sec in the average adult. Since at a speed of 0.7 inch/sec the paper bearing the finest pattern would expose a stationary eye to only 17.5 white lines/sec we were again spared the effect of a factor which would complicate the findings.

The distance of six inches was chosen because of work on visual fixation in infants performed by Ling who found that there was a period in the development of fixation when the infant was not capable of maintaining sustained fixation on the object stimulus beyond a distance of eight inches.

TEST RESULTS

In the first series using this new apparatus 100 newborns from the nurseries of the Beth Israel Hospital, Boston, were tested. They were placed in the apparatus when awake and relatively quiet. It was unnecessary to feed them because they were so young that there was not enough head movement to interfere with the examinations. The upper limit of age was 5 days. Of these there were 21 infants under 1 day; 28 from 1 to 2 days; 18 from 2 to 3 days; 18 from 3 to 4 days; and 15 from 4 to 5 days. The youngest tested was 1 hour and 20 minutes old.

The responses were graded and designated as excellent, good, fair, or negative. They were called *excellent* when nystagmus was elicited immediately or shortly after placing the infant in the apparatus, or if the pattern of nystagmus was well sustained throughout the testing after having once been elicited. They were called *good* if there were periods of well-sustained nystagmus, though interrupted by obvious conditions which might be expected to interfere with the response, such as sleepiness, crying or marked restlessness. They were called *fair* when the periods of nystagmus, although present and definitely in rhythm with the passage of lines, were short and intermittent without any obvious reason. Responses were designated as *negative* when there either was no nystagmus at all or if it was so fleeting that it could not with any certainty be attributed to the stimulus of the passing lines. Some subjects were reevaluated at other times but some were not, since the infants were not always available for retesting. A time limit of 10 minutes was placed on each observation; this was exceeded in only one or two instances. In over half the cases the examination was completed in from two to three minutes. Two infants were restless and crying throughout the entire period so that the examination was listed as entirely unsatisfactory and they were excluded from the series, two others taking their place.

The procedure which was almost invariably followed after the infant had been placed in the apparatus in his natural position of rest was that of exposing him to the passage of the finest pattern of lines (0.02) first, following with the next largest (0.06), etc. The size line at which the first positive response was elicited was noted.

Although there were variations, the usual positive response consisted of:

1. No reaction to the passage of the 0.02 pattern.

2. A sudden and marked widening of the palpebral fissures immediately upon or soon after the beginning of the 0.06 pattern coming in line with the direction of gaze.

3. A slow, smooth, following movement (corresponding approximately to the motion of the striped paper) to the limit of excursion.

4. A swift saccadic (righting) movement, the eye going back to a more central position.

The above cycle recurred rhythmically.

HIGH PERCENTAGE OF RESPONSES

Of the 100 newborns none responded to the finest pattern, 0.02. There were 93 positive responses to the 0.06 pattern; 52 excellent, 31 good, and 10 fair. However, four of those listed as positive were negative on the first examination. One response listed as negative on the fourth day became fair on the fifth; two others listed at negative on the fourth day became good and excellent respectively on the fifth; and one baby listed as negative on the third day became good when reexamined three days later. (This was the only instance in which the five-day limit was exceeded.) Of the seven subjects with negative responses only two were tested more than once, the others being unavailable for reexamination.

The percentage of excellent responses was fairly evenly distributed over the five days, there being as many on the first day—even a little more—as on the fifth.

Since this series was completed we have acquired a larger range of line patterns and have tested an additional 100 newborns, all under four days. We found that all responded to line patterns which would represent a visual acuity of approximately 20/450, and that a larger percentage of these responded to a pattern representing 20/350.

Thus it would appear that newborns have acuities which are much better than was previously believed; and that the apparatus we have demonstrated gives us a means of testing visual acuity in small infants. Its major value will be to provide the physician with a definite clue to an infant's need for more exhaustive examination and treatment.

SUPPLEMENTARY READINGS

Beasley, W. C. Visual pursuit in 109 white and 142 Negro newborn infants. *Child Develpm.*, 1933, 4, 106–120.

Chase, W. P. Color vision in infants. *J. exp. Psychol.*, 1937, 20, 203–222.

Evans, J. N. A visual test for infants. *J. Ophthal.*, 1946, 29, 73–75.

Ling, B-C. I. A genetic study of sustained visual fixation and associated behavior in the human infant from birth to six months. *J. genet. Psychol.*,
1942, 61, 227–277.

McGinnis, J. M. Eye movements and optic nystagmus in early infancy. *Genet.
Psychol. Monogr.*, 1930, 8, 321–430.

development of

brightness vision

in infants*

DIETRICH TRINCKER and INGEBORG TRINCKER

[How sensitive is the growing infant to light stimulation of different wave-lengths? This is the question to which Drs. Trincker and Trincker of the Physiological Institute of the University of Greifswald addressed themselves in this study. The response selected for study under varying conditions of light stimulation (after standardized conditions of light and darkness adaptation) was the "eye-on-the-neck-reflex." When infants are stimulated by sudden il-lumination, the head jerks backward, and the entire body takes on an opis-thotonic (S-shaped) position. The stronger the illumination, the stronger is the reflex. These investigators found that after a 15-minute period of brightness adaptation, infants during the first ten weeks of life respond to different wavelengths of light with a sensitivity that is highly similar to that of normal adults. On the other hand, after 30 minutes of darkness adaptation, it is several weeks before the infant's responses become similar to those of normal adults. On the basis of their findings and a review of the relevant histological evi-dence, Drs. Trincker and Trincker conclude that the cones (the basis of pho-topic vision) develop and become functional earlier than the rods (the basis of scotopic vision—functional under low conditions of illumination, such as at twilight).]

A. Peiper (1927) was the first to carry out systematic experiments on neonatal sensitivity to light with a physically and physiologically exactly defined method. For this purpose he used his discovery of the "eye-on-the-neck-reflex," which can be elicited in nearly all full-term and premature neonates. According to Peiper's description, "For this purpose one puts the child into an upright position, without supporting his head. On sudden

* From D. Trincker & I. Trincker. Die ontogenetische Entwicklung des Helligkeits- und Farbensehens beim Menschen. I. Die Entwicklung des Helligkeitssehens. (The ontogenetic development of brightness and color vision in man. I. The development of brightness.) *Graefes Arch. Ophthal.*, 1955, 156, 519–534.

illumination of the eyes, the head is thrown backward with a jolt, so that the entire body assumes an opisthotonic position." For his experiments Peiper first used the unfiltered white light of an electric bulb and found, through step-by-step reduction of light intensity, that the reaction is dependent on brightness and that a stimulus threshold can be ascertained with considerable accuracy. In order to ascertain the stimulus threshold and with it the relative brightness values for lights of different color he further used colored filters. Peiper undertook these experiments on neonates adapted to light or dark and found a significant difference in relative sensitivity: in light adapted neonates yellow and red had a much higher relative brightness value than in those adapted to darkness. With justification Peiper regarded these findings as proof for the existence in the neonate of Purkinje phenomenon. Unfortunately this paper of Peiper's, also important for the theory of light and color sense, is insufficiently known. It represents the starting point of our own experiments which, in principle, completely confirm it.

Almost all older papers on light and color sense of neonates, infants and children to school age fail to consider that brightness values of spectral colors in the child may not be the same as those determined for the adult. That brightness values for different age levels agree may not be taken for granted; rather, it must first be experimentally proved. Numerous experimenters have used the so-called "spontaneous tendencies" in children, i.e., looking at or grasping for a colored object. The reviews by Peiper (1926, 1949) show clearly how extraordinarily controversial are the results various authors have obtained with this method. All those authors who used grasping reactions had to omit entirely the particularly important study of neonates. Thus one must use other reactions for the investigation of light and color sensitivity in neonates. The only method yielding truly precise, dependably reproducible data is Peiper's "eye-on-the-neck-reflex" which we have therefore used for our own study.

Before beginning with the description of our experiment, we wish to call attention to a remarkable fact, which occurred to us in our work with Peiper's findings. If one compares relative brightness values of colors (red, yellow, green and blue) for light adapted, premature newborns with those obtained for adults, one finds a high degree of similarity. On the basis of the Peiper material, one must conclude that for the light adapted human eye, i.e., for photopic vision, relative brightness values remain the same from birth onward.

However, the same comparison of values obtained for dark adaptation reveals a relation that is more complicated. The transition from daylight to twilight vision that occurs in the adult eye and that takes place as a change in brightness values for colored lights is known as the Purkinje phenomenon: at the red or long-wave end of the spectrum, one finds a considerable decrease in relative brightness values, while at the blue-violet or short-wave end there is an increase in relative brightness, so that maximal brightness shifts from yellow to green. In all infants studied by Peiper there occurred under dark adaptation a strong decrease in the relative brightness of yellow and red; this agrees with the findings for adults. If, however, one compares dark adapted adults and infants on brightness value for blue and green, one misses a correspondingly significant *increase* in blue-green brightness for infants under conditions of dark adaptation.

Consequently the question arises whether the rod apparatus continues to develop after birth. Peiper's material does not provide an answer to this question. Thus, further studies were needed. From this point of view a comparison of results of repeated tests on the same individuals had to be attempted.

Our experimental work on mature and premature neonates was conducted at the Greifswalder University Clinic. The sessions were conducted in a room divided into two parts; one part served for light adaptation and the other was used for dark adaptation. This part also contained the actual testing arrangement. The apparatus consisted of a black metal wall flanked by dull black cardboard walls. A lighting device was centered in the middle of an aperture in the front wall. The aperture which measured 14 cm by 7 cm along its edges, was equipped with a light-proof frame into which the various Schott filters could be inserted. We used gray and colored filter glasses, 7 cm by 7 cm next to each other in the frame. The lighting device contained a 200 watt Osram-nitra bulb, as well as a heat filter (a 5.5 cm thick layer of water).

For reducing the initial light intensity by steps, the following Schott-neutral Glass Filters were used: Glass NG 6, thickness 1, 49 mm (reduction—20%); NG 6, 2, 91 mm (30%); NG 11, 1, 42 mm (40%); NG 11, 2, 02 mm (50%); NG 11, 2, 76 mm (60%); NG 11, 3, 46 mm (67.5%); NG 11, 4, 19 mm (74%); NG 5, 2, 48 mm (80%); NG 5, 2, 84 mm (84%); NG 5, 3, 32 mm (88%); NG 5, 3, 60 mm (90%); NG 5, 3, 98 mm (92%); NG 5, 4, 18 mm (93%); NG 5, 4, 44 mm (94%); NG 4, 2, 52 mm (95%); NG 4, 2, 70 mm (96%); NG 4, 2, 95 mm (97%); NG 4, 3, 30 mm (98%); NG 4, 3, 58 mm (98.5%); NG 4, 3, 90 mm (99%); NG 4, 4, 17 mm (99.5%).

For producing monochromatic lights, we used the following Schott filter combinations: 1. BG 12 (4 mm) + GC 15 (2 mm), 2. BG 12 (2 x 1 mm) + GG 5 (4 x 2 mm), 3. BG 18 (2 mm) + BG 20 (5 mm) + VG 3 (2 mm) + VG 3 (2 mm) + OG 5 (2 mm), 4. BG 18 (1 mm) + VG 3 (1 mm) + OG 2 (2 mm), 5. BG 17 (2 mm) + BG 20 (2 mm) + RG 5 (1 mm). The resulting spectral lights were reduced, by means of an episcotist, to identical intensity with "white" (unfiltered spectral) light of 250 lux. With this intensity they showed the following limits: 1. 430–465 mm. 2. 465–500 mm. 3. 550–560 mm. 4. 560–585 mm. 5. 645–680 mm. In order to carry out threshold determinations, the step-by-step reduction of 22 levels of intensity went to 25 lux. It was not necessary to exceed the intensity upward or downward, as all threshold values were included. The gauging, done with a two-octave-photocell (Pressler), as well as with a vacuum thermoelement for control, resulted in the following levels: 250, 205, 160, 120, 90, 65, 42, 30, 22, 16, 12, 9, 6, 4, 3, 2, 1.5, 1.2, 0.9, 0.6, 0.4, 0.25 lux.

Each session began with a 30-minute dark adaptation period; between procedures there was a readaptation period of at least 10 minutes. Adaptation took place in the dark portion of the room panelled in dull black. Initial light adaptation lasted 15 minutes; between procedures there was a readaptation period of at least 5 minutes. Brightness adaptation took place in the second part of the room, painted white. The child was prevented from falling asleep during adaptation times. In the case of brightness adaptation, a person carrying the child walked up and down at a constant distance from the almost evenly illuminated white wall; in this area, brightness at the child's eye level was measured at 1500 lux.

First tested were reactions to the five spectral lights and to the spectral, unfiltered "white" light with an initial intensity of 250 lux. At this intensity, responses inevitably occur in all healthy and normally reacting children. Further, weaker levels of intensity were sequentially tested until, at a certain level, responses were no longer elicited. Here it was especially important—most of all in premature babies—to prevent response fatigue. However, since this ordinarily occurs only with rapid repetition, we avoided it simply by inserting the long adaptation times between phases of the experiment.

The neonates' need for sleep, which often tried our patience, constituted a great difficulty in carrying out the experiment. Nevertheless, we felt that keeping the lids open artificially (by means of lid separators) should be rejected. By trying to adapt to the children's habits as far as possible, i.e., by using the children's natural "waking phases" we doubtlessly used not only the more gentle, but also the more successful method. We were able to control the children's crying quite well by carrying them around during the adaptation periods.

Due to the length of experimental time required, we usually had to work at night in order to finish the complete testing of any given child in four days at most. Thus, we were able to run several tests within the threshold range itself at any one intensity level of a given stimulus light. Following the determination of the threshold stimulus, only 10 individual tests were required; if a further response occurred, we also tested the stimulus next in sequence. For safety's sake, we also tested the next 3 levels. (We found, however, that once the response had ceased at a certain level, any weaker level did not elicit reactions.)

For a comparative evaluation of the threshold values obtained under light adaptation and dark adaptation using the eye-on-the-neck-reflex, it is practical not to use the threshold values themselves but rather, as customary, their relational values. These represent the actual goal of the tests, namely, the *relative brightness values* of the respective lights. We have designated the smallest threshold value, corresponding to maximum sensitivity, as 100% and the highest threshold value, corresponding to minimum sensitivity, as 0%. The intervening values were also calculated in percentages.

In order to compare the relative brightness values of the spectral light for neonates with those of the adult, we determined, in addition, the absolute threshold values under light and dark adaptation for the normal, color sensitive adult. The resulting relative brightness values were calculated in the same way, in terms of percentages. In the case of the adult tests the thresholds were determined by pre-level and post-level method with 20 individual tests per level of intensity.

The method described above was used with a total of 56 children. Of these a certain number were eliminated after the first test because some of them fell ill and because some were taken home by their mothers sooner than expected. Thirty-eight children remained, 18 premature and 20 full-term. Of the premature infants, two were tested five times; nine, four times; six, three times; and one, twice. Of the full-term infants, three were tested four times; 11, three times; and six, twice. The premature infants were tested in the first, second, fourth, seventh, and tenth weeks of life, while the full-term infants were tested in the first, second, fourth, and sixth week of life. We regard as reliable the data from those 31 cases in which at least three tests were possible; however, the results of the seven subjects tested only twice agree with the others.

Figure 1, with its 16 individual representations, affords an over-view of the results obtained wtih two premature (I and II) and two full-term (III and IV) children in comparison to the adult values (V). In all four children the representations designated by "1" are derived from tests undertaken in the first week of life; those designated by "2" indicate tests undertaken in the second week. In the case of the premature infants "4" indicates the results of tests made in the tenth week; in the case of one of the full-term infants (III) "4" indicates tests made in the sixth week. (In the case of the other full-term child, IV, extinction of the reflex activity, beginning in the fifth week of life, did not permit further evaluation.) All values obtained under light adaptation are shown by solid lines, and those obtained under dark adaptation, by broken lines. For clarity and ease of representation, we have used here only the relative brightness values for the five spectral lights, omitting those for spectral unfiltered "white."

If we examine the values obtained under light adaptation, the present experimental results clearly demonstrate that relative brightness values for adults are consistent with those found in full-term and premature children at all ages and developmental levels. In the case of light adaptation, we find a marked similarity in curves for adults and for all children examined. Peiper's findings, previously mentioned, are thus confirmed; since we were in a better position to control the physical characteristics of our stimulus lights, our findings are even more uniform than his. This proves that in premature neonates relative brightness values of spectral lights for the photopic or cone apparatus are already fully developed; there is no further development after birth.

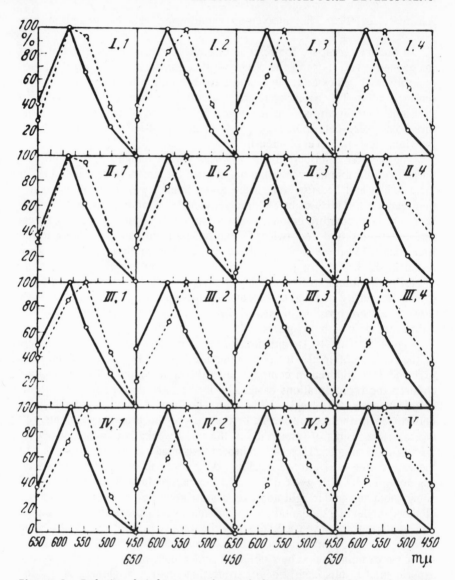

Figure 1—Relative brightness values of the spectral lights under light
adaptation (solid line) and under dark adaptation (broken line) for the
various developmental levels (1 through 4) of two premature (I and II)
and two full-term (III and IV) infants in comparison with values of the
adult (V).

Wavelengths are shown on the abscissas; relative brightness value in percentages
on the ordinate.

Of course, this finding does not say anything about color sensitivity in neonates. Whether such exists cannot, as a matter of principle, be ascertained with a method such as that used here. We will report on tests undertaken to clarify that question in a second article.

In the case of dark adaptation, if one compares the values obtained from premature children with those of the adult, one glance shows that here one cannot speak of a uniformity of curves at all. In discussing Peiper's findings, we had already pointed to the differences between darkness values in neonates and the adult values he obtained. The present experimental material clearly confirms our assumption, expressed in this connection, that conditions in the scotopic apparatus might differ considerably from those in the photopic, and that there might be postnatal change or development in cone functioning.

We find a Purkinje phenomenon in all tests, but only in the latest stages of development is it completely, or at least almost completely, identical to that of the adult. In most cases, we see a clearly recognizable, yet incompletely developed Purkinje phenomenon. For the sake of clarity we divide into three stages the course of this developmental process. Progression from stage to stage does not, of course, occur suddenly as evidenced in our material by the existence of transitional forms; yet these are less frequently observed, and we must assume that the development nevertheless proceeds in thrusts.

The first stage is characterized by the fact that the Purkinje phenomenon is limited almost entirely to the center of the spectrum, while the relative brightness values of the short- and long-wave lights as shown under light adaptation as compared to dark adaptation, scarcely differ from each other. This stage can be divided into two substages. *Stage 1a:* Although darkness values, when compared with brightness values, show a significant increase of sensitivity toward yellow-green and borderline green, a shift in maximum brightness cannot be shown, at least by our method (compare curves I, 1 to II, 1, Fig. 1). We found this level only in the first week and only in five cases of prematurely born infants who were greatly retarded developmentally.

Stage 1b: A shift occurs in maximum brightness from yellow to yellow-green. If a reduction in the relative brightness of red does exist under dark adaptation, it is small and insignificant. (In Fig. 1, compare III,1 to I,2, and II,2 to IV,1.) The five prematurely born infants at Stage 1a in the first week attained Stage 1b in the second week. Another eleven prematures and four full-term infants showed Stage 1b development during the first week of life.

Stage 2. This stage differs from the preceding one through the significant reduction in the relative brightness value of red under dark adaptation; it differs from the stages to follow in that red still has a higher value than does blue. One may define the peculiarity of this stage by stating that here the Purkinje phenomenon makes its appearance not only in the center, but also at the long wavelength end of the spectrum. At the short wavelength end the Purkinje phenomenon is still absent. We found Stage 2 most frequently; it coincides with findings of Peiper, cited above in detail. We found evidence of Stage 2 in two premature and 16 full-term infants in the first week of life and in 13 premature and all full-term infants (except for three cases of transition to the next stage) in the second week of life. All prematures had attained this stage by the fourth week.

Stage 3. In this stage, the Purkinje phenomenon appears at the short wavelength end of the spectrum, too. Blue has a higher relative brightness value than does red. Here one could also divide the stage into two sub-stages. In Stage 3a, the relative brightness of blue under dark adaptation is, however, higher than that of red and is lower than that of the adult. (In Fig. 1, compare III,3 and IV,2.) In Stage 3b, the value of blue under dark conditions is identical with that of the adult. (In Fig. 1, compare II,4, III,4, and IV,3.) Indeed, the transition from Stage 3a to 3b (in Fig. 1, I,4) occurs very gradually; an absolute separation is not possible. In no case did we find Stage 3 in the first week of life. In the second week of life, three cases had just completed transition from Stage 2 to Stage 3a, and in the fourth week all full-term infants belonged in Stage 3 (as they did also when examined in the sixth week). Of the prematures examined in the seventh week all but one child showed Stage 3 values; in the tenth week, Stage 3 was likewise found. We found no deviations from the sequence of these stages.

These tests have shown that initially brightness values of dark adapted neonates are characteristically different from those of the adult, and that in the course of about four weeks, for the full-term infant, to ten weeks, for premature children, they come to approximate those of the adult. We have further demonstrated that the course of this approximation represents an entirely lawful sequence in the middle, long and short wavelength end of the spectrum.

These findings are reminiscent of results found by G. Birukow (1949) on the development of daylight and twilight vision in the frog (*R. temporaria*) which he obtained by means of optomotoric reactions. Early larvae stages(minnows) showed a nearly complete absence of the Purkinje phenomenon. (The color brightness values in darkness adaptation were very similar to those in brightness adaptation.) With increasing development, a gradual transition to the twilight values of adult animals occurred, at first for yellow and yellow-green, then for red, and last for blue and blue-green. With reference to the works of Granit (1947), Birukow assumes a sequential maturation of *three* different types of cones. In a brief report of our results (1954) we have already pointed to the fact that in significant points Peiper's and our findings in the human and those of Birukow in frogs agree in two basic ways. First, for the cone apparatus, adult brightness values were found in all developmental stages examined. Second, cone function, both in frog and human, undergoes developmental changes; in both frog and human, adult brightness values emerge in the *same sequence* for each spectral area. However, a difference between conditions in the frog and in the human consists in the fact that, although manner and direction of the developmental process are obviously analogous, a *complete absence* of the Purkinje phenomenon exists only in the frog, not in the human.

It is reasonable to transfer Birukow's explanatory attempt to our findings. The functioning of twilight values, which we found in human ontogenesis, must be seen as a *developmental process;* the question is only, *what* proportion of development of the total optical apparatus could be quantitatively assessed. Possibly the processes primarily concern the visual substance, rhodopsin. One may further think of a maturational process of the cones, or their micro-structure, thus placing the events into the photoreceptors themselves. One may also imagine a successive activation of the function of the accessory *nerve* analyzers, in which case it may remain undecided whether one could sooner think of those parts of the central organ (or of the common system) located in the retina or of those located in the brain. (Birukow [1948] attempted to analyze more accurately the role of the central nervous factor by performing a slight incision of the intracranial part of the visual nerve. As a consequence, a shift of brightness values in the direction of twilight values was noted.) Certainly, one might also think of a progressive process of adaptation to light as the factor stimulating development, but in this case it is very difficult to come to a plausible explanation as to why the final twilight values for the different spectral ranges occur in such a characteristic temporal sequence.

In this connection, it appears important to ask whether, in the morphological development of visual cells, there exist points of reference for the fact that the cones develop faster than the rods. Chievitz (1887) first found that the cone cells in the most central area of the retina are the earliest to develop. Already in embryos of 50 to 70 mm (9th to 10th gestational week), Seefelder (1910) proved the existence on the *limitans externa* of a simple cell arrangement with "unmistakable signs of young cone cells." While definite cone cells already exist in the *area centralis* in the third embryonic month, rod development does not begin until the fifth month in the para-central zone; it continues, as does cone development, toward the periphery of the retina (Chievitz, 1887; Falchi, 1888). Similarly, Bernard (1903), Cameron (1905, 1912), Detwiler and Laurens (1921), and Saxen (1953, 1954) have found the clear priority of cone-like cells in the developing retina of amphibian animals. "In these early stages all visual cells are cone-like," Detwiler and Laurens state regarding studies of the ontogenesis of amblystoma. In contrast, mature rods appear very late.

Remarkably few relationships can be established between the anatomical and physiological findings cited, especially those reported by Peiper and ourselves, and the results of Zetterström (1951, 1952), who used the Karpe method to examine the electroretinogram in full-term and premature infants up to one year of age. In neonates either no ERG or only a very weak positive wave (b-wave) was seen.* Likewise, in three-month-old

* Editors' note. The ERG, which is a record of the changes in electrical potential of the eye induced by changes in light stimulation, is composed of "negative" and "positive" components called the "a-wave" (or initial negative dip) and the sub-

children, the b-wave amounted only to 0.10 to 0.20mV; the a-wave was still missing; latency and duration, however, approximated those of adults. At five to six months of age adult status was nearly attained, except for the absent a-wave. The a-wave appeared near the end of the first year of life in three out of thirteen cases; the b-wave was still somewhat lower than in the adult.

SUMMARY

The relative brightness values of monochromatic spectral lights for full-term premature infants during their first ten weeks of life are determined for light and dark adaptation through the "eye-on-the-neck-reflex" described by Peiper. At all levels of development the values obtained under light adaptation agree with adult values. Under dark adaptation, however, they are at first significantly different from adult values and become similar to the adult values only in the course of a developmental process which in the case of premature infants may last as long as ten weeks. The final twilight values are attained first for the middle of the spectrum (yellow and yellow-green), then for the long wave lengths (red) and last for the short wave lengths (blue-green and blue to blue-violet). Differences between daylight and twilight values in terms of the Purkinje phenomenon are found at all developmental stages of extra-uterine human ontogenesis. There is a difference between Peiper's and our findings for humans and those of Birukow for the frog: the Purkinje phenomenon is absent in the frog's earliest developmental stages, while in principle the developmental course of rod function is the same. Contrary to von Kries' assumption, in morphologic and functional development the cone apparatus has priority over the rod apparatus.

Translated by Alexandra Hendee

SUPPLEMENTARY READINGS

Chase, W. P. Color vision in infants. *J. exp. Psychol.*, 1937, 20, 203–222.
Heck, J., & Zetterström, B. Analyse des photopischen Flimmerelektroretinogramms bei Neugeborenen. (Analysis of the photopic flicker electroretinogram in neonates.) *Ophthalmologica*, 1958, 135, 205–210.
Zetterström, B. The clinical electroretinogram. IV. The electroretinogram in children during the first year of life. *Acta Ophthal.*, 1951, 29, 295–304.
Zetterström, B. The electroretinogram in premature children. *Acta Ophthal.*, 1952, 30, 405–408.

sequent "b-wave" (the positive rise). These components presumably have their origins in processes occurring in the receptor and bipolar cells of the retina. Recent consensus is that each of these wave components has both photopic and scotopic elements; however, the a-wave appears to reflect primarily cone activity and the b-wave, primarily rod activity (Spears & Hohle, in press).

pattern vision

in young infants*

ROBERT L. FANTZ

[Although the human infant's world may be a "great blooming, buzzing confusion," as William James conjectured, the infant exhibits definite preferences for viewing certain parts of his environment, even during the first few weeks of life. In the following report, Dr. Fantz, of Western Reserve University, describes his study of the infant's preference for complex stimuli. Through a tiny ¼-inch hole in a gray screen placed above the infant's head the experimenter observes the reflected images on the surface of the infant's eyeball as he gazes at one of the two available stimulus patterns. Dr. Fantz has shown that by the third to fourth week of life the human infant has definite preference in his visual fixations. This preference is, in general, for complex visual stimuli. Dr. Fantz strongly rejects the extreme empiricistic view of the development of visual organization and patterned discrimination. Nevertheless, he leaves open the question whether his findings are due principally to maturation or to prior visual experience. Dr. Fantz's work has stimulated many similar research studies that promise to give us even more information about the ways that man comes to his knowledge of the visual world.]

William James described the infant's world as a "great blooming, buzzing confusion" (1890). Two questions might be asked regarding this statement: first, what kinds of sensations are contained in the confusion, and second, is the confusion relieved by the beginnings of perceptual organization? Relative to the first question, considerable progress has been made in determining the elementary sensory dimension to which the young infant is sensitive. For example, responsiveness to the intensive and spectral features of photic radiation and to movement is present at an early age (1954). Regarding the second question, little information is available about supposedly complex functions such as form and spatial vision which involve configurations of stimuli. Since relevant data are lacking, there is a tendency to assume

* From R. L. Fantz. Pattern vision in young infants. *The Psychological Record*, 1958, 8, 43–47. (With permission.)

that visual organization and patterning are absent before considerable experience and learning have occurred. More definite information is desirable for several reasons. First, pattern and spatial vision is, in the adult, the most reliable and important source of information about the environment, so that the onset and development of this function is of great interest. Second, this topic has played a major role in theories of perception and neural functioning (Gibson, 1950; Hebb, 1949; Kohler, 1940; Lashley, 1942).

The methods available for testing young infants are limited by the lack of verbal, manual, and locomotor response indicators. However, eye activity itself, which is a prominent part of the infant's behavior, can provide a clue to what is seen and how it is organized. When under controlled conditions an infant repeatedly looks more at one target than at another, and thus shows a visual preference for certain parts of the spectrum, it may be supposed that color is seen and discriminated. In the same way, consistent visual attention to stimuli differing only in pattern, regardless of position, is evidence for form or pattern vision.

In brief, the method used in this study was that of recording the relative lengths of visual fixation by an infant of simultaneously-presented patterns. The aim was to determine whether this technique offered a solution to the difficulties in studying early visual development. A similar method, used to test a chimpanzee infant, is described more fully elsewhere (Fantz, 1958).

METHOD

SUBJECTS

The Ss were thirty infants selected from the waiting list of a university nursery school on the basis of age and availability for repeated testing. The age varied from one to fourteen weeks at the first test. Weekly test sessions were given when possible until ten records had been obtained. Eight of the thirty Ss had to be dropped before this time due to persistent crying, fussing, or sleeping in the testing situation. Most of the results are based on the remaining twenty-two infants.

PROCEDURE

The testing was carried out in the homes of the Ss in order to minimize disturbing factors. The infant was placed face up in a comfortable, form-fitting crib which prevented gross head and body movements. A uniform gray structure above the infant excluded vision of people or objects in the room and provided a background for two posterboard patterns. These patterns were located 1 ft above the infant's head and were spaced 1 ft apart. Illumination was provided from below the infant's field of view.

Four pairs of patterns were used during each test (Fig. 1). The identical triangles were included to control for the possibility of differential response

Figure 1—The stimulus patterns drawn to scale; the large squares measured five inches on a side.

Shaded areas were bright red; blank areas were gray to match the background. Adjacent patterns were presented together; the checkerboard was paired with either large or small plain square on a given exposure.

to factors other than form or pattern differences. The cross and circle were equated in area. The bull's-eye and stripes patterns were equated in area of red and in outline form. The checkerboard was paired half of the time with the plain square of equal outline size and the remaining time with the smaller square equated in area of red. A duplicate set of patterns was used for part of the testing.

Each pair was presented twice in succession, with reversed right and left positions for the second exposure. Thus eight test periods, each 30 sec long, were given during a weekly test session. The order of presentation of the four pairs was random, and the initial positions within each pair also varied randomly.

Between exposures the patterns were hidden from view by a gray shield which contained a 4-in. hole directly overhead. A test exposure did not begin until the infant was looking at this central hole. Thus, there was an equal chance of eye movements toward the two patterns when they were suddenly exposed to view. The infant's eyes were observed through a ¼-in. hole midway between the patterns. The total length of visual attention to each pattern was measured by pressing one of two telegraph keys while the corresponding pattern was fixated. Each key operated a timer. The time scores were then recorded at the end of the 30 sec exposure.

It is difficult to be certain of the direction of gaze of an infant by un-

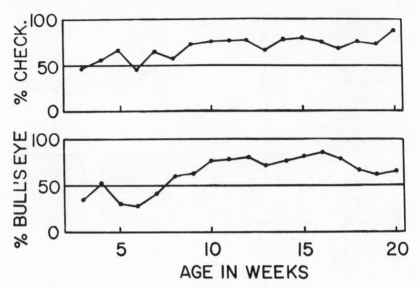

Figure 2—Developmental preference curves for two pairs of patterns: checkerboard versus plain square and bull's-eye versus horizontal stripes.

At each age is shown the relative amount of time for the two patterns out of the combined fixation time for both. Each point is the average for those *S*s tested at that age; this number varies between 5 and 20 with the higher values at the middle ages.

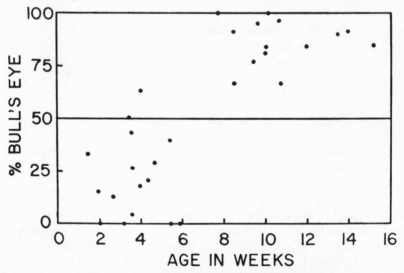

Figure 3—A scatter plot between age at first test and preference for the bull's-eye or stripes pattern.

Each point is based on the combined fixation time for the two patterns during two 30-sec exposures for a singe *S*. The *N* is 30, including those infants dropped later in the experiment.

aided observation. This problem was solved by making use of the reflected images of the patterns. These images were clearly visible on the surface of the eyeball under proper lighting conditions. When a pattern was fixated, the image of that pattern coincided with the pupil of the eye. This provided a simple and reliable criterion of fixation.

The time scores for the two exposures of a pair of patterns were summated to balance out position preferences. Non-parametric tests of significance were used.

RESULTS

Neither the control pair of triangles nor the cross and circle elicited consistent visual preferences. On the other hand, the two pairs presenting variations in type and degree of patterning gave results which were consistent both in successive tests and between Ss.

In total scores for all ten weekly sessions, nineteen infants fixated the checkerboard more than the square, compared to only three favoring the square. The results were similar for exposures using the large or small squares. Twenty Ss showed higher time scores for the bull's-eye, compared to two for the stripes. Both preferences are significant at the 0.001 level, indicating that the ability to discriminate patterns was present during the first six months of age.

Figure 2 shows developmental curves for the two pairs of patterns which gave significant overall results. An increase in the checkboard preference is evident around eight weeks. A reversal from a stripes to a bull's-eye preference was shown at eight weeks.

The latter change was an unexpected and unexplained finding, although it is one of the most consistent aspects of the results. Of the twelve infants who were first tested before eight weeks of age, eleven showed a clear reversal of preference from stripes to bull's eye. The ten older infants all showed a consistent bull's-eye preference. The change of preference could not have been caused by an unknown change in testing procedure, experimental conditions, or stimulus patterns during the course of the experiment, since it occurred at widely varying dates for different Ss, and with duplicate sets of patterns.

The preference reversal was not related to amount of testing experience, as may be seen in Fig. 3. This is a scatterplot between age and preference score for the first testing of each S. Of the sixteen Ss under seven weeks, only two fixated the bull's-eye more than the stripes, while all fourteen over seven weeks did so. The increase in checkerboard preference with age at first test was not as consistent as the other change, but still was significant at the 0.05 level. Of the sixteen infants under seven weeks, ten preferred the checkerboard; of the fourteen older infants, eleven preferred the checkerboard.

It is clear that the age trends shown in Fig. 3 are due either to maturation or general visual experience, rather than to practice effects from repeated testing. The results for checkerboard versus square alone might suggest that the change represents an improvement in pattern vision with age. However, some differential was shown during the first six weeks. The consistent preference for stripes over bull's-eye during the same period of time gives further evidence against the possibility that a process of learning to see patterns occurred during the early weeks of life. The changes at eight weeks, on the other hand, could represent a modification of the original visual behavior due to a type of early visual learning such as Hebb postulates (1949).

Similar results have been obtained from a chimpanzee infant tested from birth: consistent visual preferences were shown during the first six weeks with little opportunity for visual learning, while striking changes occurred at nine weeks which could be due either to maturation or to an intervening period of visual experience (Fantz, 1958).

CONCLUSIONS

1. Visual patterns were discriminated by infants during the first six months, as evidenced by differential fixation times.

2. Changes in the strength or direction of the pattern preferences occurred around two months of age, independently of amount of testing.

3. Consistent visual preferences were present as early as the first two months, thus arguing against an extreme empiricistic view of the development of visual organization and pattern discrimination.

4. The determination of natural visual preferences among different stimuli is a powerful method of studying early visual development which can provide data of importance to theories of perception, learning, and neural functioning.

SUPPLEMENTARY READINGS

Berlyne, D. E. The influence of the albedo and complexity of stimuli on visual fixation in the human infant. *Brit. J. Psychol.,* 1958, 49, 315–318.

Fantz, R. L. Pattern vision in newborn infants. *Science,* 1963, 140, 296–297.

Fantz, R. L., Ordy, J. M., & Udelf, M. S. Maturation of pattern vision in infants during the first six months. *J. comp. physiol. Psychol.,* 1962, 55, 907–917.

Line, W. The growth of visual perception in children. *Brit. J. Psychol., Monogr. Suppl. XV,* 1931.

Spears, W. C. Assessment of visual preference and discrimination in the four-month-old infant. *J. comp. physiol. Psychol.,* 1964, 57, 381–386.

on size perception
in children*

FRANZ BEYRL

[Adults are amused when the infant or small child reaches for the moon, which is so obviously outside his grasp. The ability to judge the size of an object, independent of its distance from the observer, or to estimate the distance of an object from the observer, independent of its size, is only gradually acquired during childhood. It may also be noted that such ability is always limited by the conditions in the overall visual environment. It is relatively easy to fool a mature person into believing that a distant object is near, or vice versa, by manipulating the texture and lighting cues of the visual surround. For example, even highly intelligent and well-trained adults continue to see the moon as being larger when near the horizon than when high in the heavens. However, grown-ups do remarkably well under most environmental conditions in estimating the sizes of different objects, independent of their distance. Franz Beyrl, from the Psychological Institute of Vienna, plots the course of the gradual acquisition of "size constancy" during the first 10 years of life. Among other things, he concludes that "size constancy" is very near its asymptote by the tenth year of life; however, being a careful investigator, he notes that this generalization is restricted to the distances and sizes of objects involved in his experiment. He also found that the child consistently exhibits superior "size constancy" judgments of three-dimensional as compared with plain surface objects. This finding is consistent with the hypothesis of many contemporary perceptual theorists that there is an intimate relationship between perceptual judgment and the manipulation of objects. Beyrl favors Karl Buehler's assumption that this difference is based on imaginary enlargements and diminutions during the so-called fairy-tale age—an assumption based on the finding that the small child finds it easier to "handle" three-dimensional rather than two-dimensional objects in his imaginary manipulations of objects in the external world.]

The capacity for size perception develops to near-perfection in the first three years of life. Thus Binet (1890) conducted tests on two young children in order to determine their ability to judge lengths. In a first series of

* From F. Beyrl. Über die Grössenauffassung bei Kindern. (On size perception in children.) Z. Psychol., 1926, 100, 344–371. (With permission.)

tests, he instructed the children to compare horizontally parallel lines of varying lengths. Both girls differentiated lengths with an accuracy of to within 1/20th of a standard size when standard and comparison stimuli were presented simultaneously. However, the method of successive presentation did not yield useful findings; the children were obviously unable to remember the length of the standard for 10 to 15 seconds. In a second series of tests, angle sizes were compared, and it was revealed that here, too, the four-year-old girl was able to detect a difference of 1/18th of the standard size. The results of both test series did not differ significantly from those obtained under the same conditions in tests with adults. Under similar circumstances, the differential threshold in adults is about four to five times as great (1/80th to 1/100th).

In a test with three- to five-year-old children, Giering (1905) obtained results similar to Binet's. Giering had the children compare (a) distances between dots (the standard distance being 30 mm). (b) distances between dashes, (c) lengths of straight lines, and—if they were unable to make these comparisons—(d) the lengths of steel rods (the standard rod being 20 cm). Briefly, the findings of Giering are as follows: Of his ten three-year-old subjects, four were able to compare lines according to size. Of the six remaining children, three perceived size differences in rods. Thus, the assumption seems justified that, as a rule, a decisive developmental phase for such abilities may be assumed to exist around the third year of life. In addition, Giering found that in regard to accuracy in size perception no further development occurs between 6 and 14 years of age.

The cases of size comparison discussed so far were simplified by the fact that the comparison objects were usually located at equal distances from the observer. To these cases one could apply the old, simple assumption that the visual angle at which certain elongations appear (and to which, after all, the size of the retinal image corresponds) is the basis, at least in part, for the comparison. However, conditions for comparison are entirely different when objects to be compared are located at unequal distances from the observer. Experience teaches that, within certain limits, we adults perceive the size of objects independently of their distance, and hence compare them with relatively great accuracy. It is not just the visual angle at which objects appear that is important for size estimation, but rather the visual angle with regard to distance. Although the process by which this occurs is not yet completely clear, distance is always taken into consideration. We call this phenomenon the size constancy of visual objects. This is how we understand the fact that we "see" familiar objects within certain common distances as remaining the same size, even though the size of the retinal images of the objects varies with their distance from the eye. In the adult this question has already been thoroughly studied (Grabke, 1924; Katona, 1925). It is the goal of this study to find how size constancy functions in the child, especially in the preschool child. This paper will attempt to determine as nearly as possible the exact values for the extent and refinement of the disposition for size constancy.

METHOD

For our main tests, we had at our disposal a total of 55 children, 25 boys and 30 girls. All of our small subjects were from the Municipal Kindergarten, Beingasse 19–21, Vienna 15, and came almost exclusively from the working class of the Viennese population. These were divided into the following five different age levels: Group I consisted of 5 boys and 9 girls between 2 and 3 years of age; Group II, 8 boys and 6 girls between 3 and 4 years; Group III, 5 boys and 5 girls between 4 and 5 years; Group IV, 5 boys and 5 girls between 5 and 6 years; and Group V, 2 boys and 5 girls between 6 and 7 years. The average age of the children in the first group was 2 years and 6 months, that of the second group 3 years and 4 months, that of the third, 4 years and 3 months, that of the fourth, 5 years and 3 months, and the average age of the fifth group amounted to 6 years and 2 months. The youngest of the tested preschool children was 2 and the oldest, 6 years and 9 months old. Because the first tests revealed that intellectual ability is not related to ability in size perception we made no division into high, average, and modestly gifted.

Since our findings show that development of the capacity for size perception (as we understand it) continues beyond the sixth year of life, we tested a few 7- to 10-year-old children (five at each age level). We also gave the same test to 5 adults.

The tests usually took place at the same hour of the day, between 9 and 11 A.M., so that consideration could be given to the physical, as well as to the mental, condition of our young subjects. The tests were conducted either in the workrooms or in the sleeping rooms of the kindergarten. These were brightly lit rooms containing no confusing or distracting objects which might divert the children's attention. All objects present were familiar, and therefore no longer provoked the children's curiosity.

The entire test was divided into two main parts. 1) Tests with cube-form wooden boxes and 2) tests with carboard discs. This division was made in order to discover in the refinement of size perception any possible difference between two- and three-dimensional stimuli. The young age of the subjects dictated the utmost simplicity of test conditions. The test design was, therefore, arranged in a way which permitted simultaneous attention to both stimuli. The diagonal distance between the boxes (or discs) never amounted to more than 20 cm.

The subject reclined on a comfortable chair which was adjusted to his physical size. The standard stimulus (box or disc) stood on a table 1 meter in front of the subject, approximately at eye level. The box or disc to be compared was presented at distances of 2, 3, 4, 5, 7, 9 and 11 meters from subject's eye. The distances were presented in random sequence; however, on any one day, the comparison stimuli were compared at one certain distance only, for instance at 2 meters.

The method of constant stimuli was used—a method that can be used with small children as long as they have some conception of "larger" and "smaller." As we were able to convince ourselves, such an understanding exists in 2- to 3-year-old children.

As the standard stimulus in the tests with boxes we chose the cube-form box with a side length of 7 cm. The boxes for comparison had side lengths of from 4–10 cm with a constant difference of 0.5 cm between adjacent boxes in the series.

In the cardboard disc tests, the standard stimulus was a disc with a diameter of 10 cm; in the comparison stimuli, the size of diameters of the discs varied between 9 cm and 23 cm. Specifically, up to 12 cm there was a serial interval of 2 mm; from 12 cm to 16 cm, an interval of 4 mm; and from 16 cm on an interval of 10 mm.

In order to obtain a sufficiently large number of judgments for valid calculation of threshold values, every comparison stimulus was compared with the standard stimulus 10 times. (For school children and adults, every comparative stimulus had to be judged five times.) But because testing time for any one subject on any one day could be stretched from 7 to 10 minutes at most, the test arrangement was changed so that on two successive days, every comparison stimulus was compared with the standard stimulus three times while on the third day there were four comparisons.

RESULTS

THE CHILDREN'S REACTIONS TO THE TEST SITUATION

The subjects expressed their judgments by stating that the comparison stimulus was "smaller" ("*kleiner*"), "same" ("*gleich*"), or "larger" ("*groesser*") than the standard stimulus. Many subjects preferred to use expressions like: "more large" ("*mehr gross*") or "more small" ("*mehr klein*"), and also understood these better. In our tests, great importance is attached to instructions for the task. As von Kuenburg (1920) notes in her work, the properly presented and accurately understood task is of fundamental importance and a major prerequisite for the success of ex-perimental test efforts in general, but especially for tests involving small children. In order to do justice to Kuenburg's demand and to our tests as well, we had to convince ourselves in prolonged pretesting, that our small subjects were really aware of the meaning of "smaller," "larger," and "same." This demand could easily be met through the investigator's inter-action with the children during their play periods. Beyond this, numerous tests were done at close range with each child. We gained the conviction that all of our subjects accurately understood the given task.

In many children the task awareness was so lively that, even on the next test day, they still knew exactly what they were to do. The instruction given to the subjects was the simple question: "Where is the larger box (disc)?"

The child pointed to one of the two objects and told the experimenter where the larger box (disc) was. We always made sure that each child could easily view the position of the objects.

Before going into presentation and discussion of our test findings, something concerning the behavior of the children should be said.

As Karl Buehler has stressed one cannot conduct self-observation experiments with children as one conducts them with adults, especially not with such very young children as those used in our tests. Therefore, special importance accrues to the observations of the experimenter. For this reason, anything unusual in the children's behavior and verbal expressions was noted. These notations constitute a valuable complement to the quantitative results obtained in our tests.

In general, we observed that the younger subjects were especially suggestible. Often one word sufficed to change the children's behavior. For example, as we were testing a child of 2 years, 8 months, an employee of the kindergarten accidentally entered the test room and heard our subject judging the larger box, which was more distant, as being smaller. The employee simply said: "*Just* the other way around." The child picked up this brief remark and from then on designated every more distant box as being larger, whether it actually was larger or not. Under these circumstances, of course, testing had to be discontinued.

Observations further showed that the children achieved comparison of the three-dimensional cubes much more easily than the two-dimensional discs. Also, the children were much more certain and confident about their judgments on the "box tests" a fact which is expressed in a more uniform pattern of judgments on those tests. Seven five- to six-year-old subjects spontaneously made such remarks as: "With the boxes one can see much better when it is larger" or "I can tell better with the boxes which is the large one," and so on. And finally there was a larger number of failures in "disc tests" than with boxes. Our pretesting had shown conclusively that all 55 subjects properly conceived and understood the task. Generally, the certainty of judgment decreased with increasing distance of the comparison stimulus.

Several 6-year-old children were encouraged to comment on the tests. As was to be expected, these comments yielded no additional insight into the pattern of psychic events; the comments were far too general for that purpose. A majority of the children questioned simply said: "I look at this box hard and then at that one there, and I can see right away which box is the larger and which the smaller"; or "I can see right away which is the larger box." These comments of the subjects revealed nothing the experimenter's observation had not already shown, namely that in the majority of cases the comparison judgment occurred immediately on sighting both comparison objects. Finally, it should be stressed that nearly all subjects undertook the tests with a great deal of joy and pleasure. No resentment was detected in any child.

THE TEST FINDINGS ON SIZE PERCEPTION

Let us continue with a discussion of the main question: With regard to development of the capacity for size perception in children, what is the picture which results from the present test findings? To answer this question, the findings of all tests were combined in 140 tables of judgments, and from these tables the threshold and equivalence values for each subject and for each distance chosen in the tests were separately calculated. For the sake of brevity we present only a few selected tables from the groups of 2- to 3-year-old subjects.

Table 1 contains an illustrative set of judgments from the tests with boxes; these judgments were made when the comparison stimulus was 2 meters distant. Table 1 shows remarkable uniformity in the judgment pat-

Table 1—Size Comparisons with Cube-Form Wooden Boxes: Height of Standard = 7x7x7 cm; Distance Between Standard and Comparison Stimuli = 2m. N = 10 Children 2–3 Years of Age. (Cell entries show the number of times each child judged the comparison stimulus to be larger than, the same size as, or smaller than the standard stimulus)

Size of comparison stimulus in cm	S #1			S #2			S #3			S #4			S #5			S #6		
	Larger	Same	Smaller	Larger	Same	Smaller	Larger	Same	Smaller	Larger	Same	Smaller	Larger	Same	Smaller	Larger	Same	Smaller
10	10			10			10			10			10			10		
9.5	10			10			10			10			10			10		
9	10			10			10			10			10			10		
8.5	8		2	10			10			10			9	1		9	1	
8	4	2	4	6		4	7	1	2	6		4	7	1	2	6	1	3
7.5			10			10	3		7			10	1	2	7			10
7			10			10			10			10			10			10

tern. Note the small number of "same" judgments. The threshold values are simply and accurately obtained through calculation according to familiar psychophysical measurement formulas (Pauli, 1923). This method of calculation yields the values reflected in Table 2. We may conclude that deviation from size constancy is still considerable at this age and that individual differences in size estimation are small.

Table 2—Mean Threshold Values for Three-Dimensional Stimuli Separated by 2 Meters

	S #1	S #2	S #3	S #4	S #5	S #6
Over-estimation	8.15	7.95	7.75	7.95	7.9	8.0
Under-estimation	8.05	7.95	7.7	7.95	7.75	7.9
Mean	8.1	7.95	7.72	7.95	7.82	7.95

Table 3—Mean Threshold Values for Three-Dimensional Stimuli Separated by 11 Meters

	S #2	S #3	S #4	S #5	S #6
Over-estimation	11.1	13.75	13.25	16.3	13.0
Under-estimation	9.4	10.4	9.8	10.1	9.55
Mean	10.25	12.08	11.52	13.2	11.28

Table 3 contains threshold values, similarly calculated, for judgments of the various size boxes when these were separated from the 7 cm standard by 11 meters. As Table 3 shows, the individual differences within this group are noticeably larger than those in Table 2. The equivalence values, too, are significantly larger. Thus, we see an even greater deviation from visual size constancy with increasing distance between the stimuli to be compared.

Table 4 presents the results obtained from the group of 2- to 3-year-olds in tests with discs. The distance of the comparison stimulus is 11 meters. The pattern of judgments is less uniform at this distance than it is when the distance between comparison and standard is smaller. This may be ascribed to the more difficult conditions of comparison.

The threshold values calculated from these data are shown in Table 5.

Table 4—Size Comparisons with Circular Discs: Diameter of Standard = 10 cm; Distance Between Standard and Comparison Stimulus = 11 m. N = 10 Children 2–3 Years of Age. (Cell entries shows the number of times each child judged the comparison stimulus to be larger than, the same as, or smaller than the standard stimulus)

Size of comparison stimulus in mm	S #1			S #2			S #3			S #4			S #5			S #6		
	Larger	Same	Smaller	Larger	Same	Smaller	Larger	Same	Smaller	Larger	Same	Smaller	Larger	Same	Smaller	Larger	Same	Smaller
23.0	10			10			10			10			10			10		
22.0	10			10			10			10			10			10		
21.0	4	3	3	10			5	2	3	10			10			10		
20.0	4	2	4	10			4	6		6	4		7	3		10		
19.0		4	6	10				3	7		3	7	3	4	3	10		
18.0			10	10				2	8	4	2	4	10			10		
17.0		4	6	1	1	8	3	2	5		3	7		3	7	10		
16.0		2	8		2	8		2	8		2	8			10		5	5
15.6			10			10			10			10			10		2	8
15.2			10			10			10			10			10		1	9
14.8			10			10			10			10			10			10
14.4			10			10			10			10			10			10
14.0			10			10			10			10			10			10

The individual differences which emerge are remarkably large. The other age groups also show these large individual differences at greater distances, even though, in general, the deviation from size constancy is much smaller for the older subjects than for the two-year-olds. (It should be noted here that there were no differences between the results for boys and girls.)

Table 5—Mean Threshold Values for Two-Dimensional Stimuli Separated by 11 Meters

	S #1	S #2	S #3	S #4	S #5	S #6
Over-estimation	21.64	17.74	21.42	20.48	20.80	16.66
Under-estimation	16.54	16.12	16.54	16.20	16.66	15.44
Mean	19.09	16.93	18.98	18.34	18.73	16.05

Table 6 summarizes the results for the three-dimensional size comparisons for all ages and all standard-comparison distances. As can be readily seen, with increasing distance there is a distinct rise in equivalence value within each of these age groups, and consequently, greater deviation from size constancy can be observed. This is especially marked in the group of two-year-olds.

Table 7 shows the average equivalence values which refer to the disc tests. Here, also, there is a strong increase in equivalence values with in-

Table 6—Three-Dimensional Stimuli: Mean Equivalence Values Obtained for All Subjects and All Standard-Comparison Distances

Subjects	Standard-comparison stimulus distances						
	2 m	3 m	4 m	5 m	7 m	9 m	11 m
2-year-olds	7.92	8.15	8.42	8.74	9.21	10.44	11.66
3-year-olds	7.72	7.89	8.07	8.16	8.43	8.92	9.12
4-year-olds	7.44	7.76	8.01	8.15	8.48	8.66	8.99
5-year-olds	7.47	7.72	8.10	8.22	8.52	9.00	9.23
6-year-olds	7.39	7.80	8.08	8.32	8.58	8.68	8.80
7-year-olds	7.20	7.20	7.34	7.46	7.57	8.02	8.02
8-year-olds	7.18	7.20	7.57	7.78	8.11	8.20	8.23
9-year-olds	7.31	7.41	7.32	7.56	7.63	7.99	7.90
10-year-olds	7.29	7.13	7.21	7.16	7.15	7.17	7.37
Adults	6.98	7.10	6.99	6.98	7.16	7.05	7.09

creasing distance. Again, this is most evident in the group of two-year-olds, while vision in terms of size constancy is completely present in the 10-year-old child.

Our tests also show what the tests by Frank (1925) have revealed: That something like size constancy exists as a predisposition in the small child. However, in comparison with Frank's tests, our tests further show that it takes several years before the efficiency of this disposition attains the perfection of that found in adults.

Our results also show that at first, solid objects are compared notice-

Table 7—Two-Dimensional Stimuli: Mean Equivalence Values Obtained for All Subjects and All Standard-Comparison Stimulus Distances

Subjects	2 m	3 m	4 m	5 m	7 m	9 m	11 m
				Standard-comparison distances			
2-year-olds	12.29	13.48	14.29	15.17	15.81	17.61	18.02
3-year-olds	10.82	11.91	12.36	13.24	14.26	15.13	15.93
4-year-olds	10.56	11.26	12.20	12.95	13.48	14.53	14.96
5-year-olds	10.36	11.12	11.91	12.25	12.84	14.46	14.93
6-year-olds	10.18	10.91	11.58	12.11	12.81	13.74	14.11
7-year-olds	10.26	10.31	10.52	10.74	11.45	11.89	12.14
8-year-olds	10.17	10.25	10.44	10.53	11.54	12.47	13.23
9-year-olds	10.40	10.50	10.27	10.54	10.46	11.61	11.81
10-year-olds	10.29	10.31	10.31	10.40	10.28	10.01	10.34
Adults	9.99	9.67	10.02	10.17	10.24	10.13	10.46

ably better than flat ones. Presumably the capacity for size constancy trains itself first on objects of the familiar environment before gradually involving more abstract objects. The precedence of the development of visual size constancy for solid objects can be integrated into a framework of general principles. Solid objects are the more natural, while two-dimensional things are more remote from the needs of the child. One might also point to the fact that solid objects offer more possibilities for manipulation to the child than do flat things. Based on our test findings, we have stated that size perception for solid objects is more exact and more accurate than that of plane sizes. It could be objected that this fact is not so much due to the kind of object involved but that perhaps the shape of the comparison object was decisive for the accuracy of size perception.

For this reason we conducted supplementary tests on the six-year-old children in which two-dimensional 10 cm squares were compared. When the distance between standard and comparison stimuli was 2 m, the mean equivalence value was 10.39; at 4 m, 11.28; at 7 m, 12.49; and at 9 m, 13.24. There is a negligible difference between these values and the corresponding values for six-year-olds' judgments of two-dimensional discs, as shown in Table 7.

Accordingly, we may say that the shape of comparison objects does not play an important role in the comparison process.

Translated by Alexandra Hendee

SUPPLEMENTARY READINGS

Cruikshank, R. M. The development of visual size constancy in early infancy. *J. genet. Psychol.*, 1941, 58, 327–351.

Frank, H. Untersuchung über sehgrössenkonstanz bei Kindern. (A study of constancy of visually perceived size by children.) *Psychol. Forschung*, 1925, 7, 137, 145.

Misumi, J. Experimental studies of the development of visual size constancy in early infancy. *Jap. J. Psychol.*, 1950, 20, 16–26. (See also Misumi, J. Experimental studies on the development of visual size constancy in early infancy. *Bull. Fac. Lit., Kyushu Univ.*, 1951, 1, 91–116.)

Peckham, R. H. Visual discrimination in preschool children. *Child Develpm.*, 1933, 4, 292–297.

Russel, A. Über Formauffassung zwei– bis fünfjähriger Kindern. (On form perception of two- to five-year-old children.) *Neue Psychol. Stud.*, 1931, 7, 1–108.

decrement and recovery

of responses

to olfactory stimuli

in the human neonate*

Trygg Engen and Lewis P. Lipsitt

[The human organism soon comes to "ignore" sustained, monotonous stimulation of moderate intensity. This phenomenon is seen by Soviet physiologists of the Pavlovian school as the product of inhibition and by American psychologists as due either to fatigue of the sensory receptors (adaptation) or, on the other side of the reflex arc, to a failure of the effectors to respond (response habituation). Drs. Engen and Lipsitt, of Brown University, addressed themselves to the very difficult question of whether or not a decrement in responsiveness to olfactory stimuli during early infancy is due to sensory adaptation or response habituation. They used differential breathing patterns following the administration of olfactory stimuli as their measure of responsiveness. Their infant subjects, who ranged in age from 27 to 77 hours, very quickly adapted or habituated to the stimulus presented first—a mixture of amyl acetate and heptanal diluted in diethyl phthalate. As soon as responsiveness to this first stimulus decreased markedly, one of the two odorants was presented in pure form. The hypothesis being investigated was that if response decrement is due to sensory fatigue (adaptation), then the change from the first (compond) stimulus to the second (pure) stimulus should not produce response recovery, i.e., a change in respiration. On the other hand, if response decrement is due to habituation, then the change from first to second stimulus should produce response recovery in the form of respiratory change. Their findings clearly support the conclusion that habituation rather than adaptation was operating. In their very interesting discussion these investigators show the similarity between their findings for very young infants and the concept of "novelty" which currently attracts the research attention of many psychologists.]

* From T. Engen & L. P. Lipsitt. Decrement and recovery of responses to olfactory stimuli in the human neonate. *Journal of comparative and physiological Psychology,* 1965, 59, No. 2, 312–316. (With permission.)

Engen, Lipsitt, and Kaye (1963) have demonstrated with recordings of activity and respiration: (a) differential reactions of human newborns to different odorants, (b) a decrement in this response after repeated stimulation by asafoetida and anise oil, and (c) recovery of the diminished response following repetitive presentation of either of these stimuli by the introduction of the other.

The decrement and recovery of such responses have been reported with olfactory stimulation in newborns by Disher (1934), who also cites Kussmaul's very early experiments, by Bridger (1961) and Bartoshuk (1962a, 1962b) with auditory stimulation, and by Bronshtein, Antonova, Kamenstskaya, Luppova, and Sytova (1958) with both olfactory and auditory stimuli. Brackbill (1962) has reported the use of the technique by Zonova for determination of color discrimination in the newborn. In these experiments, the definition of recovery involves the introduction of a different stimulus (S_2) following decrement of the response to a previous stimulus (S_1).

Engen et al. (1963, p. 76) have called attention to the distinction between sensory adaptation (fatigue of receptor organs produced by repeated stimulation) and response habituation (extinction of response to an originally effective stimulus). When recovery of response upon presentation of S_2 takes place, this could result either because sensory adaptation or response habituation has occurred to S_1. Previous studies of olfactory recovery have involved the presentation of a new or qualitatively different stimulus (S_2); consequently the recovery could not be attributed solely to sensory adaptation or to habituation. It is our purpose to demonstrate here that recovery of response may occur to an olfactory S_2 even when this stimulus is simply a component of S_1. Under such conditions, recovery of response upon presentation of S_2 would suggest that the response decrement obtained to S_1, just preceding, is more likely response habituation and less likely sensory adaptation. Our previous olfactory experiments with newborns have suggested that such component "novel" stimulation can reinstitute the diminished response.

METHOD

SUBJECTS

Seventy apparently normal infants, slightly more girls than boys were Ss. Their average age was about 55 hr with a range of 27–77 hr. Each was used only in one session and had not been an S in any other olfactory experiment.

APPARATUS

The apparatus (Lipsitt & De Lucia, 1960) and the method (Engen et al., 1963) have been described and only the pertinent details will be stressed here. Breathing was recorded on a Grass polygraph (Model 5A) from a Phipps and Bird infant pneumograph attached around the abdomen.

The odorants were anise oil (Anethol USP), tincture asafoetida, amyl acetate, heptanal, and a mixture of anise oil and asafoetida and a mixture of amyl acetate and heptanal. The diluent was diethyl phthalate. All chemicals were the purest obtainable commercially.

One cubic centimeter of each odorant was kept in a 10 x 75 mm Pyrex test tube stopped with a cork wrapped in aluminum foil. Stimuli were presented to the infant on a piece of cotton wrapped around a glass rod with the other end of the rod attached to the cork. The cotton was partially immersed in the liquid odorant when not in use.

PROCEDURE

The experiment was performed in a quiet air-conditioned laboratory room at the Providence Lying-In Hospital at a temperature of about 78°F. All infants were tested individually between 10:00 and 11:00 A.M. Infants were fed about 9:30–9:45 A.M. The infant was placed on its back in the experimental crib and the pneumograph was attached. The Es waited until the infant appeared to be asleep with no activity indicated on the stabilimeter (recorded on the polygraph), eyes closed, and a steady regular breathing. Since the infant had been fed beforehand, this condition would normally be reached within a few minutes. Less than 1 in 10 infants were discarded for failure to quiet.

A test trial consisted in holding the cotton between and about 5 mm from the infant's nostrils for 10 sec, and the duration of the trial was recorded on the polygraph. A trial was presented every minute. Occasionally it was impossible to maintain the cotton in place for 10 sec for the S responded by moving during the trial. Occasionally, also, more than a minute was required before the infant quieted to the pretrial criterion following response to the previous trial. A response was defined as a change in the regular breathing record as in a previous study (Engen *et al.,* 1963) in which reliability of Es' judgments of the records was found satisfactory.

RESULTS

EXPERIMENT 1

Ten trials were administered to each of ten infants with a 50-50% mixture of undiluted anise oil and asafoetida. Then half of the group was tested with a 50% concentration dilution of asafoetida and the other half with 50% anise oil on Trials 11 and 12. The average results are presented in Fig. 1, which shows a very regular decrement in response with the mixture over the ten trials, and a recovery of the response to asafoetida but not to anise. Average blocks of two trials present a smoother but unaltered picture of the results. The curve drawn in the figure was obtained with the method of least squares and fits the data very well as indicated by a value of r of $- 0.99$.

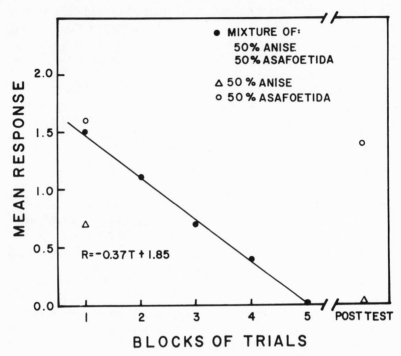

Figure 1—Average number of responses as a function of trials and
posttest stimulus presentation.

(Circle and triangle at left show level of response to odorants without prior
mixture presentation.)

To study the intensity and quality of these odorants and help clarify the
results, one of two groups of ten Ss was given two trials with the 50%
asafoetida stimulus and another group of ten Ss was given two trials with
the 50% anise stimulus. These results are also shown in Fig. 1 for the first
block of trials, and show that asafoetida is the stronger of the two stimulus
components of the mixture. Note that the response of the asafoetida component in the posttest is at a level just below its value without prior exposure to the mixture. Anise on this basis should have a value of about
0.4 in the posttest, for the slope of these decrement curves (as will be
shown below) has been found to be relatively constant with variation in
chemicals (Engen *et al.,* 1963).

It has been shown that the amount of information human *O*s are able
to transmit about multidimensional olfactory stimuli depends primarily
upon variations in quality and is not appreciably affected by the intensity
of the stimuli (Engen & Pfaffmann, 1960). To evaluate this possibility,
similarity judgments of the quality of the three odor stimuli were obtained
with the method of similarity estimation (Ekman, Goude, & Waern, 1961)
from a group of 12 graduate students in psychology. Briefly, the procedure

consisted in presenting on a rack the three possible pairs of the three stimuli used with the infants (the 50-50% mixture, the 50% anise, and the 50% asafoetida) to each individual *O*, counterbalancing the order of presentation to different *O*s. The task was to judge the similarity of the quality only of the smells of each pair on a scale from 0 ("not at all similar") to 100 ("identical") with 50 designated as halfway between these extremes, etc. The means of the judgments were: anise-mixture, 60.8; asafoetida-mixture, 39.2. That anise and asafoetida are clearly discriminable from one another was indicated by a mean value of 27.5 assigned to that comparison. The standard deviation of the judgments was about 20.0. These results show that anise was decidedly more similar subjectively to the mixture than was asafoetida. This supports the hypothesis that whether or not a posttest response occurs depends upon the similarity of the component to the mixture (i.e., the novelty of the posttest stimulus). This finding is in line with the fact that anise produced no response in the posttest while asafoetida did.

In summary, the supplementary tests suggest that another mixture with two (psycho-physical) characteristics is needed to establish recovery of response with *both* components of a two-chemical mixture. First, the components should be of equal intensity and, second, the quality of component odors should be different from each other but equally similar to the mixture. To satisfy both criteria is generally difficult, and in the case of some mixtures impossible; for example, to accomplish both conditions in the case of the mixture of anise and asafoetida would require an even smaller proportion of anise in the mixture, but that would reduce the intensity of the anise component which Fig. 1 shows was already of marginal intensity. However, satisfactory stimuli were obtained after several preliminary attempts with amyl acetate and heptanal.

EXPERIMENT 2

Twenty infants were divided at random into two groups of ten. Each group first received ten trials with a mixture consisting of 33.3% amyl acetate, 16.7% heptanal, and 50% diluent. In the posttest one group was tested with 33.3% amyl acetate, Fig. 2, and the other group with 16.7% heptanal, Fig. 3. The data were treated as above and curves fitted with the method of least squares. The curve shown in Fig. 3 is the poorer fit but is still good with $r = -0.96$ and a standard error of estimate of 0.13 which suggests that the heptanal component in posttest is a significant distance away from this regression line. A fit of the data trial by trial rather than for blocks reduces r to -0.90 but would not affect the interpretation of the results for the present purpose.

It can be observed from these figures that the slope is very similar for the three sets of data, but the *y*-intercept is higher for the two present figures which shows that even when diluted 50%, this mixture is stronger than the undiluted mixture of anise and asafoetida. In this case both components produce a response in the posttest, but more to amyl acetate (Fig. 2) than to the heptanal component (Fig. 3).

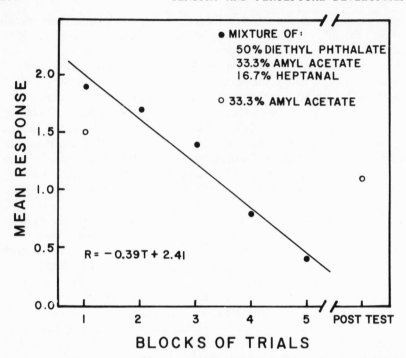

Figure 2—*Average number of responses as a function of trials and post-test stimulus.*

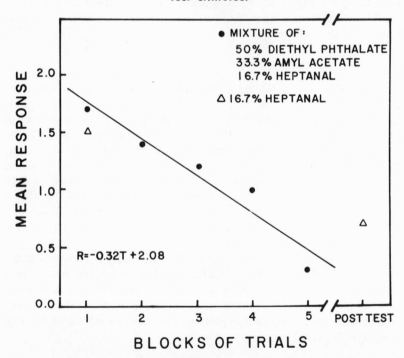

Figure 3—*Average number of responses as a function of trials and post-test stimulus.*

Again two groups of infants were used to obtain a measure of the intensity of each component without the prior exposure to the mixture. The results from these two groups are also included in Figs. 2 and 3 and indicate that the two components are of equal psycho-physical intensity, although the amyl acetate stimulus is of higher concentration. This verifies our pilot data.

A group of 12 psychology undergraduate students judged the three pairs of these stimuli as described previously. This resulted in means of 61.9 for 33.3% amyl acetate paired with the mixture, 73.3 for 16.7% heptanal paired with the mixture, and 50.9 for the pair of components. The standard deviation for a pair is about 26, and in general the data of Experiment 2 are more variable than those of Experiment 1. However, these posttest stimuli do satisfy the requirement of equal intensity and at the same time are not too different on the similarity scale, but once more the component which is more similar to the mixture (heptanal) is the less effective stimulus in the posttest. The similarity of both these components to their mixtures is greater than the similarity value for asafoetida and its mixture, and they also have lower posttest response values. Finally, the data also indicate some of the complexity of mixing odorants; this is an important psychophysical problem although not of primary interest here (cf. Geldard, 1953).

DISCUSSION

Habituation has been defined by Thorpe (1956) as the waning of a response resulting from repeated stimulation not followed by reinforcement. If the decrement is of a relatively enduring nature, and can be demonstrated to be different from sensory adaptation or fatigue, Thorpe regards the phenomenon as learned behavior. Martin (1964), on the other hand, makes a plea for the parametric study of response-decrement phenomena per se, and argues that "No useful purpose can be found for distinguishing habituation as an independent term from adaptation [p. 40]." Concerning habituation and its similarity to other response-decrement processes, Rheingold and Stanley (1963) also take the view that: ". . . any suggestion that neonatal habituation is similar to extinction, Pavlov's internal inhibition, or Hull's inhibition would be premature indeed [p. 3]." Much remains to be discovered about the neural mechanisms underlying such habituatory processes (Hernandez-Peón, 1960; Thompson & Welker, 1963).

The data of the present experiments clearly demonstrate response recovery. That is, the infant responds to a stimulus, S_2, which is a component of another stimulus, S_1, to which response decrement has just been obtained. From Thorpe's distinction, response habituation rather than sensory adaptation, or fatigue of receptors responding to S_2, accounts for our decrement, and the reactions in posttest trials constitute dishabituation. This conclusion is supported by the finding that the degree of response recovery is inversely related to the degree of similarity between S_1 and S_2, or the degree of novelty of S_2 following the exposure to S_1 (assuming congruence of similarity data of adults and infants).

Concerning the "novelty" aspects of the present data, a recent review (Cantor, 1963) of studies of attending and manipulative responses in infants and children to complex and novel stimulation stated:

> In view of the ubiquity of these types of phenomena and the relative ease with which they can be studied, it is surprising how little systematic investigation of the novelty-familiarity variable and its relation to infant or child behavior has occurred [p. 21].

Cantor cited four child studies dealing with such effects, all of these done with children of preschool age and older, and asserted that novelty cannot be considered independently of the individual organism's past experience, unlike some other stimulus attributes such as complexity. What is novel for a given S depends to some extent on the recency of his exposure to either that stimulus or one similar to it. Viewed in this way, studies of response-decrement and recovery (or habituation and dishabituation) in neonates constitute procedures for investigating effects of novel stimulation in inarticulate, immature organisms. Quantitative variations in amount of response recovery to posttest stimuli, following decrement, could yield gradients of generalization which are essentially gradients of novelty.

Under what conditions may response decrement be taken as evidence for a learning process? Another way to ask the same question is: when is response to novelty evidence for an S's having *learned not* to respond to a familiar stimulus? Thorpe (1956) seems to argue that when adaptation and fatigue have been ruled out as the basis for diminution of response to the "familiar" stimulus, learning is left.

Hinde (1954) says there may be as many as four different mechanisms underlying decrement to repetitive stimulation. When response is found to wane specifically to an evoking stimulus, when the waning seems temporary, and when the repsonse can still be evoked by other stimuli, Hinde favors calling this selective process adaptation and keeping it distinct from habituation. Martin (1964), on the other hand, asserts that *all* response decrement phenomena resulting from repetitive stimulation are of a learning nature and should not be arbitrarily separated. Bridger (1961) says that the startle decrements in neonates to tones of a given frequency are changed, do not constitute phenomena usually referred to as learning, but are rather indicative of ". . . some sort of primitive sensory discrimination [p. 994]." In contrast, Bartoshuk (1962a, 1962b) labels his heart-rate decrement to auditory stimuli, and subsequent recovery to changed stimulation, as a kind of discrimination learning. He also shows that repetitive presentation of a changing tone (from low to high frequency over an 8-sec period of stimulation) produces response-decrement and that when the change is temporally reversed (now high to low frequency over an 8-sec period), the response recovers. Barring the possibility that the auditory receptors are influenced physiologically and differentially under the two conditions of tone-order, the only determinant remaining for the recovery is novelty. Similarly, in the present study, barring the possibility that the olfactory receptors for S_2 are changed somehow by their interaction with receptors for S_1 (consisting of both stimuli), the remaining determinant for the recovery is the novelty of S_2.

Assigning the term "novelty" to a stimulus on the basis of the organism's increased reaction to it implies a preseverative effect of previous familiarization with another stimulus. Whether this familiarization effect should be regarded as a learning phenomenon or not (Lipsitt, 1963) depends upon arbitrary definitions of learning and on what particular parameters control the process that also control (other) learning processes. Since the present study rules out strictly sensory fatigue, the decrement and recovery must surely be classified as habituatory and, according to the Thorpe terminology, as a learning phenomenon.

SUPPLEMENTARY READINGS

Disher, D. R. The reactions of newborn infants to chemical stimuli administered nasally. *Ohio State Univer. Stud.*, 1934, 12, 1–52.

Engen, T., Lipsitt, L. P., & Kaye, H. Olfactory responses and adaptation in the human neonate. *J. comp. physiol. Psychol.*, 1963, 56, 73–77.

Lipsitt, L. P., Engen, T., & Kaye, H. Developmental changes in the olfactory threshold of the neonate. *Child Develpm.*, 1963, 34, 371–376.

Stirnimann, F. Versuche über Geschmack und Geruch am ersten Lebenstag. (Experiments on taste and smell on the first day of life.) *J. Kinderheilkunde*, 1936, 146, 211–227.

a study of
premature infants
fed cold formulas*

L. EMMETT HOLT, JR., EDWARD A. DAVIES,
EILEEN G. HASSELMEYER, and APOLLONIA O. ADAMS

[Modern science is committed to many different goals in carrying out its services to society. Undoutedly its most glamorous assignment is exploration of the unknown—research directed toward enlarging the perimeter of current knowledge. This highly prestigeful function may so capture the imagination that the other services of science are overlooked or undervalued. One of these most often neglected contributions relates to the continuous examination and verification of what is believed to be trustworthy knowledge. The history of science shows that today's "facts" may, indeed, become tomorrow's fictions, and that scientists must continuously be alert for the presence of floss and dross within their networks of explanation. The "old wives' tales" are a well-known source of such errors in interpretations of behavioral development and child-rearing outcomes. This is not to imply that such beliefs and practices are necessarily in error because they are based on common sense, but rather that each one must repeatedly stand the inspection of more adequate scientific theory and improved instrumentation. Sometimes common sense proves to be an uncommonly rare insight into the workings of nature but such is not always the case, as is well illustrated in the following report. Dr. Holt and his collaborators at Bellevue Hospital have collected convincing evidence that the infant's physical and psychological well being is *not* adversely affected by being fed cold formula, taken directly from a refrigerator at 39° F. These findings may constitute bad news for the manufacturers of bottle warmers, but certainly offer welcome information to mothers who need not go through the useless ritual of warming the infant's formula or feeling anxious about the adequacy of their particular wrist tests.]

* From L. E. Holt, Jr., E. A. Davies, E. G. Hasselmeyer & A. O. Adams. A study of premature infants fed cold formulas. *Journal of Pediatrics*, 1962, 61, 556–561. (With permission.)

The use of cold formulas in infant feeding is not altogether new. For some years French pediatricians (Woringer, Personal Communication) have used iced feedings in the treatment of vomiting. A single report in the American literature (Gibson, 1958) deals with the response of normal infants to cold formulas with the conclusion that such feedings are acceptable to infants and lead to no untoward results. If the traditional procedure of heating the feeding to the body temperature is indeed superfluous and carries no advantage to the infant, the saving of labor in infant care would be enormous. However, before accepting that conclusion it seemed desirable that the subject be studied in further detail and in the most critical manner possible.

The observations which we wish to report were carried out in the premature unit of Bellevue Hospital. It was thought that if any differences existed in the results of warmed and cold feedings in the case of full-term infants, these should be more conspicuous and more readily detected in premature infants. During the winter of 1958 to 1959 two studies were carried out on the premature unit with a somewhat different design. In the first study, a group of premature infants were placed for a period of four weeks on warm formulas. This was immediately followed by a similar four-week period in which cold formulas were given to all.

In this study, particular attention was focused on the behavior of the infants receiving the warm and the cold feedings. The methodologies employed were developed by the Division of Nursing of the United States Public Health Service (Hasselmeyer, 1961). A team of observers trained by the Division of Nursing, was made available, and with their aid detailed observations on sleep, vocalization, and motor behavior were made every 10 minutes around the clock for periods of about 15 seconds. Such observations were made on 261 patient days of warm feedings and 197 patient days of cold feedings. Since patients were being admitted and discharged from the unit during these two periods, it follows that for the most part the subjects on warm feedings were not the same as those who received the cold feedings. There were, however, seven subjects who were studied on both feedings; they were observed for the last three days of the warm formula period and on the succeeding three days after the changeover period to cold formulas. The data on these subjects are recorded separately. Apart from these seven subjects who were studied on both types of formulas, it was thought that more valid data would be obtained if the comparisons were made on infants of comparable age and weight. Therefore, a selection was made of infants in the medium age and weight group. This netted a group of fifteen infants fed warm formulas who were compared to a group of eleven infants fed cold formulas. The composite characteristics of these two groups is given in Table 1.

A second study was carried out with a somewhat different emphasis and design. In this study alternate babies were placed on warm and cold feedings upon which they were maintained and detailed observation were made on feeding behavior and on the body temperature before and after

Table 1—First Study

Group	Total patient days studied	Average age at onset of study (days)	Average birth weight (grams)	Average weight at onset of study (grams)	Duration of study (days)	Average daily weight gain (grams)
Warm formula (N = 15)	261	17.4	1,530	1,740	17.4	31.7
Cold formula (N = 11)	197	17.9	1,570	1,753	17.9	30.3

feeding. Measurements were made also of the temperature of the formulas as actually fed to the infants. This study was continued for 91 days, data being collected on seventeen infants fed warm formulas and sixteen fed cold formulas. Composite data of the subjects of this study are shown in Table 2.

Table 2—Second Study

Group	No. of feedings studied	Average age at onset of study (days)	Average birth weight (grams)	Average weight at onset of study (grams)	Duration of study (days)	Average daily weight gain (grams)
Warm formula (N = 17*)	2,458	16.1	1,610	1,728	22.7	30.1
Cold formula (N = 16*)	2,114	13.0	1,627	1,722	21.2	30.9

* Excluded from this study were 2 additional infants who developed intercurrent infections. One of these was on warm formula and the other on cold formula.

RESULTS

SLEEP, VOCAL, AND MOTOR BEHAVIOR

Data on the behavior of the infants from the first study is shown graphically in Fig. 1 together with the code employed in studying these phenomena. The percentages shown in the different columns represent a total of 37,584 individual observations in the warm formula group and a total of 28,368 observations in the cold formula group. The difference between the two groups is not impressive.

Statistical analyses of the figures show a significant difference at the 0.01 level in two particulars: In the cold feeding group there was a greater amount of handling and of bodily movement in the No. 2 category. We are inclined to attribute the greater percentage of wakefulness to the increased handling of the infants during the cold formula period which may have resulted from the lower census on the unit at this time, a factor which permitted more time for nursing procedures.

In Fig. 2 are shown the composite data obtained on the seven individual infants who were followed during the changeover period from warm to cold formulas. Here again no significant difference can be detected.

FEEDING BEHAVIOR

Data on feeding were obtained from the second study in which seventeen infants on warm formulas were compared with sixteen infants on cold formulas. The observations on each infant were continued for at least a ten-day period. Feeding behavior was closely followed and recorded by the nurses on a check list. Such data were obtained on 2,380 warm feedings as compared with 2,060 cold feedings. The data failed to reveal any appreciable difference in such feeding behavior as time required to feed, type of feeding, interest in feeding and behavior before and after feeding.

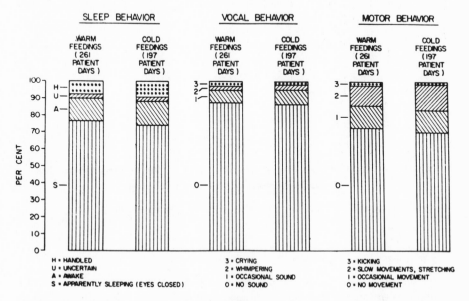

Figure 1—Sleep, vocal, and motor behavior of infants on warm & cold feedings.

FOOD INTAKE

The caloric intake of infants fed warm and cold formulas is shown in Fig. 3. The figures are most meaningful from the tenth to the thirty-first days where the sample is large enough for comparison, while above and below that range the smaller number of observations makes the result less significant. Ninety-four per cent of the feedings were given by nipple, the remainder by gavage (stomach tube).

REGURGITATION

In the warm formula group nine infants regurgitated one or more times as compared to ten in the cold formula group. The number of episodes of regurgitation was 21 in the warm formula group as compared with 36 in the cold formula group. However, 16 of these 36 episodes occurred in a single infant who had a history of regurgitation since the fourth day of life. (He was placed on cold formula on the fifteenth day of life.) His frequency of regurgitation was the same on cold as on warm formula. Less than one per cent of the feedings in both groups were regurgitated, and it does not

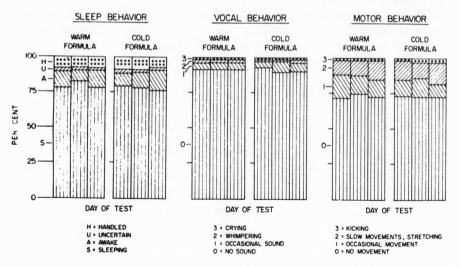

Figure 2—Sleep, vocal, and motor behavior of the seven infants during transition from warm to cold feedings.

appear that valid conclusions can be drawn from the available data on this point.

TEMPERATURE OF THE FORMULA

Observations on the actual temperatures of the formulas as fed to infants were made in 50 cases in each group. This was done by preparing

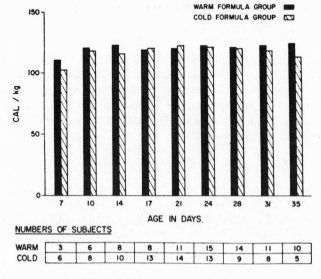

Figure 3—Average daily caloric intake on selected days of life.

duplicate bottles which were handled identically and simultaneously in precisely the manner as the bottle given to the infant. At selected times before, during, and after the feeding the temperature of the formula in the duplicate bottle was recorded. All formulas were kept in a refrigerator, the temperature of which was maintained at 4° C (39° F). The cold formulas were fed within a few minutes of being removed from the refrigerator. The warm formulas were heated by being placed in a hot water bath by the nurse; the temperature was tested in the usual way by allowing a drop to fall on the wrist. The temperature of the cold formulas at the onset of the feeding varied from 45° F to 52° F and at the end of the feeding from 48° F to 65° F. The warmed formulas showed an unexpectedly wide range —from 93° F to 124° F at the start of the feeding and from 86° F to 109° F at the end. It thus appears that the usual technique for regulating the temperature of the warmed feeding does not prevent an undesirably warm feeding being given to the infant at times.

TEMPERATURE OF THE INFANT, BEFORE AND AFTER FEEDING

It might be anticipated that the introduction of a cold feeding into the stomach of an infant might result in a reduction in body temperature. Observations were made, therefore, of the axillary temperatures before and after feeding—2,458 observations being made on infants given warm feedings and 2,114 observations on those given cold feedings. It appears that with either type of feeding the temperature may fluctuate within a range of $\pm 1.2°$ F from the preprandial figure. In the case of the warmed feedings the frequency curve of elevated and reduced temperatures was about equal, the mean temperature being the same after the feeding as before. In the case of the cold feedings the mean temperature was 0.2° F lower than that before the feeding. The variability of the temperature change was greater in the cold feeding series than in the warm feeding series ($t = 2.6$ for the warmed feedings, 47.1 for the cold feedings, both tests being significant at the 0.01 level). In neither group, however, did the variation exceed 1.2° F.

SUMMARY

The desirability of feeding infants with formulas warmed to the body temperature has been investigated in premature infants. Controlled observations have been made in which warmed formulas were compared with those fed directly on removal from a refrigerator.

Quantitative methods have been developed for assessing the behavior of premature infants—their motility, vocalization, sleep patterns, and feeding behavior.

Comparisons of warmed and cold feedings in premature infants showed negligible differences in their sleep patterns, vocalization, and motility. Significant differences in the intake of food or fluid, in the weight gain, and in the regurgitation of food were not observed.

The body temperature taken after feeding was found to vary $\pm 1.2°$ F from the temperature before the feeding in both the cold and the warm formula groups. Within this range the variability was found to be somewhat greater in the cold formula group. The average postprandial temperature in the warm formula group was the same as the preprandial temperature; in the cold formula group it was decreased by $0.2°$ F.

The observations presented in this study were submitted to statistical analysis, significant differences between the warm and the cold feeding group being found only in the case of the body temperature as mentioned above.

The experiences in this study fail to demonstrate that the traditional procedure of warming the feeding is in any way advantageous to the infant.

SUPPLEMENTARY READINGS

Cooke, R. E. The behavioral response of infants to heat stress. *Yale J. Biol. Med.,* 1952, 24, 334–340.

Jensen, K. Differential reactions to taste and temperature stimuli in newborn infants. *Genet. Psychol. Monogr.,* 1932, 12, 361–479.

Mestyan, G., & Varga, F. Chemical thermoregulation of full-term and premature newborn infants. *J. Pediatr.,* 1960. 56, 623–629.

Pratt, K. C. Note on the relation of temperature and humidity to the activity of young infants. *Ped. Sem.,* 1930, 38, 480–484.

Usoltsev, A. N., & Terekhova, N. T. Functional peculiarities of the skin-temperature analyser in children during the first six months of life. *Pavlov J. high. nerv. Act.,* 1958, 8, 174–184.

vestibular responses

to rotation in the

newborn infant*

MARGARET M. LAWRENCE and CARL FEIND

[Nystagmus—oscillation of the eyeballs from side to side following body rotation—has long been used by neurologists as an indication of proper functioning of the semicircular canals and of certain cranial nerves. Despite the fact that this is an important neurological test, little is known about the development of this response during infancy and childhood. Although several investigators have observed nystagmus in infancy, their experimental procedures have been too poorly specified and standardized to permit accurate norms and meaningful comparisons of pathological and nonpathological states. Dr. Lawrence, of Pomona, New York, and Dr. Feind, of Columbia College of Physicians and Surgeons, have developed the necessary apparatus for studying this response during early infancy—an apparatus, by the way, that could be adapted for use with older children and even adults. On the basis of their findings with 64 full-term newborn infants they conclude that during deceleration all infants show head and eye deviation opposite to the direction of acceleration. The duration of postrotational nystagmus under their standardized conditions was approximately 13 seconds. Data relevant to the normal ontogenetic development of this response have yet to be collected. This report constitutes a point of departure for a better understanding of this response, a potentially important one for neurological diagnosis.]

The need for exact knowledge of the normal vestibular response of young subjects to artificial stimulation became apparent to one of the authors while testing a group of patients with H. influenzae meningitis who had been treated with streptomycin. In addition to its importance in detecting vestibular damage caused by streptomycin, such information is of value in examining the cranial nerves of the newborn infant to identify congenital

* From M. M. Lawrence & C. Feind. Vestibular responses to rotation in the newborn infant. *Pediatrics,* 1953, 12, 300–306. (With permission.)

defects and birth injuries, and at later ages to confirm the presence of post-natal injuries and diseases.

To date, evaluation of the normal vestibular function in the newborn and young infant has been inadequate. This study is an attempt to perfect a technic or appraise the results of a simple vestibular test in infants and children.

This report concerns the vestibular response of sixty-four newborn infants to various stimuli. These infants were all healthy and were considered normal. Their ages varied from 3 hours to 10 days, and their weights between 2.2 to 4.0 kg. Sex and cultural background were disregarded. Caloric tests proved unsatisfactory at this age, because of smallness of the external canal and apparent discomfort to the infants manifested by their crying and tight closing of eyes, which made observation of nystagmus impossible. The following gives methods and results of rotation testing.

METHOD

The rotation apparatus used consisted of an electrically driven turntable actuated by a DC ¼ hp motor, capable of turning in either direction and with a rheostat speed control. With its full load it was routinely accelerated to 30 rpm in 180° and braked to a stop in 45°. This table had been used in a previous streptomycin toxicity study and was modified to accommodate a well padded baby holder. The infant was placed supine on the platform (Fig. 1), with the head over the center of rotation. The head was extended

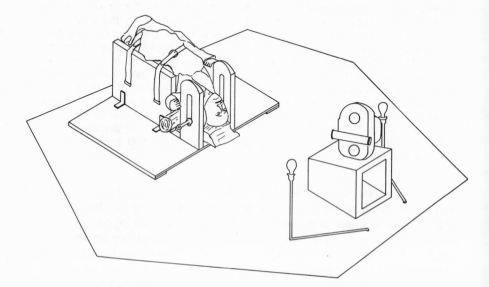

Figure 1—Male infant on turntable in position for rotation.

60° from the frontal plane of his body, so as to place the lateral semi-circular canals in the plane of rotation, and was held between 2 loose padded muffs which allowed about 45° of rotation. The babies were rotated 10 times in 20 seconds. Following a rest period of 3 to 5 minutes, rotation was repeated in the opposite direction.

The eyes were inspected before, during and after rotation. Eye deviation, nystagmus, head, neck and general body responses were noted.

RESULTS

The usual movements of the eyes before the beginning of rotation were slow and roving. Immediately after the onset of rotation the head turned in the opposite direction of rotation in all but six of the sixty-four cases. These six showed no movement. After a few turns many of the heads came back to a central position. Fifty-two of the infants kept their eyes open during the entire period of rotation. The eyes and heads of these were seen to deviate in the opposite direction to that of rotation and in this quadrant the eye exhibited a regular nystagmus with the fast component in the direction of rotation. This nystagmus started with acceleration and continued several turns. During the later period of rotating at a constant speed, the eyes in most cases returned to center or assumed their pretest roving with cessation of nystagmus. At the instant of braking (deceleration) the head and eyes rotated to the direction of turning and again nystagmus started, with the fast component now opposite to the direction of turning. Nystagmus, to acceleration and deceleration, was observed in 100% of the sixty-four cases. It was variable in rate and intensity but its direction was always parallel to the plane of rotation. Figure 2 contains a plot of the duration of postrotational nystagmus versus number of tests in sixty-four infants who were awake during the test. The duration of postrotational nystagmus varied from 3 to 35 seconds, and in any individual infant, was equal or within a few seconds in either direction except in three cases which were not further followed. It is probable that the reading of 3 seconds is inaccurate because the infant in whom it was observed had a 20 second response in rotation in the other direction, a value which according to the authors' findings is normal. The average postrotational nystagmoid response to 10 turns in 20 seconds was 13.1 seconds. Skin flushing, eructation and voiding were frequent during rotation. The above observations were checked by taking 16 mm movies of a sizeable cross-section of the babies before, during, and after rotation. The movie camera and lights were rotated with the baby and included a picture of his face. (See Fig. 1.)

Eight infants were rotated both asleep and awake. The method used to observe the eyes of all sleeping infants was as follows: An observer stood at the exact spot where the machine was stopped. The observer then separated the infant's eyelids and watched the eyes for a full minute. None of the babies who were asleep during the test had any postrotational nystag-

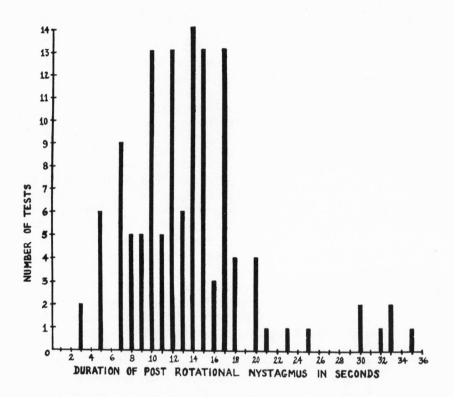

Figure 2—Duration of post rotational nystagmus in 64 newborn infants.

mus, nor did five others not included in the series of sixty-four, who were rotated asleep only. The eight infants were also described in the preceding awake group.

Failure to respond to vestibular stimulation during sleep was previously observed by one of the authors in a 4½ month old infant who did not respond to 30° or 44° C water (Hallpike Fitzgerald test), to rotation at 60 rpm, nor to 100 cc of ice water in one ear. The child remained sound asleep during all of the above procedures, but during irrigation of the second ear with ice water the child stirred and awakened. At this time, the eye under observation, which had been rolled up, came down and immediately went into regular rapid medium nystagmus. The other tests repeated while awake were all within normal limits. In the series of sixty-four, there was no difference in response in relation to age or weight.

The authors have found this method of rotation a useful one for the study of vestibular function in the newborn infant. The apparatus used is simple to construct, convenient to manage, and gives consistent results, in contrast to hand rotation using the Bárány chair.

COMMENT

Few references to vestibular responses in the newborn infant can be found in the literature and the reports are conflicting as to the presence of nystagmus. Ford (1944) states that reactions to rotation or rotary acceleration are present at birth. However, he does not describe these responses. Magnus (1924), in his description of responses to rotation in newborn animals, found that nystagmus could be observed at 18 days in the rabbit, at 4 or 5 weeks in the dog and at 6 and 7 days in the cat. Bartel (1914) described eye deviation but no fast component of nystagmus in newly born premature human infants; full term newborn infants, on the other hand, showed normal nystagmus in response to rotation. DeKleyn and Schenk in 1931 reported their findings on rotating a 1-week-old anencephalic child. Their method of rotation was to hold the infant by the trunk with his head in the upright position; the observer and the child then turned about a vertical axis. Turning to the right caused a postrotation fast component of nystagmus to the left; likewise rotating to the left resulted in nystagmus to the right. This infant, as shall be commented on later, lacked cerebral hemispheres, cerebellum, and third and fourth nerve nuclei.

McGraw (1941), as a part of a more comprehensive study, observed the postural and ocular responses of the infant to bodily rotation. This study included sixty-seven infants from birth to 2 years. The child was held in an upright position facing the experimenter, and both turned together, the experimenter pirouetting. No attempt was made to stimulate "particular vestibular canals." The speed of turning was calculated to be 0.778 rotations per second; body and ocular deviation were recorded by direct observation. Three types of response were described: A phase during which the eyes deviated laterally in the direction of rotation during the movement and in the opposite direction after rotation had ceased; this "phase" occurred in 100% of the infants under about 1 month of age. A gross oscillatory phase (Phase B) at about the fourth month in which the eyes showed coarse slow horizontal excursion during rotation, continuing for a few seconds after rotation was stopped. A fine oscillatory phase (Phase C) during rotation, occurring around the seventh month. No mention was made of how optokinetic nystagmus was eliminated during rotation in the older age group. Also there was no control of acceleration, speed or deceleration with this method.

McGraw (1932) posits that the "changing adjustments of the infant to rotation indicate reorganization of the neural system involved," and states that there is considerable doubt that the cerebral cortex exercises much influence upon these labyrinthine reflexes. Ford (1944), on the basis of the work of Langworthy (1933), states that "with some exceptions the anatomical development of the segmental apparatus is complete at birth" and that "the chief supra-segmental structures and their projection paths are still immature." We should expect, then, that vestibular responses in the newborn infant would be purely a response of the archaic motor system, a name used by Gesell for the early response systems, and that this archaic motor system would be free of cerebral inhibition. Again interpreting Langworthy's work, Ford states that the lack of cerebral function in the newborn infant is expressed in two ways: absence of true volitional activity and lack of inhibition of the segmental apparatus.

We should expect, too, that the vestibular system would be entirely capable of functioning on its own since the neurons involved are among the earliest to become myelinated, beginning as early as a fetal age of 20 to 24 weeks (Langworthy, 1933). The neurons involved in nystagmus produced by stimulation of semicircular canals are the third, fourth, sixth, and the vestibular part of the eighth cranial nerves and the median longitudinal fasciculus. Furthermore, according to Langworthy, the sequence in which tracts become myelinated is correlated with the sequence in which the function of structure develops. The anencephalic child described by deKleyn and Schenk (1931), who at one week of age exhibited both components of nystagmus, proves the ability of this archaic vestibular apparatus to function independently of cerebral influence. Only the reflex connections, labyrinths, vestibular and abducens nuclei were present; the cerebral hemispheres, cerebellum, and third and fourth nerves were absent.

The group of sixty-four newborn infants described in this report can be compared to McGraw's newborn group. As has been noted, McGraw's newborn infants were said to show "Phase A" postrotation response consisting of head and eye rotation toward the direction opposite to that of rotation. The postrotation findings of the present investigators were eye deviation to the direction of turning and a fast component (nystagmus) opposite to the direction of turning. The rotation apparatus used made it possible to observe the eye responses of infants with comparative ease and to obtain consistent results in this study. Other observers have reported eye movements in the newborn infant, in response to rotation, but they have not reported in detail concerning the presence of the fast component (nystagmus), its duration, direction and associated movements.

A careful review of the available reports on vestibular responses to rotation in adults reveals no work on an adult group comparable to that done by the present authors with newborn infants. Speed of rotation, rate of acceleration and rate of deceleration were all kept constant in the present study. None of the methods described in the rotation of adults has kept these factors constant. Because these important factors are variable, it is difficult to compare the results of these tests on adults with each other or with those done on this newborn group. Northington (1939) describes a rotation test for adults in which the same semicircular canals are stimulated as in this study. In the adult test the individual is in a face-front seated position with the head flexed 30°. In both instances the horizontal semicircular canal is in the same plane as the plane of rotation. The Bárány chair used for testing adults is rotated by hand 10 times in 20 seconds. Northington (1939) found that the duration of the postrotatory nystagmus varied from 15 to 31 seconds and in the majority from 15 to 20 seconds.

The average postrotational nystagmus is 18 seconds in duration. In adults amplitude is usually rated as fine, medium or coarse, and the frequency as fast, medium or slow. These observations are rather inaccurate and vary with the observer. It is, however, the impression of one of the authors that the response in the newborn infant is of greater amplitude, slower frequency, and shorter in duration than in adults. The need for standardized and controlled rotation tests, and permanent recordings of eye movements is great. When these improvements are worked out and normal responses are tabulated for large groups, then vestibular tests will become more meaningful as a diagnostic aid. A permanent recording of eye movements other than motion pictures, but more like an EEG or ECG will eliminate the inaccuracies of observers and give exact measurements of duration, frequency and amplitude.

SUPPLEMENTARY READINGS

Guillaume, P. Le problème de la percéption de l'espace et la psychologie de l'enfant. (The problem of the perception of space and the psychology of the child.) *J. Psychol. norm. path.*, 1924, 21, 112–134.

Heck, W. E. Vestibular responses in the newborn. *Arch. Otolaryng.*, 1952, 56, 573.

McGraw, M. B. Development of rotary-vestibular reactions of the human infant. *Child Develpm.*, 1941, 12, 17–19.

iv

Conditioning and Learning

those that do teach young babes
Do it with gentle means and easy tasks.
SHAKESPEARE, Othello, *1604.*

conditioning

gastric secretions*

HEINRICH BOGEN

[The following study is the very first one demonstrating conditioning in the human infant. It is also noteworthy as an example of a scientist's taking advantage of a variation in nature to increase human knowledge. Dr. Bogen, of the University Children's Clinic in Heidelberg, Germany, was inspired in his research by reports of Pavlov's conditioning the salivary secretion in dogs. His subject was a 3½ year-old child who had swallowed a teaspoon of lye leading to a stenosis (an extreme narrowing) of the esophagus. It was necessary to provide this boy with a stomach fistula through which he could be fed. At the time Dr. Bogen's observations were made the child could chew and swallow food but it was effectively blocked from passing into the stomach by the stenosis and was always regurgitated. The author showed that gastric secretion of hydrochloric acid (obtained from a tube inserted into the fistula while the child was in a prone position) followed the feeding of meat with a reaction time of approximately 4 minutes. He also observed that the same response appeared with about the same latency after the mere visual presentation of meat. Then he found that "psychic secretion of gastric juice" could be produced in the child by means of specific conversations (talking about food)—called "pure psychic" stimulation. His later observations involved the establishment of conditioned gastric secretion to the sound of a trumpet.]

Before presenting the tests, I should like to offer, in brief outline, the quite interesting history of the small patient on whom the experiments were made. The boy, Julius H., now 3½ years old, suffers from a stenosis of the esophagus and has a stomach fistula, through which he is fed.

On October 17, 1905, he drank a teaspoon of lye, which was immediately vomited, but did cauterize mouth, throat, and esophagus so badly that

---

* From H. Bogen. Experimentelle Untersuchungen über psychische und assoziative Magensaftsekretion beim Menschen. (Experimental tests on psychic and associative secretion of gastric juices in the human.) *Jahrbuck für Kinderheilkunde*, 1907, 65, 733–740.

dysphagia (disturbance of swallowing) resulted. The child could only ingest liquids, drank mostly milk, which also was often regurgitated. At any rate, in the middle of January, 1906, the physician is said to have been able to insert a "hose" which resulted in improvement for several days. This, however, did not last long. The stenosis symptoms became worse, so that almost nothing passed through. The child's nutritional condition deteriorated, and he was brought to our clinic on February 7, 1906.

I will here omit discussing the condition of the then very paltry child and will only mention that our soon undertaken attempts to probe (with thin and thick, with hard and soft, as well as with elastic probes) always led to negative results. Milk and tea were given as food, which did, however, not pass through the stenosized area. Therefore, on February 10th, Professor Jordan undertook, under chloroform anesthesia, a gastrotomy in order to insert a Witzel stomach tube.

After some time retrograde attempts at probing were done which, in spite of frequent repetitions, never led to a positive result. Professor Stark then tried, by means of inserting several probes at once, to succeed in possibly passing through at least one of these, again with the same failure. He did not think that esophagoscopy in this case promised anything.

Because the little one fell ill of pneumonia in the middle of May, attempts at probing could not be resumed until June; but even up to today, they have never led to any result. It was therefore decided to attempt a renewed surgical opening of the stomach on July 23, in order to overcome, through the wide cavity, the stenosis from below and to dilate it. These attempts were likewise unsuccessful, as was a probe undertaken from above with the anesthetized patient's head hanging down.

After these unsuccessful surgical efforts the patient received, every other day between August 20 and November 1, 1 cc Fibrolysin injected subcutaneously—again without yielding any success for attempts at probing.

Our frequent attempts at probing led us to the assumption that a widening had occurred above the stenosis which was located approximately 18 cm away from the row of teeth, because, first of all, the impression gained while probing pointed to such a fact, and also the hard-soft probe became lightly bent and, when removed, showed that the lower end was somewhat curved. Our assumption was strengthened by the fact that during the day, especially in the morning, great amounts of mucous, sometimes sour, sometimes alkaline, were vomited and spread an abominable odor and had obviously stagnated somewhere without having reached the stomach.

It was interesting to see how the child ate, with ravenous appetite, everything—any food he would inadvertently find—only to immediately fetch the kidney (Emerson) dish and to vomit the ingested food. Liquid food, milk also, did not pass through, a fact of which I convinced myself in the course of many probes. That such an enlargement of the esophagus does indeed exist above the stenosis is shown by X-rays which result when one feeds the child barium meal, filling the enlarged esophagus cavity.

Above the stenosis, approximately the size of a chicken egg, one clearly sees a somewhat irregularly delimited enlargement. This finding, according to Lossen (1903), is very rare.

A change in this condition occurred at the end of December last year when the child, for purposes of further tests, was given milk to drink. For some time not a trace of milk passed through the stenosized area, but then, during a test, several drops suddenly appeared at the opening of the fistula, and by now this spontaneous healing has progressed so far that the little one drinks approximately 8 to 100 cc of milk in very small swallows at each meal offered to him through the fistula, frequently without regurgitating anything at all. (N.B. X-rays now show that sometimes a drop of barium meal drops into the stomach through the opening.) Hard foods, as before, do not pass through.

The tests described in the following were made last year at a time when the esophagus was absolutely impassable for anything at all.

First, through the numerous papers from Pavlov's laboratory and also through many studies of German authors, it was shown that in the animal, especially in the dog, it is possible by means of natural or artificial (psychic) stimulation to induce saliva or gastric juice secretion. At given opportunities these tests were verified on human subjects, and the same results were found.

Since we, likewise, possessed, in the person of the sick child, a test subject, I undertook, on the suggestion of visiting Professor Dr. Tobler, similar tests with the child, partially in order to examine the results already known, partially perhaps in order to find something new. Thus tests on psychic secretions were made first, and, when these succeeded, tests on associative gastric juice secretion which were suggested by the recently appearing papers (on associative saliva secretion in dogs) originating in Pavlov's laboratory.

In order to achieve psychic and associative gastric juice secretion, it is always necessary to begin with simpler tests in which natural, i.e., un-conditioned, stimuli for gastric juice secretion are used. If it is possible in this way to induce the gastric juice secretion, one can proceed to artificial,· i.e., psychic or conditioned, stimuli.

Before presenting a description of the tests, I must touch on the preparation to the experiments with a few words. The tests were always made in the morning when the child had not yet eaten. After a small drainage tube had been inserted through the stomach fistula, the child was placed face downward on top of two suspended, wide towels, which did not quite touch in the center, thus allowing the tube to protrude from the stomach with a downward exit. This position furnished the best avenue for discharge of gastric juices. In addition, the little one did not notice the manipulations necessitated by the tests. After the boy had been turned over, a small amount of gastric juice was discharged which sometimes did and sometimes did not contain hydrochloric acid. When this predischarge was completed—it almost always occurred quickly—the actual tests were begun.

The first tests consisted in the child's being given meat to eat which reached the opening of the esophagus, from where it did not continue into the stomach, but after a short time it reappeared, together with a lot of mucous liquid, at the opening of the esophagus. Actually, this procedure represented attempts at mock feeding as are customary with patients after esophagotomy. The little one reacted to these meat feedings with rather strong secretions of gastric juice; the same result occurred when he was given milk to drink, which also was soon regurgitated. After approximately six such tests had been made, a psychic secretion of gastric juice was achieved through the mere visual presentation of meat, as well as of milk.

My observations—at first inadvertent, then intentional—showed that psychic secretion of gastric juice was a result of pure phantasy (of the meat) which was produced in the child by means of specific conversations. This secretion, which Bickel (1906) calls "pure psychic," was considered probable as a result of findings made in his laboratory. A positive result had not yet been observed there.

Attempts at association, except for experiments on lower animals, were first made in Pavlov's laboratories by Boldireff (1905, 1906) and other authors on dogs with chronic saliva fistulae. The postulates underlying these tests were as follows:

If, in numerous tests, one puts into the dog's mouth some certain food or some stimulus substance (acid, etc.), always simultaneously presenting an acoustic, optical, or olfactory stimulus, then it must finally be possible, by presenting one of the latter stimuli alone, to induce the secretion of saliva, which previously accompanied the combination of one of the first with one of the second stimuli. Actually, it was eventually possible to induce saliva secretion by purely associative means in such a way, for instance, that stimulation with some certain sound alone induced secretion.

The same basic thoughts also underlay the association tests made with our patient. It was expected that after a large number of suitable experiments, an inadequate stimulus alone would eventually induce gastric juice secretion, i.e., that gastric juice secretion would occur as a function of association. This succeeded.

For a long time—forty times in all—the child was fed with meat, while simultaneously a certain sound was produced on a small trumpet; the intention was eventually, by blowing the trumpet alone, to induce gastric juice secretion which previously occurred only on combining both stimuli —feeding and blowing. Before the final step occurred, several preparatory combinations were used—namely showing of the meat and simultaneous blowing on the trumpet, as well as stimulation with words together with the acoustical stimulus. All these tests led to a positive result; in the end seven out of ten association tests were positive, three negative.

Needless to say, in these last tests all possible external irritation was eliminated. In principle, the prescribed sequence of experiments was kept;

practically, however, several combination tests always intervened between association tests.*

The table of average values shows the findings on latent (reaction) time, amount of secretion, and hydrochloric acid content. (The stimulating substance was always meat.) The total average latent (reaction) time for meat was 4¾ minutes; on stimulation with milk, average reaction time was 9 minutes.

Table 1—Average Values for Latent (Reaction) Time, Amount of Secretion, and Hydrochloric Acid Content

Number of tests ($\Sigma = 69$)	Kind of test	Reaction time in min.	Amount of secretion in cc for each quarter hour	Hydrochloric acid content	Total acidity
5	Feeding with meat	4	10.4	0.2433	95
2	Presenting of meat	6	4.85	0.1117	—
5	"Purely psychic" secretion	4.9	2.82	0.3201	111
35	Feeding with meat; sounding the trumpet at the same time	4.57	12.2	0.2346	95.07
7	Stimulate with words; sounding of trumpet at the same time	4.5	4	0.1954	72.4
10	Stimulation only with trumpet	4.64	5.2	0.1262	69.3

Nothing can be said about the length of secretion, because in all tests only the secretion of the first quarter hour was gathered, after which the experiment was discontinued. However, I often extended the observation time and found that continued secretion occurred only on those occasions in which the natural, and not the artificial, stimulus caused the secretion.

The test did not yield conclusions on the absolute amount of secretion, for the same reason as prevailed in the case of length of secretion. At any rate, the table of average values clearly shows the great dependence of amount on the kind of preceding stimulus. We see, how with the decrease of intensity of stimulation the quantity also diminishes; how thus, in the psychic tests, the amount successively decreases from feeding to purely psychic stimulation. While the tests yielded maximally 3.6 cc of gastric juices, one associative test yielded a secretion of 18 cc. Thus, the difference between amount levels of combination and associative tests was not precisely discernable.

The total average value for hydrochloric acid content amounted to 0.2058%; in our case it was found to be lower than it is usually for normal humans (pure gastric juice approximately 0.4%), probably because our test subject secreted more alkaline stomach mucous. In spite of the commonly assumed constancy of acidity, one again sees in the tabulation how, with the exception of purely psychic secretion, acidity decreases with the

* [Several reinforced trials always intervened between test trials. Eds.]

decrease in intensity of stimulation. Should not nervous influences play a role here?

Finally, as far as the total acidity is concerned, it is analogous to the hydrochloric acid values.

Translated by Alexandra Hendee

SUPPLEMENTARY READINGS

Berkun, K. J., Kessen, M. L., & Miller, N. E. Hunger-reducing effects of food by stomach fistula versus food by mouth measured by a consummatory response. *J. comp. physiol. Psychol.,* 1952, 45, 550–554.

Engel, G. L., Reichsman, F., & Segal, H. L. A study of an infant with a gastric fistula. I. Behavior and the rate of total hydrochloric acid secretion. *Psychosom. Med.* 1956, 18, 374–398, No. 5.

Hull, C. L., Livingstone, J. R., Rouse, R. O., & Barker, A. N. True, sham and esophageal feeding as reinforcements. *J. comp. physiol. Psychol.* 1951, 44, 236–245.

Ost, J. W. P., & Lauer, D. W. Some investigations of classical salivary conditioning in the dog. In W. F. Prokasy (Ed.), *Classical conditioning: A symposium.* New York: Appleton-Century-Crofts, 1965.

the formation

of conditioned reflexes

in the young child*

N. I. KRASNOGORSKII

[The following paper, published in 1907, is the second account of the successful conditioning of a human infant. The author, Dr. Krasnogorskii, went on to a highly productive research career devoted to the conditioning of children at the Institute of Physiology named in honor of his former teacher, I. P. Pavlov. The present study, conducted with a 14-month-old infant, is as significant as Bogen's in its adaptation of Pavlovian techniques for use with human subjects. It may be recalled that Pavlov surgically diverted the salivary passage to a fistula so that he could measure the degree of salivation of his dogs. This procedure is obviously undesirable for use with human subjects. Dr. Krasnogorskii hit upon the idea of using swallowing movements to estimate the amount of salivary secretion in human subjects, estimating that approximately 0.5 cc of saliva accompanies each swallow. With all of our present knowledge about conditioning it would be easy to underestimate the significance of the author's conclusion: "There is no doubt whatsoever that the ringing of the bell after its combination with the unconditioned stimulus became a conditional stimulus, nor that I have observed in the child an artificially formed conditioned reflex." This paper is a fine tribute to the ingenuity and pioneering spirit of Pavlov's followers.]

The recent studies of Professor I. P. Pavlov and his students have opened to investigation a vast region in the psychic life of animals—a region of so-called artificial conditioned reflexes. By using a strictly objective method of research, i.e., by renouncing the imposition of his own psychic state on the object of experimentation, Professor I. P. Pavlov has succeeded in a short time in attaining interesting results and—what is more important—

* From N. I. Krasnogorskii. Opypt polucheniia iskusstvennykh uslovnykh refleksov u detei rannego vozrasta. (The formation of artificial conditioned reflexes in young children.) *Russkii Vrach*, 1907, 36, 1245–1246.

in opening a vast field for further study of complex-nervous (psychic) phenomena.

As an objective method of research I. P. Pavlov proposed using, as is well-known, the secretion of the salivary glands, having shown that the secretion of saliva has the most intimate relation with the activity of the cortex and that it serves as an index of this activity. In another publication I will review the literature that has come from Professor I. P. Pavlov's laboratory and that relates to this question. In the present article I wish only to point out the possibilities for the study of complex-nervous phenomena in infants and the related facts that have been observed in our laboratory.*

The research itself I carried out on a fourteen-month-old child always in the same isolated, quiet room, and on the same table, in an effort to preserve identity in the situation. After some trials in which the child was stimulated by feeding, I was convinced that there was the beginning of an increase in glottal movements elicited by the heightened secretion of saliva. There were also motor reactions, particularly sucking movements of the mouth, which were so clearly expressed that there is no doubt they can serve as a convenient and relatively precise measure in the study of conditioned reflexes in infants—especially since it is impossible to have an artificial salivary fistula. Since in the child a most insignificant accumulation of saliva in the mouth, 0.5 cc, accompanies the act of swallowing, then by the number of swallows one can successfully judge the strength of secretion. Our attempts gave the following results. The child, somewhat satiated, was shown a little glass with the food (milk) in it which served as a visual conditional stimulus in order to observe the increased frequency in number of swallows, sucking movements, approaches, openings of the mouth, words—in short, none other than conditioned reflexes. The number of such movements in response to the sight of the milk increased from session to session.

Table 1—Number of Swallows in Successive 3-Minute Periods

Session number	Before bell sounded	During sound of bell
1	3, 4, 2, 2, 0	6
2	3, 3, 2	5
3	5, 4, 4	8

Having obtained the conditioned reflex from stimulating the child by food shown at a distance, I tried to get it from a sound stimulus. For this purpose I combined food with the sound of a bell. After a certain number of combinations of the food with the bell I at last succeeded in that the bell alone began to elicit a clearly increased frequency of swallowing and

* In an interesting study, Bogen obtained a conditioned reflex in a child with a gastric fistula by means of repeated combinations of sound with food. The author succeeded in obtaining gastric secretion to the sound in 7 out of 10 test trials. However, aside from the exceptional rarity of such fistulas, this method is highly difficult and is not precise, owing to the absence of a section of the stomach.

motor reactions. In Table 1 are presented the results of three sessions—following the combination of food with bell and during which the child was lying quietly—showing the number of swallows for a period of time of 3 to 5 minutes up to and during the sound of the bell.

It must be noted that the excretion of saliva during the action of the conditional stimulus is, generally speaking, related in both quality and quantity to the excretion of saliva resulting from the action of the unconditioned stimulus. Therefore, if we had tried as an unconditioned stimulus a substance which produces much saliva, e.g., an acid, then we would have received, after stimulation by the conditional stimulus, a still sharper increase in the frequency of swallowing.

In order to observe the artificial conditioned reflex formed to the sound of the bell, I did the following. After a preliminary combination of food and bell we held a small glass of food in front of the child. The child began to make swallowing and sucking movements; he licked his lips (a conditioned reflex to the sight of the food), but very shortly thereafter still not having received the food, he began to cry; then little by little, he quieted down, losing interest in the glass and turning away from it. Suddenly the bell sounded. His head quickly turned toward the glass, his gaze was avidly directed toward the food, and he began to swallow and suck with energy. It is perhaps unnecessary to point out that crying is a highly inauspicious influence on the appearance of conditioned reflexes; therefore, it behooves one to carry out stimulation when the child is quiet.

There is no doubt whatsoever that the ringing of the bell after its combination with the unconditioned stimulus became a conditional stimulus, nor that I observed in the child an artificially formed conditioned reflex.

I will report at a later date evidence concerning the extinction of conditioned reflexes in children, the times of their appearance, the possibility of getting them by such stimuli as scratching, cold, warmth, light, and so on. In any event, by the method described above, it is possible with complete objectivity to study many aspects of the development of complex nervous activity in the child. I think also that for a solution to the question of the earliest time at which the child hears, sees, and so on, the method described herein, using sucking movements, will yield a more objective answer than will any other method.

Translated by Yvonne Brackbill

SUPPLEMENTARY READINGS

Krasnogorskii, N. I. Die letzten Fortschritte in der Methodik der Erforschung der bedingten Reflexe an Kindern. (Recent advances in the method of research on conditioned reflexes in children.) *Jb. Kinderheilkunde*, 1926, 114, 225–267.

Krasnogorskii, N. I. *Vysshaia nervnaia deiatelnost rebenka*. (*Higher nervous activity in the child*.) Leningrad: MEDGIZ, 1958.

Mateer, F. *Child behavior: A critical and experimental study of young children by the method of conditioned reflexes*. Boston: R. G. Badger, 1918.

conditioned leukocytosis

in newborn infants*

M. V. KRACHKOVSKAIA

[It is well nown that the normal human infant loses some body weight during the first days of life. This reflects a period of adjustment to obtaining nutrition from alimentary processes rather than from the placental blood bath. There are many physiological variables involved in the "tuning up" of the infant's digestive processes during the first few days of life. One of these is digestive leukocytosis, as reflected by an elevated leukocyte (white blood cell) count in the blood that appears about one hour after the intake of food. Most infants show this physiological response by the sixth or seventh day of life. Beginning on about the eighth or ninth day after birth most infants also show an elevated leukocyte count before as well as after feeding. There is a physiological explanation for the post-feeding leukocytosis, but there is no such explanation for the pre-feeding change. In the present report Dr. Krachkovskaia, of the I. P. Pavlov First Leningrad Institute of Medicine, interprets the latter as the formation of a conditioned interoceptive response to elapsed time as a conditional stimulus when the infant is fed on a regular schedule. She supports this inference by demonstrating a change in level of pre-feeding leukocytosis when the interval between feedings is changed. Altering the infant's feeding schedule from a three-hour to a four-hour interval soon results in an extinction of the elevated pre-feeding leukocytosis at three-hour intervals and the formation of a new conditioned leukocyte rise at four-hour intervals. As equally noteworthy as this demonstration that interoceptive conditioning can take place within the neonatal period is Krachkovskaia's further findings that intervals of time can serve as effective conditional stimuli during the first few days of life. In repeating this study, the careful investigator would want to add another group of infants switched from a four-hour to a three-hour feeding schedule.]

A study of the development of higher nervous activity in the early extra-uterine life of man is highly important if we are to understand the mechanisms that regulate the newborn infant's physiological functions.

* From M. V. Krachkovskaia. Reflex changes in the leukocyte count of newborn infants in relation to food intake. *Pavlov Journal of Higher Nervous Activity,* 1959, 9, 193–199. (With permission.)

The investigations of N. I. Krasnogorskii (1954), A. G. Ivanov-Smolenskii (1955), N. I. Kasatkin (1954), and others have revealed the basic developmental patterns of the reflex mechanisms that govern the infant's adaptation to its environment. R. P. Ol'nianskaia and her co-workers studied the natural CR originating in newborn children and animals in connection with feeding. N. A. Arkhangel'skaia and E. Ia. Poiurovskaia (1949) showed that an increased exchange of gases occurs as early as the first breast feeding of the infant. N. A. Arkhangel'skaia (1949) also discovered a CR alteration in gas exchange in response to feeding time at the end of the first week after birth. Similar results were obtained by I. S. Kanfor and A. A. Voronkova (cited in Ol'nianskaia, 1954) on changes in the sugar content of the blood. More recently, G. I. Bystroletova (1954) reported the formation of a CR to feeding time in the form of a change in the behavior of the newborn infant.

CR changes in the metabolism of newborn infants in response to feeding time support the assumption that other processes connected with the intake and digestion of food are also regulated by the central nervous system soon after birth.

Accordingly, we set out to study the leukocyte count of newborn infants in relation to food intake. Many authors have, of course, established the undoubted influence of the higher divisions of the brain on changes in the leukocyte count in the peripheral blood of adult persons and animals after eating. However, this information has not yet been fully worked out for infants. G. N. Speranskii, A. F. Tur, and others noted in children after eating both an increase and a decrease in the leukocyte count, varying with the age of the child, nature of the food, and condition of the nervous system, but the reasons for these quantitative shifts in the peripheral blood are still unclear.

We undertook to study 102 healthy nursing infants one to sixteen days old without changing the normal handling and feeding routines.

Peripheral blood leukocyte counts were made one hour before feeding, fifteen minutes before feeding, and thirty minutes, one hour, and two hours after feeding.

Our observations confirmed, first of all, that the leukocyte count in newborn infants is unstable and varies within broad limits. They further indicated that in infants up to five days old the character of the changes in the leukocyte count as related to food intake is not uniform and that at this age there is no single typical leukocyte reaction. This agrees with the findings of N. P. Gundobin (1892), A. F. Tur (1947), and others.

An increase in the leukocyte count an hour after feeding was observed in most of the children, beginning the sixth day after birth. The leukocyte count clearly rose an hour after feeding in six out of eleven children of this age; in the other five the count changed insignificantly or sharply decreased. This reaction was soon noted in the great majority of newborn infants or even in all of them (Table 1).

Table 1—Number of Newborn Infants Showing an Elevated Leukocyte Count an Hour After Feeding

Age of children	Total	NUMBER OF CHILDREN — With elevated leukocyte count after feeding
Sixth day	11	6
Seventh day	14	9
Eighth day	16	15
Ninth-tenth day	14	12
More than 10 days old	6	6

The elevated leukocyte count an hour after feeding is simply the reaction of digestive leukocytosis, i.e., an unconditioned response of the blood to the intake of food. We conjectured earlier (1954) that digestive leukocytosis might be found in eight- or nine-day-old infants; a more detailed study has shown that it is present in most children beginning as early as the sixth day after birth. An increase in the leukocyte count an hour after food intake may well occur at a later or an earlier age in some infants.

Besides the increase in the leukocyte count after feeding, we also discovered an increase before feeding, which developed in most of the experimental infants starting the eighth day after birth. Mean data on the leukocyte count in individual age groups of newborn children at various times of feeding confirm that the leukocyte count begins to rise on the sixth day after birth, an hour after feeding, and on the eighth day it rises even before feeding (Fig. 1).

The increase noted in leukocyte count before feeding indicates, as proved by further investigation, that a conditioned reflex (CR) was formed in response to the time of feeding.

To check our assumption concerning the CR mechanism in the leukocyte reaction just described, we took advantage of a change in the feeding schedule carried out in accordance with the doctor's instructions. This enabled us to make special observations of the leukocyte reaction when both the time and method of feeding were changed.

The effect of changed feeding time on digestive leukocytosis was studied in three children over one month old whose normal feeding period was altered—i.e., they were fed at four-hour rather than at three-hour intervals—after it had been established that the leukocyte count increased at the time of feeding. All three children showed regular shifts in the leukocyte reaction. For example, in infant S., sixty days old, the leukocyte count increased by 1300 per mm^3 of blood before the time of the usual feeding; a similar phenomenon was also observed the first day after the feeding time was changed, the count rising before the infant's usual nursing hour (1800 and 1200 leukocytes). However, on the second day, before the eighth feeding on the new schedule, the leukocyte count no longer increased before the feeding time on the old schedule.

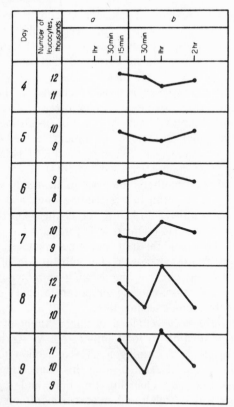

Figure 1—Leukocyte counts in infants in relation to feeding time, by age groups (mean data).

a—before feeding, b—after feeding.

Thus, whereas on the first day of the changed routine the leukocyte count rose before the usual feeding hour, on the next day the count remained virtually the same at that time; moreover, the count increased by 1100 before the feeding period (eighth in number) on the new schedule. Consequently, a conditioned increase in leukocyte count prior to the old feeding time remained for a while after the feeding schedule was changed. But since it was not reinforced, this CR to the old feeding time was extinguished on the second or third day after the change in schedule, and was replaced by a new CR to the new schedule.

To determine the effect of changing the feeding method on the leukocyte reaction, five of the infants were, with appropriate authorization, fed mother's milk from bottles instead of being nursed. Before the change, the leukocyte count in infant Gr. increased by 1800 before feeding time. After the first change from breast feeding to bottled breast milk (pasteurized), the leukocyte count fifteen minutes before the next feeding also turned out to be higher by 1300 than the count observed an hour before feeding (two hours after the previous feeding). The second day after the feeding method was changed, i.e., by the seventh feeding, the leukocyte count did not rise before feeding time or even after it. On the third day after the feeding method was changed, we observed the usual rise in leukocyte count both before and an hour after feeding.

To exclude the influence of a possible change in the quality of milk caused by pasteurization, we made similar observations of an infant fed unpasteurized bottled mother's milk in place of breast feeding. In this case the data show the usual CR to feeding time (elevated leukocyte count) before the method was changed; likewise, on the first day of the changed method of feeding the count increased by 1000 at feeding time. On the second day after bottled mother's milk was used, there were no significant changes in the leukocyte count before feeding time; and the increase after feeding was less substantial than before the change. On the third day after bottle feeding, the leukocyte count rose before and an hour after feeding. Observations on the other children yielded similar results.

These data justify the conclusion that substitution of bottled mother's milk for breast feeding changes the feeding stereotype and thereby inhibits the leukocyte reaction, causing temporary absence of elevated leukocyte count before the infant's feeding time.

Similar data have been obtained during a study of gas exchange in newborn infants in relation to food intake. N. A. Arkhangel'skaia demonstrated the possibility of forming a CR connection to feeding time in eight-day-old infants and of extinguishing this connection by changing the feeding stereotype, i.e., by changing the time and method of feeding (1949). This fact was corroborated by experiments on newborn puppies and kittens. Thus, our observations and those of other investigators have established the possibility of reflex regulation of the quantitative composition of the blood in newborn infants.

Our research and data in the literature confirm that profound transformation occurs within the infant as a result of a change in the usual feeding routine—i.e., a disturbance of the feeding stereotype—which leads to inhibition of certain physiological reactions. Hence, we draw the practical conclusion that it is important to take into account all the possible physiological variations in the blood composition of newborn infants. We believe that the data included in this report prove the existence of such variations.

SUMMARY

Most six- or seven-day-old infants show an elevated leukocyte count an hour after intake of food; beginning with the eighth or ninth day after birth, most of them show an elevated leukocyte count before feeding as well.

When the feeding time is changed, the CR elevation of leukocyte count in response to the old feeding hours is extinguished and another reflex is formed to the new hours, two or three days (eighth, fifteenth feeding) after the new schedule is inaugurated.

When the feeding method is changed, the CR component of the leukocyte reaction to the feeding time is extinguished, but is restored on the second or third day (eighth and fifteenth feeding) after introduction of the new method.

Changes in the leukocyte count in response to food intake indicate maturation of UR mechanisms in the infant's early postnatal life and rapid formation of the CR mechanisms thereafter.

SUPPLEMENTARY READINGS

Bystroletova, G. N. Obrazovanie u novorozhdennykh detei uslovnogo refleksa na vremia v sviazi s sutochnym ritmom kormleniia. (The formation in neonates of a conditioned reflex to time in connection with daily feeding rhythm.) *Zh. vyssh. nerv. Deiatel.*, 1954, 4, 601–609.

Marquis, D. P. Learning in the neonate: The modification of behavior under three feeding schedules. *J. exp. Psychol.*, 1941, 29, 263–282.

Razran, G. The observable unconscious and the inferable conscious in current Soviet psychophysiology: Interoceptive conditioning, semantic conditioning, and the orienting reflex. *Psychol. Rev.*, 1961, 68, 81–147.

Tonkova-Yampolskaya, R. V. The features of vascular conditioned reflexes in children in the third year of life. *Pavlov J. high. nerv. Act.*, 1961, 11, 89–93.

effects of
stimulus sensitization
on ease of conditioning*

K. N. IRZHANSKAIA and R. A. FELBERBAUM

[It has long been known that man has the greatest sensory awareness for stimuli importantly related to his behavior. Psychologists believe that individuals develop these sensitivities on the basis of their prior experiences. Drs. Irzhanskaia and Felberbaum, of the Krupskii Research Institute for the Protection of Mother and Child in Kharkov, asked the question whether the very young infant can be made sensitive to the significance of stimulation that is not ordinarily a normal part of his experience. They selected prematurely born infants as their subjects and the odor of mint as the stimulus to which to make the infant sensitive. From birth these infants sucked their milk through nipples which had been stored in mint and carried a mint odor. Then the investigators conditioned the infants both to mint and to anise as conditional stimuli in order to determine the speed of conditioning as a function of the infant's prior sensitization to one of these substances. Although a conditioned blinking reflex to both odors appeared in all of the infants, ". . . in practically all cases it developed more rapidly to the odor of mint than to the odor of anise." Furthermore, the conditioned reflex to mint was more stable than to anise. The authors conclude, ". . . it is apparent that conditioned reflex formation also depends on the child's capacity to differentiate among stimuli not only in terms of their physical qualities but also in terms of the degree to which they are significant for that organism." This paper was selected for inclusion by the editors for its ingenious rather than its rigorous design. The careful investigator would certainly want to add to the experimental design a control group of infants exposed to anise instead of mint prior to conditioning, as well as a group of infants who had been exposed to neither.]

* From K. N. Irzhanskaia & R. A. Felberbaum. Nekotorye dannye ob uslovnoreflektornoi deiatelnosti nedonoshennykh detei. (Conditioned reflex activity in premature children.) *Fiziologicheskii Zhurnal SSSR*, 1954, 40, 668–672.

The higher nervous activity of premature children—and particularly the activity of their analyzers—has been insufficiently studied. There are only two studies (Kasatkin, 1936, 1951) whose results show the possibility of forming conditioned reflexes by the second month of life. These studies note the weakness of these reflexes and the slowness of their development. In the past this question has not been the subject of detailed study even though its solution would prove of considerable value in our understanding of the ontogenetic development of higher nervous activity in man. Research into the higher nervous activity of premature children is of practical interest in that it is related to the rational organization of their care.

It has been shown that the strength and speed of forming conditioned reflexes in various animals depend on the biological significance or adequacy of both the conditional and unconditioned stimulus (Biriukov, 1949, 1952). Thus, for example, of many external stimuli, a splash of water elicits the clearest reaction in teal ducks. This is understandable in that the sound of splashing water is a highly significant stimulus for water birds.

The purpose of this study is to ascertain whether there is a difference among infants of varying degrees of prematurity to environmental stimuli having physical as well as biological significance for them.

METHOD

Observations were carried out on 33 children who were premature by one to two and one-half months and who ranged in age from one and one-half to two and one-half months at the beginning of conditioning.

For two weeks prior to the beginning of conditioning and during the period of conditioning itself, the children, whose only food was milk, sucked their milk through nipples which had been stored in mint and carried a mint odor.

A conditioned blinking reflex was developed in all children. The child lay supine in a laboratory crib on the back of which two rubber tubes were attached and adjusted so that the ends of the tubes were 3 cm away from the child's eyes. The other ends of the tubes joined a rubber balloon that was calibrated in such a way as to ensure identical amounts of pressure in each air puff.

On the first reinforced trials the mint or anise was presented simultaneously with the stream of air; thereafter, the UCS followed the CS by 3 to 4 seconds. At each session half the children first received combinations of air and mint followed by combinations of air and anise. For the other children this order was reversed. The presentation of the olfactory stimulus was implemented by holding a glass slide moistened with a solution of the appropriate substance—mint or anise—under the child's nose. The glass slide was not visible to the child.

It could be supposed that if the odor of mint had become a conditioned feeding stimulus, then the center of excitation in the cortex connected with this odor would be markedly stronger than the center of excitation elicited by the odor of anise—anise never having been of signal significance to the child.

RESULTS

The basic results are shown in Table 1. A conditioned blinking reflex to both odors developed in all children, but in practically all cases it developed more rapidly to the odor of mint than to the odor of anise. Only for the infants who were most premature *and* youngest at the beginning of the experiment was there no difference in speed of conditioning to mint as opposed to anise. It should also be noted that the conditioned reflexes of infants in this group were also highly unstable, but that the conditioned reflex to mint was more nearly stable then the conditioned reflex to anise.

Table 1—Number of Reinforcements Necessary to Condition a Blinking Reflex to Mint and to Anise in Children Differing in Age and Degree of Prematurity

Age in months at beginning of conditioning	Degree of prematurity					
	1 MONTH		2 MONTHS		2.5 MONTHS	
	Mint	Anise	Mint	Anise	Mint	Anise
1.5	34	49	53	68.5	63.5	63.5
2.0	12.5	31	32.5	46.5	39.5	54
2.5	6.5	19	21.5	37.5	29	45.5

1. The means in this table as well as those in Tables 2 and 3 were tabulated by the editors from data in the original text and figures.

In general, the older the infant at the beginning of experimentation, the more rapidly a condtioned reflex developed and the greater the difference in the speed of its formation to mint as opposed to anise (Table 2). The same conclusions can be drawn with respect to degree of prematurity (Table 3). It is interesting to note that the children who were premature by no more than two months showed anticipatory sucking when the odor of mint was presented to them.

All the material presented above testifies to the fact that it is possible to form defensive conditioned blinking reflexes in children who are as young as one and one-half months and who are premature by as much as two and one-half months. The process of working out these conditioned

Table 2—Number of Reinforcements Necessary to Condition a Blinking Reflex to Mint and to Anise as a Function of Age, Without Regard to Degree of Prematurity

Type of CS	AGE AT BEGINNING OF CONDITIONING		
	1.5 months	2.0 months	2.5 months
Mint	50.17	28.17	19.00
Anise	60.33	43.83	34.00

Table 3—Number of Reinforcements Necessary to Condition a Blinking Reflex to Mint and to Anise as a Function of Degree of Prematurity, Without Regard to Age

Type of CS	DEGREE OF PREMATURITY		
	1 month	2.0 months	2.5 months
Mint	17.67	35.67	44.00
Anise	33.00	50.83	54.33

reflexes depends both on age and degree of prematurity. Furthermore, it is apparent that conditioned reflex formation also depends on the child's capacity to differentiate among stimuli not only in terms of their physical qualities but also in terms of the degree to which they are significant for that organism.

Translated by Yvonne Brackbill

SUPPLEMENTARY READINGS

Gibson, E. J., & Walk, R. D. The effect of prolonged exposure to visually presented patterns on learning to discriminate them. *J. comp. physiol. Psychol.,* 1956, 49, 239–242.

Gibson, E. J., Walk, R. D., Pick, H. L., Jr., & Tighe, T. J. The effect of prolonged exposure to visual patterns on learning to discriminate similar and different patterns. *J. comp. physiol. Psychol.* 1958, 51, 584–587.

Walk, R. D., Gibson, E. J., Pick, H. L., Jr., & Tighe, T. J. Further experiments on prolonged exposure to visual forms: The effect of single stimuli and prior reinforcement. *J. comp. physiol. Psychol.* 1958, 51, 483–487.

Walk, R. D., Gibson, E. J., Pick, H. L., Jr., & Tighe, T. J. The effectiveness of prolonged exposure to cutouts vs. painted patterns for facilitation of discrimination. *J. comp. physiol. Psychol.* 1959, 52, 519–521.

the physiological mechanisms
underlying the development
of generalization
in the child*

M. M. KOLTSOVA

[Man's use of words permits him to discriminate, abstract, and generalize his experiences with a precision and a ubiquity that is distinctly unique to his species. In the present report, words are regarded as "signals of signals," the latter already possessing generalized referents. Dr. Koltsova, of the Pavlov Institute of Physiology, shows in this investigation that words develop generalizing properties among two-year-old children only when both excitatory and inhibitory processes are activated. In other words, it appears that the young child must learn not only what to include but also what to exclude as referents for a word in order for its generalizing potential to become useful and effective. The present study is a good example of the usefulness of a classical conditioning procedure in investigating the young child's acquisition of language. It is representative of current Soviet research both in terms of methodology and the subject of investigation—the ways by which man acquires his language and the influence of his language on his behavior.]

A new principle of nervous activity of man, as I. P. Pavlov demonstrated, concerns the development in him of the reflection of reality in a generalized form by means of verbal signals. The most complex form of generalization which one can successfully develop in animals is the formation of conditioned reflexes to the relationships among stimuli. In such a case there is expressed some degree of abstraction from reality as well as some degree of generalization, since the reflex is worked out not on the basis of concrete

* From M. M. Koltsova. O fiziologicheskikh mekhanizmakh razvitiia protsessa obobsheniia u rebenka. (The physiological mechanisms of development of the process of generalization in the child.) *Zhurnal vysshei nervnoi Deiatelnosti,* 1956, 6, 201–211.

phenomena but on the relations among them. However, as I. P. Pavlov emphasized more than once, that degree of abstraction from reality and that degree of generalization which characterize verbal thought are specific to the work of the human cortex. It follows that in order to understand higher nervous activity in man one must delve into the physiological study of generalization and abstraction.

In the experimental work that has come from the laboratories of A. G. Ivanov-Smolenskii and N. I. Krasnogorskii, the *word* has been studied as a "signal of signals" that already possesses a generalized referent. Analysis has centered upon the mechanism of transfer of generalization from one referent in the external environment to another—from the nonverbal stimulus to the verbal, from the verbal stimulus to the nonverbal, and from one verbal signal to another. It has also focused upon the limits of generalization as a function of the degree of abstraction represented by the referents of various verbal signals: sparrow, crow, bird, animal, and so on.

In addition, however, one must consider the very important question of the physiological mechanisms underlying the formation of words as general stimuli that stand for the specific phenomena of the outer world. Indeed, such an approach is absolutely necessary in order to clarify the physiological essence of the process of generalization itself.

Koltsova (1955) has previously shown that the physiological conditions basic to the formation of a "signal of signals" is the attachment to a word of a large number of conditioned connections. The properties of the verbal stimulus that generalize change continuously and increase in accordance with the attachment to them of new conditioned connections. However, the conditioned connections that are developed from the various analyzers are not of equal importance to this process: an especially significant role is played by the connections in which bodily movements figure. The aim of the present study was to determine the functional level of various forms of generalization and the relationships among the nervous processes by which they may be characterized.

As we know, I. P. Pavlov distinguished between two kinds of generalization. He noted first a primary, primitive generalization that may be described as a failure to differentiate among different stimuli which are in fact different and that has its physiological basis in the generalization of nervous processes. There is also a learned generalization of those stimuli *which had previously been differentiated*—the physiological basis in this case being the mechanism of "the well-trodden cortical pathways." On the basis of research carried out in Pavlovian laboratories, the characteristics of these two forms of generalization can be described as follows.

A. The primary, primitive form of generalization.

1. The physiological basis of this form of generalization is a more or less diffuse generalization of nervous processes.

2. This form of generalization is occasioned either by insufficient or extremely strong nervous processes from whence follows the weakness or absence of inductive relations between the nervous proc-

esses. The development of inductive relations between nervous processes leads to the disappearance of this form of generalization.
B. The secondary, learned, or higher form of generalization.
1. The physiological basis of this form of generalization is an extension of nervous processes according to earlier developed, "well-trodden paths."
2. A necessary condition for the appearance of this form of generalization is the presence of nervous processes that are sufficiently developed, are optimally strong, and are capable of well expressed inductive relations.
3. Another necessary condition is the availability of various forms of internal inhibition—the most important of these being differentiation.

These facts must be accepted as the starting position in any study of forms of generalization that reflect reality via the second signal system. Therefore, our first step in determining the functional level of generalization to a word was to clarify the role of external inhibition in the development of generalization. First, we studied the development of generalization to a word under conditions allowing of external and internal inhibition and compared this to its development under conditions in which inhibition was excluded. We also traced the properties of the conditioned connections in both cases.

To this end we used two groups of five children each. The children were residents of a children's home and ranged in age from two years to two years, two months.

For children in the first group the positive conditional stimuli consisted of various geometric figures—square, circle, sphere, pyramid, cone, cube, and so on. The presentation of these stimuli was always accompanied by a puff of air into the eye and repetition of the word "thing" ["vetsch"]. Various objects such as an electric key, a drumstick, and so on, served as inhibitory [negative, discriminative] stimuli. These were not combined either with the air puff or with any word. Altogether, fifteen positive and ten inhibitory stimuli were presented in mixed order to the first group of children. After a conditioned reaction had been formed and strengthened to the first stimulus, the second stimulus was introduced, and so on.

Stimuli for the second group of subjects consisted in small skeins of vari-colored yarns; the presentation of each was accompanied without exception by an air puff to the eye. In addition, the presentation of those skeins in which yellow predominated was accompanied by the word "thing" as well as by the stream of air. Thus, all stimuli presented to these children was positive and all had the same unconditioned reinforcement. Only some of the stimuli, however, were connected with the word "thing." Consequently, the conditions for developing inductive relations or some form of internal inhibition were absent for children in the second group. Table 1 gives an idea of the design and procedure for both groups of subjects.

Table 1—Sequence of Forming Conditioned Connections for Two Groups of Subjects

	Conditional stimulus	Unconditioned stimulus	Verbal signal	Type of inhibition formed
	1. Yellow wooden square	Air puff to the eye	"thing"	
	2. Skein of brightly colored yarn	None	none	Differentiation
	3. Red wooden square	Air puff to the eye	"thing"	
GROUP I	4. Electric key	None	none	Differentiation
	5. Green wooden pyramid	Air puff to the eye	"thing"	
	.			
	.			
	etc.			
	1. Thin yellow skein of yarn	Air puff to the eye	"thing"	None
	2. Thin blue skein	Air puff to the eye	none	None
GROUP II	3. Full skein of yellow with violet	Air puff to the eye	"thing"	None
	4. Full skein of green with red	Air puff to the eye	none	None
	5. Full skein of yellow with brown	Air puff to the eye	"thing"	None
	.			
	.			
	etc.			

First of all, it was necessary to compare the nature of the conditioned connections formed in the children of both groups. The differences in the experimental conditions under which temporary connections were formed had a noticeable effect on the course of conditioned reflex activity in the two groups of children.

In children of the first group, both the positive and inhibitory reflexes were clear cut. One may say, consequently, that these children showed well expressed inductive relations between nervous processes. Furthermore, the speed with which new positive and inhibitory reflexes were formed increased progressively. The data in Table 2a show that the time consumed in working out both positive and inhibitory reflexes had sharply decreased by the fifth stimulus presentation. From this point on, usually only one trial was needed to elicit either a well expressed conditioned reflex or a full inhibitory reflex.

During the entire period of study the conditioned reflexes in this group of children remained clear cut and well expressed—both during the introduction of new stimuli and during the repetition of the same stimuli. The inhibitory reflexes that had developed to the discriminative stimuli also remained clear cut throughout the period of study.

For children of the second group the development of conditioned responses proceeded in an altogether different manner. Initially, as was the case with the first group, there took place a progressive speeding up in the time required to form conditioned reflexes (Table 2b). By the time the third stimulus was introduced it was possible to obtain a conditioned reflex from the very first presentation of each new conditional stimulus. However, by the time ten positive stimuli had been introduced, the reflexes in

Table 2a—Sequence of Results for Group I (N = 5)

Stimulus presentation order	No. of that trial on which a strong CR first appeared: range for the group.	No. of that trial on which internal inhibition (discrimination) was consolidated: range for the group.
1	11–27	
2		3–10
3	10–20	
4		3–8
5	1–5	
.		
.		
.		
.		
.		
15	1	
.	Immediate formation of all CRs and differentiations	
25		

these children became weaker and less stable, notwithstanding the increased number of reinforcements. Following the introduction of the fourteenth to fifteenth stimulus, the reflexes extinguished altogether.

Table 2b—Sequence of Results for Group II (N = 5)

Stimulus presentation order	No. of that trial on which a strong CR first appeared: range for the group.	Remarks
1	10–30	
2	5–12	
3	1	
4	1	
.		
.		
10	1	Reflex somewhat weakly and irregularly expressed
.		
.		
.		
12	1	CR not very stable despite immediate formation; appears for 1 or 2 trials.
.		
.		
.		
15	Complete extinction	

Thus, it appears from these observations of the second group of children that some concentration of excitation—present initially during the working out of conditioned reflexes to the first two or three conditional signals—was subsequently replaced by generalization of excitation. In the experimental situation described above there were no conditions that allowed the subject to overcome this generalization, since there was no interference (whether by inductive relations or by any kind of internal inhibition). As a result what we have obtained is the well-known phenomenon, "extinction during reinforcement"—that form of inhibition which develops during the prolonged action of monotonous stimulation. These results indicate that the presence of process interaction between excitation and inhibition is of the utmost importance for appropriately manifested and clear-cut conditioned reflex activity. Those conditions which maximally limit the participation of the inhibitory process lead to extinction of conditioned reflexes.

Another test of generalization was carried out during the course of the experiment described above. The child was asked to take "a thing" from a larger number and variety of objects among which were placed both those objects which in the previous experiment had been connected with the word "thing" as well as objects similar to them. For example, the children saw wooden and cardboard geometrical figures of substantially larger or smaller size and of different colors than had been presented previously.

In response to the request "take a thing," children of the first group chose those geometrical figures which had been connected previously with this word, i.e., both those figures which had in fact been presented earlier and those which they were perceiving for the first time but were nevertheless geometrical figures. In other words, they generalized correctly. The other objects—toys, electrical gadgets, etc.—which were spread out before them were not chosen.

In response to the same request children of the second group chose "things" as follows. During the first ten test trials the children chose from four to six skeins of yarn without differentiating those skeins in which yellow predominated and which had been connected with the word "thing." After this they tended to choose bright objects—a block, a ribbon, and so on. The last test of this same sort was attempted after all fifteen conditional stimuli had been introduced. Now, when asked to take a "thing," the child selected the brightest and largest of the objects before him and never once chose a skein of yarn. Not even the primitive form of generalization was manifested. It is as if the word "thing" had forfeited its connection even with those stimuli on which the connection had been formed. Thus, one can consider that the process of generalization—the accretion to a word of multiple conditioned connections—is based upon a diffusion of excitation along a definite, worked out, and strengthened path. The working out of this path is accomplished only through participation of the various forms of external and internal inhibition. If conditions allow only a wide irradiation of excitation without the participation of any form of inhibition, then it is impossible to develop experimentally any higher form of generalization.

In the procedure described above, however, only extreme conditions were introduced—conditions in which the word works against a background of wide irradiation of nervous processes or in which the nervous processes were already strong, concentrated, and positive, and the inhibitory processes were very clear cut. Consequently the development of the word was compared to "a signal of signals" in the conditions under-lying the development of generalization.

Meanwhile, it is extremely important to clarify how this development is influenced by the interaction of word and conditions, and how a primitive form of generalization is changed into a higher form and vice versa. The dynamics of these changes can add considerably to a clarification of the characteristics of generalization as it develops. With this view in mind, we carried out the following observations.

In six children, all two years of age, five geometrical figures were connected with the word "thing" and with a conditioned blink reaction. In addition, differentiations were worked out on four other discriminative objects—an electric key, a drumstick, a paper chain, and an iron plate.

At this stage a test of the generalizing action of the word "thing" gave positive results: the child took all geometric figures from the total display of objects in front of him. Furthermore, both the positive, blinking reflexes and inhibitory reflexes were clear cut and stable.

At this point we began systematically to introduce only positive stimuli —fifteen more geometrical figures connected with the word "thing" and with the blinking reflex. With the introduction of the thirteenth positive stimulus, the conditioned reflex became weak and inconstant. With the introduction of the fifteenth positive stimulus, the reflex extinguished alto-gether; it was subsequently elicited only on rare occasions.

The tests which were now carried out showed that the word "thing" had forfeited its significance as a generalizing signal. The children either did not respond at all to the request "take a thing," or else they removed from the display of geometrical figures, toys, and books, one or two objects that had never been connected with the "thing." Thus, for example, Zhenia, age two years and one month, responded to the request, "take a thing," by choosing, after 20 seconds, a mechanical bird, then immediately cast it aside and turned away from the table. On the next request to "take a thing" there was no reaction at all.

The next stage in experimentation consisted in repeating the presenta-tion of four of the positive stimuli previously presented (Nos. 12–15), but with the introduction of differential inhibition this time.

After a comparatively short time conditioned blinking reactions to these positive stimuli were obtained (Table 3). The introduction of in-hibitory stimuli had led to the recovery of generalization.

At this stage a repetition of the test procedure yielded positive results.

Table 3—Reflex Activity Following the Introduction of Differentiation

Ordinal number of CS in previous phase of study	No. of CS-UCS combinations needed to obtain a CR: range for group	No. of CS-UCS combinations to a stable differentiation: range for group
12th	26–30	18–21
13th	14–15	8–10
14th	9–13	6
15th	8–10	4–6

For example, Zhenia, when asked to "take a thing," after 6 seconds selected a wooden pyramid, then a sphere, a cube, a cone, and other geometric figures—putting them all together on her knees. The results for this subject are representative of the rest of the group.

Especially interesting were the results of the first reintroduction of a positive stimulus (No. 12) when there was some weakness in conditioned reflex manifestation. Generalization at this point has a peculiar character: There was no finely differentiated selection of those objects which were previously tied to the word "thing," but, on the other hand, the children's collection of "things" was not without order. To begin with, the child correctly took one or another geometric figure, but then, in the majority of cases, he began to choose objects on the basis of color, e.g., a green sphere, a green frog, a green wire, as in Nina's case, or less frequently, on the basis of form—a rectangle, a box, a cube-shaped toy stove, a book, as in Lesha's case.

Thus, from these last observations, it appears that the degree of irradiation of nervous processes prevented at this point the realization of a highly differentiated generalization. Nevertheless, some degree of differentiation was still observed; the reaction was being carried out at a low functional level of generalization on the basis of accidental, secondary properties.

Quite similar results were obtained later in the same experimental period when the conditioned reflexes began to recover after the introduction of differential inhibition, i.e., when the previously existing irradiation of nervous processes was now somewhat restricted by the beginning of the development of inductive relations. It seems to us that such a phenomenon is exactly that which was described by Ivanov-Smolenskii as "elective" or "selective" generalization. This occurs when a conditioned response is worked out to, say, a blue light, and it turns out that the reflex is also elicited by the words "blue light," "light," "lamp bulb," and so on. The generalization may also proceed along the lines of the color (blue) when it is presented visually.

A. G. Ivanov-Smolenskii believes that reactions indicative of a high form of generalization have such an origin, and that they are based on the mechanism of elective irradiation along closed functional paths. On the basis of our present observations we consider that this form of generalization is comparatively low in terms of functional level.

The facts we have presented, it seems to us, permit us to piece together some representation of the physiological basis of the processes of abstraction and generalization. In psychology, abstraction and generalization are seen as separate "mental operations." However, the physiological characteristics of both processes are quite similar. Our results indicate that the process of generalization cannot be defined only as synthesis. Even in the most primitive form of generalization—that based on generalization of nervous processes—there is found some kind of rough analysis. For example, from studies of higher nervous activity it is known that if a conditioned reflex is worked out to a tone of one particular frequency, a tone of any other frequency is also effective initially as a conditional stimulus. However, the reflex is elicited only by tones, and not by tactile or visual stimuli. On the other hand, during the working out of a conditioned reflex to a definite rhythm of an auditory stimulus the reflex is sometimes elicited by visual and tactile stimuli presented in that same rhythm of the stimulus although the specific quality of it is still not differentiated. The higher, specialized forms of generalization are developed only in the presence of a very refined and altogether appropriate analysis of the external world, as can be seen from the data presented. Thus, the process of generalization, from the point of view of its physiological character, is an analytic-synthetic process.

Translated by Yvonne Brackbill

SUPPLEMENTARY READINGS

Ban, T. Part one: From overt behavior to neurophysiology. *Conditioning and psychiatry.* Chicago: Aldine, 1964. Pp. 1–48.
Kimble, G. A., & Ost, J. W. P. A conditioned inhibitory process in eyelid conditioning. *J. exp. Psychol.,* 1961, 61, 150–156.
Kimmel, H. D. Instrumental inhibitory factors in classical conditioning. In W. F. Prokasy (Ed.), *Classical conditioning: A symposium.* New York: Appleton-Century-Crofts, 1965.
Shepard, W. O. The effect of verbal training on initial generalization tendencies. *Child Develpm.,* 1965, 27, 311–316.

conditioning during
early postnatal development*

Hanuš Papoušek

[Several methods of conditioning can be used with infants: aversive conditioning, appetitional conditioning, and orientational conditioning. In this report Dr. Papoušek, of the Institute for the Care of Mother and Child in Prague, discusses a method of conditioning head movements which can be used with equal success for all three main types of conditioning. This method can be used for newborns as well as for older infants.

Studies of newborns are desirable because the structure of mental functions is relatively less complex in infants than in older subjects, and because inborn patterns of behavior have been less influenced by environmental variations at this time than at any other. Dr. Papoušek discusses the residential research nursery in Prague and shows that there are many methodological difficulties associated with longitudinal infant research. However, the importance of such research with young infants far outweighs these difficulties.

There is a remarkable parallel between the conditionability of the infant and the amount of time the infant spends in transitional and light sleep. The erratic conditioning records so typically obtained with infants during the first two months of life may be attributed to the great amount of time spent in a state of light sleep. This suggests the importance of obtaining accurate EEG sleep records of infants as Dr. Roffwarg has done (page 47).]

In the last few decades, some basic questions have been raised in respect to the theory of conditioning and its application to human psychology. One such question concerns the role of conditioning in learning processes, another, the relationship between conditioning and complex forms of behavior. There is no doubt that we are still just beginning to solve these problems; as a matter of fact we are still looking for adequate methodological approaches.

One methodological approach is a developmental one; for several reasons it seems particularly advantageous to analyze behavior and con-

* This is an original article reprinted with permission of the author.

ditionability from the very beginning of postnatal development, no matter how difficult it may seem to experiment with subjects as vulnerable as newborn infants. The chief advantage of studying neonates is that during this period of life different developing functions can be seen in their simplest forms—before they begin to interact or become complicated by the accumulation of experiences. There is also the advantage of being able to control a large number of external factors at this period of development.

Surprisingly enough, the conditionability of newborn infants has not yet been sufficiently explored. There are varied reasons for this, the most important ones being organizational difficulties and a lack of familiarity with infants as experimental subjects. Psychologists and physiologists interested in experimenting with animals can find detailed instructions about the establishment of animal laboratories, the design of experiments, and apparatus available to them. In contrast, there is no help for experimenters interested in the earliest development of behavior in human infants. This lack of help is especially true for longitudinal research, such as conditioning, that requires long periods of investigation.

SOME METHODOLOGICAL PROBLEMS
OF LONGITUDINAL INQUIRY

Even the establishment of a simple conditioned response takes at least several experimental days, while the study of more complex aspects of conditioning, such as extinction or conditioned discrimination may require several weeks or even months. It is, then, very advantageous, if not absolutely necessary, to keep the infants at a research unit. This kind of longitudinal experimentation presents general problems which have not been sufficiently discussed in the literature. Therefore, it may be useful to describe the ways in which these problems were solved in our own research unit at the Institute for Care of Mother and Child in Prague.

We keep our subjects at a special research unit for the first six months of life. The majority of our infants are born at the obstetrical department of our institute. Their mothers volunteer to participate for a variety of social, economical and medical reasons. They can stay with their infants at our unit, and are supplied with free meals, linen, and all necessary care. The mothers appreciate our interest in the long-term development of their children, since they are invited to consult with our pediatricians and psychologists whenever they meet major problems in the upbringing of their children. Mothers who cannot stay with their babies are replaced by specially trained nurses.

At the beginning of our research project, difficulties appeared in connection with standardizing the basic experimental conditions, and it took us a whole year of pilot experimenting to find a workable solution. The problem was to keep the basic life conditions of the subjects comparable and to maintain control over the experimental conditions in relation to the long course of conditioning. We could not, of course, ignore the individual demands of the infants and their parents by keeping the life conditions at the research unit strictly comparable, but still, it was much easier to control these life conditions, to keep them at least relatively comparable, to record them, and to analyze their influence at such a unit, than if the infants were brought up in different homes.

In our nursery, the external environment, schedule of feeding, activities during waking, and schedule of sleep are kept relatively uniform. The general state of the infants is regularly checked by pediatricians and psychologists. Records are kept showing the somatic and mental development, duration of waking and sleep, prevailing type of behavior, and daily caloric intake.

Keeping the order of sleep, feeding and waking constant and rather strictly scheduled has proved to be very useful in equating the general state of the subjects for experimental studies. Our infants first sleep, then eat, and then are exposed to social and emotional stimulation. This keeps the neonates awake for an adequate time. Naps in the fresh air throughout the whole year help to develop a very well fixed schedule by inducing deep, regular sleep. An example of scheduled care for our infants is given in Table 1. Note that the infants are divided into two groups so that one-half of them are awake at any time, thus decreasing the nurse/awake-infant ratio. Simple training of different motor skills and sensory perception are included, too.

Having assumed responsibility for the proper development of our subjects during their stay with us, we must prevent social and emotional symptoms of institutionalization, but we must also prevent contagious diseases, the risk of which can be greater in an institution than at home. While strict hygienic measures can help us prevent infectious diseases, often they are connected with a certain amount of environmental, social, or emotional deprivation, or at least with a lack of variety in external stimulation. It is, therefore, important to find a reasonable compromise between disease and deprivation.

THE USEFULNESS OF
SIMULTANEOUS INVESTIGATIONS

One way of reducing the obvious cost of such a research unit is to use the subjects for several studies simultaneously. In our case, a team of investigators uses the same subjects for different kinds of observations because we want to approach the same problems from different perspectives and by different methods so that the general applicability of our findings is increased.

The number of experiments in which the same subjects can be used is limited—especially if the experiments impose restrictions that would cause physical or mental stress. Our experience has been that two or even three different conditioning experiments do not bother the infant if their applica-

Table 1—Schedule of Care for Infants at the Research Unit at the Institute for Care of Mother and Child, Prague

Time	Group 1	Group 2
6:00 A.M.	Temperature and weight check Change of clothing and linen Experiments	
7:00 A.M.	Outdoor nap	Feeding Temperature and weight check Change of clothing and linen Experiments *Scheduled activities
8:00 A.M.		Outdoor nap
9:00 A.M.	Feeding Experiments Rounds by pediatrician and psychologist *Scheduled activities Fruit juice Outdoor nap	
10:00 A.M.		Feeding Experiments Rounds by pediatrician and psychologist Sun bath (natural or ultraviolet lamp) Outdoor nap
12:00 noon	Feeding Experiments *Scheduled activities Sun bath (natural or ultraviolet lamp) Outdoor nap	
2:00 P.M.		Feeding *Scheduled activities Fruit juice Outdoor nap
3:30 P.M.	Temperature check Bathing Feeding *Scheduled activities	
or	or	
(3:30 P.M.)	(Visits by the parents [with instruction in techniques of child care and infant gymnastics])	
5:00 P.M.	Indoor nap	Temperature check Bathing Feeding *Scheduled activities
		or
or		
(5:00 P.M.)		(Visits by the parents [with instruction in techniques of child care and infant gymnastics])
6:30 P.M.		Indoor naps
7:30 P.M.	Feeding Putting to bed for the night	

Table 1 (Continued)

Time	Group 1	Group 2
9:00 P.M.		Feeding
		Putting to bed for the night
2:00 A.M.	Feeding	
3:30 A.M.		Feeding
5:30 A.M.	Feeding	

* Scheduled activities: Play with babies, stimulating sensory perception, exercises, hardening (exposure to fresh air, washing or shower with cold water), testing psychomotor abilities.

tion is carefully organized and scheduled, and there is no limit to the number of experiments which can be used employing observational methods that do not interfere with the infant's normal freedom nor cause stress.

Another methodological problem is caused by the fact that many functions undergo dramatic developmental changes during early infancy. It is difficult to find methods for the study of conditioning abilities that are equally suitable for infants of different ages. The conditioned eye blink is one of several responses that may be studied both in infancy and adulthood. Conditioned sucking, however, is an example of a response that is limited to early infancy and, therefore, is not suitable for longitudinal developmental studies.

CONDITIONING WITH
APPETITIONAL REINFORCEMENT

Several methods of conditioning can be used with infants: aversive conditioning, appetitional conditioning, and orientational conditioning. Appetitional methods are particularly suitable for studies with newborns, since the need to satiate hunger represents a very effective motivation in newborns.

The classical method of conditioning salivary responses cannot be used with newborns since their salivary glands produce an insufficient amount of saliva at this time. Therefore, most authors have used the method of conditioned sucking, concentrating on the first appearance of this conditioned response in infants (Bekhterev & Shchelovanov, 1925; Denisova & Figurin, 1929; Ripin & Hetzer, 1930; Marquis, 1931; Wenger, 1936; Lipsitt & Kaye, 1963). Conditioned sucking has been used to investigate sensory perception and discrimination (Kasatkin & Levikova, 1935; Nemanova, 1935), the effect of hunger on conditioning (Kantrow, 1937), neonatal brain injury (Dashkovskaia, 1953), and the conditioning capacity of premature infants (Polikanina, 1955; Polikanina & Probatova, 1957).

Papoušek (1959) has described a new method of conditioning head movements that can be used for all three main types of conditioning—appetitional, aversive, and orientational. This method was originally used for infants older than one month of age but it was later modified for use with newborns, too. It is well known that head movements mature earlier than do movements of the extremities. According to Minkowski (1928), these movements appear in the human fetus by the third postconceptional month, and by birth they are fully functional. Head movements have been studied by many scientists in the form of unconditioned innate reflexes that can be elicited by various stimuli. In hungry newborns, however, they occur without any discernible external stimulation (Prechtl, 1953). Babkin (1953) distinguished an inborn rooting reflex (probably coordinated by the diencephalon) from purposive movements that develop later (probably through cortical coordination). These purposive movements appear as learned forms of orientational, aversive or appetitional behavior. Peiper (1958) observed natural conditioning of head movements to a visual bottle stimulus by the first month of life. ·

Head movements are advantageous because they can be studied earlier than can movements of the extremities. The experimenter can vary the types of reinforcement and the response requirements so that experimental models of different types of behavior can be represented. This enables the experimenter to study the gradual development of a simple inborn reflex movement to a complex, purposeful (or voluntary) response that is adjusted to fine differences in external environmental signals.

A METHOD FOR THE INVESTIGATION OF CONDITIONED HEAD MOVEMENTS IN NEWBORNS

The relatively great weight of an infant's head prevents him from moving his head while lying in a normal crib. In order to allow the head to turn easily and to record it on a polygraph, we have developed a special experimental apparatus. The most recent model used in our laboratory is shown in Fig. 1. The most important part of this crib is a special head cradle, constructed from thermoplastic styrene and lined with soft styrene foam padding, in which the infant's head is placed during an experimental session. This cradle is attached to a horizontal axis and rotates when the infant turns his head. It is necessary to be able to shift this axis in a vertical direction according to the size of the infant's head. The effect of shifting the axis of rotation is shown in Fig. 2.

If the position of the axis of rotation were extremely high (Fig. 2A), the infant would be able to keep his head in a neutral, middle position but would have difficulty turning his head to either side. If an extremely low position were used (Fig. 2B), the infant's head would fall to one side or the other and it would be difficult for the infant to maintain a middle position. This is similar to the situation in an infant's normal crib. There is a suitable position somewhere between these two extreme positions at which even a newborn can either keep his head in the middle or turn it easily to either side. This position varies from subject to subject due to differences

Figure 1—An experimental apparatus for studies of conditioned head turning.

in head size and shape, but the experimenter can easily locate the suitable axis for each infant.

This head cradle enables us to make electromechanical recordings of head turning. A potentiometer is attached to the axis of rotation and connected to an electromagnetic recording pen. Properly placed switches turn on light signals that indicate to the experimenter when the head movements exceed ±15° from midline (the limits of the neutral position of the head) or ±45° (the criterion of a positive response turn to the left or to the right). The position of the infant in the experimental crib shown in Fig. 1 simulates his normal position on his mother's lap during feeding. The main

Figure 2—The effects of shifting the axis of rotation on head turning.

A. This shows the axis in an extremely high position which makes head turning very difficult.
B. This shows the axis in an extremely low position which makes head turning easy although the maintenance of a middle position is difficult.

parts of the apparatus are attached together so that the distances between them can be adjusted to the individual subject.

CONDITIONING PROCEDURES AND MEASURES

The experimental session replaces one of the routinely scheduled late morning feedings. In newborns, we start our investigation on the second to fourth day of life and carry out five sessions per week. A baseline measure of head turning is first recorded. For the first time, or repeatedly, if necessary, infants are fed without conditioning to enable them to adjust to the experimental environment and to the kind of feeding. The presentation of milk is interrupted at irregular intervals following spontaneous decreases in sucking activity. The effects of stimuli that are to be used as conditioning signals are then tested. Five pre-experimental trials of CS_1 and five of CS_2 are presented without reinforcement. The sound of an electric bell is used for CS_1 and the sound of a buzzer for CS_2. Both sources of sounds originate from midline so that they themselves elicit no orientational head turning.

The first conditioning procedure is the establishment of a simple conditioned response. A CR to the bell is trained with reinforcement (milk) from the left side. (The left side is used because of the prevailing tendency in newborns to turn their heads to the right.) Milk is presented by the assistant who sits behind the infant's head. Milk is conveyed to the nipple from a separate thermos bottle, and its amount can be measured and controlled. Ten trials occur during one session so that each reinforcement includes approximately one-tenth of the normal portion of milk used for one feeding. The intertrial intervals last approximately one minute, but are randomly varied to avoid conditioning to time.

Unlike the classical conditioning design, the interval between conditioning stimulus and reinforcement is not constant. Milk is presented to the infant as soon as he turns his head to the left, and the bell stops ringing one or two seconds after the infant starts sucking. This arrangement makes it easier to analyze the latency of the conditioned responses. The child learns to turn his head as soon as possible since the quicker his response, the sooner he gets his milk. The gradual shortening of latency is indicative of adjustment to the experimental arrangement.

If the infant does not respond to the CS within ten seconds, the assistant tries to elicit a head turn by tactile stimulation of the left corner of his mouth with the nipple. In newborns even such tactile stimulation may be ineffective; then the assistant must turn the infant's head to the left and place the nipple in his mouth. At the end of the reinforcement, the assistant leads the infant's head back to the middle position before taking the nipple out of his mouth. In our studies, a criterion of five consecutive correct responses in one session is used to mark the establishment of a conditioned response.

Extinction, the next conditioning procedure, is carried out after the conditioning criterion has been reached. The conditioning signal is then presented for ten seconds without reinforcement. Again, ten trials are applied in one session. The final criterion in this procedure is five consecutive negative responses.

Reconditioning takes place after extinction of the conditioned response, and its form and criterion are analogous to the first conditioning procedure.

After re-establishing the conditioned response, another conditioning stimulus, a buzzer, is added and reinforced with presentations of milk from the right. This enables us to study conditioned discrimination of two different signals. The infant is now trained to turn his head to the left to the bell and to the right to the buzzer. In every session five signals of each kind are applied in random order. Six consecutive correct responses constitute the criterion for conditioned discrimination.

The next procedure is double reversal of this discrimination. The reinforcement is first reversed so that the bell is reinforced from the right, and the buzzer from the left. Next, the reinforcement is reversed again so that the signals are the same as they were in the original discrimination procedure. The criteria used for the reversal procedures are analogous to the discrimination criteria.

STATES OF ALERTNESS
AND THEIR IMPORTANCE

Pavlov believed the general state of full alertness ("a state of optimal excitability of the CNS") to be one of the basic prerequisites for successful conditioning. It is well known, however, that in newborns the state of alertness changes rather quickly, so that short periods of sleep are followed by short periods of alertness and increased motor activity, eventually accompanied by crying. It appears that simple observational methods are not reliable enough to be good evidence of short, transitional states between sleep and waking (Papoušek, 1961a, 1961b). The position of the infant's eyes is a meaningless indicator of sleeping or waking. The infant can have closed eyes and still respond to CS's (Fig. 3M) while, on the contrary, he may distinctly show a state of general inhibition while lying with open eyes, breathing slowly and very regularly, with no movements of eyes, head or extremities, and with no reactions to CS's at all.

There are, of course, precise methods available, such as electromyography or electroencephalography, which give evidence of the general state of alertness, but for daily experimenting it is preferable to use simple methods which do not require complicated preparations.

Therefore, we have used a simple pneumatic transmission method—a modified Marey capsule—to record respiration and general motor activity of our subjects during conditioning. We also record the position of the eyes, kinds of movements, and vocalizations in order to study the relationship between the general state of alertness and the course of conditioning.

THE COURSE OF CONDITIONING IN NEWBORNS

The course of conditioning in newborns differs in several ways from the course of conditioning in older infants or adults. Just as former studies have indicated, the rate of conditioning, slowest in newborns, undergoes a striking developmental change during the first half year of life (Papoušek, 1961a, 1961b).

The total duration of all basic conditioning procedures—establishment of a conditioned response, extinction, reestablishment, discrimination of two positive conditioning stimuli, and double reversal of discrimination—is given in Table 2. For newborns, the whole course took more than twice

Table 2—The Total Duration of All Conditioning Procedures

Group	Age in days at the beginning of experimentation	N	Number of experimental sessions to criterion	Statistical significance of differences
A	3.42	14	76.02	A–B: $P < .01$
B	85.78	14	47.76	B–C: $P < .01$
C	142.50	16	30.26	

the number of experimental sessions required by infants in the oldest group, who did not begin conditioning until they were five months old. Actually, for most infants in the youngest group, the establishment of the conditioned response and its extinction were the only two procedures to be completed during the first four weeks of life.

Striking individual differences appeared in the rate of conditioning. If we take into consideration only the slowest conditioners in order to estimate how many conditioning procedures could be studied during the neonatal period under optimal conditions, we find that these infants failed to reach the criterion for establishment of a simple conditioned response within the neonatal period. On the other hand, the fastest conditioners had by the end of the first four weeks achieved a discrimination between two signals as different as the sounds of a bell and a buzzer, but that even these babies did not reach the final discrimination criterion until the second month of life. This, of course, does not rule out the possibility that some newborns might have been able to reach our criterion of discrimination if we had omitted all procedures preceding discrimination and started on the conditioned discrimination procedure at the very beginning of experimentation.

Table 3 shows the number of experimental sessions required to reach criterion in the various conditioning procedures for the entire group of newborns. In general, speed of learning increased with age, but the de-

Table 3—The Duration of Individual Conditioning Procedures in the Youngest Group of Infants

Conditioning procedure	Mean number of experimental sessions to criterion	S.D.
Establishment of the conditioned response	17.71	9.34
Extinction of the conditioned response	2.68	1.29
Re-establishment of the conditioned response	4.28	2.99
Discrimination between bell and buzzer	22.35	9.92
First reversal of the discrimination	19.52	8.69
Second reversal of the discrimination	9.46	3.55

velopmental trend was not the same in every procedure. For example, we were unable to find any developmental differences in rate of extinction between neonates and three- or five-month-old infants.

The slow rate of conditioning in newborns permits us to examine the separate phases of conditioning which, in older infants, sometimes pass so quickly that they are interpreted as being accidental deviations. The stages of conditioning observed in our newborn subjects are roughly comparable to the four stages observed by Kasatkin (1948) while establishing conditioned sucking responses. He described the stage of indifference to the CS, followed by a stage of inhibition of general activity, a stage of unstable conditioned responses, and finally a stage of stable conditioned responses.

In conditioning head movements, the baseline prior to conditioning usually shows no spontaneous head movements beyond 15° from midline. Even tactile stimulation with the nipple is ineffective in the beginning. Only three of our fourteen newborns responded with head turns to the first presentation of milk from the left side. In the remaining eleven newborns from three to twenty-two trials (mean = 6.57) preceded the first response to tactile stimulation.

During the first phase of conditioning, the acoustic signal elicits nonspecific orienting behavior in the form of inhibition of general movements, a change in breathing, and perhaps wider opening of the eyes. These responses extinguish quickly, and for some time the signals elicit no obvious changes in behavior.

This phase is succeeded by the gradual appearance of the first conditioned responses. At first CR's do not appear in an integrated form; one observes a gradual coordination of partial responses, such as increased general movements, unilateral contraction of the left corner of the mouth, or the turning of the eye to the left prior to stimulation from the left side (Fig. 3A–D). Eventually these individual responses become part of the head turn to the left. However, until coordination develops completely, the

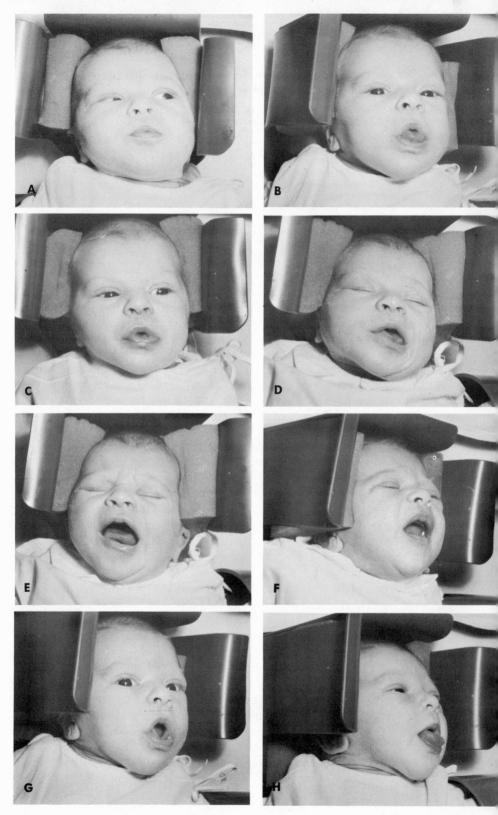

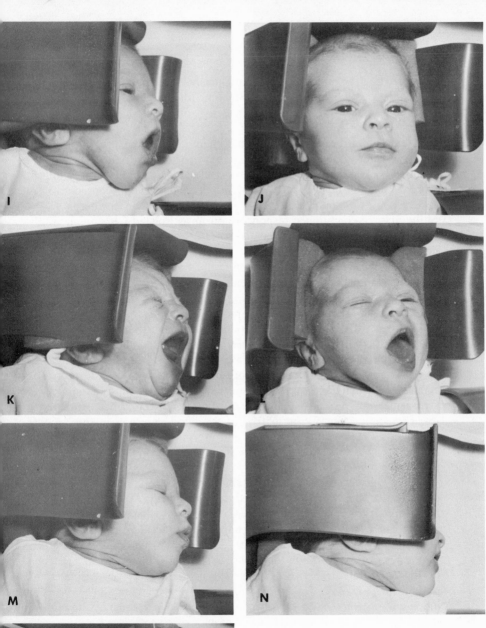

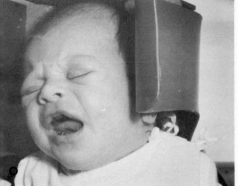

Figure 3—A photographic history of conditioning and extinction in a neonate.

This infant, a boy, was four days old at the beginning of conditioning (A) and about three weeks old by the end of the extinction procedure (O).

271

newborn may be upset, fussing and grimacing during the application of the conditioning stimulus (Fig. 3E–F). Marked signs of this lack of coordination are observed in less than 1% of the older subjects, but they are present in 50% of the newborns.

Next comes the phase of unstable conditioned responses, during which CR frequency gradually increases. The newborn is typically unable to produce very many correct responses consecutively. This inability appears to be a function of age, since older infants show several consecutive correct responses as soon as they start responding at all. In newborns, 60.7% of the first ten conditioned responses appear as isolated CR's, while 32.9% appear in groups of two consecutive correct responses, and only 6.4% in groups of three or more. The first positive responses are frequently followed by signs of generalized inhibition—slow, regular breathing and a marked decrease in general movements.

The insufficient coordination that is still present during the phase of unstable conditioning has two characteristic features: there are frequent head turns to the left or to both sides during intertrial intervals, and, in addition, the CR assumes a generalized form, including movements of both trunk and extremities ("the newborn responds with the whole body").

In Pavlovian literature, the appearance of generalized forms of responses is usually interpreted as a sign of increased irradiation of the central nervous process in the immature brain. Intertrial head turns occur less frequently in newborns (50% of the intervals) than in three-month-old infants (71% of the intervals) and are more frequently carried out to the left side, toward the source of milk. In older infants intertrial head turns are more often bilateral.

Even during the final stage, stability of the conditioned responses is only relative. The conditioned responses are quicker, stronger, and better coordinated, are carried out more economically, and have shorter and more regular latencies than in the preceding phase (Fig. 3G–I). They are no longer accompanied by signs of emotional distress; on the contrary, some positive vocalization or facial expressions may appear. Behavior during the intervals between trials is quiet, and intertrial responses do not appear (Fig. 3J). Conditioned response frequency may reach 100% in individual sessions, but a surprising decrease in this frequency may appear in any session with no obvious explanation.

In Pavlovian terms, all of these indices of characteristic age differences in the brain functions of newborns may be considered a certain confirmation of the hypothesis that the immaturity of the central nervous system manifests itself in functional inefficiency of higher centers and in instability of the basic central nervous phenomena of excitation and inhibition. Studies of the developmental peculiarities of sleep and waking states carried out in the same subjects by another member of our team (Dittrichova, 1962; Dittrichova et al., 1962) brought similar conclusions. Nevertheless, learning apparently does occur in human infants within the first days of life despite immaturity of brain functions.

THE COURSE OF EXTINCTION
IN NEWBORNS

Extinction of the conditioned head turn started at the end of the neonatal period for most of our subjects. We had no opportunity to observe evidence of earlier extinction ability because of the length of time it took the infants to reach our strict criterion for the establishment of the conditioned response. As noted earlier, we could not discern any developmental change in the rate of extinction when comparing data for age groups of one, three, and five months. Nevertheless, some developmental differences did appear in the form of the response. Both types of changes in the general state of infants that may be elicited during extinction— increased distress (Fig. 3K) or inhibition of general activity (Figs. 3L, 3M)—are more marked in newborns than in older infants.

The course of extinction is a mirror image of the establishment of the conditioned response. After a short period of stability, the frequency of appearance of the conditioned responses starts decreasing. At the same time, the responses become weaker and less coordinated, and are carried out after a long latency. They are usually accompanied by increased general movements, fussing or crying, and an increased occurrence of intertrial "spontaneous" responses often of a remarkable intensity (Fig. 3N). On the whole, this phase reminds one of unstable conditioning. Eye turns to the side at which reinforcement was formerly delivered and one-sided contractions of the corner of the mouth may remain for some time as persisting partial component responses even when head turns do not appear any more. Eye movements are usually the last to disappear.

Meanwhile, the frequency of negative responses (failures to respond) increases in a way similar to the gradual increase in positive responses during the establishment of the conditioned response. Here, as before, we can observe the infant's inability to inhibit the response in several trials consecutively. The first negative responses are usually isolated, succeeded by positive responses which sometimes have increased intensity and very short latency (Fig. 3L–N). Sometimes, paradoxical head turns to the right, instead of to the left, can be observed, even in infants in whom right turns never occurred before (Fig. 3 O).

Just as a decrease in the frequency or intensity of positive responses and a prolongation of latency may result from any accidental interruption (e.g., the slamming of a door) during the establishment of the conditioned response, an increased frequency or intensity of the no longer appropriate positive response can be caused by similar factors during extinction. In Pavlovian terms, this is the phenomenon of disinhibition.

For some time the increasing frequency of negative responses is accompanied by a generalization of inhibition. This, too, is usually more marked in newborns. After a series of several negative responses, the subject can be seen in a state resembling certain catatonic stupors. This state is characterized by slow rhythmical breathing, no movements, and open, though motionless, eyes. The conditioning stimuli, in spite of having lost their power to elicit a conditioned response, appear to be far from indifferent and are now associated wtih a distinct inhibiting power.

Finally, head turns cease both during application of the conditioned stimuli and during intertrial intervals, but in newborns, the inhibitory power of the conditioning stimuli may outlast even complete disappearance of all conditioned responses.

SUPPLEMENTARY READINGS

Dashkovskaia, V. S. Pervye uslovnye reaktsii u novorozhdennykh detei v norme i pri nekotorykh patologicheskikh sostoianiiakh. (The first conditioned reactions in newborn infants under normal and in certain pathological conditions.) *Zhurnal vysshei nervnoi Deiatelnosti*, 1953, 3, 247–259. (An English translation appears in: *The central nervous system and behavior*. Washington, D.C.: Dept. Health, Educ., and Welf., 1959. Pp. 126–146.)

Denisova, M. P., & Figurin, N. L. K voprosu o pervykh sochetatelnykh pishchevykh refleksakh u grudnykh detei. (An investigation of the first combinative feeding reflexes in young infants.) *Voprosy geneticheskoi refleksologii i pedologii*, 1929, 1, 81–88.

Kantrow, R. W. An investigation of conditioned feeding responses and concomitant adaptive behavior in young infants. *Univer. Iowa Stud. Child Welf.*, 1937, 13, No. 13.

Marquis, D. P. Can conditioned responses be established in the newborn infant? *J. genet. Psychol.*, 1931, 39, 479–492.

Warren, A. B., & Brown, R. H. Conditioned operant response phenomena in children. *J. gen. Psychol.*, 1943, 28, 181–207.

social and

nonsocial conditioning

of infant vocalizations*

PAUL WEISBERG

[Psychologists are continuously searching for those variables that serve as antecedents to the child's socialization. Vocalization is a dependent variable in early development whose antecedents are of special interest because the use of language is so important in the acculturation process. In the present report, Dr. Weisberg, of Brown University, has selected for study the influences of an adult's behavior on the vocalization responses of 3-month-old infants. He shows that vocalizing rate in these infants can be increased (operantly conditioned) by the social consequences provided by the experimenter (briefly touching the infant's chin, smiling, and "talking" to him), but not by nonsocial consequences (the ringing of a door chime), nor by the mere presence of an inactive adult. Furthermore, when the adult ceases to reinforce the infant's vocalization (starts extinction procedures), the infant's rate of talking declines. As noted by the investigator, further research is needed to identify the relative effectiveness of the different variables involved in social reinforcement. For example, is talking to the infant more effective than tactile stimulation in initiating and maintaining a high vocalization rate?]

Basic to most views on the modification of an infant's early vocalizing are the stimuli afforded by the caretaker's behavior for the control of such social behavior (Lewis, 1959; Miller & Dollard, 1941). Rheingold, Gewirtz, and Ross (1959) found that an adult's responses contingent on the vocalizing of 3-month-old infants could bring about an increase in that behavior. Subsequently, when the reinforcing stimuli (tactual contact, "tsk" sounds, and smiles) were omitted during two days of extinction, the vocal rate declined to a level about 18 per cent above the operant rate. As Rheingold *et al.* point out, however, the question of whether vocalizing was op-

* From P. Weisberg. Social and nonsocial conditioning of infant vocalizations. *Child Development,* 1963, 34, 377–388. (With permission.)

erantly *conditioned* is equivocal since the reinforcing stimuli, per se, may have acted as social releasers. The possibility exists, then, that response-independent and dependent social events may have both stimulating and reinforcing properties for infant vocal behavior. Moreover, vocalizations may be affected by the presence in the infant's visual environment of a relatively unfamiliar and unresponding adult. That is, an immobile adult may serve as a discriminative stimulus for vocal behavior. Finally, if the infant's vocalizing effects any stimulus change in his external environment, then even such physical events (as well as social ones) might reliably strengthen the behavior.

The present investigation attempted to explore these possibilities by testing the effects of a series of short term experimental manipulations on the vocal behavior of infants.

METHOD

INSTITUTION AND ENVIRONMENTAL SETTING

The institution in which the experiment was conducted was an urban Catholic orphan home equipped with fairly modern facilities for the care of children ranging from 2 weeks of age through preschool age. The infants were segregated in wards according to age group. The ward of concern here housed sixteen infants of both sexes, with a median age of 3 months. The infants were multiply cared for by full time attendants, by resident "foster mothers," and occasionally by volunteers, but usually one attendant was left in charge of the 16 infants.

SUBJECTS

Thirty-three 3-month-old full term infants, diagnosed as physically healthy, served as Ss. The groups to which the Ss were assigned (to be described below) did not differ significantly on such variables as age, birth weight, pre-experimental weight, and length of time in the institution. The ratio of males to females for each group varied from 5:1 to 3:3.

PROCEDURE

The experiment took place in a small storage room relatively free from distraction by other infants or by the personnel of the orphanage. None of the infants had ever been in this room prior to the experiment. Once an S was ready for testing, that S was carried by E to the experimental room and seated in a canvas swing (Swyngomatic). E then concealed himself behind a partition in this room and waited 30 sec before beginning an experimental session. If, within this time an S fell asleep, started to cry or to protest persistently, he was carried back to his crib and another session was attempted after half an hour had elapsed. Two 10-min. sessions were planned daily, but a session was terminated before the full 10 minutes had expired if any of these petulant behaviors appeared during the first 6 min. of a session. Thus every session reported lasted more than 6 min. without a prolonged disturbance by S. (76 per cent of all sessions ran the full 10 min.) If an S failed to complete two full daily sessions for one reason or another, that S was withdrawn from the experiment; five Ss were dropped following this criterion.

Each response consisted of a "discrete, voiced sound produced by S" (Rheingold, Gewirtz, and Ross, 1959, p. 69) appearing within each respiratory unit. Sounds classified as either "emotional" (protests, crying) or reflexive (coughs, sneezes, and certain digestive outbursts) were excluded. The phonetic topography of the response was not analyzed; the dependent variable was frequency of vocalizations made per min., i.e., rate of responding. Vocalizations and stimulus events were recorded on a kymograph. The recording speed was set at half an inch per sec, and each event could be marked by E's depression and release of a silent microswitch which was hidden from S. The median inter-observer agreement on twenty sessions between E and another person trained to discriminate vocal behavior was 97 per cent (range 67 to 100 per cent). The rank-order correlation between the mean rates of both observers was 0.99.

Vocalizations of members of six groups were recorded through eight consecutive days. Either five or six Ss were randomly assigned to each group as they became available; if an S could not complete the experiment, he was replaced by the first available S. The experimental conditions of the fifth and sixth days were the basis for naming the groups. They were: No E present; E present; Noncontingent social stimulation; Noncontingent nonsocial stimulation; Contingent social stimulation; and Contingent nonsocial stimulation. These conditions include all that appeared in any part of the experiment. After describing them, the sequences appropriate to each group, each day, will be stated, providing the full experimental procedure.

1. *No E present.* E remained behind a partition located about 5 ft to the left of S. The upper part of the partition was transparent and allowed the E to observe all of S's behavior. E stationed himself at an angle which was about 135° from S's foveal line of vision so that, if S turned his head to the left, the chances of seeing E were minimized. E, of course, minimized any auditory or movement cues that might indicate his presence. Under these conditions S oriented towards objects directly in front of himself (including parts of his body) and only occasionally turned to the left or right. S's body size and the construction of the swing prevented him from making large torso movements.

2. *E present.* E seated himself facing S approximately 2 ft away. E never smiled, frowned, or made rapid jerky movements of the head while in S's presence; he did not open his mouth and maintained a "blank expression" fixating in the vicinity of S's face. To keep his facial appearance invariant, E covertly counted numbers while fixating upon S.

3. *Noncontingent social stimulation.* Ss received stimulation on a pre-arranged schedule from *E* who was seated before them. The stimulation consisted of rubbing *S*'s chin with the thumb and forefinger followed and overlapped by an open-mouthed "toothy" smile and aspirated "yeah" sound. Each such event lasted for about 2 sec. These events were given randomly four times per min. with the restriction that the interval between one event and the onset of the next be greater than 7 sec. On occasions when social stimulation was not given, *E* reverted to the facial expression described during the "*E* present" condition.

4. *Noncontingent nonsocial stimultion.* A door chime sounded on the same schedule as that followed with noncontingent social stimulation while *E* was seated faced toward *S*. Through successive sessions, the chime sounded 3 ft to the left or right of *S* in an ABBA sequence.

5. *Contingent social stimulation.* The conditioning operations were performed by presenting the social stimulation described above immediately after each vocalization; that is, the smiles and the like were given contingent upon the infant's vocalizing. Responses made during the presentation of social stimulation were not further reinforced, and, during periods when *S* did not vocalize, *E* maintained the "blank expression."

6. *Contingent nonsocial stimulation.* The chime was sounded by *E* who was seated facing *S* immediately after each response. Vocalizations appearing during the chime's duration did not produce further auditory consequences. Spatial location of the chime also varied in an ABBA fashion from one session to the next.

The sequences through which the various Ss were run are presented in Table 1.

Table 1—Experimental Design

| | | | DAYS | |
Group	1 and 2	3 and 4	5 and 6	7 and 8
I (N = 6)	No E	No E	No E	No E
II (N = 5)	No E	E present	E present	E present
III (N = 5)	No E	E present	Noncontingent social stimulation	Noncontingent social stimulation
IV (N = 6)	No E	E present	Noncontingent nonsocial stimulation	Noncontingent nonsocial stimulation
V (N = 5)	No E	E present	Contingent social stimulation	Extinction (E present)
VI (N = 6)	No E	E present	Contingent nonsocial stimulation	Extinction (E present)

Group I controlled for changes in the operant rate of vocalizing with time in the experiment independent of an *E* being present. Group II served as a second control group, and any differences between the rates of groups I and II would indicate whether the presence of humans acted as a discriminative stimulus for vocalizations. Groups III and IV were used to determine whether the reinforcing stimuli had eliciting properties and hence to clarify whether any changes in rates observed in groups V and VI could be attributed to reinforcement (namely, social and nonsocial stimulation, respectively), *contingent* upon the occurrence of a response. Groups V and VI were used to show whether the rates of vocalizing shifted upward and downward by the imposition of reinforcement contingencies, and thus whether the behavior could be operantly conditioned.

RESULTS

CONTROL DAY ANALYSIS (DAYS 1 TO 4)

An analysis of variance of Ss' mean vocalization rates for days 1 to 4 (group variances as determined by the Bartlett test were homogeneous; uncorrected $\chi^2 = 10.65$; $P > 0.05$ with 5 df) revealed a significant day effect only ($F = 7.09$; $P < 0.001$ for 3 and 81 df). Further analysis of this day effect by t-tests for correlated means based on all groups showed that the mean rates for each of the last three days were reliably greater than those of day 1 (all P's < 0.02). Days 2, 3, and 4 (means = 0.91, 1.13, and 1.21, respectively) were not significantly different from one another. The increase in rate after the low day 1 rates (mean = 0.54) probably indicate habituation of initial response to the relatively novel stimuli in the infant's environment. The day 2 rates provide good measures of the infant's vocal behavior when a human is absent from his environment, since the mean for all Ss on day 2 are close to the mean of the daily rates for just group I (No E) on subsequent days of the experiment (means = 0.91 and 1.00, respectively). Absence of an initial selection bias is suggested by the lack of any significant group differences on these control days and the fact that the days did not discriminate among the groups.

EFFECT OF E

Upon the first introduction of E on day 3, seventeen out of twenty-seven Ss in groups II to VI (inclusive) increased in their rate over day 2 (binomial test = 1.15; $P = 0.25$, two-tailed test). The median gain for these seventeen Ss was about the same for the ten Ss who dropped in rate (medians = $+ 0.40$ and $- 0.37$, respectively). By day 4, nine out of the seventeen Ss whose rates were augmented on day 3 had declined in rate. The changes in mean rate of the six Ss in group I (No E) over this same time span were as follows: three Ss increased, one S decreased, and two Ss did not change in rate during days 2 to 3; four Ss increased and two Ss decreased in rate during days 3 to 4. Thus the presence relative to the absence of an unresponsive, immobile adult in the infant's visual environment is evidently not a releaser or discriminative stimulus for vocalizations.

TREATMENT EFFECTS

The mean rates of days 3 and 4, 5 and 6, and 7 and 8 are plotted in Fig. 1. (Pairs of treatment days were combined since each of these within-group day effects were not significantly different from each other.) Treating the different groups as blocks and any particular test of days as columns with the Ss' mean response rate as row observations, the data lent themselves to a pseudo-three way analysis of variance design (McNemar, 1955). The analysis of the mean rates for each S on the control sessions (days 3 and 4) and experimental sessions (days 5 and 6) did not indicate

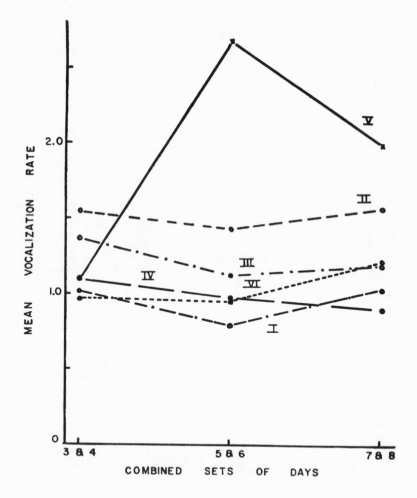

Figure 1—Group mean vocalization rates during the procedure of days 3 and 4, 5 and 6, and 7 and 8.

(See Table 1 for procedure.)

any reliable differences either between these combined sets of days ($F = 1.63$; $P > 0.20$ for 1 and 27 df) or between groups ($F = 1.14$; $P > 0.20$ for 5 and 27 df). There was, however, a significant day x group interaction ($F = 4.94$; $P < 0.01$ for 5 and 27 df). The fact that all the Ss in group V showed considerable gains in their vocal rates between these two time spans indicates that social stimulation contingent on the infant's vocalizing acted to reinforce that behavior. However, when the chime was made contingent on vocalizations (i.e., group VI), the over-all rate for this group as well as groups I–IV remained fairly stable. When a similar analysis was performed for 5 and 6 and days 7 and 8, there were no reliable differences between groups ($F = 1.65$; $P > 0.10$ for 5 and 24 df), or between the combined pairs of days ($F < 1$; for 1 and 24 df) and the day x group interaction ($F = 2.38$; $P > 0.05$ for 5 and 24 df). The reduction of the df for this analysis is due to the fact that three Ss (one from group IV and two from group VI) were not tested on days 7 and 8. However, note in Fig. 1 that, although extinction operations on days 7 and 8 decreased the vocalization rates of the socially reinforced group, that group remained the most vocal.

PERFORMANCE OF SOCIALLY REINFORCED Ss

During social conditioning sessions (days 5 and 6), the median percentage increase based on all Ss over their operant level merely with E present exceeded 282 per cent. There is no discontinuity associated with the almost 24 hour periods between sessions and the rates under reinforcement are marked by periods of response bursts and of quiescence. Although the rates were lower on extinction than on conditioning days for four out of five Ss, the median percentage drop is only 47 per cent. There seems to be a direct relation between degree of conditioning success and resistance to extinction with the highly vocal-conditioned infants (especially the two highest) failing to extinguish. Only in one case did the rate toward the end of the experiment approximate the operant level.

DISCUSSION

The fact that the group receiving noncontingent social stimulation behaved like those responding under all other conditions except for the socially reinforced group is consistent with the finding of Rheingold *et al.* (1959) that the vocalization of 3-month-old institutionalized infants can be conditioned by actions of adults.

The present study and that of Rheingold *et al.* differ in a number of ways. First, in the latter study, the infants' mean operant level (*E* present) was more than four times higher than that found here. The discrepancy is least likely due to subject differences, since both studies were done in the same institution where the caretaking activities have remained invariant over a span of years. More likely, at least three variables (or an interaction among them) may have determined the difference in rates: (a) The infants were observed in different experimental settings. In this study, responses of seated Ss to E were made in an unfamiliar room whereas in the Rheingold *et al.* study, E leaned over S's crib. Since the infants were self-nursed in *their crib* (by a propped bottle arrangement), a secondary or conditioned reinforcement (or even a secondary drive stimulus reduction) explanation cannot be ruled out. (b) The length and continuity of experimental sessions differed. Rheingold *et al.* employed blocks of three 3-min. testing sessions spaced by 2-min. "time out" or "rest" periods; this could have set up short term drive operations and allowed the response to recover between adjacent sessions. In this study in which "E present" sessions were run continuously for 6 to 10 min., the S's intrasessional response rate was frequently cyclical, suggesting that response recovery was an ongoing process. (c) The relation between the sex of E (male in this study and female in Rheingold's *et al.*) in an environment where all caretakers were female is a potentially important difference. While one can only speculate on the unknown dimensions of the human face to which infants respond, it should be pointed out that the greater opportunity for Ss to respond to "female"-like stimuli (faces, voices, etc.) would thus introduce greater "novelty" of E on S's operant level.

The results indicated that the initial presentation of an unresponding human did not serve as a discriminative stimulus (S^D) for vocal behavior. However, the relatively high resistance to extinction rates of the conditioned group suggest that the unresponding adult may have become a discriminative stimulus or, at least, a conditioned reinforcer. Admittedly, the high extinction rates could be due to the fact that not all vocalizing responses were reinforced on a continuous basis so that some of the S's responses could have been conditioned on a very low variable-ratio schedule (effectively, an interval one), thus developing high resistance to extinction. Brackbill (1958) found that several values of intermittent social reinforcement provided by an adult for smiling in 4-month-old infants produced greater resistance to extinction than that resulting from a continuous schedule. In the Rheingold *et al.* study, however, vocalizations which were socially reinforced either on the average of 72 or 94 per cent of the time failed to produce any differential effect both during conditioning and extinction sessions. Since, in the present study the extinction process was not carried to completion, further work is necessary before it can be shown that the details of E's appearance can, as stimuli, become conditioned reinforcers for infant vocal behavior.

In the Brackbill and the Rheingold *et al.* studies, an inverse relation of protest (crying) to smiling and vocal behavior was found between conditioning and extinction sessions. Protest behavior was not directly measured in this study. However, the extinction sessions did not need to be terminated any earlier than any of the other conditions because of persistent protests. During extinction sessions there was, however, a change in the topography of the vocal response. After being emitted by S

and then not reinforced by *E,* the full social response sequence on any one occasion might abruptly shift to pouts and whines only to return to smiles and the like. Both behaviors are mutually exclusive and compete with one another across time, so that, if extinction had been extended the "protest" might have gained in strength, eventually causing *E* to terminate the session and take the infant out of the situation. Substantiating evidence for this view is reported by Brackbill whose infants, after being extinguished to their operant level and below, refused to fixate to her face— "an occurrence, . . . that was in distinct contrast to *S*'s persistent fixation during conditioning" (1958, p. 120). The relation between "positive" and "negative" kinds of social behavior may be understood in terms of Estes' (1950) finding that the conditioning of one behavior is a function of the initial strength of all behaviors and of the concurrent extinction of competing reactions.

There remains the question of the unsuccessful attempts to condition vocalizing using a nonsocial stimulus as a reinforcer. Since the non-contingent and contingent nonsocial *S*s oriented towards the chime during its initial presentation, it is unlikely that the stimulus was not discriminated. The possibility exists that presenting the chime in the presence of an unresponding adult might facilitate habituation of response to it. A test of this supposition would be to compare the effects of the chime as either an evoking or reinforcing stimulus when it is given either in the absence or presence of an adult.

The results of this study should not be taken to mean that non-social stimuli are necessarily inconsequential for the prediction and control of infant social behavior. These data show only that the particular chime used, under these conditions, in infants of this age, was ineffective. Rheingold *et al.* (1962), Simmons (1962), and Simmons and Lipsitt (1961) have used nonsocial stimuli (lights and chimes) for the maintenance of behavior in older infants. The range of stimuli and subjects investigated must be extended.

SUMMARY

The vocal behavior of institutionalized 3-month-old infants in relation to manipulations in their physical and social environment through eight consecutive days was explored.

The results indicated that, after habituating to an unfamiliar setting devoid of humans, the *S*'s rate of vocalizing did not reliably increase when an unresponding adult was introduced and made part of this environment, i.e., the immobile adult was evidently not a social releaser or S^D for vocal behavior. Taking the vocalizing rate in the presence of the unresponsive adult as the operant level, it was found that the behavior could be operantly conditioned by social consequences (the adult briefly touched *S*'s chin and simultaneously smiled at and "talked" to him). Extinction operations subsequently reduced the rate but not to baseline performance.

Conditions other than social reinforcement (e.g., presenting the reinforcing stimulus noncontingent upon vocalizing and giving an auditory stimulus in the presence of an unresponding adult both independently of and contingent upon vocalizing) did not seem to control infant vocal behavior.

SUPPLEMENTARY READINGS

Jones, M. C. A laboratory study of fear: The case of Peter. *Ped. Sem.,* 1924, 31, 308–315.

Moss, F. A. Note on building likes and dislikes in children. *J. exp. Psychol.,* 1924, 7, 475–478.

Rheingold, H. L., Gewirtz, J. L., & Ross, H. W. Social conditioning of vocalizations in the infant. *J. comp. physiol. Psychol.,* 1959, 52, 68–73.

Warren, A. B., & Brown, R. H. Conditioned operant response phenomena in children. *J. gen. Psychol.,* 1943, 28, 181–207.

Watson, J. B., & Rayner, R. Conditioned emotional reactions. *J. exp. Psychol.,* 1920, 3, 1–14.

learning and maturation
in preschool children*

JOSEPHINE R. HILGARD

[Professional educators have selected the term "readiness" to designate the state of a child's being able to profit from a formally presented learning experience. It is well known that introducing the child to a learning situation that is beyond his ability may result in boredom, frustration and little progress. Some psychological theorists have suggested that when learning experiences are introduced too early (in the sense of optimal maturation and prior, related learnings) learning may progress very slowly from one trial to the next; these small increments may not be perceived by the learner as "true" progress; and, hence, may result in very low levels of motivation. On the other hand, when the child is "ready" the increments in learning are usually very large, at least to begin with, and the motivation resulting from feelings of success may be correspondingly large. The findings of the following investigation by Dr. Hilgard, of Stanford University, have been frequently quoted to support the conclusion that there is an optimal, propitious time in the ontogenetic history of children for introducing them to a given learning situation. Hilgard's procedure is an adaptation of the co-twin method developed by Gesell. (The paradigm of this method in its original form is exemplified by Strayer's study of language development, p. 309, this volume.) Hilgard concludes, not with complete justification, that when two- and three-year-old children are just on the "threshold" of ability to develop a certain motor skill, they learn slowly with even the best of educational supervision and require more training for mastering the skill than do children who are introduced to the same instruction several weeks later.]

The present study, for which a group of Merrill-Palmer nursery-school children were subjects, was undertaken in the hope that it might yield further information concerning the relative importance of maturation and practice in the development of motor skill in young children. For this purpose, it appeared that abilities which were just beginning to develop in

* From J. R. Hilgard. Learning and maturation in preschool children. *Journal of Genetic Psychology*, 1932, 41, 36–56. (With permission.)

the children offered the best opportunity for investigation. Since previous studies had shown that the abilities of buttoning, cutting with scissors, and climbing a ladder appear in children between the ages of 24 and 36 months, these three skills were selected for study. A control group and a practice group were used in order to test the effects of maturation and general practice (control group) as against the effects of intensive special training (practice group) during a three-month period.

RELATED STUDIES

It is generally recognized that the improvement of an ability with age is due both to the maturation of innate growth factors and to the cumulative effects of functional experience. To discover the role which each plays, and to estimate the degree of interdependency, is a problem which has been approached primarily from the field of animal behavior, and more recently from that of child behavior.

The classical experiments of Spalding (1875) and of Shepard and Breed (1913) on maturation in the flying of birds and the pecking of chicks are familiar. More recently, Carmichael (1926) has shown that drugged embryos of frogs and salamanders, remaining motionless during a period of growth, when denarcotized soon swam so well that there was difficulty in distinguishing them from the group which had been swimming five days. It appears that the rapid learning of the delayed group was possible because they were able to take advantage of a greater maturity.

In his careful investigations over a period of years, Coghill (1929) correlated the behavior of Amblystoma with the structural development of the nervous system. His results clearly indicated that behavior, which represents a progressive expansion of an integrated pattern, develops in a sequence of movements consistent with the order of development of the nervous system. Coghill concludes that the *form* of the behavior pattern is determined by laws of growth within the organism; the normal experience of the animal with reference to the outside world appears to have nothing specifically to do with it. On the other hand, in determining when, and to what extent, the potentiality of behavior shall be expressed, there is an interaction between the processes of growth and the experience of the individual. Thus specificity of function is fixed by the relations into which the innate elements grow, and by the excitation from the environment. Whether the conclusions drawn from the Amblystoma apply to the higher vertebrates and man is an open question. Coghill believes that it is reasonable to suppose that in their broad outlines they do.

Of environmental conditions which might be expected to influence the development of man to some extent, we distinguish, for the sake of clarity, those which offer opportunities for the general exercise of developing abilities from those which offer opportunities for the specific practice of a specific ability. Studies of the effect on development of opportunities for general exercise have been made by Blackhurst (1927), Hildreth

(1928), Goodenough (1928), and Barrett and Koch (1930). With the exception of Blackhurst, whose study was confined to the value of play apparatus for motor control, the object of these experiments was to measure the effect of nursery-school training on the intelligence test scores of young children. To what extent would the early optimal opportunities for acquaintance with many materials affect general development? The conclusions, while in general tending to minimize the influence of this training on mental test scores, are somewhat at variance. Hildreth found that children with nursery-school training, upon entering the first grade, showed only a temporary superiority, and Goodenough's results tended to confirm this. In her experiment the advantage of the nursery-school group over the control group on the second examination was slight enough to be within the limits of chance. On the other hand, Barrett and Koch, using a nursery-school group and a control group of orphan children, found that after nursery-school training the IQ's of the nursery-school group had risen from 91.71 to 112.57, while those of the control had risen from 92.59 to 97.71, or approximately half as much. An analysis of the nature of the nursery-school activities leads them to conclude that direct practice effects do not account for this rise.

Like the attempts to measure the effect of general exercise on development, a number of studies directed toward the problem of determining the effect of specific practice of a specific function have utilized certain developmental items for which standardized norms are available. This procedure seems desirable because these norms provide a fairly accurate idea of the status of the ability in question. At the same time, the experimenter may be criticizing the significance of these norms, for if practice shows much improvement in the ability tested by certain items they may prove unsuitable for inclusion in a developmental scale, in spite of age differentiation.

To test the hypothesis that intensive practice preceding full maturity may stimulate and increase the rate of growth of certain capacities, Gates and Taylor devised two tests, one on memory for oral digits (1925), which has been standardized as part of the Stanford-Binet Intelligence Test, and one on speed of tapping (Gates & Taylor, 1926). They matched a practice group of children in chronological age (four to six years), mental age, intelligence quotient, and ability in the initial performances of the activity to be tested. They found that after 78 days of practice in memory for oral digits the practice group had gained 2.07 digits, the amount gained by the average untrained child in six years, according to the Stanford-Binet Test. The control group had gained 0.67, or one-third as much. Particularly interesting is the fact that a retest four and a half months later showed that the advantage of the practice group had been entirely lost and that the two groups were as nearly equal as at the beginning of the study. Similar results were obtained in the tapping experiment. Gates and Taylor conclude that maturational processes, continuing in both control and practice groups, are not perceptibly affected by special training.

Gesell and Thompson (1929) point out the possibilities of studying maturation offered by the method of co-twin control. They report a study of monozygotic twins 46 weeks of age. For six weeks Twin T was given daily practice in climbing and cube behavior, while Twin C, the control, who had no training during that period, was given daily practice the following two weeks. At 55 weeks of age, the climbing ability of the twins was nearly the same; that is, Twin C had accomplished as much in two weeks of practice as Twin T had accomplished in six weeks. From these data Gesell and Thompson infer that the superior performance of C, with only a third the opportunity for practice, must be due to maturation of the processes involved. Further, it was impossible to demonstrate any significant influence of training upon the cube behavior patterns of Twin T. Strayer's study (1930) on the vocabulary development of the same pair of twins was interpreted to mean that, in the field of language, a maturational difference of even five weeks had a definite influence on the relative effectiveness of training.

Other studies on the efficiency of learning at different levels have dealt particularly with the development of specific skills. Goodenough and Brian (1929) tested the development of skill in throwing rings over a post in three groups of preschool children. Over a period of 50 days, Group A practiced with no instruction, Group B received some instruction, and Group C received thorough instruction. It was found that during this period Group A (ten children) had progressed only 11.5 in comparison with 17.5 for Group B (six children), while Group C (four children) had made the tremendous gain of 42.5. It would be interesting to have the results of a fourth control group having neither practice nor instruction, and also to have the results of a retest a few months later.

In a similar investigation, Hicks (1930a, 1930b) found that maturation and undirected practice in young children aged two and one-half to six and one-half years were more important in the development of the complex motor skill of hitting a moving target than was systematic, well-motivated practice once a week for eight weeks. In a parallel study the same children were given strength, perforation, and tracing path tests once during the period when the initial target tests were given and again three months later. The results showed that increase in skill on these tests without specific practice was comparable to increase in skill on the target test either with or without specific practice. The author believes, therefore, that improvement in skill may result from factors other than specific practice, such as the influence of structural maturation and of general practice.

That improvement in skill does result from factors other than specific practice there can be little doubt. The problem is one of *how much* the environmental factors can contribute. It seems now that more experimentation on abilities which are in the process of development will add to our knowledge of the total picture.

THE PROBLEM

The present experiment, which utilized a group of Merrill-Palmer nursery-school children as subjects, was attempted in the hope that it might throw further light on the problem of maturation and learning in young children. The skills of buttoning, climbing a ladder, and cutting with scissors, which previous observations had shown to be developing in children between the ages of 24 and 36 months, were chosen for study.

Clues in regard to buttoning and cutting performances at this level appear in the Merrill-Palmer Scale of Mental Tests (Stutsman, 1931). According to this scale, the age at which the average child is first able to button a one-button strip is 30.5 months; the age at which he can first button a two-button strip is 33 months; and the ability to cut gashes is an average performance for children from 24 to 29 months of age. Though few children of this age are able to make a series of successive cuts in paper, there is so striking an improvement in this ability between the ages of 30 and 35 months that 32% of fifty children of this age tested in the standardization of the scale were able to cut such strips. In contrast to buttoning and cutting, which involve the development of power and skill in fine motor coordinations, climbing brings into play gross motor coordination.

EXPERIMENTAL PROCEDURES AND MATERIALS

Two groups of fifteen children each were matched according to chronological age, mental age, sex, and approximate initial ability in the three skills: buttoning, cutting with scissors, and climbing. Because of sickness, only ten children in each group—six girls and four boys—completed the experiment. The mean chronological age of the children in the practice group was 28.3 months, and the mean mental age, 29.1 months. The mean chronological age of the children in the control group was 28.6 months, and the mean mental age, 29.9 months.

The practice group received intensive training for twelve weeks. On the average, these children had 40.7 practice periods in climbing, 28.2 in cutting, and 25.5 in buttoning. After the first three weeks of training, the group was retested, and thereafter retests were made at two-week intervals when possible. At the end of the twelve-week period the control group was retested and then received intensive training for four days. One child in the control group developed measles after the second day of training, and one was unable to return for more than one day. Eight children, therefore, completed the entire intensive training program, while the other two completed enough of the program to permit the inclusion of their data.

During this week of intensive training for the control group, the practice group received no specific training, but were tested at the beginning and again at the end of the training period.

In the following discussion of the techniques employed in testing the three skills, a description of the testing and retesting periods is in each case followed by a statement concerning the practice period.

CLIMBING

Test. This first test consisted of climbing a three-step ladder 2½ feet high, stepping on to a table at the top, and then climbing down again. On the table were various toys which might attract and please the child. These toys were changed frequently so that they did not lose novelty, and were varied to please individual children. Some of the boys, for instance, responded particularly well to engines, while other children liked toy animals. The usual formula was, "Let's see how quickly you can climb up on the table today," and "Now let's see how quickly you can climb down."

Going up the ladder, the child was timed from the second he put one foot on the first step until he had both knees or feet on top. Going down, he was timed from the second his knees were in the middle of the top of the ladder until both feet were on the floor again. The child's final score was obtained by averaging the time required for climbing up and that required for climbing down.

The pleasure the children experienced in the climbing test brought them into a cooperative frame of mind for the cutting and buttoning. They liked coming into the room to see what we had that was "new," and they particularly liked being on top of the table. After the child had examined the toy there, he was told he could hand it to the experimenter and she would put it on the little table (where he would next cut and button) while he climbed down. When this method was followed, the child would sit down at the little table ready to do the cutting and buttoning. Very often he was allowed to play with the toy for a short time before the next material was introduced. That the children retained their interest in the three tests is probably due very largely to this technique.

Only eight of the ten pairs of subjects completed this experiment. One child in the practice group was fitted with leg braces to straighten his knock-knees, and one in the control group did not take the initial test.

Practice. During the practice periods, the experimenter tried in every way to help the children eliminate wrong methods and improve the time and quality of their performance; for example, in training the child to climb faster, the experimenter showed him how to put one foot, instead of two, upon each step of the ladder. In other respects the practice periods were similar to the test period, except that the performance was not timed.

BUTTONING

Test. Usually the buttoning test was given immediately after the climbing test. In this test the child's performance was scored according to the degree of his success or the length of time he took to button strips offering different degrees of difficulty. The strip easiest to button was a folded piece of cloth with four buttons and corresponding button holes and a fifth button at the top already buttoned, so that the four buttonholes were in place over the buttons. Two of these buttons were ¾ of an inch in diameter and two ⅞ of an inch. If a child buttoned one button, he was given a score of one point; if he buttoned all four, he was given a score of two points. Performances on the other button strips have been standardized as a part of the Merrill-Palmer Scale of Mental Tests. The method of presenting the material to the child is practically identical with that used in the Merrill-Palmer Scale, and the reader is referred there for a full account (Stutsman, 1931). The folded four-button piece was presented first, and then, in turn, the one-button, two-button, and four-button strips. No assistance was ever given in a test situation. The scoring, following closely that standardized in the Merrill-Palmer Scale, considers both time and number of buttons successfully buttoned. Nine of the ten pairs of subjects were included in this test.

Practice. During the practice period the children had a wider variety of buttoning material from which to choose. A blue piece with two sizes of colored buttons down the sides made a very nice bag when all the buttons were buttoned. A red piece with black and white buttons in the form of a cross proved attractive to the children. There was also a blue folded piece with small colored buttons. During the practice period the child could select the ones he liked, though he was urged in various ways to make his choice from actual test materials. The experimenter assisted as much as was necessary and at the same time acceptable to the child.

Some of the children enjoyed buttoning; for others it was necessary to make the buttoning part of a game. One child who felt no fondness for buttons liked to put the buttoned strips into the baggage car of a toy train (secured in the climbing experiment) and send the train off on imaginary trips. Another child pretended they were blankets for the animals and after buttoning the strips put them on the animals to keep them warm. Though the interest in buttons was far from spontaneous toward the end, a fair degree of interest was maintained in ways such as these, varying much with the individual child.

CUTTING

Test. The cutting test was given after the buttoning test. To secure a measure of the child's performance and progress in this test and to provide a basis for scoring, graph paper was used for the test material. A sheet of 8 x 10½ graph paper was cut vertically into two equal parts. On one of these were drawn two vertical red lines, 10 cm high and parallel to each other; on the other a line rising to a height of 14 cm was drawn at an angle of 45° to the base of the sheet. The child was given the sheet with the two vertical red lines and told to cut as carefully as possible along one of them, the experimenter indicating the point where he was to begin.

This cutting test held considerable interest for the children. Sometimes the parallel vertical lines on the graph paper were supposed, when connected, to form a door. After the child had cut along one of the lines, the experimenter would cut across the top to the other side and fold the piece back so that it looked like an open door and supported the paper. At other times, the cut paper was called a house, the experimenter cutting a "smokestack" from the top after the child had finished cutting. Other similar devices were used to hold the child's interest.

Since there is no test sufficiently similar to this to prove of assistance in scoring the child's performance, it was necessary to devise a scoring system. On the basis of the children's performances, a scale of successive levels was devised, ranging from 100 points for the poorest performance— no cutting at all—to zero for perfect adherence to the red-line length. Deviations from the red line were computed by counting the number of 2 mm squares between the red line and the cutting. This total was then divided by the height attained. A system of weighting was soon found to be necessary, since it was obvious that the chances of any degree of deviation from the line were considerably less when the child could cut only 4 cm along the line than they were when he could cut the whole length of the line.

The data for all ten pairs of children were available in the cutting test.

Practice. During the practice period the graph sheets just described and picture pages torn from magazines proved interesting as practice material. If the child was about 24 months of age, he had to be taught how to hold the scissors and coordinate the movements of the two hands; if a little older, how to make several successive gashes in the paper; and finally, he had to be taught how to guide the scissors along the lines.

RESULTS

At the end of the 13 weeks covered by the study, when the practice group had been trained for 12 weeks and the control group had been given a final week of intensive training, the outstanding result is a marked similarity in the gains made by the two groups. Though the practice group leads in the gain made in cutting and buttoning, the groups are practically the same in climbing. In the buttoning test the practice group gained 21.4 points and the control group 15.6, or 73% as much. In cutting, the practice group gained 47.5 points and the control group 40.4, or 85% as much. The difference between the two groups in climbing is slight and unreliable—9.2 for the practice and 9.6 for the control.

It is evident that the two groups were very evenly matched in all three initial skills. However, after the 12 weeks of intensive practice, there is a reliable difference between the two groups in all skills. At the time of the final retest the practice group has an apparent lead over the control in cutting and buttoning, but the difference in climbing is negligible.

Table 1—Mean Scores for Practice and Control Groups in Climbing, Buttoning, and Cutting

Task and group	Initial test, December	After 12 weeks of practice for practice group	After 1 week of practice for control group	Total gains
Climbing* (N = 8/group)				
Practice group	17.8	8.8	8.6	9.2
Control group	18.4	12.9	8.8	9.6
Buttoning (N = 9/group)				
Practice group	6.6	30.5	28.0	21.4
Control group	7.7	19.0	23.3	15.6
Cutting* (N = 10/group)				
Practice group	64.3	19.3	16.8	47.5
Control group	73.6	40.3	33.2	40.4

* Lower scores indicate greater improvement.

Certainly, the remarkable relative gains of the control group, with so limited an amount of training, suggest that factors other than specific training contributed to the development of these three skills. This is borne out by the fact that between the initial test and the first retest in April, before the week of specific training, the control group had gained 57.3% of its total score in climbing, 72.5% of its total in buttoning, and 82.4% of its total in cutting. A comparison of the total gain made by the control group with the gain made by this group during the one week of intensive training also throws some light on the nature of the factors involved. We find that in climbing 42.7% of the total gain comes during this week; in buttoning, 27.5%; and in cutting, 17.6%. These gains are all considerably in advance of those made by the practice group during any one week of its 12-weeks' training period. In fact, the practice group in climbing required all of the previous month to make 42.7% of its total points, a feat accomplished by the control group in one week. Thus, it would appear certain that the rate of learning was accelerated toward the close of the 13-week period covered by the investigation.

The learning curves for climbing (Fig. 1) are particularly significant in offering clues for the interpretation of the gains. An examination of the curves reveals positively accelerated learning for the practice group up to the last retest in March, learning being much more rapid toward the end of the period. On the supposition that the control group lags behind the practice group throughout (a fair assumption because it is behind on every test), it follows that the curve of improvement for the control group is also positively accelerated between the initial trial and the first retest, for without positive acceleration it would not cut across the practice curve, as in the figure. This positive acceleration shared in by both practice and

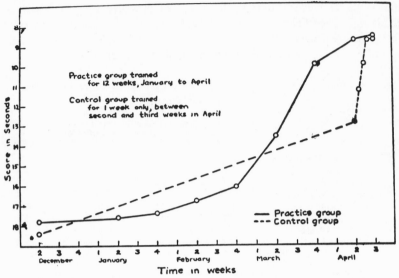

Figure 1—Mean learning curve for the two groups in climbing (N = 8/group).

control groups we may interpret as signifying more favorable maturation and general developmental potentiality for climbing toward the end of the period. The practice group has taken a pronounced lead by the second week in April, showing that training effectively capitalizes this potentiality, and the very rapid improvement of the control group during the following

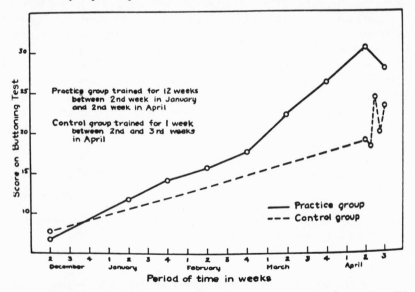

Figure 2—Mean learning curve for the two groups in buttoning (N = 9/group).

week is further evidence in the same direction. That the two groups at the end are almost identical in their mean scores, the one after 12 weeks of practice, the other after one week of practice, shows the importance of the underlying factors. These curves therefore demonstrate more clearly than the others both the importance of the underlying factors and the temporary acceleration which can be introduced by special training. The decrease in acceleration of the practice group after the end of March suggests that there may be a limit to improvement during any given developmental stage, which is, of course, to be expected.

A consideration of the data on buttoning (Fig. 2) and cutting (Fig. 3) yields some information concerning the values of these two items as part of a mental test battery. As was mentioned earlier, even though certain

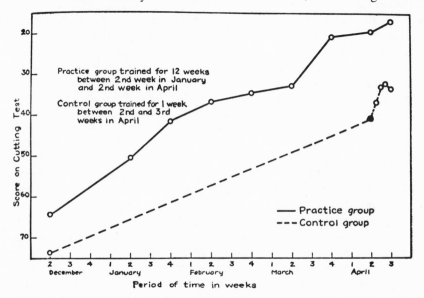

*Figure 3—Mean learning curve for the two groups in cutting (N =
10/group).*

skills show age differentiation, they may not be desirable in such a battery if, at the same time, they are much affected by special training. If it had been possible to retest the practice and control groups at a later period the results bearing on this point would be more clear cut. Nevertheless, it is evident from the slight differences between the two groups at the end of the experiment that special training, though it had some effect, was far outweighed by the general developmental factors. The fact that the curve for buttoning had already started to decline lends credence to the view that the slight superiority attained in this skill may have been temporary.

In interpreting the findings of this experiment it must be remembered that the control group was given a retest and four training periods during the one week of intensive training, while the practice group averaged only two training periods a week during 12 weeks; consequently, the frequency of the practice periods may be one factor in determining the increase in the rate of learning evident at the close of the study. It is impossible, also, to eliminate the factor of specific practice in interpreting the gain made by the control group during the period of no specific training. Yet children from 23 to 34 months of age are unlikely to be required to button their own clothes, and they are too young to take much interest in cutting unless they have considerable supervision and assistance. Climbing is usually a favorite activity, but whether a child does much of it at home depends on a number of conditions, such as the kind of play space available and the attitude of the parents toward allowing the child to climb.

In all skills, however, even though we can say that it is unlikely that the children have had much practice in these specific skills in the home, we cannot rule out, as Carmichael did by drugging his frog and salamander embryos, the factor of constant practice in related manipulatory activities. The child is continually handling objects and gaining greater skill in co-ordinating the fingers and the two hands as well as gaining skill in gross motor movements. Consequently, when he is retested after four months, it is to be expected that he will have made progress quite aside from the specific training he has been given. Whether or not we shall term this progress "maturation" depends largely on our definition of the word. Gesell and Thompson concluded, from the results of their study of twins (1929), that maturation was the dominant factor in the climbing ability of the twins; but, of course, the twin observed as a control, like the children of the control group in the present study, was gaining much general practice in activities related to his learning to climb at a later time—kicking, balancing, and the like.

In this experiment, we certainly cannot distinguish between the gain to be attributed to maturation alone and that due to maturation plus practice in activities related to the specific skills studied. What does appear is that maturation, plus this related general practice, accounts for the great gain made between the initial test and the initial retest of the control group, and that specific training throughout the twelve-week period was a far less important contributing factor in the development of these three abilities than was this general developmental trend.

SUPPLEMENTARY READINGS

Graham, F. K., Ernhart, C. B., Craft, M., & Berman, P. W. Learning of relative and absolute size concepts in preschool children. *J. exp. child. Psychol.*, 1964, 1, 26–36.

Hicks, J. A., & Ralph, D. W. The effects of practice in tracing the Porteus Diamond Maze. *Child Develpm.*, 1931, 2, 156–158.

Hill, S. D. Chronological age levels at which children solve three problems varying in complexity. *Percept. mot. Skills*, 1962, 14, 254.

Ling, B-C. Form discrimination as a learning cue in infants. *Comp. Psychol. Monogr.*, 1941, 17, No. 2.

Melcher, R. R. Children's motor learning with and without vision. *Child Develpm.*, 1934, 5, 315–350.

V

From Vocalization
to Functional Language

*the Egyptian King Psammetichus took two children of the common
sort, and gave them over to a herdsman to bring up at his folds, strictly
charging him to let no one utter a word in their presence, but to keep
them in a sequestered cottage, and from time to time introduce goats to
their apartment, see that they got their fill of milk, and in all other
respects look after them. The herdsman obeyed his orders for two years,
and at the end of that time, on his one day opening the door of their
room and going in, the children both ran up to him with outstretched
arms, and distinctly said "Becos." Psammetichus learnt that "becos" was
the Phrygian name for bread. In consideration of this circumstance the
Egyptians yielded their claims and admitted the greater antiquity of the
Phrygians. The Greeks, among other foolish tales, relate that
Psammetichus had the children brought up by women whose tongues he
had previously cut out; but the priests said their bringing up was such as
I have stated above.* HERODOTUS, *History.* 5th Century B.C.

acceleration

of infant speech

by story-reading*

ORVIS C. IRWIN

[In our society we are politically and philosophically committed to offer opportunities for self-fulfillment to all, regardless of social or economic class. At the
time of this writing we have just embarked on an economic opportunity program (more commonly known as an antipoverty program), a part of which
involves providing enriched verbal experiences for the preschool children of
economically underprivileged families. Visitors to the homes of these children
have been impressed with the extreme dearth of reading and pictorial materials
and with the relatively low frequency of verbal interaction between these
parents and their small children. The working hypothesis of the current program of social reform is that such children's verbal skills can be improved by
immersing them in a richer language environment. The findings of the present
investigation by Dr. Irwin, of the Institute of Logopedics, Wichita, provide
some supporting evidence for this hypothesis now being tested in a national
program of social reform. Dr. Irwin's findings clearly show that daily reading
sessions with preschool-aged children from lower socioeconomic homes significantly increase vocalization rates in children between 17 and 30 months of
age. The difference in scores between the experimental group whose mother
read to them from 15 to 20 minutes each day and the control group who did
not have this experience is substantial.]

In a previous study (Irwin, 1948) it was found that differences in the
speech sound status of two groups of infants exist when they are categorized according to the occupational level of their fathers. The fathers of
one group of babies were in business and the professions, the fathers of
the other group were skilled, semiskilled, or unskilled workers. The influence of occupational level was found to be negligible during the first year

---

* From O. C. Irwin. Infant speech: Effect of systematic reading of stories. *The
Journal of Speech and Hearing Research,* 1960, 3, 187–190. (With permission.)

and a half, but during the period from about 18 months to 30 months the speech sound superiority of the former group of infants over the latter was statistically significant.

The present study was designed to test the hypothesis that in the homes of working families systematic reading of stories to infants during the year-and-a-half period between the ages of 13 and 30 months will increase the amount of their phonetic production.

SUBJECTS

Two groups of infants were selected from families whose fathers were engaged in occupations which fall into the following categories: day laborer, truck driver, fireman, policeman, mechanic, delivery man, electrician, printer, ambulance driver, nurseryman, tavern keeper, carpenter, barber, tentmaker, and butcher. The experimental group included 24 infants, the control group 10. All of the children were considered physically normal; all were from Iowa City homes which, with only a few exceptions, were monolingual.

METHOD

Mothers of the 24 infants in the experimental group were instructed to spend 15 or 20 minutes each day reading stories to their children from illustrated children's story books ("Little Golden Books"), pointing out the pictures, talking about them, making up original, simple tales about them, and in general furnishing materials supplemental to the text so that the speech sound environment impinging upon the children would be enriched. In order to assure that the regimen was carried out by the parents, frequent consultations were held with them. Two or three books were brought into each of the homes during each two-month period beginning when the child was 13 months of age and continuing until he was 30 months old.

Books were not furnished to the parents of the 10 children in the control group and no reading regimen was prescribed for the group. This of course does not mean that the control group children did not receive the customary stimulation characteristic of these homes.

The children of both groups were regularly paid an afternoon visit during each two-month period and their spontaneous speech was recorded by paper and pencil in the international phonetic alphabet rather than by a tape recorder. As a rule one parent was present. No effort was made to stimulate the child's vocalization. It has been demonstrated (Irwin, 1947; Irwin & Chen, 1946) that infants' articulation may be measured in terms of phoneme type or frequency. A phoneme type is one of the individual sounds listed in the international phonetic alphabet. Phoneme frequency is defined as the total number of times a particular type occurs in a given speech sample. An infant who vocalizes a single phoneme would receive a type count of one and a frequency count equal to the number of productions of that type. The present report is concerned with the amount of vocalization as measured by the total phoneme frequency of all types. It has been found (Irwin, 1945) that a satisfactory unit for observing phoneme frequency is one breath. The reliability of the observer who recorded the sounds live by paper and pencil in the international phonetic alphabet has been demonstrated and reported elsewhere (Irwin, 1957; Irwin, 1948). The vocalizations of sounds on 30 breaths constituted the sample taken at each visit. The phoneme frequency score for each child at each age was his total score at that age.

RESULTS

Data were grouped into two-month age levels for analysis. Mean phoneme frequency scores (Table 1 and Fig. 1) show that from the thir-

Table 1—Comparison of Mean Phoneme Frequency Scores of Two Groups of Infants at Two-Month Intervals During Study of Effect of Systematic Reading of Stories on Their Speech Sound Production. The Experimental Group (E) of 24 Children Was Under a Regimen of Enriched Reading; The Control Group (C) of 10 Children Was Not

Age in months	Group	Mean	SD	Diff.	t^*	P
13–14	E	78.7				
				−2.5		
	C	81.2				
15–16	E	84.5				
				−1.7		
	C	86.2				
17–18	E	90.9	12.1			
				6.2	2.21	.02
	C	84.7	11.3			
19–20	E	93.9	12.9			
				9.7	3.62	.01
	C	84.2	11.2			
21–22	E	107.8	29.2			
				12.0	1.77	.10
	C	95.8	18.4			
23–24	E	117.2	29.3			
				16.4	2.13	.05
	C	100.8	15.4			
25–26	E	131.1	32.0			
				25.4	2.73	.01
	C	105.7	21.1			
27–28	E	144.3	40.9			
				36.7	4.03	.005
	C	107.6	11.6			
29–30	E	152.5	30.1			
				31.1	4.26	.005
	C	121.4	12.5			

* One-tailed test. Beginning with the 21-22-month level a modified *t* test which allows for unequal variances was used.

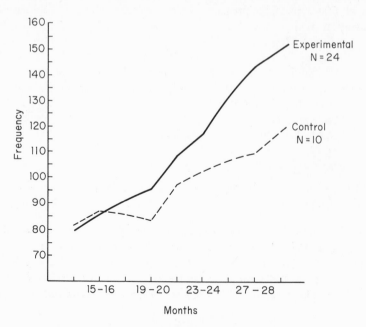

Figure 1—Graphic presentation of mean phoneme frequency scores of two groups of young children.

Children in experimental group were under a regimen of enriched reading. Children in control group were not.

teenth until about the seventeenth month there is little difference between the experimental and control groups. Soon after the seventeenth month the curves for the two groups separate and thereafter the means of the experimental group consistently exceed those of the control group until the age of two and a half years, the age at which the experiment was terminated.

Table 1 gives the phoneme frequency scores for the two groups and the significance of the differences between them. Except for the first two age levels all differences are in favor of the experimental group. (The differences at the first two age levels were not tested.) A one-tailed t-test was applied. It will be noted that for the experimental group not only the means but also the variances increase with increase in age, while the variances for the control group remain about the same. The effect is to render the variances for the two groups unequal beginning with and after the 21–22 month level. For evaluation of differences beginning with the 21–22-month level it was thus necessary to use a modified t-test (Cochran and Cox, 1950, p. 451) which can be applied regardless of the sizes of the variances. All differences are significant at or beyond the 5% level except that of the 21–22-month age. The differences between the experimental and control groups increase markedly after this period.

The results of this study suggest that systematically increasing the speech sound stimulation of infants under two and a half years of age in homes of lower occupational status by reading and by telling stories about pictures will lead to an increase in the phonetic production of these infants over what might be expected without reading enrichment.

SUMMARY

This study was designed to test the effect which systematic reading of stories would have on phonetic production of very young children. Subjects were 34 children; the experiment began in their thirteenth month and ended in their thirtieth month. During this period books were furnished weekly and a regimen of reading was prescribed for the children in the experimental group ($N = 24$), but not for the children in the control group ($N = 10$). Spontaneous vocalization of each of the 34 children was recorded by paper and pencil in the international phonetic alphabet in home visits during each two-month period throughout the experiment.

Little difference was found between the groups in the mean scores for phoneme frequency until about the seventeenth month; from then on the difference increased consistently with the experimental group having higher scores than the control group.

SUPPLEMENTARY READINGS

Jenkins, J. J., & Palermo, D. S. Mediation processes and the acquisition of linguistic structure. *Monogr. Soc. Res. Child Develpm.*, 1964, 29, 141–169.

Lewis, M. M. *Infant speech: A study of the beginnings of language.* (2nd ed.), New York: Humanities Press, 1951.

Sapir, E. The psychological reality of phonemes. In D. Mandelbaum (Ed.), *Selected writings of Edward Sapir.* Berkeley: Univ. California Press, 1949, Pp. 46–60.

Valentine, C. W. *The psychology of early childhood. A study of mental development in the first year of life.* Cleveland: Sherwood Press, 1942, Pp. 392–448.

influence of

early language experience

on later learning*

HAROLD E. BURTT

[There is mounting evidence in psychology that mere exposure to certain sensory experiences during the early stages of an organism's life enables it to respond more adaptively to these stimuli during a later developmental period. For example, recent evidence shows that exposing white rats to "meaningless" geometric forms in their cage environments enables them during their later development to learn to discriminate between these stimuli more quickly than can animals who did not have this early experience. In a now classic investigation, Dr. Burtt, Professor Emeritus of Psychology at Ohio State University, demonstrated this phenomenon in a developmental study involving his own child. Each day Dr. Burtt read 20-line selections of Greek drama to his son, beginning at the age of 15 months. "Every three months a different set of similar selections was used as material and this procedure was continued until the age of three." When his son was 8½ years of age he learned the original material by a modified prompting method and at the same time learned other similar material *de novo*. It took the boy an average of 435 repetitions per selection to learn the new material but only 317 to learn the material to which he had been exposed as an infant. This represents a saving of 27 per cent. The experiment was repeated when his son was 14 years old, and a corresponding saving in trials to learn was found to be only 8 per cent. When the last set of materials was learned at the age of 18 there was no saving at all.

[The reader will notice that despite many differences in methodology, the issue Burtt investigated is basically the same as that studied by Irzhanskaia and Felberbaum (p. 246, this volume).]

The present study is a continuation of one reported earlier (Burtt, 1932, 1937) in which nonsense material presented systematically to the subject in infancy was learned at a later age and the rate of learning compared

* From H. E. Burtt. An experimental study of early childhood memory: Final report. *Journal of Genetic Psychology,* 1941, 58, 435–439. (With permission.)

with the rate of learning new material of similar nature. The previously reported learning experiments began at the ages of 8½ and 14 respectively; the present one at the age of 18. The material consisted of selections from Sophocles *Oedipus Tyrannus* in the original Greek which was tantamount to nonsense material. Each selection included approximately 20 lines or 240 syllables of iambic hexameter. The subject was a boy with an IQ of approximately 130. Beginning at the age of 15 months three of these selections were read to him once daily for a period of three months—a total of 90 repetitions. At the age of 18 months these selections were discontinued and three others read daily for three months. This procedure was continued until the subject was three years old and twenty-one selections had been presented. The 8½ year experiment utilized one-third (seven selections,—one from each three-month period) of the available material which had been presented in infancy plus three new, matched selections for control. The 14-year experiment utilized another third, and the present and final experiment used the last seven selections plus three new controls. It was thus possible to compare the "saving" at the three ages.

The procedure in the present case was practically identical with that in the previous experiments. Two trials were given daily and this schedule was maintained with very little variation. A minor difference was the relearning of two selections which had served as controls in the two previous series. The twelve selections under comparison were always given in one trial and their order from trial to trial was rotated systematically. The selections as in the earlier experiment, were merely read to the subject for the first 18 trials. Beginning with the nineteenth, every third trial used the prompting method in which the selection was read slowly and the subject anticipated any syllables which he could. These syllables were underlined in the text and the date noted at which they had first been anticipated correctly. This procedure was continued until every syllable in a selection, except for the initial cue words, had been anticipated and the requisite number of trials constituted one item of score. The repetitions were continued as necessary until the subject could recite the entire selection without prompting and the number of trials up to this point constituted the other item of score. Motivation in the present instance was apparently about the same as in the second experiment. A variable which could not be controlled, of course, was the occasional tendency to think of words or phrases between trials. This was marked with reference to Selection D (below) but otherwise the tendency was negligible. In a few instances while listening to a selection when he was not supposed to recite, the subject did speak it softly to himself. On the occasions when there was an apparent tendency to depart from the regular program in the way of reciting between trials, no comment was made and the practice seldom persisted. With the exception of Selections A and D, which had served as controls in the two earlier series, the subject apparently had no notion as to which were original and which were control selections.

Table 1—Number of Trials Necessary at Three Age Levels to Learn New Material as Compared to Material to Which S Had Been Exposed as an Infant

	Age in months at original reading	Selections learned at age 8	Trials to learn	Selections learned at age 14	Trials to learn	Selections learned at age 18	Trials to learn
Previously presented material	15–18	No. 3	382	No. 2	142	No. 1	202
	18–21	No. 6	253	No. 5	139	No. 4	190
	21–24	No. 9	385	No. 8	169	No. 7	181
	24–27	No. 12	379	No. 11	151	No. 10	220
	27–30	No. 15	328	No. 14	145	No. 13	160
	30–33	No. 18	226	No. 17	169	No. 16	175
	33–36	No. 21	265	No. 20	127	No. 19	193
Mean, 3 earlier selection			340		150		191
Mean, 4 later selections			299		148		187
Mean, all 7 selections			317		149		189
New material		A	409	D	169	G	205
		B	451	E	151	H	193
		C	445	F	166	J	175
Mean, control selections			435		162		191
% Savings in learning "old" material			27%		8%		—

The main results together with some data from the earlier experiment by way of comparison are given in Table 1. The first column gives the age at which the original reading took place. The numbers in the next column are the arbitrary designations of the selections used in the 8-year experiment. The next column gives the number of repetitions necessary before the subject recited the selection verbatim without prompting. The data were analyzed from two standpoints, the number of repetitions necessary before each word in the selection had been anticipated and the number of repetitions required for reciting it verbatim without prompting. Previous analysis indicated, however, that there was little choice between these two methods of scoring and for the remainder of the discussion the data will be confined to the last method, viz., the number of trials necessary for a complete verbatim recital without prompting. Such scores for the 8-year experiment occur in the third column. The next two columns give similar data for the 14-year experiment and the last two columns for the present experiment. The lower portion of the table gives data for the control selections, i.e., those which were learned *de novo*. Those were arbitrarily designated by letters rather than by numbers. In the last two columns Selections A and D appear a second time. They were included at the 18-year level to determine the difficulty of relearning a selection of this type which had been mastered ten or four years previously.

The most general notion of the results may be obtained from the averages. It required 189 repetitions for a correct recital of the average selection in the present learning experiment whereas for the corresponding control selections the average is 191. The difference obviously is negligible and of no statistical significance. By the other method of scoring—not shown in Table 1—the corresponding averages are 172 and 175. The absence of any saving in the present case may be compared with the 27 per cent at 8 years (30 per cent by the other method of scoring) and 8 per cent at 14 years by either scoring method. Apparently the last four years were sufficient to eradicate completely any trace of the original stimulation in infancy.

As in the previous experiments, the selections were grouped and averaged so that the three which were presented earlier in infancy constituted one group and the four in later infancy a second group. The difference between these averages obviously is not significant in the present series.

The gross number of repetitions necessary in the present study was much less than in the 8-year but slightly greater than in the 14-year experiment. The former difference is presumably due to greater maturity, better motivation and an appreciation of the scientific importance of the experiment. The reason for the latter is less clear. It cannot be attributed to the mere lapse of time since the reading in infancy, because it characterized control as well as experimental selections. The subject reported occasional confusion of groups of syllables with similar groups which he remembered vaguely. It is quite possible that such similar groups were carried over from the 14-year experiment and caused this confusion. Indications of this carry-over may be seen in the fact that Selection D which had been learned to the point of complete recitation at age 14 was relearned at age 18 in 37 repetitions, and on the 19th trial, which was the first one on which he was allowed to attempt recitation, the subject repeated 182 out of the 240 syllables. (Incidentally, on the second trial with that selection the subject stated that it sounded familiar and thereafter was suspicious that he had experienced it more recently than infancy. However, quite early with Selection G [control] he stated that some words were vaguely familiar.) Selection A was relearned in 112 trials.

On the whole the experiment suggests that the effect of presenting nonsense material in infancy was very clearly manifest in terms of differential learning efficiency at the age of 8½, traces were still apparent at the age of 14, but by the age of 18 the effect had completely disappeared.

SUPPLEMENTARY READINGS

Norcross, K., & Spiker, C. C. Effects of mediated associations on transfer in paired-associate learning. *J. exp. Psychol.*, 1958, 55, 129–134.

Shepard, W. O. The effect of verbal training on initial generalization tendencies. *Child Develpm.*, 1956, 27, 311–316.

effects of the
differential timing
of early
language experiences*

LOIS C. STRAYER

[Identical twins are produced from one fertilized ovum and have identical genetic characteristics. It is easy to see why they have frequently been preferred subjects for psychological and sociological experiments designed to test the effects of different environmental conditions on behavior and later development. In the usual study, one of the identical twins is provided with special experiences, while the other twin, who serves as a control, is not permitted these experiences. One of the earliest psychological studies of identical twins was sponsored by Dr. Arnold Gesell, who was for many years associated with Yale University. The twins *T* and *C* (*T* for trained, and *C* for control) were the subjects for many investigations conducted by Dr. Gesell and his colleagues. The present investigation, conducted by Dr. Strayer at Yale University, involved a study of the effects of short periods of language training on the verbalizations of these identical twins. At 84 weeks of age twin *T* was presented with various objects and toys along with appropriate verbalizations by the experimenter. During the five-week period of training twin *T* was encouraged to name the objects. The training sessions also included less formalized inducements to verbalization. During this training period twin *C* lived in a nonverbal environment attended by two adults who did not speak in her presence. (The effects of this deprivation on her verbal and nonverbal behavior are of interest in themselves.) When the identical twins were 89 weeks of age the conditions were reversed, and twin *C* received four weeks of special instruction. Although these training periods were admittedly brief in duration, they did produce differential verbal behavior in the identical twins. The most important finding is that the later specialized training of four weeks was almost as effective as the earlier training of five weeks.]

* From L. C. Strayer. Language and growth: The relative efficacy of early and deferred vocabulary training, studied by the method of co-twin control. *Genetic Psychology Monograph*, 1930, 8, 209–319. (With permission.)

The purpose of the present investigation is to compare language development at two developmental levels, during a given length of time, by an
experimental analysis of the influence of vocabulary training in relation to
maturity.

The method employed is that of co-twin control, as presented in a
recent monograph by Dr. Arnold Gesell and Dr. Helen Thompson (1929).
By this method one of a pair of identical twins is trained experimentally,
and the other reserved as a control. The subjects in the present investigation are the same pair of identical twins described in that monograph.

The results of the study made by Gesell and Thompson in the field of
locomotion and of prehension and manipulation point consistently to the
preponderant importance of maturational factors in the determination of
infant behavior pattern. It seemed pertinent, then, to test these factors in
another field—that of word learning. An experiment was devised, therefore, in which Twin *T* of the first study was again the trained twin, and
Twin *C* was reserved as a control.

The experimental period was directly preceded by a developmental
examination of the twins at the nursery home, when they were 84 weeks
of age. The results of this examination again emphasized the remarkable
similarity of their behavior patterns. As had been the case consistently
throughout their history, the final ratings for both indicated identical
developmental levels. As regarded language, specifically, responses to
language as well as spontaneous vocalizations showed a high degree of
similarity. Both children handed a box to the experimenter on command
without gesture, both put the pellet in the bottle on command, and both on
command with gesture withdrew the rod from one hole of the performance
box, and put it to another. During the course of the examination, Twin *C*
vocalized somewhat more frequently than did *T*, but *T*'s vocalizations were
more apt to have a social reference. In spite of this slight difference of
emphasis, neither child vocalized in a situation in which her twin did not
also vocalize at some time during the afternoon. No difference could be
detected in the variety of sounds produced.

At the time of this examination, both twins were known to have
acquired the word "up" and to use it at appropriate times. Both definitely
made some attempt to imitate words repeated to them, but, except for the
word "up," no other word was definitely established.

METHOD

Through the cooperation of the superintendent and staff of the nursery
home in which the twins lived, a set-up was arranged in which it was possible to maintain continuous experimental control. The experimenter, with
the twins and an assistant nurse, was established in a suite of rooms in
which there could be complete isolation from other individuals as well as
isolation of twin from twin.

Twin *C*'s training was as nearly identical with Twin *T*'s as it was possible to make it. Daily routine, time and place of training, objects used, and words taught were the same, and the method of training was duplicated as closely as possible. The one difference was the greater age of Twin *C* at the beginning of training.

To insure comparative control, the environment and opportunities of the twins were kept as identical as possible, except that vocabulary training was completely deferred for Twin *C*. She was isolated from Twin *T* and every other individual except the nurse and the experimenter, both of whom refrained from verbal language in her presence. In order that even incidental training might be entirely dependent on the experimenter, and thus subject to control, the nurse maintained complete silence with both children. This rule of silence was relaxed for Twin *T* with regard to a few established commands after her training was complete. It was maintained for Twin *C* throughout the entire period of investigation. It became evident at once that Twin *C*'s joy in life was in no way curtailed by her being deprived of our conversation. She retained opportunity for expression through gesture and vocalization. Gesture was employed by the nurse and the experimenter in certain natural situations, and both made use of humming and wordless singing in which Twin *C* took keen delight. Vocalization was not discouraged by social disapproval, nor encouraged by any practical response. Like Twin *T,* she was freely encouraged in games and activities by demonstration, dramatic presentation, and the like, but without verbal vocalization.

In order to reduce to a minimum the possibility of sounds from one child being overheard by the other, the twins were kept as widely separated as the suite of rooms permitted. When one twin was on the porch or in Room A, her co-twin was kept in Room 1, shut off by two sets of doors, rather than in Room 2. Thus, although absolutely sound-proof rooms were not available, careful investigation showed that under the arrangement adopted, vocalizations of one child could not be heard by the other. This precaution was necessary to insure complete independence in language development, in order that the control twin might not be affected in any way by Twin *T*'s training.

The training can be considered under two main classes: (a) formal, in the sense of following systematically a definite, intensive procedure in which the child's attention and interest were persistently directed to the training materials or activities; (b) informal, or incidental, in which the training was a function of the child's daily routine. Each of these may now be considered more specifically.

FORMAL TRAINING

The principal formal training period was a period of an hour and a quarter in the morning. It took place in a room which was furnished at that time with the child's crib, a child's wicker arm chair, a toilet chair, a chair for the examiner, and a dictaphone machine. Into this standard setting were introduced various objects and toys which were used in the training.

The method consisted of presenting to the child an object or toy, naming it, and attempting to secure from her some repetition of the word. As learning progressed, the object was presented with the question, "What is it?" If it were not named, or were incorrectly named, the word was supplied by the examiner, and the procedure repeated. After some degree of learning had been evidenced, an opportunity was usually given for the child to correct her own error. Throughout the period, every effort was made to keep the training in the nature of a game. Frequent shift of material was made, as well as slight variations of presentation, in order to maintain the child's interest. In teaching the word "ball," for example, teacher and pupil played ball vigorously, the ball being held poised for throwing but not thrown by the experimenter until it was named. Later, the child herself initiated play with the objects, in which spontaneous naming was prominent. That the training period was an enjoyable one for the subjects was indicated by the excited way in which they hurried ahead of the experimenter into the training room and by the evident anticipation which they showed, as well as by their obvious interest throughout the period.

It should be pointed out that differences in the frequency of repetition of a given word did occur between T and C. After careful consideration, it was decided that in an experiment of this kind any attempt to hold the number of repetitions entirely constant would create a highly artificial situation. With length of training time and forms of training kept constant, number of repetitions depended on the child's own receptivity. If Twin C showed a capacity to progress faster, it did not seem justifiable to limit arbitrarily her tendency to do so. There was a certain minimum of drill which remained constant for both subjects. Variations in excess of that were a function of the child's own responsiveness. This excess, in turn, could not be so great as to cause any marked discrepancy of drill between the two subjects because of the definite time limitation of the training period.

The procedure adopted was further justified by evidence which had not been anticipated but which became apparent as the experiment progressed. This was the tendency to self-initiated practice which was observable in both T and C. Very frequently the subject would continue to repeat a given word long after the experimenter would have changed the subject. On Day 7 of C's training, for example, she showed the keenest enjoyment of the hand-shaking, with its accompaniment of "How do you do," and initiated it repeatedly by reaching for the experimenter's hand and shaking it.

Besides drill in the naming of objects, training was given by means of directions concerning the same objects. The commissions were very simple, being for the most part simply "Bring the —— to me," or "Put the —— on the chair." They involved the selection of the correct object, however, from a group of several objects. As in the case of object-naming, the experimenter gave opportunity for a correction whenever there was failure or an error, and demonstrated if the error persisted. Towards the end of the experimental training, more complexity was introduced into the directions by such commissions as, "Put the —— on the bed; in the wagon; in the basket"; etc.

At the end of the first week of training for both subjects, a picture book was introduced, and daily training given in picture pointing. The experimenter named a picture, secured some attempt at repetition on the part of the child, and then tested her ability to point to that picture on request, both in its original setting and in others. The direction given was, "Show me the ——," or "Put your finger on the ——," or "Where is the ——?"

Throughout the whole formal training period, a complete record was kept of the language of the experimenter and of the child. Besides this record by the examiner, daily phonetic records were made on the dictaphone of the child's responses to a series of stimulus words.

The order of events in the training period followed a definite sequence, as follows: A test for object names; drill in the repetition of a given list of words with the responses recorded on the dictaphone; a series of directions or commissions involving the test objects; and picture-pointing. With the exception of the dictaphone recording, the events were repeated as often as time permitted.

INFORMAL TRAINING

By informal training is meant that which was a function of the child's daily routine. While, in most cases, it was no less regular than the formal training, it was not so intensive. It was, perhaps, more natural in that it made use of the manifestly absorbing activities of dressing and eating, as well as of spontaneous play situations.

Informal training took place chiefly during dressing, at two meals, during the daily walk, and during certain periods of free play under standardized conditions. For example, during dressing, it consisted of brief drill in naming shoes, stockings, dress, pins, etc.

In order to have further check on object-naming besides the daily checks of the examiner, Twin *T* was tested in another environment (the Yale Psycho-Clinic) and by another individual (A.G.), at the end of four weeks of training, and again at the end of five weeks of training. On both of these occasions an attempt was made (by A.G.) to teach a new word to both *T* and *C,* separately, for comparative purposes. At the end of *C*'s training a similar test was given her, a retest was given *T,* and both subjects were again taught a new word.

Separate developmental examinations were conducted at the end of *T*'s training (which, of course, marked the beginning of *C*'s). The examination for *C* was conducted silently, and results were noted by a second observer in order to eliminate the customary dictation on the part of the examiner. At the end of *C*'s training period, a simultaneous back-to-back developmental examination was given both.

While Twin *T* was being trained, Twin *C* was by no means neglected. Although her vocabulary training was being deferred, care was taken that her social and expressional experience should be rich in other directions. The experimenter spent about half as much time with her as with her co-twin. During the time spent with her, many of the same games which were played with her twin were played with her, except that they were silent. Vigorous games of ball, peek-a-boo, and hand-shaking (the last initiated at first by *C* herself) were favorites. Music, in various simple forms, was introduced. Both nurse and experimenter made use of humming in situations annoying to the child (face-washing, nose drops, and the like), in which they would ordinarily have talked to her. The experimenter made somewhat more definite use of it in a given play situation. One of Twin *C*'s favorite games was to rock the experimenter as she sat in a rocking chair. The experimenter entered into the game by humming, in rhythm to the rocking, the tune of the nursery song, "See Saw, Marjorie Daw." This was done consistently whenever *C* initiated the rocking, and resulted in an interesting development which will be described later.

A harmonica was supplied, and, after wordless demonstration, *C* learned to blow it. She had a small Swiss music-box which was played by turning a handle and around which a number of activities were developed. Although it could hardly be called musical, a crying doll was given her at certain periods. It might be noted in passing that we found no evidence of imitation of its wail!

Expressive gesture was used by both the nurse and the experimenter, such as nodding and smiling for approval, head-shaking in places where "No, no" was used for Twin *T,* and beckoning and pointing in simple wordless directions.

During the subsequent training of Twin *C,* Twin *T*'s training was discontinued, but she remained in a relatively normal language environment. The experimenter talked to her as she had throughout the experiment, but gave no drill and did not stimulate the use of words by questioning. No new words were given or used even when there was opportunity for them. The nurse did not talk to her, except for a minimal use of the following expressions: "Come," "No, no," "Stand up," "Sit down," "Toilet," and the child's name. A record of *T*'s language and the situation in which it occurred was kept as in the training period.

RESULTS

The results of the experiment will be considered in three sections: the behavior of Twin *C* while she remained in a non-verbal environment; a comparison of the language behavior and development of Twin *T* and Twin *C* from the point of view of comparable days of training; and the behavior and language development of Twin *T* in the four-weeks' period subsequent to her training.

TWIN C: NON-VERBAL CONTROL PERIOD

The reactions of Twin *C* to the conditions of the control environment were from the beginning gratifying and reassuring. These conditions were carefully safe-guarded to insure her social experience, emotional life, and self-expression. Neither the writer nor an independent observer (A.G.) noted any adverse effects in the postponement of the vocabulary training. There was a gradual shift or modification in behavior which seemed to result from the non-verbal environment, but at no time was any problem presented.

At the beginning of the experimental period, Twin *C*'s vocalizations could not be distinguished from her co-twin's, either in variety, inflection, or in amount. As the experiment progressed, however, differences in vocalizations could be noted as well as in what may be more generally termed language behavior.

As has been mentioned before, Twin *C*'s vocalizations, although not discouraged, were not specifically encouraged by social approval or by making any observable response to them. She very soon, therefore, adopted other means of attracting attention. Grunting, coughing, and throwing kisses appeared, as well as a highly artificial "laugh." This last was the most persistently used, and appeared on the sixth day of the experiment, continuing throughout the rest of the period and even into the training period when language was encouraged. Although its origin probably lay in a true laugh, it soon ceased to be recognizable as one. It was a rough "heh-e-heh-e-heh" sound, produced by a vocalized breathing in and out. It seemed to have no emotional content. At first it was used following a vocalization to which the examiner had paid no attention, but later it came to be used alone as definitely as any verbal summons.

Approval was given Twin *C* by means of nodding and smiling, and by the middle of the third week this form of expression had become very prominent in *C* herself. She nodded when commendation was due her for success in toilet-training, when she had succeeded in following the experimenter's demonstration in play with the blocks, when she handed an object to the experimenter to be repaired, and when the repaired object was returned to her. The nodding frequently appeared during meals when she had finished her food. On a few occasions the nodding was accompanied by vocalization, but usually there was only smiling with occasional pointing. Twin *C* responded as well to a head shake as her co-twin did to "No, no." On several occasions, however, there was some silent arguing with the experimenter. The first time it occurred, Twin *C* was engaged in a forbidden activity, and the experimenter, having attracted her attention, shook her head in disapproval. *C* hesitated a moment, then with a mischievous grin nodded emphatically several times and continued, entirely unconvinced! Later the same day there was more agreement. The experimenter shook her head at *C* for pouring her milk on the table. *C* at once began to shake her own head and continued for some time to do so whenever the experimenter looked at her.

Although there was little evidence that the total amount of Twin C's vocalizations became less as the experiment proceeded, there is abundant evidence of modification as to the situations in which it appeared, and of increasing disparity between her vocalizations and Twin T's, as the latter's training progressed. As has been mentioned, by the sixth day C was attracting the experimenter's attention by "laughing" instead of vocalization. Jargon of a conversational type, and even simple vocalizations directed to the experimenter, showed a steady decline. During the first week of the period, the child always vocalized to the experimenter when handing her an object. During the second and third weeks she was sometimes silent, merely nodding. By the fourth week she was as likely to be silent as to vocalize; but by the fifth week she vocalized in only about a third of the occurrences, the other two-thirds being silent presentations. Even as early as the eleventh day there is evidence that the experimenter's silence in her presence was having a noticeable effect. On that day, the experimenter, going into Room I to investigate the switching on and off of the light, found a twin standing up, playing with the light cord. Twin T should have been having her nap there, and, without investigating, the experimenter said, "No, no; lie down." The child showed such evident surprise that it was suspected that a mistake had been made. Inquiry revealed that an unexpected shift of rooms had been made, and that the twin addressed had been Twin C. (It is quite certain that no other mistakes of a like nature were made!)

On the eighteenth day, the following summary appears in the notes: "Whether or not the absolute amount of vocalization at this time is different in T and C, it seems evident that there is a well-defined difference in kind. Twin T shows a characteristic tendency to turn to the experimenter with vocalizations of a questioning nature or with a series of syllables suggesting a statement of fact, and to use less often than C the purely sound-play type of vocalization. Even when there is no change of situation, she is apt to point and vocalize, looking at the experimenter. She is tending now, also, to use some of her drill words in vocalization when she is alone.

"Twin C, on the other hand, is apt to vocalize at any change. Her sounds tend to be of an exclamatory and sound-play type. She vocalizes to the experimenter only rarely, and never has the questioning intonation. Her sounds are more staccato than T's, generally, with fewer liquid sounds, and are more apt to be repetitive. Usually when specifically engaged in play with the experimenter she is entirely silent, merely nodding. Such vocalizations as she does use during these situations seem to be called forth by a sudden change or event such as a dropped block."

The mimetic tendency of Twin C during the control period was extremely interesting. This tendency was much more marked for C than it was for T at any time in the experiment, and outside the vocal field was greater than it was for C during her subsequent training period. Her nodding and smiling in the same way the experimenter did has already been noted. On Day 18, the experimenter observed Twin *C* holding a folded piece of paper in front of her, moving her lips silently as though reading, and nodding from time to time. No immediate explanation could be given for this new game, but inquiry revealed the fact that the nurse, when reading in *C*'s presence, moved her lips silently. *C* had adopted this new activity entirely spontaneously.

Although *C*'s world was devoid of word language, it was not devoid of sounds, and she showed a marked tendency to imitate certain of them. The experimenter and the nurse had adopted a code of whistles for communication in the presence of Twin *C*, and by the twelfth day *C* was definitely imitating the whistle with an "ōo-ōo" vocalization in which the pitch was identical with that of the whistle. On Day 18, she imitated with surprising accuracy the yelp of a dog outside. She definitely awaited his yelp, and followed it each time with her own imitation. On Day 28, a fire engine with siren sounding passed outside, and *C*, running to watch it, gave several recognizable vocal imitations of the siren.

While it would be unjustifiable to place too much emphasis on such evidences of imitation, nevertheless, the fact that they were prominent only during the control period suggests that they were to some degree a substitute activity; that there was a certain readiness to respond imitatively, which found expression later in a language situation.

A COMPARISON OF THE TWIN'S LANGUAGE DEVELOPMENT DURING THE TRAINING PERIOD

The next step in the presentation of the experimental results is a comparison of the language behavior and development of Twin *T* and Twin *C* from the point of view of comparable days of training. Throughout this section, day numbers refer to *days of training*. For Twin *T*, days of training correspond in number to experimental days. For Twin *C*, of course, 35 must be added to the number of the training days in order to obtain the number of experimental days.

The general procedure and method of training has already been described. One variation in the training conditions for Twin *C* must be noted, however. On Day 3, Twin *C* developed an infection which necessitated medical as well as experimental isolation for several days.

Something should be said here concerning the selection of the words used for training. As will appear later, a great many of them are object names. A comparatively large number of the words taught were more or less spontaneously selected by Twin *T*. That is, her natural interests were followed as a guide for the addition of new words. Twin *C*, on the other hand, was taught *only those words which had been used in Twin T's training,* and any different interests of *C* were disregarded. This again served to increase the severity of conditions for Twin *C*.

A study of the records of *T* and *C* revealed the fact that certain well-defined stages of development could be observed in their learning. These stages were remarkably similar in kind and in order of appearance, though there were differences in relative time of appearance. A brief description of the steps will be given, therefore, before we turn to a discussion of actual vocabulary.

At first it was necessary, in the cases of both T and C, to repeat a stimulus word many times before the child made any attempt to repeat it. Although this tendency reappeared from time to time throughout the course of the experiment in the case of new words, it was not characteristic of Twin T after the first week, nor of Twin C after the second day.

After the initial stage in which there was marked reluctance of response, there appeared a willingness to make a sound in response to "Say," but the response was largely undifferentiated. That is, there was a tendency to say repeatedly a word which had just been drilled, even though the stimulus word had been changed, or to respond with what seemed to be a generalized response word. For Twin T the generalized response was an indefinite "kgn"; for Twin C it seemed to be "daty." The marked readiness of response began for Twin T on Day 8, and for Twin C on Day 6. About Day 12 for Twin T and Day 11 for Twin C persistence in an undifferentiated response began to decline. It never entirely disappeared for either child, but tended to be prominent whenever a new word was introduced.

Both children apparently attempted to attract the experimenter's attention by running through the list of learned words—Twin T by Day 18, and Twin C by Day 7, after the latter had first been unsuccessful with a "laugh" characteristic of the silent period. Both, in attempting to name a given object, would give several words in succession if approval were not given for the first one. At times, when the naming was entirely spontaneous, the child gave every outward appearance of searching for the right word. The first words were said hesitatingly and with no evidence of conviction. When the correct word was finally said, however, it was uttered forcefully, usually with a smile, and was then usually repeated again in a firm manner.

Very early in their training both T and C pointed to objects and, turning to the experimenter, vocalized inquiringly. The inquiry had a fairly constant form and was typical for each twin. These questions were usually satisfied by the experimenter's naming the object pointed out. Later, Twin C followed her own questioning jargon by naming the object immediately herself. This did occur with Twin T by Day 30, but never became prominent.

By Day 17, Twin T was occasionally naming an object encountered in play without any reference to the experimenter, and by Day 25 this had become quite usual. Twin C's object-naming, on the other hand, maintained quite definitely its personal reference, any object met with in play being brought to the experimenter and named, or named after her attention had been secured. Both twins at times spontaneously brought all of the training objects to the experimenter in rapid succession, naming them voluntarily. This occurred first with Twin *T* on Day 30, and with Twin *C* on Day 22.

In the case of both twins, the usual level of responsiveness to the language training was broken by a sudden marked increase of interest. There was almost continuous vocalization involving, for the most part, a proper use of training words. Each word was repeated 10 or 12 times in succession, often actually shouted, and there was a rapid transition from one word to another. There was almost a frenzy of gleeful speech, as the child picked up one object after another, named it repeatedly, and insistently drew the experimenter from her frantic recording to some objective acknowledgment of her pupil's prowess. This sudden spurt occurred for Twin *T* on Day 22; for Twin *C* on Day 26.

We can turn now to a consideration of actual vocabulary acquired. As has been noted before, any sound used consistently in response to a given stimulus or in a given situation was considered a word, for the purposes of this experiment, even if the sound were not phonetically accurate. An object name was considered learned if it were correct in 100% of the opportunities given. Words such as "dirty," "all gone," "bang," and the like, are considered learned if they were used correctly by the child without the aid of a repetition by the experimenter. While the 100% criterion for object names seems somewhat stringent, it was adopted in order to keep those words closely comparable to other words which were dependent on situations. That is, a word such as "dirty" or "all gone" either appeared or did not appear, and could not be correct only a part of the time.

Table 1 gives a daily comparison for Twin *T* and Twin *C,* on the basis of number of learned words. It includes all of the words acquired, and is not limited to those which were a function of any one phase of training.

A comparative study of the daily vocabulary material reveals some interesting facts. In the first place, Twin *C* began to acquire words earlier in the training than did Twin *T*. Throughout the four weeks of her training period, her daily vocabulary total always exceeded Twin *T*'s on comparable days of training, by from 1 to 13 words. At the end of *C*'s training, she had 7 more words than Twin *T* on the 28th day—a more impressive fact when one considers that it represented about 30% of Twin *T*'s total vocabulary at that time.

While it can never be shown conclusively that the disadvantages under which *C* worked—the five weeks of silence preceding training, *C*'s illness during the training period, and the use of non-spontaneous training material—could offset any unconscious improvement in the training of Twin *C,* it seems to the experimenter that the weight of evidence favors the conclusion that there was no advantage in Twin *C*'s training conditions which would account for her consistent superiority, and that any difference in training conditions lay rather on the side of greater severity. It would appear, then, that the more rapid attainment of Twin *C* in the field of language was in some way a function of her greater age at the time of training.

Table 1—Number of Words in Vocabulary

Day of training	Twin T	Twin C
1	0	0
2	0	1
3	0	1
4	0	1
5	0	2
6	1	2
7	2	4
8	2	8
9	2	5
10	2	7
11	3	7
12	5	13
13	5	13
14	6	14
15	8	15
16	7	15
17	7	18
18	10	15
19	11	19
20	8	21
21	10	23
22	13	26
23	12	24
24	18	26
25	21	27
26	21	28
27	22	29
28	23	30
29	23	
30	26	
31	29	
32	33	
33	34	
34	34	
35	35	

Twin C was also superior to Twin T in generalization, i.e., the total number of training word extensions. She attained by Day 28 a total number of extensions greater by four than Twin T had attained by Day 35. In the use of two-word sequences, however, Twin T showed to better advantage than Twin C, making combinations with two words, while Twin C made them with only one. In phonetic accuracy, also, Twin T showed a slight advantage. It is suggested that in this connection the factor of length of practice is of importance, and that to this may be due her slight superiority. (This suggestion is further confirmed by evidence from the post-training period of Twin T.)

From the data on response to commands in regard to the training objects, it appears that Twin C was markedly superior to Twin T, not only in ability to execute a commission, but in ability to select correctly the object named in the commission. For example, Twin T never learned to discriminate among the duck, cat, and rabbit, while Twin *C* was making no errors after Day 22.

In picture-pointing, Twin *C*'s advantage was even more marked. By the end of her training, Twin *C* was making no errors in pointing to the ball, the spoon, the chair, the teddy-bear, the duck, and the table, on request, while for Twin *T* definitely correct responses had not been established for a single picture, even by Day 35.

It seems to the experimenter, then, that in spite of the exceptions noted in Twin *T*'s favor (two-word sequences and phonetic accuracy), the weight of the evidence is decidedly toward the conclusion that Twin *C*'s advancement in language behavior was more rapid than Twin *T*'s, and that after 28 days of training she was equal, if not superior, to Twin *T* after 35 days of training. Under the conditions of the experiment, we must account for this superiority on the basis of the greater maturity of Twin *C* at the time her training was begun.

A COMPARISON OF THE TWIN'S LANGUAGE DEVELOPMENT DURING THE POST-TRAINING PERIOD

In the four weeks during which Twin *C* was being trained, Twin *T,* although she was not receiving any training, showed a marked absorption in language. Her use of words, far from showing any falling off, continued to increase. Her typical behavior when with the experimenter was to hold up her toys one by one, naming each in rapid succession, with numerous repetitions of each word. Unless the experimenter accorded her a sufficient amount of acknowledgment, the repetitions reached an almost unbelievable crescendo of volume and rapidity. She talked continuously, mixing a conversational jargon with the recognizable words, and often after she was put to bed for the night she could be heard practicing almost her entire vocabulary for some minutes before she went to sleep. During this period an increased inflectional quality was noticeable in her jargon, as well as in certain words. "All gone," for example, came to be said in an expressively mournful tone.

The daily vocabulary of Twin *T* during the period subsequent to her training is shown in Fig. 1. Although specific training had been eliminated, Twin *T*'s vocabulary continued to grow slowly during this time. The increase was due in part to an elimination of errors in words already taught, and in part to the fact that a few words were spontaneously acquired. In the latter class, for example, appear "hot," "now," "comb," and "good girl."

After the close of Twin *T*'s training, she was allowed to play with all but three of the training objects. The cat, the train, and the basket were reserved in order to see what result an interval during which she did not see the objects would have on the object-name. On Day 63, she was retested on all of the training objects, including the cat, the cat's tail, the train, and the basket. None of the names which had been established during training

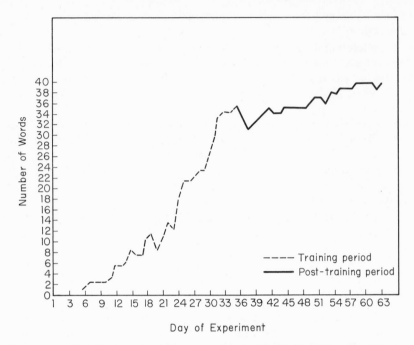

Day of Experiment

Figure 1—Vocabulary-learning curves for Twin T during training and post-training periods.

were lost for objects with which she had been allowed to play during the intervening period, but none of the other four were retained.

The post-training results for Twin *T* for other measures than vocabulary may be summed up briefly as follows. The extensions of applications of words showed themselves to be much less dependent on drill than was vocabulary; they increased almost as rapidly as in the training period. Not only did number of applications increase, but in some cases the broadening of use definitely suggested an approach to a true concept. Two-word sequences were used more frequently than in the training period, and the number of words involved in combinations with object names was increased from two to four. Phonetic accuracy for words already learned increased somewhat, and several new words became phonetically consistent, some of them being rather easily recognizable. Twin *T*'s pronunciation at the end of the experiment was noticeably better than Twin *C*'s at the end of her training, suggesting the importance of length of practice in that connection. Finally, although Twin *C* had reached a higher level of accomplishment in the field of language at the end of four weeks of training than Twin *T* had attained after five weeks of training begun at a chronological age earlier by five weeks, she had by no means caught up to Twin *T* in final accomplishment at the close of the experiment. It seems safe to assume that eventually differences in language behavior would be entirely eliminated as increasing chronological age lessened the proportional importance in total life span of the few weeks of training. Indeed, during the present experimenter's further contacts with the twins, a period of about three months, there was evidence that differences were disappearing if not entirely gone.

CONCLUSIONS

The findings in the present experiment seem to indicate rather consistently in the field of language that a maturational difference of even five weeks has a definite influence on the relative effectiveness of language training. Gesell and Thompson found much the same results for the effectiveness of training in the locomotor field (stair-climbing), although they are careful to point out that the appearance of the activity seems not to be a function of training but of maturational level (1929, p. 114ff.): In the present experiment, of course, readiness for the acquisition of language was already obvious in the case of both twins. The data bear, then, not on the appearance of an activity, but on the effectiveness of training at two maturational levels, and on the pattern of response to training. Not only was training which was begun with a maturational advantage of five weeks more effective than earlier training, but the pattern of response was more mature. Twin *C,* although her acquisition of vocabulary had been deferred, showed, when opportunity for advance was finally given, a more rapid elimination of such infantilisms as the need for several repetitions of a given word before a response was made, the doubling of a syllable (ba-ba for ball) in response to a one-syllable word, and the need for a definite question by an adult to elicit the use of a word. There was less interference of association; she incorporated the new words more quickly into her spontaneous jargon, and extended their application earlier and more widely, using them more often. Such tendencies seem to be relatively independent of training, and to be rather a function of maturational level. That training cannot transcend maturational level is obvious from the fact that in spite of intensive drill and training, neither of the two subjects was able to attain a vocabulary equal to that of the average child of their chronological age, a result to be expected in view of their consistent degree of retardation rated as sub-average normality.

To summarize briefly, then, the factor of maturation influences not only the effectiveness of training in vocabulary but the general pattern of behavior. Training, although it cannot transcend maturational level, is to some degree effective in increasing vocabulary.

SUPPLEMENTARY READINGS

Dawe, H. C. A study of the effect of an educational program upon language development and related mental functions in young children. *J. exp. Educ.,* 1942, 11, 200–209.

Milner, E. A study of the relationships between reading readiness in grade I school children and patterns of parent-child interaction. *Child Develpm.,* 1951, 22, 95–112.

Sommer, A. T. The effect of group training upon the correction of articulatory defects in pre-school children. *Child Develpm.,* 1932, 3, 91–107.

conflicts between

the first and second

signal systems[*]

E. I. LEBEDINSKAIA and A. G. POLIAKOVA

[When a mother tells her small child that he is not to do something he very frequently assents, says "no," and then without hesitation proceeds to carry out the prohibited action. This lack of concordance between actions and verbalizations is the focus of the present study by Drs. Lebedinskaia and Poliakova, of Moscow University and the Soviet Academy of Medical Sciences. They found that this phenomenon exists in children up to four years of age and is largely absent in children over that age. Their experimental conditions involved an adult's suggesting to the child that he had not actually performed a given action (rolling a ball). Small children's inadequate responses to leading questions (e.g., "You did not just roll the ball!") are interpreted as ". . . the primitive, ontogenetically earliest verbal reactions of the echolalic type." Providing the small child with reinforcement of the "action-word" association reduces the influence of the adult's verbalization; however, this influence is completely dissipated over a 2–3 hour rest period. These findings are interpreted along conventional Pavlovian theoretical lines, as a lack of concordant activity of the first and second signal systems. The authors infer that with increasing age children learn to rely on their own experiences (both motor and verbal) and become resistant to an outsider's verbal influence on their own verbalizations. Some of the findings of recent experiments by social psychologists show that even adults remain somewhat influenceable in their verbal responses by erroneous information given to them under "prestige" conditions.]

The studies of the I. P. Pavlov school have shown that concordant activity of the first and second signal systems develops gradually in the child and that the two systems function in intimate and indivisible association

---

[*] From E. I. Lebedinskaia & A. G. Poliakova. Certain age modifications of the interaction of the first and second signal systems in children two to seven years of age. In: *The Central Nervous System and Behavior*. Washington: National Institutes of Health, 1960. Pp. 488–499.

with one another (Krasnogorskii, 1954; Ivanov-Smolenskii, 1930, 1940). However, the development of the conjoint operation of both signal systems has still been inadequately studied.

In the process of investigating conditioned reflexes in children we observed that under the influence of the form and tone of the adult's question, a child sometimes gives incorrect responses as to what he has done.

An example illustrating this statement:

Vitia S. (Koltsova, 1953), after the elaboration of a visual conditioned reflex, responded to the questions of an adult in the following way:

"When the light was on, did you open the box?"
"Yes, I did."
"When the bell rang, did you open the box?"
"Yes, I did." (He had not opened the box.)
"And when the horn blew, did you open it?"
"Yes." (He had not opened the box.)
"And when you saw the little bird, did you also open it?"
"Yes, I also opened it then." (There wasn't any bird, and he had not opened the box.)

A description of similar phenomena is encountered in the works of various psychologists who have undertaken to explain this phenomenon. Thus, Binet after giving children a number of "leading questions" established the dependence of incorrect responses on the age and degree of development of the child: The younger and less developed the child the more often were incorrect responses observed (1910).

Rosengart-Pupko noted that the child often "even in spite of his own wishes" answers a question in the words of the adult (1948). This investigator believes that it is one phase of normal speech development for a child in the second year of life to try out the effects of the adult's speech before developing his own.

Various authors have limited themselves to noting this phenomenon without explaining its nature. The purpose of the present article is to explain to what extent the given phenomenon operates according to rules, what the conditions of its occurrence and disappearance are, and its physiological aspects.

METHODOLOGY

During the experiment the child and experimenter were alone in the same room. The experimental conditions conformed as far as possible to play activity most typical for children of this age. The experiment was conducted in the form of play with a ball. It should be noted that in a previous experiment these actions had already been mastered by the child and to some extent were associated with the words denoting various aspects of this play.

The experiment included three phases in all. In the first phase, after a single demonstration of how the ball should be rolled, the child was told to perform this action 3 times after which he was asked questions about the action that he had just performed. If the child gave to even one question an answer that was inappropriate to the action, then a second series of experiments was conducted on him.

In the second phase, play with the ball was continued until the child's responses to all the questions put to him were appropriate to the preceding action. After every 20 rolls of the ball the children were questioned about the preceding accomplished actions.

The third phase was conducted 3–4 hours after termination of the first two phases and was so constructed that the children were questioned according to the same plan as in the preceding series, but without showing the ball or performing any action with it.

After the action was completed, the child was asked a number of questions. The questions which were asked may be divided into 2 groups: questions which did not contradict the action performed by child (e.g., "Did you just roll the ball?") and questions making the child's action doubtful or plainly negating it (e.g., "Did you really just roll the ball?", "You didn't roll the ball, did you?").

The sequence of questions was kept constant. When the child did not answer the questions, a 10-second pause was observed. The answers of the children, the latency of verbal reaction, the number of trials needed to obtain correct answers to all questions, and general behavior of the child during the experimental session were recorded.

The investigation was conducted on 75 children of 5 age groups (2–3, 3–4, 4–5, 5–6, and 6–7 years), with 15 children in each age group. The experiment was conducted in the nursery school and kindergarten of the Division of Development and Training of the Institute of Pediatrics of the Academy of Medical Sciences, USSR.

RESULTS

In each age group the number of children responding inadequately to the questions is unequally distributed, as is shown in Table 1. In the first phase of the experiment (rolling the ball 3 times) inadequate responses were noted in almost all children of 2–3 years and in the majority of the 3–4-year-old children when leading questions were asked by the experimenter. Such responses were sometimes accompanied by a clearly manifested, negative emotional reaction.

In children of the 4–7 age group (with the exception of one child of 4 years, 1 month) no responses inadequate to the action were noted in the first phase. Hence the children of these age groups did not participate in the second series.

The second phase (further exercises with the ball) was conducted only

Table 1—Number of Children Who Gave Answers Inadequate to the Action Performed in Various Series of Experiments

Age of children	FIRST PHASE: Rolling Ball 3 Times		SECOND PHASE: exercises with ball						THIRD PHASE: Final Test	
			After Rolling Ball 20 Times		After Rolling Ball 40 Times		After Rolling Ball 60 Times			
	No. taking part	No. giving inadequate response	No. taking part	No. giving inadequate response	No. taking part	No. giving inadequate response	No. taking part	No. giving inadequate response	No. taking part	No. giving inadequate response
2–3 years	15	14	14	10	10	4	4	—	15	12
3–4 years	15	10	10	4	4	—	—	—	15	10
4–5 years	15	1	1	—	—	—	—	—	15	2
5–6 years	15	—	—	—	—	—	—	—	15	2
6–7 years	15	—	—	—	—	—	—	—	15	—

with those children 2–4 years of age who had given inadequate responses in the first phase. The greatest number of trials needed for obtaining the correct responses occurred in children 2–3 years of age (up to 60 rolls). Fewer trials were needed for children 3–4 years of age (up to 40 rolls).

In the third phase (final test 3–4 hours after completion of the first 2 phases) the number of children answering incorrectly in the 3 older age groups was small (2 children each). In children 2–3 and 3–4 years of age the number of incorrect responses occurring in this phase was almost the same as in the first phase (Table 2).

With the aim of elucidating the regularities of the phenomenon studied, an analysis was made of the quality of the responses of the children and of the changes in the latent periods of these responses to each question. In

Table 2—Dependence of the Character of Children's Responses and the Increase of Latent Periods on the Form of the Questions in the First and Third Series of Experiences

	Answer	Did you just roll the ball?	Did you really just roll the ball?	You didn't roll the ball, did you?	You did not just roll the ball!
		FIRST SERIES			
2–3 years	Correct	15	15	4	1
	Incorrect	—	—	11 (5–7")	14
	Silence	—	—	—	—
3–4 years	Correct	15	6 (5–6")	7	5 (5–6")
	Incorrect	—	4 (5–6")	7	10
	Silence	—	5	1	—
4–5 years	Correct	15	14 (2–4")	14	14 (5–6")
	Incorrect	—	1	1	1
	Silence	—	—	—	—
5–6 years	Correct	15	15 (5–6")	15	15 (3–4")
	Incorrect	—	—	—	—
	Silence	—	—	—	—
6–7 years	Correct	15	15 (3–4")	15	15 (2–3")
	Incorrect	—	—	—	—
	Silence	—	—	—	—
		THIRD SERIES			
2–3 years	Correct	15	15	5	2
	Incorrect	—	—	9 (4–5")	12 (4–5")
	Silence	—	—	1	1
3–4 years	Correct	15	14	6	4
	Incorrect	—	— (5–6")	8 (7–10")	9 (7–10")
	Silence	—	—	1	2
4–5 years	Correct	15	15	14	13
	Incorrect	—	—	1	2 (5–7")
	Silence	—	—	—	—
5–6 years	Correct	15	15	15	13
	Incorrect	—	—	—	2 (1–2")
	Silence	—	—	—	—
6–7 years	Correct	15	15	15	13
	Incorrect	—	—	—	2 (1–2")
	Silence	—	—	—	—

Note: Increase in latent period (in seconds) is noted in parentheses.

the first series, children 2–3 years of age answered the first and second questions correctly; children 3–4 years of age gave answers which were adequate to the action performed only to the first (non-leading) question. To the remaining questions the children gave answers which were inadequate to the action. The greatest number of such answers was evoked by the fourth question. An increase in latency was observed in children 3–7

Table 3—Dependence of the Character of Responses and Increase of Latent Periods of Children's Responses on the Form of the Questions in the Second Series of Experiments

	Answered	Did you just roll the ball?	Did you really just roll the ball?	You didn't roll the ball, did you?	You did not just roll the ball!
No. of children 2–3 yrs. old, who after rolling ball 20 times	Correct	14	14 (3–4")	6	4
	Incorrect	—	—	8 (1–2")	10
	Silent	—	—	—	—
No. of children 2–3 yrs. old, who after rolling ball 40 times	Correct	10	10 (2–3")	7	5
	Incorrect	—	—	3 (2–3")	4 (2–3")
	Silent	—	—	—	1
No. of children 2–4 yrs. old, who after rolling ball 20 times	Correct	10	8	8	6
	Incorrect	—	1	2	4
	Silent	—	1	—	—

Note: Increase in latent period (in seconds) is noted in parentheses.

years who answered adequately, in children 2–3 years who answered the second and fourth questions inadequately, and in children 3–4 years who answered the fourth question inadequately.

In the second phase—in which only children 2–3 and 3–4 years of age who had responded inadequately in the first phase participated—the responses of the children to the experimenter's questions after they had rolled the ball 20 times were of approximately the same character as in the first series. An increase in latency occurred only in children 2–3 years of age whose responses to the second question were appropriate to the action and whose responses to the third question were inappropriate. After rolling the ball 40 times, responses were inadequate only in certain children 2–3 years of age and only to leading questions. After 60 rolls, which was done only with those children 2–3 years of age, there were no negative responses nor did latency increase.

In the third phase (final test, 2–3 hours after conclusion of the first 2 series) children 3–4 years of age gave inadequate responses to leading questions nos. three and four. Also in this phase there first appeared incorrect responses to the fourth question in a few children 4–7 years of age. In all age groups there was some increase in latency of response to the leading questions.

EVALUATION OF RESULTS

The experimental results show that in the first phase of the experiment many of the youngest children reacted to the verbal influence of an adult and gave answers which were inadequate to the action performed. This phenomenon is observed when the action is still inadequately elaborated. After reinforcement of the action the inadequate responses disappear completely. Thus, from comparison of the form of the question and the character of the responses of children in the first and second phases of the experiment it is seen that in children 2–3 years of age with direct and leading questions the responses are often of an echolalic character, i.e., the child in his response repeats what the adult has said. (First question: "Did you roll the ball?" Answer: "Yes, I did.") The latency of these answers is short. The same responses to the questions with the word "really" and without it are evidently explained by the fact that children of this age do not differentiate the two verbal complexes represented in the first and second questions. The meaning of the word "really" is still not understood by them, and hence in the second question, "Did you really roll the ball?" they perceive only the second part—"Did you roll the ball?"

Echolalic responses are also observed to the leading questions. (Third question: "You did not roll the ball, did you?" with interrogative intonation. Answer: "I did not." And especially the fourth question: "You did not roll the ball!" with exclamatory intonation. Answer: "I did not.")

The fact that negative responses to the fourth question are encountered somewhat more often than to the third in the presence of the same content of these leading questions is evidently explained by the greater degree of positiveness of the fourth question (exclamatory) compared with the third (interrogatory). As past studies have shown (Kaverina, 1950; Koltsova, 1953), conditional associations in ontogenesis are elaborated more quickly in response to intonation than to the thought aspect of the word.

Children 3–4 years old answer the third and fourth leading questions in about the same manner. However, there is an increase in the latent period of the response to these questions, which indicates that their responses are no longer purely echolalic.

When in the first and second series all the children gave correct answers to the leading questions, as did also the children 3–4 years of age to questions with the word "really," we may say that the association between the action and the word designating it is adequately consolidated.

Direct questions play a different role. They do not disturb the "action-word" association; rather they reinforce it, making it still more stable. Therefore there were no incorrect responses to the first question in the children 2–4 years of age.

What causes the children to respond inadequately? Very probably the responses of children 2–4 years old which are inadequate to the action performed and which are given under the verbal influence of an adult, depend on a still insufficient concordance between the first and second signal systems in their stabilization and formation. The entire activity of a child of early age is directed toward adults. Starting with the second year of life of the child, the basic method of influencing the child is a verbal one; hence the word of the adult is an especially strong stimulus for children. On the other hand, as a result of their own activity a definite system of associations is formed in children which permits them to reflect adequately the surrounding reality.

In our experiments the verbal reactions of children were conditioned by both these circumstances—the verbal influence of the adult and the consolidated personal action of the child, which gives a stable system of associations between the action and the word designating it. If the action of the child is still not consolidated then the word of the adult which denies this action (leading question) is a very strong stimulus. Hence, in the cortex there is formed a stronger focus of excitation than that which was created from the still unreinforced action of the child. The latter focus of excitation is weak, inadequately concentrated, and therefore the "action-word" association is itself unstable. This leads to inductive inhibition of the weaker focus of excitation by the stronger focus. Thus, a leading question elicits a primitive reaction of the echolalic type, which I. P. Pavlov considered the elementary, ontogenetically earliest verbal association.

Consolidation of the child's action makes the focus of cortical excitation from this action stronger and more concentrated, exceeding in strength the focus of excitation from the verbal action of the adult. Thus, with repeated trials the relative strength of the two foci changes; a strengthening occurs in the focus of excitation because of the child's action. Now the word of the adult does not inhibit the consolidated "action-word" association.

The results of the third phase of the experiment are interesting in this connection because in that phase the majority of children aged 2–4 once again gave the incorrect responses which had previously been removed in the second phase series by reinforcement of the action of rolling the ball. In the older children (4–7 years) incorrect responses in the deferred test were very rare (2 responses in each age group). This fact points to the lesser stability of associations which had been consolidated in our experiments compared with associations which had already been formed and reinforced ontogenetically.

CONCLUSIONS

Analysis of experimental results shows that the character of responses of children 2–7 years old relating to actions performed by them depends to a great degree on the form of the adult's question. Sometimes the verbal influence of the adult, constituting a denial of the action just performed by the child, evokes in the child a response which negates the given action. This phenomenon exists in children 2–4 years old and is absent at older ages (in children 4–7 years old); it occurs because the action of the young child is still inadequately consolidated. Responses of children that are inappropriate to their actions, given under the verbal influence of an adult, are explained by inadequately concordant, unstable interaction of the two signal systems. Inadequate responses to leading questions asked by an adult are the primitive, ontogenetically earliest verbal reactions of the echolalic type. The mechanism behind them is that the focus of excitation created in the cortex by the still unconsolidated "action-word" association is easily inhibited by the stronger cortical focus resulting from the adult's question.

Having the child repeatedly perform an action leads to reinforcement of the "action-word" association. The focus of cortical excitation from the child's own action becomes strong and concentrated, exceeding in strength the focus of excitation stemming from the adult's verbal influence, and therefore cannot be inhibited by this influence. The consequence is an adequate verbal reaction in the child.

SUPPLEMENTARY READINGS

Koltsova, M. M. O vozniknovenii i razvitii vtoroi signalnoi sistemy u rebenka. (The appearance and development of the second signal system in the child.) *Trud. Fiziol. Instit.*, 1949, 4, 49–102.

Luria, A. R. The directive function of speech in development and dissolution. *Word*, 1959, 15, 341–352.

Luria, A. R., & Yudovich, F. *Speech and the development of mental processes in the child*. London: Staples Press, 1957.

Vygotsky, L. S. *Thought and language*. Cambridge, Mass.: M. I. T. Press, 1962.

the young child:

a linguistic genius*

KORNEI CHUKOVSKY

[Authors of poems and stories that will be enjoyed by children must have a deep understanding of the subtle nuances of the language usage and thought processes of the young. They must be able to adopt an expository form that blends the logical and the illogical, the real and the unreal, the factual and the imaginary. Few adults have the talent required for this type of creative writing. The following discussion was written by a master artist in the field of children's literature, Kornei Chukovsky. Over forty million copies of his children's books have been published in the Soviet Union alone, and a large number of them have been translated into and published in several other languages. As may be judged from the following excerpt from his volume *From Two to Five,* here is a children's author who not only listens to children but who also appreciates the subtleties of their efforts to master a language. The scientist who aspires to gain some understanding of the young child's perceptions or cognitive processes does well to listen closely to the child's verbalizations.]

FROM CREATIVITY TO IMITATION

"My daddy himself told me this . . ."

"My mommy herself told me that . . ."

"But my daddy is himselfer than your mommy—my daddy is much more himselfer . . ."

. . . .

"Isn't there something to eat in the cupboard?"

"There's only a small piece of cake, and it's middle-aged."

. . . .

"Can't you see? I'm barefoot all over!"

. . . .

"Daddy, you look how your pants are sulking!"

. . . .

It seems to me that, beginning with the age of two, every child be-

* From K. Chukovsky. *From two to five.* (Translated and edited by Miriam Morton.) Berkeley: Univer. Calif. Press, 1963. Pp. 25–32. (With permission.)

comes for a short period of time a linguistic genius. It is a pleasure to find out from young kids that a bald man has a barefoot head, that a mint candy makes a draft in the mouth, that the husband of a grasshopper is a daddy-hopper. Later, beginning with the age of five to six, this talent begins to fade. There is no trace left in the eight-year-old of this creativity with words, since the need for it has passed; by this age the child already has fully mastered the basic principles of his native language. If his former talent for word invention and construction had not abandoned him, he would, even by the age of ten, eclipse any of us with his suppleness and brilliance of speech. Not in vain did Leo Tolstoy, addressing himself to adults, write: ". . . (the child) realizes the laws of word formation better than you because no one so often thinks up new words as children."

Even the original words invented by children, which do not yet exist in the language, seem almost real. They could have come into being, and their absence from the language seems to be merely fortuitous. One somehow reacts to such words as to old acquaintances, feeling that one has already heard them somewhere, at some time. I heard, for instance, a three-year-old in the Crimea spontaneously use the word "bulleting," and he "bulleted" from his tiny rifle all day long, not even suspecting that this word has been thus used for centuries in the far away Don region.

Having been told by a little boy that a big horse "hoofed" (kopytnula) him, I used this word, "hoofed," at the first opportunity in a conversation with my young daughter. Not only did she understand at once the meaning of the word, but she did not even suspect that it did not exist, for it seemed to her completely normal. And, in a sense, such words *are* normal; at times they are even more "normal" than conventional ones. Why, one might ask, do we call a full-sized horse a "horsie" when speaking to a small child? To a tiny tot a horse must seem enormous. Can we expect him to use a diminutive word for so huge a creature? Sensing the falseness of this diminutive, the child transforms the word "horsie" into "big-horse" [*loshada*], thus underscoring the hugeness of the animal. [The Russian word for an average-sized horse is *loshad*.]

Of course, when we speak of the creative powers of the young child, of his keen sensitivity to language, of his genius, we do not consider these words sentimental hyperboles. But we must not, just the same, forget that the basis for all the linguistic aptitude attributed to the child "from two to five" is imitation, since every new word he invents he creates in accordance with the norms made known to him through adult speech. However, he does not copy adults as simply (and as docilely) as it seems to the casual observer. In another section of this chapter, "Children as 'Critics' of Adult Speech," a large amount of evidence is available to show that in the process of assimilating his native spoken language the child, from the early age of two, introduces a critical evaluation, analysis, and control.

To be sure, many neologisms of the child are often evidence of his inability to make himself conversant, in his early attempts to speak the language, with this or that exception to a grammatical norm. At times a word or a locution "invented" by the child, which seems to us so original, has occurred to him actually only because he has applied to it, too directly, some "grammatical" rule, unaware of any exception to the rule. Despite this, I am convinced of the tremendous speech-giftedness of the preschool child.

This giftedness consists not only in his early ability to classify word endings, prefixes, and suffixes, a process he accomplishes unconsciously in his two-year-old mind, but also in the divination with which he chooses them when he creates a new word, imitating and using for such a word an appropriate model. Imitation itself is in this way a creative act.

It is frightening to think what an enormous number of grammatical forms are poured over the poor head of the young child. And he, as if it were nothing at all, adjusts to all this chaos, constantly sorting out into rubrics the disorderly elements of the words he hears, without noticing, as he does this, his gigantic effort. If an adult had to master so many grammatical rules within so short a time, his head would surely burst—a mass of rules mastered so lightly and so freely by the two-year-old "linguist." The labor he thus performs at this age is astonishing enough, but even more amazing and unparalled is the ease with which he does it.

In truth, the young child is the hardest mental toiler on our planet. Fortunately, he does not even suspect this.

We have said earlier that by the time the child reaches his eighth year his keen sensitivity to his language is dulled. However, it does not follow that his linguistic development suffers to any extent from this loss. Having lost his recent giftedness to improvise original word structures, he replaces this lack a hundredfold with valuable new qualities of his linguistic growth. The linguistic work of the child has now switched to new rails. Using his achievements of the earlier period, he now equips himself for more intricate and varied communication with others.

It has been established for a long time that at the age of about one year the child knows less than ten words; at the end of two years his vocabulary has grown to two hundred and fifty or three hundred words, and by the end of his third year it is in the thousands—that is, in only a year's time the child builds up his basic word "reservoir," and after this accumulation of new words proceeds much more slowly. The same is true of the grammatical forms that the child learns in the same period. I once tried to make a list of these forms (declensions, conjugations, the use of prefixes and suffixes). I noted down not less than seventy. Most of these "generalizations" that are formed in the child's brain forever, for his entire life, are established between the ages of three and four, when the linguistic giftedness seems to be particularly strong.

CHILDREN AS "CRITICS" OF ADULT SPEECH

Unfortunately, we are not yet rid of those "theoreticians" who continue to maintain that in respect to language the child is a mere automaton who imitates adult speech without discrimination or analysis. This notion is declared even in learned articles—it is thus "declared" precisely because it cannot be proved. One need only observe closely the speech of young children to notice that they imitate at the same time as they examine and analyze. Is there a child who has reached his fifth year without having repeatedly bothered his mother with questions that revealed his strict and even disparaging criticism of the way adults use certain words and expressions?

"Why do you say penknife? It should be pencil-knife," a little boy objected.

When their grandmother said that winter was coming soon, her grandchildren laughed and wanted to know:

"Do you mean that winter has legs?"

The logic of four-year-old rationalists is merciless. They admit no exceptions. Every liberty taken with words seems to them arbitrary. One might say in conversation, for instance:

"I'm dying to hear that concert!"

"Then why don't you die?" a child would ask sarcastically.

A saleswoman said one day after returning home from her job:

"The devil only knows what goes on in our store."

"Well, what goes on there?" her husband asked.

Their five-year-old son objected to the question and remarked instructively:

"She just said that the devil only knows. Is mama a devil? She doesn't know!"

The fact is that adults think in terms of allegories and metaphors, whereas children think in terms of objects perceived in their world of objects. Their thinking is limited during the first years to images of things; this is why they object so strongly to our symbolism.

A woman, for example, asked her four-year-old Natasha:

"Tell me, what does it mean to say that a person is trying to drown another in a spoonful of water [a Russian expression]?"

"What did you say? In what kind of spoon? Say that again."

The mother repeated the adage.

"That's impossible!" Natasha said categorically. "It can never happen!"

Right there and then she demonstrated the physical impossibility of such an act; she grabbed a spoon and quickly placed it on the floor.

"Look, here am I," and she stood on the spoon. "All right, drown me. There isn't enough room for a whole person—all of him will remain on top. . . . Look for yourself . . . the foot is much larger than the spoon!"

And Natasha expressed scorn for such an absurd idea conceived by grownups, saying:

"Let's not talk about it any more—it's such nonsense."

Other children, endowed with a sense of humor, often pretend that they cannot understand this or that adult idiom and try to "train" us to observe more closely the rules that we ourselves have taught them. If you complain in the presence of a child that your head is splitting, he might say:

"Then why can't I hear it split?"—he would thus underscore his negative attitude to the odd way adults express their thoughts metaphorically, a way so unlike the obvious.

After a long separation, a mother said to her little girl:

"How thin you've become, Nadiusha. All that's left of you is one little nose."

"Well, Mommie, did I have more than one nose before you left?"

When a child heard that a woman "fell into a faint," she asked, with a noticeable twinkle in her eye:

"Who dragged her out of it?"

Her father said to Maniusha: "Come on, skate out of my room! I have work to do." ["Skate out" is a polite, Russian way of saying "Scram!"]

"I'll not skate out—I have no roller skates."

Playing with his son's toy soldiers, the father suggested that one of them would stand watch. They boy picked up the toy soldier and, laughing, ran to the wall clock to place it there, knowing quite well what "stand watch" meant.

However, these polemics with adult speech are not always carried on in jest. I know a four-year-old child who gets furious whenever she hears an adult speak about ladyfinger biscuits:

"They are not made out of fingers, they're made out of dough!"

Most often the criticism is caused by the child's confusion about the way adults use words. The child whom we ourselves have trained to see sense in every word cannot forgive us the "senselessness" that we introduce into some of our expressions. It is difficult for the preschool child to understand even simple idioms and figurative expressions.

"I'll never go to school," five-year-old Seriozha announced. "They cut [flunk] children there."

A visitor asked about his baby sister: "Does your little Irishka go to sleep with the roosters?"

"No, she doesn't go to bed with the roosters. They scratch! She sleeps in her cradle."

At times this childish inability to understand figurative expressions causes adults considerable embarrassment.

Four-year-old Olia, who came with her mother to visit a Moscow aunt, looked closely at this aunt and her husband as they were all having tea, and soon remarked with obvious disappointment:

"Mama! You said that uncle always sits on Aunt Aniuta's neck but he has been sitting on a chair all the time we've been here."

I am sorry, but I cannot repeat what the mother said in reply.

This reminds me of an incident in an American family:

"Betty, why didn't you provide a knife and fork for Mr. White?"

"Because I thought he didn't need them—daddy said he ate like a horse."

An exasperated mother said to her son: "Some day you'll lose your head, so help me God!"

"I'll never lose *my* head," was the reassuring reply, "I'll find it and pick it up."

The child reacts with such innocence to idioms because he takes them literally.

A critical attitude toward the meaning and the use of words is observable not only in gifted children but in almost all children. And the same criticisms and objections and the same word adaptation and word inventions recur among children in different geographic regions and in different generations.

SUPPLEMENTARY READINGS

Berko, J., The child's learning of English morphology. *Word,* 1958, 14, 150–177.

Brown, R. W., & Hildum, D. C. Expectancy and the perception of syllables. *Language,* 1956, 32, 411–419.

Werner, H., & Kaplan, E. Development of word meaning through verbal context: An experimental study. *J. Psychol.,* 1950, 29, 251–257.

the preschool child

learns to read and write

in the autotelic

responsive environment*

Omar Khayyam Moore

[In the conventional schools of our culture there is usually a standard curriculum that is geared to the interests and abilities of the mythical "average child." Pupils whose interests and abilities fall outside the middle of the very wide range of human talents are usually taught in special classes for "slow learners," "intellectually gifted," and so on. This is admittedly a compromise solution to a very difficult problem. Dr. Moore presents a fresh and interesting approach to the solution of this vexing problem. He has proposed what he calls an "autotelic responsive environment" as being optimal for the acquisition of new language skills. This environment is designed to maximize motivation for language learning: It permits the learner free exploration, self-pacing, full use of his capacity for discovering relations, possibilities for interconnected discoveries, and immediate information about the consequences of his actions. That part of Dr. Moore's work that has attracted the greatest attention is his "talking typewriter"; however, he is quick to point out that special instrumentation of this type is only a very small part of his total program. He proposes to use mechanical devices as teaching aids only when they contribute uniquely and significantly to the overall educational effort. Unobtrusive guidance of the teacher or supervisor is emphasized throughout his special program, and a unique plan for the optimal development of each pupil is the primary focus of his interest.]

In every society there are those who fail to learn the things which are held to be essential for carrying out the role of a competent adult, or who learn so slowly that they are generally out of phase with the age-graded societal demands imposed upon them. Slow learners are apt to be problems to

* From O. K. Moore, *Autotelic responsive environments and exceptional children.* Responsive Environments Foundation Incorporated, 1963. (With permission.)

themselves and to their friends. It is recognized, in scientific circles at least, that there are many and diverse causes for failure to learn at the socially prescribed rate: brain damage, emotional disturbance, social-cultural deprivation, and the like.

What is not perhaps so generally recognized is that prodigies are sometimes out of phase with societal demands also; they tend to make people as uncomfortable as retarded children do. Both retarded children and prodigies unwittingly violate social expectations—they need help if they are to reach their full potential. Both the ultrarapid and the ultraslow are *exceptional* children. The main topic of this paper is to describe some methods whereby the acquisition of complex skills can be accelerated, for both ultraslow and ultrarapid learners.

For a number of years my staff and I have been conducting studies of early learning in prenursery, nursery, kindergarten and first grades, where children are in the process of acquiring complex symbolic skills. In the course of this work I formulated the notion of a responsive environment and decided to act on the assumption that an *autotelic responsive environment* is optimal for acquiring such skills. I will now try to make clear just what this assumption means.

I have defined a *responsive environment* as one which satisfies the following conditions:

(1) It permits the learner to explore freely.
(2) It informs the learner immediately about the consequences of his actions.
(3) It is self-pacing, i.e., events happen within the environment at a rate determined by the learner.
(4) It permits the learner to make full use of his capacity for discovering relations of various kinds.
(5) Its structure is such that the learner is likely to make a series of interconnected discoveries about the physical, cultural or social world.

My colleague, Alan Ross Anderson, and I have defined an activity as *autotelic* (Anderson & Moore, 1959) if engaging in it is done for its own sake rather than for obtaining rewards or avoiding punishments that have no inherent connection with the activity itself. The distinction between autotelic and nonautotelic activities is somewhat vague, but it can be applied in some cases without difficulty.

LABORATORY — PHYSICAL DESCRIPTION*

The Responsive Environments Laboratory is located in Hamden Hall Country Day School, Hamden, Connecticut, a few yards from the Hamden

* The Responsive Environments Laboratory described here served as the model for four other laboratories. Two of the laboratories operate under my personal direction —the others work cooperatively with me.

In order to avoid confusion, everything that is said here pertains to the Hamden Hall Laboratory.

Hall preschool classrooms. It consists of two adjoining prefabricated metal sheds, each 20' x 40', set on concrete foundations. One shed is windowless and the other has windows only in a small office area; they are centrally heated and air conditioned.

The parts of the laboratory used by children are windowless—windows are an open invitation to digress. The absence of windows also increases the children's sense of privacy. (It is important to note that children spend only a small fraction of their day in this laboratory. It is not suggested here that gay designs and intriguing novelties are not appropriate in many other contexts.) One-way windows, camera ports, semiautomatic motion-picture controls, and the like, make it possible to observe and document children's behavior without intruding upon them.

The staff seeks to make the laboratory a child-centered milieu. Even the introduction of a child to the laboratory is done by another child rather than an adult. A child guide takes the newcomer through the laboratory (equipment is turned off—the introduction to its operation is made later). Sometimes three introductory visits are needed before a newcomer seems to be at ease—although one visit is sufficient for most children. The guide also explains some of the relevant rules: (1) that he need not come to the laboratory unless he wants to, (2) that he can leave whenever he wishes, (3) that he must leave when his time is up (30 minutes maximum stay), (4) that he need not explain his coming or going, (5) that he go to the booth to which he is assigned for the day, (6) that if he says he wants to leave, or starts to leave, he can come back again the next day (but not the same day). Newcomers have the opportunity to explore every nook and corner of the laboratory. The guide watches this activity but does not interfere. After a while newcomers seem to feel satisfied that they have seen everything and are ready to leave.

The laboratory staff is carefully instructed about treating the children. The import of the rules is that we want children to initiate activities. The staff is to respond to them rather than to teach them. Those who are in daily interaction with the children are not permitted to see the background information gathered by the project's professional staff; for example, the operating personnel do not know IQ test scores. Operating personnel are randomly assigned to booths every day. (There are two kinds of booths, automated and nonautomated. In nonautomated booths an adult is with the child.) Every effort is made to maintain a setting in which "kibitzing" by parents and friends of the children is virtually impossible. (There is a rule against their visiting and the physical arrangement ensures privacy vis-a-vis the "significant persons" in the child's life.)

The Hamden Hall children leave their classrooms (nursery, kinder-garten and first-grade) to come to the laboratory every school day. When it is a child's turn to come, his classroom teacher lets him know. He then either accepts or rejects his turn for the day. If he decides to come he takes his "pass" and goes by himself the few yards to the laboratory where he is checked in and goes to the booth assistant to whom he has been assigned. One of the most remarkable things about this environment is that, day in and day out, children elect to come to it—sometimes several months go by without one child of the current group (which numbers 60) refusing his turn. However, it frequently happens that a child does not want to leave when his time is up—in which case he is gently picked up and told that another child is waiting.

My objective in formulating a curriculum was to design an environment, within the microworld of the booths, in which children would learn their native language in its written form. This enterprise presupposes that, in the broadest sense, spoken English and written English are isomorphic. From this standpoint, we can think of written English as visible speech and spoken English as audible writing. It is true that written English is a very imperfect phonetic transcription of speech; nevertheless, in planning this environment, I decided to work on the assumption that the spoken and written forms of English are *sufficiently* isomorphic to enable children to find for themselves some set of rules which would permit them to move back and forth between these two linguistic forms.

Speaking and writing are active processes and listening and reading are passive ones. An attempt is made to tie each of these four activities (or passivities) to the others, not only maintaining a balance between active and passive processes, but also avoiding the pitfalls of under-emphasizing or overemphasizing any one of them at the expense of the others. The overall objective is to develop higher-order intellectual abilities which may be thought of as ranging over this complex of linguistic processes.

In order to determine whether such overall abilities are developing and at the same time, to facilitate their development, it is necessary to set some task for the children which involves all four of the processes. There are many jobs which would do the work. The one which was chosen as a part of the laboratory curriculum was publishing a newspaper. The first-grade class publishes its own newspaper (there are also contributions by nursery and kindergarten children) and the four processes (speaking, writing, listening and reading) are subordinate to the superordinate skill of *publishing a newspaper.* A child may begin a newspaper story by speaking into a microphone; later, he will type his own story from dictation—this means that he goes directly from the spoken word to the written word. After he has completed his transcription he may then read it critically before turning it over to one of the other children who is an editor. The editor first proofreads the copy, perhaps reading it aloud to a fellow editor, and then the suggested changes are discussed with the author. Then the children type it on stencils along with other stories. Finally, they mimeograph, collate, staple and distribute the paper. If they wish to discuss the newspaper in their regular classroom, they may do so with their teacher's permission. It is also permissible to take the newspaper home where it is sometimes subject to further discussion.

LEARNING IN THE AUTOTELIC RESPONSIVE
ENVIRONMENT

PHASE 1. FREE EXPLORATION

Now let us turn our attention to the interior of a booth and imagine that a child, already introduced to the laboratory in the manner previously explained, is ready for his first booth session. This is the beginning of Phase 1, *Free Exploration*. For convenience of exposition pretend that he is to begin learning in an automated booth. The booth assistant helps him get into the elevated chair, turns one switch, tells the child to enjoy himself and to raise his hand if he wants anything. Without further comment the assistant leaves the booth, closes the booth door and then goes to a control panel mounted on the exterior wall of the booth, presses appropriate buttons, and begins to watch the child through a one-way window located just below the control panel (Fig. 1).

The child is alone in the booth confronted with what may appear to him to be a typewriter with colored keys. Prior to entering the booth his fingernails have been painted with nontoxic water colors. There is a match between the nail colors and the colored typewriter keys so that striking keys with matching fingers constitutes correct fingering. Also, there is a noticeable difference in pressure between the left-hand and the right-hand keys to help the child orient his hands. Behind the keyboard is a lucite housing which permits him to see everything in front of him, but which keeps his fingers out of the moving parts of the typewriter. Whether or not he believes that the object in front of him is some kind of typewriter, as a matter of fact, he is in charge of much more than an electric typewriter—he is at the controls of a computer in-put and read-out device, three distinct memory systems, an audio-recording system, and two visual exhibition systems, all of which are integrated by a central electronic logic and control system. Nevertheless, the operation of this complex instrument is under his management.

Of course, not all of the abilities of the instrument are needed for the child's first session. The booth assistant has set the instrument so that the child can explore the keyboard freely. Whenever a key is struck, E.R.E.* types the letter, in large type, and pronounces the name of the character that has been typed. The "reaction time" of E.R.E. time to a key operation averages 1/10th of a second. When a key has been depressed and released no key can be operated for about one second—this gives E.R.E. time to pronounce the name of the character. No two keys can be depressed simultaneously. This makes it impossible to jam keys or to garble pronunciations. The moment any given pronunciation is completed, the keyboard is automatically unlocked so that the child can go on exploring.

---

* E.R.E., the Edison Responsive Environment, is our name for the equipment. It is the product of a three-year collaborative effort with an engineering team of the Thomas A. Edison Research Laboratory of West Orange, New Jersey, a division of the McGraw-Edison Company.

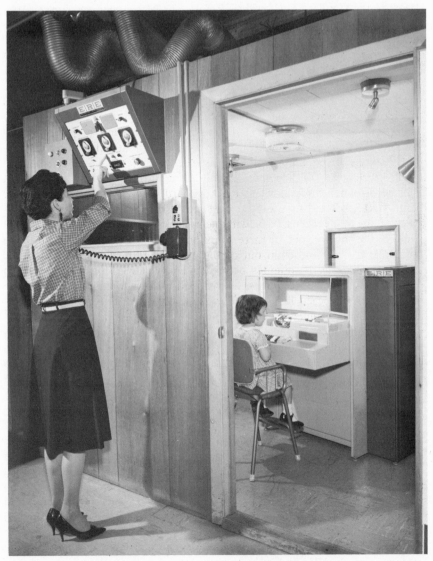

Figure 1—The child is shown at her "typewriter" while the booth assistant observes her through a one-way window.

Because the standard keyboard of E.R.E. has both upper and lower cases, and the young child probably does not know this, there are small lights next to the upper and lower-case keys to show which case is operative. If the child were to play by himself with an ordinary typewriter he might get "stuck" at the end of a line because he does not know about the carriage return. E.R.E. automatically returns the carriage at the end of a line even though there is a carriage return key whose function the child will catch on to sooner or later. His exploration will not be interrupted by using up a sheet of paper—E.R.E. has a fan-folded tape of paper several thousand feet long. It should also be mentioned that E.R.E. is rugged—it withstands the pounding it sometimes receives.

Returning to the hypothetical child, the intriguing question is, What will he do when he is alone at the keyboard of the "talking typewriter"? Until he strikes the first key he does not even know that the typewriter talks. One thing we can say with near certainty about our hypothetical child is that he will not sit there for a half an hour simply looking at the instrument. Only one child out of the 102 children whom I had studied sat for as long as 10 minutes before striking a key. Most children begin immediately using fingers, fists, elbows and an occasional nose. There are children who proceed in a very thoughtful way; looking, listening, repeating what the instrument says, reflecting—in brief, they explore systematically. Some notice at once the relation between their colored fingernails and the colored keys and painstakingly match fingers to keys. If, at first, a finger is wayward, they use their other hand to guide it. Some children go on exploring for their full 30 minutes; others raise their hands and want to leave after a few minutes.

A daily record is kept of each child's performance in the laboratory. Some parts of this cumulative record are quite objective—E.R.E., for example, keeps track of the time the child spends in the booth and his stroke count, i.e., the number of times he depresses keys. Other aspects of the record are less objective—for instance, booth assistants' notes about a child's attitude. There is a daily staff conference at which each child's performance is reviewed. It is the laboratory supervisor's responsibility to decide when a child is beginning to lose interest in any given phase of the curriculum. There are children who will go on happily in Phase 1, Free Exploration, for a number of weeks, whereas others' interest in this phase declines rapidly after as few as two sessions. Sooner or later every child's interest in Phase 1 will wane (at least every child the laboratory has encountered behaved this way) and before his interest completely disappears, he must be shifted to the next phase. If a child were permitted to completely exhaust his interest, he might very well not return to the laboratory. Quite clearly, the decision as to when to shift a child from one phase to another still is a matter of experience and judgment. In the early days of this research I had to make this decision. Later, I trained supervisors who now are fully capable of performing this task. For the most part, the more objective indicators of declining interest are a sufficient basis for judgment

—for example, a child's sessions become markedly shorter and his stroke count drops off. Sometimes a child will simply say that he is tired of what he is doing—his opinion counts! As a general rule, it is safer to err on the side of shifting the child too soon. It will be made clear below that explicit provision is made for regressing from advanced phases to more elementary ones, and since no significant persons in his life are there to see this regression, there is little stigma attached to it. Every child I have studied has regressed from time to time. The children call Phase 1 (Free Exploration) "plain typing." It is not unusual for even a gifted child to say with a little laugh, "Today I just want to plain type."

PHASE 2. SEARCH AND MATCH

When the laboratory supervisor makes the decision to shift a child from Phase 1 to the next phase, the learner rceives no warning—he has to discover for himself that he is playing a new game with new rules. Phase 2 is called *Search and Match*. In order to understand what this involves, let us imagine a close-up view of E.R.E. "opened up." There is a picture of a barn on a rear-view projection screen—the projector is loaded through an open panel to its right. To the left of the barn is an illuminated rectangular window—exhibitor cards can be inserted into this space through the open door on top. On the upper right side of E.R.E. is a triangular shaped open panel—this exposes controls for some of E.R.E.'s functions which are set by the booth assistant.

In Phase 2 the exhibitor system on which the picture of a barn is projected is not used. The only new thing about this phase, in terms of visual display, is the use of the rectangular window. In this window characters can be exhibited in four different ways: (1) one character at a time with a red arrow pointing down to it; (2) a cumulative exhibit in which the red arrow points to a newly exposed character while all previously exposed characters on the same line remain visible; (3) all characters on one line are visible with the red arrow pointing to the one to be typed; and (4) all characters on the four lines in the rectangular window are exposed, again with the red arrow pointing to the one to be typed.

In Phase 2, unlike Phase 1, E.R.E. takes the initiative in starting the game. All typewriter characters appear in the rectangular exhibitor window one at a time in random order. When a character appears with the red arrow pointing to it, E.R.E. automatically locks the keyboard with the exception of the appropriate matching key and pronounces the name of the character. If the child wants to get a response from E.R.E., he must find the right key. As soon as he strikes the matching key which causes the character to be typed, E.R.E. repronounces the character and then covers it up before exposing a new one. The game becomes a little more difficult when the new character is in a different case—under this circumstance, E.R.E. first says "upper case" or "lower case" (as the case may be), the appropriate case light flickers, and the keyboard must be changed to the proper case (when this is done it repronounces it) before the matching character is named by E.R.E. and can be struck by the child. It should be mentioned that if a child is fast enough at pressing the appropriate key, he can cause E.R.E. to speed up by omitting redundant pronunciations. If a child's attention has wandered so that he missed the first pronunciation, or if he has forgotten it, there is a repeat cycle which the booth assistant can start, using a delay appropriate for the given child. A dial can be set which will delay E.R.E.'s repronunciation in order to give the child a chance to speak first. E.R.E. is not restricted to pronouncing the names of characters—it also can give phonetic values for them (or, for the linguistic purist, hints as to phonetic values).

What has just been described is the simplest version of Phase 2, Search and Match. As interest wanes in this first version of Phase 2, the booth assistant can make the game more challenging in many ways. For example, the assistant can cause E.R.E. to omit its first pronunciation of characters, or the second, or both. The window display can be changed to show characters cumulatively, one line at a time, or four lines at a time. A blank card can be used in the window so that the match is solely between pronunciations and keys.

I have found that adults, as well as children, like to play with E.R.E. in both Phase 1, Free Exploration, and the various versions of Phase 2, Search and Match. These activities are especially interesting to adults when E.R.E. is switched to a foreign language—one unfamiliar to the players. Of course, for children who are learning to read, the written form of English is a new language. Both children and adults discover that they always can succeed in finding the appropriate key in Search and Match by the simple-minded expedient of trying each key. This is a tedious and boring way to go at it on a continuing basis; both children and adults prefer to learn the characters.

PHASE 3. WORD CONSTRUCTION

When a child has eliminated nearly all of the "search" from the Search and Match game, it is time to shift to Phase 3 of the curriculum, *Word Construction*. There are two forms of this game. One form leads to reading, the other to writing, i.e., writing in the sense of composing original stories. We will designate the former as "WC-Reading" (Word Construction-Reading) and the latter as "WC-Writing" (Word Construction-Writing). When a child has been shifted to Phase 3 he alternates during his booth sessions between these two forms of the game. Let us take up WC-Reading first.

Word construction-reading. Up to this point, the child has been dealing exclusively with the building blocks or primitive elements of the written language. He has been exposed to and can discriminate among the basic set of elements from which all meaningful written expressions are formed. He is in a position to begin to get some sense of the formation rules of the written language. Now other of E.R.E.'s abilities can be brought into play.

Imagine that a child, who has become quick at finding individual characters, is confronted without notice with several of them at a time, isolated either by a margin and a space or by spaces. For instance, the first letters might be *b-a-r-n*. So, the child types *b-a-r-n*. E.R.E. pronounces these letters before and after each is struck and then, following the pronunciation of *n,* it calls for a space. A light flickers just under the space bar, and after the bar is pressed, E.R.E. says, "Space, *b-a-r-n,* barn." E.R.E. may also exhibit a barn on the projector as shown in Picture 3. (As a matter of fact, pictures have been used very sparingly because they can be quite misleading in the early phases of learning to handle written symbols. The referent of many important words such as "if," "then," "either," "or," "some," etc., cannot be pictured in the same way that the referent of the word "barn" can be. Other words which are relational, but not obviously so, such as "mother," "father," "sister," etc., are not as easily denoted through pictures as some writers of children's primers seem to think. The use of pictures comes into its own when E.R.E. is "teaching" foreign languages or in Phase 4 where content, e.g., maps for geography, is important.)

From the standpoint of planning the curriculum, WC-Reading offers an indefinitely large number of choices with respect to the selection of a beginning or basic vocabulary. The question is, What words should come first? Faced with the problem of selection, I preferred a direct solution, namely, to choose those words which are constituents of interesting stories —that is, stories which have proved to be intriguing to children and adults over a long period of time, for example, *Aesop's Fables.* Many children can be expected to have lost interest in WC-R long before they have mastered a vocabulary large enough to enable them to read a wide variety of stories. Therefore, it is essential to be able to shift them to at least some stories, but they only can do this if they have mastered enough of the words to get started reading them. If the stories are of some intellectual and aesthetic value, it is highly probable that the words out of which they are composed will offer a sufficient basis for making sound inferences about the relations between letters and sets of letters, on the one hand, and appropriate verbalizations, on the other.

Word construction-writing. The form of the Word Construction game explained above is somewhat arbitrary from a child's standpoint. The experimenter has decided, in advance, what is good for him. It is especially important, from the point of view of sustaining children's interest, to let them take the initiative. It is also important to see to it that at times there is an almost perfect correspondence between their verbal skills and the written symbols with which they will be dealing. WC-Writing serves these purposes. The first step in this activity is to have the child go to the Transfer Room where he is encouraged to talk—he may talk about anything he pleases—and everything he says is recorded. Later, an analysis is made of his utterances, and a list is compiled consisting of those words which are constituents of coherent statements on some topic in which he was engrossed. The next step is to program this word list in E.R.E. The child is virtually certain to find some of his own words meaningful.

An alternative version of WC-Writing involves the use of a standard recording-reproducing unit attached to E.R.E. or to an electric typewriter. This version does not require programming. The child simply talks into a microphone and then takes his own dictation, word by word. In this version of the game, he responds to his own voice. Interestingly enough, from a social-psychological perspective, some children reject their own voice, but will type other children's dictation. Some three-year-olds have learned to be very skillful in taking dictation.

This second version of WC-Writing eliminates the presentation of written symbols, since the child goes directly from verbal utterances to the corresponding written symbols. Visitors who have watched this process are often surprised by children's ability to spell new words that are non-phonetic or markedly irregular. Indeed, this is extraordinary! I have concluded that there must be some subtle lawfulness holding between the spoken and written forms of English; otherwise young children would not spell as well as they do in this version of WC-Writing. This should give pause to enthusiasts for spelling reform. In any case, this relation seems worthy of serious study.

PHASE 4. READING AND WRITING

Anyone who has followed children's progress from *Free Exploration* to *Search and Match* and on through *Word Construction* easily can see that the shift to Phase 4 comes very naturally. E.R.E. is at its best here. It can read a sentence, a paragraph, or tell a story before or after a child types, while at the same time it can continue to respond to individual characters and words. In sum, it can deal with higher-order units while exercising all of the abilities previously described with reference to the earlier learning sequences.

E.R.E., of course, can ask questions, just as teachers do. The questions may pertain to what is visually exhibited in the rectangular window or on the projection screen—the questions may call for subtle interpretations. Answers can either be typed out or expressed verbally on E.R.E.'s own recording-reproducing unit.

The material programed for E.R.E. can be as banal as the dullest courses in school or it can be as stimulating as the best of new programs, for example, some in modern mathematics or science. (It should be noted that E.R.E. can handle many aspects of mathematics and of science programs—numbers and some arithmetic symbols are on the keyboard.)

Every effort is made to select materials which give children a chance to make imaginative interpretations. As a general principle, it seems advisable to select materials which permit several levels of interpretation. A good case in point is Alice's Adventures in Wonderland. Retarded, normal, and gifted children can all begin reading this story with enjoyment just because it starts off with a little girl and an extraordinary rabbit.

Even though gifted children like the manifest content of Alice's adventures, at the same time, they can begin to get glimpses of deeper meanings. A serious objection to many stories found in beginning readers is that they confine children to one interpretation since the manifest content of such stories is all there is to them.

It is in Phase 4 that the methodology presented in this paper must come to terms with the traditional school curriculum. The bridging mechanism between the laboratory booths and the school class-room is the Laboratory's Transfer Room. Here, children who have been working alone have an opportunity to engage in cooperative activities, for example, publishing a newspaper, under the guidance of a teacher. Discipline emerges from the interaction of the children with each other.

When children go to first grade, having reached Phase 4 both in reading and composing original stories, a new curriculum is needed. Most of the things which ordinarily are taught in first grade lie far behind them. (This year at the end of first grade, the Hamden Hall Country Day School children who had been in the program at least two years, read, on the average according to the Metropolitan Achievement Test, at the beginning sixth-grade level.) Their competence in composing original stories can be judged by examining their newspaper, and, in conclusion, I have included a few examples of the children's stories for the newspaper. They clearly demonstrate the originality and skill with which young children can use written English.

FIRST GRADE

Camping in Maine (by Tamara Plakins). We are going to Maine, and we are going camping. I think the whole family is going. We have a dog who barks at strangers; we hope he can come too. We hope to live in a lean-to. A lean-to is a kind of a cave, only there are no bears in it. We will have a lot of fun!

KINDERGARTEN

Mother (by Helen Greenspan). Mother is well now. The cast is off her leg. Now she can drive me to school. I am glad.

Susan squirted me (by Pam Malley). My friend Susan squirted me with water on my new dress. Susan had to put her head down.

NURSERY SCHOOL

Fishing (by Edgar Smith). Taffy and Marmalade and the mouse went fishing.

Typing (by Larry Batter). I want to type like my brother. It is fun typing like my brother. He types in script. I love my family.

Lisa (by Lisa Carpenter). Lisa has two cats.

Pam (by Melanie Canadeo). Pam, you could be a nurse someday. But when you be a nurse, you can not scream like you do now.

Fishing (by Larry Batter). I went fishing with my father and my brother and we caught a goldfish and a whale.

Radishes (by James Taylor). I have radishes to plant today.

I Like School (by Carissa Whitcomb). I paint at Sharon's house. I like Ricky. I like God. He makes us healthy.

Feeding an Ape (by April Palm). Come Ape, come to April. April wants to feed you.

Baby (by Melanie Canadeo).

> Baby, baby
> You're the best.
> Do you like
> Your baby nest?

SUPPLEMENTARY READINGS

Jeffrey, W. E. The effects of verbal and non-verbal responses in mediating an instrumental act. *J. exp. Psychol.,* 1953, 45, 327–333.

Staats, D. K., & Staats, A. W. Meaning established by classical conditioning. *J. exp. Psychol.,* 1957, 54, 74–80.

Terman, L. M. An experiment in infant education. *J. appl. Psychol.,* 1918, 2, 219–228.

syntactic structures

in the language

of children*

PAULA MENYUK

[It is both amusing and instructive to observe the growing child's efforts to master the verbal arts necessary for acceptable communicative skills in a civilized society. For a long time it has seemed clear to perceptive observers that the child learns this art by something more than sheer imitation of a rote-learning type. At a very early age the young preschool-aged child produces phrases and other syntactic structures that lead observers to infer that he is utilizing his own set of transformation rules. This inference is reinforced when one observes the young child's redundant use of conflicting rules, as in the phrase "he stooded up." During recent years many linguists have developed elaborate logical models for the analysis of the syntactic structures found in language usage. The model developed by Dr. Chomsky has proved to be particularly useful in linguistic analysis and has helped to create an area of psycholinguistics in which psychologists have attempted to identify some of the antecedent developmental and learning conditions for certain stages of language growth. In the present report, Dr. Menyuk, of Massachusetts Institute of Technology, has used Chomsky's model of syntactic structures as a schema for analyzing the verbalizations of preschool and first grade children. She found that all the basic structures used by adults to generate their sentences were found in the grammar of nursery school and first grade children. As might be expected, she also found that more of the nursery school children omitted obligatory rules in their verbalizations. It is of some interest that her findings have confirmed those of an earlier study by Dr. Mildred Templin in noting no sex differences in these aspects of language usage. For readers with no previous background in modern linguistic analysis the examples in the materials appended to this report provide an introduction to the fundamentals of one of the modern linguistic models.]

Any technique used to describe a child's grammar must permit us to (a) examine language at particular times in its development as a self-contained

* From P. Menyuk. Syntactic structures in the language of children. *Child Development*, 1963, 34, 407–422. (With permission.)

system and (b) describe the changing processes of this system as the child matures. Such a technique is provided by a generative model of syntactic structures. Although a description of the syntactic structures in the child's language does not give a total account of his language development, it may go beyond the quantitative measure of percentages of adult usage and can encompass the interrelationship of various previously compartmentalized measures of grammar. It may, in addition, provide "a hypothesis concerning the specific nature of the innate intellectual equipment of the child" (Chomsky, 1957, p. 36).

Chomsky (1961) gives us a technique for describing the rules or categories from which the child may generate the sentences in his language. This model of a grammar is analogous to a categorization theory of learning. The rules formulated for generating possible sentences in a language are the categories of grammatical structure in the language (the negative sentence, the imperative sentence, etc.). It is hypothesized that the attributes of a given category are memorized and the child can then produce new instances of the category. In using this technique to analyze the language of children, we may identify the grammatical categories of their language and determine which categories are acquired at an earlier or later age. In addition, this descriptive technique encompasses previously compartmentalized measures by allowing us to describe sequentially (a) the underlying structure of each sentence, (b) the structural changes necessary to derive other sentences from this basic sentence, and (c) the morphological changes which occur because of the previous sequences. In this way the child's grammar can be described as a structural whole rather than in segments.

Chomsky's model has not as yet been used to describe the grammar of children. It was for the purpose of exploring the efficacy of this technique for such a description that this study was undertaken.

TECHNIQUE

The generative model considers grammar as having a tripartite structure; a phrase structure level, a transformation level, and a morphology level. Each of the three levels of grammar has a sequence of rules which generate the form of sentences within the level. (Examples of the rules are given in the Appendix.)

The syntactic structures described at the phrase-structure level are the parts of speech used to formulate simple-active-declarative sentences of the type "I play." Chomsky calls these sentences terminal strings (or sentences in a transitional state), and they form the basis for all other sentences.

The more complex sentences are formulated by a sequence of rules at the second level of the grammar which Chomsky has termed transformational rules. At this level of grammar the rules change the order of the symbols in the terminal string or allow symbols to be deleted or added. The transformational rules are of two kinds, optional and obligatory. The optional rules are chosen by the speaker. He can choose to formulate an affirmative sentence, a negative sentence, or an imperative sentence. Once having chosen a form, there is a set of obligatory rules which must be followed to produce sentences which will be accepted by the listener as grammatical. These sentences are of the type: "I did play" (affirmative), "I did not play" (negative), "Play" (imperative). The transformational rules carry strings with phrase structure into new strings to which the rules at the third or morphological level can apply. Transformations are derived from either one phrase structure string (simple transformations) or from two or more phrase structure strings (general transformations).

At the third level of grammar there is a sequence of inflectional rules from which the actual sounds of speech are derived. These structures formulate, for example, the third person singular present of the verb and the past of the verb.

PROCEDURE

The population was composed of 48 private nursery school children and 48 first grade children. There were 24 girls and 24 boys in the nursery school group and 25 boys and 25 girls in the first grade group. All the first grade children included in the sample had attended nursery school and kindergarten. The age range of the nursery school group was from 3 years, 1 month, to 4 years, 4 months, and the age range of the first grade group was from 5 years, 11 months, to 7 years, 1 month. There was no significant difference in the mean age of males and females in either group. The nursery school group's mean age was 3 years, 8 months, and the first grade group's mean age was 6 years, 5 months.

The population did not include children with a physical disability which impaired speech, or those with an IQ under 90 as measured by the Full Range Picture Vocabulary Test (Ammons & Ammons, 1948). There was no significant difference between mean intelligence of nursery school children and first grade children or between males and females. Intragroup analyses comparing IQ of males and females within the two age levels also showed no significant differences. The nursery school children's mean IQ was 130.3 (SD = 11.2), and the first grade children's mean IQ was 132.0 (SD = 13.4).

Seventy-nine per cent of the nursery school children's parents were in the occupational categories of professional or semiprofessional and managerial, and eighty-three per cent of the first grade children's parents were in these same occupational categories. The remainder were in the occupational category of clerical, skilled trades, and retail business. Thus, parental occupation for all the children in both groups falls within the upper twenty-four per cent range of a middle-class population.

Speech was tape recorded in three stimulus situations. The first situation was spontaneous speech responses to the projective test, The Blacky Pictures (Blum, 1950). The second was conversation with an adult (the experimenter) generated by some of the questions suggested in the test manual and additional questions introduced by the experimenter. Each child was asked the same questions. The third situation was conversation with peers generated by role playing in a family setting. Each group was composed of three children (two girls and a boy or two boys and a girl). The situation was introduced in the following manner:

"You are going to pretend that you are a family. I have some things here which will help you to pretend." The play objects were then handed out. The children were then told, "Pretend that you've just gotten up in the morning and you're going to get ready for the day." The experimenter did not participate unless a question was directly asked, and then only a direct answer was given. The play situation was recorded for a period of 15 minutes.

The entire speech output of each child was recorded in a single day and was transcribed on the same day. Those children who produced less than 50 sentences were eliminated from the sample population. The mean number of sentences produced by nursery school children was 82.9 (SD = 16.7), and the mean number produced by first grade children was 95.7 (SD = 15.2). The t-test showed that this difference was significant ($P < 0.01$). There was no significant difference in the mean number of sentences produced by males and females or children above and below the mean IQ within the two age levels or between them.

In addition to the above, the children were observed in their classrooms and written recordings were made of their speech. This was done for the purpose of cross-validation, to determine if there were some syntactic structures which were used in the classroom situation and not in other situations. The children were observed in each classroom for a period of two hours. The language sample contained 8574 sentences obtained in the tape recorded situations and 1009 obtained in the classrooms.

The language sample of each child and of the classroom groups was analyzed using Chomsky's technique. A grammar was written which included all the rules used at both age levels to generate all the sentences obtained (Menyuk, 1961). Using the chi square technique, comparisons of the number of children using structures which are grammatically acceptable were made between (a) nursery school and first grade groups, (b) all males and females and males and females within the nursery school and first grade groups, and (c) all children above and below the mean IQ and children above and below the mean IQ within the nursery school and first grade groups. The same comparisons were made of the usage of structures which are grammatically unacceptable or, in other terms, restricted to a children's grammar.

RESULTS

At the phrase structure level of grammar (rules for simple-active-declarative sentences) and the morphology level of grammar (inflectional rules), all children used all the structures in a grammatically acceptable form. Therefore, no comparisons were made of the usage of these structures, but only of transformational rules where differences in usage were found. Simultaneously, structures restricted to a children's grammar were used by varying numbers of the children at all three levels of grammar, and therefore comparisons of the usage of all these structures were made. The rules described at the morphology level of the grammar in this study were limited to those structures in which forms restricted to a children's grammar occurred: third person singular and plural in the present tense of verbs, past tense of verbs, singular and plural of nouns, and possessive pronouns and adjectives. An example of each transformation and each structure restricted to a children's grammar (taken from the children's language sample) is presented.

TRANSFORMATIONS

SIMPLE TRANSFORMATIONS

1. *Passive*—He was tied up by the man.
2. *Negation*—I am not.
3. *Question*—Is he sleeping?
4. *Contraction*—He'll choke.
5. *Inversion*—Now I have kittens.
6. *Relative question*—What is that?
7. *Imperative*—Don't use my brushes.
8. *Pronominalization*—There isn't any more.
9. *Separation*—He took it off.
10. *Got*—I've got a book.
11. *Auxiliary verb*
    a. *be*—He is not going to the movies.
    b. *have*—I've already been there.
12. *Do*—I did read the book.
13. *Possessive*—I'm writing daddy's name.
14. *Reflexive*—I cut myself.

GENERALIZED TRANSFORMATIONS

15. *Conjunction*—They will be over here and momma will be over there.
16. *Conjunction deletion*—I see lipstick and a comb.
17. *Conditional*—I'll give it to you if you need it.
18. *So*—He saw him so he hit him.
19. *Causal*—He won't eat the grass because they will cry.
20. *Pronoun in conjunction*—Blacky saw Tippy and he was mad.
21. *Adjective*—I have a pink dog.
22. *Relative clause*—I don't know what he's doing.
23. *Complement*
    a. *Infinitival*— I want to play.
    b. *Participial*—I like singing.

24. *Iteration*—You have to clean clothes to make them clean.
25. *Nominalization*—She does the shopping and cooking and baking.
26. *Nominal compound*—The baby carriage is here.

STRUCTURES RESTRICTED TO A CHILDREN'S GRAMMAR

PHRASE STRUCTURE

1. *Verb phrase*
   a. *Omission*—The momma'll.
   b. *Redundancy*—He'll might get in jail.
   c. *Substitution*—Say the story.
2. *Noun phrase*
   a. *Omission*—Want it.
   b. *Redundancy*—She took it away the hat.
3. *Preposition*
   a. *Omission*—I want to go New York.
   b. *Redundancy*—You shop in over there.
   c. *Substitution*—Daddy took me at the train.
4. *Article*
   a. *Omission*—Giant wakes up.
   b. *Redundancy*—His name is a teddy bear.
   c. *Substitution*—I see a teeth.
5. *Particle*
   a. *Omission*—Put the hat.
   b. *Redundancy*—Take it in in there.

TRANSFORMATIONS

6. *Double negation*—You can't put no more water in it.
7. *Contraction deletion*—They sleeping.
8. *Inversion restrictions*
   a. *Subject-object*—Brother and sisters I have.
   b. *Verb number*—There's three strings.
9. *No question*—What that is.
10. *There substitution*—It isn't any more snow.
11. *No separation*—You pick up it.
12. *Reflexive 3rd person*—He's licking hisself.
13. *Tense restriction*—They get mad and then they pushed him.
14. *Pronoun restriction*—Mommy was mad so he spanked Blacky.
15. *Adjective restriction*—I write that numbers.
16. *Relative pronoun restriction*—I see a dog what's white.

MORPHOLOGY

17. *Verb form*
   a. *Omission*—He wash.
   b. *Redundancy*—He liketed it.
   c. *Substitution*—He growed.

18. *Noun form*
   a. *Omission*—I have two necklace.
   b. *Redundancy*—Where are the childrens?
   c. *Substitution*—We have childs in this school.
19. *Possessive*—Hims stomach hurt.

COMPARISON OF THE USAGE OF TRANSFORMATIONS

Some transformations were used by significantly more of the first grade children than by the nursery children, whereas the inverse was never true. Evidence of this maturation in grammatical development is given in Table 1, where it is seen that the passive transformation, use of the auxiliary verb *have,* conjunctions with *if* and *so* as introductory segments, and the nominalization transformations were used by significantly more children

Table 1—Comparison of the Usage of Transformations by Nursery School and First Grade Children

| | NUMBER OF CHILDREN | | |
Transformations	Nursery school N = 48	First grade N = 48	P*
1. Passive	23	41	.05
2. Negation	48	48	
3. Question	44	48	
4. Contraction	48	48	
5. Inversion	45	48	
6. Relative question	47	47	
7. Imperative	35	42	
8. Pronominalization	16	26	
9. Separation	41	44	
10. Got	48	48	
11. Auxiliary			
a. be	48	48	
b. have	8	20	.05
12. Do	48	48	
13. Possessive	48	48	
14. Reflexive	29	44	
15. Conjunction	41	48	
16. Conjunction deletion	40	47	
17. If	12	30	.01
18. So	12	29	.01
19. Because	30	46	
20. Pronoun	48	48	
21. Adjective	48	48	
22. Relative clause	37	46	
23. Complement			
a. Infinitival	48	48	
b. Participial	19	31	
24. Iteration	5	13	
25. Nominalization	6	24	.01
26. Nominal compound	48	48	

*P values were obtained by chi square evaluations.

in the first grade population than in the nursery school population. Figures of the significance of the differences are given in the last column of the table only when $P < 0.05$.

Many of the transformations which show significant maturation effects from nursery school to first grade have not yet been completely acquired by the first grade population. Although acquisition of the passive trans-

Table 2—Transformations Used by Significantly Less Than 100 Per Cent of First Grade Children

Transformations	FIRST GRADE CHILDREN N = 48		
	Number	Per cent	P
Pronominalization	26	54	.05
Auxiliary verb	20	42	.01
If	30	63	.05
So	29	60	.05
Participial complement	31	65	.05
Iteration	13	27	.01
Nominalization	24	50	.01

formation has essentially been accomplished by the first grade, use of the auxiliary verb *have,* conjunctions with *if* and *so,* and the nominalization transformation still show significant departures from complete acquisition by the first grade group. This is also true of the pronominalization, participial complement, and iteration transformations. The latter two, namely participial complement and iteration, were used by more of the first grade children at a level approaching significance ($P < 0.10$).

A chi square evaluation of the data considering the effects of IQ and sex upon transformation usage showed no significant difference in usage of transformations between males and females or between all children above and below the mean measured intelligence. Comparisons of the usage of transformations by males and females and by children above and below the mean measured intelligence within the nursery school and first grade levels were also made, and no significant differences were found. The results indicate that there is no difference between the sexes in the acquisition of syntactic structures. This is a finding noted in other studies using different means of describing children's grammar (Templin, 1957). Although no significant differences were found for those above versus those below the mean in intelligence, the results should be viewed with some reservations since the comparison made was coarse and since all of those below the mean of this group were above average in intelligence.

COMPARISON OF THE USAGE OF STRUCTURES
RESTRICTED TO A CHILDREN'S GRAMMAR

As previously stated, all the rules found in phrase structure and the rules described at the morphology level of grammar were used by all the children in the sample population. Simultaneously, forms restricted to a children's grammar existed at all three levels. Therefore, comparisons were made of the usage of these unique forms at all three levels of the grammar.

The numbers of children in nursery school and first grade using the various unique structures are given in Table 3. The chi square technique with Yates' correction for small cells was used to compare these figures. There were significantly more children in the nursery school group who omitted prepositions and articles in phrase structure. Also, there were significantly more children in the nursery school group who could perform

Table 3—Comparison of Usage of Structures Restricted to Children's Grammar by Nursery School and First Grade Children

| Structures | NUMBER OF CHILDREN | | |
	Nursery school $N = 48$	First grade $N = 48$	P
1. Verb phrase			
a. Omission	5	0	
b. Redundancy	5	3	
c. Substitution	16	9	
2. Noun phrase			
a. Omission	19	19	
b. Redundancy	24	40	.05
3. Preposition			
a. Omission	14	3	.05
b. Redundancy	20	10	
c. Substitution	16	8	
4. Article			
a. Omission	16	2	.01
b. Redundancy	9	7	
c. Substitution	4	2	
5. Particle			
a. Omission	9	2	
b. Redundancy	2	1	
6. Double negation	4	4	
7. Contraction deletion	42	29	
8. Inversion restrictions			
a. Subject-object	8	7	
b. Verb number	17	12	
9. No question	18	2	.01
10. There substitution	8	1	.05
11. No separation	4	0	
12. Reflexive 3rd person	10	8	
13. Tense restriction	11	17	
14. Pronoun restriction	12	11	
15. Adjective restriction	15	2	.01
16. Relative pronoun restriction	5	4	
17. Verb form			
a. Omission	29	20	
b. Redundancy	16	7	
c. Substitution	15	5	.05
18. Noun form			
a. Omission	10	6	
b. Redundancy	9	4	
c. Substitution	5	2	
19. Possessive	7	0	.05

only the first steps in the following transformations: relative question, pronominalization, and adjective. That is, they could not bring them to correct completion. They could perform the optional steps in the transformation but, once having chosen a structure, they did not observe the additional obligatory restrictions. At the morphological level, there were significantly more children in the nursery school group who omitted the irregular past form of verbs and substituted regular past forms. In general, one can term all the unique forms noted here as omissions of restrictions which are obligatory once a structure has been optionally chosen.

Unique forms, however, occurred infrequently as compared to structures that follow the rules to completion. All omissions, redundancies, and substitutions at the phrase structure and morphology levels are categorized together, as are all omissions of restrictions on the transformation level in order to compute the frequency of occurrence per sentence of the total number of restricted forms. There was no significant difference between the two groups in the total numbers of the various unique forms used. Contraction deletions accounted for 0.04 of the total per sentence unique forms used at the nursery school level and 0.02 at the first grade level. It was the most frequent restricted form found in the children's grammar. Contraction was almost always chosen in using the auxiliary verbs and modals, and this is consistent with adult usage.

In addition to the trends noted above, significantly more first grade children used redundant noun phrases in their sentence formation. Redundancies in other forms existed at the phrase structure and morphology levels. There seems to be a developmental trend which resembles a damped oscillatory function rather than an asymptotic approach toward a zero usage of restricted forms. At the phrase structure and morphology levels of the grammar, the children used rules with omissions, then rules with redundancies, with decreasing maximum amplitude. The decreasing amplitude indicates a gradual lessening in fluctuation toward a static point which may be considered an adult grammar. Since these restricted forms occurred with such infrequency in the language sample, no quantitative statement about this trend can be made.

Comparisons of the usage of structures restricted to the children's grammar were made between males and females and between children above and below the mean IQ. There were significantly more females in the total population who did not always use the pronoun restriction in conjunction and conjoining sentences ($P < 0.05$). There were no significant differences between males and females within the nursery school or within the first grade populations. In comparing the total population above and below the mean IQ, significantly more children below the mean substituted verb forms at the morphology level ($P < 0.05$). Within the nursery school population, significantly more children above the mean IQ used articles redundantly ($P < 0.05$). These measurements indicate that there is little significant difference between the sexes or between children above and below the mean IQ in the use of restricted forms. It should be noted, however, that in those instances in which significant differences occurred, the children above the mean IQ (at the nursery school level) used a redundant form, and the children below the mean omitted an obligatory rule. The previously stated reservations concerning the possible effect of intelligence on the usage of transformations apply to the usage of restricted forms as well.

DISCUSSION

The basic structures which generated all the sentences in the total language sample could be described within the framework of the Chomsky model. These syntactic structures include those found in both children's and adults' grammar and those which are restricted to a children's grammar. Thus, the technique is capable of describing a stage of development of children's grammar as a self-contained system.

All the basic structures used by adults to generate their sentences can be found in the grammar of the nursery school children. Mean sentence length has long been used as a valid quantitative measure of increased verbal maturity. In this study it was found that in the same stimulus situations the total sentence output increases significantly with age, and that as the child matures, syntactic structures are added to syntactic structures leading to increased length, but without adding to the basic structures used. For example, we find constructions such as conjunction plus conjunction plus conjunction ("I have a big, big teddy bear and I have a little doggie and he's named Blacky/Whitey and there's this big dog and he's named Peppermint"). The addition of structures to structures does not necessarily indicate that any new basic structures have been acquired.

In comparing the number of children in the nursery school group and in the first grade group who used each syntactic structure, it was found that most of the structures are used at an early age and are used consistently. If we look at the nature of the structures which are used by *all* of the children (for example, negation, contraction, auxiliary *be,* etc.), it would seem that the theory of Piaget and others, which states that language is an expression of children's needs and is far from a purely imitative function even at a very early age, is valid. A need for social instrumentation and a method of categorizing the environment would motivate the usage of these structures. The particular constraints of the language shape the parameters of these structures. With those structures which show significant maturational changes in a comparison of nursery school and first grade children, there are indications that further significant changes occur beyond the 7-year level.

The structures which are restricted to a children's grammar occurred infrequently in the total language sample. It was found that significantly more children at the nursery school level omitted rules which are obligatory once a structure has been optionally chosen. In addition, at the phrase structure and morphology level, a damped oscillatory function was observed in the course of the maturational development toward a zero usage of restricted forms. The data is limited by the infrequency of occurrence of such forms. The possibility that such a function exists fits in well with an information theory conceptual framework. By using symbol patterns in a redundant fashion, we make it likely that an error will transform this pattern into some highly improbable pattern and thus enable us to detect a mistake. When the child begins to use the irregular form of verbs, for example, past experience tells him that the addition of "ed" is the rule for transforming present to past. If he is trying out a new verb in past form, he may use the regular past form and produce the verb "standed." He may then use the irregular past form plus the regular past to insure its "correctness." For example, he says "stooded." After repeated trials he may acquire the concept that past forms of some verbs do not require the regular inflectional ending, and he finally can produce "stood." All three stages of past tense verb formation exist in children's grammar.

One reservation to be kept in mind in looking at the results of comparisons of usage of all transformations is the presumption that *all* the transformations would be used by an adult in like stimulus situations.

SUMMARY

The purpose of this study was to use an explanatory model of grammar, Chomsky's model of syntactic structures, to determine if it was capable of describing a children's grammar as a self-contained system and of indicating developmental trends.

Language was elicited and tape recorded in three stimulus situations: (a) spontaneous speech in response to The Blacky Pictures, (b) conversation with an adult (the experimenter) and (c) conversation with peers. For cross validation purposes, the language used in the classrooms of the sample population was transcribed. The language sample of each child and of the classroom groups was analyzed using Chomsky's technique.

It was found that the basic structures which generated all the sentences obtained could be described within the framework of the Chomsky model. A children's grammar was written which included all the rules used at both age levels to generate structures consistent with adult usage and those which, presumably, are not. All the basic structures used by adults to generate their sentences were found in the grammar of the nursery school group. In comparing the number of children at the two age levels who used these structures, it was found that most of the structures were used at an early age and used consistently. Structures which were still in the process of being acquired by the nursery school group were also still in the process of being acquired by the first grade group. Structures inconsistent with adult usage occurred infrequently. Significantly more of the nursery school children omitted rules which are obligatory once a structure has been optionally chosen. There were few significant differences in the usage of all structures between males and females or between children above and below the mean IQ.

APPENDIX

The rules at the phrase structure level of the grammar are all of the type X becomes Y with the restrictions that only a single symbol can be replaced in a single rule and that X is not Y. The following is a partial listing of the rules:

X	becomes $\longrightarrow$	Y
Sentence	$\longrightarrow$	Noun phrase + Verb phrase + (Adverbial phrase)
Noun phrase	$\longrightarrow$	(Article) + Noun + (Prepositional phrase)
Verb phrase	$\longrightarrow$	Verb + (Noun phrase)
Adverbial phrase	$\longrightarrow$	Adverb
Adverbial phrase	$\longrightarrow$	Prepositional phrase
Prepositional phrase	$\longrightarrow$	Preposition + Noun phrase
Article	$\longrightarrow$	The, an, a
Noun	$\longrightarrow$	Man, ball, it, etc.
Verb	$\longrightarrow$	Hit, feel, etc.
Preposition	$\longrightarrow$	Of, for, in, etc.

To derive the particular sentence "The man hit the ball," the following rules are used:

Sentence
Noun phrase + Verb phrase
Article + Noun + Verb phrase
Article + Noun + Verb + Noun phrase
Article + Noun + Verb + Article + Noun
The + Noun + Verb + Article + Noun
The + man + Verb + Article + Noun
The + man + hit + Article + Noun
The + man + hit + the + Noun
The + man + hit + the + ball

By repeating the rules, endless strings of words may be derived. This is in keeping with the fact that no language places an upper limit on the length of sentences, although all actual sentences are finite.

The following are examples of some simple transformational rules which are used to derive various sentences from the single terminal string sentence "The man hit the ball."

From phrase structure, where person, number, and tense are chosen, we derive the following form:

Sentence
Noun phrase   Verb phrase
Article Noun Verb + present Article Noun + plural
The   man   hit + present   the   ball + plural

If we replace each symbol in this sample sentence with a number, transformations can be derived in the following manner:

Transformations

1. Affirmation

   The man do hit + present the ball + plural
    1   2   3 4 +   5   6   7 +   8

                   Becomes ⟶

   The man do + present hit the ball + plural
    1   2   3 +   5   4 6   7 +   8

2. Question

   The man do + present hit the ball + plural
    1   2   3 +   5   4 6   7 +   8

                   ⟶

   Do + present the man hit the ball + plural
    3 +   5   1 2 4 6 7 + 8

3. Negative

   Do + present the man hit the ball + plural
    3 +   5   1 2 4 6 7 + 8

                   ⟶

   Do + present not the man hit the ball + plural
    3 +   5   9 1   2 4 6   7 + 8

4. Do + present not the man hit the ball + plural
    3 +   5   9 1   2 4 6   7 + 8

                   ⟶

   Do + present n't the man hit the ball + plural
    3 +   5   9 1   2 4 6   7 + 8

By one of the final obligatory transformations, the grammatical operators act upon the words in the sentence.

5. Affix

   Do + present n't the man hit the ball + plural
    3 +   5   9 1   2 4 6   7 + 8

                   ⟶

   Present + do n't the man hit the plural + ball
    5   + 3 9 1   2 4 6   8   + 7

The following are some examples of morphophonemic rules applied to the sentences obtained from transformational rules:

Morphophonemic Rules

	becomes	
Third person singular present + hit	⟶	hits
Third person singular present + do	⟶	does
Plural + ball	⟶	balls

From the above rules, the following sentences are derived:
1. The man does hit the balls.
2. Does the man hit the balls?
3. Does not the man hit the balls?
4. Doesn't the man hit the balls?

SUPPLEMENTARY READINGS

Brown, R. W., & Fraser, C. The acquisition of syntax. *Monogr. Soc. Res. Child Develpm.*, 1964, 29, 43–79.

Brown, R. W., Fraser, C., & Bellugi, U. Explorations in grammar evaluation. *Monogr. Soc. Res. Child Develpm.*, 1964, 29, 79–92.

Miller, W., & Ervin, S. The development of grammar in child language. *Monogr. Soc. Res. Child Develpm.*, 1964, 29, 9–34.

social influences

on the language usage

of preschool children*

RUTH M. WILLIAMS and MARION L. MATTSON

[The very young preschool-aged child is frequently observed talking to himself, to his toys, or to imaginary playmates, as he practices and perfects the art of verbal expression. During the third and fourth years of life the preschool-aged child spends less and less time in verbal monologue and more time attempting to communicate with other children and with adults. The social conditions that stimulate the development of the need and the skills for verbal communication are of great interest to psychologists and educators. In the present study, Drs. Williams and Mattson manipulated the size and composition of small groups of mature 3-year-olds in order to study the effects of such conditions on their verbalizations and communicative overtures. Within the limits of the variables manipulated in this investigation, it would appear that the presence of one adult and two children favors more talking, more words per sentence, and more "friendly intercourse" than smaller or larger groups. When the child is alone with an adult, he asks more questions than under the other conditions, a finding noted by several other investigators. It seems probable that this questioning may be a social tool, the most effective one available to the child to attract and sustain the attention of the adult. When the group is increased in size to one adult and three children, there is an increase in friendly communication, and a decrease in dual monologue (communication with an outsider who is expected neither to hear nor to understand what is said). The authors suggest that children of this age may have difficulty in "handling" social communication in a group this large. Although our confidence in the generalization of these findings is limited by the small number of subjects studied, the experimental procedures are ones that could be put to good use in evaluating the many educational programs now being designed to stimulate the language and communication skills of children reared under intellectually impoverished conditions.]

* From R. M. Williams & M. L. Mattson. The effect of social groupings upon the language of preschool children. *Child Development,* 1942, 13, 233–245. (With permission.)

Children's language development has been studied from many angles but there has been little work done on the important factor of the relationship between children's verbal responses and the number of child and adult companions. Since language is primarily a response to a social situation, and is intended to convey meaning to some other person, the presence of other people in the environment would seem to have an influence upon the quantity and maturity of language activity.

This study is an attempt to determine what is the effect of increasing the size of the play group of nursery school children upon their language.

PREVIOUS INVESTIGATIONS

In order to study the social behavior of children which is expressed by language, various experimental methods have been worked out. Piaget (1926) made an intensive study of the language of 2 children under ordinary home conditions where there was no attempt to control the situation. The language records of these children were classified according to different types of social and egocentric speech. McCarthy (1930) recorded 50 verbal respones for each of 140 children when they were exposed to the same play materials in an experimental situation. In this study a modified form of Piaget's classification was used.

Fisher (1934) analyzed stenographic records of large samples of language expression of 72 children in a natural nursery school situation. When acceptably high reliability on the Piaget classification could not be obtained, a special classification was worked out by dividing language into the four following categories: self as the subject, other person as the subject, a thing as a subject, and non-verbal language. Fisher found that the use of structurally complete sentences increased rapidly up to the beginning of the fourth year, thereafter the ratio of complete and incomplete sentences remained constant.

Studies have been made in which all-day conversations were analyzed according to parts of speech. Investigators generally agree that there is a marked decrease in the percentage of nouns and a corresponding increase in percentage of verbs during the preschool years. Verbs increase from 14 to 25 per cent; adjectives almost double; adverbs show no consistent tendency with age never exceeding 9 per cent. Pronouns gain from 10 to 20 per cent up to the age of 30 months and then remain constant. Prepositions and conjunctions appear late and do not form an important part of the child's vocabulary (McCarthy, 1931).

METHOD

SUBJECTS

Subjects were 6 children attending the nursery school at Purdue University. The group consisted of 3 boys and 3 girls, who ranged in age at the beginning of the experiment from 43 to 46 months and with IQ's from

104 to 116 on the Minnesota Preschool Scale. These children had all been in nursery school the previous year so were familiar with the environment and each other. They were accustomed to being invited into the experimental room to "play games," a procedure to which they usually looked forward with eagerness.

RECORDING MACHINE

Ten-minute language records were secured by means of a Fonda Recorder* which transcribed upon acetate tape all verbal responses that occurred within the room. It was thus possible to obtain an accurate record of the language responses of the entire group of subjects at the same time. In order to check the accuracy of the record transcribed from the acetate film the investigator, after an interval of 3 months, again transcribed all of the records of a single child in the study and found a 93 per cent agreement with her first record for that child.

EXPERIMENTAL SET-UP

An experimental play situation was set up in a small room adjoining the nursery school. This was equipped with a low table and chairs and a cabinet containing such toys as a small doll family, rubber animals and trucks, blocks, pencils and pads, toy telephone and picture books. It was felt that such a wide range of play materials would hold interest for each child. There were also pictures on the wall and a bowl of goldfish. The recorder was placed behind a screen in such a way that it could be operated by the experimenter but was not visible to the subjects.

Each child had a turn to play freely with these materials alone, alone with the experimenter, and in a group composed of one other child and the experimenter, and also in a group composed of two other children and the experimenter. As all possible combinations of children were utilized each child was in the play situation for 17 different ten-minute periods. In all, there were 47 ten-minute language records, or a total of 470 minutes of language records.

ANALYSIS OF LANGUAGE RESPONSES

The language responses were transcribed on paper and arranged into sentences, a natural pause on the record indicating what constituted a sentence. The language responses were then analyzed according to the four following classifications: type of sentence, parts of speech, social usage, and a modification of Piaget's functional analysis.

ANALYSIS I — TYPE OF SENTENCE

1. For this study, a complete sentence was defined as any sentence which has a complete meaning for the child. It may be structurally incomplete.

* Manufactured by the Fonda Corporation, New York City. This was an experimental design and is not in commercial production.

2. Each sentence was classified either as a complete sentence or an incomplete sentence. At the same time, the number of words in the sentence was counted.

3. Contractions were considered as one word.

4. Dashes indicated pauses.

5. Names of people, such as John Smith, were one word.

6. Hyphenated words were one word.

7. Infinitives and participles were counted as one word.

ANALYSIS II — PARTS OF SPEECH

The definitions for the parts of speech were taken from a standard English text book (Canby, Opdyke, & Gillu, 1934).

ANALYSIS III — SOCIAL USAGE

1. Parallel speech: A child talks to himself when someone else is in the room. When a child telephones to someone else outside the room, it is a parallel speech.

2. Social speech: One child talks to another, exchanging ideas, asks a question and either gets or receives an answer, etc. When a child talks on a telephone to someone in the room, it is social speech.

3. Monologue: One child talks to himself as if thinking out loud. No one else is in the room.

4. Each sentence was classified as parallel speech, social speech, or monologue.

5. Each sentence received only one classification.

ANALYSIS IV — PIAGET'S ANALYSIS

A. Socialized Speech
1. Friendly intercourse is an exchange of thought or ideas of two or more people. It is a friendly conversation directed to someone or giving out information for the benefit of someone.
2. Criticism includes all remarks about the behavior of a thing or person.
3. Commands, requests, and threats are all wishful words.
4. Questions are any remarks that definitely require an answer from the hearer.
5. Answers are all answers to real questions or commands.

B. Egocentric Speech
1. Repetition is the repetition of words or syllables for the pleasure of talking, with no thought given of talking to anyone.
2. Monologue occurs when a child talks to himself as though thinking out loud.
3. Dual or collective monologue occurs when an outsider is associated with the action or thought of the moment, but is ex-

pected neither to hear nor to understand what is said (Piaget, 1926).

RELIABILITY

RELIABILITY OF SCORING

To test the reliability of the scoring of the various categories into which language responses were divided, six persons, all members of the Nursery School staff, rated one-tenth of the records after a brief practice period. The transcribed sentences were analyzed individually by each one of the raters who followed the same directions that the experimenter had used.

The scores of the six judges were arranged in rank order and, by use of the Spearman rank method, each rater's score was correlated with that of every other rater. The resulting reliability coefficients were high for the most part. Of the 33 median coefficients 27 were 1.00 and only four fell below 0.85.

Fisher (1934) had rejected the classifications of dual monologue and monologue in Piaget's analysis because her judges were so unreliable. Median correlation of the judges of the present study range from + 0.90 to + 1.00 which seems sufficiently high to permit the use of Piaget's intensive interpretation.

RESULTS

ANALYSIS I—TYPE OF SENTENCE

Table 1 is based on records for the ten-minute periods regardless of whether or not conversation occurred.

Table 1—Type of Sentence

(A)	Alone with experimenter (B)	Two children and experimenter (C)	Three children and experimenter (D)
Total number of children participating	6	6	6
Number of situations	6	15	20
Average number of words for the ten minute period per child	126	127	116
Average number of words per sentence	4.07	4.18	3.99
Average number of complete sentences	28.66	29.87	22.78
Average number of incomplete sentences	.16	.35	.21
Average total number of sentences	28.82	30.53	22.99

In evaluating Table 1 it should be pointed out that percentages in column D were somewhat lowered because two of the children did not talk at all during 4 of 20 ten-minute periods. In all other periods in this study, every child spoke at least a few words.

From an examination of Table 1 one can see that the largest average number of sentences, 30.53, occurred when two children were in the experimental room with the observer. We find that the highest average number of words in a sentence, 4.18, also occurred when two children and an observer were together. The average number of words per sentence remains almost constant as the size of the group is increased and is in substantial agreement with other studies. Smith (1926) found an average of four words per sentence at the age of 3½ years; while Strang (1938) reports an average of three and seven-tenths words at the same age.

The greatest amount of talking occurred when there were one or two children in the room at the same time. While the differences are not great, the analysis reveals a slight tendency for the group of two subjects and an adult to be more talkative. In this combination it is interesting to note that every child talked some; whereas in the largest group, 36 per cent of the time, a child did not talk at all.

In an effort to determine whether the differences among the means of the various sized groups were significant, t-tests were calculated for each difference. From observing Table 2, we notice that the t ratios for "average number of words per sentence" and "average number of incomplete sentences" are not reliable but that the results of the other categories are highly reliable.

Table 2—Statistical Significance of Analysis of Type of Sentence

	B-C		B-D		C-D	
	t	P	t	P	t	P
Average No. of words for the ten minute period per child	4.01	.01	3.35	.02	2.54	.05
Average No. of words per sentence	.13	NS	.2	NS	.3	NS
Average No. of complete sentences	3.34	.02	3.56	.01–.02	2.43	NS
Average No. of incomplete sentences	.3	NS	.13	NS	.13	NS
Average total No. of sentences	3.32	.02	3.34	.02	2.00	NS

ANALYSIS II — PARTS OF SPEECH

This study agrees with previous studies in the frequency of the different parts of speech used. Nouns and pronouns when added together were most frequent, verbs came next, adverbs and adjectives followed. The other parts of speech were of minor importance in the vocabulary of this group of children 3½ years old. Percentages of the various parts of speech remained relatively constant regardless of the size of the group except in the case of adjectives which decreased and adverbs which increased as the size of the group increased. Apparently children of this age describe action more than things as the size of the group increases. The averages for the remaining parts of speech seem to be quite consistent for the various sized groups. This is reflected in lack of statistical significance between means obtained under the different situations.

Table 3—Parts of Speech

(A)	Alone with experimenter 6 situations (B)	Two children and experimenter 15 situations (C)	Three children and experimenter 20 situations (D)
Pronouns	20.78%	20.26%	18.99%
Nouns	8.97%	9.92%	13.99%
Total of nouns and pronouns	29.75%	30.18%	32.98%
Verbs	28.73%	27.93%	27.23%
Adverbs	10.02%	17.05%	17.52%
Adjectives	19.00%	10.31%	9.53%
Prepositions	2.10%	4.39%	3.81%
Articles	4.67%	4.99%	4.52%
Interjections	3.85%	2.37%	2.90%
Conjunctions	2.38%	1.26%	1.02%
Play words	.23%	2.38%	1.30%

ANALYSIS III—SOCIAL USAGE

The greatest amount of social talking, 78.17 per cent, occurred when two children were in the experimental room with the observer. This indicates that children 3½ years old talk more and are more sociable in small groups. From general observation we know that there is a tendency for large groups to baffle a young child.

Parallel speech occurred when a child talked to himself when someone else was in the room. The most favorable situation for this type of speech was found to be when one child was in the experimental room with an uninterested observer. Larger groups seemed to inhibit parallel speech and to stimulate social speech. Parallel speech often occurred when a child was putting the puzzle together and talking to himself about it without expecting or getting any verbal response from other children in the room who were playing with other materials.

The figures on Table 5 show that differences obtained during social

Table 4—Social Usage

(A)	One child with experimenter 6 situations (B)	Two children with experimenter 15 situations (C)	Three children with experimenter 20 situations (D)
Sentences that were monologue	0%	0%	0%
Sentences that were parallel speech	39.87%	21.83%	33.39%
Sentences that were social speech	60.13%	78.17%	66.61%

Table 5—Statistical Significance of Percentages on Social Usage

	B–C		B–D		C–D	
	t	P	t	P	t	P
Monologue	2.45	.02–.05	2.30	.02–.05	.09	NS
Parallel speech	3.98	.01–.02	4.03	.01	3.75	.01–.02
Social speech	3.76	.01–.02	3.32	.02	3.65	.01–.02

speech and parallel speech are highly reliable. This is true of only two of the three differences obtained during monologue speech.

ANALYSIS IV — PIAGET'S FUNCTIONAL ANALYSIS

Table 6 shows that children engaged in more friendly conversation as the size of the group increased. There was less criticism and commanding when a child was alone with an observer than in any other social situation.

Table 6—Piaget's Functional Analysis

	Alone with experimenter 6 situations (B)	Two children with experimenter 15 situations (C)	Three children with experimenter 20 situations (D)
Per cent of sentences which were:			
Friendly intercourse	13.49%	22.25%	24.09%
Criticism	.52%	1.71%	2.97%
Command	0%	7.05%	7.84%
Questions	27.68%	16.96%	16.67%
Answers	0%	5.30%	6.10%
Repetition	.52%	5.37%	3.47%
Monologue	37.55%	19.18%	27.49%
Dual monologue	20.04%	18.86%	11.31%

Table 7—Statistical Significance of Percentages on Piaget's Functional Analysis

	B–C		B–D		C–D	
	t	P	t	P	t	P
Friendly intercourse	4.00	.01	4.01	.01	2.23	NS
Criticism	1.06	NS	4.03	.01	4.00	.01
Command	4.03	.01	3.30	.02–.05	3.26	.02–.05
Questions	2.33	NS	2.33	NS	4.03	.01
Answers	4.02	.01	4.03	.01	1.32	NS
Repetition	2.32	NS	4.02	.01	4.02	.01
Monologue	4.00	.01	4.03	.01	4.10	.01
Dual monologue	2.76	.02–.05	1.92	NS	3.56	.01–.02

This situation in which the adult was present was not a natural one, because as was pointed out before, the adult was an observer only and discouraged social approaches. When other children were added to the group, there was more criticism, commanding, and answering questions and commands.

It is also interesting to note that four of the categories according to

Piaget's functional analysis; friendly intercourse, questions, monologue, and dual monologue, have the highest averages regardless of the size of the group.

SITUATIONS WHEN A CHILD WAS ALONE

Because every child reacted as if he were in a social situation when he was alone with the observer, it was decided to try each child in the play-room entirely alone; with the observer hidden behind an observation screen.

In this situation only one of the six children used verbal language. She talked continuously while she was playing, using a total of 60 sentences. The range of average number of words per sentence for the three social groupings, 3.99, 4.07, 4.18, dropped to 2.75 when the child was entirely alone. The percentage of various parts of speech which the child used in the situation when she was entirely alone was substantially the same as that for children in social groupings.

According to Piaget's analysis 88 per cent of the sentences of this child were repetition. She repeated "Bunny rabbit" many times as she played with the rabbit puzzle. In this case language was an accompaniment to play activity rather than a means of communication. Twelve per cent of the sentences were classified as monologue. Examples of this type of speech are: "It is hot in here," "I don't need this," and "This is going to be a big building." There was no criticism or commanding when the child was alone, a fact to be expected since criticism and commands are usually directed toward other people and are functions of the social group.

SUMMARY AND CONCLUSIONS

An attempt has been made in this experiment to investigate the changes in various phases of the preschool child's language when the size of the group is increased. Six children of the Purdue Nursery School, whose chronological ages ranged from 3 years, 5 months to 3 years, 10 months, served as subjects.

The children were invited into a controlled play situation, in different sized groups, and records were made of the language that occurred during ten-minute periods. The data were analyzed under four classifications: type of sentence, parts of speech, social usage, and Piaget's functional analysis. The differences indicated are for the most part statistically significant.

Analysis of the data regarding *type of sentence* leads us to the following conclusions. Most talking occurs when two children are in the play situation with the experimenter. The average number of words per sentence remains practically constant for the three social situations and agrees substantially with other investigations. (For the 3½-year-old child it is about 4.06.) Only one of the six children talked when alone in the play situation. Speech was largely repetition—an accompaniment to activity—rather than a means of communication.

When data were analyzed according to parts of speech, it was found that nouns and noun substitutes are most used, verbs are second in frequency, and adjectives and adverbs are third most frequent. Other parts of speech form a minor part of the child's vocabulary and remain relatively constant as the size of the group changes. It was also found that children apparently describe action more than things as the size of the group increases.

The analysis of social usages revealed that when the child is alone, the total speech is monologue with no social or parallel speech. Social speech occurs most often when two children and an adult are in the room together. The most favorable situation for parallel speech occurs when one child and an observer are in the experimental room. When the data are analyzed according to Piaget's classification, several definite trends are apparent. First, as the group becomes larger the language used by children becomes more sociable and less egocentric. There is also slightly more criticism as the size of the group increases. There are no commands when children are alone or with an adult, and the number of commands is relatively constant when other children are added to the group. There are no answers to questions or commands when children are alone or with an adult; answers and questions are more frequent for groups and are relatively constant when other children are added to the group. There are more questions when one child is with an adult than in any other social situation studied. The amount of repetition is high in the single child situation but decreases when other children are added to the group. Finally, there is a considerable amount of monologue and dual monologue even when several children are in a group together.

Of the social groups investigated, this study points out that the combination of two children and an adult results in more talking, more words per sentence, and more "friendly intercourse" than any other size of group which was included in this study. Whether this would be true of other ages or larger groups is a question for further investigation. Because social growth is of prime importance in the life of the child, every opportunity for such experiences should be provided. From the findings of this study, we see that small social groups are the most favorable for verbal language of $3\frac{1}{2}$-year-old children.

SUPPLEMENTARY READINGS

Bernstein, B. Aspects of language and learning in the genesis of the social process. *J. Child Psychol. Psychiat.*, 1961, 1, 313–324.

Chapin, A. B., & Corcoran, M. A program for the speech inhibited child. *J. Speech Disorders*, 1947, 12, 373–376.

Hahn, E. Analysis of the content and form of the speech of first grade children. *Quart. J. Speech*, 1948, 34, 361–366.

Hymes, D. H. The ethnography of speaking. In T. Gladwin & W. C. Sturtevart (Eds.), *Anthropology and human behavior*. Washington, D. C.: Anthropol. Soc., 1962, Pp. 13–53.

vi

Intellectual Growth

. . . as the soul and body are two, we see also that there are two
parts of the soul, the rational and the irrational, and two corresponding
states—reason and appetite. And as the body is prior in order of
generation to the soul, so the irrational is prior to the rational. The proof
is that anger and wishing and desire are implanted in children from their
very birth, but reason and understanding are developed as they grow
older. Wherefore, the care of the body ought to precede that of the soul,
and the training of the appetitive part should follow: nonetheless our
care of it must be for the sake of the reason, and our care
of the body for the sake of the soul.

ARISTOTLE, *Politica*, 4th Century B.C.

infant development under

environmental handicap*

WAYNE DENNIS and PERGROUHI NAJARIAN

[What are the necessary experiential antecedents of "normal" intellectual development during infancy and early childhood? Several prominent theorists in psychology, such as Freud, Hebb, and Piaget, have postulated a *sequential* patterning of developmental processes, with the present building on, integrating with, and sometimes transforming what has gone before in the life history of the organism. This type of theorizing is not inconsistent with the currently popular "critical periods" hypothesis, various deprivation hypotheses, and the notion of primary and secondary learning periods. Are there some absolute essentials in early experiences without which intellectual growth is irreparably retarded? Spitz's research on the anaclitic depression has suggested that removing the infant's mother during the second six-months of life and failing to provide a stable substitute is catastrophic and permanently damaging if the haphazard interchanging of mother figures is prolonged into the second year of life. In the following research, Dr. Dennis, of Brooklyn College, and Dr. Najarian, of the American University of Beirut, present data related to a similar, but slightly different, question: what happens to the psychological development of infants who have been reared *from the time of birth* by a number of different, interchangeable mothers? Information related to this question has obvious practical, as well as theoretical, significance. These investigators found that "minimum mothering" (adult-child ratio of one to ten) was associated with perceptual-motor retardation between three and twelve months of age but not with later intellectual development between 4½ and 6 years of age. The early retardation is attributed to lack of learning opportunities, and the overall findings are interpreted as not supporting "the doctrine of the permanency of early environmental effects." In other words, there appear to be *some* early deprivations whose effects can be offset, or corrected, by subsequent experiences. Of course this does not necessarily imply that such is the case for *all* early deprivations. Theories related to the "permanency of early environmental effects" are still robustly viable in contemporary psychology.]

* From W. Dennis & P. Najarian. Infant development under environmental handicap. *Psychological Monographs,* 1957, 71, No. 7, 1–13. (With permission.)

381

Ribble (1943, 1944) and Spitz (1945, 1946a, 1946b, 1949, and 1951) have proposed that if certain stimulus deprivations occur in early childhood the consequences are drastic and enduring. These views have arisen largely from observation of infants in institutions. The supporting evidence has consisted in part of scores of institutional subjects on infant tests and in part upon general impressions of the emotional states of the children.

This report is concerned with behavioral development in an institution whose care of infants is in some respects identical with, and in some respects quite different from, that described in other studies.

The data were obtained in a foundling home in Beirut, Lebanon, which, because of inadequate financial support, is able to provide little more than essential physical care. We will report upon the developmental status of two age groups of children in this institution: those between two months and twelve months of age and those between four and one-half and six years of age. After describing the environmental conditions and presenting the data we will discuss the relationship of this study to previous studies, and to theories of child development.

METHOD

THE CRECHE

The institution in which the study was conducted will be called the Creche, although this is not the formal name of the home. The Creche is a home for infants and young children operated by a religious order (of nuns). All children in the Creche are received shortly after birth. They arrive via two routes. The majority come from a maternity hospital operated by the religious order referred to previously. An unmarried woman being attended by this hospital may arrange to have her infant taken to the Creche. In so doing she relinquishes claim to the infant and may not see or visit it thereafter. The remainder of the Creche population consists of infants left upon the doorstep of the institution. Nothing is known definitely concerning their parents, but it is likely that the majority of these infants, too, are illegitimate.

The Creche is nearly 30 years old but it has a new building which was completed in the spring of 1955, and for which the order is still indebted. The building is an excellent one, being fireproof, sunny, and airy. The infant beds and other pieces of equipment are new and modern. The appearance of the institution fails to reveal that it exists month after month upon inadequate and uncertain contributions. The feeding, clothing, and housing of the children have the first claim upon the Creche's meager income. The most stringent economy must be exercised in regard to expenditures for personnel. For this reason the number of persons taking care of the children is extremely limited. Understaffing is the direct cause of whatever deficiencies may characterize the child-care practices to be described later.

Naturally the number of children in the institution varies from time to time with the advent of new arrivals, departures due to deaths, or transfer to other institutions to which the children are sent at about six years of age. The size of the staff, too, is subject to some variations. However, estimates made at two periods separated by five months agree in showing that for each person directly concerned with the care of the children—i.e., those who feed the children, change diapers, bathe and clothe them, change their beds, nurse them when they are ill, supervise their play, and teach them— there are 10 children. Clearly this is an extremely limited staff and the essential functions of child-care can be accomplished only by means of hurried procedures and long hours of work.

From birth to one year there is no assignment of individual children to particular attendants. Rather, a room of children is assigned jointly to several caretakers and observation showed no consistent relationships between attendants and children. At later ages, each group of children is assigned most of the day to a supervisor and an assistant.

During the first two months of life the infant is taken out of his crib only for his daily bath and change of clothes. He is given his bottle while lying on his back in his crib, because ordinarily no one has time to hold it. The nipple is placed in his mouth and the bottle is propped up by a small pillow. Bathing and dressing are done with a maximum of dispatch and a minimum of mothering. In conformity with a widespread Near Eastern practice, the infant is swaddled from birth so that his arms and legs are enclosed in tight wrappings. While no fixed schedule is followed in regard to freedom from swaddling, in general the hands are freed at about two months of age, and swaddling is ended at about four months. Each crib has a covering around the sides so that the child is protected from drafts. Another consequence of this practice is that the child can see only the ceiling and the adults who occasionally come near him. Adults seldom approach him except at feeding times and even then they do not usually speak to him or caress him. When two or three persons are feeding twenty infants, many of them crying, there is no tendency to dally.

At about four months of age the child is removed to a room for older infants. He is placed in a larger crib, but for several further months his care remains much the same as it has been. A toy is usually placed in each crib, but it soon becomes lodged in a place inaccessible to the child and remains there. The child remains in this second crib until he begins to pull to the edge of the crib and faces some danger of falling out. At this point, he is usually placed during his waking hours with one or two other children in a play pen. Sometimes he is placed in a canvas-bottomed baby chair, but this is usually done only for short periods of time. The older child takes his daytime naps in the play pen, but is returned to his crib at night and tightly tucked in. The child graduates from room two to another room at one year of age or slightly thereafter.

The introduction of cereals and other semi-solid food begins at four months. Depending upon the preferences of an attendant, a child is sometimes fed while held in arms, sometimes while sitting in chairs, and sometimes lying down. Toilet training is begun between ten and twelve months.

Children are weighed at weekly intervals and, while serious efforts are made to give special feeding to infants who are not gaining properly, staff limitations make it difficult for an attendant to spend much time with any one child. The average weight during the first six months, based on records of the infants we tested, is appreciably below what is ordinarily considered desirable. Comparable data are not available for other Lebanese children, however.

From about one to three years the children spend much of the day in play groups of about twenty children with a supervisor and an assistant. Equipment is limited to a few balls, wagons, and swings. From three to four years of age much of the day is spent seated at small tables. The children are occupied in a desultory way with slates, beads, and sewing boards. At about four years they are placed in kindergarten within the Creche where training in naming objects and pictures, writing, reading, and numbers is begun. Instruction is given in both Arabic and French.

Diet and medical care are under the supervision of a physician who devotes, gratis, about one hour per day to the Creche, whose population is about 140 children. During the winter months colds are common, and pneumonia occasionally occurs. The usual childhood illnesses occur. When a contagious disease enters the Creche it is likely to become widespread since there are no facilities for isolation of infectious cases. We do not have adequate statistics on mortality. It is our impression that it is high in the first three months of life, but not particularly high thereafter. Mortality seems especially high among those infants who are found on the doorstep, many of whom are suffering from malnutrition, exposure, or disease upon admission. In evaluating institutional mortality it should be noted that in some areas of Lebanon the crude death rate in the first year among children in homes is as high as 375 per 1000 (Khamis & Powers, 1955).

THE COMPARISON GROUP

For comparison with behavioral records of the Creche infants, data were obtained from children brought to the Well Baby Clinic of the American University of Beirut Hospital. All well babies of appropriate age who were brought to the clinic on certain days were tested. They were from among the poorer, but not the poorest, segments of the Beirut population.

All children tested were living at home and were brought to the clinic by their mothers. The majority were being breast fed. We did not obtain detailed data on swaddling, but typically the younger babies were brought in swaddled and the older ones unswaddled. It is our impression that swaddling customs among the poorer half of the Beirut population approximate those of the Creche. This conclusion is supported by a study by Wakim (1956). Other comparison data were provided by American norms and certain Lebanese norms to be described later.

THE TESTING PROGRAM

For the subjects under one year of age, the Cattell infant scale was employed (1940). This scale was selected because among available tests it seemed to offer the most objective procedures for administration and scoring. It provides five items for each month from two to twelve months of age, with one or two alternate items at each age level. The procedures described in the test manual were carefully followed. They call for testing each infant at a level at which he passes all tests, at a level he fails all tests, and at all intermediate levels. Several items on the test were not applicable to the Creche group because they require the examiner to obtain information from the mother or other caretaker and attendants at the Creche could not supply this information. Among such items are babbles, anticipates feeding, inspects fingers, says "dada," etc. For this reason, "alternate" items provided by Cattell and based on direct observation were regularly substituted for these items. In the case of the comparison infants all age-appropriate items, including all alternates, were administered, but in computing developmental scores for comparative purposes identical items were used for the Creche and the comparison groups.

At the four and one-half- to six-year level the tests used were the Goodenough draw-a-man test, the Knox cube test, and the Porteus maze test. These were chosen because it was judged that they might be but little affected by the environmental handicaps of the Creche children. They have the further advantage of requiring a minimum of verbal instructions.

In giving and scoring the draw-a-man test, Goodenough procedures were followed (1926). For the other two tests the procedures and norms employed were those given in the Grace Arthur Scale of Performance Tests, Revised Form II (1947).

SUBJECTS

We tested all subjects who fell into our age categories upon two series of testing dates. The only exceptions consisted of children who were ill or who had just undergone serious illness. The infant tests were given to 49 Creche infants and the 41 comparison cases. Since rather few of the Creche infants were above six months of age at the time of our first period of testing, during our second testing period we tested all infants who were six months of age and over even though this meant retesting in 13 cases. For this reason the number of *test scores* for the 49 Creche infants is 62.

In the four and one-half- to six-year group, Goodenough tests were given to 30 subjects, and the Knox cube test and the Porteus maze test were each given to 25 subjects. None was retested.

RESULTS AND DISCUSSION

For the infants, Table 1 indicates by age levels the score earned on each test. The Creche scores are shown by 0-symbols, the comparison scores by X-symbols. Scores are grouped by step intervals of ten points. Thus, examining the figure by beginning at the top of column one, one finds that between 2.0 and 2.9 months of age one comparison infant had a developmental quotient between 140 and 149, two comparison infants had quotients between 130 and 139, etc.

Examination of Table 1 shows that at the two-months age level there

Table 1—Individual Infant Scores by Age: Creche Infant Scores Are Indicated by 0; Comparison Infants by X

Scores	2	3	4	5	6	7	8	9	10	11
					AGE IN MONTHS					
140–149	X									
130–139	XX		X							
120–129	X	X					X			
110–119	00		X		XX	XX		X		
100–109	00XX	XXXX	X	XX		X	XX	X	XX	
90–99	00	0		XX		0X				0
80–89	00X	0X	XXXXX			0		0		
70–79		00	00X		00			0	00	0
60–69		0	000000	00000	0	X	0	0	0	
50–59	X	00	000	00	0	0			00	00
40–49			0		00	000		00	0	

is little if any difference between the two groups. The mean of the Creche group is 97, that of the comparison group 107. These means, each based on only 8 cases, are not significantly different from each other or from the American norms. However, at all ages beyond 3.0 months the Creche infants score definitely lower than either the comparison or the normative groups, whose records are indistinguishable.

If all scores from two to twelve months are averaged, the Creche mean is 68, the comparison mean 102. For the three- to twelve-month period the mean of the Creche scores is 63, $(SD$ 13), that of the comparison group 101 $(SD$ 15), a difference of 38 points. This is a very large and highly significant difference $(P < 0.001)$. In this age range all of the comparison infants tested above the mean of the Creche subjects and all of the Creche subjects were below the mean of the comparison group. No· Creche baby between three and twelve months had a DQ above 95.

Before discussing the results of the infant tests we turn now to the tests given to Creche children between 4.5 and 6 years of age. We note first that there are reasons to believe that the subjects tested at 4.5 to 6.0 years of age performed, as infants, at the same level as did the children whose test results have just been presented. Because procedures of admission to the Creche have not changed in recent years the two groups of infants can be assumed to be genetically similar. Since practically all infants who enter the Creche remain for six years, there are no selective influences between admission and six years. The only qualification of this statement regards infant mortality, whose selective action so far as psychological tests are concerned is unknown, here as elsewhere. According to the supervisory staff there have been no changes in child care within the past six years.

The results of the performance tests are shown in Table 2. Two things should be noted concerning the data in this table. First, in regard to the Porteus Maze, four children earned fewer than 4 points, which is the minimum score for which Arthur gives a mental age. Since the lowest MA given by Arthur is 4.5, these children were arbitrarily given a mental age of 4 years and DQ's were computed accordingly. Obviously these scores affect the mean and *SD* but not the median.

Second, on the Knox cube test, 11 of the 25 subjects scored below the 4.5 MA, the lowest age for which Arthur gives norms. Because of the large number below 4.5 no arbitrary scores were given. Of the 14 subjects who earned MA's of 4.5 and above, one had a DQ of 80 and two of 100. The remaining scores ranged from 101 to 165. The median of 100 seems representative.

Table 2—Results of Performance Tests

			VARIOUS "DQ" SCORES		
Test	N	Range	Median	Mean	SD
Goodenough	30	58–136	93	93	20
Porteus maze	25	69–150	89	95	20
Knox cube	25		100		

In general, the data reported in Table 2 agree remarkably well in showing that on these tests the development of the Creche children is only about 10 per cent below the norms of American home-reared children. In a separate report (Dennis, in press) it has been shown that on the Goodenough test Lebanese children at the five-year level make scores equivalent to the American norms. No Lebanese norms are available for Knox cube or Porteus maze tests but there is no reason to believe that they would be higher than the published standards. In other words, there is evidence that the environment of the Creche produces only a slight retardation among four- and five-year-olds on these tests.

In summary, the data show that, with respect to behavioral development, children in the Creche are normal during the second month of age, are greatly retarded from 3 to 12 months of age, and almost normal on certain performance tests between 4.5 and 6 years of age.

To a reader acquainted with the numerous and ofter divergent opinions concerning the effects of early environment, the results just reported may, on the surface, only serve to confuse further the already unclear picture. We believe, however, that we can show that these data and others can be fitted into a coherent view.

The fact that the Creche subjects had DQ's of approximately 100 during the second month, and presumably during the first month also, should not be surprising. It has not been shown that any stimulus deprivation will affect infant behavioral development during the first two months. The twins reared under experimental conditions by Dennis and Dennis (1951) made normal progress during this period. The infants tested by Spitz (1945) had a mean developmental quotient of 130 during the second month. (The supernormality of this score was probably due to the inadequacy of test norms rather than to institutional influence.)

If it is true that restricted stimulation has little or no effect upon early behavioral development, this can be due to at least two different causes. One explanation would be in terms of maturation. Perhaps growth of the nervous system, apart from sensory stimulation, is alone responsible for postnatal behavioral growth during the first two months. A second explanation lies in the possibility that sensory experience is essential, but that for the tests presented to him the infant even when swaddled hand and foot and lying on his back obtains sufficient stimulation.

For the Cattell infant tests the second interpretation is not altogether unreasonable. Of the five tests which we employed at the two-months level, four are given to the infant while lying on his back, and the responses required are visual. These are "inspects environment," "follows moving person," "follows moving ring vertically," and "follows moving ring horizontally." Since the infants spend nearly 24 hours per day in a supine position in a well lighted room, and some movement occurs near them there is considerable opportunity to practice visual pursuit movements.

The fifth item among the two-months tests is lifting head when prone. The Creche infants are placed on the abdomen for a short time daily while being bathed, dried, and dressed. For this reason, lifting the head while in this position can be practiced and direct observation shows that it is practiced. Possibly the Creche infants respond normally to the items given them at two months because the required responses are well practiced. However, the possibility that maturation alone is sufficient for the development of the items is not ruled out.

Beyond the two-months level the majority of items on the Cattell scale require that the infant be tested in a sitting position while being held on the lap of an adult. Sitting is a position to which the Creche infants under about ten months of age are relatively unaccustomed. They are neither propped up in their beds nor placed in chairs before that age. The first occasion for placing the infants in a sitting position may come with the introduction of semisolid foods, but we have noted that some of the infants are given these while lying down. Perhaps as a consequence of inexperience in being held upright, the infants as a group make a poor record on the test item which involves holding the head erect and steady. This unsteadiness of the head, plus general unfamiliarity with sitting, may account in part for the low scores earned on certain purely visual items. These are "regards cube," "regards spoon," "follows ball," and "regards pellet."

Many of the remaining items involve not only sitting but in addition manual skills directed by vision. Among the items are "picks up spoon," "picks up cube," "grasps pellet," "grasps string," "lifts cup," "takes two cubes," "exploits paper," "pulls out peg," etc. Between ages five and seven months (the age placement given these items), the infants have little opportunity to practice visuo-manual coordinations in a sitting position and, further, visuo-manual coordinations are not required or encouraged even in a lying position.

Analysis of other items whose placement is between three and twelve months reveals that practically all of them require manual skills and require adjustment to visually presented objects. It is suggested that the relationship between the items and the environmental restrictions experienced by the children account for the low scores made by the Creche subjects.

We examined the records made by the Creche children aged three months and above on each item, expecting that one or two items might be found in regard to which their performance is normal. We were able to find none, but we were also unable to find an item in this age range on which the subjects were judged to receive a normal amount of relevant experience.

It is interesting to note two items on which the subjects are very deficient even though the motor component of the item is clearly present. These involve turning to sound. In one of these items, the child, sitting on the lap of an adult, is required to turn toward the experimenter who stands by the shoulder of the seated adult, and calls the infant's name. The second item is similar but a small hand-bell is used instead of the voice. The first item has an age placement of four months, the second, five months. Of thirty-six children tested between 4.0 and 10.0 months of age only one turned to the voice and only four turned to the bell.

Now all of the children turned to and followed a moving person in the field of view. The difficulty of the item apparently lies in the subject's lack of associations with sounds. We have noted that in approaching a child or providing services for a child the attendants seldom speak to him. This seems to be due partly to the fact that the attendants are too busy. A second relevant fact is that, with twenty children in a room, and the windows open to rooms containing one hundred additional children, it is seldom quiet enough at feeding times and bathing times to encourage verbal greetings. So far as we could determine no events which happens to a Creche baby is consistently preceded by a sound signal. These conditions seem to explain the findings that the infants seldom turned to a voice or a ringing bell only a few inches from their ears.

From the preceding discussion it will be obvious that we tend to attribute the retardation of Creche subjects between three and twelve months of age to a lack of learning opportunities relative to the Cattell test items.

As far as the four- and five-year-olds are concerned, we have no doubt that on many tests they would be retarded, perhaps to a marked degree. We think this would be particularly true in regard to tests involving more than a very modest amount of language comprehension and language usage. The language handicap of institutional children with limited adult contact has been sufficiently demonstrated (McCarthy, 1954).

It is likely that on some performance tests the Creche children also would score below available norms. On the Healy Picture Form Board, for example, most of the incidents represented are outside the experience of Creche children. We assume that the older Creche children are retarded on some tests, but we wish to determine whether retardation is general or whether it is related to specific environmental handicaps.

We chose the draw-a-man test, the Knox cube test and the Porteus maze test because it was thought that the Creche environment might affect these tests less than other tests. So far as the Knox cubes are concerned, it is difficult to imagine how one can deprive a child of the experience of visually remembering just-touched objects, except through loss of sight. So far as the Goodenough is concerned, both human beings and two-dimensional representations of them were familiar to the subjects. They were also familiar with the idea of drawing and with the use of pencils. Knowledge of the use of pencils may also play a part in the Porteus maze test. It is uncertain what other experience may play a role in this test.

The results show clearly that on these tests the Creche children approximated the performance of children in normal environments. In other words, the retardation which was found to exist between three and twelve months of age did not produce a general and permanent intellectual deficit. It is possible for infants who have been retarded through limitations of experience at an early age level to perform normally, at least in some respects, at later age periods. The assumption that early retardation produces permanent retardation does not receive support from our data.

In conclusion, we would like to emphasize the following interpretations of these data. First, it is uncertain whether the normality of behavior at two months shows that maturation plays a major role in early development, or whether experience, limited as it was, provided the essential requirements for learning the responses which were tested. Second, the retardation prevailing between three and twelve months of age seems to be due to lack of learning opportunities in situations comparable to the test situations. It is possible that an observational approach in the day-by-day situation might reveal that some behaviors developed normally. Third, the Creche infants did not undergo loss of an emotional attachment. There is nothing to suggest that emotional shock, or lack of mothering or other emotion-arousing conditions, were responsible for behavioral retardation.

Retardation in the last nine months of the first year to the extent of a mean DQ of 65 does not result in a generally poor performance at four and one-half to six years, even when the child remains in a relatively restricted environment. The study therefore does not support the doctrine of the permanency of early environmental effects.

It is believed that the objective data of other studies, as well as this one, can be interpreted in terms of the effects of specific kinds of restrictions upon infant learning.

SUPPLEMENTARY READINGS

Ainsworth, M. D. Effects of maternal deprivation: A review of findings in the context of research strategy and controversy. *Public Health Papers,* No. 14. Geneva: World Health Organization, 1962.

Casler, L. Maternal deprivation: A critical review of the literature. *Monogr. Soc. Res. Child Develpm.,* 1961, 26, No. 2.

Skeels, H. M., & Fillmore, E. A. The mental development of children from under-privileged homes. *J. genet. Psychol.,* 1937, 50, 427–439.

Skeels, H. M., Updegraff, R., Wellman, B. L., & Williams, H. M. A study of environmental stimulation; an orphanage pre-school project. *Univer. Iowa Stud. Child Welf.,* 1938, 15, No. 4.

inheritance of behavior
in infants*

D. G. FREEDMAN and BARBARA KELLER

[Psychological research, as well as common observation, supports the conclusion that identical twins who are reared together grow up to be very similar in ability, temperament, and general personality functioning. However, the findings of Freeman, Newman, and Holzinger suggest that when identical twins are separated in early infancy and reared under very different environmental conditions, they may demonstrate substantially different levels of intelligence. The generalization that *both* environment and inherited organismic structures influence the behavior of the individual is amply supported by many different psychological investigations. In the present report, Dr. Freedman, of the University of Chicago, and Mrs. Keller, of Berkeley, California, ask the question: "Does heredity, in a general sense, play a role in the development of abilities and personality?" For their subjects they selected 20 pairs of infant twins of the same sex, and examined their performance on the Bayley Mental and Motor Scales at monthly intervals during the first year of life. The zygosity status of these twins was not known either to the investigators or to the parents until the end of the experiment at which time it was established on the basis of non-concordance or concordance on 13 blood-group factors. Happily for this study, there turned out to be 11 fraternal and 9 identical pairs of twins in the sample. These scientists found that, "Within-pair differences were significantly greater within fraternal twins on all tests and rating scales." They also discovered that motor behavior was most effective in differentiating within-twin pairs, but attributed this as probably being due to the greater objectivity in scoring these items on the Bayley Scales.]

The majority of longitudinal studies of infants and children has indicated that there is consistency in personality within individuals over the years (Neilon, 1948; Thomas, Chess, Birch & Hertzig, 1960), but the role that heredity has played in this can only be surmised. We have applied the twin method to a longitudinal study in order to investigate the role of heredity.

* From D. G. Freedman & B. Keller. Inheritance of behavior in infants. *Science,* 1963, 140, 196–198. (With permission.)

Twenty pairs of twins of the same sex were examined on a monthly basis in their own homes in their first year. Zygosity was determined at the end of the study on the basis of non-concordance or concordance on 13 blood-group factors. We found an N_1 of eleven fraternal pairs and an N_2 of nine identical pairs. All families entered the study voluntarily, apparently because of an interest in gauging development of their twins. None was paid. Most were middle class and represented a variety of racial and cultural backgrounds.

The tests included the Mental and Motor Scales and the Infant Behavior Profile developed by Nancy Bayley at the National Institute of Mental Health. Our report is based on the scores of these instruments which are in current use in the nationwide "collaborative study" sponsored by the National Institute of Neurological Diseases and Blindness. Standard scores on the Mental and Motor Scales are based on norms given by Nancy Bayley for *The California First Year Mental Scale* and *The California Infant Scale of Motor Development* (University of California Syllabi Nos. 243 and 249, 1933 and 1936). The Infant Behavior Profile consists of twenty-one items covering 12 categories of behavior: social orientation (two items), object orientation, goal directedness, attention span, cooperativeness, activity (four items), sensory reactivity, tension, fearfulness, general emotional tone, endurance, and sensory mode (six items). Each item is rated along a scale from deficient to overendowed with five steps specifically spelled out; a nine-point scale was obtained by adding half-steps. An unpublished study of tester-observer reliability resulted in a median 70 per cent full agreement on these items, with an interquartile range of only 6 per cent.

The present approach has several advantages: (1) According to Piaget, deferred imitation of other children, that is, imitation independent of immediate perception, starts after the first year (Piaget, 1951). Such imitation was not observed in our group. Our observations also bear out Ahrens' findings that infants have little interest in one another before the 10th month, after which interest gradually increases (Ahrens, 1954). Thus, mutual imitation and "contagion" within pairs can be ruled out as factors in our results. (2) Differential treatment of identical and fraternal twins by parents can also be effectively ruled out as a contaminating factor. Neither examiners nor parents were certain of zygosity, since determinations were made only at the end of the study. Parents who ventured an opinion tended to believe their twins were fraternal; hence parents of fraternals were correct, and parents of identicals were incorrect in six out of the nine pairs. Obstetricians were of little help in determining zygosity, for they were incorrect nine out of nineteen times. (Our observations and careful discussions with parents indicated that, as a rule, differential behavior of infants drew different rather than the same responses from parents. In no case did a parent "create" differences where none previously existed.) (3) Two investigators worked independently, each seeing approximately half the twin pairs. Their data formed similar distributions on all measures used and suggests that the results are readily reproducible.

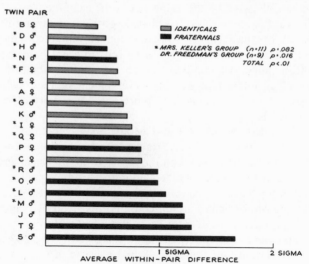

Figure 1—The Bayley Mental and Motor Scales averaged to form a single distribution.

Average within-pair differences in the first year, based on 8 to 12 monthly administrations.

Figure 1 shows the distribution of intra-pair differences on the combined Mental and Motor Scales, and it is clear that identical pairs and fraternal pairs form two distinct but overlapping populations ($P < 0.01$). (All P values are based on one-tailed tables of the Mann-Whitney nonparametric test.) The Mental Scale ($P < 0.10$) and the Motor Scale ($P < 0.005$) follow a similar order when plotted individually. Figure 2 illustrates the distribution of intra-pair differences on the Infant Behavior Profile, where once again fraternal pairs exhibit greater differences ($P < 0.001$).

The extent of within-pair consistency over the first year is indicated by the following: On the Mental Scales, in identical twins within-pair changes in superiority occurred in 37 per cent of the tests administered; fraternal twins switched positions on 23 per cent of consecutive tests. Likewise, on the Motor Scales, identical pairs switched positions on 35 per cent of the tests compared to 15 per cent in fraternal pairs. Ranking indicated that fraternal pairs exhibited significantly fewer changes vis-á-vis each other on both the Mental Scales ($P = 0.05$) and Motor Scales ($P = 0.005$).

Similar results were obtained on the 21-item Infant Behavior Profile. Fraternal pairs averaged 4.36 items on which no more than one switchover in relative position occurred over the first year and on which there was an average within-pair difference of two or more points, that is, items in which intra-pair differences were decidedly persistent and large; identical twins averaged 1.12. Ranking on this basis again differentiated identical from fraternal twins ($P < 0.025$). Items rated on the basis of motor activity

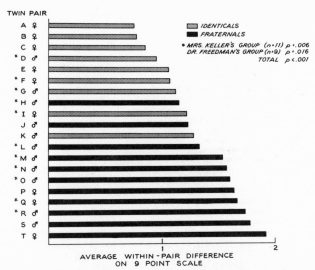

TWIN PAIR

IDENTICALS
FRATERNALS

* MRS. KELLER'S GROUP (n=11) p=.006
DR. FREEDMAN'S GROUP (n=9) p=.016
TOTAL p<.001

AVERAGE WITHIN-PAIR DIFFERENCE
ON 9 POINT SCALE

Figure 2—The Bayley Infant Behavior Profile, a rating scale consisting of 21 items covering 12 categories of behavior.

Average within-pair differences in the first year, based on 8 to 12 monthly administrations.

most often met the above criteria although other categories of behavior proved equally discriminating in particular pairs.

Judgment of behavior from films is perhaps the best-controlled aspect of this study. Monthly motion pictures were taken in which each twin of a pair was filmed separately in the same situations. At the end of the study, the films of one twin were shown to a group of four professionals who had worked with infants, and the films of the other were shown to a second comparable group. In this way we avoided a possible "halo" effect. The judges rated each child on the Infant Behavior Profile, and the scores were averaged for each infant. The difference within each pair was ascertained, the differences ranked, and again intrapair differences among fraternal twins were distinctly larger ($P < 0.005$). The rank order correlation between the distributions in Figs. 2 and 3 is 0.44 ($P < 0.03$).

The distribution of within-pair differences on the Infant Behavior Profile reflects our experiences in recording data after visits to the homes of identical pairs A, B, C, and D. In each of these pairs the personalities merged into a single picture after a few hours, and unless our impressions of differences were recorded immediately, it became impossible to do so later. This merger could not be ascribed to similar appearance, for there was no difficulty in recording other identical looking pairs who exhibited some clear-cut behavioral differences.

Consistent behavioral differences within some identical pairs deserves special attention. In pair E, following normal births, only the second-born was startled by noises in the first two months, cried at the jack-in-the-box

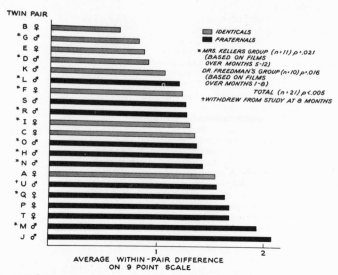

Figure 3—Within-pair differences on the Bayley Infant Behavior Profile, based on 8 consecutive months of filmed behavior (either months 1 to 8, or months 5 to 12).

at three months, and became extremely fearful of strangers during the last half of the first year. In pair K, the second-born twin, after a traumatic breech birth, slept much of the time over the first one and one-half months. Then he began smiling at people more readily than did his brother whose delivery had been normal, and at five months he wanted to be picked up by any newcomer. Thereafter he remained more immediately outgoing to people than his twin. Our observations and interviews with the parents suggested that differential treatment played no role in producing these differences, and obstetrical and pediatric records yielded no clues. The following categories were examined, and none could be reasonably associated with such differences: birth order, traumatic delivery, large differences in birth weight, Apgar ratings (an assessment of viability at birth), and monochorionic versus dichorionic embryogenesis.

Although motor behavior was most effective in differentiating within twin-pairs, perhaps because it was most objectively scored, we cannot estimate heritability for specific aspects of behavior, nor was this our aim. Our question was rather: Does heredity, in a general sense, play a role in the development of abilities and personality? An affirmative answer would appear to be warranted.

SUPPLEMENTARY READINGS

Bayley, N., & Jones, H. E. Environmental correlates of mental and motor development: A cumulative study from infancy to six years. *Child Develpm.*, 1937, 8, 329–341.

Kallmann, F. J. *The genetics of schizophrenia.* New York: Augustine, 1938.

Kallmann, F. J. The genetics of psychoses: Analysis of 1,232 twin index families. *Amer. J. Hum. Genet.,* 1950, 2, 385–390.

Newman, H. H., Freeman, F. N., & Holzinger, K. J. *Twins; a study of heredity and environment.* Chicago: Univer. Chicago Press, 1937.

Wellman, B. L. IQ changes of preschool and nonpreschool groups during the preschool years: A summary of literature. *J. Psychol.,* 1945, 20, 347–368.

Woodworth, R. S. *Heredity and environment; a critical survey of recently published material on twins and foster children.* New York: Soc. Sci. Res. Council, 1941.

the growth
of intelligence*

NANCY BAYLEY

[One of the baffling problems in modern science is how to enjoy the gains of specialization without losing the insights that sometimes come only from a broader, more general knowledge. The complexities of modern science demand an ever greater degree of specialization, so there is always the danger that important information may fall in between the arbitrary partitions that segment the overall endeavor. It is a truism that the significance of parts can sometimes only be evaluated within the perspective of the embracing whole. The following report by Dr. Nancy Bayley, of the University of California, on the growth of intelligence over the life span does much to outline the grand design of intellectual functioning in its broadest perspective. Dr. Bayley marshals a variety of research evidence to support the generalization that there is a changing organization of intellectual factors during development. This paper is a scholarly review of what is known about the development of intelligence at the midpoint of the 20th century, after some 50 years of research. This summary also illustrates the difficulties involved in collecting longitudinal data during a period when new and improved instruments are continuously being developed. Of special interest to the readers of this volume will be Dr. Bayley's conclusions that there is a decisive "break" between the kinds of intellectual functions measured during infancy and during the school-age years.]

One of the primary objectives of the Berkeley Growth Study (Jones & Bayley, 1941) has been to study the processes of the development of intelligence as measured by tests. During the 25 years since the study was started, there has been continual change in psychologists' ideas and theories about intelligence. As a result, some of the changing theories and emphases are reflected in the series of reports that have been made on the growth of intelligence in these children. What is more, by their very nature these

* From N. Bayley. On the growth of intelligence. *American Psychologist,* 1955, 10, 805–818. (With permission.)

longitudinal studies have themselves contributed something to our knowledge of, and theories about, intellectual development and functioning.

I should like here to review the data from the Berkeley Growth Study, together with some related material, as they bear on our knowledge of the growth of intelligence.

THE CONCEPT OF THE CONSTANT IQ

In early studies the intelligence quotient was found to be very practical: it served as an easily understood index of a child's relative ability, an index by which he could be compared wtih other children the same age or in the same grade at school. It was found that as a rule the IQ changed very little when a child was retested a week or a month or a year or two later. This gave people great confidence in the IQ's "constancy." Furthermore, there are advantages in being able to classify a child and have him remain as classified. But this very stability of scores over certain short periods of the life span led to the assumption that intelligence is a basic entity which changes only by accretions and decrements in quantity with childhood growth, adult stability, and senescent decline. Of course this is an oversimplified extreme position, though it seems to have been (and still often is) held by many people who have used "IQ Tests" in education and in practice. It is not, however, a position held for long by those who have been actively engaged in studying the nature of intelligence and its growth.

Another result of the concept of the constant IQ has been its extrapolation, both forward and backward from the school age child, to include all ages, from birth to senescence. If the IQ is constant, then we should be able to classify a child in infancy according to his intellectual potential. We can plan his education, we can make better foster home placements, we can put the feeble-minded into custodial care very young, and so on.

THE SELECTION OF INFANT TESTS

Although the Binet-Simon tests and Kuhlman's American revision included items for the first year of life, little had been done on tests of infants before Gesell set up a normative study at Yale in the early 1920's. When the Berkeley Growth Study started in 1928, we searched the literature for descriptions of infant behavior that would be suitable for evaluating intellectual development during the first year. The list tentatively compiled for our mental tests was heavily loaded with items from Gesell's norms, in their first formulations as published in 1925. Many of these items were closely similar to those listed in other sources, but Gesell had assembled an excellent set of materials on which to test these behaviors. He was also one of the few who had actually tested a fair sample of infants, thus furnishing good preliminary norms. We selected from both the test materials and test items as first described by Gesell, adding items from other sources. In many instances we found it necessary to work out our own standard procedures and criteria of success or failure.

These tentative schedules we applied to the 61 babies of the Berkeley Growth Study, each infant being brought in at monthly intervals, starting at approximately one month of age. Ratings and descriptions were made on each child's responses during the testing situation. The items finally included in the California First Year Mental scale were selected after analysis of their adequacy according to the usual criteria. These criteria include: their occurrence in all or most of the infants; the increasing percentage of success on them with increasing age, for appropriate developmental stages; their internal consistency and correlation with the total behavioral criterion; and their apparent relevance as intellectual, or adaptive, functions.

PREDICTION FROM SCORES IN INFANCY

At the outset we had accepted the findings based on school age children and assumed that IQ's were constant at all ages. Consequently we were amazed at the precocity of some of the babies whose mothers seemed not very bright, and embarrassed at the poor records of other babies who, by the laws of inheritance, should have done better. But we soon found that our embarrassments and amazements were alleviated with time: a slow baby would forge ahead and redeem his inheritance, a precocious infant often seemed to rest on his laurels while the others caught up with him. We were not too surprised, therefore, when the statistical treatment of the test scores revealed that there was no relation between performance in the first few months of life and scores earned at the end of the first year.

When the report on the mental scores of the Berkeley Growth Study children during their first three years (Bayley, 1933) was published, it was met by many with scepticism. However, in spite of their failure to conform with established theory, these Berkeley children continued to develop in their own individual ways. What is more, we have corroborative evidence from the records of the children in the Guidance Study, as reported by Honzik (1938), and more recently by Honzik, Macfarlane, and Allen 1948). Furthermore, these irregularities in mental growth were found to occur in other than Berkeley children. Whenever careful statistics have been applied to comparisons of repeated test scores on infants and very young children the correlations between tests separated by a year or two are low. It is now well established that we cannot predict later intelligence from the scores on tests made in infancy (J. Anderson, 1939; Goodenough, 1949). Scores may be altered by such conditions as emotional climate, cultural milieu, and environmental deprivation, on the one hand, and by developmental changes in the nature and composition of the behaviors tested, on the other. These latter factors are the primary concern in this paper.

As the Berkeley Growth Study children grew older we continued to record their progress by successive tests at frequent intervals. We have from time to time reported the results of these tests, along with efforts to find relationships between mental growth and other factors (Bayley, 1940b). When the children were 8 years old a study of the individual growth records showed that only a fifth of the group had maintained any stability in their relative status over the eight-year span (Bayley, 1940a). Even these few had unstable Standard Scores during the first two years.

This lack of stability in infant test scores has resulted in various efforts to supplement and to correct the infant tests to make them more predictive. It has been suggested that the scales are not composed of the right kind of test items. However, efforts to devise other, more adequate scales, invariably run into the hard fact that infants exhibit a very limited range of behaviors that can be observed and recorded. The various scales of infant intelligence have a remarkable similarity of content. At first there is little to note beyond evidences of sensory functioning in reacting to appropriate stimuli. One can observe that the one-month-old looks momentarily at a dangling ring, rattle or other small object; or one can vary the source of the sharp sound that will make him start to blink. A little later the responses are evidenced in motor coordinations: the six-month-old may pick up a one-inch cube or a teaspoon placed in easy reach. There are some early evidences of adaptation to the presented stimuli, of memory from a past experience: the seven-month-old, for example, looks "aware" that a fallen toy is no longer there, and when a little older he may turn to look for it on the floor. One can note the progression of vocalizations as they become more complex and then as they are used meaningfully. There is also a developing ability to discriminate differences, to be aware of new situations, to recognize differences between members of the family and strangers, and so on.

The question is: Which, if any, among these is the forerunner of later intellectual functions? Which, if any, will predict the individual differences found in school age children?

One method of testing and selecting predictive items has been to use a later (or "terminal") measure of intelligence as the criterion. Scores earned by infants or very young children on individual test items have been correlated with their later IQ's. Those items showing the highest r's with the criterion have in some instances been combined into scales. Theoretically, if other items of similar nature are then devised and added, such a scale can be expanded into an adequate predictive test. This method has been tried on infant scales by L. D. Anderson (1939) and by Nelson and Richards (1940). They compared successes on items under one year with retest criteria at ages 2 to 5 years. Maurer (1946) compared scores on items in tests given children at 3 to 5 years with their scores at 15 years as a criterion. More recently Hastings compared preschool test items with 14- to 18-year scores from our studies at the Institute of Child Welfare (1952). In all of these studies some items have proved to be better predictors than others. Hastings selected items from the Guidance Study records and validated them on the Berkeley Growth Study (19 boys and 18 girls). His predictive items were good for boys, but not for the girls in the validating sample. These boys had a wide range of ability, and thus an unusually large SD of scores. Their 2-year performance on a scale made up of good predictors correlated 0.67 with scores at 16–17 years. The same comparisons for the girls gave an r of 0.34. In general the predictions were better at the later preschool ages.

We have tried to find predictive items from the First Year Scale on the Berkeley Growth Study children. Several years ago, using the six children at each extreme of intelligence as measured at the 14 to 16 year tests, we went through the First Year Scale item by item, noting the age at which each of these twelve children first passed each item. We were able to select 31 items in which the six high-scoring teenagers had, as infants, been two months or more advanced over the six low-scorers. These items were an odd assortment, and there was no evident reason for their superiority over other items. Most of the items occur in the second half year, where there is a fair amount of range in scores. In the first few months very few items had a range of more than two months in age at first passing.

Recently we computed scores for the total Berkeley Growth Study sample on this 31-item scale for three ages: months 6, 9, and 12. The r's of these new point scores with the mean of the intelligence sigma scores at ages 16, 17 and 18 years (for 45 cases) are 0.09 at six months, 0.32 at 9 months, and 0.30 at 12 months. We were unable to get significant correlations even though our sample was composed in large part of the cases on whom the items were selected, including all of the extreme cases that would determine a relationship.

So far, none of these efforts has been successful in devising an intelligence scale applicable to children under two years that will predict their later performance. The moderate successes of Maurer and of Hastings have been on items at the two-year level of difficulty or older. Even here the r's are not high enough for accurate prediction on individual children. As far as I know, no one has used these items to set up and standardize an expanded scale. There does seem to be some coherence in the types of function tested by the predictive items. It is interesting to note, too, that those items which are good predictors are often not the items that best characterize a child's current stage of development. It has even been suggested that a scale should combine both types of items and then be scored in two ways—one score for evaluating present status and one for predicting future development.

These findings give little hope of our ever being able to measure a stable and predictable intellectual factor in the very young. I am inclined to think that the major reason for this failure rests in the nature of intelligence itself. I see no reason why we should continue to think of intelligence as an integrated (or simple) entity or capacity which grows throughout childhood by steady accretions.

THE CHANGING ORGANIZATION OF INTELLECTUAL PROCESSES

Intelligence appears to me, rather, to be a dynamic succession of developing functions, with the more advanced and complex functions in the hierarchy depending on the prior maturing of earlier simpler ones (given, of course, normal conditions of care). The neonate who is precocious in the developing of the simpler abilities, such as auditory acuity or pupillary reflexes, has an advantage in the slightly more complex behaviors, such as (say) turning toward a sound, or fixating an object held before his eyes. But these more complex acts also involve other functions, such as neuromuscular coordinations, in which he may not be precocious. The bright one-month-old may be sufficiently slow in developing these later more complex functions so as to lose some or all of his earlier advantage. This is the kind of thing that does seem to happen. Scores on tests given a month apart are highly correlated, but the longer the time interval between these baby tests the lower the intertest correlation.

If intelligence is a complex of separately timed, developing functions, then to understand its nature we must try to analyze it into its component parts. One approach to this process has been by factor analysis. Of the two main theories resulting from factor analysis, our data would seem to fit better into some variation of a multiple-factor than a two-factor theory. Or perhaps they fit better a theory that is intermediate, somewhere between the two.

The program of the Berkeley Growth Study has not been carried on in such a way as to make factor analysis on this material practicable. For one thing, the number of cases is too small for the usual factorial procedures. Also, for such a purpose one might have chosen a different or a more extensive series of tests. (As it is, the children have tolerated an amazingly large amount of testing and measuring!)

Nevertheless, some of our findings should point the way to new areas where factorial or other kinds of analysis would be fruitful. I should like to know, for example, where to look for *g* in the infant scales. One might expect *g* to be that factor on which prediction could be based. If *g* is not present at first, then what and how does it appear? Or does *g* itself change as it grows more complex? How do factor loadings distribute themselves in infant scales? Does a heavily-loaded first factor show a characteristic developmental process of change?

Richards and Nelson (1939) using the Gesell items, at 6, 12, and 18 months, obtained two factors which they called "alertness" and "motor ability." They found age changes in communality of the tests that were in part due to restrictions in the type of items included in the scales at the older ages. This very fact reflects the relatively undifferentiated nature of behavior in the very young. It may be a mistake to try to call any infant behavior before 6 months more characteristically "mental" than, for example, motor. In spite of progressive selection of behaviors observed in intelligence tests, the evidence of a motor factor persists in the early ages of the Stanford-Binet, according to McNemar's factor analysis (1942). These studies only scratch the surface of what needs to be done to gain real understanding of the nature of early mental processes.

If the word "intelligence" is best used as a broad general term that we apply to a great variety of mental functions, then we will want to investigate the nature of these functions, their interrelationships and the changes that take place in mental organization with growth. We should expect a given "factor" of intelligence to be more important at one stage of development than at another. As Garrett (1946), has shown, in a summary of factor analyses, there is evidence of increasing independence of mental factors as children grow older. Does this trend continue indefinitely? Or do some of these factors become functionally reintegrated as they mature? The studies of Thurstone and others can be most valuable in yielding information on this point. Let us hope they will be continued, over the entire life span, with careful attention to the problem of selecting items to test all relevant mental functions at all ages.

The very fact that the scores of mental growth in individual children tend to exhibit gradual shifts in relative status supports the theory that a changing organization of factors is in process. Something akin to g, or a high first-factor loading, must appear soon after the second or third year. The correlations of tests at these ages become positive with the later test scores. After 5 or 6 years children can be reliably classified into broad categories of normal, defective, and bright.*

PROBLEMS ENCOUNTERED IN CONSTRUCTING CURVES OF GROWTH IN INTELLIGENCE

The use of intelligence quotients, or standard scores, in studying growth changes in children is helpful in showing a child's shifts in status relative to the norms. But a child's progress, in relation to his own past, is better represented if we can use scores that measure increments or *amounts* of intelligence. Here we run into the problem of comparable units. Lacking absolute units for measuring intelligence, we must settle for some measure of greater or lesser difficulty, or degree of complexity of intellectual functioning. The first, and perhaps still most generally used unit of intelligence is mental age. Such a unit tends to force the same value on a mental age increment of (say) a month, whether it occurs at 6 months of age, at 6 years or 16 years. Thurstone (1925), Thorndike (1926), and others have tried by various devices to set up units that approximate equality of dif-

* Since this paper was read, Hofstaetter has made a factor analysis using the 18-year consistency correlations of my data (Bayley, 1949). He obtained three distinct factors: the first is predominant for the first two years, the second between 2 and 4 years, and the third accounts for almost the entire variance after 4 years. He names them: I, Sensory Motor Alertness; II, Persistence; and III, Manipulation of Symbols. This latter is most likely the general intellectual factor that most intelligence tests are designed to measure. These are, of course, global, or total-test characterizations, but they illustrate the complete break between the kinds of function measured in infants and in school-age children (Hofstaetter, 1954).

ficulty at all levels of complexity. This is done usually by comparing the overlapping distributions of scores earned by children of successively older ages. Such units would vary with the test and with the normative sample. In any event, they remain only approximations. When we accept and label them as such, however, they become useful in comparing age changes in ability.

Thurstone applied his method to the Berkeley Growth Study scores on the California First Year and Preschool Scales for the first two years (Bayley, 1933). We later extended the scaling through five years, and obtained a curve which is positively accelerated for a few months and then settles into a consistent rapid growth for almost a year, after which there is a gradual slowing down in the rate, though growth continues to be fairly rapid. The curve makes sense in the light of ordinary observations of children's early development. It seems to be a useful approximation, even though one cannot claim absolute equivalence of difficulty of the units at different levels.

Problems of equating different scales. When the children grew older, and an extension of the scale was in order, we ran into another problem. We had to find new tests, adapted to the children's increased mental capacities. At the beginning of the study there had been no well-standardized infant and preschool scales, and we had found it necessary to develop our own. However, good standard tests were available for school age children. The 1916 revision of the Stanford-Binet was given at 6 years. Since that time we have consistently used standardized tests of intelligence, including the 1916, and both forms of the 1937 Stanford Revision of the Binet, the Terman-McNemar Group test, and the Wechsler-Bellevue Adult Intelligence Scale, Form I. But shifts in scales, with their different norms and units of increment, have complicated the problem of setting up a single continuous scale of mental growth units. This problem has not been solved, but I have approached it tentatively in several ways.

A few years ago, in presenting some data on mental growth for the first 18 years (Bayley, 1949), I transposed the early scores into mental age equivalents. These scores, together with the Stanford-Binet mental ages, give us age units from birth to 17 years. The mean mental age curve of the Berkeley Growth Study children is shown in Fig. 1. At 17 years, the latest available Stanford-Binet M.A. score for this group, the scores were continuing to increase. However, the rate of growth as expressed in M.A. units has diminished at the later ages. The standard deviations, shown in the lower part of Fig. 1, do not increase at a constant rate but are relatively large around 10 to 12 years. Similar trends in variability may be found in other samples, and for other tests. This, I have argued (Bayley, 1949), reflects a true state of increased variability in intelligence during early adolescence.

The curve of the mean mental ages is in many ways similar, for the same age intervals, to curves constructed by other investigators, using other units of mental growth. The general similarity holds whether the scores are based on longitudinal or cross-sectional samples.

Accordingly, I felt justified in using this longitudinal M.A. curve in conjunction with the Jones and Conrad (1933) curve based on cross-sectional data and standard score units, to construct a theoretical curve of the probable course of intelligence from birth to 60 years (Bayley, 1951). This curve is shown in Fig. 2. It is similar to curves offered by Miles (1942), Wechsler (1944), and others. However, more recent data on the Berkeley Growth Study, together with data from other studies, raise questions concerning the representativeness of this curve.

The data on the Berkeley Growth Study do not stop at 17 years. The

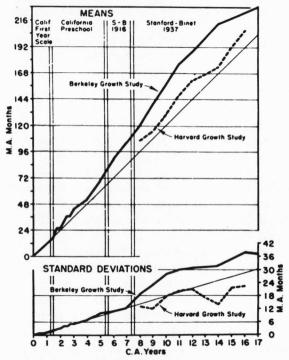

Figure 1—Curves of means and SD's of mental ages, 1 month to 17 years, Berkeley Growth Study.

From Bayley (1949).

Wechsler-Bellevue Adult intelligence scale was given at 16, 18, and 21 years, and we are currently repeating the test at 25 years. A study of the growth of intelligence between 16 and 21 years, as measured by these tests is now in press (Bayley, 1957). The scores were found to increase through 21 years. This was true for each category, at least to 18 years, and for the Efficiency Quotients based on the total test. It was even true of the IQ's. These trends are shown clearly in the curves of the means. The weighted category scores are given in Fig. 3; all but one or two are still increasing at

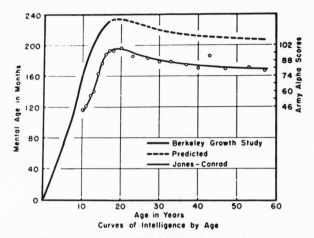

Figure 2—Curves of intelligence by age based on data from the Berkeley Growth Study, and from Jones and Conrad (1933).

From Helson (1951).

21 years. The total scores in Fig. 4 are expressed as quotients: total IQ, and EQ, and Verbal and Performance EQ. (The EQ expresses the deviation of the weighted score from the norm for 20–24-year-olds [Wechsler, 1944]). The gains occurred at all levels of ability within the group. All but one of the 33 subjects made some gain in total weighted score over the five-year period.

These data are in agreement with other investigators' findings on retests of the same individuals. Freeman and Flory (1937) and Thorndike

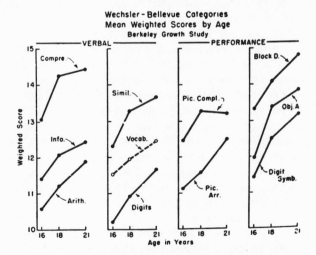

Figure 3—Curves of mean Wechsler-Bellevue category scores, 16, 18 and 21 years, Berkeley Growth Study.

From Bayley (1957).

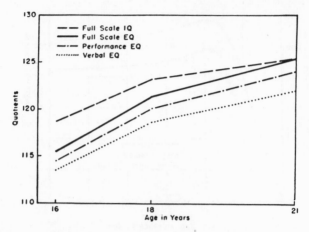

Figure 4—Age curves of Wechsler-Bellevue IQ's and EQ's, Berkeley Growth Study.

From Bayley (1957).

(1948) have found for different samples, and for different tests, that intelligence scores continue to increase at least to 21 years. Dearborn and Rothney (1941) have fitted the Harvard Growth Study data to a curve that, by extrapolation, indicates mental growth would continue to 30 years.

The general appearance of the Wechsler-Bellevue weighted score curve for the Berkeley Growth Study gives the impression that it could very well fit on as a continuation of the 17-year mental age curve. But to put the two curves into a single continuum would require transposing the scores into comparable units. This I have attempted to do, in the hope that it will give at least a rough approximation of the direction of mental growth.

The construction of the 16D Scale. The Berkeley Growth Study tests were scheduled so that alternating forms of the Stanford-Binet were given annually through 12 years and again at 14 and 17 years. The Terman-McNemar Group test was given individually, Form C at 13 years and Form D at 15. The Wechsler-Bellevue was thus dovetailed in, having been given at years 16, 18, and 21. If we assume that the 16-year Wechsler-Bellevue scores earned by these subjects are equivalent in difficulty to a mental age at the 16-year point on their Stanford-Binet mental age curve, we can start at 16 years as a basis for equating the two sets of scores. At the adjacent ages the Stanford-Binet M.A.'s have standard deviations averaging 34 points, while the Wechsler-Bellevue SD's were about 20 and the Terman-McNemar SD's about 19 points.

With these data, starting with the Means and SD's of the 16-year scores, we have constructed a method of transposing the scores from all tests into what may be called 16D Scores. That is, each child's scores at all ages are expressed in terms of the 16-year standard deviations from the mean score at 16 years.

To do this, a table of equivalents was made by extrapolating the

Terman-McNemar scores and interpolating the Stanford-Binet scores to obtain a 16-year mean, or assumed mean, score for this sample on all three tests. To get comparable standard deviations for the three tests, the Stanford-Binet M.A. units were reduced by the fraction 20/34, and the Terman-McNemar units were increased by the fraction 20/19. Then, taking an arbitrary score of 140 to represent the 16-year mean, the three scales were related to this new 16D scale, point for point so that the 16-year mean would equal 140, while plus and minus one SD at 16 years would equal 160 and 120 respectively. This scale can be extended in either direction. All scores for all ages are expressed as deviations from the 16-year level.

The resulting curve, based on the means and SD's of the 16D scores, is shown in Fig. 5. Whether or not it is a legitimate construct, it looks reasonable, and not too far from the probable trends of growth in intelligence. It would have been better to construct the curve on a more nearly average sample, but at least we may be justified in using the 16D scores to apply to the members of the Berkeley Growth Study as one way of expressing their progress toward, and development beyond, their status at 16 years.

Sixteen years has no particular significance as a point of reference: it was chosen because it was the only age at which the three scales we had used could be approximately equated for this sample. It would have been more satisfying if we could have started at a terminal point, say, conception, or birth, or the age at which scores stop increasing. However, 16 years is one age that has been considered a terminal point, or at least the age beyond which the ratio IQ cannot be used without modification.

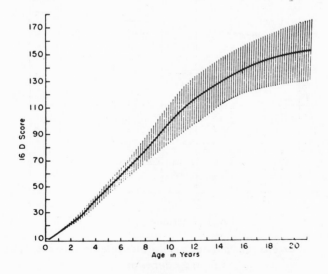

Figure 5—Curves of means and SD's of Intelligence by 16D units, birth to 21 years, Berkeley Growth Study.

The score of 140 at 16 years was chosen because, from this figure when the curve is extrapolated downward from the mean score obtained at month one, the curve approximates zero at conception.

THE VALUES AND LIMITATIONS OF STANDARD SCORES AND INCREMENT SCORES

In our comparisons with such things as emotional and environmental factors that could affect test scores, we have found the Standard Scores to be of value. For example, we have correlated the children's Standard Scores on intelligence at successive ages with the amount of schooling achieved by their parents. The age-changes in correlation (as expressed in Z scores) for this comparison are shown in Fig. 6. The infants' scores at first are independent of parental status or negatively correlated, but after 18 months the r's become positive, and by 5 years are about 0.55. Individual curves in Fig. 7 illustrate differences in the ages at which children's scores approach the level of their parents' educational status as expressed in standard scores (Bayley, 1954).

Standard scores have been used to correlate mental ability with emotional factors. For example the r's between children's standard scores and the amount of time they spent crying during the period of observation and measurement were at the zero level during the first year. Then, too, the repeated standard scores obtained for one child on intelligence can be correlated with repeated scores on other variables, using the repeat observa-

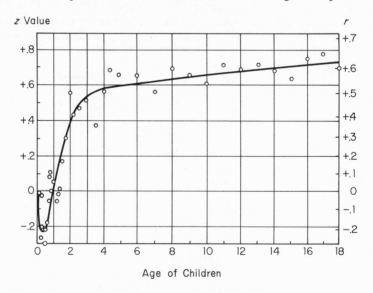

Figure 6—Correlations between children's intelligence scores and parents' education.

From Bayley (1954).

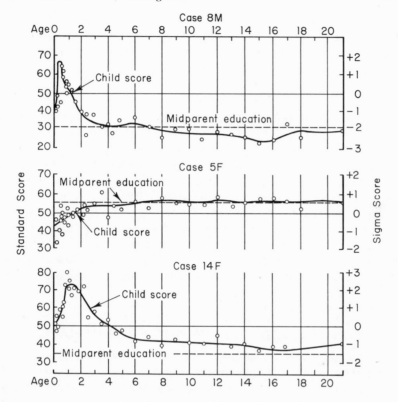

Figure 7—*Individual curves of intelligence scores, showing differences in ages at approaching parents' educational level.*

From Bayley (1954).

tions on a single child as a population. For example, I obtained an "Optimal" score for each testing by combining 8 ratings that were indicative of the babies' responsiveness, or attitudes that might affect their performance on the tests (Bayley, 1940a). The r's between these Optimal scores and intelligence at any one age were close to 0.30. Twenty of the children had Optimal scores available for from 12 to 15 test ages each, for the age-span between 6 months and 3 years. Using the rank difference method of correlation, rho's were computed for each child between his mental standard scores and his corresponding Optimal scores. These rho's ranged from + 0.77 to − 0.33. For similarly-constructed "Attitude" scores based on ratings made between 2 and 7 years of age, the individual children's rho's ranged from + 0.76 to − 0.46.

The wide range of correlations obtained corroborates the impression that observable emotional factors and attitudes (seen also in age curves of the different variables) rated at the time of the test, are to some extent related to the test scores, and evidently serve to help or to hinder the child's intellectual functioning. But other factors are also operative in determining a child's shifts in scores. These other factors may, in some cases, be so strong as to override the effects of emotional attitudes, resulting in negative correlations between mental performance and the child's observed responsiveness to the testing situation.

It becomes evident that the intellectual growth of any given child is a resultant of varied and complex factors. These will include his inherent capacities for growth, both in amount and in rate of progress. They will include the emotional climate in which he grows: whether he is encouraged or discouraged, whether his drive (or ego-involvement) is strong in intellectual thought processes, or is directed toward other aspects of his lifefield. And they will include the material environment in which he grows: the opportunities for experience and for learning, and the extent to which these opportunities are continuously geared to his capacity to respond and to make use of them. Evidently all of these things are influential, in varying amounts for different individuals and for different stages in their growth. Many of these factors can be studied by observing concomitant variations in Standard Scores.

INDIVIDUAL DIFFERENCES IN GROWTH RATES

But Standard Scores, and other measures of relative status, have limited usefulness in the study of individual differences in rates of growth. Relative scores tend to make us forget that intellectual growth is a dynamic ongoing process in which both averages and standard deviations in scores are related to the age of the subjects. It is worthwhile, therefore, to try to present individual curves of growth in units that will emphasize a child's change in relation to himself. Growth curves will enable us to observe a child's periods of fast and slow progress, his spurts and plateaus, and even regressions, in relation to his own past and future.

Such a growth curve for the first five years based on absolute scale units, is shown in Fig. 8. In addition, Fig. 8 shows two individual curves, superimposed on the curves of the mean and SD's. Both of these boys tend to score above average during their first 18 months. Then case 9M becomes outstandingly superior for a year or two, while 8M suddenly lags behind. Study of the complete sample of individual curves reveals a great variety. There may be plateaus, periods of no growth, and occasionally actual decrements—or there may be rapid forging ahead. Each child appears to develop at a rate that is unique for him.

TEMPORAL CHANGES IN ADULT INTELLIGENCE

The few 25-year scores so far available indicate that the intellectual processes measured by these tests have not yet reached a ceiling. Fourteen out of fifteen subjects tested show continued increments. If these are

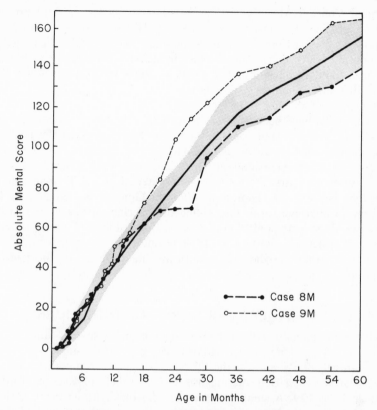

Figure 8—Individual curves of growth of intelligence in absolute scale units, showing contrasting patterns.

From Peterson, Marzolf, and Bayley (1948).

typical cases, what, then, may we venture to predict for the years ahead? The alternative explanation of practice effects from repeating the same test might be offered. But the intervals between repeats on the Wechsler-Bellevue are 2, 3, and 4 years. These are rather long times to remember much about the specific items. Nevertheless, there is probably some residual memory for, or vague familiarity with, the task and the type of solution found at the previous testings. At present we must assume that these factors account for part of the increment.

On the other hand, we have some recent evidence that some intellectual functions do continue to improve with age in adults. When the same individuals are retested after long intervals on the same test or on an alternate form of a test, the scores on the retests are significantly higher. These retests were carried out on superior adults, and their patterns of mental change may be different from those of less able persons.

In a recent study of the adult intelligence of the subjects of the Terman Study of Gifted Children, Bayley and Oden (1955) found that scores on the difficult Concept Mastery test increased on a second testing. For a population of over a thousand, composed of Gifted Study subjects and their spouses, comparisons were made between two tests that had been taken about 12 years apart. The increase in scores on the retest averaged about half a standard deviation. The subjects ranged in age from about 20 to about 50 years. When they were grouped into 5-year age intervals, the test-retest scores of all age groups increased.

Similar results have been reported by Owens (1953) who repeated the Army Alpha test at 50 years on 127 men who had first taken the test as 19-year-old freshmen at Iowa State College. Their scores improved by 0.55 SD's over the 31-year interval. One can hardly claim practice effects after a lapse of 31 years. Even the 12-year interval of the Terman study is rather long for any such claim; in addition the Gifted Study subjects were retested on an alternate form, thus ruling out specific memories of items. Furthermore, there were control groups consisting of those who were tested only once, at either the 1940 or the 1951 testing. The differences in mean scores of these groups at the two testings are the same as for the twice-tested groups.

A SUGGESTED FIFTY-YEAR CURVE OF INTELLIGENCE

I have experimented with using the data from these two studies of adults to extend the 16D growth curve to 50 years. The subjects of the Berkeley Growth Study are, on the average, a somewhat superior group. Their 16-year Wechsler-Bellevue mean is 117, and their 17-year Stanford-Binet mean IQ is 129. A small group of 25-year-olds who have taken the Concept Mastery earned scores close to the average for the spouses of the Terman subjects at that age. We may assume, then, that this sample is rather similar to the Iowa State Freshmen and to the spouses of the Gifted Study subjects in its general level of test performance. It has, therefore, seemed reasonable to join the data from the Berkeley Growth Study directly to the scores of either of the other studies in extending the curve which is shown in Fig. 9.

This joining of the curves has been done for the Iowa study simply by placing the 19-year initial point at 19 years on the 16D curve and the 50-year point at the equivalent on the 16D scale of an increase of 0.55 standard deviations.

For the Gifted Study spouses, the process was a little more complicated, but it has yielded a series of intermediate points which give some indication of the probable shape of the curve. To obtain these points, I plotted a series of SD increment curves, placing the successively older ages at points on the curves of the younger groups in such a way as to take into account the growth already attained at any new starting age. That is, the youngest group was tested at 20 years and again at 32, with a gain of 0.4 SD. The 25-year initial score of the next older group was then plotted at the 25-year point on the first curve (or at 0.19 SD) and their gain at 37 years was

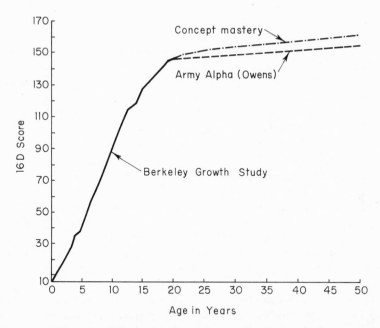

Figure 9—A proposed age curve of intelligence, birth to fifty years.

Based on data from the Berkeley Growth Study, the Terman Gifted Study and Owen's Iowa Study.

plotted as 0.33 *SD* above this point (or at 0.52 *SD*), and so on for successively older groups. From these series of overlapping curves, a smoothed curve was drawn and equivalent 16*D* scores were read off at 5-year intervals.

The resulting two-pronged curve for the 50-year span shows a more modest increment for the Alpha scores of the Iowa men. The Concept Mastery scores of Gifted Study spouses gain a full standard deviation, or about twice as much. Of course, since both of these curves are only approximations, neither may be more correct than the other. The differences are probably due, at least in part, to differences in the testing instrument. For example, the Concept Mastery scale has far more top than the Alpha and allows for much greater expansion upward.

We have here evidence that tested intelligence, as measured by verbal concepts and abstractions, continues to grow when populations composed primarily of superior adults are retested. Intelligence may also continue to increase in the less bright. Certainly, the less favored members of the Berkeley Growth Study are still improving their scores at 25 years. Others have obtained similar results. Freeman and Flory (1937), for example, divided the children in their study on the basis of scores at 12, 13, and 14, into low and high scorers. At the later ages, 16 and 17 years, the low-scoring group was continuing to improve at a faster rate than the high-scoring group. A recent study by Charles (1953) reports retest IQ's for 20 adults who had been diagnosed in childhood as feeble-minded. Their mean childhood IQ on a Stanford-Binet, 1916, was 58 and their mean adult Wechsler-Bellevue IQ was 81. Charles accounts for this difference in two ways: errors of diagnosis in childhood, and evidence from other studies that people who score low on the Binet test tend to make higher scores on the Wechsler. Similar explanations have been offered for similar findings in other studies. But a mean increase of 23 IQ points amounts to 1.5 *SD*'s of either of the tests used. This is a rather large shift to be attributed to test differences in restriction of scores, to regression phenomena, or to errors in the original test. All 20 individuals improved on the retest. It seems to me quite possible that these people did continue to improve in their mental ability.

There are many gaps in our knowledge of the nature of intelligence, and many questions remain unanswered concerning age changes in mental organization. In the curve presented in Fig. 9, there remains an unanswered discrepancy between the adult portion and data for these ages presented presented by earlier investigators, who have found decrements in scores with increasing age after about 21 years. In the earlier studies some types of functions held up better than others. Owens found that those abilities that had held up best on the cross-sectional samples were the same ones that increased the most on his retests. The real difference between the conflicting findings seems to lie in the longitudinal as opposed to the cross-sectional method of obtaining scores for successive ages. In the former we have a constant sample whose life experiences, age for age, will have been similar in pervasive environmental conditions, such as wars, technological advances, and methods of education.

If, after taking adequate account of practice effects, the increases still remain, then the next question is to inquire into the nature of the tests, and the extent to which they measure intellectual abilities. Do such tests as the Army Alpha and the Wechsler-Bellevue, for example, measure intelligence in adults? Or do they tend to reflect continued experience in an increasingly enriched environment? Do the younger generations have more opportunity to develop their intellectual capacities than did their parents, or even their older brothers and sisters? Or are we just measuring the effects of increasingly widespread informal education made possible by radio, television, and other modern means of communication?

If, regardless of the cause of the improved scores, they reflect actual degrees of competence outside of the testing situation, then these scores continue to have practical value. Another practical question is: What norms should be used in measuring deterioration resulting from brain injury, or from senescence? Perhaps it will be necessary to compare a present 50-year-old man's score with norms for, say, those who are 50 in 1954, rather than with 50-year norms for other decades.

What normal age changes should be expect in mental organization? The curve presented here is a composite. The forms of growth curves vary according to the functions measured. We should expect differences in the steepness of increment and decrement in growth curves of the different functions, and differences in the ages at highest efficiency. These differences have been found consistently in cross-sectional studies. The question raised here is whether more adequate studies, of the same individuals through time, will not show that the age of highest intellectual capacity is later than we thought, and that the decrements in abilities are, correspondingly, deferred.

This curve is offered as an alternative to previously published age-curves of intelligence. I should like to see it tested with further research that would refine, modify, and extend it into a more complete and accurate representation of intellectual changes over the entire life span.

SUPPLEMENTARY READINGS

Bayley, N., & Schaefer, E. Correlations of maternal and child behaviors with the development of mental abilities: Data from the Berkeley growth study. *Monogr. Soc. Res. Child Develpm.*, 1964, 29, No. 97.

Bradway, K. P. Predictive value of Stanford-Binet preschool items. *J. educ. Psychol.*, 1945, 36, 1–6.

Bradway, K. P. An experimental study of factors associated with Stanford-Binet IQ changes from the preschool to the junior high school. *J. genet. Psychol.*, 1945, 66, 107–128.

Bradway, K. P., Thompson, C., & Cravens, R. B. Pre-school IQs after 25 years. *J. educ. Psychol.*, 1958, 49, 278–281.

Cavanaugh, M. C., Cohen, I., Dunphy, D., Ringwall, E. A., & Golber, I. D. Prediction from the Cattell Infant Intelligence Scale. *J. consult. Psychol.*, 1957, 21, 33–37.

Jones, H. E. The environment and mental development. In L. Carmichael (Ed.), *Manual of child psychology*. New York: Wiley, 1954. Pp. 631–696.

Kagan, J., Sontag, L. W., Baker, C. T., & Nelson, V. L. Personality and IQ change. *J. abnorm. soc. Psychol.*, 1958, 56, 261–266.

MacRae, J. M. Retests of children given tests as infants. *J. genet. Psychol.*, 1955, 87, 111–119.

parent-child resemblances

in intelligence*

MARJORIE P. HONZIK

[Children reared by their own parents tend to resemble them in intelligence, although the correlation of approximately 0.50 is only modestly predictive. Social scientists have naturally asked what would happen if children born to parents of below-average intelligence were reared by foster parents of above-average intelligence. This is exactly the question that was asked in the well-known investigation by Skodak and Skeels. The results of their study were both encouraging and discouraging for the social reformer. Although the children as a group continued to test above average in intelligence during the first 14 years of life, their IQ's were still significantly correlated during later childhood with those of their true mothers—even though they had not seen or been in contact with their true mothers from earliest infancy. In the present report, Dr. Honzik, of the University of California at Berkeley, compares the Skodak-Skeels data on parent-child resemblance in intellectual ability with longitudinal data obtained from children living with their true parents. The developmental pattern and the magnitude of the two sets of correlations are remarkably similar: essentially zero at two years of age and then quickly rising to a statistically significant relationship by four years of age. Dr. Honzik concludes: ". . . obtained parent-child correlations reflect individual differences which are largely genetically determined."]

A number of developmental studies have reported that the mental test scores of children under two years have little or no relationship to parental ability as measured by the number of years of schooling, ratings of intelligence, or test scores (Bayley, 1954; Honzik, 1940; Skodak & Skeels, 1949). When these same children are retested at later ages, their mental test scores are found to be significantly correlated with parental ability. A crucial question is the extent to which these age changes in relationship are due to environmental factors, or to intrinsic differences in the patterns of

* From M. P. Honzik. Developmental studies of parent-child resemblance in intelligence. *Child Development,* 1957, 28, 215–228. (With permission.)

mental growth. One way in which this increasing resemblance can be evaluated is by comparing the age changes in the correlations which occur
among children reared by their own parents in contrast to those reared
apart from their parents.

In this report we shall compare the age changes in relationship for
two distinct groups, each of over 100 children, who were tested at various
ages between twenty-one months and sixteen years; and then contrast this
trend with that reported by Skodak and Skeels for 100 adopted children
who were tested four times between their second and fourteenth year
(1949).

In the Guidance Study at the University of California Institute of Child
Welfare, a sample of 252 children who were representative of those born in
Berkeley during an 18-month period were divided into equivalent subsamples called the "Guidance" and "Control" groups. This division of the
main sample was made on the basis of certain socioeconomic variables
before the mental testing program was begun (Macfarlane, 1938). The
children in the two groups were first brought to the Institute for mental
tests at the age of twenty-one months. The tests used at this age level and
at the subsequent testings during the preschool years were the California
Preschool Schedules (Table 1). Beginning at six years, the 1916 Stanford
Revision of the Binet Scale was the test used, with a shift to the 1937 Revision at age eight. The parents were not given intelligence tests but the
number of years of schooling is known for both parents. In addition, in
the Guidance group, ratings (on a seven-point scale) of the mothers' intelligence were made when the children were between three and one half
and four and one half years by staff members who had had many hours
of discussion with the mothers. The correlation between these ratings of
the mothers' intelligence and the number of years of schooling of the
mothers is + 0.73. In fact, in this study all measures which reflect the
ability of the parents were intercorrelated to about the same extent (socioeconomic status correlates with both mothers' and fathers' schooling
+ 0.73; mothers' and fathers' schooling correlate + 0.74). The relationship between these indices of parental ability and the children's mental
test scores was reported earlier for the age period twenty-one months to
eight years (Honzik, 1940).

The correlation between the education of the mothers and the children's
mental test scores at twenty-one months was negligible but between three
and three and one-half years, the relationship became significant (Table
1). To check the validity of this age trend, correlations were computed
separately for the two subsamples of the total Guidance Study sample. The
results of this comparison are shown in Table 1. The finding that these
subsamples exhibit essentially the same age changes in relationship suggests
that the trend is a valid one and would be duplicated in comparable developmental studies; in fact, Bayley (1954) has reported a similar trend in
the Berkeley Growth Study.

In a study of 100 adopted children, Skodak and Skeels report that

Table 1—Correlations of the Children's Mental Test Scores With Mothers' Education and Ratings of Mothers' Intelligence

Age in years	CORRELATIONS WITH MOTHERS' EDUCATION			CORRELATIONS WITH RATINGS OF MOTHERS' INTELLIGENCE	Type of test given children
	Guidance group	Control group	Combined groups	Guidance group	
1¾	.13 (N=117)	.00 (N=117)	.06 (N=234)	.11 (N=117)	California Preschool
2	.07 (N=113)	...	.07 (N=113)	.08 (N=113)	California Preschool
2½	.10 (N=114)	...	.10 (N=114)	.06 (N=114)	California Preschool
3	.10 (N=116)	.08 (N=113)	.09 (N=229)	.17 (N=116)	California Preschool
3½	.27** (N=107)	.25** (N=108)	.26** (N=215)	.39** (N=107)	California Preschool
4	.22* (N=105)	.25** (N=106)	.23** (N=211)	.38** (N=105)	California Preschool
5	.45** (N=104)	.25** (N=106)	.35** (N=210)	.53** (N=104)	California Preschool
6	.27** (N=109)	.37** (N=102)	.32** (N=211)	.40** (N=109)	Stanford-Binet (1916)
7	.35** (N=104)	.33** (N=104)	.33** (N=208)	.51** (N=104)	Stanford-Binet (1916)
8	.34** (N=100)	.32** (N=98)	.33** (N=198)	.54** (N=100)	Stanford, Form L
10	.33** (N=105)	.34** (N=92)	.34** (N=197)	.52** (N=105)	Stanford, Form L or M
12 or 13	.38** (N=98)	.38** (N=94)	.38** (N=192)	.54** (N=98)	Stanford, Form L or M
14 or 15	.39** (N=90)	.30** (N=78)	.35** (N=168)	.59** (N=90)	Stanford, Form L or M

* Significant at the 5 per cent level.
** Significant at the 1 per cent level.

adopted children whose true mothers tested quite low in intelligence earned mental test scores which were substantially higher than those of their mothers (1949). In addition, these authors report the relation of various indices of ability of the true mothers to the mental test scores of their children at four successive age levels. It is these correlations which interest us and which we wish to compare with the relationships obtained in the Guidance Study for children reared by their own mothers.

Regardless of the index used (IQ or number of years of schooling), Skodak and Skeels found that the correlation between the *true* mother's ability and her child's mental test scores at approximately two years of age is insignificant. By the time the adopted children reached four years on the average, the correlations between their IQs and the true mothers' education and intelligence are $+ 0.31$ and $+ 0.28$, respectively. These correlations are significant at the 5 per cent level. In contrast these authors found *no* relationship at any age between the mental test scores of these same children, who were adopted in the first months of life, and their *foster,* or adopting, mothers' education. These highly significant results are especially interesting when compared with the findings for the groups of children who have always lived with their own parents (Bayley, 1954 and Honzik, 1940).

In Fig. 1, the mother-child correlations for the total Guidance Study sample (combined Guidance and Control groups) are compared with those reported by Skodak and Skeels for the adopted children. The true mother-child correlational age trends in their study and ours are as alike

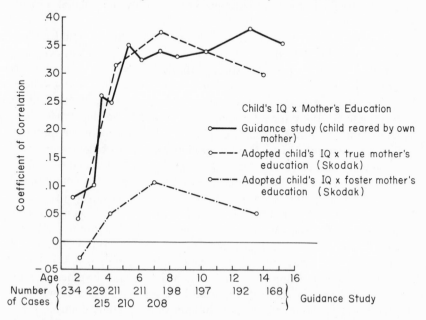

Figure 1—*Education of mother in relation to child's IQ.*

as are the two subsamples of our group. The similarity in the changing relationships with age for the Guidance Study group who always lived with their parents as compared with the Skodak-Skeels group who never lived with their parents is impressive. However, the final correlations between the index of maternal ability (number of years of schooling) and the children's mental test scores is only + 0.35 for the children reared by their true parents; and + 0.32 for the children not reared by their true parents, indicating that less than 15 per cent of the variance in the children's scores can be accounted for by this very rough index of the true mother's ability.

It should also be noted that the individual differences in the adopted children's mental test scores are not related to the foster mothers' education at any age. This finding is surprising since the average IQ of the adopted children at thirteen and one half years was 106, while the average IQ of their true mothers was reported as only 86. A regression upward toward the mean is to be expected but not beyond the mean. Our interpretation of these findings is that the educational level of the true mother roughly indi-cates her intellectual capacity and this capacity is at least somewhat deter-mined by genetic factors which she, in turn, transmits to her children. The difference in the level of ability of the adopted children and their true mothers may be due in part to systematic undermeasurement of the true mothers' intelligence and in part to the generally favorable environment provided by the foster families. It is conceivable, and it seems to us prob-able, that in this sample certain unmeasured family variables such as the affection and emotional support given the foster children were as important as purely intellectual stimulation in nurturing the mental growth and performance of these foster children.

A better indication of the age changes in the mother-child resemblance would probably have been obtained if optimal test scores had been available for the mothers in these two studies. In the Skodak-Skeels investigation, 63 of the mothers were given individual mental tests but these mothers were tested shortly after the babies' births "usually after the mother had decided to release the baby for adoption." The authors note that "these IQs were consistent with other evidence of the mental adequacy of the mothers" and "tests were never given when the mother was ill or obviously upset," but it is unlikely that these IQs reflect the optimum performance of which these mothers might have been capable under more favorable conditions. How-ever, even these IQs showed age trends in relationship to the mental test scores of the children which were similar but tended to run a little higher than those obtained for the mothers' education. The mother-child correla-tions in the Guidance Study are higher when based on ratings of the mother's intelligence than when education is used as an index of the mother's ability (Table 1). They are, in the former instance, comparable with the correlation of 0.49 reported by Jones in a study in which testing procedures for both parents and children were carefully controlled (1928).

In Fig. 2, the age change in mother-child resemblance in intelligence reported by Skodak and Skeels for 63 of the adopted children is compared

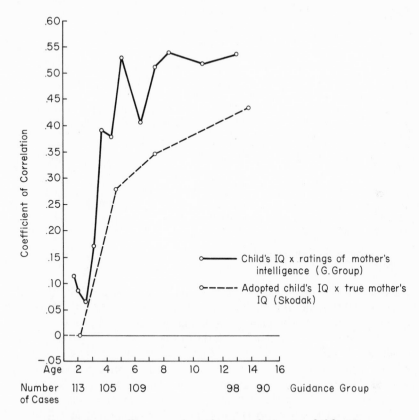

Figure 2—Intelligence of mother in relation to child's IQ.

with the findings for the Guidance group where the measure of maternal intelligence was an averaged rating. The correlations obtained in the Guidance group are higher than those reported for the adopted children. This latter difference may be due to differential environmental stimulation by the more intelligent mothers in the Guidance group but there is also the likelihood in the Skodak-Skeels study of an unequal effect of stress on the mothers' IQs. These findings certainly suggest that the variations in the magnitude of the correlations depend somewhat on the sensitivity of the measures of maternal intelligence, but the question of whether the differences in the correlations shown in Fig. 2 are entirely attributable to differences in the validity of the measures of mothers' intelligence cannot be answered by these studies.

The correlations between the number of years of schooling of the father and the children's mental test scores at successive ages are reported for the Guidance and Control groups separately and combined in Table 2. Although there are a few coefficients in this table which appear too high or too low in relation to the trend (e.g., the correlations of + 0.40 at five years for the Guidance group and + 0.43 for the Control group at seven years),

Table 2—Correlations of the Children's Mental Test Scores with the Fathers' Education

CORRELATIONS

Age in years	Guidance group	Control group	Combined groups	Type of test given children
1¾	.10 (N=117)	.06 (N=117)	.07 (N=234)	California Preschool
2	−.05 (N=113)	. . .	−.05 (N=113)	California Preschool
2½	.03 (N=114)	. . .	.03 (N=114)	California Preschool
3	.01 (N=116)	.19 (N=113)	.11 (N=229)	California Preschool
3½	.17 (N=107)	.25** (N=108)	.21** (N=215)	California Preschool
4	.17 (N=105)	.30** (N=106)	.24** (N=211)	California Preschool
5	.40** (N=104)	.19* (N=104)	.29** (N=208)	California Preschool
6	.24* (N=109)	.36** (N=102)	.30** (N=211)	Stanford-Binet (1916)
7	.37** (N=104)	.43** (N=104)	.40** (N=208)	Stanford-Binet (1916)
8	.37** (N=100)	.34** (N=98)	.35** (N=198)	Stanford, Form L
10	.36** (N=105)	.32** (N=92)	.34** (N=197)	Stanford, Form L or M
12 or 13	.45** (N=99)	.33** (N=94)	.39** (N=193)	Stanford, Form L or M
14 or 15	.48** (N=90)	.26* (N=78)	.37** (N=168)	Stanford, Form L or M

* Significant at the 5 per cent level.
** Significant at the 1 per cent level.

the age changes are similar to those found between the mental test scores of these children and the mothers' education. The relationship between the number of years of schooling of the father and the children's test scores is negligible at twenty-one months (+ 0.07) and three years (+ 0.11) but is significant at the 5 per cent level at three and one-half years (+ 0.21) and reaches a high of + 0.40 at seven years, thereafter ranging from + 0.34 to + 0.39. The trend of the age changes in relationship between the children's mental test scores and the fathers' schooling is similar in the two groups (Guidance and Control) in spite of the above mentioned inconsistencies. In Fig. 3, the correlations for these two groups combined are compared with the findings for adopted children in relation to the education of their true fathers. The correlations between the mental test scores of the adopted children and the education of their true fathers were computed from the raw data presented by Skodak and Skeels (Table 3). The impressive fact shown by Fig. 3, is that the trend in relationships for the adopted children resembles so closely that found for the children reared by their own parents. Since the relationships obtained in the Guidance Study are no higher than those found for the adopted children, we may infer that the more highly educated fathers do not offer differentially more stimulating environments to their children. This inference is confirmed by the findings for the foster fathers shown in Table 3.

The mental growth patterns for individual children have been considered in relation to the parental ability. The method used was to convert both the children's mental test scores and the average of the number of years of schooling of the parents into standard scores, and to note the age level at which the child's mental test SD score reaches the parental SD score with respect to educational level. Using this technique, Bayley presents three cases from the Berkeley Growth study in which the mental test SD

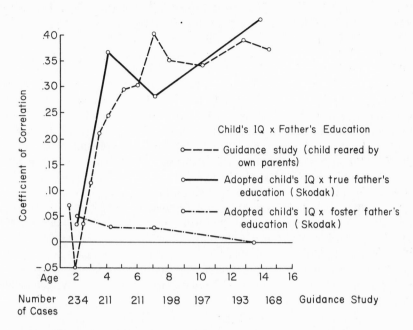

Figure 3—Education of father in relation to child's IQ.

scores of the children reached the parents' relative educational level at ages four, eight, and sixteen years, respectively, after a period of scoring above or below the parental status (1954). Inspection of individual mental growth records in the Guidance Study also suggests that there are marked differences in the ages at which the children's scores reached the parental level of ability, as indicated by their education.

SUMMARY AND CONCLUSIONS

The increasing parent-child resemblance in mental ability found for two groups of children reared by their own parents has been compared and found to be similar to that reported for a group of children reared

Table 3—Correlations Between the Children's Mental Test Scores and the Fathers' Education (Skodak-Skeels Data)

Average age of adopted children in years and months	Correlation between true father's education and child's IQ* (N=60)	Correlation between foster father's education and child's IQ (N=100)	Mental test given children
2–2	+.03	+.05	Kuhlman or Stanford-Binet (1916)
4–3	+.36**	+.03	Stanford-Binet (1916)
7–1	+.28**	+.03	Stanford-Binet (1916)
13–6	+.42**	+.00	Stanford-Binet (1937)

* These correlations were computed from the original data published by Skodak and Skeels (1949).
** Significant at the 1 per cent level.

from early infancy by foster parents (Skodak & Skeels, 1949). The ability measures used in both studies were, for the children, individually administered intelligence tests, and for the parents, the number of years of schooling; and additionally for the mother, test scores and ratings. The finding that the parent-child resemblance in ability follows the same age changes in the two studies, even though the true parents did not rear the children in the Skodak-Skeels group, suggests that the existing relationship is largely due to genetic factors which tend to become manifest in the child during the later preschool years. Although the group age trends in relationship for both the adopted and non-adopted children are similar, the extent of the relationship is of low predictive value. There were wide individual differences in the ages at which children achieved mental test standard scores which were comparable with their parents' standard scores.

The fact that the parent-child resemblance is no greater for children reared by their own parents and the further fact reported by Skodak-Skeels of no relationship between the children's mental test performance and the foster parents' ability suggest that the education of the parents per se is not an environmentally important factor and that the obtained parent-child correlations reflect individual differences which are largely genetically determined.

SUPPLEMENTARY READINGS

Bayley, N. Some increasing parent-child similarities during the growth of children. *J. educ. Psychol.*, 1954, 45, 1–21.

Kagan, J., & Moss, H. A. Parental correlates of child's IQ and height: a cross-validation of the Berkeley growth study results. *Child Develpm.*, 1959, 30, 325–332.

Snygg, D. The relation between the intelligence of mothers and of their children living in foster homes. *J. genet. Psychol.*, 1938, 52, 401–406.

Thurstone, L. L., & Jenkins, R. L. *Order of birth, parentage, and intelligence.* Chicago: Univer. Chicago Press, 1931.

the limitations
of infant and preschool
intelligence tests*

JOHN E. ANDERSON

[Nowhere in psychology have points of view differed more widely than in assessing the relative effects of "nature and nurture" on human intelligence. The discoveries of the early geneticists swayed the pendulum to an extreme heritability position, and strongly influenced such psychological pioneers as Goddard and Terman. More refined studies of genetic transmission in the 1920's and 1930's showed that genetic predispositions in organisms are still substantially influenced during development by variations in the environment. These events gradually pushed the pendulum to an extreme of environmental primacy, perhaps culminating in the position of the Russian geneticist Lysenko. Psychologists were caught up in the swing that emphasized environmental influence and began looking for data supportive of this interpretation. The data were, of course, found and the ensuing argument became the "nature-nurture controversy" of the late 1930's and early 1940's. Many of the questions raised during that controversy have yet to be answered some 25 years later. Dr. Anderson, who was for many years Director of the Institute of Child Welfare at the University of Minnesota, questions in the following report whether psychologists have really done their best in constructing tests to measure human intelligence. He reasons that intelligence tests should "tap to a greater degree an inherent organization of abilities" if they are to differ significantly from achievement tests. He appears appropriately depressed that psychologists have made so little progress in instrumentation since the early contributions of Binet and Spearman at the turn of the century. His suggestion that tests should be developed to maximize correlations with terminal measures of human intellectual abilities constitutes a serious challenge to psychometric specialists. Whether or not this is the most promising line of scientific inquiry is, of course, not known, thereby reflecting the ever present uncertainty of what constitutes the next best move in expanding any domain of scientific knowledge.]

* From J. E. Anderson. The limitations of infant and preschool tests in the measurement of intelligence. *Journal of Psychology,* 1939, 8, 351–379. (With permission.)

The practical application of intelligence tests and the scientific and theoretical problems opened up by them, have been so valuable that they constitute one of the greatest achievements in the modern study of man. Recently, however, some of the assumptions of modern test theory have been called into question. Wellman (1932a, 1932b, 1934, 1937), Skeels (1936, 1937, 1938), and Skodak (1938, 1939), in a series of articles, state that scores on intelligence tests are determined by environmental opportunities and imply that inherited factors are of little or no weight. According to these studies, children with nursery school experience made better scores on subsequent intelligence tests than did children without such experience. Foster children tested in infancy increased in test score when placed in good homes. Children in a good orphanage environment increased in test score over those in a poor orphanage environment. These results, all of which are based on infant or preschool tests as origins, are interpreted to show that a favorable environment produces great changes upward and an unfavorable environment great changes downward in *true* intelligence.

It is not the purpose of this paper to analyze these studies in detail, but to concern itself with certain problems of theory which raise the question as to the reliance to be placed upon infant and preschool tests as measures of the function later known as intelligence. Because early tests may measure different functions than do those given later in the developmental sequence, it is possible that the prediction from early scores of both terminal status and the final series of interrelations with other factors is hazardous. If to this hazard there is added that of constant errors arising out of the emotional reactions of the child, the prediction of ultimate interrelations becomes doubly hazardous.

The traditional criteria for the standardization of intelligence tests have been: first, increase in score with chronological age; second, the correlation of test performance with ratings of brightness; third, the correlation of test performance with composite academic achievement; and fourth, the correlation of items with total score, i.e., internal consistency. Of these, the first and the second were used by Binet, and the third and fourth by subsequent investigators. In the derivation of intelligence test scales for young children, only one of these criteria—that of progression with chronological age—has been consistently used.

THE CRITERION OF TERMINAL STATUS

Because of the use of the criterion of age progression, infant scales consist very largely of motor items. It has long been known that the total scores based on infant scales show zero or very low positive correlations with intelligence test scores at later ages (Bayley, 1933; Furfey & Muehlenbein, 1932). Recently Richards and Nelson (1938, 1939) found that the items in infant scales correlate in different degrees with total intelligence test scores at two and three years and suggest that by item analysis and weighting through partial correlation the correlations of infant scales with later measures may be raised. Unfortunately, their reported increases could not be checked on a separate group from that on which the validation was done, and so few items were available that a final answer on the possibilities of weighting and item selection could not be obtained. In any event, however, their results suggest the possibility of developing infant scales of greater predictive value if the techniques of item analysis are applied to the selection of individual items and if performance at later age levels can be used as a criterion against which to check items at earlier levels. The criterion suggested in this paper, then, is that of evaluating items in terms of a later or final mental status.

In spite of the Wellman and Skeels results, intelligence tests will continue to be used for practical and predictive purposes. What is it that we wish to measure? Is it present standing or the level that will be reached when development is complete? Strong arguments could be made for either position. *This paper, however, assumes that in making the best possible prediction of terminal status, we will also make the best measurement of present status, insofar as our concern is with potentiality rather than achievement.* When tests are used in clinic or court, interest is in terminal status, i.e., at the age of nine years, we wish to forecast status at twelve or sixteen years. If this reasoning is sound, measuring instruments should be developed for the highest possible prediction of final standing and, in addition to the criteria ordinarily used, items should be selected in terms of their correlation with final status. With the use of this criterion, some of the items now included in our scales might be eliminated, and others now on the borderline with respect to present criteria might be included.

The use of this criterion would impose upon a series of subtests and items a selective device related in some respects to the criterion of internal consistency. It should result in tests that are more homogeneous in terms of content and underlying psychological functions and in a clear delimitation of that which is now defined as intelligence. So far as our present infant and preschool tests are concerned, it would involve a thorough reworking of the field. The problems here raised grow out of longitudinal studies, and would not have arisen in that period when cross-sectional studies held the stage.

CORRELATIONS BETWEEN INITIAL AND TERMINAL STATUS

A number of investigators have commented on the decrease in the correlations of successive measures with an initial measure. It is especially evident in the Bayley studies (1933) of growth in mental functions. Honzik (1938) made a very interesting analysis of the relation between mental test constancy and the interval between changes. She obtained an age ratio by dividing chronological age on the first test by chronological age on the second test and then correlated this ratio with the correlation co-

efficients obtained between the tests. She finds the correlation between 22
age ratios and the corresponding *r*'s for *California* I to be + 0.92 ± 0.02.
For *California* II, the figure is 0.78 ± 0.06. Thus higher correlations are
found between those separated by longer intervals.

Honzik also finds that a test at twenty-one months gives a negligible
prediction of success on the Stanford-Binet at six or seven years, and
that later tests are increasingly predictive of such success. She interprets
her results as suggesting the impossibility of making an accurate prognosis
of the future ability of a child on a single mental test before the age of two.
Her data are so important that a detailed analysis of them is made later by
means of the methods developed in this article. Although somewhat less
attention has been paid to the increase in the correlation of successive
measures with terminal status, it is an equally marked phenomenon in
longitudinal studies.

In the Bayley study (1933), the correlations of mental tests at successive periods from one to thirty-six months show a striking decrease
(from 0.57 to − 0.09) as we move away from initial status and a striking
increase (from − 0.09 to 0.80) as we move toward terminal status (Table
1). Similar coefficients were found in the Honzik study (1938) in which
once again the phenomenon of progressive decrease in correlations with
initial status and progressive increase in correlations with terminal status
are apparent.

Table 1—Results Found by Bayley (1933)

Age at testing	Correlation with initial status 1, 2, and 3 mos.	Correlation with final status 27, 30, and 36 mos.
1, 2, and 3 mos.		−.09
4, 5, and 6 mos.	.57	.10
7, 8, and 9 mos.	.42	.22
10, 11, and 12 mos.	.28	.45
13, 14, and 15 mos.	.10	.54
18, 21, and 24 mos.	−.04	.80
27, 30, and 36 mos.	−.09	

I was unable to find longitudinal studies on older children which
presented correlations at successive ages with initial and terminal status.
However, Hirsch (1930) presents the intelligence quotients for each child
in his study for six successive retests at yearly intervals, starting with a
group that originally was between six and eight years of age. The correlations obtained from reworking his data and including only the 150 cases
that had the entire six tests are presented in Table 2. It should be noted
that the span covered at each successive yearly measurement is three years
of chronological age, rather than one year or less, as is true of the other
data in this paper. In this table the correlations of intelligence quotient with
initial status decrease from 0.868 to 0.80, while those with final status increase from 0.800 to 0.902 over a five-year span.

From the data of the Harvard Growth study (Dearborn, Rothney, &

Table 2—Recalculated Data From Hirsch Study

Age	Mean	σ	Correlation of IQ with first test 6–8 yrs.	Correlation of IQ with final test 11–13 yrs.
6–8 yrs.	102.91	13.55		.800
7–9 yrs.	106.74	12.95	.868	.770
8–10 yrs.	106.75	14.39	.824	.773
9–11 yrs.	107.01	16.46	.787	.828
10–12 yrs.	107.79	19.00	.839	.902
11–13 yrs.	111.46	19.51	.800	

Shuttleworth, 1938), I selected 135 boys and 130 girls, on which 10-year records were complete and calculated the correlation coefficients for mental age at each year level with the mental age at seven years as initial status and with mental age at sixteen years as terminal status. Unfortunately, the children in this study were not given the same mental tests year after year. This operates to reduce the correlations by decreasing their reliability so that the data become less satisfactory for our purposes than data obtained from test scales which are the same from year to year. In spite of this deficiency a trend is clear which justifies further analysis. The results are presented in Tables 3 and 4.

Table 3—Recalculated Data on 135 Boys, Harvard Growth Study

Mean chronological age	Mean mental age	SD mental age	Proportion initial of later measurements	Proportion earlier of terminal measurement	Correlation with initial status	Correlation with terminal status
7.44	90.98	14.88		46.2		.582
8.43	103.39	16.98	88.0	52.5	.735	.641
9.42	113.11	19.45	80.4	57.4	.697	.581
10.43	128.79	23.56	70.6	65.4	.726	.744
11.42	146.69	24.87	62.0	74.5	.670	.752
12.42	159.36	23.26	57.1	80.9	.642	.790
13.41	163.81	20.52	55.5	83.1	.659	.778
14.41	169.33	22.62	53.7	86.0	.653	.829
15.42	185.13	28.65	49.1	49.0	.606	.901
16.42	197.02	31.03	46.2		.582	

Table 4—Recalculated Data on 130 Girls, Harvard Growth Study

Mean chronological age	Mean mental age	SD mental age	Proportion initial of later measurements	Proportion earlier of terminal measurement	Correlation with initial status	Correlation with terminal status
7.41	94.74	12.07		45.7		.542
8.40	108.35	16.41	87.4	52.3	.651	.584
9.40	117.98	18.01	80.3	56.9	.604	.533
10.40	133.95	20.15	70.7	64.6	.719	.700
11.40	148.75	22.29	63.7	71.8	.668	.728
12.39	161.56	22.92	58.6	78.0	.655	.776
13.39	166.98	19.21	56.7	80.6	.642	.812
14.39	175.08	20.78	54.1	84.5	.632	.822
15.39	194.37	28.58	48.7	93.8	.569	.906
16.39	207.22	29.63	45.7		.542	

For the boys the correlations with initial status decrease from 0.735 to 0.582, while those for the girls decrease from 0.651 to 0.542. For the boys the correlations with terminal status increase from 0.582 to 0.901, while those for the girls increase from 0.542 to 0.906. In connection with these tables it should be noted that a mental age standardization forces the results into a linear framework with equivalent increments of mean mental age and standard deviation for each chronological year.* Examination of the columns in Tables 3 and 4, presenting the means and standard deviations of mental age at each year level, reveals this to be approximately the case, though the increments from year to year vary enough to indicate some inaccuracy in standardization. They are probably more irregular than they would have been had the same scale been used throughout.

In Table 5, the correlations from the Honzik data and the Harvard Growth Study are compared over a six-year span; the correlations for initial status being with 1.9 and seven years, respectively.

Table 5—Correlations with Initial Status at Different Age Levels

HONZIK DATA: CORRELATIONS BETWEEN MENTAL AGE AT 1.9 YEARS AND MENTAL AGE AT LATER AGES		HARVARD DATA: CORRELATIONS BETWEEN MENTAL AGE AT 7 YEARS AND MENTAL AGE AT LATER AGES		
Age		Age	Boys	Girls
2 yrs.	.68	8 yrs.	.735	.651
3 yrs.	.47	9 yrs.	.697	.604
4 yrs.	.46	10 yrs.	.726	.719
5 yrs.	.32	11 yrs.	.670	.668
6 yrs.	.30	12 yrs.	.642	.655

In Table 6, similar data for terminal status are presented, the correlations being with seven and sixteen years, respectively. Although the data are not as perfect or as comparable as one would wish, nevertheless it is clear that the coefficients obtained later in the developmental course are significantly higher than those obtained earlier and that the correlations

* The linearity imposed by mental age scaling becomes of some importance for the subsequent discussion, since it proved difficult to interpret the correlations which were also calculated with initial and terminal measurements for height and weight at successive year levels. The facts that the growth curves for height and weight are sigmoid in character and that different individuals reach their final heights at different ages result in increments at some levels that are negatively correlated with previous status. Hence the curves for the relation between successive correlations with initial and terminal status for height and weight at different levels and the proportion of growth attained calculated directly from the measurements, possess peculiar characteristics which deserve more extensive analysis and treatment in another article. But the coefficients do decrease away from initial status and increase toward terminal status. Thus for the boys the correlations for height with initial status at seven years decreased from 0.982 to 0.876, while those for the girls decreased from 0.988 to 0.799. For the boys the correlations for height with terminal status at sixteen increased from 0.876 to 0.967, and for girls the increase is from 0.799 to 0.994. For boys' weight the correlations with initial status decrease from 0.906 to 0.740, and for girls' weight decrease from 0.923 to 0.734. For boys' weight the correlations with terminal status increase from 0.740 to 0.921, while for girls' weight the increase is from 0.734 to 0.956.

Table 6—Correlations with Terminal Status at Different Age Levels

HONZIK DATA: CORRELATIONS BETWEEN MENTAL AGE AT 7 YEARS AND MENTAL AGE AT EARLIER AGES		HARVARD DATA: CORRELATIONS BETWEEN MENTAL AGE AT 16 YEARS AND MENTAL AGE AT EARLIER AGES		
Age		Age	Boys	Girls
2 yrs.	.46	11 yrs.	.752	.728
3 yrs.	.56	12 yrs.	.790	.776
4 yrs.	.66	13 yrs.	.778	.812
5 yrs.	.73	14 yrs.	.829	.822
6 yrs.	.81	15 yrs.	.901	.906

with initial status drop much more rapidly in the earlier ages. Correlations with terminal status build up more rapidly in the earlier ages, but do not reach as high a level within a comparable span. It is unfortunate that a complete series from two to sixteen years on the same children is not available. Such a series would make possible a much more adequate check of the principle involved.

THE CONCEPT OF OVERLAP

Obviously we deal here with a phenomenon in which we are basing our prediction of final status upon a larger and larger proportion of that which is included in the total, i.e., scores at ten years include a larger proportion of that which is present at sixteen years, than do scores at three years. We can then inquire into the nature of the relation between an earlier and a later measure when successive measurements include a larger and larger part of that which makes up final status and a smaller and smaller part of that which makes up initial status. In order to arrive at the determining principle, two packs of playing cards from which the Kings had been removed were thoroughly shuffled. The numbers on the face of the cards were then recorded at face value, calling the Jacks elevens and the Queens twelves. The cards were again shuffled and the figures obtained added in succession to the results of the first shuffle, then the cards were again shuffled and the results obtained added to the sum of the previous two shuffles, and so on for 16 shuffles. This procedure gave scores for 96 cases, which cumulated from the first to the sixteenth shuffle. The cumulated scores at each shuffle were then correlated successively with initial score and with final score. A similar procedure was followed using the Tippett (1927) tables of random numbers to make up a series of 300 scores, cumulated from the first score to the sixteenth.

The characteristic of each series is determined by the fact that the increments were uncorrelated and have a uniform mean standard deviation. As a result the means at successive levels resulting from the cumulation of the increments increase by a constant amount, while the standard deviations increase in systematic fashion. By obtaining the ratio of the means at each successive level to the initial mean and terminal mean, the proportionate amount of overlap can be obtained, and the correlations obtained can be plotted against these percentages or proportions.

The formula for handling the problem of overlapping is found in the coefficients of determination and non-determination, which measure the amount of association between two measures, or the extent to which the variance in one variable is determined by that in the other variable (Ezekiel, 1930; Guilford, 1936; and Nygaard, 1926). Since $r^2 + k^2 = 1$, r^2 becomes a coefficient of determination and k^2 a coefficient of non-determination. The per cent of overlapping is given by:

$r^2 =$ per cent overlap or $r = \sqrt{\text{per cent overlap}}$.

$k^2 =$ per cent non-overlap or $k = \sqrt{\text{per cent non-overlap}}$.

In Fig. 1, the curve obtained by plotting the correlation of each successive measure with the terminal measure against per cent of overlap is presented, together with the data obtained in the playing card and Tippett number series. With a one-half or 50 per cent overlap, r is the square root of 0.50 or 0.707, with a one-fourth overlap r is the square root of 0.25 or 0.50, etc. It is clear that the results obtained with the playing card series and the random numbers fit the formula. The cumulation, however, fits least well as we move farthest from the terminal measure in Fig. 1. Obvi-

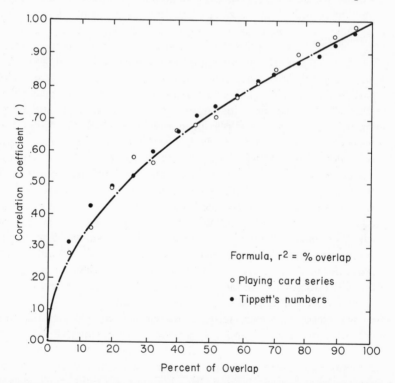

Figure 1—Curve obtained by plotting the correlation of each successive measure with the terminal measure against per cent of overlap.

ously the chance variation between single sortings of cards or single series of random numbers is greater than between cumulations. Thus the relation between the first sorting and the cumulation of 16 sortings is less stable than the relation between the cumulation of 15 sortings and the cumulation of 16 sortings.

We may then suggest the principle that the earlier in a developmental series a measurement is taken the less predictive it will be of final status and the later it is taken the more predictive it will be, and inquire as to the conditions under which the principle will hold. It may hold only if the increments, as in the playing card series or random number series, are uncorrelated or if the increments correlate with previous position in varying but moderate degrees. If the increments are perfectly uniform, it will not hold because the relative positions at successive periods will be unchanged as a constant will be added uniformly to each score. Neither will it hold if the increments are differential with respect to original scores and always perfectly correlated with them, because only a fanning out of the individual growth curves will result. If, then, correlations with terminal and initial status for mental test data show the characteristics of the curves obtained from the use of playing cards and random numbers, it would appear that the process of mental growth is one in which the increments either are not exactly constant or proportional to the original measures from which they start, or one in which that which is measured at different periods is composed of different elements or functions which overlap the initial and the terminal measures in content and function to different degrees. It is likely that both of these alternatives are characteristic to some extent of mental growth as measured by intelligence tests.

If now we ask what a measurement of a living organism, such as one of height, is, we see that it is a composite, i.e., total body length includes leg, trunk, and head length, each of which proceeds at a different rate and reaches its points of flexion and terminus at different times. The head grows rapidly in infancy and slowly in adolescence, legs grow slowly at first and more rapidly later. Weight is again a composite made up of the weights of skeleton, muscle, body organs, etc., each with its own characteristic growth pattern. If we think of intelligence in somewhat similar terms, we see it likewise as a composite of many different functions, each with its own characteristic growth pattern. It is unfortunate that, because we lack the means of measuring in absolute units these functions and their total, we must throw our measurements into a mental age standardization with its framework of linearity. Nevertheless we are led to a concept of the prediction of final status in terms of overlapping elements in earlier measures, and of a progressive differentiation of the structures and functions which go to make up the composite whole. We deal ultimately then not with increments of a single function, but with the resultant or combination of a series of increments spread over a variety of changing and growing functions. In this sense, the intelligence quotient as a measure of rate is an abstraction, which in so far as it shows constancy measures elements that are common to a number of functions. Moreover, at any particular level the intelligence quotient measures present status, and gains its predictive value only from the fact that positive and high correlations have been shown to hold for successive determinations.

We may now ask whether or not the coefficients obtained for mental test results at successive periods in longitudinal studies fit the formula given for determining overlap. The two sets of data analyzed in this study are the Honzik data, otbained in the early years, for which reliability coefficients are available, and the Harvard Growth data at later age levels for which reliability coefficients are not available.

In Fig. 2, the curves for the decrease in coefficients with successive measurements are plotted in terms of the proportion the initial measure is of later measures. For the Harvard Growth study data these proportions could be calculated directly from the material presented in Tables 4 and 5. For the Honzik material, since the actual results are not available, the mean mental age at any level was assumed to correspond to the chronological age, and the chronological age at the time of the first measurement was divided by the chronological age at later levels of measurement. This is the same ratio that Honzik herself used, and is probably not as accurate for the problem of this paper as actual mental age figures would be. I suspect that the curve for the Honzik data lies too far to the left, and that the fit would be closer had the actual mean mental ages been available. The Honzik data has been corrected for attenuation. In examining Fig. 2, the reader should keep in mind that the initial measurement for the Honzik data is at 1.9 years and the terminal measure at seven years, while the initial measure for the Harvard data is at seven years and the terminal measure at sixteen years.

For the Harvard Growth data, the original coefficients from Tables 4 and 5 were used, together with the same series of coefficients corrected for attenuation, by assuming the reliability at age seven to be 0.85, age eight, 0.86, and so on, adding 0.01 to the reliability with each year of age. This makes the assumed reliability at the terminal measure 0.94.

I also corrected the coefficients of the Harvard data for attenuation by assuming reliabilities of 0.95, 0.09, and 0.85 throughout the whole age span. The effect of correcting for attenuation is to move the curves upward, nearer the curve given by the formula. On the whole, the best assumption seemed to be that of a slight increase in reliability with increase in age. Except for raising the whole level of the curves, the effect of correction upon the form of the curve is negligible.

It is clear from Fig. 2 that in general form the curves obtained approximate the curve for the formula, but that they lie under it. The Harvard Growth curves are approximately 10 points of r under the curve, the Honzik data approximately 15 points of r under it. With corrections for attenuation the Harvard data from the 9-year level on, come close to the formula. The data in the Harvard series for the 7- and 8-year measure-

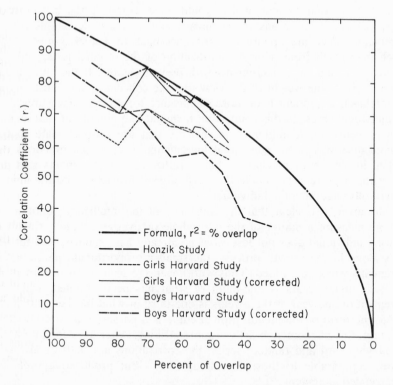

Figure 2—Curves for the decrease in coefficients with successive measurements.

ments, when the Dearborn group Test *A* was used, are erratic in both curves and tables.

Whatever question may be raised with reference to the accuracy with which the data obtained fit the formula, it is clear that the phenomenon of the increase and decrease of correlation coefficients as we move toward terminal status or away from initial status is one that is related to the per cent of overlap between the measures. Since the formula gives the curves for this relation when increments are uncorrelated, the question why the curves for the obtained data fall below rather than above the formula curve can well be raised. At the present time this cannot be answered. If there were consistent increments from age to age, plus commonalty of factors in the tests, the coefficients would tend to lie above the formula curve. If the increments were uncorrelated with previous status, but were of the same order from year to year, i.e., possessed identical means and standard deviations, the situation that exists in the playing card series and the random number series would hold and there should be close approximation. Since the curves lie under the expected curve the factors that are to be sought are (a) unreliability of the measures, which we know if corrected, brings the curves nearer expectancy; (b) differences or variations in the content of the tests from year to year, which would serve to reduce the intercorrelations; (c) small variations in the means and standard deviations of the increments which are apparent if one goes back to Tables 3 and 4 and which may result from poor standardization of the original tests, and (d) negative correlations of increments with previous status. If the latter holds it would give some weight to the view that the concept of the constancy of the intelligence quotient is of more significance for grouped measures than for individual cases. In this connection it should be pointed out that mental growth seems not a matter of increments that are proportionate to the original measures in the sense that increments occur in the functions described in physics or mechanics, but is rather one of increments that are differential with respect to both the stage of growth reached and the unique pattern of variation in the individual.

Moreover, it is clear that the constancy of the intelligence quotient is in large measure a matter of the part-whole or overlap relation, since the growing individual does not lose what he already has attained. The farther he is along in the growth process, the smaller proportionate part are the increments which are added. Thus with linear age scaling, an increment of one year at ten years is one-tenth of what has been attained, while an increment of one year at three years is one-third of what has been attained. If the true form of the mental growth curve is a parabola, as some writers maintain, this phenomenon is even more striking. After 10 cumulations in the playing card and random series, the correlations are 0.80 or above— figures comparable to those for mental tests—but produced entirely by uncorrelated increments.

Certainly these data suggest the desirability of a re-examination of the whole problem of individual increments in intelligence quotient in longitudinal series, using accurately standardized tests and the best possible conditions of testing. If this paper leads those who have or are in a position to secure extensive longitudinal series of data on children to a re-examination of the problem of constancy in the light of the concept of overlap and age increments, it will have fulfilled its purpose.

RELATION TO OUTSIDE FACTORS

The relation between a measure of intelligence and measure of any other functions at successive intervals may change in accordance with the principle of overlap. Thus a relation may be high in the early years and decrease, or be low early and increase with development. Successive measures, then, can be viewed as indicators of more or less of that which is associated with the outside variable. A striking example is furnished in the study by Bayley and Jones (1937), in which scores on mental tests at successive age levels were correlated with measures of parental and socioeconomic status. Table 7 presents in shortened form several series of the relations they report.

The correlations of mental test score with mother's education, father's

Table 7—Correlations Between Mental Score and Different Measures:
(from Bayley and Jones, 1937)

Age in months	Mother's education	Father's education	Father's occupation	Total SES Scale
1, 2, 3	− .15	− .07	− .12	.12
4, 5, 6	− .23	− .26	− .26	− .10
7, 8, 9	− .01	− .09	− .05	− .04
10, 11, 12	.06	− .06	.01	.05
13, 14, 15	.03	− .11	− .09	− .10
18	.12	− .10	− .06	− .10
21	.37	.19	.16	.15
24	.52	.39	.35	.34
36	.46	.28	.23	.04
48	.50	.37	.31	.22
60	.48	.53	.43	.36
72	.58	.50	.38	.41

education, father's occupation, and standing on the socioeconomic scale are predominantly zero or negative up to the age of 21 months and then become positive and increase in size until a maximum seems to be reached. The tests seem to measure a factor which is increasingly associated with these other variables. How are these results to be interpreted?

THE USE OF AN EARLY SCORE AS AN ORIGIN

We may regard *true* intelligence as a parameter which is approximated by actually measured intelligence in terms of a particular test at any particular time. The problem of the age level at which this approximation is the most accurate indication of *true* intelligence then arises. But this is a double problem. First, does true intelligence change with age and, second, do tests given at particular age levels approximate more or less the intelligence parameter than do tests given at other ages of developmental periods?

To the first of these questions there is no clear answer at the present time. That there is absolute growth in intelligence cannot be doubted. But is this growth an increase in level, i.e., quantitative, or is it both an increase in level and a change in kind, i.e., qualitative as well as quantitative? Thurstone's attempt to determine primary mental abilities and to study their age relations may make a significant contribution. To the second of these questions, the answer given by this paper is that measurement later in the developmental sequence gives a closer approximation than does an earlier determination. This is precisely the opposite of the assumption made by Wellman and Skeels, who match children with respect to intelligence on the basis of early tests, and who also consistently use test results obtained in infancy or early childhood as the origin from which to make calculations of increments and gains. While it may be said that this is the only possible procedure that can be followed in a longitudinal study, nevertheless *the adequacy with which a particular test measures what it purports to measure, has to be determined in terms of its correlation with tests at later ages before it can be used as an origin, in those instances in which an attempt is made to measure a particular function, and it is assumed that the changes that occur take place only in that function.* A low correlation between the initial test and the terminal test in a series would tend to make both unsatisfactory as origins, whereas a high correlation would make both satisfactory. To some extent the case that Wellman and Skeels make for gains breaks down if the principle is accepted that the earlier a measurement is made the less predictive it is of final status and the more it is subject to both constant and random errors and it is assumed that the same function is tested throughout. Because of the extraordinary importance of the first measurement when it is used as an origin in a series, every precaution should be taken to insure its validity and reliability and the avoidance of constant errors. The latter would involve the use of several tests or forms rather than one or the repetition of the test after a short interval of time, discounting any gains made during that interval.

The problem of the use of early tests as origins from which to calculate gains or losses is closely related to the problem of whether or not they are adequate measures for attacking the heredity-environment problem. If correlations with later tests are of the zero order, and if correlations with measurements of the true mother or with secondary measures such as mother's education or father's occupational status known to be of some size later on are of zero order, the question of the validity of an early test as an origin from which to calculate gains or as a device to measure the inheritance of intelligence must be met, since the zero order relations may result from deficiencies in the measuring instrument itself.

THE PROBLEM OF PAIRING AT EARLY AGES

Suppose that two groups of children are paired on the basis of infant or preschool test performance and that these scores show decreasing correlations with subsequent test performances. What are the chances that the two groups will be equivalent at subsequent periods? This is an important question in the set-up of a longitudinal experiment. If other factors, such as the hereditary factors, have not been controlled in the sampling, they may operate in successively greater amounts to produce differentiation between the groups, i.e., it is perfectly possible that there may be a spurious matching of the groups and that later on they may diverge quite widely irrespective of the type of training received. Thus, if we suppose that two groups are matched at the age of one year with the coefficients with initial status decreasing by 10 points each year, the amount of overlap may be indicated by the formula for determination as follows:

At three years, the correlation would be 0.90 and the overlap, 81 per cent; at five years, 0.70 and 49 per cent; and at seven years, 0.50 and 25 per cent. There would seem to be no quarantee that the groups matched at three years will still be matched at six or seven. Thus it is quite possible that matching children on the basis of an initial score will not produce matching at any subsequent period for characteristics or traits that are subsequently differentiated on the basis of maturation.

If the principles brought out in this paper hold, it should be possible to do a much more effective job of matching from the measurements of children's intelligence at seven or eight years, when the correlation coefficients with final status are of the order of 0.60 or more, than from measurements prior to three years when the coefficients with a measure of terminal status, such as that at seven years, are around 0.40, or below. The value of the matching procedure will increase as the measurements are taken later in the age sequence and the more effectively the infant and preschool tests predict final status. Further, if correlations with initial status decrease, it will always be possible to select a number of striking individual cases which will show consistent gains or losses from an early determination as a base, and in extreme cases, gains and losses of very large amounts.

It is also likely that the results obtained from the use of matching or control group techniques in which other variables, such as mother's education or mother's intelligence quotient, are used for selecting the groups will be affected. Thus, if one were to select a group of mothers of low intelligence quotients and a group of mothers of average intelligence quotients and measure the mental level of their children at successive ages, the phenomenon described in this paper would result in a series of decreasing intelligence quotients for the children of the mothers with low intelligence quotients, while the intelligence quotients of the children from mothers of average intelligence quotients would show little or no change with age. On the basis of regression the mental level of the children of the mothers of low intelligence quotients would fall halfway between the mean mental level of the mothers and that of the general population. But if the original tests measure little of that which is finally measured in an intelligence test, the earliest measures of the children from the mothers of low mental level would tend to fall about the mean of the population, and then as intelligence is measured more and more accurately, to move from that position to the true intermediate position. Irrespective of other factors, this trend would appear. This downward trend is quite apparent in Fig. 1 of Skodak's study (1939, p. 307) or Fig. 12 (1939, p. 90). Likewise, children from an hereditary background of high level would fall near the mean of the population on early tests and show a marked upward trend as intelligence was measured more and more accurately. Perhaps also this phenomenon explains why early training *seems* to be so much more important in producing the desirable effects found in the Iowa studies than is late training.

THE EFFECT OF CONSTANT ERRORS

Throughout this paper the early tests in a series have been assumed to be reliable. When reliability coefficients were available, it was found that correcting for attenuation there was closer approximation to the formula for overlap or determination. When, however, a factor is present which produces large errors and these errors are in a constant direction, the correlations with both terminal and initial status and with any outside measure would be seriously affected. While no data is available which enables me to evaluate such errors in terms of initial and final status, many investigators have raised the question as to the effects of resistance or negativism upon the determination of the intelligence quotient of young children. Resistance is a much greater problem at the preschool than at the older age levels. Modern scales have taken some account of this factor by eliminating those items and tests which children often refuse and substituting those which have more intrinsic interest. The Merrill-Palmer Scale includes a method of correcting for refusals which clearly recognizes the existence of this factor. One of the most interesting investigations of the phenomenon was made by Rust (1931), who gave three-year-old children both Kuhlman-Binet and Merrill-Palmer tests, repeating those tests which were refused (not those failed) on successive days a second, a third, and fourth time, etc., until the children either definitely passed or failed them. The results from this study, as presented in Table 8, indicate significant changes in intelligence quotient level, as a result of recording on the basis of ultimate success or failure on the items.

Table 8—Number of Children Whose Intelligence Quotient Increased as a Function of Repeating Items Initially Refused (from Rust, 1931)

No. of points by which IQ increased	Kuhlman-Binet	TYPE OF TEST Merrill-Palmer (not corrected for refusals)	Merrill-Palmer (corrected for refusals)
25–35	7	2	0
15–24	18	3	0
5–14	26	38	3
1–4	14	14	26
Unchanged	31	42	70
Total N	96	99	99

On the Kuhlman-Binet only 31 out of 96 intelligence quotients were unchanged, and in 51 out of 96 cases the change upward in the intelligence quotient ranged from 5 to 35 points. Somewhat similar, but not as striking results were obtained for the Merrill-Palmer, when the scores were not corrected for refusals. When corrected for refusals the changes were slight, as shown by the last column in the table.

On the basis of this study negativism seems to result in a constant error in the direction of lowering the intelligence quotient. If such a factor is present the relations of preschool tests to terminal mental level will be seriously affected. In formulating criteria for the selection of tests and test items, then, some account must be taken of the emotional reactions elicited by the tests. It is likely that many items in which this factor is pronounced would be automatically eliminated by the application of the criterion of relation to terminal status, because of the low relationships that will inevitably result. But despite this, in preparing and standardizing tests for young children, it would seem to be both profitable and necessary to subject items to rather rigorous selection in terms of the emotional reactions and resistance they elicit. And it may also be pointed out that we must be very careful in interpreting the results of examinations which were given many years ago when tests were markedly subject to this constant error.

Since the constant errors arising out of test refusals and negativism are in the direction of a lowered score, and the regression effect is for the low intelligence quotient group to be in the direction of a spuriously high score, the interpretation of the trends in curves showing change in mental level with age becomes difficult. For here are two phenomena which may mask one another, or so distort the relations found in any particular study that any correct determination of the inter-relationships of factors cannot be made.

SUMMARY: PRECAUTIONS IN THE USE AND INTERPRETATION OF EARLY TESTS

From the principles brought out in this paper several general precautions to be observed in the practical or theoretical use of measurements can be formulated. These are:

1. The earlier in the developmental course measurements are made, the less reliance can be placed on a single measurement or observation, if that measurement or observation is used for predicting subsequent development.

2. The earlier in the developmental course measurements are made, the greater care should be taken to secure accuracy of observation and record and to follow standardized procedures.

3. The earlier in the developmental course measurements are made, the more account should be taken of the possibility of disturbing factors, such as negativism and refusals, which operate as constant errors to reduce score. On young children, in particular, two tests separated in time are superior to a single test for determining status.

4. Since development is a timed series of relations or sequences, there are for many functions periods below which only a small portion of the function can be measured and above which a progressively larger portion can be measured. Hence, the possibilities of prediction are limited and progression with age is not an infallible indicator of the value of a measurement. Every effort should then be expended to secure the most accurate and predictive tests by standardizing tests against multiple rather than single criteria.

SUPPLEMENTARY READINGS

Buros, O. K. *The sixth mental measurements yearbook.* Highland Park, New Jersey: Gryphon Press, 1965. Pp. 514–542.

Cronbach, L. J. *Essentials of psychological testing.* (2nd ed.) New York: Harper, 1960. Pp. 208–212.

Escalona, S. K., & Moriarity, A. Prediction of school-age intelligence from infant tests. *Child Develpm.,* 1961, 32, 597–605.

Illingworth, R. S. The predictive value of developmental tests in the first year, with special reference to the diagnosis of mental subnormality. *J. child Psychol. Psychiat.,* 1961, 2, 210–215.

Pease, D., Rosauer, J. K., & Wolins, L. Reliability of three infant developmental scales administered during the first year of life. *J. genet. Psychol.,* 1961. 98, 295–298.

hypothetical structures
of abilities during
the preschool years[*]

C. E. MEYERS and HARVEY F. DINGMAN

[There have been periods in almost all of the sciences during which investigators have been so intent on one line of research inquiry that they have ignored, or discarded, equally important information that appeared as a by-product of their studies. As later history has shown, the neglected data were often related to questions more important than the one that guided the original research. For example, alchemists, attempting to find a way to convert lead into gold, developed some of the basic techniques and gathered some of the necessary information for the gradual emergence of chemistry. It is also well known that the early astrologers, who searched for ways of predicting the future from the positions of the stars in the heavens, recorded data on which astronomy would later build. There may be something of a parallel in psychologists' search for tests to measure "general" intelligence. There seems to be little doubt that the field of intelligence testing has been dominated almost exclusively by this interest in "general" ability during the entire 20th century. The fact that "intelligence" tests administered during infancy are not highly predictive of later measured intelligence has discouraged a good many psychologists from doing further research on tests of infant intelligence. Drs. Meyers and Dingman, of the University of Southern California and the Pacific State Hospital, suggest in the following report that psychologists may have been asking the "wrong" questions about the infant's psychological abilities. They further suggest that factor analysis may make us sensitive to new dimensions in the infant's behavior that will permit prediction of later achievements in life that are equally as important as academic success. Their very careful review of the related research literature shows that much research will have to be conducted to test the importance of their suggested points of departure. This paper is also an excellent review of the psychometric properties of those tests that have already been developed to assess the psychological abilities of infants and preschool-aged children.]

* From C. E. Meyers & H. F. Dingman. The structure of abilities at the preschool ages: Hypothesized domains. *Psychological Bulletin*, 1960, 57, 514–532. (With permission.)

This paper discusses the possibilities for factorial descriptions of the abilities of the infant and young child. It brings forth the practical and theoretical need for test reconstruction and shows the potentials for doing so which reside in the current repertory of test materials. Finally the paper hypothesizes a series of factors which may ultimately be identified at the late preschool level, with some speculations regarding the early appearance of the hypothesized factors.

CHARACTERISTICS OF ABILITY EXAMINATIONS FOR INFANTS AND YOUNG CHILDREN

Most of the instruments in current use for appraisal of the abilities at the preschool ages were constructed after the prototypes of Binet and Gesell. In both instances these pioneers faced a need to describe a child in direct terms and for practical usage. They took the easiest approach possible. The examined child was tried out on the behaviors of his own and other age groups, and was then described in terms of the age norms of the test items he passed.

The test construction and reporting of results so developed are illustrated in the construction and use of the popular instruments in contemporary clinical practice. Today's age-scale construction also employs the two technical criteria for selective retention of tried-out test items, age-progression and internal consistency. Inasmuch as the "common" behavior of young children changes with growth, the employment of these technical criteria sharpens any age-to-age difference in the abilities sampled at different levels of the examination, and narrows the spectrum of abilities sampled at any one level.

Table 1 lists a series of standarized examining instruments available for use at the various preschool ages. Most of the instruments were constructed on Binet-type principles and procedures, and yield an "age score" as a test result. The tests apparently satisfy enough of the clinical need to describe a child as he is now, in terms of age norms.

It can be shown that the instruments are not the best conceivable ones for certain other purposes. One such purpose is that of clinical prediction. Over a dozen studies have demonstrated that baby tests and early preschool tests do not predict later intelligence very well (most recently, Cavanaugh, Cohen, Dunphy, Ringwall, & Goldberg, 1957; Wittenborn, 1956). It is also shown that the best items for predicting future status may be poor items on a criterion of internal consistency at the level where they are placed (Nelson & Richards, 1938, 1939). All such studies (except those of Gesell) were preoccupied with the prediction of future "intelligence," the criterion variable being a later Binet or other IQ. Little has been done by psychologists on the prognostic value of early testing for other variables of social and theoretical interest. Will the motor subscale in Gesell and Amatruda (1947) tell of later athletic prowess or the age of

Table 1—Illustrative Current Ability Measures with Notations on Item Selection and Age-Scoring

Type of instrument and stated or implied scope	Preschool ages tested	Bases for item selection	Kind of score yielded
A. General behavioral development			
1. Gesell & Amatruda (1947) "Gesell Schedules"	1 month up	Age-normal behavior	DA (by median success level)
2. Griffiths (1954) Abilities of Babies	1–24 months	Age-normal behavior; "G" broadly conceived	Cumulated MA
B. General intelligence			
1. Cattell (1940) Infant Intelligence Scale	3–24 months	Age-normal behavior; some selection by face validity for intelligence	Cumulated MA
2. Shotwell, Dingman, & Tarjan (1957) Number Concept Test	3 years up	Quantitative tasks, progression with MA	Cumulated MA
3. Terman & Merrill (1937) Stanford-Binet	2 years up	r with 1916 SB; face validity, age progression, internal consistency	Cumulated MA
4. Valentine (1950) Intelligence Tests for Children	2 years up	Age-normal; face validity	Cumulated MA
5. Ammons & Ammons (1948) Picture Vocabulary	2 years up	Age-suitable recognition vocabulary, r with SB	MA from points; centiles
C. General intelligence by non-language, culture-free means			
1. Arthur (1947) Point Scale	4½ years up	Face validity for intelligence; r with other tests	MA from points
2. Burgemeister, Blum, & Lorge (1954) Columbia Mental Maturity	3 years up	Nonverbal, ease of resp., suitable to age, face, r with other tests	MA from points
3. Leiter (1948) International Performance Scale	2 years up	Age-suitable culture-fair, face validity for G	Cumulated MA
D. Purposes other than to measure intelligence			
1. Bayley (1935) California Motor Scale	1–50 months	Age-normal motor	Points; sigma for age
2. Doll (1953) Social Maturity Scale	1 year up	Age-normal, self-help, culture-required conduct	Social age by points
3. Sloan (1955) Lincoln-Oseretsky Motor Tests	4 years up	Motor, selected from Oseretsky by objectivity, age progression	Points to centiles by age and sex

ambulation in handicapped children? Do the personal-social items in Griffiths (1954) predict leadership in the fifth grade? Surprisingly little is available. Neilon (1948) reported good consistency in general behavior descriptions between infancy and adolescence in Shirley's (1933) famous subjects, and provides a good review of available literature.

Gesell (e.g., Gesell, Castner, Thompson, & Amatruda, 1939; a summary in Gesell 1954) found consistency within broad categories of diagnosis, such as mentally deficient or palsied, and some intriguing instances of temperamental consistency in normals as well. Escalona (1950) and Gallagher (1953) demonstrated that prediction from infant testing gave better results if subject testability was adequately attended to. Neither found a degree of improvement that altered the general conclusion on predictability.

There have been three efforts to identify test items having forecasting value. In the Fels series (Nelson & Richards, 1938, 1939; Richards & Nelson, 1939) the Gesell items on alertness and perception at 6, 12, and 18 months had promising correlations with later IQ and were superior to the whole scale in this. The Berkeley data (Hastings, 1952; Pinneau, 1953; summary by Bayley, 1955) have similarly been analyzed, yielding little of value before 18 months. After 2 years the prediction becomes surer. Tasks which are verbal or complex seem best. A third such study comes from Catalano and McCarthy (1954), where measures of infant consonantal differentiation correlated about 0.40 with Binet later on, the magnitudes being little reduced when age of phonemic' recording or of testing was partialed out.

The above paragraphs suggest that precious little developmental test work has come forth in either concept or practice in the ability testing of the young since the time of Binet. Ability testing, preoccupied with technical purity of verbal and nonverbal G, has chosen to eschew the imitative, psychomotor, and other functions which do not correlate well "with later IQ," omitting large areas of human competence which might have values in their own rights. The elegant simplicity of the age-scale notion served the needs well for several decades. It is, however, no longer possible to defend narrow spectrum G testing. Voices have appealed for change (Bayley, 1955, 1956; Sarason & Gladwin, 1958; Thurstone, 1956). But the only energies exerted toward new scales which the present writers have knowledge of seem limited to those of students of Kirk and Osgood at Illinois (e.g., Sievers, 1955).

POTENTIAL CONTRIBUTIONS
OF FACTORIAL STUDY

Beyond the need for greater clinical breadth and prediction, the growth studies could very well use some instruments which provide whatever continuity is available from one age to another in the functions tested. Even more intriguing than continuity is the emergence and differentiation of those abilities which one calls "factors" when the child grows up.

The study of abilities at older levels has enjoyed considerable sophistication. A fairly stable structure of human competencies is taking form in replicated works (Fleishman, 1957; French, 1957; Guilford, 1956, 1957, 1958). Factorial study is not in its infancy. Its contributions no longer need to be in the form of scattered dramatic discoveries, but are systematic, stepwise contributions. Not all the expected factors of adulthood have yet been operationally described, nor have all the questions one raises about them or the structure they fit been answered. Whether the many factors have market value or how they emerge as nature-nurture products, are questions which for the moment are beside the main issue. If factorial descriptions of man's abilities are available, one can make efficient measurement of whatever attributes one chooses or needs for a specific purpose. Further, it should be of advantage to seek for continuities between the established factor structure for young adults and the rather bulky amount of information which is available from the observations and experimental study of the infant and young child.

PREVIOUS FACTOR STUDIES

Attention is first given to those factorial studies of abilities known to have been performed at preschool ages. Only five, all of them American, have been found. A perusal of British summaries of factor literature (e.g., Thomson, 1950; Vernon, 1950) did not reveal evidence of any other preschool analyses. The findings of these studies are presented not to claim that some group factors have been discovered, replicated, and accepted, which is hardly the case, but only to show that something beyond a general factor can be found.

Richards and Nelson (1939) analyzed the interitem tetrachoric *r*'s of the Gesell items in the Fels data.

Clearly emerging on the centroid extractions at 6, 12, and 18 months were two factors labeled "alertness" and "motor." At 12 months there was a hint of a third factor.

McNemar (1942) reported on the standardization of the 1937 Stanford-Binet. Included were analyses which, unlike most factor efforts, were designed to disclose whether the item selection of the famous scale was carefully enough done to have avoided group factors. The unrotated centroid analyses demonstrated at most age levels the excellence of item selection from the viewpoint given: a first loading accounted for most of the common factor variance at nearly all age levels. Exceptions included 2–0 and 2–6, at which there were two apparently unimportant loadings of unclear meaning, evident in the identifying, memory span, and movement items.

Hofstaetter (1954) analyzed a matrix of interage test correlations. The results showed a "sensorimotor" alertness with best loadings in the first 2 years, "persistence" from 2 to 4, and "intelligence" from 3 years on. Thus a sophisticated treatment confirms what is seen in the inspectional analysis of test content and the study of age-to-age intercorrelations.

The above-mentioned three studies were analyses of already existing data. Only Kelley's and the Thurstones' analyses sought for factors. Kelley (1928) was the pioneer and provided factor reports for seventh grade, third grade, and kindergarten children. With a highly rational but painstaking and difficult method no longer used, he reported on the upper two groups a pattern that we today would identify as verbal, numerical, spatial, etc., with loadings also on what he prefers to call "maturity heterogeneity" rather than G. Only his kindergarten array is of interest here. The original table is substantially reproduced in Table 2.

The findings deserve some discussion. First, Kelley was one of the few in his day in resisting G, believing the British data for it to be due to insufficiently controlled variability in sex, age, and background of subjects and to unrealistic treatment of error in residuals. Kelley labels his own first factor as maturity-heterogeneity (his age range at kindergarten was 3–6 to 6–3). Second, what he called "verbal" should be called "memory span," or "immediate memory," as the items required only serial recital

Table 2—Final Factor Values for the Population of 107 Kindergarten Children at Close of Forty-Eighth Successive Approximation*

Tests used	Maturity, heterogeneity, etc.	Verbal	Memory	Spatial No. 1	Spatial No. 2	Control of meaningless content
1. Memory for meaningful forms	.79		.13			
2. Control of meaningful visual memory images	.71			.27		−.18
3. Memory of meaningless forms	.62		.18	.27	.50	
4. Control of meaningless visual memory images	.63				.15	.42
5. Memory for verbal material	.49	.61	.50			
6. Divided Forms Test	.52				.58	−.24
7. Knox Cube Test	.62		.36		.13	

* From Kelley (1928), with slight modification.

after one hearing, not semantic interpretation. This "verbal" (or memory) is found for only one entry in the matrix.

Leaving aside the characteristics of the work in today's terms, the Kelley report is not contradicted by later data. There is replication to the extent the Thurstones, with group tests, explored down to age 5½. The Kelley study remains the best available model for anticipation of factors.

The second and remaining analysis-for-factors' sake at preschool ages was the work of the Thurstones leading to the Primary Mental Abilities tests (Thurstone & Thurstone, 1953) which included a level for ages 5–7. According to the publisher, (personal communication), the factorial analysis of 5–7 age group has not been published; the norms for the published tests were established on a new group. The 5–7 PMA has this array: motor, perceptual-speed, verbal, spatial, and quantitative (replaced by N at higher levels). "Motor" is tested by requiring the drawing of pencil lines between dots and compares to "dynamic precision" at higher levels. It is not in the array of the PMAs for older subjects. Regarding the Q or quantitative, the Thurstones point out that N and R evolve from Q sometime after the kindergarten-primary level.

While the original factor study was not published, the Technical Supplement to the Manual provides some information on groups of pupils utilized for correlational studies. There is less evidence of factor clarity at 5–7 compared with the higher ages. Intercorrelations were 0.50 and up. With an age range of only 5–9 to 6–8, the prospect of reduction by partial r is small. Another table shows rs with Binet; only motor is below 0.50.

The PMAs cannot be considered replications of specific Kelley factors, but the two reports do reinforce the conviction that factors can be found. Note that Kelley had a first loading called maturity-heterogeneity and the Thurstones found considerable interfactor correlation. To label either result the consequence of G is as unwarranted at this time as to conclude the cause is differential testability or variance due to testing conditions. The McNemar report had little common factor variance beyond the first loading, but in this instance "purity" was built into the test material by preliminary steps. The general conclusion, therefore, is that factors will emerge once appropriate test materials are made available.

PROBLEMS IN CONDUCTING FACTORIAL STUDIES WITH THE YOUNG

That only five studies have been done is not entirely due to lack of interest. The problems of testability at preschool ages are discouraging. It is not until fourth or fifth grade (age 9 or 10) that a typical group of children have enough reading ability and conformity to be tested easily in full class groups. In second and third grades (and some fourth) one must read directions aloud with the children and provide monitors; even so, only 30 minutes of adequately controlled testing are accomplished. One who watches the process might challenge the word "adequately." At kindergarten it is the custom to do readiness evaluation in groups not exceeding four or five. School psychologists are not at all sure that even this situation gives control over testing circumstances, especially when other personnel than themselves do the administering. It is almost certain that individual differences in conformity and distractibility, broken pencils, and the like have contributed to variance and lie behind the larger test and factor intercorrelations found in the younger level when different levels have been compared. The skeptic should watch the PMA being administered even to a small, well-motivated kindergarten-primary group. Below kindergarten, of course, no useful testing other than individual can be accomplished, and the cost factor becomes significant.

HYPOTHESIZED FACTORS

It is convenient to return briefly to the issue of prediction from an early to a later age. The discovery of factors at age 5 is of merit in itself, whether or not what is found had continuity with abilities at other levels. Relation with findings at higher age levels can be taken for granted. It is another matter with respect to extension downward from age 5 to infancy. There is little guarantee that any particular ability seen at age 5 is represented at 3 or earlier. In other words, the lack of prediction from baby tests, previously discussed, may not entirely be due to poor instrumentation; to some degree, qualitative differences exist between infant and child. The issue of whether abilities emerge via differentiation or via consolidation certainly enters. Bayley (1955, 1956) provides a good discussion of this. But answers to these and related questions cannot be produced till the instrumentation capable of detecting what exists has been created.

A further introductory note is required. The word "ability" needs more than an implicit definition. It is here regarded as that functioning which does *not* include (a) the so-called vestigial reflexes such as the plantar; (b) the vegetative responses even if they can be volitionally controlled at times, such as sphincter activity; (c) random, apparently unaimed "emitted" movement of the skeletal sets, such as the arm and leg motions of the infant.

It is more difficult to say what *is* included, but tentatively, it is behavior change which is guided by current or previous sensorial input. For example, cessation of movement at a sound is regarded here as an ability. This breadth of concept is wanted in order to include within the scope of human "adaptive ability" for any movement, change in movement, cessation of movement, readiness for movement, etc., when such conduct is performed in direct or delayed consequence of experiencing with the senses. Of necessity, such movements and their attributes must include such nonintellectual dimensions as strength, simple reaction time, and the like.

For clarity's sake, the above discussion and the test items to be mentioned might be thought of in the traditional expression: S-O-R. As usual, the term S represents the stimulus situation or any portion of it we choose to center upon, current or past. As usual, R represents a response, a muscular activity or change in same, of any recordable or observable sort. Discussion of O is postponed for the moment.

In the use of a test of perceptual functioning, it is hoped the obtained individual differences were due to perception, not to O or R. A response must be made by the subject, of course. But the examination process provides that there is simplicity and ease in the means of response. Hence in a perceptual task a subject signifies his recognition or discrimination by a gesture, a lever depression, a word, or a pencil mark. On the other hand, if one seeks individual differences in response speed, strength, dexterity, sentence length, imaginativeness, or other quality, then the input factors should bring no differential difficulty to the subjects.

With respect to the O term above, the present paper needs to presume no special theoretical position. The intermediation between input and response can stand for "mind" or physiology. The expression "thinking factors" is utilized below, and refers without commitment to whatever intermediates. Test items which have their difficulty in "mental" or thinking intermediators should put no burden upon the perceptual or response operations of the examinees. Hence, one uses a time or space gap between S and R; one requires the subject to draw a conclusion on similarity or difference, to extrapolate, to find a rule, to make a judgment, to find new uses or combinations.

The hypothesized factors now presented are grouped, to some extent, on the grounds just presented.

Table 3 presents domains and hypothesized factors within them, for ages 4–6. It also shows estimated ages of emergence of the proposed abilities as identifiable factors. The table also lists sources in the literature which implicitly or explicitly support certain of the differentiations assumed in the array.

Three domains ought to be fairly certain of existence: psychomotor, perceptual, and psycholinguistic. The seven which are specified result from the separation of auditory from visual perception, the separation of gross-body psychomotor from hand-eye, the separation of receptive from expressive psycholinguistics, and the differentiation of mental or thinking from all of these.

It is not claimed that all the hypothesized factors can be found. No immediate claims about orthogonality can be made. Until the first few simple matrices are analyzed, one can make only guesses.

THE MOTOR DOMAINS

Two general groups of motor factors are presumed: (a) the whole-body, in which gravity is defined in postural and locomotor achievements and (b) the hand-eye or manipulational. The developmental psychologist will quickly note that the motor items in baby scales, in the Bayley-California (1935) and the Oseretsky (Sloan, 1955) can be easily sub-divided into whole-body and hand-eye items. Gesell did this a generation ago in separately listing motor and adaptive, while Griffiths (1954) utilized similar rubrics. In a more sophisticated way, Guilford (1958) provides a structure which distinguishes "gross" psychomotor factors from those of specified parts of the body.

Taking useful reaction to gravity as the first expression of psychomotor ability, then the earliest response occurs in the first month. The normal baby shows momentary maintenance of head posture when held erect, and can lift his face from prone and turn it so as to breathe. The onward development includes postural and locomotor achievements against gravity. Whole-body motor differentiated from hand-eye within the first year, with low congruence believed to occur before two years. Among whole body-activities, the antigravity and the locomotor are different by "face" appearance, and clearly separate in adulthood (Guilford, 1958). This distinction appears in the words "static" and "dynamic" in Table 3. Within each of the whole-body and hand-eye domains, differentiation should be easily observable before school age. In fact, perusal of Table 3 shows that greater differentiation is predicted in the psychomotor than in other domains. This particularization is suggested by the low intercorrelations of various motor tests (Jones & Seashore, 1944). Adult motor abilities are surprisingly specific (Seashore, 1951) and differentially trainable (Fleishman, 1957).

To sum up on motor factors, whole- vs. part-body should be evident within 2 years; a nearly full display like the adult structure of Guilford is expected by 5 years of age.

Table 3—Factors Hypothesized in Seven Domains with Related Information

Early appearance	Hypothesized factors, CA 4–6 years	Age of emergence of factors	Tests & items	Test & item sources	Bibliography pertaining to domain
DOMAIN 1: Psychomotor, whole-body					
1 month: Earliest antigravity, chin-up; momentary head control	1.1 Postural balance	1½ years	Heath rail walk; toe-balance; chalk walk	Bayley (1935), Glanville & Kreezer (1937)	Bayley (1935), Fleishman (1953, 1957), Guilford (1958), Jones (1949), Jones & Seashore (1944), McCloy & Young (1954)
5 months: Rolls over	1.2 Dynamic balance	1½ years	Hop-skip; one-foot hop; jump-balance	Bayley (1935), Heath (1953), Hempel & Fleishman (1955)	
7 months: Erect sitting	1.3 Impulsion	2½ years	Standing broad jump & high jump; football kick	McCloy & Young (1954), Metheny (1941)	
8 months: Crawling progress	1.4 Coordination	2½ years	Hurdle jump; cable jump; rotary pursuit	Sloan (1955)	
12 months: Standing alone	1.5 Flexibility	3 years	Back-down-wall; toe-touch; amplitude of joint movement		
12–15 months: Walking	1.6 Strength	3 years	Dynamometer; abduction of leg; push-ups		
24 months: Up and down stairs					
DOMAIN 2: Psychomotor, hand-eye	2.1 Static precision	3 years	Steadiness-aim; track tracing	Bayley (1935), Glanville & Kreezer (1937), Heath (1953), Hempel & Fleishman (1955)	Bayley (1935), Fleishman (1953, 1957), Guilford (1958), Jones (1949), Jones & Seashore (1944), McCloy & Young (1954), Seashore (1951)
3 months: Retentive grasp	2.2 Dynamic precision	3 years	Rotary pursuit; pursuit-aiming; circle dotting; hole punching		
4 months: Grasps and secures	2.3 Reaction time	3 years	Auditory & visual RT	McCloy & Young (1954), Metheny (1941)	
7 months: Drinks from cup	2.4 Dexterity	3 years	Tweezer tasks; cube stacking; nut stacking	Sloan (1955)	
10 months: Pulls toy by string	2.5 Speed	4 years	Dot tapping; finger tapping; articulation speed (also see 6.1)		
30 months: Buttoning					

Domain	Category	Age	Description	References	
DOMAIN 3: Visual perception 1 month: Awareness—pursuit movements 5 months: Recognition of parents, differentiation from strangers 6 months: Other percepts	3.1 Perceptual speed	18 months	Thurstone PMA tests; readiness items; letter and word discrimination; Leiter items; Columbia items; (Burgemeister)	Burgemeister et. al. (1954) Lee & Clark (1951) Leiter (1948) Monroe (1935) Templin (1957) Terman & Merrill (1937) Thurstone & Thurstone (1953)	French (1957) Gollin (1956) Guilford (1956, 1958) Munn & Steining (1931) Thurstone (1948) Thurstone (1956) Thurstone & Thurstone (1953)
	3.2 Space	36 months	Thurstone PMA tests; space items in readiness tests	Terman & Merrill (1937) Thurstone & Thurstone (1953)	Osgood & Sebeok (1954) Sievers (1955) Templin (1957)
DOMAIN 4: Auditory perception 1 month: Awareness 5 months: Auditory localization 6 months: Identification of mother, bottle sounds, voices 9 months: Word sound discrimination; differential reaction to sounds, voices, tone of voices	4.1 Auditory discrimination	1½ years	Identification of common sounds; phoneme discrimination; discrimination learning	Lee & Clark (1951) Monroe (1935) Sievers (1955) Templin (1957) Terman & Merrill (1937)	
	4.2 Auditory localization	1½ years	Indicating sound sources		
DOMAIN 5: Receptive psycholinguistics 1 month: Quieted by voice 3 months: Responsive vocalization to voice 8 months: Responds to name and "no" 18 months: Identifies pictures by name	5.1 Auding	1 year	Ammons vocabulary; Stanford-Binet identifying items; use identification items; directions tests; sentences with prepositional instructions	Ammons & Ammons (1948) Gollin (1956) Hildreth & Griffiths (1949) Monroe (1935)	Brown (1954) Caffrey (1955) Eisenson (1954) Gewirtz (1948a, 1948b) McCarthy (1954) Osgood & Sebeok (1954) Sassenrath & Holmes (1956)
	5.2 Verbal comprehension	5 years	"Preliterate" items; recognition of own name; address; meaning of common signs, symbols, numbers at "readiness" level; Thurstone street-gestalt; Sievers object-picture differential vocabulary	Sievers (1955) Stutsman (1931) Templin (1957) Terman & Merrill (1937) Thurstone (1948)	

Early appearance	Hypothesized factors, CA 4–6 years	Age of emergence of factors	Tests & items	Test & item sources	Bibliography pertaining to domain
DOMAIN 6: Expressive psycholinguistics 1 month: Noncrying vocalization 6 months: Babbling 12 months: First spoken word	6.1 Articulation	1½ years	Speed of repetitive pronunciation different phonemes	Gewirtz (1948a, 1948b) Monroe (1935) Sievers (1955) Stutsman (1931) Templin (1957) Terman & Merrill (1937)	Eisenson (1954) Gewirtz (1948a, 1948b) McCarthy (1954) Osgood & Sebeok (1954) Thurstone (1948)
	6.2 Semantic fluency	2 years	Naming or use vocabulary, thing names, food names, child names, etc.; picture description; Templin sentence complexity; action agent; uses of objects; Sievers picture vocabulary; Binet picture vocabulary; how many? items		
	6.3 Symbolic fluency	3 years	Sievers nonsense imitation; alliteration; rhyming; word-sound games		
DOMAIN 7: Mental (memory & thinking) 8–9 months: Piaget's "fourth stage" 10 months: Imitation 15 months: Discrimination learning (Munn & Steining, 1931) 30 months: Rotated form board	7.1 Memory span	2½ years	Digit span; word span; sentence memory; Sievers nonsense grammatical mimicry; Knox cubes, Binet picture memory and design memory; Verbal analogies; sorting; transfer tasks	Gollin (1956) Keller (1954) Monroe (1935) Sievers (1955) Stutsman (1931) Terman & Merrill (1937)	Bayley (1955, 1956) Garrett (1946) Gollin (1956) Keller (1954) McCarthy (1957) Maurer (1946) Piaget (1952) Thurstone (1948) Thurstone (1956) Werner (1948)
	7.2 Abstracting	3 years	Kohs blocks; Rutgers drawing; bead chain;		
	7.3 Reproduction of visual models	3 years	Thurstone pattern completion and pattern copying		

VISUAL PERCEPTION

The utilization of exteroception and somesthesis is observed within the first weeks of life. One may see primitive awareness or discrimination at 1 month or earlier, in a change in conduct at a change in the stimulus field (visual pursuit, cessation of movement at a sound, etc.). At 3 or 4 months the primitive awareness has become recognitive, perhaps only at a conditioning level, by the criterion of anticipatory behavior at the sight of bottle or mother. The word "percept" is deserved at 6 months if not earlier in that the infant seems to be able to carry a recognition past the immediate time or space. Discriminating, recognizing, and percept building must precede, in all logic, the use of receptive input when that use is more than reflexive. The order of items in the Gesell scale, for example, shows recognitive behavior before adaptive positive response.

A distinction between perception and spatial ability should be evident at 3 years, according to Thurstone (1948). Kelley's study identified two visual factors, one probably spatial, in subjects whose ages reached down to 3½. The Merrill-Palmer (Stutsman, 1931) and the Stanford-Binet (Terman & Merrill, 1937) have items which appear to be both of the speedy differentiating kind and of the visualization sort at several levels. In a study relating reading to various Thurstone perceptual tests, Goins (1958) identified two factors. The first appeared mainly in the timed tests while the second might be called spatial, as it appeared on untimed tasks of pattern completion, copying, reversals, etc.

In summary, therefore, it is proposed that visual perception will be seen as noncongruent with motor and other abilities at 6 months and that by 3 years will differentiate into separably measurable if not orthogonal perceptual vs. space factors.

AUDITORY PERCEPTION

It is necessary to point out that the distinction made here between visual and auditory perception is on theoretical grounds. The classic Thurstone (1938) work on perception was exclusively on visual. The subject of channel differences intrigues the communication people (Osgood & Sebeok, 1954) and was suggested by Thurstone himself (1948).

Evidence for more than reflexive use of auditory input can be detected as early as evidence for similar use of visual input. That is, within the first month, a normal baby is quieted by sound or otherwise changes his activity. However, it is less clear how auditory skills proliferate for the necessary testing confuses auditory discriminatory skills with word semantics. While a child who selects "bear" separately from "pear" in a "spondee test" clearly shows ability to distinguish the two initial sounds, one cannot tell how early this perceptual distinction occurs by simple testing before a good "auding" vocabulary has been acquired. It is necessary to use differential

conditioning or discrimination learning. It is therefore necessary, in practical testing, to ignore auditory figural discrimination vs. auditory semantic
factors at their earliest and to limit present predictions of high refinement of
factors to about second grade testability.

But if the resources for extensive investigation become available, it is
predicted that such factors analogous to the visual can be detected by 2
years and before: space orientation via sound, differential reaction to word-
sound phonemes apart from meaning, pitch discrimination, and many
others.

LINGUISTIC

Receptive. The distinction between receptive and expressive language
was known in the literature of aphasia before Thurstone distinguished W
from V (cf. French's review, 1951). The distinction is demanded in com-
munications theory (e.g., Osgood & Sebeok, 1954). In addition, channel
differences are also suggested by these theorists as well as by the auding
literature from educational psychology (Brown & Caffrey, 1952; Caffrey,
1955; Sassenrath & Holmes, 1956) and experience with slow learners
(Durrell & Sullivan, 1958; Kirk & McCarthy, 1950). Thus, one must not
yet assume that an auding factor in prereading ages is congruent with later
V developed with printed tests.

Receptive factors are hypothesized as shown in Table 3. The auditory
channel includes a factor of speech-sound perception. Difficulties in testing
for it were mentioned just above. One might anticipate it at those levels at
which it must be presumed present—before 1 year of age when a child
shows evidence of differential understanding of words before he can use
them expressively. The hypothesized visual comprehension factor would be
only primitive as yet. Its origins may be detectable at ages 5 and up by
items from readiness tests in which meaning is obtained, for example, in
specifying the significance of a traffic signal. Note that both auditory and
visual perceptive factors are located in both linguistic and the perceptual
domains.

Expressive. The array here also distinguishes the vocal from the graphic-
gestural modes of expression. Since the age of interest here is preschool,
the written language could at best be rudimentary; at kindergarten the
ability to hold a pencil, use it, and print one's name is generally expected,
little more. Psychomotor factors which are listed under appropriate head-
ing are repeated here.

THINKING

Referring back to the S-O-R discussion, "thinking" refers to that which
is intermediate between discrimination of the stimulus matrix and the
making of the response. The intermediation may be memory or visualization, rule-finding or abstracting. In any case, a test item needs to have its

difficulty in O and not in stimulus discrimination or response refinement, and certainly not in word knowledge as such. For children of 5 or 6, the verbal problem is best avoided by simple omission. The choice of item content is limited largely to elemental figural materials among which discriminations are known to be made in the first year of life.

Hypothesized are memory span, abstracting, and reproduction of figural models. The last-mentioned is probably complex; in adult work the Kohs and the pattern copying tasks are loaded on space but also on reasoning, perceptual, verbal, and specific factors (French, 1951). Obviously it is going to cause some problems to separate space from thinking and perhaps this task cannot be accomplished so long as figural materials are used.

Memory span of course is easily obtained by both verbal and gestural means, provided the contents are "easy" to begin with. Digit span for the normally cultured child is satisfactory. The Knox cubes provide another span-measuring process of reasonably apparent purity.

Further speculation about the thinking factors is probably premature. There is insufficient experience at preschool ages with analogs of, for example, what Guilford would call productive thinking. Existing Binet and WISC items are of three main sorts: immediate memory span; perceptual discriminations and identifications; and information "bits" brought forth by items of the sort, What should you do when, Which is prettier, How many, etc.

It is not till the age levels of 6 and 7 that the Stanford-Binet uses productive thinking items. At these age-levels one finds verbal analogies, picture absurdities, and similarities and differences. Defining thinking as the processing of information to produce a conclusion, then thinking is so introduced. Such items are concerned with semantic content. Symbolic content also is rare at younger levels. It was already pointed out that one competent team found no "number," a symbolic ability, in the age bracket 5 to 7 years (Thurstone & Thurstone, 1953). The making of rhymes, which would be another ability in symbolic content is called for in the Stanford-Binet at the 9-year level.

The WISC (Wechsler, 1949) is another scale in common use which, like the Binet, essentially lacks thinking items, as above described, below the mental-age equivalent of about V. The first items in the Arithmetic subtest require only counting. But the WISC has some verbal analogies with mental-age values at around 5 and 6 years.

Hence the preschool age-levels of popular batteries are barren of thinking items; the speculator has few reference points on which to develop a system. The many observations of Piaget should not be ignored, nor those of American investigators on problem solving in the young (a recent example, Braine, 1959). But the aggregate of items and ideas from these scattered sources is not large. A considerable amount of inventive elaboration is required if even a modest 6-year-old model of adult-level structure is wanted.

SUMMARY

This paper has reviewed the situation of ability testing at the infant and preschool ages. The available instruments have, on the one hand, failed to predict "later IQ," for whatever value later IQ has as a criterion. On the other hand, the spectrum of abilities tested, which if anything should broaden as the child grows, is caused to narrow down by the use of technical criteria of age-progression and internal consistency in item selection. The previous factorial studies at preschool ages, of which only one (Kelley's) may be regarded as of quality, give reason to believe that carefully prepared testing could demonstrate that more than a G is present. Finally, a series of factors is hypothesized, representing seven domains of whole-body and hand-eye psychomotor, visual and auditory perception, receptive and expressive psycholinguistics, and thinking or mental. The hypotheses are made for ages 4–6 years, with some speculations as to age of earliest emergence of the factor. Illustrative item-types and supporting literature are given.

SUPPLEMENTARY READINGS

Cattell, R. B. Factor analysis: An introduction to essentials. *Biometrics,* 1965, 21, 190–215.

Cureton, E. E. The principal compulsions of factor analysts. *Harvard Educ. Rev.,* 1939, 9, 287–295.

McNemar, Q. The factors in factoring behavior. *Psychometrika,* 1951, 16, 353–359.

Thurstone, L. L. *Multiple-factor analysis.* Chicago: Univer. Chicago Press, 1947.

piaget's theory

of cognitive development*

D. E. BERLYNE

[Periods of dramatic change in conceptualization are marked in the history of the well-established physical sciences by the names of men who possessed broad vision and unusually creative talents. For example, scientific progress in physics is closely linked to the personalities of Galileo, Newton, and Einstein. Personalities are equally important during the infancy of a science, although one must wait for history to document their enduring influence. Experimental psychology, which has not as yet celebrated its first centennial, appears to have been most strongly influenced by the contributions of Pavlov. And it now appears that developmental psychology may well be given a strong forward thrust by the theoretical formulations of Piaget. This highly productive Swiss psychologist has proposed a truly developmental model for psychological man. Up until recent years it has been difficult for American psychologists to secure a broad picture of Piaget's comprehensive theory, because his writings are scattered across literally hundreds of scientific reports and books (many of which have yet to be translated into English). During the last few years this communicative problem has been partially solved by Flavell's book on *The Developmental Psychology of Jean Piaget,* summarizations by Inhelder, and the following overview by Dr. Berlyne of the University of Toronto. As this report indicates, Dr. Piaget is fully committed to the generalization that "the infant is father to the man." His emphasis on the psychological functions of "accommodation" is not new in psychology, but is, perhaps, an often forgotten perspective among some of the extreme behaviorists.]

Piaget is known to English-speaking psychologists mainly for his early writings, with their thought-provoking but, according to some critics, disputable accounts of the quaint notions of young children. Doubts have been expressed about the validity of the method of interrogation used for these studies and about the generality of the findings. Repetitions with other populations have not always produced the results that Piaget's works

* From D. E. Berlyne. Recent developments in Piaget's work. *British Journal of educational Psychology,* 1957, 27, 1–12. (With permission.)

would lead one to expect. At least one writer was moved to dismiss his "subjective approaches to the analysis of child behavior" as "little removed from ordinary literary speculation" (Pratt, 1933).

Since the 1930s, however, Piaget's researches have been undergoing some gradual but profound changes. He has been turning to more exact and behaviouristic methods of collecting data: close observation of the infants, setting older children practical tasks or putting precise questions to them about events enacted in front of them, and psychophysical experiments with both child and adult subjects. His theory has become more detailed and more ambitious in scope, drawing on his knowledge of biology, logic and history of science, all of them fields to which he has contributed. These developments can be summed up by saying that he has changed from one of the most celebrated *developmental* psychologists into one of the most important of contemporary *general* psychologists. But this does not mean that his work has lost any of its importance for those faced with the practical problems of childhood in their everyday work.

Like most contemporary psychologists, Piaget starts from the biological concept of "adaptation." He sees adaptation as an interplay of two complementary processes, which he calls *"assimilation"* and *"accommodation."* Assimilation occurs when an organism uses something in its environment for some activity which is already part of its repertoire. At the physiological level, it is exemplified by the ingestion of food, and at the psychological level it embraces a variety of phenomena. Piaget sees assimilation at work, for example, whenever a situation evokes a particular pattern of behaviour because it resembles situations that have evoked it in the past, whenever something new is perceived or conceived in terms of something familiar, whenever anything is invested with value or emotional importance. Accommodation, on the other hand, means the addition of new activities to an organism's repertoire or the modification of old activities in response to the impact of environmental events.

Psychologists accustomed to other conceptual schemes may wonder whether it really helps to group together such multifarious processes under the same rubrics. Is the role played by a cow which a child confuses with a horse really analogous to that played by a cow appearing as roast beef on the child's dinner plate? Although Piaget discusses assimilation and accommodation at great length, some readers may feel that the concepts need to be analyzed more minutely before they can yield unequivocal predictions rather than describing facts already discovered. At all events, assimilation seems to include what learning theorists call "generalization" and "discrimination," processes determining which response a particular stimulus will elicit, while accommodation covers "differentiation of responses" and the learning of new responses.

As the child's development proceeds, a more and more complete balance and synthesis between assimilation and accommodation is achieved. The child is able to take account of stimuli more and more remote from .

him in space and time, and to resort to more and more composite and indirect methods of solving problems.

Piaget agrees with many other theorists in distinguishing "affective" and "cognitive" factors. The former release energy, while the latter determine how the energy will be applied. Piaget's writings have concentrated on the "cognitive" aspect of behaviour rather than on motivation and emotion, but he insists that neither aspect must be overlooked. The child does not undergo separate intellectual and emotional developments. The most dispassionate pursuit of knowledge must be driven by some motive, and the directions in which drives and emotions impel behaviour must depend on the structures made available by the growth of intelligence.

THE PERIOD OF SENSORI-MOTOR INTELLIGENCE (BIRTH TO TWO YEARS)

During his first two years, the child gradually advances towards the highest degree of intelligence that is possible without language and other symbolic functions. He begins life with innate reflexes, but these are, from the start, modified and made more effective by learning. New responses are soon acquired, and then complex solutions to problems are achieved by piecing together familiar responses in novel combinations. By the end of the second year, the first signs of the human capacity for symbolization appear: he invents new patterns of behaviour which show him to be representing the results of his actions to himself before they occur. In short, the sensori-motor period sees attainments comparable to the highest found in subhuman animals.

This growing ingenuity in the face of practical problems goes hand in hand with the formation of a less "egocentric" and more "objective" conception of the world. For some weeks after birth, the world must consist of a succession of visual patterns, sounds and other sensations. The infant comes naturally to pay attention to those external events which are associated with satisfactions or which are brought about by his own actions. Gradually, he builds up a view of the world as a collection of objects continuing to exist even when they are out of his sight and generally preserving the same sizes and shapes, despite the changes in their appearance that come with changes in position. Whereas no distinction between himself and what is outside him can have any meaning for him at first, he comes to conceive of himself as one object among the many that people the world, most of them unaffected by his activities.

The concept of an *object* is bound up with objective notions of *space, time* and *causality,* which the child does not possess as part of his native endowment but has to build up gradually through interaction with the world. After learning to select appropriate spatial directions and temporal successions for his actions, he comes to respond to the positions and times of occurrence of events outside himself, using his own body and his own actions as reference-points. Finally, he conceives of a space and a time in which both he himself and external objects are located. He learns, for example, to distinguish occasions when objects are moving independently of him from occasions when they merely appear to be changing positions because he is moving among them. Similarly, he progresses from an understanding of the relationship between his responses and their consequences to an understanding of the causal influence inanimate objects can exert on one another and even on him.

THE ORIGIN OF SYMBOLIC PROCESSES

Anything the child has achieved during the sensori-motor period is dwarfed by the prospects introduced by signs and symbols, particularly words and images. They expose him to a world of real and imaginary entities extending far beyond his momentary range of vision or even his life-span. It is a stable and consistent world, whereas the objects he perceives come and go.

Piaget deprecates the long-established belief that images are mere reactivations of traces of past experiences, passively registered by the nervous system. He insists that imagery is an extremely complex and active process, as can be seen from the time it takes to appear after birth. It grows out of the child's imitative capacities and is, in fact, "internalized imitation." The gradual extension of imitation during the sensori-motor period proceeds from a tendency to reproduce sounds and visual effects which have just been produced by the infant himself or by somebody else to an ability to copy an increasing range of new responses from an increasing range of models. It reaches its climax and the point at which it can perform symbolic functions with "deferred imitation," the imitation of the behaviour of an absent person of whom the child is "reminded."

Inanimate objects also can evoke imitation, as, for example, when a child opens his mouth on finding it difficult to open a match-box. Imagery consists of just such symbolic imitation "internalized" i.e., so reduced in scale that only the subject himself is aware of it. It consists, in other words, of what behaviourists call "implicit" or "fractional" responses. When the first indications of imagery emerge about the middle of the second year, the child is beginning, significantly enough, to turn from "practice" games, in which pleasure is derived from exercising simple activities, to "symbolic games," which involve make-believe or role playing. The child understands, however, the nature of the relation between a symbol and what it signifies; he knows that the doll is not really a baby or that he is not really a cowboy.

Having learned to use actions and images as symbols and having by now acquired a sufficient vocabulary, he finds himself using words in a similar way. But words, more than images, are responsible for the progressive socialization of thought. Words and the concepts corresponding to them are taken over from the social group. They are, therefore, bound to edge the child's thoughts into line with those of other persons. He can influence and be influenced by, benefit from or suffer from, the beliefs and values of other members of his group and so arrive at an equilibrium and harmony with his social as well as his physical environment.

RELATIONS BETWEEN PERCEPTION AND THOUGHT

In recent years, Piaget has been spending a great deal of time, together with Lambercier and other collaborators, on the painstaking investigation of visual illusions and related phenomena. This area of research, a time-honoured preserve of the more prosaic type of experimental psychology, may seem remote from the work for which he is best known. It has, nevertheless, given rise to some of his most original and comprehensive ideas, forming the kernel of his whole theory of intellectual functions. Whereas writers influenced by Gestalt psychology or by certain trends in American social psychology have tended to lump all "cognitive" processes together, Piaget finds the differences between perceptual and conceptual processes illuminating.

There are two obvious ways in which perception contrasts with thought. One arises from the fact, emphasized by the Gestalt school, that the perceived properties of a stimulus vary according to the pattern of which it is a component. The concepts participating in thought do not share this instability. The essential nature of a number does not change, no matter what the structure into which a mathematician fits it. A journey between two towns may seem longer or shorter in different circumstances, but the distance separating the towns according to our knowledge or our calculations does not fluctuate.

Secondly, perceptions are notoriously variable from person to person and from moment to moment. If we take 1,000 subjects, show them a line three inches long and another two inches long, and ask them to select a third line equal in length to the two combined, we shall expect a distribution of results with a high variance. We shall even expect each subject's response to vary from trial to trial, especially if the two lines are shown in different arrangements. On the other hand, if we take the same 1,000 subjects, show them the figure 2 and the figure 3, and ask them to select a third figure, equal to the sum of the two, the uniformity of the responses will be remarkable.

These differences can be traced back to two related factors which inevitably distort all perception. First, perception is always "centred" (*centré*). Sense organs have to be oriented in one direction at once, and the optical apparatus in particular is so constructed that the centre of the visual field is seen more clearly and in more detail than other parts. As some of Piaget's psychophysical experiments show, the size of a fixated object is over-estimated in comparison with the sizes of peripheral objects. The various parts of the visual field expand and shrink in turn as the gaze wanders from one point to another. The second source of error is the fact that larger portions of a figure are likely to catch the eye more often than others, with the result that the distortions that arise when they are the centre of attention play a disproportionately large part in the net impression of the figure. What we have is, in fact, a biased sample of all possible fixations. From these assumptions, Piaget has derived a formula predicting the direction and extent of "primary" visual illusions, i.e., those which are found in infants and lower animals as much as, if not more than, in adult human beings and which can be ascribed to the inherently "probabilistic" nature of perception.

Perception is analogous to certain processes in physics, notably in statistical mechanics, which are likewise governed by probability. These processes are irreversible, since they always lead from a less probable to a more probable state. For example, when a hot body is brought into contact with a cool body, heat is transmitted from the former to the latter and not *vice versa*. A spoonful of sugar diffuses evenly through a cupful of tea, but particles of sugar in a mixture do not forgather at one spot. Similarly, the distortions to which perceived figures are subject work predominantly in one direction. They cannot be relied on to balance out.

Thinking can escape from these limitations, because it is comparable with physical systems of a different type, namely those possessing *reversibility*. An example is a balance with equal weights in the two pans. The depression of one pan is followed by an upward swing which restores the original situation. Such systems are in stable equilibrium precisely because a change can be cancelled by an equal change in the opposite direction. A balance, however, is inflexible in the sense that there is one state to which it invariably reverts. Thought processes require structures which permit of more mobility without threatening disequilibrium. They must be free to flit rapidly from one idea to another and to arrange ideas in new combinations. But systems of concepts must preserve their organization, despite this mobility, if thoughts are to be consistent and if they are to produce a stable conception of the world. The "dynamic equilibrium" which Piaget attributes to thought can perhaps best be compared with that of a lift and its counterweight. The lift can move freely up and down, and the system remains intact and in equilibrium, no matter what floor is reached. This is because of its reversibility: any movement of the lift is compensated by an equal and opposite movement of the counterweight, and it can also be nullified by an equal and opposite movement of the lift.

The reversibility of logical thought is acclaimed by Piaget as the acme in which the growth of intelligence culminates. The spoken word and the performed action can never be recalled. The influence of something which has been perceived and then disappears from view lingers to infect subsequent perceptions. But a thought can be entertained and then unthought, and everything is as if it had never occurred. We are consequently able to conceive possible solutions for problems which it would be costly, dangerous or impossible to test by action. And no matter how extravagant an idea is considered and then rejected, the coherence of conceptual systems is not threatened. The world represented by thought, unlike that presented by perception, is relatively free from "centring" (*centration*). It does not change with the location of the thinker or the direction of his attention.

These contrary characteristics are found in a pure form only in the naive perception of the infant on the one hand and in the rigorous thought of the scientist, mathematician or logician on the other. The principal merit of this part of Piaget's work, as far as child psychology is concerned, is the light it sheds on certain processes forming compromises between perception and thought. As we shall see when we return to the chronological sequence, the first attempts at thinking are still contaminated with the short-comings of perception. And perception, after the first months of life, is usually accompanied by "perceptual activities," which mitigate its imperfections. There is no way of removing distortion completely from perception, but one distortion can be set against another. The focus of attention can be systematically varied, so that information from a succession of fixations is compared and collated to yield something approaching an objective impression. What appears from one point of view can be related to the perseveration or anticipation of what has been or will be seen from a different angle. "Perceptual activities" thus contribute to the "decentring" (*decentration*) of perception and the achievement of "semi-reversibility," so called because errors are not corrected exactly but merely tend to cancel out in the long run. Although these activities generally enhance accuracy of perception, they can on occasion lead to "secondary illusions," which are less pronounced in younger than in older children. An example is the "size-weight illusion," which makes a small object seem heavier than a larger one of equal weight.

THE PERIOD OF PRECONCEPTUAL THOUGHT
(TWO TO FOUR YEARS)

Before his use of symbolic processes can reach fruition, the child has to re-learn on a conceptual level some of the lessons he has already mastered on the sensori-motor level. For instance, he may have learned to recognize transient stimulus-patterns as shifting appearances assumed by enduring objects. But this does not immediately make him at home with the *concept* of an object. Adults are familiar with the concept of a particular *object* ("*this table*," "*Socrates*"), with the concept of a class ("*all four-legged tables*," "*all men*") and with the relation of *class-membership* which joins them ("*This is a four-legged table*," "*Socrates is a man.*"). These underlie our deductive reasoning, since having, for example, placed Socrates in the class of men, we can infer that Socrates has all the properties characteristic of this class.

The three-year-old child still lacks this equipment and has to use something midway between the concept of an object and that of a class, which Piaget calls the "pre-concept." On a walk through the woods, for example, he does not know whether he sees a succession of different snails or whether the same snail keeps on re-appearing. The distinction, in fact, means nothing to him; to him they are all "snail." Similar phenomena are, in some hazy way, identified, so that a shadow under a lamp in a room has something to do with the shadows under the trees in the garden. Contrariwise, a person in new clothes may be thought to require a new name.

Unlike adults, who reason either *de*ductively from the general to the particular or *in*ductively from the particular to the general, the child at the pre-conceptual stage reasons *trans*ductively from the particular to the particular. It is a form of argument by analogy: "A is like B in one respect, therefore A must be like B in other respects." Transduction may often lead to valid conclusions, e.g., that if Daddy is getting hot water he must be going to shave, since he shaved after getting hot water yesterday. But it will at other times lead the child into errors of a sort said to be common in psychotics but certainly not unknown in intellectual circles.

THE PERIOD OF INTUITIVE THOUGHT
(FOUR TO SEVEN YEARS)

When the child's reasoning has overcome these deficiencies, other limitations remain, mainly because thought has not yet freed itself from perception and become "decentred." Intuitive thought can best be understood from an experiment Piaget is fond of quoting. The child sees some beads being poured out of one glass into a taller and thinnner glass. It is made clear to him that all the beads that were in the first glass are now in the second; none has been added or removed. He is asked whether there are now more or fewer beads in the second glass than there were in the first. The usual answer at this stage is either that there are more (because the level has risen) or that there are fewer (because the second glass is narrower).

To explain such errors, it may be worth asking why we, as adults, are able to avoid them. The first reason is that we are told by our thought processes that the number of objects in a set, if nothing is added or subtracted, must necessarily remain the same. We usually regard our thought processes as more trustworthy than our perceptions whenever the two conflict. At a conjurer's performance, for example, we do not really believe that the rabbit has been created *ex nihilo* or the lady has been sawn in half. The child at the intuitive stage is, on the other hand, still dominated by his perceptions. His conclusions are still at the mercy of the changes resulting from successive "centrings." The second reason is that we take into account several aspects of the situation at once or in turn. We can see that the height of the column of beads has increased and that the width has decreased just enough to compensate for the increase in height. But the child focusses on one aspect and overlooks others. In his reasoning as in his perception, "centring" causes one element to be overemphasized and others to be relatively ignored. The instructiveness of such examples for adults, who might smile at the child's mistakes in the bead experiment but be liable to precisely the same sort of misjudgment in relation to, say, political or social problems, needs hardly be laboured.

CONCLUSIONS

It is evident that Piaget's latest work will not silence his critics altogether. He still does not pay much attention to questions of sampling. Some projects, e.g., Inhelder's on adolescents, seem to have used a large part of the school population of Geneva. The data on the sensori-motor period, on the other hand, come mainly from observation of Piaget's own three children, hardly the children of the Average Man! But Piaget might well retort, like Kinsey, that such bodies of data, however imperfect, are all we have of comparable density.

Except for some means and mean deviations in his reports of perceptual experiments, he provides few statistics. There are generally no measures of variance, which one suspects must be considerable, no tests of significance, just a categorical statement that at such an such an age children do such and such, with a few specific illustrations. He is not much affected by the growing vogue for rigorous theories, with precise statement of assumptions, derivation of predictions and operational definition of concepts.

Be that as it may, Piaget is, without any doubt, one of the outstanding figures in contemporary psychology, and his contributions will eventually have to be reckoned with much more than they are both in the management of children and in many areas which may not seem directly connected with child psychology. His ideas are closely tied to observation of behaviour, and this makes them the sort of psychology which moves science forward because it is testable by reference to the facts of behaviour. At the same time, it goes beyond the facts just sufficiently to open up new lines of research and to attempt the sort of synthesis which is one of the chief aims of science.

Not the least reason for paying attention to Piaget's work is the relation it bears to trends followed by English-speaking psychologists. At times, his conclusions parallel those reached independently by other investigators; at other times, they serve to correct or supplement what psychologists with other approaches have to say. Like those influenced by Gestalt psychology, Piaget affirms that perceptions and thought cannot be understood without reference to the wholes in which they are organized. He disagrees with them in denying that wholes are unanalyzable into component relations and in insisting that the wholes figuring in thought are radically different from those figuring in perception. There are, throughout his writing, many reminders of psycho-analytic concepts—the "omnipotence" and "oceanic feeling" of infancy, "functional pleasure," the formation of the ego and the super-ego, the advance from the pleasure principle to the reality principle. But he makes many detailed criticisms of psycho-analytic theories, and the child as described by him certainly seems tranquil and studious by comparison with the passion-torn "polymorphous pervert" that emerges from Freudian writings.

But Piaget's closest affinities are undoubtedly with the neo-behaviourists. He does not hold with early attempts to explain everything by "conditioned reflexes" or "association." But many of his observations and many aspects of his theory harmonize extremely well with conceptions of learning based on studies of what has come to be called "instrumental" or "operant conditioning." The sequences of more and more complex behaviour patterns which he depicts as outgrowths of simple reflexes and habits parallels Hull's list of progressively more intricate adaptive behaviour mechanisms, "found in animals." And Piaget's view of images and thought operations as "internalized" overt responses approximates very closely to the view prevalent among stimulus-response learning theorists.

One body of work which has grown up in Great Britain and the U.S.A. and which Piaget is eagerly endeavouring to bring into relation with his own findings is that centering on cybernetics, information theory and game theory. But it is to be hoped that the other common ground between his psychology and others with different starting points will be explored. It is certainly high time that the national self-sufficiencies which disfigure psychology in contradistinction to other branches of science were left behind.

SUPPLEMENTARY READINGS

Mays, W. Professor Piaget's épistémologie génétique. *Proc. II. Int. Congr. Phil. Sci.,* 1954, 5, 94–99.
Piaget, J. *The origin of intelligence in the child.* London: Routledge and Kegan Paul, 1953.
Piaget, J. *The child's construction of reality.* London: Routledge and Kegan Paul, 1955.
Piaget, J. *Play, dreams and imitation in childhood.* London: Heinemann, 1951.
Piaget, J. *The psychology of intelligence.* London: Routledge and Kegan Paul, 1950.

vii

Socialization and the Development of Social Behavior

When the infant attempts to sit and to stand, one should help it in its movements. For if it is eager to sit up too early and for too long a period it usually becomes hunchbacked (the spine bending because the little body has as yet no strength). If, moreover, it is too prone to stand up and desirous of walking, the legs may become distorted in the region of the thighs. This is observed to happen particularly in Rome; as some people assume, because cold waters flow beneath the city and the bodies are easily chilled all over; as others say, because of the frequent sexual intercourse the women have or because they have intercourse after getting drunk—but in truth it is because they do not make themselves fully acquainted with child rearing. For the women in this city do not possess sufficient devotion to look after everything as the purely Grecian women do.

SORANUS, *Gynecology.* 2nd Century B.C.

trends in

infant care*

MARTHA WOLFENSTEIN

[Conscientious and loving parents face a horrendous problem for which there is no completely satisfactory solution. They hope, and are expected, to rear their children toward happy and successful patterns of living, to help them acquire the necessary skills for adjusting and contributing to the welfare of their present and future affiliates. The goals for this most important undertaking can be only vaguely defined because the demands and expectations of modern society are in a state of continuous change. The child-rearing practices that would be most effective in permitting progress toward these poorly delineated goals are, as yet, largely unknown. Nevertheless, psychologists, psychiatrists, and pediatricians have from time to time offered specific advice to parents, sometimes reluctantly, but at other times with apparent confidence or even bravado. These recommendations have varied widely during the last 40 years, as interestingly illustrated in the following report by Dr. Wolfenstein, of the Albert Einstein College of Medicine. It seems abundantly clear that parents cannot be taught the fundamentals of child-rearing in the same ways that one might teach them how to repair a leaky faucet. Psychologists are now aware that parents have unresolved childhood problems and unconscious longings that serve as an effective filter for what they hear and that frequently stand in the way of their attempts to transduce available precepts into optimal child-rearing practices. Although this state of affairs is discouraging to professional workers who are committed to programs of immediate social action, it is not especially surprising or demoralizing to those scientists who appreciate the complexity of the assignment. Looking into the future, one can predict with great confidence that advice to parents will continue to follow the different styles and fads initiated and sustained by an evolving culture.]

In our culture where we tend to believe persistently that the latest is the best, we often fail to reckon sufficiently with the residues of the past. We behave as if convictions of a year or two ago had been banished without a

* From M. Wolfenstein. Trends in infant care. *American Journal of Orthopsychiatry*, 1953, 23, 120–130. (With permission.)

trace once they have been contradicted by the most recent discovery. This is particularly so with our ideas about child training. We rarely pause to look back (no one likes to recall past errors) to realize the tremendous changes which have taken place in these ideas in the last few decades. But overlooking does not abolish the things that are thus passed over. In all of us—parents, teachers, pediatricians, child psychologists, therapists— there are the accumulated ideas of a number of periods which have passed in rapid succession. And these ideas, insofar as they are not sorted out, cause considerable uncertainty and conflict.

In the fall of 1951, the United States Children's Bureau issued a new edition of the bulletin *Infant Care,* which first appeared in 1914 and which subsequently underwent several drastic revisions. This would seem to be a good occasion for surveying the changes which have appeared during these years in this most widely circulated child care publication.

I shall deal here mainly with the trends in severity and mildness in handling the impulses of the child, as manifested in the areas of thumb-sucking, weaning, masturbation, and bowel and bladder training. I shall not undertake to judge the correctness of the procedures recommended at one time or another. Nor shall I attempt to trace the various influences (of behaviorism, Gesell, psychoanalysis, etc.) which may be observed. What I wish to bring out are facts of social history. I should like to show the sharp contrasts between what mothers of the twenties and those of the forties were told about the best way to bring up their babies (for instance, in the twenties bowel training was to be completed by eight months; in the forties it was to be begun at eight months or later). Marked shifts have also occurred in much shorter periods of time (in 1938, the bulletin still showed a stiff cuff that could be bound on the baby's arm so that he could not bend his elbow to get his thumb in his mouth; in 1942, mothers were told that thumb sucking is a harmless pleasure that should not be interfered with). It would require further research to determine to what extent mothers were influenced by these ideas (from mother to daughter, or the same mother with an older and a younger child). However, we may suppose that a considerable number of mothers have participated in these changing attitudes. I shall try to show that the fluctuations of opinion in this field are related not only to advances in knowledge, but also in part to unresolved conflicts in our feelings about the child's impulses.

Let me indicate first the main trends through time which we may observe in various editions of *Infant Care.* (This account is based on the editions of 1914, 1921, 1929, 1938, 1942, 1945 and 1951. I omit those of 1926 and 1940, which I was unable to obtain.) In the first period, 1914–21, the danger of the child's autoerotic impulses was acutely felt. Thumb-sucking and masturbation, if not promptly and rigorously interfered with, would grow beyond control and permanently damage the child. While he was in bed, he was to be bound down hand and foot so that he could not suck his thumb, touch his genitals, or rub his thighs together.

In the next period, 1929–38, the focus of severity shifts. Autoerotism seems less dangerous. Now it is bowel training which must be carried out with great determination as early as possible. Severity in this area increases as compared with the previous period. This is accompanied by a pervasive emphasis on regularity, doing everything by the clock. Weaning and the introduction of solid foods are also to be accomplished with great firmness, never yielding for a moment to the baby's resistance. The main danger which the baby presented at this time was that of dominating the parents. Successful child training meant winning out against the child in the struggle for domination.

In 1942–45, all this was changed. The child became remarkably harmless, in effect, devoid of sexual or dominating impulses. His main active aim was to explore his world; autoerotism was an incidental by-product of such exploration. When not engaged in his exploratory undertakings, the baby needs attention and care; and giving these when he demands them, far from making him a tyrant, will make him less demanding later on. At this time mildness is advocated in all areas: thumb-sucking and masturbation are not to be interfered with; weaning and toilet training are to be accomplished later and more gently.

In 1951 there is an attempt to continue this mildness, but not without some conflicts and misgivings. Autoerotic activities become even more harmless and negligible. Sucking is a permissible though low-grade pleasure (a poor substitute for being held or fed or talked to) and the pacifier (explicitly taboo, 1914–38; not mentioned, 1942–45) is now restored. Rocking and head-banging (not masturbation) are the puzzling things which babies may do in bed and from which they seem to get some satisfaction; perhaps they do it out of boredom. Masturbation is mentioned only in connection with toilet training. While on the toilet, the baby may touch his genitals. This does not amount to anything (not even pleasure), but if it bothers the mother she may give the child a toy. Here the tolerance for autoerotism seems to require increasing denial of its nature. Requirements in toilet training become even more easygoing than in the preceding period. But the anxiety of 1929 that the child may dominate the parents reappears. If one picks up the child whenever he cries, he may become a tyrant. And in the area of toilet training, gentleness is urged out of the consideration that if the mother tries to be tough she cannot win. If she seems to be fighting the child, he can really hold out against her. Thus we get, if we compare 1929 with 1951, the same anxiety about the child's possible domination combined with extremely polarized approaches toward toilet training, on the one hand very strict, on the other, very mild. Neither the problems of the child's autoerotism nor of his possible domination seem to have been quite solved.

To document the foregoing points: In the 1914 edition of *Infant Care* (p. 62), masturbation is called an "injurious practice"; it "easily grows beyond control . . . children are sometimes wrecked for life." "It must be eradicated . . . treatment consists in mechanical restraints." In the 1921 revision (pp. 45–46), this is already toned down a bit: "a common habit

. . . it grows worse if left uncontrolled." The mechanical restraints are slight moderated; the nightgown sleeves must still be pinned down, but it is no longer specified (as it was in 1914) that the child's legs should be tied to opposite sides of the crib. In 1929, the atmosphere is much more relaxed: this "early period of what may be called sex awareness will pass away unless it is emphasized by unwise treatment on the part of adults." Physical restraints are now considered of little value. "Occupation and diversion" are the best treatment. The baby may be given a toy to hold until he goes to sleep (1929 ed., pp. 60–61). The 1938 revision (p. 49) anticipates the exploratory theme which subsequently becomes central: children "discover accidentally" that they can get pleasure from touching their genitals. The point about spontaneous recovery is repeated. In 1942, we are told: "Babies want to handle and investigate everything that they can see and reach. When a baby discovers his genital organs he will play with them. . . . A wise mother will not be concerned about this." Also, "see that he has a toy to play with and he will not need to use his body as a plaything" (1942 ed., p. 60). There is no change in 1945. In the 1951 edition (p. 87), we read: "Sometimes a baby handles his genitals when he is sitting on the toilet, or at other times when he is undressed. This is a common thing, and usually will not amount to anything if let alone. But sometimes it is disturbing to mothers, so if you feel uncomfortable about it you can try giving him a toy to hold while he's on the toilet seat. Don't confuse him by saying, 'No, No.' " The increased moderation in handling masturbation in the course of these years is accompanied by an increasingly diluted version of the activity. From expressing an urgent and dangerous impulse of the child, masturbation becomes an act about which the child has no feelings and which is only inexplicably embarrassing to the mother.

The alarm about thumb-sucking is somewhat less extreme than that about masturbation in the beginning, but it persists longer. Thus while mechanical restraints in connection with masturbation are abandoned in 1929, such restraints are still recommended to combat thumb-sucking as late as 1938. In 1914–21, mothers are cautioned that thumb-sucking deforms the mouth and causes constant drooling. "Thumb or finger must be persistently and constantly removed from the mouth and the baby's attention diverted to something else." Thus diversion, a relatively mild technique which is not yet envisaged in the case of masturbation, is considered at least partially effective against thumb-sucking. However, it is not enough; sleeves should also be "pinned or sewed down over the offending hand for several days and nights or the hand put in a cotton mitten." The zeal of the mother to keep the child's hand inaccessible is considered so great that the following caution is added: "The baby's hands should be set free now and then, especially if he is old enough to use his hands for his toys, and at meal times to save as much unnecessary strain on his nerves as possible, but with the approach of sleeping time the hand must be covered" (1914 ed., p. 61; no change in 1921)! At this time also the use of a pacifier is called a "disgusting habit" which the adults are to blame for introducing. The pacifier "must be destroyed." "Thumb and finger sucking babies will rebel fiercely at being deprived of this comfort when they are going to sleep, but this must be done if the habit is to be broken up" (1914 ed., pp. 58 and 61; 1921 is about the same). Thus in the period of open struggle against the baby's oral pleasures the ferocity of this drive is fully acknowledged.

In 1929–38, thumb-sucking retains the same hazards and is to be treated by the same methods. However, it is described in a more reassuring way. "When the baby first discovers his finger or thumb he naturally starts sucking it." "It is a natural habit . . . it should not excite parents unduly." While mechanical restraints are still recommended, there is a greater emphasis on diversion: "The best way to break up the habit is to keep the hands occupied with some toy" (1929 ed., pp. 59–60). In 1942–45, the exploratory motive becomes central; thumb-sucking like masturbation becomes an incident in the baby's exploration of his world. "A baby explores everything within his reach. He looks at a new object, feels it, squeezes it, and almost always puts it in his mouth." The baby "knows how to suck because he has learned to get food that way, and naturally he sucks on anything he puts in his mouth." No interference with thumb-sucking is required: "Usually children will outgrow the habit unless too much fuss is made . . . as he grows older other interests and pleasures take the place of sucking" (1942 ed., pp. 59–60; 1945 ed. is the same). Oral drives have now lost their fierce tenacity; they are easily outcompeted by other interests. The baby is now much more attracted by things around him than by his own body.

In 1951, thumb-sucking has become even more permissible and even more devalued as a satisfaction. When the baby is "tired or hungry or doesn't have anything interesting to watch or do, he may try to get a little pleasure out of his thumb or fingers. Sucking is a poor substitute for being held, or talked to, or fed; but it is better than nothing." Where the motivation for pleasure sucking had been first a fierce specific urge, later a more bland diffuse exploratory impulse, it is now more apt to arise from "loneliness or boredom." Thus as the attitude toward the child's impulses becomes increasingly permissive these impulses are depicted as increasingly weak and weary. It is now a matter for wonder that thumb-sucking was ever objected to. "Why do so many of us have this strong feeling against what is so perfectly natural for babies to do?" Why such a strong feeling against such a trivial impulse? Even the pacifier is now permitted. The damaging effect of early sucking on jaw formation is denied (1951 ed., pp. 56–57).

From 1914 through 1945 breast feeding was emphatically recommended. However, from 1921 on there was an increasing implicit apprehension that mothers did not want to breast-feed their children. This was expressed in warnings against too early weaning, review and refutation of an increasing number of arguments which mothers might give for early weaning, and the assertion that only a very few extreme circumstances could justify it. Concurrently with these doubts about the mother's willingness to nurse, there developed, however, an increasingly severe attitude toward the child who was to be weaned. Weaning, once the time had come to initiate it, was to be carried out according to a strict schedule and no backsliding was to be permitted. The mother was to refuse the breast and later the bottle with great firmness; the baby would yield and take the proffered substitutes. This trend was reversed in 1942–45, when the temporal pace of weaning was to be adapted to the baby's needs in such a way that the experience would be one of glad growing up and not of deprivation. The anxiety about the mother's unwillingness to nurse continued, however, at this time. It is only in 1951 that mothers are granted an honorable exemption from breast feeding if they prefer it that way. "If a mother isn't happy nursing her baby, and does it only because she thinks it is her duty, it may be better all around for her baby to be bottle fed. Mothers who find bottle feeding easier should feel comfortable about doing it that way" (1951 ed., p. 17). The adaptation of weaning procedure to the baby's needs continues to be recommended. Thus in the latest period both mother and baby are treated indulgently in this area.

In 1914 there seemed to be little anxiety that mothers would wean the babies too soon. However, there was great stress on gradualness in weaning. No precise time schedule was given. A first bottle might be introduced at five months to give the baby plenty of time to get used to it; weaning might be completed by one year (1914 ed., pp. 55–56). In 1921 the anxiety about too early weaning set in. Where previously mothers were told that the baby might be weaned by one year, they are now warned that he should not be weaned before six months. Attention is focused on the minimal nursing period. After six months a normal baby can be weaned if necessary, though preferably weaning should be postponed till about nine months. Once initiated, it "need not take more than two weeks." The mother is advised to persist in getting the baby to take the artificial food even if he refuses it at first: "the child will finally yield" (1921 ed., pp. 58–59). This anticipates the struggle for dominance of the next period. Some fairly serious disturbance about the breast seems indicated in 1921. This is suggested by the only two illustrations in this edition: one a close-up of a breast from which milk is being expressed by hand, the other a diagram of the baby's teeth. If one may speculate on these two images, they would seem to say that the breast had better be preserved from the infant's destructive jaws. We may recall in passing that in the twenties the preferred female body image was one in which the breasts were unnoticeable. There would seem to have been a marked conflict at this time about both the erotic and the material uses of the breast. In *Infant Care,* this is reflected in the apprehension that women will not want to breast-feed their children. It is stressed that there are few legitimate excuses for not nursing the child (although the illustrations unwittingly tell a different story). However, once it is time to wean the baby, the mother can be very firm about withholding the breast.

In the 1929 edition (pp. 74–76), we find a further elaboration of in-adequate reasons which are often given for too early weaning. "Many babies are weaned unnecessarily because the breast milk looks blue or is thought to be 'too thin.' " That is, the mother is dissatisfied with what her breasts can produce. Mothers are urged to continue breast-feeding their babies until they are seven or eight months old "even if only one or two feedings a day are given and the other feedings are artificial." Weaning, once begun, should follow a strict schedule, and is to be completed by the end of the ninth or beginning of the tenth month. The dominant orienta-tion of this period is evident in the way that weaning is to be carried out. "If the baby refuses the bottle or cup the mother must not give in and allow him to nurse." She must offer the cup or bottle regularly according to the weaning schedule. "Soon the baby will give in and take the cup or bottle. The mother must not get excited or upset if the baby refuses, be-cause he will finally yield." The 1938 revision continues and even slightly intensifies this rigor.

In 1942–45 for the first time the emotional impact of weaning on the baby was acknowledged. Giving up the breast "is a big step for the baby in growing up. Later steps will be easier if the baby finds this one pleasant." If the transition to the bottle is sufficiently gradual, "he will take the step forward gladly. If the change is made suddenly he may resist it." Thus instead of firmly overriding the baby's resistance, the mother should now avoid rousing it. The tempo of weaning is to be adapted to individual needs rather than following a preconceived schedule. The transition from the bottle to the cup is "also a big problem for the baby. . . . Let him take his time. . . . It makes little difference at exactly what age bottle feeding is given up for good. It makes a great deal of difference to the baby's mental and emotional health that he does not feel cheated out of something im-portant to him, but that he does feel that he is giving up a baby way for a grown-up way" (1945 ed., pp. 47–50). A new consideration is introduced in connection with weaning: the mother may want to wean the baby sooner than she would otherwise in order to return to work. However, she is advised to discuss this with the father; perhaps they can arrange for her to stay home and "nurse their baby, especially when they realize what a good start in life breast feeding will give the baby" (pp. 70–71). This invocation of the father as the arbiter over the breast, the one who is to grant and ensure the baby's right to it, suggests that both the erotic and maternal associations of the breast have been re-established.

In 1951 the long-term intransigence about breast feeding is relaxed: the mother should not feel guilty if she prefers to bottle-feed her baby from the first. However, sometimes a mother who really wants to breast-feed her baby is prevented by the doctor. "Sometimes doctors and hospitals take very lightly a mother's earnest insistence that she intends to nurse her baby" (1951 ed., p. 17). It is now the doctor rather than the father who becomes a more impersonal and also more grudging arbiter over the breast. It is again stressed, as in the preceding period, that weaning should be gradual and adapted to the readiness of the individual child to give up the pleasure of sucking. The child should be compensated by "a little extra attention" for the loss of this satisfaction. While there is "no set time at which the baby should be drinking his milk from a cup," there is now some anxiety that the transition to the cup may be too long postponed. The situation may arise where mothers "are at a loss what to do when their baby gets so used to the bottle that at 18 or 20 months, or even later, when he's fast getting beyond seeming like a baby, he still insists on having the bottle" (pp. 43–44). This expresses a conflict which pervades the 1951 edition. The view had been advanced in 1942–45 that early full gratification facilitates later acceptance of limitations. In 1951 doubts about this have rearisen. May not continued gratification lead to addiction and increasingly intensified demands? Thus while on some points (notably thumb-sucking and acceptance of the baby's preferences in solid foods) it is held that indulgence will not spoil the baby but just the reverse, on other points (continued bottle feeding, picking up the baby when he cries) there is the apprehension that gratification will intensify the baby's demands. Also a new issue is now raised about weaning to the cup: Should not the breast-fed baby be weaned directly to the cup rather than through a transitional stage of bottle feeding? It would seem that there has been a displacement of conflicting feelings here. Up till this time there was the troubled issue whether to breast-feed or bottle-feed in the first place, with heavy arguments for breast feeding. Now the uncertainty attaches to the question whether to wean to the cup or to the bottle. In other words the issue breast versus bottle has been replaced by bottle versus cup. (Such displacements as an indication of unresolved problems are frequent in this literature. Thus for instance in 1929, when a more easygoing line was being advanced on masturbation, the danger of obsessive preoccupation was displaced to the toy which was to be given the child to keep his hands occupied in bed. It was feared he might become excessively attached to one toy, and parents were advised to vary these bedtime distractions [1929 ed., pp. 60–66].)

Recommended procedures in bowel training have shown sharp fluctuations. In the twenties there was increasing severity. Subsequently there was a trend in the opposite direction; from 1938 through 1951 increasing mildness has been recommended. Thus where in 1921 the mother was to take up the task of bowel training as soon as she recovered from her confinement, in 1951 the mother is told: "Many babies are not ready to start learning bowel control by the end of the first year" (p. 86). In this latter phase flexibility has replaced rigidity in the training schedule. In the earlier period the value of regular bowel habits for health and character was emphasized. Now what is stressed is the negativism which the mother risks provoking in her child if she tries to force him to be trained against his will.

In 1914 bowel training was to be begun "by the third month or even earlier." The mother was to use "the utmost gentleness. . . . Scolding and punishment will serve only to frighten the child and to destroy the natural impulses, while laughter will tend to relax the muscles and to promote an easy movement." The chamber was to be presented "persistently each day" at the same hour. It is emphasized that establishing bowel regularity will be a great saving of trouble to the mother and "of untold value to the child, not only in babyhood, but throughout the whole of life" (1914 ed., p. 51). Increased severity is evidenced in the 1921 revision (pp. 42–44) in demanding an earlier beginning of bowel training: "as early as the end of the first month and as soon as the mother takes charge of the baby after her confinement she should begin upon this task." The time for the completion of bowel training is now specified: almost any baby can be trained so that there are no more soiled diapers after the end of the first year. The time that the baby is to be placed on the chamber each day is specified more rigidly: "not varying the time by five minutes." Gentleness and laughter are no longer mentioned; the warning against scolding and punishment drops out. The nuisance for the mother in training the child is expressed more strongly. Where in 1914 this training required "much time and patience" from the mother, it now takes "unlimited patience." The value of establishing and maintaining bowel regularity is that it prevents "endless misery from constipation in the adult."

In 1929 the demand for bowel control is most rigorous. "Almost any baby can be trained so that there are no more soiled diapers to wash after he is six to eight months old." The requirement of absolute regularity, not varying the time for the movement by five minutes from one day to the next, continues (1929 ed., pp. 57–58). The demand for regularity, doing everything "by the clock" now pervades the daily routine. In 1938, there is a reverse in the trend. We hear no more about beginning bowel training at one month. Now it may be begun "as early as six months" (the time when the mother in 1929 might already expect the baby to be completely trained). The time for completion of training is now put at one year. The specification about not varying time by five minutes drops out, and instead we find that the baby should be put on the chamber "each day for a short period" (1938 ed., pp. 47–48). Correspondingly the general clock-boundness of 1929 is moderated. The lifelong value of good bowel habits is not explicitly asserted in 1929 or 1938. Instead there is a general statement that training in regularity of eating and elimination is also character building.

In 1942–45 bowel training is to commence still later, "usually at eight or ten months," and the time for completing it is left indefinite. The baby can not really cooperate in the training until his muscles have matured. If one waits until this time training becomes easy. Efforts of the mother to catch the baby at the right moment, before he can actively participate, are disparaged; it is the mother, not the baby, who is trained in this case. Bowel training should not be begun at the same time as weaning since one or the other may be hard for the baby to accept (1945 ed., pp. 53–54). Neither the lifelong value of bowel regularity nor its indirect relation to character building is mentioned any more. All that remains is a very general statement (carried over since 1929) that early habits form the basis for later health, happiness and efficiency.

As we have noted, in 1942–45 the handling of the infant in all areas has become very gentle. This tendency is continued and even carried further in 1951. The advocacy of increased leniency is most marked in respect to bowel training. This is also the aspect of the mother-child relation which is seen as most fraught with emotional hazards. "Why do we stress this bowel training so much? Because you can so easily make trouble for yourself and the baby if you start training too early. A child can get to feeling that his mother is his enemy if she urges on him things he is not ready for. . . . Let him sit on his toilet chair only a few moments the first few times. . . . As he gets used to his new seat, you can keep him on a little longer, but never more than five minutes." (Note how the theme of "five minutes" recurs, but in a very different way from the twenties' "not varying the time by five minutes.") "You don't want him to hate this new routine. Much of the trouble mothers have . . . comes because the babies get the idea this is a battle. . . . This is once when a baby has the upper hand. No mother can make her child move his bowels. . . . A lot depends on her not letting him get to feel this is a hateful bore. . . . What you're after is not having fewer diapers to wash, but having a baby who feels like working with you instead of against you." In view of all this the commencement of bowel training is postponed to a considerably later time. "Most babies are not ready to start learning bowel control by the end of the first year. One and a half or two years is a much more common time for them to learn willingly" (1951 ed., pp. 86–87).

The handling of bladder training is not correlated exactly with that of bowel training. In 1929 when severity in bowel training was at its height, severity in bladder training decreased as compared with the preceding period (1921 ed., pp. 42–45; 1929 ed., pp. 58–59). Urination here seems to have more a genital than an anal association. (We may recall that severity toward masturbation also decreased at this time. Masturbation was explicitly associated with bed-wetting in the 1929 revision [pp. 60–61] as an early habit which would be easily outgrown. Incidentally, masturbation was associated with thumb-sucking in 1942–45, and with defecation in 1951.) Intolerance toward wetting was most intense in 1921; from 1929 on the attitude became steadily gentler.

The increase or decrease in severity in the various areas which we have considered may be roughly indicated in Table 1.

Table 1

Severity in the handling of:	From 1914 to 1921	From 1921 to 1929	From 1929 to 1938	From 1938 to 1942–45	From 1942–45 to 1951
Masturbation	Decreases	Decreases	Constant	Decreases	Constant
Thumb-sucking	Constant	Decreases	Constant	Decreases	Decreases
Weaning	Increases	Increases	Constant	Decreases	Constant
Bowel-training	Increases	Increases	Decreases	Decreases	Decreases
Bladder-training	Increases	Decreases	Decreases	Decreases	Decreases

In respect to masturbation and thumb-sucking the curve of severity shows a consistently declining direction. In weaning and bowel training we find a curve, rising in the twenties and subsequently declining. However, this refers only to the overt procedures which are recommended (when to begin toilet training or weaning, whether to use mechanical restraints against thumb-sucking or masturbation, etc.). It does not indicate the range of conflicting emotional attitudes which are expressed in more subtle ways (as in the altered conception of autoerotic drives, etc.).

The problem of making scientific insight widely accessible is nowhere more pertinent than in child training. The efforts of the authors of the *Infant Care* bulletins illustrate the difficulty of the undertaking. In the last decade, they have been telling mothers to behave with great tolerance toward the child's autoerotic impulses, his urge to suck, his soiling and wetting. But what has become of the feelings which not so long ago were being expressed with a clear conscience in strenuous struggle against these same impulses in the child? These feelings have certainly not been worked through or transformed, but seem much more to be suppressed or repressed. The mother of 1914 or 1921 was supposed to know that children masturbate in bed, and was told to eradicate this wickednes. The mother of 1951, who is told that masturbation does not amount to anything, is not supposed to know that children masturbate in bed, but may only notice that they sometimes touch their genitals while on the toilet. She is permitted to feel uncomfortable when she observes this and may give the child a toy to relieve her own feelings. But the mother who feels uncomfortable and so must distract her baby may convey, albeit covertly and indecisively, considerable disapproval. And so with other things; changes in behavior too quickly superposed on less quickly alterable feelings may fail to obtain the hoped-for results. The problem remains of how to help people to face the realities of human nature and yet to treat it gently.

SUPPLEMENTARY READINGS

Ariès, P. *Centuries of childhood.* New York: Knopf, 1962.

Bronfenbrenner, U. Socialization and social class through time and space. In E. Maccoby, T. Newcomb, & E. Hartley (Eds.), *Readings in social psychology.* (3rd ed.) New York: Holt, 1958. Pp. 400–425.

Bronfenbrenner, U. The changing American child—a speculative analysis. *J. soc. Issues,* 1961, 17, 6–18.

Mace, D., & Mace, V. *The Soviet family.* New York: Doubleday 1963.

Stendler, C. Sixty years of child training practices. *J. Pediat.,* 1950, 36, 122–134.

Waters, E., & Crandall, V. J. Social class and observed maternal behavior from 1940 to 1960. *Child Develpm.,* 1964, 35, 1021–1032.

White, M. Social class, child rearing practices and child behavior. *Amer. sociol. Rev.,* 1957, 22, 704–712.

young children in

wartime: traumatic effects

of separation from parents[*]

DOROTHY BURLINGHAM and ANNA FREUD

[The bombing of London during World War II exposed the children of that great city to all of the stresses of modern warfare: large scale destruction of property by explosions and fire, dislocation of families whose homes were destroyed, physical loss of parents for some and prolonged separation from parents for others, separation from playmates, disruptions of sleeping and eating routines, and living amidst the anxieties and fears of adults who were almost continuously threatened with physical destruction. Many parents, through private arrangements or through agencies especially established for the purpose, were able to have their young children evacuated from the city to foster homes or child care centers in the rural section of England, such as the one administered under the supervision of Dorothy Burlingham and Anna Freud.

The following report by these authors is a psychological analysis of the adjustment difficulties experienced by these displaced children, some observations of children's perceptions of, and adjustments to, death and destruction during the "blitz," and an extremely interesting discussion of the consequences of separation anxiety during different developmental levels. One of the most widely quoted observations made by these investigators is the finding that continual bombing is much less traumatic for the child's psychological developmental than separation from parents. The destructive influence of being an "artificial war orphan" was aptly expressed in one five-year-old's self-description: "I am nobody's nothing." The authors of this report also conclude that children are more resilient to the ravages of war than are adults. This is, of course, only one of many findings in developmental psychology pointing to the superior flexibility of the less mature organism.]

[*] From D. Burlingham and A. Freud. *Young children in war-time: A year's work in a residential war nursery.* London: Allen & Unwin, 1942. (With permission.)

In this war children are frequently to be found directly on the scenes of battle. Though here in England they are spared the actual horror of seeing people fight around them, they are not spared sights of destruction, death, and injury from air raids. Even when removed from the places of the worst danger there is no certainty, as some of our cases show, that they will not meet new bombing incidents at places to which they were sent for safety. General sympathy has been aroused by the idea that little children should thus come into close contact with the horrors of the war. It is this situation which led many people to expect that children would receive traumatic shock from air raids and would develop abnormal reactions very similar to the traumatic or war neurosis of soldiers in the last war.

We can only describe our observations on the basis of our own case-material, which excludes children who have received severe bodily injuries in air raids, though as mentioned before it does not exclude children who have been bombed repeatedly and partly buried by debris. So far as we can notice there were no signs of traumatic shock to be observed in these children. If these bombing incidents occur when small children are in the care either of their own mothers or of a familiar mother-substitute they do not seem to be particularly affected by them. Their experience remains an accident, in line with other accidents of childhood. This observation is borne out by the reports of nurses or social workers in London County Council Rest Centres where children used to arrive, usually in the middle of the night, straight from their bombed houses. They also found that children who arrived together with their own families showed little excitement and no undue disturbance. They slept and ate normally and played with whatever toys they had rescued or which might be provided. It is a widely different matter when children during an experience of this kind are separated from or even lose their parents.

It is a common misunderstanding of the child's nature which leads people to suppose that children will be saddened by the sight of destruction and aggression. Children between the age of 1 and 2 years, when put together in a play-pen will bite each other, pull each other's hair and steal each other's toys without regard for the other child's unhappiness. They are passing through a stage of development where destruction and aggression play one of the leading parts. If we observe young children at play we notice that they will destroy their toys, pull off the arms and legs of their dolls or soldiers, puncture their balls, smash whatever is breakable, and will only mind the result because complete destruction of the toy blocks further play. The more their strength and independence grow the more they will have to be watched so that they may not do too much damage, nor hurt each other or those weaker than themselves. We often say half jokingly that there is continual war raging in a nursery. We mean by this that at this time of life destructive and aggressive impulses are still at work in children in a manner in which they only recur in grown-up life when they are let loose for the purposes of war.

It is one of the recognized aims of education to deal with the aggressiveness of the child's nature, i.e., in the course of the first four or five years to change the child's own attitude towards these impulses in himself. The wish to hurt people and later the wish to destroy objects undergo all sorts of changes. They are usually first restricted, then suppressed, by commands and prohibitions; a little later they are repressed, which means that they disappear from the child's consciousness—he does not dare any more to have knowledge of these wishes. There is always the danger that they might return from the unconscious; therefore all sorts of protections are built up against them: the cruel child develops pity, the destructive child will become hesitant and over-careful. If education is handled intelligently the main part of these aggressive impulses will be directed away from their primitive aim of doing harm to somebody or something and will be used to fight the difficulties of the outer world; to accomplish tasks of all kinds, to measure one's strength in competition, and to use it generally to "do good" instead of "being bad" as the original impulse demanded.

In the light of these considerations it is easier to determine what the present war conditions with their incidents of wholesale destruction may do to a child. Instead of turning away from them in instinctive horror, as people seem to expect, the child may turn towards them with primitive excitement. The real danger is not that the child, caught up all innocently in the whirlpool of war, will be shocked into illness. The danger lies in the fact that the destruction raging in the outer world may meet the very real aggressiveness which rages in the inside of the child. At the age when education should start to deal with these impulses, confirmation should not be given from the outside world that the same impulses are uppermost in other people. Children will play joyfully on bombed sites and around bomb craters with blasted bits of furniture, and throw bricks from crumbled walls at each other. But it becomes impossible to educate them towards a repression of or a reaction against destruction while they are doing so. After their first years of life they fight against their own wishes to do away with people of whom they are jealous, who disturb or disappoint them or who offend their childish feelings in some other way. It must be very difficult for them to accomplish this task of fighting their own death wishes when at the same time people are killed and hurt every day around them. Children have to be safeguarded against the primitive horrors of the war, not because horrors and atrocities are so strange to them but because we want them at this decisive stage of their development to overcome and estrange themselves from the primitive and atrocious wishes of their own infantile nature.

Children never feel friendly towards new-born additions to their family. They sometimes pretend to do so; at other times they are mollified by the smallness and complete helplessness of the newcomer. The newly billeted foster-brother on the other hand is very often neither small nor helpless. He usurps rights which the other child is unwilling to give up. The billeted newcomer, for his part, is deeply conscious of his second-rate position and is embittered by it. There are certainly all the elements for jealousy and discomfort given in the situation.

These reactions are interesting enough to have been made the subject of surveys carried out by child guidance clinics set up in reception areas and by consulting psychologists attached to County Medical Offices. These keep an eye on trouble in the billets, smooth out difficulties and remove the worst billeting misfits. They have a unique opportunity for studying the situation (especially the situation of the school children).

The Government scheme for evacuation of unattended children was never meant to include children under school age, with the exception of some little ones who were taken along with evacuation parties as younger brothers and sisters. Evacuation of unattended children under 5 was rightly considered a difficult undertaking. They were supposed to stay with their mothers and only to be evacuated with them when necessary. When the percentage of mothers who were unwilling to leave London and stay in billets was rather large, a scheme for under-fives was added to the other. These under-fives, whose mothers had to have a good reason for staying behind, were sent out unattended, either to nurseries or to selected billets. The difficulty remained that vacancies under this scheme were scarce compared with the onrush of mothers who were eager to send their small children to some place of safety.

In a London Nursery like ours there is little opportunity for collecting evidence about the successful billeting of under-fives. Children who are happy in their billets, i.e., who find a foster-mother ready to 'adopt' them, stay in the country and little more is heard about them. 'Billeting-failures,' on the other hand, wander backwards and forwards between London and the country. Some of them may settle down in the end in residential nurseries. As mentioned in our statistics, more than 20 per cent of our cases are billeting failures of various types.

We should be more inclined to hold the billets responsible for the inability of such a large number of children to adapt themselves to the new conditions if we did not possess first-hand evidence of the difficulties involved from our own observations of children after their first separation from their families.

It is true that not many children present as frightening a picture as Billie (3½), who found himself reduced to a state in which compulsive formulas and symptomatic actions played the largest part; or Beryl (4) who sat for several days on the exact spot where her mother had left her, would not speak, eat, or play, and had to be moved around like an automaton. Even apart from these unusual cases we have seen long-drawn-out states of homesickness, upset, and despair which are certainly more than the average inexperienced foster-mother can be expected to cope with. We certainly see no similar states of distress in children when we make the round of London shelters and find them sleeping on the platforms next to their mothers. Our own feeling revolts against the idea of infants living under the conditions of air raid danger and underground sleeping. For the children themselves during the days or weeks of homesickness this is the state of bliss to which they all desire to return.

There are so many obvious reasons why small children should not stay in London shelters that it is not easy to pay equal attention to the emotional reaction of the individual child against evacuation. A child who is removed from London to the country is certainly removed from a state of greater danger to a lesser one; he exchanges unhygienic conditions of life for more hygienic ones; he avoids the possibilities of infection which multiply where thousands of individuals are massed together. If the child goes to a residential nursery he will be better fed than before; he will be given proper occupation and companionship and will be spared the dreariness of an existence where at the worst periods he was dragged to and fro between home and shelter with long and empty hours of queuing up at a Tube Station. It is difficult to realize that all these improvements in the child's life may dwindle to nothing when weighed against the fact that he has to leave his family to gain them.

This state of affairs is still more difficult to understand when we consider that many of the mothers concerned are not "good mothers" in the ordinary sense of the word. We deal with a large majority of mothers who are affectionate, intelligent, hardworking, ready to make every possible sacrifice for their children; but there is a minority of mothers who are none of these. They may be lazy and negligent, hard and embittered and unable to give affection. There are others who are over-strict in their demands and make the life and upbringing of the child extremely difficult. It is a known fact that children will cling even to mothers who are continually cross and sometimes cruel to them. The attachment of the small child to his mother seems to a large degree independent of her personal qualities and certainly of her educational ability. This statement is not based on any sentimental conception of the sacredness of the tie between mother and child. It is the outcome of detailed knowledge of the growth and nature of the child's emotional life, and of the structure of his mind, in which the figure of the mother is for a certain time the sole important representative of the whole outer world.

DEVELOPMENT OF THE MOTHER-RELATIONSHIP AND THE EFFECT OF SEPARATION FROM THE MOTHER AT VARIOUS STAGES

In the relationship of the small child to its mother there are definite main phases to be distinguished from each other. *The first phase,* which comprises the first few months of life, is characteristically selfish and material. The small baby's life is governed by sensations of need and satisfaction, pleasure and discomfort. The mother plays a part in it so far as she brings satisfaction and removes discomfort. When the baby is fed, warm and comfortable, he withdraws his interest from the outer world and falls asleep. Whe he is hungry, cold and wet, or disturbed by sensations in his own intestines, he cries for attention.

It is certain that care and attention given by the mother, i.e., in a special atmosphere of affection which only the mother can supply, is more satisfactory to the baby than more indifferent and mechanical ministrations to his needs. But the fact is that a baby who at this time of life is separated from his mother will accept food and care from a mother-substitute. His needs are overwhelming, his helplessness is extreme, and his distinction between one person and another is still in the beginning stage. Babies of this age who are left with us by their mothers will usually have a short time of upset, may cry a while, have more difficulty in falling asleep, and show some irregularity in their digestion for a day or two. We still have to learn exactly how much of this upset is due to the disturbance of routine and how much to the change away from the individual handling and from the particular atmosphere of intimacy created by the mother.

The upset caused is, of course, of a far more serious nature and of longer duration in cases where the mother has been breast-feeding the baby and weaning has to occur simultaneously with the separation. Weaning in itself acts on the child as a loss of satisfaction and a separation from the mother in an important sense. When the mother who has left reappears after a few days, the baby at this stage will probably not show signs of recognition.

The second phase starts in, roughly, the second half of the first year of life. The material relationship to the mother still exists. The mother remains, as she will remain for several years, the instrument of satisfaction for the child. But out of this ignoble beginning of a human relationship something different begins to grow. The baby begins to pay attention to the mother also at times when there is no urgent necessity for him to be attended to. He likes his mother's company, enjoys her fondling, and dislikes to be left alone. So far the absence of the mother has only been a potential danger: some inner need might arise and there might be nobody outside to fulfill it. Now, in this later phase, the mother is already appreciated or missed for her own sake. The child is conscious of her presence, follows her round with his eyes, can answer her smile and is, as described above, moved by her moods. His need for her affection becomes as urgent for his psychological satisfaction as the need to be fed and taken care of is for his bodily comfort.

Disturbance after parting from the mother will last somewhat longer at this stage. Babies of this age are sometimes off their feed when left with us. Many show signs of restlessness during sleep and often seem unfriendly or rather withdrawn from contact with the outer world. Smiles, friendliness, playfulness will only reappear after the bodily functions have returned to normality. This interruption of psychological contact with the outer world is *not* simply the consequence of the bodily discomfort which the baby experiences; when once used to us, the same baby will not cut off his contact with the nurse who handles him even in times of illness. But at this period of separation he repeats what he did in the beginning of his mother-relationship; he establishes personal contact with the mother-substitute only on the basis of the fulfilment and satisfaction provided for his bodily needs.

The personal attachment of the child to his mother, which starts in this manner in the first year of life, comes to its full development in the second. It was said before that the child is attached to his mother; it can now be safely said that he loves her. The feelings for her which he is able to experience acquire the strength and variety of adult human love. This love makes demands and is possessive. All the child's instinctive wishes are now centred on the mother. While she is breast-feeding him, he wants to 'eat' her; later on he will bite her, handle her, and whatever impulse starts up in him will try to find satisfaction on her person.

This relationship between small child and mother might be a happy one except for two reasons. The child's demands are too great; he is virtually insatiable. However long the mother may have fed him at the breast, he will express by his resentment at weaning-time that it was not long enough; however much time she spends near him, he will still bitterly resent being left alone at other times. Also the child soon becomes aware of the fact that there are other people in the world besides him and his mother. He realizes the presence of brothers and sisters who claim equal rights and become his rivals. He becomes aware, sometimes at a very early age, of the presence of the father and includes him in his world. He recognizes him as a dangerous rival (where family life is normal). He loves him at the same time. With this conflict of feelings he enters into the whole complicated entanglement of feelings which characterizes the emotional life of human beings.

Reactions to parting at this time of life are particularly violent. The child feels suddenly deserted by all the persons in this world to whom he has learned to attach importance. His new ability to love finds itself deprived of the accustomed objects and his greed for affection remains unsatisfied. His longing for his mother becomes intolerable and throws him into states of despair which are very similar to the despair and distress shown by babies who are hungry and whose food does not appear at the accustomed time. For several hours, or even for a day or two, this psychological craving of the child, the "hunger" for his mother, may override all bodily sensations. There are some children of this age who will refuse to eat or to sleep. Very many of them will refuse to be handled or comforted by strangers.

The children cling to some object or some form of expression which means to them at that moment memory of the material presence of the mother. Some will cling to a toy which the mother has put into their hands at the moment of parting; others to some item of bedding or clothing which they have brought from home. Some will monotonously repeat the word by which they are used to call their mothers, as, for instance, Christine (17 months), who said, "Mum, mum, mum, mum, mum, . . ." continually in a deep voice for at least three days.

Observers seldom appreciate the depth and seriousness of this grief of a small child. Their judgment of it is misled for one main reason. This childish grief is short-lived. Mourning of equal intensity in an adult person would have to run its course throughout a year; the same process in the child between 1 and 2 years will normally be over in 36 to 48 hours. It is a psychological error to conclude from this short duration that the reaction is only a superficial one and can be treated lightly. The difference in duration is due to certain psychological differences between the state of childhood and maturity. The child's life is still entirely governed by the principle which demands that he should seek pleasure and avoid pain and discomfort. He cannot wait for the arrival of pleasure, and bear discomfort, in the idea that in this way ultimate pleasure may again be reached.

An adult person may find himself in the same situation of being suddenly cut off from all the people he loves, and will also experience intense longing. But his memories of the past and his outlook into the future will help him to maintain an inner relationship to the loved objects and thus to bridge the time until reunion is possible. The psychological situation of the child is completely different. A love-object who does not give him immediate satisfaction is no good to him. His memories of the past are spoilt by the disappointment which he feels at the present moment. He has no outlook into the future, and it would be of no help to him if he had. His needs are so urgent that they require immediate gratification; promises of pleasure are no help.

The little child will, therefore, after a short while, turn away from the mother-image in his mind, and, though at first unwillingly, will accept the comfort which is offered. In some cases acceptance may come in slow stages. Christine, for instance, would at first only let herself be fondled or held by an unseen person. She would sit on somebody's lap, turn her head away, enjoy the familiar sensation of being held, and probably add to it in her own mind the imaginary picture of her own mother. Whenever she looked at the face of the person who held her, she began to cry. There are other children who are spared these violent reactions. They seem placid, dazed, and more or less indifferent. It takes a few days or even a week before this placidity is disturbed by a realization of the fact that they are among strangers; all sorts of slighter depressive reactions and problems of behaviour will then result. All children of this age, those with the violent reactions as well as those whose reaction is delayed, will show a tendency to fall ill under the new conditions; they will develop colds, sore throats, or slight intestinal troubles.

That the shock of parting at this stage is really serious is further proved by the observation that a number of these children fail to recognize their mothers when they visit after they have 'settled down' in the new surroundings. The mothers themselves realize that this lack of recognition is not due to any limitation of the faculty of memory as such. The same child who looks at his mother's face with stony indifference as if she were a complete stranger, will have no difficulty in recognizing lifeless objects which have belonged to his past. When taken home again he will recognize the rooms, the position of the beds, and will remember the contents of cupboards, etc.

Fathers are treated better in this respect. The children were always more or less used to their coming and going and not dependent on them for their primitive gratifications. Consequently parting from them is no real shock and their memory remains more undisturbed. Failure to recognize the mother occurs when something has happened to the image of the mother in the child's mind, i.e., to its inner relationship to her. The mother has disappointed the child and left his longing for her unsatisfied; so he turns against her with resentment and rejects the memory of her person from his consciousness.

PRACTICAL CONCLUSIONS

At first glance it seems from this material that small children have little chance to escape unharmed from the present war conditions. They either stay in the bombed areas with their parents, and, quite apart from physical danger, get upset by their mothers' fears and excitements and hardened and brutalized by the destruction which goes on around them and by shelter life. Or they avoid these dangers, are evacuated to the country and suffer other shocks through separation from the parents at an age which needs emotional stability and permanency. Choosing between two evils seems to be all that war-time care is able to accomplish for them.

Yet we should not be too quick in drawing such conclusions. That evacuation under present conditions is as upsetting as bombing itself is no proof that methods of evacuation could not be found which would guard the children's lives and bodily health and at the same time provide the possibility for normal psychological development and steady progress in education.

Our case-material shows that it is not so much the fact of separation to which the child reacts abnormally as the form in which the separation has taken place. The child experiences shock when he is suddenly and without preparation exposed to dangers with which he cannot cope emotionally. In the case of evacuation the danger is represented by the sudden disappearance of all the people whom he knows and loves. Unsatisfied longing produces in him a state of tension which is felt as shock.

If separation happened slowly, if the people who are meant to substitute for the mother were known to the child beforehand, the transition from one object to the other would proceed gradually. If the mother reappeared several times during the period when the child has to be weaned from her, the pain of separation would be repeated but it would be felt each successive time in smaller doses. By the time the affection of the child has let go of the mother the new substitute-object would be well known and ready at hand. There would be no empty period in which the feelings of the child are completely turned inward and consequently there would be little loss of educational achievement. Regression happens while the child passes through the no-man's land of affection, i.e., during the time after the old object has been given up and before the new one has been found.

Two of our children have expressed this state of mind in their own words, Georgie (3¾) when he said: "I don't like you. I don't like anybody, I only like myself"; and John (5) when he said: "I am nobody's nothing."

Mothers are commonly advised not to visit their children during the first fortnight after separation. It is the common opinion that the pain of separation will then pass more quickly and cause less disturbance. In reality it is the very quickness of the child's break with the mother which contains all the dangers of abnormal consequences. Long-drawn-out separation may bring more visible pain, but it is less harmful because it gives the child time to accompany the events with his reactions, to work through his own feelings over and over again, to find outward expressions for his state of mind, i.e., to abreact slowly. Reactions which do not even reach the child's consciousness can do incalculable harm to his normality.

SUPPLEMENTARY READINGS

Heinicke, C. M. Some effects of separating two-year-old children from their parents: A comparative study. *Hum. Relat.*, 1956, 9, 105–176.

Hellman, I. Hampstead Nursery follow-up studies. I. Sudden separation and its effect followed over twenty years. *Psychoanalyt. Stud. Child*, 1962, 17, 159–174.

Howells, J. G., & Layng, J. Separation experiences and mental health. *Lancet*, 1955, 269, 285–288.

Roudinesco, J., David, M., & Nicolas, J. Responses of young children to separation from their mothers. *Courrier*, 1952, 2, 66–78.

an experiment

in group upbringing*

ANNA FREUD with SOPHIE DANN

[Within the limits of recorded history the sensibilities and morality of civilized man have provided a generally supportive environment for the rearing of infants and small children. Although mythology includes numerous accounts of human infants being abandoned by their human caretakers and then nurtured by wild beasts, these stories remain as myths, sometimes half-believed but always mistrusted. For it is true, almost without exception, that children are reared by nurturant adults, either by their true parents or by surrogate wards appointed and supported by benevolent agencies in the larger society. The psychological limits of childrearing are usually much more restricted by the dictates of modern civilization than would be required for the sheer physical survival of infants and small children. Occasionally fate intervenes, as by war and its aftermath, to extend the range of circumstances under which children are reared.

The following report by Anna Freud and Sophie Dann tells with sympathy and an unusually high degree of insightfulness what happened to a group of six preschool-aged children who were deprived by Nazi brutality of their true parents immediately after birth, were buffeted about (*but as a group*) from one concentration camp to another, and were finally brought (*again as a group*) to the stable adult care of a nursery in England when they were between three and four years of age.

Clinical observations of these six children showed them to be similar to identical twins in the closeness of their social and emotional ties to each other. ". . . the feelings of the six children toward each other show a warmth and spontaneity which is unheard of in ordinary relations between young contemporaries." It is interesting to see the gradual dilution of these extraordinarily strong intragroup attachments as ties between each of the six children and a particular adult begin to form and to become stronger little by little.]

The experiment to which the following notes refer is not the outcome of an artificial and deliberate laboratory setup but of a combination of fateful outside circumstances. The six young children who are involved in it are

* From A. Freud with S. Dann. An experiment in group upbringing. *Psychoanalytic Study of the Child*, 1951, 6, 127–168. (With permission.)

German-Jewish orphans, victims of the Hitler regime, whose parents, soon after their birth, were deported to Poland and killed in the gas chambers. During their first year of life, the children's experiences differed; they were handed on from one refuge to another, until they arrived individually, at ages varying from approximately six to twelve months, in the concentration camp of Tereszin, in Moravia. There they became inmates of the Ward for Motherless Children, were conscientiously cared for and medically supervised, within the limits of the current restrictions of food and living space. They had no toys and their only facility for outdoor life was a bare yard. The Ward was staffed by nurses and helpers, themselves inmates of the concentration camp and, as such, undernourished and overworked. Since Tereszin was a transit camp, deportations were frequent. Approximately two to three years after arrival, in the spring of 1945, when liberated by the Russians, the six children, with others, were taken to a Czech castle where they were given special care and were lavishly fed. After one month's stay, the six were included in a transport of three hundred older children and adolescents, all of them survivors from concentration camps, the first of one thousand children for whom the British Home Office had granted permits of entry. They were flown to England in bombers and arrived in August 1945 in a carefully set-up reception camp in Windermere, Westmoreland, where they remained for two months. When this reception camp was cleared and the older children distributed to various hostels and training places, it was thought wise to leave the six youngest together, to remove them from the commotion which is inseparable from the life of a large children's community and to provide them with peaceful, quiet surroundings where, for a year at least, they could adapt themselves gradually to a new country, a new language, and the altered circumstances of their lives.

This ambitious plan was realized through the combined efforts of a number of people. A friend of the former Hampstead Nurseries, Mrs. Ralph Clarke, wife of the Member of Parliament for East Grinstead, Sussex, gave the children a year's tenancy of a country house with field and adjoining woodland, "Bulldogs Bank" in West Hoathly, Sussex, containing two bedrooms for the children, with adjoining bathrooms, a large day nursery, the necessary staff rooms, a veranda running the whole length of the house and a sun terrace.

The children arrived in Bulldogs Bank on October 15, 1945. The personal data of the six, so far as they could be ascertained, were the following:*

* Nothing has been changed for the purpose of publication except the children's names. According to a Nazi rule, all Jewish children had to bear names out of the Old Testament. These have been replaced here by another set of biblical names. On immigration the official register of the children contained nothing beyond their names, birth-dates and birthplaces. Some additional information concerning the six Bulldogs Bank children was supplied later by letter by Mrs. Martha Wenger, herself a concentration camp victim who had been in charge of the children in the Ward for Motherless Children in Tereszin.

Name	Date and Place of Birth	Family History	Age at Arrival in Tereszin	Age at Arrival in Bulldogs Bank
John	December 18, 1941 Vienna	Orthodox Jewish working-class parents. Deported to Poland and killed.	Presumably under 12 months	3 years, 10 months
Ruth	April 21, 1942 Vienna	Parents, a brother of 7 and a sister of 4 years were deported and killed when Ruth was a few months old. She was cared for in a Jewish Nursery in Vienna, sent to Tereszin with the Nursery.	Several months	3 years, 6 months
Leah	April 23, 1942 Berlin	Leah and a brother were illegitimate, hidden from birth. Fate of mother and brother unknown. Brother presumed killed.	Several months	3 years, 5 months. Arrived 6 weeks after the others, owing to a ringworm infection.
Paul	May 21, 1942 Berlin	Unknown	12 months	3 years, 5 months
Miriam	August 18, 1942 Berlin	Upper middle-class family. Father died in concentration camp, mother went insane, was cared for first in a mental hospital in Vienna, later in a mental ward in Tereszin where she died.	6 months	3 years, 2 months
Peter	October 22, 1942	Parents deported and killed when Peter was a few days old. Child was found abandoned in public park, cared for first in a convent, later, when found to be Jewish, was taken to the Jewish hospital in Berlin, then brought to Tereszin.	Under 12 months	3 years

Meager as these scraps of information are, they establish certain relevant facts concerning the early history of this group of children: (i) that four of them (Ruth, Leah, Miriam, Peter) lost their mothers at birth or immediately afterward; one (Paul) before the age of twelve months, one (John) at an unspecified date; (ii) that after the loss of their mothers all the children wandered for some time from one place to another, with several complete changes of adult environment. (Bulldogs Bank was the sixth station in life for Peter, the fifth for Miriam, etc. John's and Leah's and Paul's wanderings before arrival in Tereszin are not recorded.); (iii) that none of the children had known any other circumstances of life than those of a group setting. They were ignorant of the meaning of a "family"; and

(iv) that none of the children had experience of normal life outside a camp or big institution.*

BEHAVIOR TOWARD ADULTS ON ARRIVAL

On leaving the reception camp in Windermere, the children reacted badly to the renewed change in their surroundings. They showed no pleasure in the arrangements which had been made for them and behaved in a wild, restless, and uncontrollably noisy manner. During the first days after arrival they destroyed all the toys and damaged much of the furniture. Toward the staff they behaved either with cold indifference or with active hostility, making no exception for the young assistant Maureen who had accompanied them from Windermere and was their only link with the immediate past. At times they ignored the adults so completely that they would not look up when one of them entered the room. They would turn to an adult when in some immediate need, but treat the same person as nonexistent once more when the need was fulfilled. In anger, they would hit the adults, bite or spit. Above all, they would shout, scream, and use bad language. Their speech, at the time, was German with an admixture of Czech words, and a gradual increase of English words. In a good mood, they called the staff members indiscriminately *Tante* (auntie), as they had done in Tereszin; in bad moods this changed to *blöde Tante* (silly, stupid auntie). Their favorite swearword was *blöder Ochs* (the equivalent of "stupid fool"), a German term which they retained longer than any other.

GROUP REACTIONS

CLINGING TO THE GROUP

The children's positive feelings were centered exclusively in their own group. It was evident that they cared greatly for each other and not at all for anybody or anything else. They had no other wish than to be together and became upset when they were separated from each other, even for short moments. No child would consent to remain upstairs while the others were downstairs, or vice versa, and no child would be taken for a walk or on an errand without the others. If anything of the kind happened, the single child would constantly ask for the other children while the group would fret for the missing child.

This insistence on being inseparable made it impossible in the beginning to treat the children as individuals or to vary their lives according to their special needs. Ruth, for instance, did not like going for walks, while

* An attachment to a mother substitute is recorded of one child only. Martha Wenger, in the letter mentioned above, writes concerning Ruth: "Ruth was passionately attached to me and maltreated me accordingly. When somebody else had night duty with the children, she slept soundly; when it was me, she would stay awake, cry, and force me to sit with her." No similar relationships are mentioned with regard to the other children.

the others greatly preferred walks to indoor play. But it was very difficult to induce the others to go out and let Ruth stay at home. One day, they actually left without her, but kept asking for her until, after approximately twenty minutes, John could bear it no longer and turned back to fetch her. The others joined him, they all returned home, greeted Ruth as if they had been separated for a long time and then took her for a walk, paying a great deal of special attention to her.

It was equally difficult to carry out measures for the children's health, so far as they did not apply to everybody. When the children arrived, they were in fairly good physical condition, though somewhat pale, flabby, with protruding stomachs and dry, stringy hair, cuts and scratches on their skin tending to go septic. All the children were given codliver oil and other vitamins which were taken easily and liked by everybody. But it was nearly impossible to keep individual children in bed for small ailments, or for instance to give Miriam and Peter, who needed it, an afternoon nap while the others had no wish to rest. Sometimes those two children would fall asleep exhaustedly in the middle of the noise made by the others. At night, all children were restless sleepers, Ruth being unable to fall asleep, Paul and Peter waking up in the night crying. Whoever was awake naturally disturbed the sleep of the others. The upset about separation was so great that, finally, children with colds were no longer kept upstairs. The only child who was in bed once, for two days with a slight bronchitis, was Paul. Another time three children had to be isolated for several days with stomatitis. The only other child in need of individual physical treatment was Leah. She had a bad squint, her eyes were treated daily but the operation was postponed for six months to give her time for better adjustment to a renewed separation.

Inability to be separated from the group showed up most glaringly in those instances where individual children were singled out for a special treat, a situation for which children crave under normal circumstances. Paul, for example, cried for the other children when he was taken as the only one for a ride in the pony cart, although at other times such rides were a special thrill to him as well as to the others. On another, later, occasion the whole group of children was invited to visit another nursery in the neighborhood. Since the car was not large enough to take everybody, Paul and Miriam were taken earlier by bus. The other four, in the car, inquired constantly about them and could not enjoy the trip nor the pleasures prepared for them, until they were reunited.

TYPE OF GROUP FORMATION

When together, the children were a closely knit group of members with equal status, no child assuming leadership for any length of time, but each one exerting a strong influence on the others by virtue of individual qualities, peculiarities, or by the mere fact of belonging. At the beginning, John, as the oldest, seemed to be the undisputed leader at mealtimes. He only needed to push away his plate, for everybody else to cease eating. Peter, though the youngest, was the most imaginative of all and assumed leadership in games, which he would invent and organize. Miriam too played a major role, in a peculiar way. She was a pretty, plump child, with ginger hair, freckles and a ready smile. She behaved toward the other children as if she were a superior being, and let herself be served and spoiled by them as a matter of course. For example, Miriam dropped her towel, turned around and said: "Pick it up, somebody." Leah picked it up for her. She would sometimes smile at the boys in return for their services, while accepting Leah's helpfulness toward herself without acknowledgment. But she, too, did not guide or govern the group. The position was rather that the other children sensed this need and did their best to fulfill it.

The children's sensitiveness to each other's attitudes and feelings was equally striking where Leah was concerned. Leah was the only backward child among the six, of slow, lower average intelligence, with no outstanding qualities to give her a special status in the group. As mentioned before, Leah's arrival in Bulldogs Bank was delayed for six weeks owing to a ringworm infection. During this period the five other children had made their first adaptation to the new place, had learned some English, had established some contact with the staff and dropped some of their former restlessness. With Leah's coming, the whole group, in identification with her, behaved once more as if they were all newcomers. They used the impersonal *Tante* again instead of first names for the members of staff. They reverted to talking German only, shouted and screamed, and were again out of control. This regression lasted approximately a week, evidently for the length of time which Leah herself needed to feel more comfortable in her new surroundings.

POSITIVE RELATIONS WITHIN THE GROUP.
ABSENCE OF ENVY, JEALOUSY, RIVALRY,
COMPETITION

The children's unusual emotional dependence on each other was borne out further by the almost complete absence of jealousy, rivalry and competition, such as normally develop between brothers and sisters or in a group of contemporaries who come from normal families. There was no occasion to urge the children to "take turns"; they did it spontaneously since they were eager that everybody should have his share. Since the adults played no part in their emotional lives at the time, they did not compete with each other for favors or for recognition. They did not tell on each other and they stood up for each other automatically whenever they felt that a member of the group was unjustly treated or otherwise threatened by an outsider. They were extremely considerate of each other's feelings. They did not grudge each other their possessions, on the contrary lending them to each other with pleasure. When one of them received a present from a shopkeeper, they demanded the same for each of the other children, even in their absence. On walks they were concerned for each other's safety in traffic, looked after children who lagged behind, helped each other over ditches, turned aside branches for each other to clear the passage in the woods, and carried each other's coats. In the nursery they picked up each other's toys. After they had learned to play, they assisted each other silently in building and admired each other's productions. At mealtimes handing food to the neighbor was of greater importance than eating oneself.

Behavior of this kind was the rule, not the exception. The following examples merely serve the purpose of illustration and are in no way outstanding. They are chosen at random from the first seven months of the children's stay in Bulldogs Bank:

November 1945.—John refuses to get up in the morning, lies in his bed, screams and kicks. Ruth brings his clothes and asks: "Willst Du anziehen?" ("Don't you want to put them on?") Miriam offers him her doll with a very sweet smile. John calms down at once and gets up.

December 1945.—Paul loses his gloves during a walk. John gives him his own gloves, and never complains that his hands are cold.

May 1946.—A ladybird is found by the children, sitting on a nettle. John wants to have it but is warned that the nettle will sting. Shortly afterward John appears with the ladybird and Paul reports beaming with pride: "Ich (I) step on stinging nettle for John and and and John got the ladybird and stinging nettle did not hurt and Paul step on it for John."

AGGRESSIVE REACTIONS WITHIN THE GROUP

With the exception of one child the children did not hurt or attack each other in the first months. The only aggressiveness to which they gave vent within the group was verbal. They quarreled endlessly at mealtimes and on walks, mostly without any visible provocation. The disputes ended sometimes in a general uproar, sometimes in a concerted attack on any adult who had tried to interfere and appease the quarrel; mostly the quarrel merely petered out when some new event distracted the children's attention.

After the children had entered into more normal emotional relationships with the adults and had become more independent of each other, word battles diminished and were replaced to some degree by the fights normal for this age. This second phase lasted approximately from January to July, when the relations between the children became peaceful again on a new basis.

The only child whose reactions did not fit in with the general behavior of the group was Ruth. She behaved like the others so far as being inseparable from the group was concerned, did not want to be left alone and worried about absent children. She also did her share of comforting others or of helping Leah, the latter especially after Leah began to call her "my Ruth." But apart from these reactions, she was moved by feelings of envy, jealousy and competition, which were lacking in the other children and which made her actions stand out as isolated instances of maliciousness or spitefulness. In this connection it is interesting to remember that Ruth is the only child among the group who has a recorded history of passionate attachment to a mother substitute. The evidence is not sufficient to establish with certainty that it is this past mother relationship which prevented her from merging completely with the group, and which aroused normal sibling rivalry in her. On the other hand, the difference between her and the other children's behavior together with the difference in their emotional histories seems too striking to be a mere coincidence.

AGGRESSIVENESS TOWARD THE ADULTS

The children behaved with strong and uncontrolled aggression toward the adults from their arrival. This aggression was impersonal in its character, not directed against any individual and not to be taken as a sign of interest in the adult world. The children merely reacted defensively against an environment which they experienced as strange, hostile and interfering.

On arrival it was striking that the form of aggressive expression used by the children was far below that normal for their age. They used biting as a weapon, in the manner in which toddlers use it between eighteen and twenty-four months. Biting reached its peak with Peter, who would bite anybody and on all occasions when angry; it was least pronounced with Leah who showed very little aggression altogether. For several weeks John and Ruth would spit at the adults, Ruth also spitting on the table, on plates, on toys, looking at the adults in defiance. Similarly, Peter, when defying the staff, urinated into the brick box, on the slide, into the toy scullery, or wetted his knickers.

After a few weeks, the children hit and smacked the adults when angry. This happened especially on walks where they resented the restrictions imposed on them in traffic. Shouting and noisy behavior was used deliberately as an outlet for aggression against the adults, even though the children themselves disliked the noise.

Toward spring these very infantile modes of aggressiveness gave way to the usual verbal aggressions used by children between three and four years. Instead of hitting out, the child would threaten to do so, or would say: "Naughty boy, I make noise at you," and then shout at the top of their voices. Other threats used by the children were: "Doggy bite you." Paul once used: "Froggy bite you." After a visit to Brighton in April, where Peter had been frightened of the waves, a new threat was used by them: "You go in a water." They sometimes tried to find a water so as to carry out the threat.

FIRST POSITIVE RELATIONS WITH THE ADULTS

The children's first positive approaches to the adults were made on the basis of their group feelings and differed in quality from the usual demanding, possessive behavior which young children show toward their mothers or mother substitutes. The children began to insist that the members of the staff should have their turn or share; they became sensitive to their feelings, identified with their needs, and became considerate of their comfort. They wanted to help the adults with their occupations and, in return, expected to be helped by them. They disliked it when any member of staff was absent and wanted to know where the adults had been and what they had done during their absence. In short, they ceased to regard the adults as outsiders, included them in their group and, as the examples show, began to treat them in some ways as they treated each other. For example, when Mrs. Clarke, who had been visiting left, Ruth demanded to be kissed. Then all the children had to be kissed. Then John and Ruth called out: "Kiss for Sophie."

SECOND PHASE OF POSITIVE RELATIONS TO ADULTS. PERSONAL RELATIONSHIPS

Several weeks after arrival in Bulldogs Bank the first signs of individual personal attachments to adults appeared, alongside with and superimposed on the relationships based on community feelings. These new attachments had many of the qualities which are well known from the relationship of young children to their mothers or mother substitutes. Attitudes such as possessiveness, the wish to be owned, exclusive clinging, appeared, but they lacked the intensity and inexorability which is one of the main characteristics of the emotional life at that age. During the year's stay at Bulldogs Bank these ties of the children to the adults in no way reached the strength of their ties to each other. The children went, as it were, through the motions and attitudes of mother relationships, but without the full libidinal cathexis of the objects whom they had chosen for the purpose.

EXAMPLES OF CONFLICTING RELATIONSHIPS

Several children had considerable difficulties in choosing their mother substitutes, their positive feelings wavering uncertainly between the adult figures. John, after being left by Maureen, attached himself to Sister Gertrud, and shortly afterward became fond of Sister Sophie. Neither relationship was exclusive or very passionate and consequently he seemed to have no difficulties in maintaining both simultaneously. In contrast to this, Miriam, who was attached equally to Sisters Sophie and Gertrud, suffered badly from the consequent conflict of feeling. She lived in a constant state of tension without finding relief and satisfaction in her relationships. During Sister Sophie's absence, she "wrote" and dictated long letters to her and she was full of happiness on Sister Sophie's return. But the preference for Sister Sophie, which seemed established at the time, gave way once more to a preference for Sister Gertrud in the course of a few weeks.

EXAMPLE OF FULL CATHEXIS
OF A MOTHER SUBSTITUTE

The only child to choose a real mother substitute was Ruth, an exception which is easily explainable on the basis of her former attachment to the superintendent of the Children's Ward in Tereszin. She chose as her object Sister Gertrud, and developed toward her the same demandingness, aggressive possessiveness and wish for exclusive attention which had characterized her earlier relationship, a mixture of emotions which is well known from children in the toddler stage and at later ages from those who have gone through the experience of loss, separation, rejection and disappointments in their earliest object relationships. Ruth's lack of satisfaction and insecurity expressed itself with regard to Sister Gertrud in the constantly repeated phrase: "And Ruth? And Ruth?"

ORAL EROTISM. MASTURBATION

There was a further factor which accounted for the children's diminished capability to form new object relationships. As children for whom the object world had proved disappointing, and who had experienced the severest deprivations from the oral phase onward they had had to fall back to a large degree on their own bodies to find comfort and reassurance. Therefore oral-erotic gratifications persisted with each child in one form or another. Ruth, besides, had a habit of scratching herself rhythmically until she bled, and of smearing with the blood. One child, Paul, suffered from compulsive masturbation.

Peter, Ruth, John and Leah were all inveterate thumb-suckers, Peter and Ruth noisily and incessantly during the whole day, John and Leah more moderately, gradually reducing it to bedtime only. Miriam sucked the tip of her tongue, manipulating it with her teeth until she fell asleep. With Peter, sucking changed in spring to "smoking" carried out with match sticks, twigs, grass blades, then again to sucking his thumb when cross, angry, or at bedtime only. With Ruth sucking persisted even while she was carrying out interesting activities such as threading beads or playing with plasticene.

Since the children's sucking was noisy and obvious they often heard remarks from passers-by or in shops that they should stop or that "their thumbs would be cut off." Contrary to their usual oversensitiveness they remained completely indifferent on such occasions, not even needing reassurance. Sucking was such an integral and indispensable part of their libidinal life that they had not developed any guilt feelings or conflicting attitudes concerning it.

That the excess of sucking was in direct proportion to the instability of their object relationships was confirmed at the end of the year, when the children knew that they were due to leave Bulldogs Bank and when sucking in daytime once more became very prevalent with all of them.

This persistence of oral gratifications, more or less normal under the circumstances, which fluctuated according to the children's relations with the environment, contrasted strongly with Paul's behavior, where compulsive sucking and masturbation manifested themselves as a complicated and, at the time, inaccessible symptom.

Paul, in his good periods was an excellent member of the group, friendly, attentive and helpful toward children and adults, and capable of friendship. Though not aggressive himself, he was always ready to come to another child's rescue and take up arms against an aggressor. But when he went through one of his phases of compulsive sucking or masturbating, the whole environment, including the other children, lost their significance for him. He ceased to care about them, just as he ceased to eat or play himself. He did not bother to take part in his favorite communal activities such as sorting the laundry or lighting fires. He did not defend himself, or anybody else, merely cried passively when something or somebody made him unhappy. These spells attacked him at any time of the day, while playing, when eating at the table, and during work. He was only free of masturbation on walks, when he sometimes sucked his thumb but otherwise showed a completely changed, cheerful and interested attitude.

EATING HABITS

Since a child's enjoyment of food is based in the first instance on satisfying experiences in the oral phase, undisturbed by violent changes and upheavals, it was not surprising that all the six Bulldogs Bank children were bad eaters. Moreover, in Tereszin, they had been fed almost exclusively on soft, dull starchy food, with the sole exception of an occasional sweet received as comfort after a medical inspection or injection. Consequently, they were uninterested in their food, reluctant to chew and unwilling to try new tastes and dishes. On arrival and for several months afterward they refused all but starchy foods. Meat, fish, vegetables and cheese were picked out by them and thrown on the ground.

With the exception of Paul, whose ambivalence toward food expressed a deeper underlying conflict, the children acquired gradually a moderate enjoyment of new dishes. A decisive intermediate step toward this aim was the gratification of their craving for sugar which may have had physical as well as mental reasons. There is no doubt that under concentration camp rations their diet had contained an insufficient amount of sugar. Simultaneously the craving for an excessively sweet taste may have been the expression of their never-satisfied longing for oral satisfactions. In any case, a covering with sugar enabled the children to approach new foods such as raw vegetables and salads. They even put sugar on meat, fish, cheese and eggs for a period.

On the other hand, mealtimes were by no means dull occasions. Though interest in food was reduced and conflicting, passionate interests were attached to apparently minor factors, such as the details of serving, sitting arrangements, the cutlery, etc.

After a first week of riotous meals, when everybody refused to sit down and cutlery and crockery were thrown about, one of the children's group attitudes came to the help of table manners. Since they were concerned that everybody should have his turn, they began to enjoy a routine of passing on plates. Any child would interrupt his meal, even a favorite dish, to pass on what his neighbor needed.

After several weeks, advances in skill came to the help of mealtimes. The children enjoyed helping themselves from the dishes and would sometimes taste new foods for the sake of this enjoyment. They were specially interested in sugaring the food on their plates themselves, an occasion where the liking for the taste of the food combined successfully with the interest in carrying out the desired activity.

Since mealtimes were the setting for most word battles, and fights broke out frequently about the spoons,* eating was not a peaceful process. The custom developed gradually of letting children who had been the victim of attacks by others, sit next to the adult who shared the nursery meal, a practice which fitted well with the children's initial restlessness and disinclination to sit in one place for any length of time. Meals occurred where seats were changed so often that finally no child sat in the place where he or she had begun their meal.

It is well known from other observations of children's eating habits and difficulties that, where the initial oral pleasure in food and in the gratification of hunger are disturbed, interests and conflicts are displaced to the subsidiary outward arrangements of the meal (sitting arrangements, color and form of cups, table manners, etc.).

TOILET HABITS

According to the report from Tereszin, all the children had undergone, and successfully completed, an elaborate process of toilet training while in the Ward for Motherless Children. Martha Wenger attributed the length and difficulty of this procedure, which included taking up some of the children two or three times every night, to the "watery diet." The present authors recognize this protracted battle for cleanliness as characteristic for institutional children who do not acquire bowel and bladder control on the basis of an exclusive relationship with their mothers or with a stable mother substitute. According to Martha Wenger, the six children were finally completely and reliably clean and dry during day and night from the spring of 1945 until their liberation.

* The significance of the spoons remained a puzzle until an eyewitness from Tereszin reported that in the camp spoons were the only personal possessions of the children as well as adults. Each inmate had a spoon which had his initials (in the children's case their sign) scratched into the handle. Many of the bigger children used to carry their spoon around from morning to night. The "little things" therefore were for the children symbols of their otherwise forgotten past.

It bears witness to the disturbing effect of their subsequent changes of environment that with four of the children the result of this toilet training was wholly or partially undone. As usual, there was no simple direct correspondence between the extent of emotional disturbance and the loss of cleanliness. The two most deeply disturbed children, Paul and Ruth, remained clean, without relapses, manifesting their conflicts and abnormalities through other channels. John, Leah and Peter wetted regularly at night with frequent accidents in daytime; Leah and Peter even regressed to soiling for short periods. Miriam merely lost her reliability in toilet matters and had frequent accidents.

The close connection of wetting with the relationship to the adult world was demonstrated most convincingly by Peter's behavior. He used urination quite deliberately in defense against and in defiance of the staff, and as the expression of emotions such as anger, or a feeling of frustration. Characteristically enough for children with this type of wetting, a decisive turn in his toilet habits followed a present of new trousers with braces from his American foster parents. He was very excited about this personal gift, was very careful not to wet these trousers and, on the basis of these positive feelings, reacquired his lost bladder control.

DEVIATIONS FROM THE NORM IN EGO ATTITUDES

In Tereszin, i.e., up to the ages of three to three and one-half, the children had led the existence of inmates of a Ward, within a restricted space, with few or no toys, with no opportunities for moving about freely, for contact with animals, for observing nature. They had not shared or observed the lives of ordinary people and, in the absence of strong emotional ties to the people who looked after them, they had lacked the normal incentives for imitating the adults and for identifying with them. Consequently, their knowledge of the external world, their ability to understand and to deal with it, were far below the level of their ages and of their intelligence.

INDOOR AND OUTDOOR ACTIVITIES

During their first weeks in Bulldogs Bank, the children were unable to use play material. The only toys which attracted their attention from the start were the soft toys, dolls and teddy bears which were adopted as personal possessions and not so much played with as used for autoerotic gratification (sucking, masturbation), or in replacement of it. All the children without exception, took their dolls or teddy bears to bed with them. When a child failed to do so in the evening, it would invariably wake up in the middle of the night, crying for the missing object.

The first play activity, which the children carried out with passionate eagerness, was the pushing of furniture, the usual favorite occupation of toddlers who have just learned to walk. They began their day in the morning with pushing chairs in the nursery and returned to this activity at intervals during the day, whenever they were free to do so. After they had learned to play in the sandpit, they used sand for the same purpose, pushing a supply of it along the whole front of the veranda by means of an inverted chair. They would revert to pushing furniture even on coming home from long walks, or when tired.

Gradual progress in their physical ability to handle objects and to manage their own possessions coincided with the growth of the children's emotional interest in the adult world. This led to the wish to "help," to share the work of the adults and, as described above, to fetch and carry, to set chairs and tables, etc., activities which were carried out surprisingly well. For a short while, the wish to be equal to the adults in these matters led to a frenzy of independence, as the following example shows:

In November, the children are taken for their first bus ride. The situation has been explained to them beforehand, also that the ride will be short and that they will have to get out quickly at the bus stop. They have promised to cooperate, and they leave their seats without protest at the appointed time. But when the conductor and a passenger try very kindly to help them down the steps, they push them away, and shout and scream that they want to do it alone. Finally Miriam lies on the road, her face almost blue with fury, Paul sits next to her, kicking and screaming, the others cry and sob.

While such a phase of independence brought marked increases in the skill and range of the children's activities, in periods of an opposite emotional nature the advances seemed to be lost once more. In January all the children went through a phase of complete passivity, and dependence on the adults, corresponding to the change of their relationships with them from the more impersonal community feelings to warmer personal attachments. During this time they refused to do anything for themselves, wanted to be fed, dressed, etc., and did not cooperate in work. Their ambivalent attitude toward the adults, the outgoing and withdrawal of emotion toward them, was reflected in the sphere of activities by violent demands to be helped and looked after like a helpless infant, coupled with an equally violent refusal to accept the care. In such moods the children would run away from being dressed, push the tables and chairs away when they had been set for a meal, refuse to carry even their own belongings, etc.

After approximately six months stay in Bulldogs Bank, these violent upheavals gave way to more ordinary and stable modes of progress.

In March 1946 the children began to lose interest in their soft toys and took picture books to bed with them for "reading." For some time each child was content to have any book. From April onward the children demanded books in which they were particularly interested.

When Miriam received her postcard from Mr. E. and "wrote" her answer on it before going to sleep in the evening, "reading" came to an end and "writing" took its place. Several children had received letters and parcels from their American foster parents and "wrote" to them in bed.

At first they used pencils indiscriminately, after a while they chose their colors. The imaginary letters written at that time dealt with matters such as Sister Sophie's absence, news about animals, flowers, etc., i.e., interests in the external world which had taken the place of the exclusive autoerotic activities of the bedtime hour.

In the second half of their year in Bulldogs Bank, the children became increasingly interested in the usual nursery school occupations. At the end of the year they had become able to concentrate on an occupation for as much as an hour. They had become able to handle scissors, pencils, paint brushes, blunt needles, and enjoyed painting, cutting out, doing puzzles and threading beads. Even then they preferred "grownup work" to nursery occupations and carried it out very efficiently.

After the beginnings, which had shown the children to be backward in their play by as much as eighteen months or two years, it was all the more impressive to watch the speed with which they passed through consecutive stages of play activity making up for development which had been missed.

Absence of adequate experience with consequent backwardness in understanding and behavior was even more striking outdoors than indoors. The children lacked both the city child's knowledge of traffic, shops, busy streets, etc., and the country child's familiarity with animals, trees, flowers and all types of work. They knew no animals except dogs, which were objects of terror. They did not know the name of a single plant and had never picked or handled flowers. They seemed to know no vehicles and were completely oblivious of the dangers of the road. Consequently their walks on the country road, through the village or the lanes and paths were exciting events during which innumerable new impressions crowded in on them.

Parallel to the speed of their development in the sphere of play, the children passed rapidly through the various stages of experience and behavior with regard to outdoor events, which are usually gone through between the ages of two and four. Their interest in animals, once awakened, was accompanied by the usual animal play, identification with animals and observation of animals. Interest in cars went from an initial terror of being "made too-too by a car" to a pride in being able to manage crossings, to admonish others to do so, and to distinguish between the types of car. Before they left Bulldogs Bank the children had acquired the experience normal for country children of their age. They knew most trees and practically all the common flowers by name and asked for information when meeting new specimens. They distinguished weeds from plants; they picked flowers with long stems instead of tearing their heads off as at first. They were greatly helped in making up for lost time by the interest of the village people who showed them their animals, permitted them to come into their gardens, gave them flowers, explained their tools, allowed them to look inside their vans or behind counters, all of it new experiences of unique importance for the children.

RETARDATION IN MODES OF THINKING

In dealing with the mass of experience which crowded in on them, the children revealed, during the first weeks, some characteristic peculiarities which are worth noting in individuals of their ages.

A first perception of an object, or the experiencing of an event, together with the naming of it, left an impression on their minds far overriding all later ones in strength and forcefulness. This was clearly demonstrated on several occasions.

A pony in the field had been introduced to the children as a donkey by mistake, and the first ducks which they met had been misnamed geese. In both cases it took several weeks to undo the wrong connection between object and word. In spite of repeated efforts at correction, the children clung to the names connected with their first image of the animal.

The first leaf shown to the children was an ivy leaf. For a whole month every green leaf was called ivy leaf.

When the children noticed a plane overhead for the first time and asked where it was going, they were told that it was going to France. "Going to France" remained a fixed attribute of every plane from then onward. During the whole year they called out: "Aeroplane going to France," whenever they heard a plane overhead.

The first time that letter writing had come into the children's lives was on the occasion of Sister Sophie's absence. All later letters, imagined or dictated by them retained the opening phrases which they had used then: "Dear Sophie in London in a Miss X's house. Miss X all better," regardless of the fact that Sister Sophie had returned long ago and that the letters were addressed to other people.

The first English song which the children learned in Bulldogs Bank was "Bah bah black sheep." Though they learned and sang many other nursery rhymes during their stay, "Bah bah black sheep" remained in a class of its own. They would sing it when cheerful or as a treat for somebody on special occasions.

When talking of people the children would name them according to their most interesting attribute or possession, or would name these objects after them. Mrs. Clarke, for example, had two small dogs which were the first friendly dogs known to the children and played an important role in helping them to overcome their terror of dogs. In December all children called Mrs. Clarke: "Miss Clarke's doggies." Objects given by her to the children were called by the same name. A big electric stove which came from her house was called by Peter: "Miss Clarke's doggies." Green porridge bowls given by her as a Christmas present were called Mrs. Clarke by everybody. For example, when washing up, John said: "You wash Mrs. Clarke. I dry Mrs. Clarke. Look at that, Mrs. Clarke all dry."

The examples quoted in this chapter reveal primitive modes of thinking which are shown by children in their second year of life. The overwhelming strength of a first link between an object or event and its name is characteristic for the time when children first learn to speak, or—to express it in metapsychological terms—when word representations are first added to the images (object representations) in the child's mind. The inability to distinguish between essential and nonessential attributes of an object belongs to the same age (see example of aeroplanes). Instances of naming where this is directed not to a single limited object but to a whole idea related to it (for example, "Miss Clarke's doggies") are forms of "condensation," well known from the primary processes which reveal themselves normally in dream activity, and continue in the second year of life as a mode of waking thought.

That these infantilisms in the sphere of thinking were not based on a general mental retardation with the children under observation was borne out by their adequate, adapted reasoning and behavior in situations with which they felt familiar (such as household tasks, community affairs, etc.); that they were not merely a function of the reversal in their emotional development is suggested by the fact that they overcame them before their libidinal attachments had changed decisively. That the rapid growth of life experience brought about an equally rapid advance in the modes of dealing with it mentally, suggests rather that it was the extreme dearth of new perceptions and varied impressions in their most impressionable years which deprived the children of the opportunity to exercise their mental functions to a normal degree and consequently brought about a stunting of thought development.

FEARS AND ANXIETIES

The children had grown up in an atmosphere laden with fear and anxiety. Tereszin was a transit camp, and though some people remained there from their arrest to the end of the Nazi regime, thousands of others, adults as well as children, passed through it on their way to the extermination camps in Poland, their stay in Tereszin lasting days, weeks or months. To be called up for further transport, which was equivalent to a death sentence, was the constant terror of the camp population, from which no inmate was exempt. Arrivals and departures took place continually, especially at nighttime. Inmates who escaped transportation themselves lost parents, husbands, wives, and children. It was a daily happening for members of the community to disappear, not to be seen again, especially in the last year before the liberation when the camp was cleared of tens of thousands of its inmates in the course of several months. Besides, during the whole time, there was a large death roll owing to epidemics, other illnesses, weakness, and old age, and burials were the order of the day.

There were several thousand children of all ages in Tereszin who lived a comparatively protected life in packed dormitories, cared for by their own compatriots. The Ward for Motherless Children was one of these hostels. Though the workers did their best to shelter the children from the unrest and the miseries of concentration camp existence, the excitements, fears, sorrows and losses cannot but have penetrated into their nursery atmosphere. The children, and the adults who looked after them, lived together in such close proximity that there was no room for privacy. In the yard, the children met the inmates of other hostels, adults and children, and must have heard their talks. Though they had no conscious memories of these matters, some of their attitudes seemed to bear witness to the impressions made on them.

ANXIETIES

Apart from particular fears—of dogs, of feathers, of flying—the children showed the usual variety of transient individual anxieties which are the manifest expression for the underlying conflicts and difficulties normal for their ages. There were instances of fear of darkness (Miriam), of flies (Paul), of waves (Peter), of crossing bridges, of finding fluff in the bathwater or in the food (Paul). Apart from the fear of dogs, there was no fear of big animals, horses, cows, pigs, etc. Surprisingly enough, these common forms of anxiety were not more noticeable and widespread than with children who grow up under normal conditions; they were, if anything, less in evidence.

It remains an unanswered question why the atmosphere of anxiety and terror in which the children had spent their first years, had not predisposed them to more violent anxiety states of their own. Infants and young children are, as we know, deeply affected by their mothers' conscious and unconscious fears and anxieties. The explanation may be that these young infants, though they lived in closest proximity with their adult guardians, did not have the intimate emotional contact with them which provides the path for the contagion of feeling between mother and child. Perhaps the fact that they had never known peaceful surroundings rendered them more indifferent to the horrors happening around them. A further possible explanation may be connected with the fact that the children possessed strong defenses against anxiety in their close relationship to each other which acted as reassurance and protection. This latter point is borne out by the fact that they became insecure and anxious as soon as they were separated from each other.

A better answer to this question will, the authors hope, be provided in time by the future analysis of these children or others who have undergone experiences of this nature.

CONCLUSION

"Experiments" of this kind, which are provided by fate, lack the satisfying neatness and circumscription of an artificial setup. It is difficult, or impossible, to distinguish the action of the variables from each other, as is demonstrated in our case by the intermingled effects of three main factors:

the absence of a mother or parent relationship; the abundance of community influence; and the reduced amount of gratification of all needs, from the oral stage onward. It is, of course, impossible to vary the experiment. In our case, further, it proved impossible to obtain knowledge of all the factors which have influenced development. There remained dark periods in the life of each child, and guesswork, conclusions and inferences had to be used to fill the gaps.

Under such circumstances, no claim to exactitude can be made for the material which is presented here and it offers no basis for satistical considerations. Though an experiment staged by fate, in the sense that it accentuates the action of certain factors in the child's life (demonstrated through their absence or their exaggerated presence), it has little or nothing to offer to the experimental psychologist. What it helps to do is to create impressions which either confirm or refute the analyst's assumptions concerning infantile development—impressions which can be tested and in their turn confirmed or rejected in detailed analytic work with single individuals.

According to the results of child analysis and reconstruction from the analyses of adults, the child's relationship to his brothers and sisters is subordinated to his relationship to the parents, is, in fact, a function of it. Siblings are normally accessories to the parents, the relations to them being governed by attitudes of rivalry, envy, jealousy, and competition for the love of the parents. Aggression, which is inhibited toward the parents, is expressed freely toward brothers and sisters; sexual wishes, which cannot become manifest in the oedipal relationship, are lived out, passively or actively, with elder or younger brothers and sisters. The underlying relationship with siblings is thus a negative one (dating from infancy when all siblings were merely rivals for the mother's love), with an overlay of positive feelings when siblings are used for the discharge of libidinal trends deflected from the parents. Where the relations between the children of one family become finally manifestly positive, they do so according to the principles of group formation, on the basis of their common identification with the parents. The rival brother is tolerated as belonging to the mother; in special cases—which lead to later homosexual attitudes—the rival brother even becomes an object of identification as the mother's favorite. The child's first approach to the idea of justice is made during these developments of the brother-sister relationship, when the claim to be favored oneself is changed to the demand that no one should be favored, i.e., that there should be equal rights for everybody. Since contemporaries outside the family are treated like the siblings, these first relationships to the brothers and sisters become important factors in determining the individual's social attitudes.

It is well in line with these views when our material shows that the relations of the Bulldogs Bank children to each other were totally different from ordinary sibling attitudes. The children were without parents in the fullest sense of the word, i.e., not merely orphaned at the time of observation, but most of them without an early mother or father image in their unconscious minds to which their earliest libidinal strivings might have been attached. Consequently, their companions of the same age were their real love objects and their libidinal relations with them of a direct nature, not merely the products of laborious reaction formation and defenses against hostility. This explains why the feelings of the six children toward each other show a warmth and spontaneity which is unheard of in ordinary relations between young contemporaries.

It merely bears out this theory to find that attachments to a mother figure in single instances disturb these positive relations, such as in Ruth's case. Or when John, in his mourning for Maureen, turned against his companions and began to hurt them. In these instances the positive libidinal attachment was directed toward the adult; the other children were thereby changed from the position of friends and love objects to that of enemies and rivals.

When working with the children of the Hampstead Nurseries (Freud & Burlingham, 1944), one of the authors has described certain attitudes of helplessness, cooperation, identification and friendship which appeared in a group of toddlers (between fifteen months and two and one half years of age) who had been temporarily deprived of their mothers' care. The six Bulldogs Bank children, as the observations prove, show these attitudes in excess, the quantitative difference between them and the Hampstead Nursery group corresponding to the difference between total and partial absence of a parent relationship.

The high degree of identification with each other's needs is known from one other relationship in early years, that of identical twins to each other. In a recent study of the subject Dorothy Burlingham (1951) demonstrates the emotional importance of twins to each other, the way in which the twin is treated as an extension of the self, cathected with narcissistic as well as object love. Identification with the twin prospers on the basis of common needs, common anxieties, common wishes, in short, on the similar reactions of two beings of the same age living in close proximity under the same external conditions. While in the case of twins the twin relationship conflicts with and has to adapt itself to the parent relationship, the attitude to the companion within our age group of orphans reigned supreme.

That the children were able to attach their libido to their companions and the group as such, bypassing as it were the parent relationship which is the normal way to social attitudes, deserves interest in relation to certain analytic assumptions. In recent analytic work the experiences of the first year of life, the importance of the relationship to the mother during the oral phase and the linking of these experiences with the beginnings of ego development have assumed great significance. Explorations in these directions have led to the belief, held by many authors, that every disturbance of the mother relationship during this vital phase is invariably a pathogenic factor of specific value. Grave defects in ego development, lack or loss of speech in the first years, withdrawnness, apathy, self-destructive attitudes, psychotic manifestations, have all been ascribed to the so-called "rejection" by the mother, a comprehensive term which includes every disturbance within the mother relationship from loss of the mother through death, permanent or temporary separation, cruel or neglectful treatment, down to lack of understanding, ambivalence, preoccupation or lack of warmth on the mother's part.

The six Bulldogs Bank children are, without doubt, "rejected" infants in this sense of the term. They were deprived of mother love, oral satisfactions, stability in their relationships and their surroundings. They were passed from one hand to another during their first year, lived in an age group instead of a family during their second and third year, and were uprooted again three times during their fourth year. A description of the anomalies which this fate produced in their emotional life and of the retardations in certain ego attitudes is contained in the material. The children were hypersensitive, restless, aggressive, difficult to handle. They showed a heightened autoerotism and some of them the beginning of neurotic symptoms. But they were neither deficient, delinquent nor psychotic. They had found an alternative placement for their libido and, on the strength of this, had mastered some of their anxieties, and developed social attitudes. That they were able to acquire a new language in the midst of their upheavals, bears witness to a basically unharmed contact with their environment.

SUPPLEMENTARY READINGS

Faigin, H. Social behavior of young children in the Kibbutz. *J. abnorm. soc. Psychol.*, 1958, 56, 117–129.

Makarenko, A. S. *Learning to live.* (Originally titled, *Flags on the Battlements.*) Moscow: Foreign Languages Publ. House, 1953.

Makarenko, A. S. *A book for parents.* Moscow: Foreign Languages Publ. House, undated.

Rabin, A. I. Behavior research in collective settlements in Israel. Infants and children under conditions of "intermittent" mothering in the Kibbutz. *Amer. J. Orthopsychiat.*, 1958, 28, 577–584.

Rabin, A. I. *Growing up in the Kibbutz.* New York: Springer, 1966.

Spiro, M. *Children of the Kibbutz.* Cambridge: Harvard Univer. Press, 1958.

the later effects

of an experimental

modification of mothering*

HARRIET L. RHEINGOLD and NANCY BAYLEY

[Many infants who have lost or have been rejected by their true parents are reared in institutions or shuttled about from one foster home to another. The sometimes indifferent and varied "mothering" received by these infants is a continuous source of concern to humanitarians. This concern was heightened some years ago by Dr. Spitz's findings that infants reared by institutional personnel during the second six months of life often fall into an anaclitic depression of withdrawn apathy and high mortality risk. Social scientists have naturally been concerned with the generality of Dr. Spitz's findings, because institutional agencies and foster homes are notoriously variable in the quality of "mothering" provided to infants and young children. In the following report, Dr. Rheingold, of the University of North Carolina, and Dr. Bayley, of the University of California, report findings that are somewhat reassuring to personnel involved with the care of institutionalized babies. Infants who had spent on an average of about nine months in an institution appeared to be perfectly normal in social responsiveness and psychological development when they were observed and tested at about twenty months of age in the homes where they had been placed or adopted. In an earlier report, Dr. Rheingold had shown that these same infants became more socially responsive between the sixth and the eighth months of life when they received more attentive care than that ordinarily provided within the institutional routines. However, this follow-up study failed to show any difference between the infants who had received the special care some ten to twelve months earlier and infants in a control group. In their general evaluation of research related to maternal deprivation, these investigators wisely note that such effects ". . . will depend upon the age of the child, the nature and duration of the deprivation, and the experiences prior to and subsequent to it."]

* From H. L. Rheingold & N. Bayley. The later effects of an experimental modification of mothering. *Child Development*, 1959, 30, 362–372. (With permission.)

An extensive literature in psychology attests to the effect of early experience upon later behavior. For the human infant an important determiner of early experience is maternal care. Some of the dimensions of maternal care thought to be of consequence are amounts and kinds of care, interruptions of care, the number of persons giving care, as well as their attitudes. There is not yet, however, any considerable *experimental* literature on the effects of these variables upon the later behavior of children. The present study reports an attempt to discover the presence, a year later, of a change in behavior brought about in a group of infants by an experimental modification of maternal care (Rheingold, 1956).

Sixteen children, living in an institution for approximately the first nine months of life, were the original subjects of study. From the sixth through the eighth month of life, half of them, the experimental group, were cared for by one person alone, the experimenter, for 7½ hours a day. They thus received more attentive care than the control subjects who were completely reared under institutional routine; and of course the number of different persons from whom they received care was markedly reduced. As a result the experimental babies became more responsive to the experimenter almost at once, while with time they became more responsive to other persons as well. They did not however do reliably better than the control subjects on the Cattell Infant Intelligence Scale or on tests of postural development and cube manipulation. At the conclusion of the study the experimental subjects returned to the full-time care of the institution. Details of the institutional care, of its experimental modification, of the tests used, and of the results may be found in the report referred to above.

One by one, all but one of both the experimental and the control subjects were placed outside the institution—in their own homes, or in adoptive or boarding homes. Approximately a year after the conclusion of the study, the children, then about eighteen months of age, were seen again, in an attempt to detect the effects of the earlier treatment. Since the only clear difference between the groups at the time of the study had been an increase in social responsiveness among the experimental babies, it would be here that one would expect a difference, if any, to persist. Still, the possibility existed that differences might appear later as new functions matured. On the other hand, the subsequent, and more recent, experience of several months' duration in different life situations might reduce the chance of finding a difference.

The effects of experimental treatment were sought in two areas of behavior, the social and the intellectual. Would the experimental subjects be more socially responsive, that is, more friendly and outgoing than the control group to two examiners who visited the home? Would the experimental subjects, in addition, be more responsive to the original experimenter than to another person? If not, the variable under test is really their responsiveness to strangers. Second, would the experimental subjects now do better on a test of developmental progress?

It was planned, in addition, to use the retest data to explore the effect of type of home placement, as well as to evaluate the performance of the whole group considered as a sample of institutionalized children.

PROCEDURE

SUBJECTS

Fourteen of the original sixteen children were located and tested; one from the experimental group and one from the control group could not be found.

The mean age of the experimental group was 19.8 months (range, 17.6–22.1), of the control group, 20.1 months (range, 17.5–21.7). The experimental group had spent an average of 9.2 months in the institution before being placed in homes (range, 4.0–13.6); for the control group the mean time was 10.4 months (range, 6.5–18.1). If the control subject who was still in the institution was omitted from the calculations, the average stay for the control group became 9.2 months (range, 6.5–12.2). In respect, then, to age and to duration of stay in the institution both groups were similar.

The children left the institution at different ages. Two experimental subjects left after only three weeks of treatment. One control subject left in the sixth week of the study, another in the seventh week. All the other subjects stayed at least through the eight weeks of treatment.

The home placements were varied. Three experimental and two control subjects returned to their own homes. With one exception, the own parents of these five subjects were of foreign birth and the homes were marked by poverty. Two of the experimental and four of the control subjects were in adoptive homes which, in general, were superior to the own homes in socioeconomic status. Two experimental subjects were living in boarding homes, pending a release for adoption. And one control subject, a Negro boy, remained in the institution only because a home could not be found for him. Furthermore, there was no difference between the experimental and the control groups in the intellectual stimulation provided by the homes or in the friendliness of the mothers, according to ratings made by the Experimenter and the Examiner after each visit. In type of home placement, therefore, there appeared to be no major difference. Rather, the difference between homes within each group appeared to be larger than any difference between the groups.

THE TESTS

Each child was seen in his own home. The homes were scattered widely through Chicago, its suburbs and neighboring cities, with one home in another state. Two persons, the original Experimenter and an Examiner visited the homes together, with one exception: the child who lived out of the state was examined by the Experimenter alone. The Experimenter knew all the children but, of course, had been especially familiar with the experimental subjects. She served *only* as a stimulus person in the social tests. The Examiner had no previous acquaintance with any of the children and did not know which had been the experimental subjects. She also served as a stimulus person in the social tests, but it was she alone who recorded the children's responses to both the Experimenter and herself, and who administered the test of developmental progress.

The social test resembled those reported in the first study, but was made more suitable for older children. It was composed of three parts, each of which set up a rather natural situation between adult and child, with an easy transition between the parts. In the first part, the responses to the stimulus person in the first few minutes after her entrance into the home were recorded. During this time the stimulus person did not talk to or approach the child but sat at some distance from him and talked to the mother, occasionally smiling at the child. The Examiner recorded the child's responses to whichever stimulus person happened first to engage his attention, then to the other person. At an appropriate moment one of the persons smiled and spoke warmly to the child, saying, "Hi (child's name), come to me," accompanying her words by stretching out her arms in invitation. This constituted the second situation. In the third situation, the stimulus person actually approached the child, smiling, talking, and gesturing as in the second situation. After the child's responses had been recorded, the other stimulus person presented herself to the child similarly. The order of stimulus persons was determined by the convenience of the moment: whoever was closer to the child or was receiving more glances was the first stimulus person.

The child's responses were recorded on a checklist under these categories: *positive facial expression,* which included seven items of behavior ranging from "stares with expression" to "laughs"; *physical approach* with nine items ranging from "shows toy" through "makes physical contact" to "makes social overtures while in the stimulus person's lap"; *vocalizations* for which a child received a score of one for each part of the test in which he vocalized, whether he said discrete sounds, jargon, or words; *negative facial expression,* which included eight items ranging from "a fleeting sober expression" to "cries"; *physical retreat* with six items ranging from "hangs head" to "leaves room"; and *response to mother* (during the social test period) which included a series of six items, from "turns toward mother" to "stays in contact with mother."

Within each category, items of behavior were thus arranged in what seemed a reasonable progression in terms of duration or amplitude of response. Each item within a category was arbitrarily assigned a value of one. Because the items were arranged in ascending order, the score for any item was one plus the value of all other items below it in that category. The scores for the categories of positive facial expression, physical approach, and vocalizations were summed to yield a measure of *positive social responsiveness.* Similarly, the sum of both negative categories gave a measure of *negative social responsiveness*. The sum of these two measures was the measure of *total social responsiveness*. The category of "reponse to mother" was calculated separately and not included in the other measures.

After the social tests, the Cattell Infant Intelligence Scale (Cattell, 1940) was administered by the Examiner, with the Experimenter *not* present. Lastly, the number of words in the child's vocabulary was calculated from his performance on the language items of the Cattell and from the mother's report.

RESULTS

THE EFFECT OF TREATMENT

Table 1 shows that both the experimental and the control subjects responded similarly to the Experimenter and to the Examiner. The close agreement of all means, and of the ranges, is apparent in the part, as well as in the total, scores. The only difference of any size between the two stimulus persons appeared in the experimental group's response to mother.

Table 1—Means and Ranges of the Social Test

Subjects	EXPERIMENTER Mean	Range	EXAMINER Mean	Range	Combined score mean
Experimental group*					
Total social responsiveness	32.1	27–39	30.9	27–38	31.6
Positive	17.4	2–30	16.0	2–37	16.7
Negative	14.7	1–37	14.7	3–29	14.7
Response to mother	2.3	0–16	5.7	0–19	4.0
Control group†					
Total social responsiveness	28.0	14–39	28.3	22–44	28.4
Positive	19.8	5–32	20.2	4–37	20.1
Negative	8.2	3–12	8.2	2–18	8.0
Response to mother	4.5	0–11	4.8	0–10	5.4

* N is 7.
† N is 6 for responses to Experimenter and to Examiner, but 7 for combined score. See text for explanation.

But since only one subject of the seven gave a response to the mother when the Experimenter was the stimulus person, and only three subjects of the seven, when the Examiner was the stimulus person, this difference, as all the others, was not statistically significant. From the results we conclude that the experimental subjects did not appear to remember the Experimenter.

Furthermore, since the experimental and the control groups gave similar scores to both persons, it was assumed that they were of approximately equal stimulating value. Therefore, a combined score for each subject (the average of a subject's responses to both stimulus persons) was used in the analyses which follow. This procedure made it possible to add to the control group the subject who was seen by the Experimenter alone. If every other subject responded similarly to both stimulus persons, it may be assumed that this subject would too. (It will be seen in Table 1 that the addition of this subject to the control group made the combined means slightly different from the separate means.)

The combined scores showed that the experimental subjects were more responsive to both persons than the control subjects, but the difference was not statistically significant. The part scores, further, revealed that the control group gave more positive responses, the experimental group, more negative responses. Again, the differences were not statistically reliable. Moreover, inspection of the data revealed that the negative responses of only two of the seven experimental subjects were responsible for the difference between the groups. The findings therefore do not warrant the conclusion that the experimental subjects were either more or less responsive to the stimulus persons, positively or negatively.

Because some of the subjects made no response to their mothers during the social tests, the means for this category of behavior were not subjected to test. Only three of the seven experimental subjects and five of the control subjects made some contact with the mother during social stimulation by one or the other of the stimulus persons, a difference which permits no conclusive statement of difference.

Although vocalizations had been included in the measure of positive social responsiveness (as explained above), a measure which did not differentiate the groups, they were also analyzed separately. Inspection showed that five of the seven experimental subjects vocalized to one or the other of the stimulus persons but only one of the control subjects did. The difference was significant by the Fisher exact probability test at $P = 0.051$ (one-sided), a finding in agreement with the original study in which, at the end of the experimental treatment, the experimental subjects also vocalized more than the control subjects.

On the Cattell Infant Intelligence Scale the mean IQ for the experimental group was 97.4 (range, 82–110); for the control group it was 95.4 (range, 83–122). More attentive care given during a limited period in the first year of life therefore appeared to produce no difference in IQ on retest a year later.

The experimental subjects had a larger spoken vocabulary than the control subjects (17.9 and 13.7 words), but the difference was again not statistically significant.

THE EFFECT OF HOME PLACEMENT

It early became clear that the adoptive homes were of a higher socioeconomic level than the own homes, and therefore it seemed desirable to look for differences in the performance of the children in these two types of home placement. The adoptive homes were also ranked higher than the own homes by the investigators on the basis of the friendliness of the mother during the visit and of the intellectual stimulation the home seemed to offer the child.

On the social test the children in adoptive homes gave more positive responses than those in own homes; the means were 21.6 and 15.6, respectively, but the difference was not statistically significant. It should be noted, however, that one subject in a boarding home and the subject still in the institution made higher positive scores than the mean of the adoptive home group.

Similarly, the mean IQ of the children living in adoptive homes was higher (98.8) than that of those living in own homes (95.4), but the difference was not reliable. The two children living in boarding homes had IQs of 95 and 102. And, while the child still in the institution obtained an IQ of only 83, two children in own homes had lower IQs, one of 79 and one of 82, and one child in an adoptive home had an IQ of 84.

Finally, the children in adoptive homes had a larger vocabulary than the children in own homes (means were 18.6 and 13.4, respectively), although again the difference was not significant.

In summary, there was no reliable evidence that the children in adoptive homes were more socially responsive or more developmentally advanced than those in own homes.

THE GROUP AS A WHOLE

We may now evaluate the performance of the group as a whole ($N = 14$), representing as it does a sample of children who spent approximately nine months of the first year of life in the care of an institution and who then experienced a major change in life situation.

In general, the group was marked by a friendliness which seemed warm and genuine. Eleven of the fourteen subjects not only approached the stimulus persons but also allowed themselves to be picked up and held. Only two subjects, both boys, presented a different social response: they clung to their mothers and cried when the stimulus persons approached them. No comparable data are available for children who have lived all their lives in own homes, but in preliminary testing of the social test on three such children not one approached the examiners. Instead, they looked at the examiners from behind their mothers' skirts and retreated whenever the examiners moved in their direction.

On the Cattell Infant Intelligence Scale the mean IQ of the group was 96.4. At six months of age the mean IQ for these fourteen children was 93.8; at eight months it was 94.3. They continue therefore to score in the normal range. Furthermore, the mean number of words in their vocabulary was 15.5, which compares favorably with Gesell's (Gesell and Amatruda, 1941) norms of 10 words at eighteen months and 20 words at twenty-one months. Certainly, the group showed no sign of mental dullness or of language retardation.

No child, furthermore, showed the marked apathy or attention-seeking behavior believed by some to characterize the behavior of children reared in institutions. Differences there were, to be sure, between the children, but none seemed to depart markedly from the normal in temperament or personality. In fact, several of the mothers spontaneously commented upon how easy these children were to handle in comparison with their other children. They mentioned, specifically, their good eating and sleeping habits and their ability to amuse themselves.

DISCUSSION

The discussion will take up three separate points: (a) the effect of the experimental treatment, (b) the effect of own home versus adoptive home placement, and (c) the characteristics of the whole group considered as a sample of institutionalized children.

On the basis of the changes in social behavior produced at the time of treatment, one might have expected that the experimental subjects on retest would have been more responsive to the Experimenter than to the Examiner. Instead, no reliable difference was found in their responses to either person. The Experimenter was not remembered. Further, we did not find, except in the vocalizing of the children, any evidence that the experimental subjects were more responsive than the control subjects. It seems therefore, that the experiences provided by the more attentive mothering were not great enough to maintain the experimentally produced difference over a year's time, except in one class of behavior.

The findings give rise to several speculations. First, it is possible that the verbal behavior of young children is more sensitive to changes in the environment than are other classes of behavior. In this connection, the responsiveness of vocalizations to conditioning in the three-month-old infant has already been demonstrated (Rheingold, Gewirtz, and Ross, 1959). Second, differences between the experimental and control groups may well have existed but in some untested area of behavior. Third, the expected (or some other) differences may make their appearance in the future in some more complex behavior incorporating the experiences of treatment. Finally, serious limitations to the study were imposed by the small number of subjects and by the diversity of home placements within each group. Differences would have to be very large indeed to surmount these limitations.

That no difference was found between the experimental and control groups in developmental status is not surprising, considering that no difference was found at the end of treatment. Some of the speculations about the course of social responsiveness may apply here, too.

We turn now to a consideration of the effect of home placement. The adoptive homes in general were of a higher socioeconomic level, the mothers were more sociable, and the homes were judged to offer more intellectual stimulation. For these reasons we would have expected the children in adoptive homes to be more socially responsive and more advanced in developmental status. But significant differences were not found. Possible explanations are that the differences between the two groups of home may have been not as great as they seemed, or that the number of cases was too small.

Lastly, the characteristics of the group as a whole may be assessed for the effects of a life experience usually thought of as deprived. All the children had been cared for in an institution for the first half of their lives, all but one had experienced a major "separation" in going from one life situation to another, and, furthermore, three children were now living in depressed socioeconomic environments, two were in boarding homes, and one was still in the institution. Yet, as a group, the children were healthy, of normal intelligence, and they appeared to be making a satisfactory adjustment. In addition, they seemed to be more friendly to strangers than children who have lived all their lives in own homes and, according to mothers' reports, were more adaptable than their other children. In no way, then, did they resemble the emotionally disturbed and mentally retarded children described in studies of the effect of institutional or hospital life or of separation from the mother. They did not show apathy or the inability to form relationships or make excessive bids for attention. Even earlier, at the beginning of the study when the infants were still in the institution, they were physically robust, mentally alert, and socially responsive.

It is true that in kind and duration of experience they resemble exactly no other group of children reported in the literature. There is a tendency among workers, however, to lump together studies of children who actually differ in age and experience and to generalize from them to all children who have experiences which may be similar in only one of many possible respects. It is to be hoped that as more prospective (in contrast to retrospective) studies are carried out, the dimensions of deprivation and of its effects can be clarified. Certainly, we may expect to find that the effects will depend upon the age of the child, the nature and duration of the deprivation, and the experiences prior to and subsequent to it (Ainsworth & Bowlby, 1954). The present study of the effects of early experience, limited as it is, emphasizes the need for more precise measurement both of deprivation and of its effects.

SUMMARY

The present study reports an attempt to discover the presence, a year later, of a change in behavior brought about in a group of infants by an experimental modification of maternal care.

Sixteen babies, living in an institution for approximately the first nine months of life, were the original subjects of study. Half of them, the experimental subjects, received more attentive care by one person, the Experimenter, from the sixth through the eighth month of life. As a result they became more socially responsive than the control group who were cared for under the usual institutional routine. They did not, however, do better upon tests of developmental progress.

Subsequently all but one of the children were placed in homes. A year later, when the children were about nineteen months old, fourteen of the original sixteen subjects were located, and tested for their social responsiveness and developmental progress.

The results did not reveal any statistically significant differences between the experimental and the control groups except that more of the experimental subjects vocalized during the social tests. It is concluded therefore that the experience provided by the more attentive mothering, while great enough to produce a difference at the time of study, was not great enough to maintain that difference over time, except in one class of behavior. It is possible that the verbal behavior of young children is more sensitive to changes in the environment than are other classes of behavior.

No statistically significant differences in social responsiveness and developmental status were found between children living in own homes and in adoptive homes, although the adoptive homes were of higher socioeconomic status.

Finally, the group as a whole was friendly, of normal intelligence, and apparently was making a satisfactory adjustment. They did not resemble the emotionally disturbed and mentally retarded children described in studies of the effects of institutional life or of separation from the mother.

SUPPLEMENTARY READINGS

Ourth, L., & Brown, K. B. Inadequate mothering and disturbance in the neonatal period. *Child Develpm.*, 1961, 32, 287–295.

Rheingold, H. L. Mental and social development of infants in relation to the number of other infants in the boarding home. *Amer. J. Orthopsychiat.*, 1943, 13, 41–44.

Rheingold, H. L. The effect of environmental stimulation upon social and exploratory behavior in the human infant. In B. Foss (Ed.), *Determinants of infant behaviour*. London: CIBA Foundation, 1959.

Skeels, H. M., Updegraff, R., Wellman, B. L., & Williams, H. M. A study of environmental stimulation; an orphanage preschool project. *Univer. Iowa Stud. Child. Welf.*, 1938, 15, No. 4.

environmental influences

on physical growth*

J. W. B. DOUGLAS and J. M. BLOMFIELD

[Psychologists have long emphasized the importance of the child's environment upon his emotional development. It is less well appreciated that environmental factors greatly influence the child's physical development as well. The following report by Dr. Douglas, of the Medical Research Unit at the London School of Economics, and Miss Blomfield suggests that socioeconomic factors may be better predictors of a child's height than is his mother's height. Their data clearly demonstrate the importance for the child's physical growth of such demographic factors as social class (as indexed by parental occupation), parents' educational level, region of residence, rural-urban background, and number of siblings. (First-born children, though smaller than their later-born sibs at birth, eventually surpass them in size.) All these environmental correlates are more marked for girls' heights than for boys'. According to these National Survey data, which are based on measurements of more than 4000 British children followed from birth, the tall child is most likely to be the first-born child of well-educated, professional parents who live in a county, or rural area, in England (rather than in Wales or Scotland). All of these differences increase noticeably with age. It is interesting to speculate at what age environment-related differences in physical growth stop increasing. According to Oppers' data on the heights of Dutch military recruits, differential physical growth continues beyond adolescence.]

GROWTH

The survey children were measured at 2 and 4¼ years by health visitors, usually at Infant Welfare Centers, though a few were measured at home or at chemists'. Both heights and weights were taken but only the former are considered here because nearly half the survey children were weighed in their clothes; moreover, we have found that children living in widely different home circumstances show relatively small differences in weight.

* From J. W. B. Douglas & J. M. Blomfield. *Growth. Children under five.* London: George Allen & Unwin, 1958. Pp. 55–62. (With permission.)

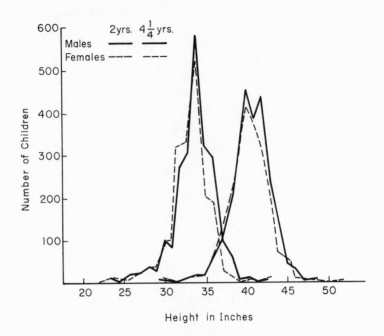

Figure 1—Distribution of heights of girls and boys ages 2 years and 4¼ years.

Some of the children were measured several months after the date fixed for the survey and so have been excluded from the following discussion. We are left with 4037 children measured at 2 years, 4298 at 4¼ years and 3589 at both ages. There is no reason to believe that the children excluded were in any way unrepresentative; for example, the average height at 2 years of those excluded at 4¼ was 33.6 inches as compared with 33.5 inches for those who were measured in both years.

The average height of 2-year-old boys was 33.7 inches and of 2-year-old girls 33.3 inches; at 4¼ years it was 40.7 inches for boys and 40.4 inches for girls. The averages for both sexes together at these ages were 33.5 inches and 40.5 inches respectively. The distributions of heights of boys and girls are shown in Fig. 1.

Regional differences in the heights of 4¼-year-old children are shown in Table 1. Those living in the counties were generally taller than those living in the towns. This holds whether we compare the average for all counties with the average for all towns, or whether we compare the towns with their surrounding rural areas. Wales was different; here the county children were shorter than those in the towns. In the North the advantage of the county children was small. London was virtually the only town with children whose heights were above the national average, but even here they were shorter than children from the surrounding counties.

English children from both town and county were taller than Scottish

Table 1—Average Heights at 4¼ Years of Children in Counties and County Boroughs in Different Parts of Great Britain

	AVERAGE HEIGHT (IN INCHES*) OF CHILDREN IN	
Region	Counties	County boroughs and large burghs
South-East	40.72 ± 0.07	40.18 ± 0.17
London	————	40.52 ± 0.12
North	40.25 ± 0.09	40.17 ± 0.17
Midland	40.67 ± 0.10	40.08 ± 0.13
East and South-West	40.47 ± 0.13	39.97 ± 0.26
Wales	40.08 ± 0.16	40.35 ± 0.27
Scotland	40.13 ± 0.13	39.74 ± 0.14

* Adjusted for sampling.

children, and those in the South of England were taller than those in Wales or the North.

As will be seen in Table 2 and Fig. 2, the children of agricultural workers were not appreciably taller than those of the semi-skilled manual workers, the majority of whom lived in the towns, and there is no reason to believe that rural life of itself favours the rapid growth of children. The

Table 2—Average Heights at 2 & 4¼ Years of Children in Different Social Groups

	AVERAGE HEIGHT (IN INCHES) AT	
Social group	2 years	4¼ years
Professional and salaried	33.89 ± 0.08	41.16 ± 0.08
Black-coated	33.70 ± 0.07	40.77 ± 0.07
Skilled manual	33.35 ± 0.06	40.27 ± 0.06
Semi-skilled manual	33.21 ± 0.12	40.13 ± 0.12
Agricultural	33.42 ± 0.11	40.08 ± 0.10
Unskilled manual	32.98 ± 0.16	39.81 ± 0.16
Self-employed	33.66 ± 0.18	40.57 ± 0.16

regional differences are explained by the fact that the county areas contained a relatively high proportion of black-coated and professional workers whose children were taller than those in the other social groups.

At both 2 and 4¼ years the poorest children were the shortest. But they were less handicapped in this respect at the younger age and it appears that the gap between the rich and poor families has widened during the survey period.

After allowing for variations in education, the considerable difference in height of the professional and salaried as compared with the black-coated worker groups vanished. When the parents had had a secondary education the average height of the child was 41.4 inches for the professional, 41.1 inches for the salaried and also for the black-coated. When the parents had had elementary schooling only, the average heights were 40.9 inches, 40.6 inches and 40.7 inches in the three groups respectively. Whether the relationship between parents' education and height of off-

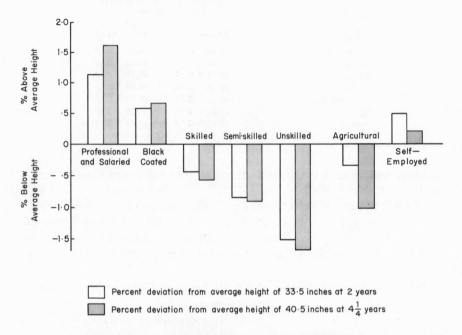

Percent deviation from average height of 33·5 inches at 2 years

Percent deviation from average height of 40·5 inches at $4\frac{1}{4}$ years

Figure 2—Social group differences in heights of children at ages 2 and 4¼ years.

spring was the result of more intelligent care or better economic circumstances we cannot say.

The children whose parents had moved into self-employment were superior in height, in each social group, to all the others—even those from families moving upwards in the social scale. For example, in the skilled manual workers the average height of first-born children from these families was 41.0 inches as compared with 40.4 for the families moving upwards, 40.2 for those moving downwards and 40.5 for those remaining stable.

The influence of social group on height was different in the two sexes, being greater for girls than boys. Table 3 gives the gains in height made by boys and girls in each of the social groups between the ages of 2 and 4¼. It will be seen that in the most prosperous groups the girls gained more than the boys, while in the least prosperous groups they gained less.

First-born children were considerably taller than second, and second than third, but after this differences were small. For example, the mean height of first-born boys of manual workers at 4 years was 40.7 inches, of second-born 40.4 inches, of third-born 39.7 and of fourth-born 40.2, and of later than fourth-born 39.9 inches. The position of first-born children is interesting because they were smallest at birth. It has, of course,

Table 3—Average Gains in Height Between 2 and 4¼ Years of Boys and Girls in Different Social Groups Gain in Height (in inches)

	Boys	Girls
Non-manual workers		
Professional and		
salaried	7.06	7.50
Black-coated	6.95	7.21
Manual workers		
Skilled	6.89	6.96
Semi-skilled	6.88	6.97
Agricultural	6.76	6.66
Unskilled	7.05	6.62
Self-employed	6.31	7.49

been known for a long time that they catch up and eventually surpass those of higher birth rank, but it has never been made clear whether this is due to biological superiority or to better environment. It appears from Table 4 that the latter is the more probable explanation since among non-manual workers there were no significant differences in the height of first and later-born boys, while among the manual workers, both skilled and unskilled, the differences were large. For girls significant differences were found in all groups.

Table 4—Average Heights at 4¼ Years of First-Born and Later-Born Boys and Girls in Different Social Groups

Sex	Social group	AVERAGE HEIGHT (IN INCHES)	
		First-born	Later-born
	Non-manual	41.06 ± 0.11	40.92 ± 0.09
Boys	Skilled manual	40.72 ± 0.14	40.29 ± 0.10
	Semi-skilled, unskilled		
	and agricultural	40.72 ± 0.16	40.10 ± 0.06
	Non-manual	41.14 ± 0.11	40.63 ± 0.09
Girls	Skilled manual	40.40 ± 0.13	39.85 ± 0.11
	Semi-skilled, unskilled		
	and agricultural	40.16 ± 0.18	39.54 ± 0.12

We have divided the children in the family into those younger than the survey child and those older, in order to get a better picture of the relation between family size and growth. When this was done it appeared that the child with younger sibs was more handicapped than the child with older ones. For example, the first-born child with younger sibs in the semi-skilled and unskilled workers' families was 0.4 inches shorter than the first-born child without them. Similarly, the later-born child with younger sibs was 0.6 inches shorter than the later-born child with older sibs only. The explanation of these differences is not necessarily economic; it may be that the older child suffered because his mother had less time to provide meals and see that he ate them.

An earlier study (Hewitt & Stewart, 1952) suggested that the effects of environment on height were reduced, or even eliminated, when allowances were made for the varying sizes of the parents. We obtained the heights of the mothers of 3689 of the children and found them to be significantly correlated with the heights of their children, but the degree of correlation was small and only about 6 per cent of the variation in children's heights could be explained in terms of their mothers' heights. (Correlation coefficient $+0.23$ for boys and $+0.25$ for girls.) When the heights of the children were adjusted to a common maternal height, social class differences were slightly reduced but still highly significant.

The nutrition of a child will be affected by the conscientiousness of his mother in providing suitable food and seeing that he eats it and, in the poorer families, on her ability to lay out the limited money available to the best advantage. We therefore expected that the growth of the survey children would be related to the standard of their mother's care. Table 5 shows that this was so, but only in certain social groups.

Table 5—Average Heights at 4¼ Years of Children in Different Social Groups with Different Standards of Maternal Care (Average Height in inches)

	NON-MANUAL WORKERS			MANUAL WORKERS			
Standard of maternal care	Professional and salaried	Black-coated	Skilled	Semi-skilled and unskilled	Agri-cultural	Self-employed	All groups*
Best	41.21	40.99	40.65	40.04	40.97	41.04	40.88
Intermediate	41.12	40.79	40.13	40.07	40.15	40.16	40.46
Worst	41.25	40.49	39.99	40.03	39.92	40.31	40.20

* Adjusted for sampling.

The two groups where maternal care appeared to have no effect on growth were at either end of the social scale, i.e., the professional and salaried and the semi-skilled and unskilled manual workers. It is possible that when a certain level of material prosperity is reached in the family the nutrition of the child is likely to be adequate whatever the capacity of the mother. Below a certain level, on the other hand, even the best manager cannot provide an adequate diet for her child with the money available unless, as may be the case among the agricultural workers, the family income can be supplemented by garden produce.

If this explanation were correct we should expect no relationship between maternal care and height in the *most* favourably placed of the black-coated workers' families (e.g., those with few children) and in the *least* favourably placed of the skilled manual workers' families (e.g., those with many children). The figures in Table 6 support this view.

It is of interest that even in the professional and salaried group maternal care seems to become of importance in relation to the growth of fourth—or later-born children. With black-coated workers it only *becomes* of importance after the first child, whereas with skilled manual workers it *ceases* to be important after the third. With semi-skilled and unskilled

Table 6—Average Heights at 4¼ Years of Children of Different Birth Rank in Different Social Groups with Different Standards of Maternal Care

Social group	Average height in inches for children differing in ordinal position	STANDARD OF MATERNAL CARE		
		Best	Intermediate	Worst
Professional	First child	41.23	41.42	41.60
and salaried	Second or third child	41.19	40.82	41.12
	Fourth or later child	41.21	41.29	40.77
Black-	First child	41.11	41.15	40.90
coated	Second or third child	41.02	40.48	40.33
	Fourth or later child	40.54	40.84	39.88
Skilled manual	First child	40.92	40.51	40.25
workers	Second or third child	40.70	39.87	39.81
	Fourth or later child	39.74	39.97	39.84
Semi-skilled	First child	40.48	40.46	40.26
and unskilled	Second or third child	40.12	39.65	40.02
workers	Fourth or later child	38.62	40.39	39.45

workers, maternal care does not appear to be related to the growth of children of any birth rank, though there is a suggestion that first-born children in this group may be stunted when maternal care is worst.

So far we have only considered the average height of the children and it is of some interest to see whether the social differences were less or more marked if we took only those who were consistently tall or consistently short during the survey period. For our tall children we have taken those who were 43 inches or more at 4¼ years and 36 inches or more at 2 years, and for our short children those who were 32 inches or less and 31 inches or less at these ages. There were 256 "tall" and 161 "short" children and in Table 7 they have been grouped according to sex, position in family and social group. There were more consistently tall and fewer consistently short boys among the non-manual workers, especially

Table 7—Frequency of Consistently Short and Consistently Tall Boys and Girls in Various Social Groups (Tabular entries are percentages)

	FIRST-BORN		LATER-BORN	
	Non-manual	Manual	Non-manual	Manual
Boys				
Short	1.9	2.7	3.2	5.5
Tall	13.8	10.1	9.0	5.7
Girls				
Short	2.7	3.9	2.8	10.2
Tall	10.9	2.9	7.3	2.3

the later-born. The only significant differences, however, were among the girls. The proportion of first-born girls who were tall was less in the manual than in the non-manual worker group, but the proportion who were short was the same in both. It was only with later-born girls that there was a high proportion who were short among the manual workers.

It appears, then, that the first effect of an adverse environment on girls is to reduce the proportion of tall girls; as conditions further deteriorate so the proportion of short girls increases.

SUPPLEMENTARY READINGS

Meredith, H. V. The stature and weight of U.S. children as influenced by racial, regional, socio-economic and secular factors. *Amer. J. Dis. Child.*, 1941, 62, 909–932.

Meredith, H. V. Physical growth from birth to two years. I. Stature. *Univer. Iowa Stud. Child Welf.*, 1943, 19.

Oppers, V. M. *Analyse van de Acceleratie van de Menselijke Lengtegroei door Bepaling van het Tijdstip van de Groeifasen. (Analysis of the acceleration of human growth through the determination of the time of the growth spurts.)* Amsterdam: Univer. Amsterdam Press, 1963.

Sanders, S. *Environment and growth.* Baltimore: Warwick and York, 1934.

some social antecedents

of imitative behavior*

ALBERT BANDURA, DOROTHEA ROSS, and SHEILA A. ROSS

[The dynamic interplay of those social-psychological forces that Freud placed under the rubric of *identification* provides a series of convenient shortcuts to the socialization process. Under normal developmental conditions little boys identify with and imitate many of the masculine behavior sequences of the father; little girls imitate the feminine activities of the mother. These imitative responses permit the rapid acquisition of fairly complex chains of behavior and associated personality attributes. Socialization is thereby significantly advanced, even though many of these imitative actions may be subsequently altered, or inhibited, by societally-administered rewards and punishments.

Sometimes the normal identification-imitation process fails to occur, or it is inverted so that little boys and girls identify with and imitate behavior patterns of the parent of the opposite sex. What social-psychological variables are related to the usual, and the unusual, in this important dimension of social learning? In the following report, Dr. Bandura, of Stanford University, and his research colleagues show that the imitative behavior of preschool-aged children can be studied under the controlled conditions of the psychological laboratory and that the adult model chosen to imitate is significantly determined by the model's social role preceding the choice. In this "prototype of identification" the children clearly preferred to imitate the adult who possessed rewarding power rather than the one who received rewards in competition with the child subjects. This outcome favors the "social power" as contrasted with the "status envy" theory of identificatory learning. These investigators have also noted that their subjects "exhibited a relatively novel pattern of behavior representing an amalgam of elements from both models." In other words, imitation is selective, and it seems unlikely that any existing theory of identification is sufficiently comprehensive to encompass all of the relevant antecedent-consequent relationships.]

* From A. Bandura, D. Ross, & S. A. Ross. A comparative test of the status envy, social power, and secondary reinforcement theories of identificatory learning. *Journal of Abnormal and Social Psychology*, 1963, 67, 527–534. (With permission.)

Although it is generally assumed that social behavior is learned and modified through direct reward and punishment of instrumental responses, informal observation and laboratory study of the social learning process reveal that new responses may be rapidly acquired and existing behavioral repertoires may be considerably changed as a function of observing the behavior and attitudes exhibited by models (Bandura, 1962).

The latter type of learning is generally labeled "imitation" in behavior theory, and "identification" in most theories of personality. These concepts, however, are treated in the present paper as synonymous since both encompass the same behavioral phenomenon, i.e., the tendency for a person to match the behavior, attitudes, or emotional reactions as exhibited by actual or symbolized models. While the defining properties of identification are essentially the same in different personality theories, a host of divergent learning conditions have been proposed as the necessary antecedent variables for matching or identificatory behavior (Bronfenbrenner, 1960; Freud, 1946; Freud, 1924, 1948; Kagan, 1958; Klein, 1949; Maccoby, 1959; Mowrer, 1950; Parsons, 1955; Sears, 1957; Whiting, 1960).

In the experiment reported in this paper predictions were derived from three of the more prominent theories of learning by identification, and tested in three-person groups representing prototypes of the nuclear family. In one condition of the experiment an adult assumed the role of controller of resources and positive reinforcers. Another adult was the consumer or recipient of these resources, while the child, a participant observer in the triad, was essentially ignored. In a second treatment condition, one adult controlled the resources; the child, however, was the recipient of the positive reinforcers and the other adult was assigned a subordinate and powerless role. An adult male and female served as models in each of the triads. For half the boys and girls in each condition the male model controlled and dispensed the rewarding resources, simulating the husband dominant family; for the remaining children, the female model mediated the positive resources as in the wife dominant home. Following the experimental social interactions the two adult models exhibited divergent patterns of behavior in the presence of the child, and a measure was obtained of the degree to which the child subsequently patterned his behavior after that of the models.

According to the *status envy theory* of identification recently proposed by Whiting (1959, 1960), where a child competes unsuccessfully with an adult for affection, attention, food, and care, the child will envy the consumer adult and consequently identify with him. Whiting's theory represents an extension of the Freudian defensive identification hypothesis that identificatory behavior is the outcome of rivalrous interaction between the child and the parent who occupies an envied consumer status. While Freud presents the child as in competition with the father primarily for the mother's sexual and affectional attention, Whiting regards any forms of reward, material and social, as valued resources around which rivalry may develop. The status envy theory thus predicts that the highest degree of imitation by the child will occur in the experimental condition in which the rivalrous adult consumes the resources desired by the child, with the consumer adult serving as the primary object of imitation.

In contrast to the envy theory, other writers (Maccoby, 1959; Mussen & Distler, 1959; Parsons, 1955) assume that the controller, rather than the consumer, of resources is the main source of imitative behavior. The *power theory* of social influence has received considerable attention in experimental social psychology, though not generally in the context of identification theories.

Social power is typically defined as the ability of a person to influence the behavior of others by controlling or mediating their positive and negative reinforcements. French and Raven (1959) have distinguished five types of power based on expertness, attractiveness, legitimacy, coerciveness, and rewarding power, each of which is believed to have somewhat differential effects on the social influence process. For example, the use of threat or coercion, in which the controller derives power from his ability to administer punishments, not only develops avoidance behavior toward the controller but also decreases his attractiveness and hence his effectiveness in altering the behavior of others beyond the immediate social influence setting (French, Morrison & Levinger, 1960; Zipf, 1960). The use of reward power, in contrast, both fosters approach responses toward the power figure and increases his attractiveness or secondary reward value through the repeated association of his attributes with positive reinforcement. Attractiveness is assumed to extend the controller's power over a wide range of behavior (French & Raven, 1959).

In the present investigation power based upon the ability to dispense rewards was manipulated experimentally. In accordance with the social power theory of identification, but contrasting with the status envy hypothesis, one would predict that children will reproduce more of the behavior of the adult who controls positive reinforcers, than that of the powerless adult model, and that power inversions on the part of the male and female models will produce cross-sex imitation.

The *secondary reinforcement theory* of identification, which has been alluded to in the discussion of social power through attractiveness, has been elaborated in greatest detail by Mowrer (1950, 1958). According to this view, as a model mediates the child's biological and social rewards, the behavioral attributes of the model are paired repeatedly with positive reinforcement and thus acquire secondary reward value. On the basis of stimulus generalization, responses which match those of the model attain reinforcing value for the child in proportion to their similarity to those made by the model. Consequently, the child can administer positively conditioned reinforcers to himself simply by reproducing as closely as possible the model's positively valenced behavior. This theory predicts that the experimental condition in which the child was the recipient of positive reinforcements will yield the highest imitation scores with the model who dispensed the rewards serving as the primary source of imitative behavior.

METHOD

SUBJECTS

The subjects were 36 boys and 36 girls enrolled in the Stanford University Nursery School. They ranged in age from 33 to 65 months, although the variability was relatively small with most of the ages falling around the mean of 51 months.

An adult male and female served as models in the triads so as to reproduce possible power structures encountered in different types of family constellations. A female experimenter conducted the study for all 72 children.

DESIGN AND PROCEDURE

The subjects were assigned randomly to two experimental groups and one control group of 24 subjects each. Half the subjects in each group were males, and half were females.

High rewarding power was induced experimentally through the manipulation of material and social reinforcements, and the use of verbal structuring techniques. While accompanying the child to the experimental room, for example, the experimenter informed the child that the adult who assumed the role of controller owned the nursery school "surprise room," as well as a fabulous collection of play materials. After introducing the child to the controller, the experimenter asked whether the child may play in the surprise room. The controller explained that he was on his way to his car to fetch up some of his most attractive toys, but the experimenter and the child could proceed to the room where he would join them shortly. As the controller left, the experimenter commented on how lucky they were to have access to the controller's play materials.

On the way to the experimental room they met the other adult who insisted on joining them but the experimenter informed her that she would have to obtain permission from the controller since he owned the room, and it was doubtful whether sufficient play materials were available for both the adult and the child. This brief encounter with the other adult was designed primarily to create the set that rewards were available to one person only and thereby to induce rivalrous feelings over the controller's resources.

As soon as the experimenter and the child arrived in the experimental room, they sat down at a small table and played with the few Lincoln Logs and two small cars that were provided. A short time later the other adult appeared and announced that the controller also granted her permission to play in the room.

The controller then entered carrying two large toy boxes containing a variety of highly attractive masculine and feminine toys, a colorful juice dispensing fountain, and an ample supply of cookies. As soon as the controller appeared on the scene, the experimenter departed.

For children in the Adult Consumer condition, the adult who assumed the role of consumer requested permission to play with the articles and the controller replied that, since the child appeared to be occupied at his table, the consumer was free to use the play materials. This monopolistic move by the consumer adult left the child stranded at a table with two relatively uninteresting toys.

During the 20-minute play session, the controller offered the consumer, among other things, miniature pinball machines, mechanical sparkling toys, kaleidoscopes, dolls, and actively participated with the consumer in dart games and other activities. To add to the credibility of the situation, both the controller and consumer devoted most of their attention to articles, such as the pinball machine and dart game, which could be used in adult appropriate activities. Throughout the interaction the controller was most helpful, supportive, and generous in dispensing social reinforcers in the form of praise, approval, and positive attention. The consumer, in turn, commented frequently on the controller's highly attractive resources so as to further enhance the controller's rewarding status. The consumer also verbalized considerable positive affect characteristic of a person experiencing positive reinforcements.

Approximately half way through the session, the controller remarked, "Say, you look hungry. I have just the thing for you." He then brought forth the soda fountain dispenser, poured colorful fruit juices into paper cups and served them to the consumer along with a generous supply of cookies. While the consumer was enjoying his snack, the controller turned on a "TV-radio" that played a nursery melody while a revolving dial displayed a series of storybook scenes.

Toward the end of the session, the controller informed the consumer that he will be leaving on a shopping trip to San Francisco that afternoon, and asked the consumer if there was anything special she would like him to buy for her. The consumer requested a super two-wheel bicycle, a high status object among the nursery school children. The controller promised to purchase the bicycle along with any other items the consumer might think of before the controller departed for the city.

The procedure for the Child Consumer condition was identical with that described above except the child was the recipient of the material rewards and the social reinforcement. During the session the other adult sat at the opposite end of the room engrossed in a book, and was totally ignored by the controller. In discussing the prospective San Francisco shopping trip, the controller mentioned to the child that he was planning to visit some toy stores in the city that afternoon, and asked for suggestions of attractive toys he might purchase for future play sessions with children.

For half the boys and girls in each treatment condition the male model controlled and dispensed the resources, simulating the husband dominant family; for the remaining children the female model mediated the positive resources as in the wife dominant home.

At the completion of the social interaction session the controller announced that he had a surprise game in his car that the three of them could play together. The controller then asked the other adult to fetch the experimenter to assist them with the game, and as soon as the adult departed, the controller removed the toys and assembled the imitation task apparatus.

IMITATION TASK

The imitation task was essentially the same two-choice discrimination problem utilized in an earlier experiment (Bandura & Huston, 1961), except the response repertoires exhibited by the models were considerably extended, and the procedure used in the acquisition trials was somewhat modified.

The apparatus consisted of two small boxes with hinged lids, identical in color and size. The boxes were placed on stools approximately 4 feet apart and 8 feet from the starting point. On the lid of each box was a rubber doll.

As soon as the other adult returned with the experimenter, the controller asked both the child and the experimenter to be seated in the chairs along the side of the room, and the other adult to stand at the starting point, while the controller described the game they were about to play. The controller then explained that the experimenter would hide a picture sticker in one of the two boxes and the object of the game was to guess which box contained the sticker. The adults would have the first set of turns, following which the child would play the guessing game.

The discrimination problem was employed simply as a cover task that occupied the children's attention while at the same time permitted observation of the models as they performed divergent patterns of behavior during the discrimination trials in the absence of any set to attend to or learn the responses exhibited by the models.

Before commencing the trials, the controller invited the other participants to join him in selecting a "thinking cap" from hat racks containing two identical sets of four sailor caps, each of which had a different colored feather. The controller selected the green feathered hat, remarked, "Feather in the front," and wore the hat with the feather facing forward. The other model selected the yellow feathered hat, commented, "Feather in the back," and placed the hat on her head with the feather facing backward. The child then made his choice from the four hats in the lower rack and it was noted whether he matched the color preference, hat placement, and the verbal responses of the one or the other model.

The models then went to the starting point, the child returned to his seat, and the experimenter loaded both boxes with sticker pictures for the models' trials.

During the execution of each trial, each model exhibited a different set of relatively novel verbal and motor responses that were totally irrelevant to the discrimination problem to which the child's attention was directed. At the starting point the controller stood with his arms crossed, but at the experimenter's warning not to look, the controller placed his hands over his eyes, faced sideways, and asked, "Ready?" The other model stood with his arms on his hips, then squatted with his back turned to the boxes, and asked, "Now?"

As soon as the experimenter gave the signal for the first trial, the controller remarked, "Forward march," and began marching slowly toward the designated box repeating, "March, march, march." When he reached the box he said, "Sock him," hit the doll aggressively off the box, opened the lid and yelled, "Bingo," as he reached down for the sticker. He then remarked, "Lickit-sticket," as he pressed on the picture sticker with his thumb in the upper-right quadrant of a 24 x 24 inch sheet of plain white paper that hung on the wall immediately behind the boxes. The controller terminated the trial by replacing the doll facing sideways on the container with the comment, "Look in the mirror," and made a final verbal response, "There."

The other model then took her turn and performed a different set of imitative acts but equated with the controller's responses in terms of number, types of response classes represented, structural properties, and interest value. At the starting point, for example, she remarked, "Get set, go," and walked stiffly toward the boxes repeating "Left, right, left, right." When she reached the container she said, "Down and up," as she lay the doll down on the lid and opened the box. She then exclaimed, "A stickeroo," repeated, "Weto-smacko," and slapped on the sticker with the open hand in the lower-left quadrant of the sheet of paper. In termination of the trial, the model lay the doll on the lid of the container with the remark, "Lie down," and returned with her hands behind her back, and emitted the closing remark, "That's it."

The two sets of responses were counterbalanced by having the models display each pattern with half the subjects in each of the three groups.

The models performed alternately for four trials. At the conclusion of the fourth trial the controller explained that he had to check some materials in his car and while he and the other model were away the child may take his turns. Before they departed, however, the experimenter administered a picture preference test in which the models were asked to select their preferred picture from six different stickers pasted on a 5 x 8 inch card, after which the child was presented a similar card containing an identical set of stickers and requested to indicate his preference.

In addition to the introductory block of four trials by the models, the child's fifteen total test trials were interspersed with three two-trial blocks by the models. The models were always absent from the room during the child's test series. This procedure was adopted in order to remove any imagined situational restraints against, or coercion for, the child to reproduce the models' responses. Moreover, demonstrations of delayed imita-

tion in the absence of the model provides more decisive evidence for learning by means of imitation.

The models always selected different boxes, the right-left position
varying from trial to trial in a fixed irregular order, and the controller
always took the first turn. Although the models received stickers on each
trial, the child was nonrewarded on one-third of the trials in order to maintain his interest in the cover task.

At the beginning of each of the blocks of subjects' trials, the experimenter administered the picture preference test and the selection of stickers
that matched the models' choices was recorded. In addition, on the eighth
trial the models removed their hats and hung them in different locations
in the room. If the child removed his hat during the session and placed it
alongside one or the other of the model's hats, this imitative act was also
scored.

At the completion of the imitation phase of the experiment, the children were interviewed by the experimenter in order to determine whom
they considered to be the controller of resources, and to assess their model
preferences. The latter data were used as an index of attraction to the
models. In addition, for the children in the adult consumer condition, the
session was concluded by providing them the same lavish treatment accorded their adult rival.

Children in the control group had no prior social interaction with the
models but participated with them in the imitative learning phase of the
study. The experimenter assumed complete charge of the procedures and
treated the models as though they were naive subjects. This control group
was included primarily to determine the models' relative effectiveness as
modeling stimuli. In addition, the models alternated between subjects in
the order in which they executed the trials so as to test for the possibility
of a primacy or a recency of exposure effect on imitative behavior.

IMITATION SCORES

The imitation scores were obtained by summing the frequency of occurrence of the postural, verbal, and motor responses described in the
preceding section, and the hat, color, and picture preferences that matched
the selections of each of the two models.

The children's performances were scored by three raters who observed
the experimental sessions through a one-way mirror from an adjoining
observation room. The raters were provided with a separate check list of
responses exhibited by each of the two models, and the scoring procedure
simply involved checking the imitative responses performed by the children
on each trial. In order to provide an estimate of interscorer reliability, the
performances of 30% of the children were recorded simultaneously but
independently by two observers. The raters were in perfect agreement on
95% of the specific imitative responses that they scored.

RESULTS

The control group data revealed that the two models were equally effective in eliciting imitative responses, the mean values being 17.83 and 20.46 for the male and female model, respectively; nor did the children display differential imitation of same-sex $(M = 22.30)$ and opposite-sex $(M = 18.50)$ models. Although children in the control group tended to imitate the second model $(M = 22.21)$ to a somewhat greater extent than the one who performed first $(M = 16.08)$ on each trial, suggesting a recency of exposure effect, the difference was not of statistically significant magnitude $(t = 1.60)$.

Table 1 presents the mean imitation scores for children in each of the

Table 1—Mean Number of Imitative Responses Performed by Subgroups of Children in the Experimental Triads

Subjects	OBJECTS OF IMITATION			
	MALE Controller	FEMALE Consumer	FEMALE Controller	MALE Consumer
Girls	29.00	9.67	26.00	10.00
Boys	30.17	18.67	22.33	16.17
Total	29.59	14.17	24.17	13.09
	Controller	Ignored	Controller	Ignored
Girls	22.00	16.17	31.84	22.17
Boys	29.17	16.67	26.83	34.50
Total	25.59	16.42	29.34	28.34

two experimental triads. A 2 x 2 x 2 x 2 mixed factorial analysis of variance was computed on these data in which the four factors in the design were sex of child, sex of the model who controlled the resources, adult versus child consumer, and the controller versus the other model as the source of imitative behavior. As shown in Table 2, the findings of this study clearly support the social power theory of imitation. In both experimental treatments, regardless of whether the rival adult or the children themselves were the recipients of the rewarding resources, the model who possessed rewarding power was imitated to a greater degree than was the rival or the ignored model $(F = 40.61, P < 0.001)$. Nor did the condition combining resource ownership with direct reinforcement of the child yield the highest imitation of the model who controlled and dispensed the positive rewards. The latter finding is particularly surprising since an earlier experiment based on two-person groups (Bandura & Huston, 1961), demonstrated that pairing of model with positive reinforcement substantially enhanced the occurrence of imitative behavior. An examination of the remaining significant interaction effects together with the post-experimental interview data suggest a possible explanation for the discrepant results.

The differential in the controller-other model imitation was most pro-

Table 2—Summary of the Analysis of Variance of the Imitation Scores

Source	df	MS	F
Between subjects	47	310.17	
Sex of subjects (A)	1	283.59	<1
Sex of controller model (B)	1	128.34	<1
Adult versus child consumer (C)	1	518.01	1.61
A X B	1	23.01	<1
A X C	1	1.76	<1
B X C	1	742.59	2.31
A X B X C	1	21.10	<1
Error (b)	40	321.49	
Within subjects	48	113.24	
Controller versus other model (D)	1	2,025.84	40.61***
A X D	1	297.51	5.96*
B X D	1	237.51	4.76*
C X D	1	396.09	7.94**
A X B X D	1	256.76	5.15*
A X C X D	1	19.52	<1
B X C X D	1	23.02	<1
A X B X C X D	1	184.00	3.69
Error (w)	40	49.88	

* $P < .0.05$
** $P < 0.01$
*** $P < 0.001$

nounced when the male model was the controller of resources ($F = 4.76$, $P < 0.05$), particularly for boys. In fact, boys who were the recipients of rewarding resources mediated by the female model tended to favor the ignored male as their object of imitation. In the postexperiment interview a number of boys in this condition spontaneously expressed sympathy for the ignored male and mild criticism of the controller for not being more charitable with her bountiful resources (for example, "She doesn't share much. John played bravely even though she didn't even share. . . . She's a bit greedy.").

As a partial check on whether this factor would tend to diminish the differential imitation of the two models, six children—three boys and three girls—participated in a modified Child Consumer treatment in which, halfway through the social interaction session, the ignored adult was informed that he too may have access to the playthings. He replied that he was quite content to read his book. This modified procedure, which removed the rivalry and the exclusion of the model, yielded four times as much imitation of the controller relative to the model who was ignored by choice.

The significant triple interaction effect indicates that the differential in the controller-other model imitation was greatest when the same-sex model mediated the positive reinforcers, and this effect was more pronounced for boys than for girls.

The data presented so far demonstrate that manipulation of rewarding power had produced differential imitation of the behavior exhibited by the two models. In order to assess whether the dispensing of positive reinforcers in the prior social interaction influenced the overall level of matching responses, the imitation scores in each of the three groups were summed across models and analyzed using a Sex x Treatment design.

The mean total imitative responses for children in the Child Consumer, Adult Consumer, and the Control group were 50.21, 40.58, and 37.88, respectively. Analysis of variance of these data reveals a significant treatment effect ($F = 3.37$, $0.025 < P < 0.05$). Further comparisons of pairs of means by the t-test, show that children in the child rewarded condition displayed significantly more imitative behavior than did children both in the Adult Consumer treatment ($t = 2.19$, $P < 0.05$), and those in the Control group ($t = 2.48$, $P < 0.02$). The Adult Consumer and Control groups, however, did not differ from each other in this respect ($t = 0.54$).

The model preference patterns were identical for children in the two experimental conditions and consequently, the data were combined for the statistical analysis. Of the 48 children, 32 selected the model who possessed rewarding power as the more attractive, while 16 preferred the noncontrolling adult. The greater attractiveness of the rewarding model was significant beyond the 0.05 level ($x^2 = 5.34$). The experimental triad in which boys were the recipients of positive reinforcers while the male model was ignored, and the female consumer-girl ignored subgroup, contributed the highest preference for the non-controlling adult.

In addition to the experimental groups discussed in the preceding section, data are available for 9 children in the Adult Consumer condition, and for 11 children in the Child Consumer treatment who revealed, in their postexperiment interviews, that they had actually attributed rewarding power to the ignored or the consumer adult despite the elaborate experimental manipulations designed to establish differential power status. A number of these children were firmly convinced that only a man can possess resources and, therefore, the female dispensing the rewards was only an intermediary for the male model (for example, "He's the man and it's all his because he's a daddy. Mommy never really has things belong to her. . . . He's the daddy so it's his but he shares nice with the mommy. . . . He's the man and the man always really has the money and he lets ladies play too. John's good and polite and he has very good manners.") This view of resource ownership within the family constellation was often directly reinforced by the mothers (for example, "My mommy told me and Joan that the daddy really buys all the things, but the mommy looks after things."). Children who attributed the resource ownership to the consumer or ignored female model had considerable difficulty in explaining their selection (for example, "I just knowed it does. . . . I could tell, that's how."), perhaps because the power structure they depicted is at variance with the widely accepted cultural norm.

As shown in Table 3, models who were attributed rewarding power were perceived by the children as possessing no control over the rewarding elicited approximately twice as many matching responses as models who resources. Because of the small and unequal number of cases in each cell,

Table 3—Imitation as a Function of Attributed Rewarding Power to the Models

Treatment condition	OBJECTS OF IMITATION			
	Female controller	Male noncontroller	Male controller	Female noncontroller
Adult consumer	24.0	12.3	29.8	14.6
Child consumer	18.2	6.7	35.5	16.2

these data were not evaluated statistically. The differences, however, are marked and quite in accord with those produced by the experimentally manipulated variations in power status.

DISCUSSION

To the extent that the imitative behavior elicited in the present experiment may be considered an elementary prototype of identification within a nuclear family group, the data fail to support the interpretation of identificatory learning as the outcome of a rivalrous interaction between the child and the adult who occupies an envied status in respect to the consumption of highly desired resources. Children clearly identified with the source of rewarding power rather than with the competitor for these rewards. Moreover, power inversions on the part of the male and female models produced cross-sex imitation, particularly in girls. The differential readiness of boys and girls to imitate behavior exhibited by an opposite-sex model are consistent with findings reported by Brown (1956, 1958) that boys show a decided preference for the masculine role, whereas, ambivalence and masculine role preference are widespread among girls. These findings probably reflect both the differential cultural tolerance for cross-sex behavior displayed by males and females, and the privileged status and relatively greater positive reinforcement of masculine role behavior in our society.

Failure to develop sex appropriate behavior has received considerable attention in the clinical literature and has customarily been assumed to be established and maintained by psychosexual threat and anxiety reducing mechanisms. Our findings strongly suggest, however, that external social learning variables, such as the distribution of rewarding power within the family constellation, may be highly influential in the formation of inverted sex role behavior.

Theories of identificatory learning have generally assumed that within the family setting the child's initial identification is confined to his mother, and that during early childhood boys must turn from the mother as the primary model to the father as the main source of imitative behavior. However, throughout the course of development children are provided with ample opportunities to observe the behavior of both parents. The results of the present experiment reveal that when children are exposed to multiple models they may select one or more of them as the primary source of behavior, but rarely reproduce all the elements of a single model's repertoire or confine their imitation to that model. Although the children adopted many of the characteristics of the model who possessed rewarding power, they also reproduced some of the elements of behavior exhibited by the model who occupied the subordinate role. Consequently, the children were not simply junior-size replicas of one or the other model; rather, they exhibited a relatively novel pattern of behavior representing an amalgam of elements from both models. Moreover, the specific admixture of behavioral elements varied from child to child. These findings provide considerable evidence for the seemingly paradoxical conclusion that imitation can in fact produce innovation of social behavior, and that within the same family even same-sex siblings may exhibit quite different response patterns, owing to their having selected for imitation different elements of their parents' response repertoires.

The association of a model with noncontingent positive reinforcement tends to increase the incidence of imitative behavior in two person groups (Bandura & Huston, 1961), whereas the addition of a same-sex third person who is denied access to desired rewards may provoke in children negative evaluations of the rewarding model and thereby decreases his potency as a modeling stimulus. These two sets of data demonstrate how learning principles based on an individual behavior model may be subject to strict limitations, since the introduction of additional social variables into the stimulus complex can produce significant changes in the functional relationships between relevant variables.

SUPPLEMENTARY READINGS

Bandura, A. Influence of models' reinforcement contingencies on the acquisition of imitative responses. *J. Pers. soc. Psychol.*, 1965, 1, 589–595.

Bandura, A., & Kupers, C. J. Transmission of patterns of self-reinforcement through modeling. *J. abnorm. soc. Psychol.*, 1964, 69, 1–9.

Bandura, A., Ross, D., & Ross, S. A. Transmission of aggression through imitation of aggressive models. *J. abnorm. soc. Psychol.*, 1961, 63, 575–582.

Bandura, A., Ross, D. & Ross, S. A. Imitation of film-mediated aggressive models. *J. abnorm. soc. Psychol.*, 1963, 66, 3–11.

Bandura, A., & Walters, R. H. *Social learning and personality development.* New York: Holt, Rinehart, & Winston, 1963.

influence of different
nursery school experiences
on social development*

GEORGE G. THOMPSON

[In what some sociologists have called our "other-directed" society it seems especially important that children become sensitive and responsive to the expectations and demands of their contemporaries. Social learning during the childhood years provides some of the necessary preparatory experiences for achieving the social skills required for happiness and success during adult life. Some educational philosophers believe that many children, especially those from the lower socioeconomic stratum of our society, who are socially handicapped at an early age will continue to be seriously handicapped in the development of those abilities necessary for coping with the social and intellectual demands of modern society.

If normal schooling is to be extended downward to three- and four-year-old children, what should be the curriculum for these young pupils? There will obviously never be a simple or perhaps even uniform answer to this question. Moreover, at the present time, there are extremely few guide lines by which to design suitable learning experiences for these "preschool" scholars. One of the few experimental studies conducted in this area is the investigation by Dr. Thompson, of Ohio State University. The findings of this research showed that young children need, and profit from, sympathetic adult guidance in solving their social problems. It seems obvious that more of this type of controlled research is needed if we are to profit from the outcome of education for the socially and culturally underprivileged preschool-aged child, the so-called "head start" program now being promoted and subsidized by the federal government.]

The present research is an experiment that attempts to study the effects of different nursery school curricula on the social and emotional development of young children at a more "micro-level" and in a more "restricted set-

* From G. G. Thompson. The social and emotional development of preschool children under two types of educational program. *Psychological Monographs*, 1944, 56, No. 5, 1–29. (With permission.)

ting" than previous studies of the effects of nursery school experience (e.g., Jersild & Fite, 1937; Page, 1936; Skeels, Updegraff, Wellman, & Williams, 1935).

METHOD

SUBJECTS

The subjects for this experiment were twenty-three children enrolled in the four-year-old group of the Iowa Child Welfare Research Station's preschool laboratories. These children were divided into two groups after the first week of preschool attendance and equated as nearly as possible on chronological age, intelligence, socioeconomic status of parents, and on pretest scores for the principal dependent variables of the study: constructiveness, ascendance, social participation, leadership, and nervous habits. Twelve of the children were assigned to environment A; these children attended preschool only in the afternoon, playing from one until three o'clock and resting from three until five o'clock. Eleven of the children were assigned to environment B; these children attended preschool only in the afternoon, playing from three until five o'clock and resting from one until three o'clock. Both groups of children met in the same preschool building and played with the same materials at different times in the afternoon.

As so often happens in longitudinal studies, there was a loss of subjects over the period of study. In group A, the final $N = 11$, and in group B, the final $N = 8$.

TWO NURSERY SCHOOL CURRICULA

The most important and the only two fundamental differences in the programs are these:

First, in program B the teacher not only acts as an understanding, dependable, interested guide, immediately ready in case of appeal and a secure bulwark in situations of danger and extreme difficulty (as in A), but there is between each child and his teacher a particular friendship. This friendship is based upon (1) interchanges in conversation of a somewhat personal sort, (2) an evident enjoyment by the teacher of each child, (3) a real meaningful contact between the home and the school and (4) the probable increase in contacts which will be due to the teacher's part in many activities as they develop.

Second, in program B the children's activities are not dependent entirely upon a child's remembering or seeing a certain piece of equipment or activity, all of which are in readiness (as in A), but are influenced (*not* by verbal suggestions of the teacher) (1) by her skillful obtaining and arrangement of equipment to give the children ideas for activities and (2) her ability through her information, enthusiasm and cooperation to capitalize on these activities (in response to children's questions and their expressed ideas) so that she can help the children enlarge and develop them. She is *not* to suggest activities directly, impose her ideas verbally or produce products or activities which are heavily dependent upon teacher participation. Her aim is to guide the child's thinking into channels in which he may produce ideas; it is also to help the child to take over self-control, aware of reasoned principles of action.

The materials are the same for programs A and B. In program A they are not conspicuously arranged, but the child is aware of possibilities in the way of materials to be used. In program B, arrangement of the materials is such as to suggest activity, and the child is aware of other available materials.

The children were exposed to the two programs for a period of eight months. An attempt was made to equate for the two groups the possible differential effects of teacher personalities. The head teacher taught in both groups for the entire school year. The assistant teacher who taught in group A for the first half of the school year was transferred to group B for the remainder of the school year. Unfortunately it was necessary to replace the assistant teacher who taught in group B for the first half of the school year with a newly appointed teacher. The new assistant teacher taught in group A during the last half of the school year.

All of the observational and experimental measures of social and emotional development used in this study have been employed in previous studies. They are measures of social participation, leadership, ascendance, nervous habits, and constructiveness when faced with possible failure.

An attempt was made to have the number of indoor and the number of outdoor observations proportional to the relative amounts of time that the children spent in both places.

Initial and terminal measurements of social and emotional development were taken. The initial measurements were started November 1 and were completed by December 15; the terminal measurements were started April 15 and were completed by May 30.

An observational technique was constructed to measure the types and number of teacher and other-child environmental impacts received during four hundred minutes of observation for each child distributed over the preschool year.

OBSERVATIONAL MEASURES OF SOCIAL AND
EMOTIONAL GROWTH

Social participation. This method of measuring social participation was devised by Parten (1932–33a) from observations made during the free play of young children. Parten defined and observed the following types of social behavior: unoccupied behavior; onlooker; solitary, independent play; parallel activity; associative activity; and cooperative or organized supplementary play. Arbitrary weights were assigned to each category of behavior; these weightings ranged from − 3 for unoccupied behavior to

+ 3 for cooperative or organized supplementary behavior. The algebraic sum of a series of observations gave the score for each child observed. Parten stated that 20 one-minute observations on 42 children resulted in an odd-even correlation of + 0.90 for the reliability of the sampling. Her average observer-reliability with three other observers was 89 per cent. The combined ratings of five teachers on social participation correlated + 0.88 with her social participation scores secured by this method on 60 observations; this provided the only known criterion for validity.

Parten's scale was adopted for this study, as presented in the literature, with the exception that 30 one-minute observations were taken instead of 20. The agreement for two observers on 50 one-minute observations was 98 per cent.

Leadership. The method used to observe manifestations of leadership in young children was also devised by Parten (1932–33b); the records for leadership were taken at the same time as the records for social participation. The behavior of the children for the one-minute samplings was recorded by the observers as one of the following types of leadership or non-leadership: following; independently pursuing his own ends; both directing and following; reciprocally directing; and directing. Four other observers recording with Parten obtained an average of 89 per cent agreement with her in recording these types of leadership. Arbitrary weights were assigned to the different types of behavior; these weights ranged from a − 2 for following to a + 3 for directing. The total score was secured by adding these scores algebraically for a series of observations. The odd-even correlation of scores for 42 children was + 0.73 for 30 observations. Combined ratings of five teachers on leadership correlated with leadership scores on 60 children to the extent of + 0.81; this served as the criterion of validity.

This scale was employed in the present study with one modification. The category of reciprocally directing seemed to occur so infrequently in the present study that it was combined with the category directing and a + 2 was assigned to this category as a weighting; hence the weightings ranged from a − 2 to a + 2. The agreement for two observers on 50 one-minute observations was 90 per cent.

Nervous habits. A measurement of nervous habits was taken by the observational method patterned after Carr's (1938) modification of Olson's (1929) method. In the present experiment 30 one-minute observations were taken of the following nervous habits: oral, nasal, hirsutal, genital, orbal, and aural. The odd-even correlation of 30 observations as computed by the experimenter was + 0.86. In this method the child was watched for one minute; if during this period the child exhibited any one of the six nervous habits listed he was given a score of one; nervous habits in addition to this one, if occurring during the one minute, were not recorded. The agreement for two observers for 50 one-minute observations was 95 per cent.

EXPERIMENTAL MEASURES OF SOCIAL AND EMOTIONAL GROWTH

Ascendant behavior. Jack (1934) studied ascendant behavior by using a sand box that contained three small animals, two small cars, and a group of sand toys; two children were introduced into the room containing this sand box and these toys and the following behavior was recorded for both children: verbally attempts to secure materials; forcefully attempts to secure materials; succeeds in securing materials; defends, snatches back materials; verbally attempts to direct child's behavior; companion complies to directions; forbids, criticizes, reproves companion; and provides pattern which companion imitates. This behavior of the children was observed through a one-way-vision screen. Jack made ten pairings for each child (each pairing lasting five minutes) and secured an odd-even correlation of + 0.80 on ten partial scores versus ten. She reported a 95 per cent agreement with one other observer on one hundred minutes of observation. She also secured correlation of + 0.81 between total ascendance score and a composite of three teachers' ratings on ascendance.

In the present study, Page's (1936) modification of Jack's procedure was adopted and each child was paired with five other children. Each child's score was the total number of times in five five-minute pairings that he (1) attempted to secure play materials from his companion, (2) attempted to direct or criticize his companion, (3) was successful in directing, in providing a pattern of behavior for his companion, or in defending his own play materials. The agreement of two observers for one hundred minutes of observation was 95 per cent.

Reaction to failure. Keister (1937) devised two test situations to measure the behavior of young children in failure: (1) a weighted-box test and (2) a puzzle-box test; these tests were possible to solve, but solution was not probable by young children. During the fifteen minutes of the puzzle-box experimental situation the following types of performance or verbal behavior were checked during each half-minute: attempts to solve alone; no overt attempt; asks another to solve; asks help; stops trying; destructive behavior; and rationalizes (indifference, distaste, postponement, shift of responsibility, and blame).

Also, during each half-minute the following types of emotional behavior were observed and checked: interest; no emotional manifestations; indifference; smiles; laughs; sulks; cries; whines; yells; and motor manifestations of anger.

Keister reports (personal communication) that there was more than 90 per cent agreement between two observers for this experimental situation.

A partial test of the validity of procedure was worked out by showing the percentage of agreement between those subjects who manifested one or more types of immature responses on the tests and scores of 6 or more on teachers' ratings of two items of behavior maturity; this percentage of agreement was 56.

In the present study the experimenter decided to make some modifications in Keister's procedure of scoring for the puzzle-box test. Using only the types of behavior listed as performance or verbal, it was decided that each half-minute in which the child exhibited *only* that behavior classified as "attempts to solve alone" would be considered as a positive unit of "constructiveness"; and that each half-minute in which the child exhibited any of the other possible types of behavior listed under the category of performance or verbal (even though this half-minute also included "attempts to solve alone") would be considered as a negative unit of "constructiveness." The criterion score was then obtained by calculating the algebraic sum of the negative and positive units of behavior. For this type of observation the percentage of agreement between two observers for 90 minutes of observation was 92.

OBSERVATIONAL MEASURES OF ENVIRONMENTAL IMPACTS

By the use of a week's preliminary observation of the diary type, during which the children were adjusting to the preschool situation and before they were assigned to the two experimental groups, two experimenters set up a large list of behavior items, including: (1) environmental impacts from the teachers and other children on the observed-child, (2) behavior overtures of the observed-child toward the teachers, and (3) behavior reactions of the observed-child. This list included actually-recorded examples of child and teacher behavior under each category that the experimenters felt appropriate to be listed under that title. This reference list served as a basis for the later observations and their subsequent analysis.

It was decided that the diary type of observation was the best method for this research, since the experimenters were entering a relatively unexplored area and did not know a priori what variables in the environment were going to be fruitful in differentiating the two curricula.

Twenty 20-minute observations were taken on the activity of each child during the course of the year. These observations were roughly distributed over the school year and were representative samples of the amount of time spent in indoor- and outdoor-play.

The percentage of agreement between two analysts in placing the behavior items from five diary records in the various categories was 85 for 100 minutes of observation.

As was expected some of the items of behavior were ill-chosen; some of them occurred very infrequently, hence it was impossible to secure reliability of sampling. In the final analysis the following numbers and types of behavior categories were retained: eighteen teacher and other-children environmental impacts on the observed-child; four behavior categories of the observed-child; and five types of observed-child's initiated overtures toward the teachers. These behavior categories are as follows:

Teacher impacts.

1. The teacher gives social and objective information to the observed child. (Reliability of sampling = + 0.83.)

2. The teacher gives the observed-child verbal and/or physical help. (Reliability of sampling = + 0.46.)

3. The teacher makes a structuring suggestion about the observed-child's present and/or future activities and behavior. (Reliability of sampling = + 0.89.)

4. The teacher asks an objective and/or social leading question. (Reliability of sampling = + 0.83.)

5. The teacher is friendly with the observed-child. (Reliability of sampling = + 0.83.)

6. Teacher ascendance to observed-child to stop behavior. (Reliability of sampling = + 0.81.)

7. Teacher is stern. (Reliability of sampling = + 0.89.)

8. Teacher ignores child approach. (Reliability of sampling = + 0.87.)

Other-child impacts.

1. Observed-child is given information. (Reliability of sampling = + 0.97.)

2. Observed-child is given help. (Reliability of sampling = + 0.92.)

3. Observed-child is rejected by other children. (Reliability of sampling = + 0.91.)

4. Observed-child is refused or ignored by another child or by a group of children. (Reliability of sampling = + 0.97.)

5. Observed-child is given materials by another child. (Reliability of sampling = + 0.84.)

6. Other children comply to observed-child's requests. (Reliability of sampling = + 0.96.)

7. Other children develop a social situation with the observed-child. (Reliability of sampling = + 0.94.)

8. Observed-child is hit, shoved, or grabbed-at. (Reliability of sampling = + 0.95.)

9. Observed-child is persecuted by other children. (Reliability of sampling = + 0.96.)

10. Observed-child is threatened by other children. (Reliability of sampling = + 0.86.)

Observed-child behavior.

1. The observed-child makes rationalizations. (Reliability of sampling = + 0.78.)

2. Observed-child engages in destructive behavior. (Reliability of sampling = + 0.92.)

3. Observed-child engages in property-rights conflicts. (Reliability of sampling = + 0.90.)

4. Observed-child gets equipment for equipment's sake. (Reliability of sampling = + 0.93.)

Observed-child's initiated contacts with the teachers.

1. The observed-child makes a bid for the teacher's attention. (Reliability of sampling = + 0.86.)

2. The observed-child makes unfriendly approaches to the teacher. (Reliability of sampling = + 0.73.)

3. The observed-child requests help from the teacher. (Reliability of sampling = + 0.91.)

4. The observed-child requests information from the teacher. (Reliability of sampling = + 0.95.)

5. The observed-child requests materials from the teacher. (Reliability of sampling = + 0.78.)

SUMMARY OF ENVIRONMENTAL IMPACTS ON THE OBSERVED-CHILD

I. (1) All of the differences between groups A (the group with little guidance) and B (the group highly guided) in frequency of occurrence of *teacher extensive contacts* are highly significant statistically. In every case group B received more extensive teacher contacts than did group A.

(2) None of the differences between group A and group B is statistically significant in frequency of occurrence of *teacher restrictive contacts*. Only one category of teacher restrictive environmental impacts approaches significance; this category is "teacher is stern"; for this category the mean of group A is higher than the mean of group B.

II. (1) None of the differences between groups A and B is statistically significant in frequency of occurrence of *other-child extensive contacts*.

(2) All of the differences between groups A and B in frequency of occurrence of *other-child restrictive contacts* are highly significant statistically.

One may conclude from these findings that the only systematic variables that were different for groups A and B (of those variables that were measured observationally) are environmental impacts included in the two constructs: (1) teacher extensive contacts and (2) other-child restrictive contacts. Group B (theoretically, the highly-guided group) received *more* teacher extensive contacts than did group A and *fewer* other-child restrictive contacts than did group A.

The experimenter presents the observed-child's initiated contacts with the teacher not because they throw any light on the number and types of environmental impacts experienced by the observed-child, but because they are interesting in and of themselves.

The following tabulation shows that there was no difference between the two groups in any of the following types of overtures toward the teacher:

(1) The observed-child makes bids for the teacher's attention.

(2) The observed-child makes unfriendly approaches toward the teacher.

(3) The observed-child requests help from the teacher.

(4) The observed-child requests information from the teacher.

(5) The observed-child requests materials from the teacher.

RESULTS

There were, of course, no significant differences between groups A and B on any of the initial measurements for which they were matched. The results of analyses of covariance for terminal measurement of the dependent variables are as follows. There was a significant difference between the means of groups A and B in constructiveness when faced with possible failure ($F = 49.00$, $P < 0.001$). Group B, the highly-guided group, was significantly more constructive than group A, the group with little guidance.

Table 1—Results for Groups A and B on the Dependent Measures of the Study

Dependent measure

Group	CONSTRUCTIVENESS WHEN FACED WITH POSSIBLE FAILURE		ASCENDANCE		SOCIAL PARTICIPATION		LEADERSHIP		NERVOUS HABITS	
	Initial Mean	Final Mean*	Initial Mean	Final Mean*	Initial Mean	Final Mean*	Initial Mean	Final Mean*	Initial Mean	Final Mean
A	35.18	26.47	50.00	42.79	42.00	36.91	28.72	34.30	19.00	21.36
B	31.75	46.69	46.62	60.17	44.25	69.13	26.12	62.30	20.50	17.00

* Adjusted for difference in initial values.

Group B was also significantly more ascendant than group A by the end of the experiment. The respective means are significant at the 0.02 level of confidence ($F = 7.10$). Group B also showed significantly greater social participation than group A ($F = 26.30$, $P < 0.001$) and significantly greater leadership ($F = 7.38$, $P = .02$). Although there was a trend toward fewer nervous habits shown by subjects in group B, the difference was not significant. Neither were there significant differences between the two groups in extent of IQ change from fall to spring, number of property rights conflicts, or in rationalizations, although subjects in group A did engage in a significantly higher number of acts of destructive behavior.

From these results it seems appropriate to conclude that in preschool environments with personal guidance as the major aim of the curricula, development in ascendance, social participation, leadership, and constructiveness when faced with possible failure is an increasing function of "teacher extensive" environmental impacts, as defined in this study and a decreasing function of "other-child restrictive" environmental impacts.

Furthermore, the construct of "other-child restrictive" environmental impacts is a decreasing function of "teacher extensive" environmental impacts.

Last, it appears that development in the reduction of nervous habits or change in IQ is not a measurable function of "teacher extensive" environmental impacts and/or "other-child restrictive" environmental impacts.

The experimental findings demonstrate that, with other variables being equal between two groups of children and with a sufficiently large difference between the relative amounts of teacher guidance directed at meeting the children's social and emotional needs in two groups, the highly-guided group will show a significantly different development in ascendance, social participation, leadership, and constructiveness when faced with possible failure than a group with little teacher guidance.

It follows from the findings of this study that those experimenters wishing to discover environmental factors related to intellectual growth or reduction of nervous habits must look to other sources than the personal guidance program as defined and set up in this experiment. It is beyond the scope of this study to formulate hypotheses as to the nature of the environmental factors that may be related to intellectual growth or development in the reduction of nervous habits.

For those readers wishing to generalize the findings of this study to specific preschool situations the author would like to emphasize that his generalizations are limited to preschool environments with personal guidance as the major aim of the curricula, and as defined in this study. There has been no experimental evidence presented either in the research literature or in this study to indicate the manner in which the constant variables of this experiment, if permitted to vary considerably, might mask or modify differences in social and emotional development produced by differences in the amount of teacher guidance.

SUPPLEMENTARY READINGS

Isaac, S. *Social development in young children: A study in beginnings.* New York: Harcourt, Brace, 1933.

Montessori, M. *The Montessori method.* Cambridge, Mass.: Robert Behtly, 1964.

Sears, P. S., & Dowley, E. M. Research on teaching in the nursery school. In N. Gage (Ed.), *Handbook of research on teaching.* Chicago: Rand McNally, 1963. Pp. 814–864.

Swift, J. W. Effects of early group experience: The nursery school and day nursery. In M. L. Hoffman, & L. W. Hoffmann (Eds.), *Review of child development research. Vol. I.* New York: Russell Sage Foundation, 1964. Pp. 249–288.

social interaction in an

interracial nursery school*

HAROLD W. STEVENSON and NANCY G. STEVENSON

[The major question of our time is "How can man learn to live with his fellow man in peace and with mutual understanding?" This issue has such vast ramifications that scientists are generally reluctant to anchor the problem to the study of small groups in social psychology. Despite this understandable reluctance, social psychologists are impelled to do what they can, in whatever ways possible, to shed light on this human dilemma. For example, it has been shown that children's prejudices against members of other social and religious groups is more significantly related to the biases of their parents than to actual experiences in interacting with children of minority groups. It has also been shown that prejudices may be intensified during a period of interracial camp experiences for those children who enter the camping experience with a relatively poor psychological adjustment status and with pronounced needs for aggression. Social scientists, sensitive to the tragedy of interracial prejudices and conflicts, are eager to apply their theories and research crafts to the solution of this complex problem, but they are always aware that the required knowledge will not come easily.

In the following report, Drs. Stevenson and Stevenson, of the University of Minnesota, show that some of the antecedents of racial awareness emerge slowly during the early preschool years and seem to be closely related to the young child's search for his own identity. These investigators conclude their report with a most provocative suggestion ". . . it seems likely that the discovery of physical differences between the races may disturb the process of self-identification in some children." The more recent findings by Dr. Kenneth Clark suggest that self-identification may be slower and less certain to emerge among children of a minority group whose members do not enjoy all the rights and privileges of the majority.]

This is a report of a study of the social behavior of young children in a southern interracial nursery school. The study was undertaken because the nursery school provided a unique opportunity for investigating inter-

* From H. W. Stevenson & N. G. Stevenson. Social interaction in an interracial nursery school. *Genetic Psychology Monographs*, 1960, 61, 41–75. (With permission.)

racial behavior; here for the first time in their lives southern Negro and white children found themselves in contact with members of the other race. It was recognized from the beginning that the small size of the nursery school would limit the generalizations which could be made from the results of the investigation. Consequently, the project was designed as an intensive study of a few children, and was regarded as a pilot or exploratory study. The purpose was not to draw definite conclusions about interracial behavior, but to suggest hypotheses for further study.

METHOD

SUBJECTS

The subjects for the study were ten two- and three-year-old children attending an interracial nursery school in Austin, Texas. The children had had minimal previous interracial experience, and their parents considered themselves relatively free of racial prejudice. The children in the group studied were selected to meet the following qualifications: (a) that there be an equal number of Negro and white children (five of each race); (b) that the sex ratio be the same in each race (three girls, two boys); (c) that the children not have previously attended nursery school; and (d) that the children be between two and one-half and three and one-half years of age. The children came primarily from southern families and the educational and socioeconomic levels of both the Negro and white families were comparably high. The median Stanford-Binet IQ of the Negro children was 100 and that of the white children, 109. None of the children had previously had interracial group experience and, although none of the Negro children had previously played with white children, two white children had played with Negro children. This play had been infrequent and had occurred at home with children of part-time maids. The children's contacts with adults of the other race were primarily of an impersonal nature, such as encounters with salesmen, delivery men, etc. None of the white families had Negro friends, but one Negro parent had several white friends who visited her home.

The Negro children varied from light to dark skin color and from moderate to marked Negroid features. The white children were all light complexioned and varied in hair color from blonde to brunette. The two groups of children did not differ in other features related to physical appearance. There were no general differences between the two groups in height or physique, physical attractiveness, grooming, or type of clothing worn.

PRESCHOOL

The privately operated nursery school was open from 9 A.M. to 12 P.M. five days a week. The children were divided into two age groups, a younger group from two and one-half to three and one-half and an older group from three and one-half to four and one-half. The younger group was supervised by a white teacher and the older group by a Negro teacher. One of the mothers acted as a participating mother each morning, and was available to both groups to help with routines and to assist the teachers in other activities.

The nursery school offered a relatively unstructured program, with a great deal of time being spent in free play or small group activities. The only routine activities were toileting, juice, and rest, which lasted for the younger group from around 9:50 to 10:20 every morning. Observations were made during these periods, but because of the restricted nature of social interaction during routine activities, these portions of the observations were not analyzed. The younger group spent the first half of the morning indoors and the second half outdoors.

There were frequent opportunities in the school for all the children to encounter other members of each race in addition to the children in their group. Such encounters were with the two teachers, with the participating mothers, and with children in the older group during brief daily contacts. At the time of the study there were three Negro and six white children in the older group. The policy of the nursery school was to avoid any teaching about race. The teacher made no references to race and she did not introduce the topic of racial differences to the children. She showed neither approval nor disapproval of any behavior related to race. When it was necessary for her to interfere with conflicts that were related to racial matters she did not verbalize the racial aspects of the problem, but merely attempted to interest the children in some other activity.

OBSERVATIONS

For this study fourteen 45-min. observations of each child were made at the beginning of the nursery school year, and six at the end of the year. The observations were concentrated at the beginning of the year since it was felt that the recognition of and reaction to interracial factors in social interaction would be most likely to occur during this period. The second set of observations was included to provide information about changes in behavior which might occur with time. The observations were analyzed according to eight categories of behavior, and according to the race and sex of the other children with whom each child interacted. Comparisons were made of own-race and other-race interaction and of the relative frequency of each type of behavior in each racial group. As a possible aid in interpreting the behavior of the children, the parents were interviewed twice during the course of the study.

Five observers, all graduate students in psychology, were employed in the study. Each observation consisted of a running description of all aspects of the behavior of an individual child during a continuous 45-min. period. Social interaction was recorded in detail, including the behavior and verbalization of the child or children with whom the subject was interacting.

The observations were taken in a shorthand fashion, and at the end of the 45-min. period the observer transcribed his notes on an electrical recorder in the nursery school office. Observers were present at the nursery school from the opening day, Sept. 19, 1955. Group observations were made until Oct. 10, by which time the enrollment was complete. Fourteen individual observations were made of each child during the 10 weeks following October 10. The second set of six observations was scheduled so that the last observations could be completed approximately a month before the end of the nursery school. For the observation of each child the time of day, day of the week, and observer were randomized. The observations were randomly assigned for analysis to the same five individuals who had observed.

The unit of analysis was called a behavior unit and was defined as a change in the relationship between S's behavior and his environment. The behavior unit is determined primarily by changes in S's overt behavior; however, a behavior unit may also occur when there is an observable change in S's environment followed by no change in S's overt behavior. There are three ways in which the relationship between S's behavior and his environment may change, creating new behavior units:

(a) There is a change in S's behavior following an observable change in S's environment.

Example. The S and another child have been playing in the sandbox. Suddenly the child pours sand in S's hair and S cries loudly. The behavior unit consists of an observable change in S's environment—the child's pouring sand in S's hair—and a change in S's behavior—S cries.

(b) There is a change in S's behavior with no observable change in S's environment.

Example. A child and S have been playing in the sandbox. Suddenly S throws sand at the child. The behavior unit consists of the unchanged environment—the child's continued play in the sandbox—and S's change in behavior—his throwing sand at the other child.

(c) There is no change in S's behavior following an observable change in S's environment.

Example. The S and another child have been playing in the sandbox. Suddenly the other child pours sand in S's hair, following which S continues making sand-pies as before. The behavior unit consists of the observable change in S's environment—the child's pouring sand in S's hair—and S's unchanged behavior—continued playing in the sand.

A change in behavior occurs when S makes a new response, or modifies a previous response by using new materials, by making a new use of the same materials, by changing the manner in which he performs the response, or by interacting with or responding to new persons. The term "response" indicates a molar act, such as swinging, making a remark to another person, drawing, etc. This is contrasted with the molecular components of an act, such as moving one's arms, lifting a pencil, etc.

An observable change in environment consists of a change in people, objects, or events which is of sufficient proximity or intensity that it can be assumed to be perceived by S.

The method of dividing behavior into behavior units and scoring behavior units on behavior categories proved to be a feasible means of obtaining quantitative measures of children's social behavior. Reliable scoring was done on the categories analyzed in the reliability study. It is difficult, however, to generalize too broadly from such reliability studies. The reliability is a function of a number of conditions, and an analysis of each set of conditions would be desirable. For example, the reliability of division and scoring undoubtedly differs for observations made indoors, where the child's play space is more constricted and his conversations can be more easily understood, than for observations made outdoors. The reliability differs for different children. For inactive, averbal children, it is undoubtedly higher than for children who are hyperactive and constantly talking. In general, however, the method can be used reliably by trained workers.

This type of study has the disadvantages inherent in any application of the naturalistic method of observation—it is expensive and time-consuming. However, in any study where extensive and detailed information about the social interaction of individual children is desired, the observational method, in spite of these disadvantages, remains the best means of collecting data.

DEFINITIONS OF BEHAVIOR CATEGORIES

The initial step in the analysis was to divide the observational record into behavior units as described above. Following or simultaneously with the division, each unit was examined to determine the type of behavior included within it. Eight categories of behavior were defined. In addition to the eight categories, the behavior units were scored for contacts with adults, and routine and group activities. The definitions of these categories follow:

(a) *Social participation.* The S has physical or verbal interaction with another child, or his activity is influenced by that of another child, as in parallel play. The S is involved in another child's activity to the extent that he attempts to change the child's behavior, or his own behavior varies with changes in the other child's activity. Behavior units scored for social participation often are scored also for one or more of the other categories of behavior which involve interaction with other children. No scoring can be made on the other categories unless the behavior unit is first scored for social participation or lack of it.

(b) *Lack of social participation.* The S has no physical or verbal contact with another child in a situation where there are opportunities for social interaction. The S observes another child's play without making contact, withdraws from other children without making contact, or remains by himself.

A score on lack of social participation sometimes occurs together with a score on one or more of the other behavior categories involving interaction with other children, usually the negative or "reactive" ones, such as Unfriendliness and Response to Aggression.

(c) *Social control.* The S tries to influence, direct, or dominate another child to achieve his own ends or to attain a position of superiority. The S tries to get a specific type of response from another child, employing techniques for leadership, dominance, or attention-getting. Rejection of another child is included if S's attempt is primarily to control or dominate, rather than to be rid of, another child.

(d) *Response to social control.* The S responds to another child's attempt at social control.

(e) *Initiation of aggression.* The S makes a physical or verbal attack on another child or object. Aggression may be aimed directly at another child or it may be deflected through objects or activity. The S may try to get others to attack or punish for him or may talk about future aggression toward others.

(f) *Response to aggression.* The S responds to another child's initiation of aggression toward himself.

(g) *Friendliness.* The S expresses verbally or through physical demonstrativeness a positive feeling tone toward another child, or indicates a desire for close personal relations with another child indirectly by doing favors, seeking close physical contact, or by friendly smiling.

(h) *Unfriendliness.* The S expresses either verbally or physically a disinterested or negative feeling tone toward another child, or indicates a desire to alienate another child or to discourage social interaction. In order for initiation of aggression to be scored for unfriendliness it must express a wish to alienate or eliminate the other child from contact, rather than merely to punish or gain control.

OTHER CATEGORIES

(a) *Contacts with adults.* This category includes all behavior in which S has individual contact with an adult. It is scored when S asks an adult for help, comfort, support, or direction, when S initiates or responds to conversation with an adult, or when there is an individual exchange within routines or adult-led group activities. Interaction with an adult as a member of the group, as in the observance of routines, is not included. If S is interacting simultaneously with an adult and with another child, the behavior unit is scored for contact with adults and for social participation. If S is interacting primarily with an adult while another child is present— that is, if S is drawn to the scene because of the adult's presence—the unit is scored only under adult contact. Similarly, if S is interacting primarily with another child, even though an adult may be present, the unit is scored only under social participation.

(b) *Routine or group situation.* A routine situation exists whenever S is occupied in juice, toilet, or rest periods, or in the adult-directed intervals immediately prior or subsequent to these periods. A group situation exists whenever S is responding as a member of a group to adult leadership in non-routine activity. Situations where there is continuous adult supervision are included under group activities which are set up by an adult but given no further adult impetus except for help sought by the children are not included under group. The routine or group situations usually preclude social participation by reason of their restrictive nature; however, scoring on other categories may at times be made during a routine or group situation. In tabulating the results all units which were scored for routine or group were eliminated since it was felt that these scores would have had to be weighted differently from the others.

RESULTS

RELIABILITY OF THE METHOD

A question that should be discussed before the results of the analysis of the observational records are presented concerns the reliability with which the method can be used. Several studies have already been performed which indicate that the general method employed in this study can be used by different individuals with satisfactory reliability. In two reliability studies, Stevenson and Stevenson (1953, 1957) have found that the division of observations into behavior units and the analysis of behavior units according to behavior categories can be done by trained individuals with high reliability. In a more recent reliability study involving simultaneous observation, division and rating of behavior units by three persons, coefficients of concordance (Walker & Lev, 1953) from 0.80 to 0.90 were obtained for categories similar to social participation, lack of social participation and adult contact.

The above studies have indicated that the method can be used reliably. It was decided to check the reliability of scoring in this study by an analysis of the scoring of the two categories, social participation and lack of social participation. These categories were chosen because of their importance for the study and because they were scored more frequently than the other categories. Kendall's coefficient of concordance (W) was used to evaluate the reliability of scoring with these two categories. In computing W, the proportions, social participation per behavior unit and lack of social participation per behavior unit for each of the 140 observations made during the fall, were classified by scorers (N = 5) and subjects (N = 10). The obtained values of W for the two measures, 0.86 and 0.82 respectively, indicate that the scoring was done with high reliability.

ANALYSIS OF OBSERVATIONAL RECORDS

A total of 188 observations was analyzed in the study. These consisted of the 14 observations made of each of the ten children during the fall and the 6 observations of each of the eight children remaining at the nursery school during the spring.

There were large individual differences among Ss in the average number of behavior units for each 45-minute observation. Nevertheless, there were no differences between the Negro and white Ss in the average number of behavior units during the fall or spring. When the behavior units were broken down into the proportion of total behavior units for each S which had been scored for social participation, lack of social participation and adult contact, it was apparent that there was a high degree of consistency between fall and spring in Ss' scores on social participation and adult contact. There were no consistent differences, however, among the proportions of behavior units in which the Ss in each racial group were scored for social participation, lack of social participaiton, and adult contact.

The proportion of his total social participation in which each S interacted with an individual child of his own race varied greatly among Ss during the fall, but the variability decreased during the spring. There was little correlation between the proportions of own-race choices in the fall and spring for individual Ss.

The values indicate the average proportions of social participation for play with an individual child, with more than one child, and with racially mixed groups. There are no consistent trends distinguishing the two races. Interaction with individual Ss constituted the most frequent type of interaction. The mixed-race group interaction was small during the fall but in the spring it constituted 15 per cent of the Negro Ss' social participation and 10 per cent of the white Ss' social participation. The rise in proportion of mixed-race group social participation was characteristic of all but one child.

In computing the results for the other behavior categories, the number of behavior units scored for each category was divided by S's total number of social participation units. The frequency of behavior of the types encompassed by these categories is a function of the frequency of social participation; hence the use of proportions has the effect of partialling out differences in frequency of social participation among the Ss. An examination of the proportions of each S's social participation scored for each of the remaining categories revealed no consistent tendencies for the two racial groups to be separated.

For each S the scores on the remaining categories were tabulated by

Table 1—Analysis of Own-Race and Other-Race Social Participation

| | SOCIAL PARTICIPATION AVERAGE PROPORTION OF Ss' TOTAL | | | |
| | WHITE | | NEGRO | |
Type of interaction	Fall	Spring	Fall	Spring
Own race (individual)	.45	.42	.48	.34
Other race (individual)	.45	.45	.45	.45
Own race (group)	.01	.01	.01	.02
Other race (group)	.03	.01	.01	.04
Mixed race (group)	.06	.10	.05	.15

the race of the child or children with whom S interacted. The averages across Ss for own-race and other-race scores on each category were determined. Mixed-race interactions were omitted. As an aid in indicating trends, a separate ratio for Negroes and whites on each category was computed of own-race contacts divided by other-race contacts.

The proportions as seen in Table 2 are relatively the same for Negroes and whites and the values from fall to spring are relatively consistent. Only in Response to Aggression and Response to Social Control do the white children appear to have notable changes from fall to spring, and the changes show an increase of own-race scores.

Table 2—Analysis of Own-Race and Other-Race Ratings on Other Scales

	$\dfrac{\text{OWN-RACE}}{\text{OTHER-RACE}}$ RATINGS			
	WHITE		NEGRO	
Scale	Fall	Spring	Fall	Spring
Social control	1.0	.6	1.7	1.0
Response to social control	1.5	5.0	.6	1.0
Initiation of aggression	.8	1.0	.8	1.2
Response to aggression	1.0	4.0	.7	.5
Friendliness	.7	1.0	.7	1.0
Unfriendliness	2.0	1.5	1.0	1.0

Although the study was not designed to investigate sex differences and although the number of boys and girls was not the same, it is of interest to examine certain of the data to determine whether trends might emerge which would differentiate the behavior of boys and girls.

There was a tendency for the boys and girls to differ in their average numbers of behavior units; there was some overlap in the ranges of behavior units for boys and girls in the fall, but there was no overlap during the spring. There was also a tendency for the boys to have more social participation and less lack of social participation than the girls. There was no overlap in the range of proportions of social participation per behavior units for the boys and girls in the fall, and in the spring only one girl was in the boys' range. The analysis of the other behavior categories, with the exception of the fall scores on social control, does not reveal such clear sex differences. The girls in the fall all had higher social control scores than the boys.

DISCUSSION

The majority of the Ss showed some indication of racial awareness. Two Negro and three white children verbalized the differences between the two races or categorized people by race, and two Negro and one white child identified some distinguishing features of his own or the other race without noting differences between the races. Only one Negro and one white child gave no indication of racial awareness.

The indications of such awareness at nursery school did not appear until after the children had been in attendance for several weeks. The question arises as to whether the delay indicated gradual learning on the part of the children, or whether it may have been due to the fact that the racial characteristics of the children were of minor importance in comparison with other characteristics of the new situation in which the children found themselves on entering nursery school. The adjustment to the new routine, the new locale, the new equipment, and the teacher may have provided dominant stimuli during the first weeks of attendance, and only after these had become familiar to the children could responses to racial stimuli become manifest.

Racial awareness did not result in the children's showing negative behavior toward members of the other race. All combinations of awareness and behavior were found, ranging from one subject's lack of any indication of awareness and lack of differential response to Negroes and whites, to another's clear differentiation between the two races and his preference for play with children of the other race, to still another's negative verbalizations regarding racial differences and his tendency in the spring to prefer interaction with children of his own race.

The children did show some concern about their own racial status, as indicated by the questions they asked their parents. In view of this, it seems likely that the discovery of physical differences between the races may disturb the process of self-identification in some children. It is interesting that in this study, while the discovery of race differences tended to create concern in several children about their own physical characteristics, it did not in general extend to negative interaction with the racially different children. Perhaps in a less neutral environment for interracial interaction the children's anxiety would have been reflected in more negative interracial behavior.

The results indicate no general differences in the behavior of the two racial groups. There were no consistent differences between the two races in the types of behavior shown, or in the relative amount of the time spent in own-race and other-race interaction. For this group of children it was of little or no importance to which race an individual child belonged in the determination of his social role. As one visitor put it: "They might as well all be blue."

There are several alternative interpretations of these results. First, the results cannot, as discussed above, be attributed to the children's lack of racial awareness. Second, it is possible that personality characteristics of certain outstanding children might have suppressed racial differences which might otherwise have appeared. The two most outgoing, socially aggressive children were two boys, one white and one Negro, who may have led the children into interracial interaction to a greater extent than they otherwise would have ventured. One of these, Lyle (white), the most popular child and the most socially active member of the group, had a large amount of interaction with both races from the very beginning; the other, Hugh (Negro), consistently had among the highest proportions of interracial interaction. To what degree they may have set the pattern for the group cannot be known. With a small sample it is impossible to determine whether other personality constellations among the children might have produced different results.

A third possible explanation of the results is that too long a time interval (10 weeks) was used in the analysis of the fall results. The use of this long a period may have obscured differences in behavior related to race occurring at different times during this period. In order to test this possibility a complete analysis of the data was made in which the fall observations were broken down into two successive five-week periods. No trends which differed from those found in the analysis of the 10-week period were found. For example, the average proportions of social participation involving own-race interaction for the two five-week periods were 0.44 and 0.42.

The interpretation of the results which seems most probable is that under neutral conditions young children do not react to each other primarily in terms of differences in racial characteristics. In this study the parents had either a positive wish for good relations with the other race for their children, or had no expressed negative feelings toward the other race. The teacher and other adults attempted not to introduce the topic of race or to follow actions of the children related to race with either approval or disapproval. Finally, the two groups of children did not seem to differ in such characteristics as personality, grooming, or physical attractiveness. It is assumed, therefore, that the children entered nursery school with no previously acquired responses which would determine their reactions to members of each race, and had no basis other than the physical differences related to race for responding to each other as members of a racial group rather than as individuals. The children did show evidence of responding to the physical characteristics associated with race, but these responses were not under these conditions reflected in the children's general behavior. The interaction among the children may be assumed, therefore, to have developed as it does in any nursery school, according to the degree to which the relationship between any two children satisfied the needs of each child. In short, these were two groups of children who did not differ significantly from each other except in certain physical characteristics and who responded to each other as individuals and not as members of a racial group.

The most striking positive finding was the consistent separation of the sexes on some of the behavior categories. The boys on the average had more behavior units and more social participation in relation to behavior units than did the girls. The boys had less lack of social participation and adult contact per total number of behavior units than did the girls. These results, although based on a small number of Ss, warrant further study, especially in the light of a more recent study involving two other groups of nursery school children (Stevenson, 1957). In these groups the boys also had a higher proportion of social interaction and tended to have a lower proportion of adult contacts.

SUPPLEMENTARY READINGS

Jersild, A. T., & Markey, F. V. *Conflicts between preschool children.* New York: Bureau of Publications, Teachers College, 1935.

Riessman, F. *The culturally deprived child.* New York: Harper & Row, 1962.

Wolman, T. G. A preschool program for disadvantaged children. *Young Children,* 1965, 21, 98–111.

viii

Emotional Responses and the Developing Personality

That the chief expressive actions, exhibited by man and by the lower animals, are now innate or inherited—that is, have not been learnt by the individual—is admitted by everyone. So little has learning or imitation to do with several of them that they are from the earliest days and throughout life quite beyond our control; for instance, the relaxation of the arteries of the skin in blushing, and the increased action of the heart in anger. We may see children, only two or three years old, and even those born blind, blushing from shame; and the naked scalp of a very young infant reddens from passion. Infants scream from pain directly after birth, and all their features then assume the same form as during subsequent years. These facts alone suffice to show that many of our most important expressions have not been learnt; but it is remarkable that some, which are certainly innate, require practice in the individual, before they are performed in a full and perfect manner; for instance, weeping and laughing.
DARWIN, *The expression of the emotions in man and animals*, 1872.

psychoanalytic theory

of psychosexual

development*

OTTO FENICHEL

[Over the centuries of recorded history man has taken diverse attitudes toward such hedonistic pleasures of bodily activities as eating and experiencing sexual gratification. The Greek Epicureans proposed that these pleasures be enjoyed as frequently as possible; the Stoics advised their denial; the middle Christians were persuaded that such pleasures were base and sinful; the Victorians were inclined to deny their existence. Sigmund Freud risked social ostracism to introduce this rejected area of human behavior to his psychological colleagues. It may be recalled that scientific psychology emerged as a separate discipline during the Victorian era when discussions of sensual pleasures were generally taboo. It was obviously desirable and necessary that psychologists concern themselves with this important domain of human living. But who would take the first step? Freud's observations on the developing organization of erogenous zones related to hedonistic pleasures and the details of his theory of psychosexual development were, of course, scattered over many years and fragmented in many scientific papers. The following report by Fenichel, one of the most highly regarded interpreters of Freud's writings, presents the framework of classical psychoanalytic inferences as they relate to the development of sexuality.]

INFANTILE SEXUALITY

The characteristics of the polymorphous perverse infantile sexuality are well known from Freud's *Three Contributions to the Theory of Sex* (1910). Infantile sexuality differs from adult sexuality in several respects. The most impressive difference lies in the fact that the highest excitation is not necessarily located at the genitals, but that the genitals, rather, play the part of *primus inter pares* among many erogenous zones. The aims,

* From O. Fenichel. *The psychoanalytic theory of neurosis.* New York: Norton, 1945, 61–69. (With permission.)

too, are different; they do not necessarily lead toward sexual intercourse but linger at activities that later play a role in forepleasure. Infantile sexuality may be *autoerotic,* that is, take the child's own body or parts of it as its object. The components, which are directed toward objects, bear archaic features (incorporation aims and ambivalence). When a partial instinct is blocked, "collateral" partial instincts become correspondingly strengthened.

The small child is an instinctual creature full of polymorphous perverse sexual drives or, to put it more correctly, full of a still undifferentiated total sexuality which contains all the later "partial instincts" in one. Reality seems to be judged at first only as to whether it is compatible with instinct satisfaction. Reality, as conceived of by the primitive ego, is colored by the status of its sexual aims. Every kind of excitation in the child can become a source of sexual excitement: mechanical and muscular stimuli, affects, intellectual activity, and even pain. In infantile sexuality excitement and satisfaction are not sharply differentiated although there are already orgasmlike phenomena, that is, pleasureful sensations that bring relaxation and the end of sexual excitation. In time, however, the genitals begin to function as a special discharge apparatus, which concentrates all excitation upon itself and discharges it no matter in which erogenous zone it originated.

It is called genital primacy when this function of the genitals has become dominant over the extragenital erogenous zones, and all sexual excitations become finally genitally oriented and climactically discharged. The antithesis to genital primacy is the earlier pregenital period, when the genital apparatus has not yet assumed dominance, and as a result the relaxation achieved is never complete. The road from the early pregenital strivings to genital primacy can be described from two different points of view: from that of the change of the leading erogenous zones, and from that of the types of object relationships.

First of all it must be emphasized that the concept of developmental phases is a relative one, serving as a better means of orientation only. Practically, all phases gradually pass into one another and overlap.

When one attempts to organize the abundance of phenomena in infantile sexuality, one is struck by a period in which these phenomena are relatively few and the number and intensity of direct sexual manifestations are diminished. This is the so-called period of latency, extending from the sixth or seventh year of life until puberty. It is true that sexual manifestations never completely disappear; cultures have been described in which a period of latency seems to be lacking, and even in our culture there are many children who do not renounce their masturbation during these years; but even in these cases, sex is less in the foreground than it is earlier and later. Freud was of the opinion that the occurrence of the period of latency is a characteristic of the human species. The early blossoming of infantile sexuality is, as it were, "doomed to destruction" by nature, and this fact is a biological precondition for repression and thus for neuroses (Freud,

1936). Other authors have pointed out that since among some primitive tribes a latency period never appears, cultural restrictions must be responsible for the renunciation of sexual wishes (Malinowski, 1929; Reich, 1932). However, there is no clear-cut contradiction between "biologically" and "socially" determined phenomena. Biological changes may be brought about by former external influences. It may be that the latency period is a result of external influences that have been in effect long enough to have left permanent traces; perhaps at this point we are watching external influences becoming biological. At any rate, during this period the forces operative against instinctive impulses, such as shame, disgust, and so forth, develop at the price of instinctual energies.

Thus preadult sexuality generally can be divided into three major periods: the infantile period, the latency period, and puberty. The beginning and the end of the infantile period are very well known today, whereas that which lies in between is still in need of much research. It is possible that in this in-between stage accidental variations are of greater import than they are in the beginning and end phases.

THE ORAL STAGE

The beginning is the oral (more correctly the intestinal) stage of organization of the libido (Abraham, 1927a; Freud, 1910). In discussing the development of the ego, factors were brought out as to how the knowledge of reality comes about in connection with experiences of hunger and satiation. Further, it was evident that the first perceptions were connected with a kind of oral incorporation, and that the first judging was the decision whether or not a substance was edible. These findings may now be supplemented by a discussion of the autoerotic phenomenon of thumbsucking. Thumbsucking is already evident in the newborn child and can, of course, be considered an innate reflex. That does not prevent us from noting that this reflex is concerned with a type of stimulation that usually is tied up with the function of nourishment but has become independent of it. Thumbsucking shows that the pleasure gained from breast or bottle is based not alone on the gratification of hunger but on the stimulation of the erogenous oral mucous membrane as well; otherwise the infant would disappointedly remove his thumb, since it produces no milk. There, sexual excitement has originally leaned upon the need for nourishment; in a similar way early sexual excitement has also leaned upon other physiological functions, upon breathing and cutaneous sensations and upon the sensations of defecation and urination.

It is not necessary to go into detail here about the many phenomena in which oral eroticism is still retained in the adult: kissing, perverse practices, drinking and smoking customs and many eating habits. One must not forget, however, that in drinking and smoking we are not dealing only with oral eroticism. Alcohol and nicotine are also toxins, which by chemical means produce wished-for changes in the balance of instinctual conflicts.

These changes diminish inhibitions, heighten self-esteem, and ward off anxiety, at least for a short time and to a certain extent.

The aim of oral eroticism is first the pleasurable autoerotic stimulation of the erogenous zone and later the incorporation of objects. Animal crackers, loved by children, are significant remnants of early cannibalistic fantasies (Boehm, 1935). The appearance of an especially intense greed, either manifest or, after its repression, in the form of derivatives, is always traceable to oral eroticism. Many peculiarities of persons fixated at this level can be explained by realizing that in this period objects are not looked upon as individuals but only as food or providers of food. By incorporating objects one becomes united with them. The "oral introjection" is simultaneously the executive of the "primary identification." The ideas of eating an object or of being eaten by an object remain the ways in which any reunion with objects is thought of unconsciously. The magical communion of "becoming the same substance," either by eating the same food or by mixing the respective bloods, and the magical belief that a person becomes similar to the object he has eaten are based on this fact. Abundant evidence of this is to be found in experiences ranging from religious rites to everyday habits. Handshaking means that union is sealed by letting one's body substance flow into the other person's. And a companion is still a "com-panion," a person whose bread is identical with ours.

Corresponding to the specific aims of oral eroticism and in accordance with the principle of animistic misunderstanding, we find specific oral fears, especially the fear of being eaten (Fenichel, 1929; Freud, 1936).

> Analytic experience shows that the fear of being eaten often serves as a cover for a more deeply hidden castration anxiety (Freud, 1924a, and 1924b). This is not to be taken as an objection to the archaic nature of this fear. The distortion, which aids in the defense against castration anxiety, may operate through regression.

Of course, the idea of being eaten is not only a source of fear but under certain circumstances may also be a source of oral pleasure. There is not only a longing to incorporate objects but also a longing to be incorporated by a larger object. Very often, the seemingly contradictory aims of eating and of being eaten appear condensed with each other. In the chapter on the ego the longing to be rejoined with an object to which one had yielded one's omnipotence was described. This rejoining, too, is unconsciously thought of as a kind of being eaten by a larger, more powerful object; it depends on individual circumstances whether this idea is met with positive longing or with anxiety (Graber, 1937).

Clinical experience shows that aims of oral incorporation often assume a sadistic character. This probably occurs under the influence of unknown constitutional factors or as a reaction to frustrations. Psychoanalysis of persons suffering from depressions or addictions shows that actually the sadistic character of the incorporation fantasies did not become added on later but was actually operative at the time of the oral phase. However, that is certainly no reason for assuming that every infant sucking at his mother's breast has the desire to kill and destroy her in a sadistic manner. The clinical material of British analysts who hold this point of view (Klein, 1932, 1938; Rickman, 1936) certainly should not be doubted. What is doubtful, however, is that the cases described are typical; they represent, rather, pathological cases with special oral-sadistic fixations (Benedek, 1936; Fenichel, 1937).

However, incorporation destroys the object objectively. This fact gives all the aims of incorporation a more or less "ambivalent" character. It has already been stated that this ambivalence does not exist from the very beginning. As long as there is no conception of objects, it is meaningless to talk about ambivalence. However, as soon as a conception of objects is developed, the objectively destructive character of the incorporation facilitates a connection of ideas of incorporation with sadism, especially if definite frustrations have been endured (Abraham, 1927d).

The oral-sadistic fantasies, reconstructed in the analysis of orally fixated patients (*cf.* Bergler, 1933) and sometimes manifest in orally oriented psychoses, are so fantastic that certain authors are even of the opinion that real experiences are not at all important for their formation. (Riviere, 1927). Actually, however, these "fantasies" express the ways in which an undeveloped archaic ego perceives (and misunderstands) a frustrating reality.

Abraham differentiated two subphases of the oral stage: a preambivalent one in which subjectively no object exists and only pleasurable sucking is sought, and an **ambivalent** phase, appearing after the eruption of teeth, which has the aim of biting the object (Abraham, 1927d). Analysis of sadistic perverts often reveals that at the bottom of their symptoms there is a fixation on the oral sexual aim of biting (Ophuijsen, 1929). This coordination of sucking and the phase before the establishment of objects, and of biting and oral-sadistic drives, does not entirely fit, however; often oral-sadistic sucking fantasies directed against objects can be observed (vampire).

Of the neuroses, the manic-depressive cycle and the addictions present manifestations of fixation on the oral level. However, since in mental development earlier developmental levels still persist behind the more mature ones, oral-erotic characteristics are also present in all other neuroses.

Because of their significance for the later development of neuroses, it is advisable to elaborate again upon the concepts of fixation and regression which were discussed in another chapter. It was stated that in mental development the progress to a higher level never takes place completely; instead characteristics of the earlier level persist alongside of or behind the new level to some extent. Disturbances of development may occur not only in the form of a total arresting of development but also in the form of retaining more characteristics of earlier stages than is normal. When a new development meets with difficulties, there may be backward movements in which the development recedes to earlier stages that were more successfully experienced. Fixation and regression are complementary to each other. Freud used the simile of an advancing army in enemy territory leaving occupation troops at all important points. The stronger the occupation troops left behind, the weaker is the army that marches on. If the latter meets a too powerful enemy force, it may retreat to those points where it had previously left the strongest occupation troops (Freud, 1920). The stronger a fixation, the more easily will a regression take place if difficulties arise.

What are the factors responsible for evoking fixations? Unquestionably there are hereditary tendencies that account for the various erogenous zones being charged with different amounts of cathexis or different degrees of ability for discharge. Little is known about such constitutional factors. Psychoanalysis did succeed, however, in studying the kinds of experience that favor the development of fixations.

1. The consequence of experiencing excessive satisfactions at a given level is that this level is renounced only with reluctance; if later, misfortunes occur, there is always a yearning for the satisfaction formerly enjoyed.

2. A similar effect is wrought by excessive *frustrations* at a given level. One gets the impression that at developmental levels that do not afford enough satisfaction, the organism refuses to go further, demanding the withheld satisfactions. If the frustration has led to repression, the drives in question are thus cut off from the rest of the personality; they do not participate in further maturation and send up their disturbing derivatives from the unconscious into the conscious. The result is that these drives remain in the unconscious unchanged, constantly demanding the same sort of satisfaction; thus they also constantly provoke the same defensive attitudes on the part of the defending ego. This is one source of neurotic "repetitions."

3. One frequently finds that excessive satisfaction as well as excessive frustrations underlie a given fixation; previous overindulgence had made the person unable to bear later frustrations; little frustrations, which a less spoiled individual could tolerate, then have the same effect that a severe frustration ordinarily has.

4. It is understandable, therefore, that abrupt changes from excessive satisfactions to excessive frustrations have an especially fixating effect.

5. Most frequently, however, fixations are rooted in experiences of instinctual satisfaction which simultaneously gave reassurance in the face of some anxiety or aided in repressing some other feared impulse. Such simultaneous satisfaction of drive and of security is the most common cause of fixations.

THE ANAL-SADISTIC STAGE

The analysis of compulsion neuroses enabled Freud to insert between the oral and phallic periods another organizational level of the libido, namely, the anal-sadistic level (Freud, 1924). Anal pleasure certainly is present from the beginning of life. However, in the second year of life the anal-erogenous zone seems to become the chief executive of all excitation which now, no matter where it originates, tends to be discharged through defecation. The primary aim of anal eroticism is certainly the enjoyment of pleasurable sensations in excretion. Later experience teaches that stimulation of the rectal mucosa may be increased by holding back the fecal mass. Anal-retention tendencies are a good example of combinations of erogenous pleasure with security against anxiety. Fear of the originally pleasurable excretion may lead to retention and to the discovery of retention pleasure. The possibility of achieving a more intense stimulation of the mucous membrane, and with it a more intense sensation through the increased tension of retention, is responsible for the tension pleasure which is greater in anal eroticism than in any other eroticism. Persons who, in their pleasures, seek to prolong the forepleasure and to postpone the end pleasure are latently always anal erotics.

The origin and character of the connection between anal and sadistic drives, hinted at in the terms of the organization level (anal sadism) is analogous to the discussed connection between orality and sadism. It is due partly to frustrating influences and partly to the character of the incorporation aims. However, two factors must be added. First, the fact that elimination objectively is as "destructive" as incorporation; the object of the first anal-sadistic action is the feces themselves, their "pinching off" being perceived as a kind of sadistic act; later on, persons are treated as the feces previously were treated. Second, the factor of "social power" involved in the mastery of the sphincters: in training for cleanliness, the child finds opportunity effectively to express opposition against grownups.

There are physiological reasons for the connection of anal eroticism to ambivalence and bisexuality. Anal eroticism makes the child treat an object, namely feces, in a contradictory manner: he expels the matter from the body and retains it as if it were a loved object; this is the physiological root of "anal ambivalence." On the other hand the rectum is an excretory hollow organ; as an excretory organ it can actively expel something; as a hollow organ it can be stimulated by an entering foreign body. Masculine tendencies are derived from the first faculty, feminine tendencies from the second; this is the physiological root of the connection between anal eroticism and bisexuality (Jekels, 1913).

The first anal strivings are, of course, autoerotic. Pleasurable elimination as well as (later) pleasurable retention can be attained without any object. The fact that this pleasure is experienced at a time when the primary feelings of omnipotence are still operative can be seen in the magical narcissistic overvaluation of the power of the individual's bowel movements; this finds expression in many neurotic and superstitious remnants (Abraham, 1927b). Though the pleasure is attained by the stimulation of the rectal mucous membrane, the feces, as the instrument by which this pleasure is attained, also become a libidinal object. They represent a thing which first is one's own body but which is transformed into an external object, the model of anything that may be lost; and thus they especially represent "possession," that is, things that are external but nevertheless have ego quality. The impulse to coprophagia which certainly has an erogenous source (representing an attempt to stimulate the erogenous zone of the mouth with the same pleasurable substance that previously stimulated the erogenous zone of the rectum) simultaneously represents an attempt to re-establish the threatened narcissistic equilibrium; that which has been eliminated must be reintrojected. A similar attempt at cutaneous reintrojection is represented by the impulse to smear (Lewin, 1930). Thus the feces become an ambivalently loved object. They are loved and held back or reintrojected and played with, and they are hated and pinched off.

Certain anal pleasures are first perceived in the sensations accompanying the mother's care when diapers are changed. This care and, later on, conflicts aroused by the child's training toward cleanliness gradually turn the autoerotic anal strivings into object strivings. Then, objects may be treated exactly like feces. They may be retained or introjected (there are various types of anal incorporation) as well as eliminated and pinched off (Abraham, 1927c, 1927d). The training for cleanliness gives ample opportunity for sensual and hostile gratifications. The "narcissistic overvaluation" (Abraham, 1927b) expresses itself now in a feeling of power over the mother in giving or not giving the feces. Other anal tendencies directed at objects are the impulses to share anal activities with somebody else: to defecate together, to watch and exhibit anal activities, to smear together, to defecate on another person or to have another person defecate on oneself. All these anal object strivings are ambivalently oriented. They may express tenderness in an archaic way, as well as, after their condemnation, hostility and contempt ("to play a dirty trick on somebody") (Ferenczi, 1926; Lorand, 1931).

Abraham took this contradictory attitude of the anal erotic toward the object world as a starting point for his suggestion to subdivide the phase of anal organization of the libido into an earlier period having a sadistic aim in excretory pleasure without consideration for the object, and a later period characterized by a prevalent retention pleasure where the object is conserved (1927d). The consideration of the object's well-being, which constitutes love, probably starts in this second anal phase; its first manifestation is the readiness to sacrifice the feces for the object's sake.

Just as frustrations in the oral period through animistic misunderstanding lead to the formation of specific oral anxieties, so do frustrations in the anal period form specific anal anxieties. As a retaliation for anal-sadistic tendencies, fears develop that what one wished to perpetrate anally on others will now happen to oneself. Fears of physical injury of an anal nature develop, like the fear of some violent ripping out of feces or of body contents.

The other erogenous zones and partial drives are somewhat neglected in analytic literature since they do not become leading executive zones. Nevertheless, conflicts around them often play as decisive a role in the genesis of neuroses and in character formation as oral and anal eroticisms do.

SUPPLEMENTARY READINGS

Abraham, K. Contributions to the theory of the anal character. In *Selected papers*. London: Hogarth Press, 1927.

Abraham, K. *Selected papers on psychoanalysis*. New York: Basic Books, 1953.

Blum, G. S., & Miller, D. R. Exploring the psychoanalytic theory of the oral character. *J. Pers.*, 1952, 31, 287–304.

Brill, A. A. Anal eroticism and character. *J. abnorm. soc. Psychol.*, 1912, 7, 176–203.

Hetherington, E. M., & Brackbill, Y. Etiology and covariation of obstinacy, orderliness, and parsimony in young children. *Child Develpm.*, 1963, 34, 919–943.

early personality

development as viewed

by john b. watson*

JOHN B. WATSON

[During the third decade of the 20th century two major educational prophets appeared on the American scene. John Dewey, drawing upon the philosophical position so clearly stated by Rousseau and adding a generous dash of American pragmatism, proposed that the infant and child be given a considerable amount of freedom to find his own way to maturity. He proposed doing what came naturally to both children and adults. In sharp contrast, John B. Watson, setting his course along the lines proposed by John Locke and Pavlov, suggested that it was the responsibility of adults to train infants and small children according to explicit, prearranged educational plans. Both philosophical stances are still very much alive among contemporary psychologists who offer words of advice for the rearing of our young. The Dewey-Rousseau heirs still emphasize the broad goals of self-determination, while the Watson-Locke lineage specializes in advice on the most economical methods of fostering human skills and of eliminating undesirable behaviors. The time was right in American psychology for an influential spokesman like Watson, a psychologist who could offer a detailed philosophical structure consistent with our pragmatic heritage. He became an influential figure because he spoke and wrote clearly, confidently and persuasively on the details of "proper" child-rearing practices. The following excerpt illustrates his recommendations for rearing children: "Let your behavior always be objective and kindly firm. Never hug and kiss them [your children], never let them sit on your lap. If you must, kiss them once on the forehead when they say goodnight. Shake hands with them in the morning." This was, and is still, repugnant advice to most American parents who center so many of their family activities around the nurturance and amusement of their children. For the reader who may be attracted to Watson's philosophical position and who wishes a more modern, though substantially unchanged, version, we recommend Skinner's *Walden Two*.]

* From J. B. Watson. *Psychological care of infant and child*. New York: Norton, 1928, 41–44 and 80–84. (With permission.)

We are forced to believe from the study of facts that forms of behavior such as imitation, fear, cleanliness and love are *built in* by the parent and by the environment which the parent allows the child to grow up in. There are no instincts. We build in at an early age everything that is later to appear.

This doctrine is almost the opposite of what is taught in the schools at the present time. Professor John Dewey and many other educators have been insisting for the last twenty years upon a method of training which allows the child to develop from within. This is really a doctrine of mystery. It teaches that there are hidden springs of activity, hidden possibilities of unfolding within the child which must be waited for until they appear and then be fostered and tended. I think this doctrine has done serious harm. It has made us lose our opportunity to implant and then to encourage a real eagerness for vocations at an early age. Some few thousands of undergraduates have passed through my hands. Only in the rarest of cases have I found a senior college student with his mind made up as to what vocation he will enter when he leaves college. There is no white heat for a certain type of career and no organization developed for seeing that career through. The young graduate today is almost as helpless as the straw tossed by the wind. He will take any kind of a job that chance may offer him in the hope that his special bents and aptitudes will show them-selves. There is no reason why he shouldn't pick out his career at the age of 12 or earlier.

The behaviorists believe that there is nothing from within to develop. If you start with a healthy body, the right number of fingers and toes, eyes, and the few elementary movements that are present at birth, you do not need anything else in the way of raw material to make a man, be that man a genius, a cultured gentleman, a rowdy or a thug.

So much for general behavior, the behavior that you can directly observe in your children. But how about the things you cannot observe? How about *capacity, talent, temperament, personality,* "mental" constitu-tion and "mental" characteristics, and the whole inward emotional life?

Let us take fear and timidity for a moment. It has been demonstrated that the only thing the child is afraid of at birth is either a loud sound or the loss of support. Everything else the child may fear is built in, is the result of the environment we let him grow up in. Until you have studied how all this comes about no one could expect you to know you are com-pletely responsible for all the other fear reactions your child may show. Does he avoid dark rooms, animals, strange people, strange situations? Is he timid and shy? Have you handicapped his whole future by making him shun new situations and new people?

How about temper, anger, rage? Only one simple situation will evoke temper, anger or rage, namely, *restraint of the child's movements.* Temper and rage displayed in any other situation is home made. Parents do not realize that when they or their nurses are dressing their child badly, putting it in tight clothes, teasing it by holding its hands, or putting it in narrow quarters for punishment, they are organizing it in such a way that it will show throughout its life fits of anger and temper tantrums. A calmer mode of behavior would enable the child, and the adult it is to become, to conquer the environment instead of being overwhelmingly conquered by it.

How about its loves—its affectionate behavior? Isn't that "natural"? Do you mean to say the child doesn't "*instinctively*" love its mother? Only one thing will bring out a love response in the child—stroking and touching its skin, lips, sex organs and the like. It doesn't matter at first who strokes it. It will "love" the stroker. This is the clay out of which all love—material, paternal, wifely or husbandly—is made. Hard to believe? But true. A certain amount of affectionate response is socially necessary but few parents realize how easily they can overtrain the child in this direction. It may tear the heart strings a bit, this thought of stopping the tender outward demonstration of your love for your children or of their love for you. But if you are convinced that this is best for the child, aren't you willing to stifle a few pangs? Mothers just don't know, when they kiss their children and pick them up and rock them, caress them and jiggle them upon their knee, that they are slowly building up a human being totally unable to cope with the world it must later live in.

The mother coddles the child for two reasons. One, she admits; the other, she doesn't admit because she doesn't know that it is true. The one she admits is that she wants the child to be happy, she wants it to be surrounded by love in order that it may grow up to be a kindly, good-natured child. The other is that her own whole being cries out for the expression of love. Her mother before her has trained her to give and receive love. She is starved for love—affection, as she prefers to call it. It is at bottom a sex-seeking response in her, else she would never kiss the child on the lips. Certainly, to satisfy her professed reason for coddling, kissing the youngster on the forehead, on the back of the hand, patting it on the head once in a while, would be all the petting needed for a baby to learn that it is growing up in a kindly home.

But even granting that the mother thinks she kisses the child for the perfectly logical reason of implanting the proper amount of affection and kindliness in it, does she succeed? The fact that we rarely see a happy child is proof to the contrary. The fact that our children are always crying and whining shows the unhappy, unwholesome state they are in. Their digestion is interfered with and probably their whole glandular system is deranged.

There is a sensible way of treating children. Treat them as though they were young adults. Dress them, bathe them with care and circumspection. Let your behavior always be objective and kindly firm. Never hug and kiss them, never let them sit in your lap. If you must, kiss them once on the forehead when they say good night. Shake hands with them in the morning. Give them a pat on the head if they have made an extraordinarily good job of a difficult task. Try it out. In a week's time you will find how easy it is to be perfectly objective with your child and at the same time kindly. You will be utterly ashamed of the mawkish, sentimental way you have been handling it.

If you expected a dog to grow up and be useful as a watch dog, a bird dog, a fox hound, useful for anything except a lap dog, you wouldn't dare treat it the way you treat your child. When I hear a mother say "Bless its little heart" when it falls down, or stubs its toe, or suffers some other ill, I usually have to walk a block or two to let off steam. Can't the mother train herself when something happens to the child to look at its hurt without saying anything, and if there is a wound to dress it in a matter of fact way? And then as the child grows older, can she not train it to go and find the boracic acid and the bandages and treat its own wounds? Can't she train herself to substitute a kindly word, a smile, in all of her dealings with the child, for the kiss and the hug, the pickup and coddling? Above all, can't she learn to keep away from the child a large part of the day since love conditioning must grow up anyway, even when scrupulously guarded against, through feeding and bathing? I sometimes wish that we could live in a community of homes where each home is supplied with a well-trained nurse so that we could have the babies fed and bathed each week by a different nurse. Not long ago I had opportunity to observe a child who had had an oversympathetic and tender nurse for a year and a half. This nurse had to leave. When a new nurse came, the infant cried for three hours, letting up now and then only long enough to get its breath. This nurse had to leave at the end of a month and a new nurse came. This time the infant cried only half an hour when the new nurse took charge of it. Again, as often happens in well-regulated homes, the second nurse stayed only two weeks. When the third nurse came, the child went to her without a murmur. Somehow I can't help wishing that it were possible to rotate the mothers occasionally too! Unless they are very sensible indeed.

Certainly a mother, when necessary, ought to leave her child for a long enough period for over-conditioning to die down. If you haven't a nurse and cannot leave the child, put it out in the backyard a large part of the day. Build a fence around the yard so that you are sure no harm can come to it. Do this from the time it is born. When the child can crawl, give it a sandpile and be sure to dig some small holes in the yard so it has to crawl in and out of them. Let it learn to overcome difficulties almost from the moment of birth. The child should learn to conquer difficulties away from your watchful eye. No child should get commendation and notice and petting every time it does something it ought to be doing anyway. If your heart is too tender and you must watch the child, make yourself a peephole so that you can see it without being seen, or use a periscope. But above all when anything does happen don't let your child see your own trepidation, handle the situation as a trained nurse or a doctor would and, finally, learn not to talk in endearing and coddling terms.

SUPPLEMENTARY READINGS

Becker, W. C. Consequences of different kinds of parental discipline. In M. L. Hoffman & L. W. Hoffman (Eds.), *Review of child development research.* New York: Russell Sage Foundation, 1964. Pp. 169–208.

Broadbent, D. E. *Behavior.* New York: Basic Books, 1961.

Bronfenbrenner, U. Socialization and social class through time and space. In E. Maccoby, T. Newcomb, & E. Hartley (Eds.), *Readings in social psychology.* New York: Holt, 1958. Pp. 400–425.

Caldwell, B. M. The effects of infant care. In M. L. Hoffman & L. W. Hoffman (Eds.), *Review of child development research.* New York: Russell Sage Foundation, 1964. Pp. 9–87.

Child, I. L. Socialization. In G. Lindzey (Ed.), *Handbook of social psychology, Vol. II.* Reading, Mass.: Addison-Wesley, 1954. Pp. 655–692.

Orlansky, H. Infant care and personality. *Psychol. Bull.,* 1949, 46, 1–48.

Skinner, B. F. *Walden Two.* New York: Macmillan, 1948.

early personality
development as viewed
by harry stack sullivan*

PATRICK MULLAHY

[A wag once said that psychology first lost its soul and then its mind. Certainly it is true that there are relatively few psychologists today who are concerned about man's "inner experiences." The inferential links between "consciousness" and observable behaviors are as yet so obscure that psychologists have gone on to less complex problems for which the available conceptual models seem more adequate. Despite their many defeats, psychologists continue to return to questions about the "self." Developmental psychologists have been especially interested in the growth of self-awareness. What neurological and experiential events lie behind the layman's conviction that he is a unique person with a varied and exciting "inner life"? No one has written more candidly or confidently in response to this question than the renowned American psychiatrist Harry Stack Sullivan. For him the modes of human experience were developmentally tripartite: the prototaxic, parataxic, and syntaxic. Whether or not one agrees with this largely intuitive leap into the child's mental world, he will, nevertheless, be impressed with the freshness of Sullivan's approach. The following report is a summary from Mullahy's *Oedipus Myth and Complex*. This sample may whet the reader's appetite for some of Harry Stack Sullivan's original writings, which are often obscure but always entrancing.]

THREE MODES OF EXPERIENCE

All experience occurs in one or more of three "modes"—the prototaxic, parataxic, and syntaxic. As the Greek roots of this horrendous term indicate, the prototaxic mode refers to the first kind of experience the infant has and the order or arrangement in which it occurs. As grown-ups, we experience things in terms of time and space, of here and "out there," of

* From P. Mullahy. *Oedipus myth and complex.* New York: Hermitage Press, 1948. Pp. 286–299. (With permission.)

before and after. We break up our experience, so to speak, into constituent elements for the purposes of getting along in the world. Furthermore, our experience, or at least much of it, is referable to a self who does the experiencing, the self being a center of reference. "I went for a walk in the park at four o'clock." These are examples of every day distinctions we make. Others, of course, are much more subtle and refined.

Now in the beginning, the infant, Sullivan hypothecates, makes no such distinctions for a variety of reasons. Aside from structural and functional limitations, the organism at birth has had, of course, no direct experience with the cultural heritage. We shall avoid saying he has no mind as yet— for we shall not deal here with the problem of the nature of mind nor with the problem of what he inherits from his life in the womb, concerning which apparently not a great deal is known, at least regarding mind.

According to Sullivan's hypothesis all that the infant "knows" are momentary states, the distinction of before and after being a later acquirement. The infant vaguely feels or "prehends" earlier and later states without realizing any serial connection between them. He has no ego in any distinctive sense because the self has not yet developed. For such reasons, he has no awareness of himself as an entity separate from the rest of the world. In other words, his felt experience is all of a piece, undifferentiated, without definite limits. It is as if his experiences were "cosmic." This mode of experience is often marked in certain schizophrenic states.

The terms "parataxic" and "syntaxic" also are etymologically related to the order and arrangement of experience. At the risk of confusion, we shall remind the reader that parataxic (like syntaxic) is a grammatical term as well, which refers to the ranging of clauses or propositions one after another without connectives such as "and," "or," "since," etc. to show the relations between them.

Gradually the infant learns to make some discrimination between himself and the rest of the world. As Sullivan puts it, he no longer reaches out to touch the moon. In other words he gradually learns to make elementary differentiations in his experience.

> We learn in infancy that objects which our distance receptors, our eyes and ears, for example, encounter, are of a quite different order of relationship from things which our tactile or our gustatory receptors encounter. That which one has in one's mouth so that one can taste it, while it may be regurgitated to the distress of everyone is still in a very different relationship than is the full moon which one encounters through one's eye but can in no sense manage.

As the infant develops and maturation proceeds, the original undifferentiated wholeness of experience is broken. However, the "parts," the diverse aspects, the various kinds of experience are not related or connected in a logical fashion. They "just happen" together, or they do not, depending on circumstances. In other words, various experiences are felt as concomitant, not recognized as connected in an orderly way. The child cannot yet relate them to one another or make logical distinctions among them. What is experienced is assumed to be the "natural" way of such occurrences, without reflection and comparison. Since no connections or relations are established, there is no logical movement of "thought" from one idea to the next. The parataxic mode is not a step by step process. Experience is undergone as momentary, unconnected states of being.

The parataxic mode of organizing experience occurs mainly through visual and auditory channels. Dreams are often examples of this mode of experiencing. But it occurs a good deal of the time in waking life. In other words, we do not—and cannot—always organize our experience into a logically connected, related totality, in which the various elements are compared, contrasted, and ordered in a precise fashion. Ordinarily we do not indulge in careful ratiocination as we dress in the morning, proceed to work, and so on. It is not necessary, and in any case there is not enough time.

As the infant learns the rudiments of language, he is said to pass into the "epoch" of childhood. And here we introduce another term, the "autistic." The autistic is a verbal manifestation of the parataxic. But the capacity for verbal communication is just beginning to be manifested, and the tools, vocabulary, grammar, etc. are scarcely formed and learned. Because of the child's limited equipment and experience with the symbol activity and experience of others, his own symbol activity is arbitrary, highly personal, unchecked and untested. Hence his imagination is not curbed to conform to everyday "reality." Autistic symbols, however, are useful in recall and foresight.

Let us take an example of a child who has been given a picture book also containing words, say, to name or describe the pictures. It will have a picture of a cat, and below or above or somewhere on the page there is written what the child eventually learns is c-a-t. Then, too, to complete the example, the animal who runs around the house also is referred to by the same name as that of the colored or black and white pattern in the book. Sullivan comments on the significance of such a frequent phenomenon in our culture as follows:

> I am sure no child who can learn has not noticed an enormous discrepancy between this immobile representation in the book which, perhaps, resembles one of the momentary states that kitty has been in on some occasion. I am certain that every child knows that there is something very strange in this printed representation being so closely connected with the same word that seems to cover adequately the troublesome, amusing, and very active pet. Yet, because of unnumbered, sometimes subtle, sometimes crude experiences with the carrier of culture, the parent, the child finally come to accept as valid and useful a reference to the picture as "kitty" and to the creature as "kitty."

> The child thus learns some of the more complicated implications of a symbol in contradistinction to the actuality to which the symbol refers, which is its referent; in other words, the distinction between the symbol and that which is symbolized. This occurs, however, before verbal formulation is possible.

From the picture book and the spoken word in this culture one progresses to the printed word and finally discovers that the combination of signs, c-a-t, includes "kitty" in some miraculous fashion, and that it always works. There is nothing like consistent experience to impress one with the validity of an idea. So one comes to a point where printed words, with or without consensually valid meaning, come to be very important in one's growth of acquaintance with the world.

There was first the visually and otherwise impressive pet, which was called "kitty" (an associated vocalization): then came the picture of the kitten; now comes the generic *cat* which includes kitty, picture of kitten, a kitten doll, and alley cats seen from the windows. And all this is learnt so easily that—since no one troubles to point it out—there is no lucid understanding of the sundry types of reality and reference that are being experienced. Familiarity breeds indifference in this case. The possibilities for confusion in handling the various kinds of symbols, naturally, remain quite considerable.

The child gradually begins to catch on to patterns of relationships, to the grammatical structure of the language, and to the usual relationships and distinctions obtaining in his society. There is a more discriminating realization of the other fellow, the responder. The child now more clearly realizes that, for example, when he cries "dada," the other person responds in a more or less characteristic fashion. And so the child learns to anticipate the responses of others. These responses become associated with the use of certain words and gestures. In other words, the characteristic reactions of the other people give meaning to the language, a meaning that is thus implicitly agreed upon. Of course, the child does not set out systematically to learn the everyday meaning of the language. He learns by the trial and error method. Hence, he also learns that not only one's own experience is important, but that of others. He also learns to use verbal symbols as an economical way to get a lot to happen in a short time, with little use of energy.

Of course, there is a great deal more than this to be said about the learning process, but this sketch may indicate some of the ways by which, according to Sullivan, a child learns to use language with an interpersonal reference.

In any case, the child gradually learns the "consensually validated" meaning of language—in the widest sense of language. These meanings have been acquired from group activities, interpersonal activities, social experience. Consensually validated symbol activity involves an appeal to principles which are accepted as true by the hearer. And when this happens, the youngster has acquired or learned the syntaxic mode of experience.

But the learning process is not always consistent—because the significant others are not always consistent in their behavior. Furthermore, as we know, people do not always take the trouble to teach the child the distinctions between various symbols and that to which they refer. The trial and error method by which a good deal of learning necessarily occurs is not ideally suited for acquiring precise distinctions. For such reasons, language thus comes to have a double meaning—a personal meaning and a consensually validated meaning or a blend of both. In this way, among others, people come to maintain a wide margin of misinformation and illusion about others, themselves, and the world.

Tension, when it occurs in connection with needs, such as those of food and sex, is experienced in the syntaxic and parataxic modes. The tension of anxiety, however, is experienced by grown-ups mainly in the parataxic mode.

THE MEANING OF DYNAMISM

Before taking up an exposition of the self dynamism (or self system or, simply, self), we must try to indicate what the term "dynamism" means. It has been defined as "a relatively enduring configuration of energy which manifests itself in characterizable processes in interpersonal relations." In other words dynamism refers to the way energy is organized and channeled in the human organism. Dynamism implies only a relatively enduring capacity to bring about change. It is analogous to any structure or organization of processes which always contains numerous sub-structures.

For Sullivan energy always means physical energy. He rejects the notion of "psychic energy."

THE EVOLUTION OF THE SELF

As everyone knows, certain restraints are put on the young offspring's freedom which are or are considered to be necessary for his socialization, for training him and making him the sort of person considered right and desirable in the society in which he will live and have his being. These restraints, above everything else, bring about the evolution of the self dynamism. In this evolution, other aspects of the personality, such as *the selectively inattended* and *disassociated* processes, those which occur outside of self-awareness, are also developed.

We shall begin our exposition of Sullivan's theories concerning the evolution of personality wtih the "epoch" of infancy. Infancy refers to the period from birth to the maturation of the capacity for language behavior. During this period certain of the attitudes of the parent or nurse are said to be conveyed empathically. Suppose the mother is tired or upset or angry when she is in close contact with the infant, let us say, when she nurses or bathes him. Something of her attitude is then conveyed to him. His sense of well-being, his euphoria, is markedly decreased. The mother who observes or at least senses this gets anxious, which state is then communicated to the infant, further lowering his feeling of well-being, further increasing his insecurity. And so the process goes on. It is "dynamic."

Euphoria and anxiety are, conceptually, direct opposites, "polar constructs." In actuality there is no such thing as "pure" euphoria, in which there is no tension and therefore no action, something like an empty state of bliss. Perhaps the nearest approximation to euphoria in the "ideal" sense is deepest sleep. Nor is there any actual state of absolute anxiety. In the state of terror—in which there is a complete but temporary disorganization of personality—the most extreme degree of tension ordinarily observable occurs. Euphoria and anxiety are inversely related.

It is not difficult to see that a chronically hostile mother will induce an intense and more or less chronic anxiety in the offspring. Furthermore, such a mother will deprive him of the experience of tenderness—a deprivation which will have fateful consequences for his future well-being and happiness.

One of the characteristics of anxiety is that it interferes with observation and analysis, with the acquisition of information and understanding and with recall and foresight. It interferes with alertness to the factors in a situation that are relevant to its occurrence. Therefore it interferes with effective action.

Sooner or later the infant is recognized as educable. And when this happens, there is said to be a restriction of tender cooperation. The exhibition of tenderness by the parents tends to be modified so that it will be used more on "suitable" occasions. The mother, for example, begins to train the child in the "proper" toilet habits, those considered proper in the society in which she lives. She will express or withhold tenderness and approval as the child learns to conform or not to her desires and methods in this matter. Thus, training involves the expression of tenderness and approval for some acts and disapproval and the withholding of tenderness for others. In other words, some performances bring tenderness and approval wtih the consequent increase of euphoria, while others bring disapproval and hence anxiety. These experiences of rewards and punishments come to be regarded as something special. Gradually the child catches on to the fact that they are related to his feelings of euphoria and anxiety. The more or less abrupt supervention of anxiety gradually teaches or forces him to focus awareness on the performances which bring approval and disapproval. He learns, for example, to recall incidents occurring before anxiety. After a while a forbidding gesture will be sufficient to change his behavior. In other words, as his observation improves, his grasp on the patterns of approval and disapproval becomes more refined. He learns that when anxiety is present and something is done which brings tenderness and approval, the painful discomfort is assuaged or banished.

Hence, the child gradually learns to focus attention on behavior which brings approval and disapproval in order to win rewards, tenderness and approval, and escape punishment, disapproval and disapprobation.

In infancy a vague idea of "my" body arises. From the sentience of the body as a basis, there gradually evolve three "personifications" of "me"—"good me," "bad me," and "not-me." The "good me" is an organization of experiences of approval, tenderness, and general good feeling. The "bad me" is an organization of experiences related to increasing anxiety states. The "rudimentary personification" of "not-me" evolves very gradually. The processes labeled "not-me" belong to the most poorly grasped aspects of living and refer to "uncanny" experiences like horror, dread, loathing, awe. What these uncanny experiences are about is not known, but they seem to originate in the experiences of anxiety in infancy, "primitive anxiety." They occur in the parataxic mode. The personification, "not-me" is not constituted by communicative processes and hence not much can be said about it. Nightmares and certain schizophrenic experiences are examples of uncanny experiences of the "not-me."

The "personifications" of "good me" and "bad me" belong to the self system. In other words, to put this crudely, there are times when "I" am "good me" and times when "I" am "bad me." Whether or not the self is predominantly one or the other depends on the course of experience, especially in early life. But the "good me" is essentially desirable, for it is organized on the basis of experiences of security. Hence "I" shall tend to regard "my" self as essentially the "good me" at least unless my life experience has been extraordinarily unfortunate.

We can now state in general terms the origin, nature, and function of the self dynamism. It has its basis in the need for alertness to approval, tenderness and disapproval. We should like, too, to call attention to its *restrictive* function.

> The self-dynamism is built up out of this experience of approbation and disapproval, of reward and punishment. The peculiarity of the self-dynamism is that as it grows it functions, in accordance with its state of development, right from the start. As it develops, it becomes more and more related to a microscope in its function. Since the approbation of the important person is very valuable, since disapprobation denies satisfaction and gives anxiety, the self becomes extremely important. It permits a minute focus on those performances of the child which are the cause of approbation and disapprobation, but, very much like a microscope, it interferes with noticing the rest of the world. When you are staring through your microscope, you don't see much except what comes through that channel. So with the self-dynamism. It has a tendency to focus attention on performances with the significant other person which get approbation or disfavor. And that peculiarity, closely connected with anxiety, persists thenceforth through life. It comes about that the self, that to which we refer when we say "I," is the only thing which has alertness, which notices what goes on, and, needless to say, notices what goes on in its own field. The rest of the personality gets along outside awareness. Its impulses, its performances are not noted.

Among the peculiarities of anxiety is the fact that it is always "at 180° to any other tension with which it coincides." In other words, it directly opposes the tensions of somatic needs and thereby prevents or hinders the satisfaction of somatic needs. An extremely anxious person cannot obtain proper sexual satisfaction or may be prevented from enjoying food by nausea, vomiting, etc. While all other tensions are followed by activities, either overt or covert, which resolve the tensions and satisfy the needs, the tension of anxiety, in Sullivan's language, does not result in energy transformations directed to its relief by the removal of the situational factors obviously concerned in its provocation. The tension of fear, on the other hand, is often manifested in activities which remove the situational factors provoking fear, escapes them, neutralizes their importance or defers being afraid until the near future when the real or apparent danger is over.

As one grows, one learns, if only in a dim way, how to avoid most situations which provoke intense anxiety, but the capacity for it remains. And it will manifest itself throughout life. In this respect, the difference between the "normal" person and the "neurotic" is only one of degree.

Because experiences of approbation and disapproval occur long before one can think, long before one can discriminate what occurs, the earliest attitudes, and the most "deep seated" and pervasive, are acquired unthinkingly, with little or no discrimination. Furthermore, the infant, and to a large extent also, the child, is biologically and psychologically helpless. Not only does he depend on the parents for the necessities of life itself, but he has no or only an incipient ability to think and no or insufficient social experience. Hence, in earliest years the attitudes, codes, and behavior of the parents and their surrogates are necessarily accepted without criticism or discrimination. In Sullivan's language he is still pretty much restricted to the parataxic mode of experience. Later, at least to some degree, he will develop the ability to question, compare and relate his experiences.

The "facilitations and deprivations," that which is approved and disapproved by the parents and others close to the child, becomes the source of the material built into the self dynamism. By and large their behavior will be sufficient consistent to give the self-system a form and direction which it will maintain throughout life. Any experience which promises to threaten the form and direction of the self will provoke anxiety. When this happens, the person will not clearly notice what is happening; its significance will not be realized. And he will usually, without being aware of it, indulge in behavior calculated to nullify the experience or its importance.

Thus, anxiety is the instrumentality by which the self limits and restricts awareness. It functions so as to maintain its own form and direction.

> Even when the self is a derogatory and hateful system it will inhibit and misinterpret any disassociated feeling or experience of friendliness toward others; and it will misinterpret any gestures of friendliness from others. The. direction and characteristics given to the self in infancy and childhood are maintained year after year, at an extraordinary cost, so that most people in this culture, and presumably in any other, because of inadequate and unfortunate experience in early life, become "inferior caricatures of what they might have been." Not only the family, but various other cultural institutions less directly, all combine, more or less unwittingly, to produce this effect.

Actions, including thinking, phantasy, and emotions and feeling, if they are to occur within self-awareness, must conform to the characteristics of the self. Otherwise they are "disassociated" or "selectively inattended."

The self may be said to be made up of or at least circumscribed by *reflected appraisals*. The child lacks the equipment and experience necessary for a careful and unclouded evaluation of himself. The only guide he has is that of the significant adults who take care of him, and who treat and regard him in accordance with the way in which they have developed from their own life experience. Hence, the child experiences himself and appraises himself in terms of what the parents and others close to him manifest. By empathy, facial expression, gestures, words, deeds they convey to him the attitudes they hold toward him and their regard or lack of it for him.

These he "naturally" accepts because he is not yet a questioning, evaluating being. If the significant people express a respecting, loving attitude toward him, he acquires a respecting, loving attitude toward himself. If they are derogatory and hateful, then he will acquire a derogatory and hateful attitude toward himself. Throughout life, save perhaps for the intervention of extraordinary circumstances and allowing for some modification through later experience, he will carry the attitudes toward himself he learned in early life around with him just as surely as he will carry his skin.

Sullivan suggests, however, that the controlling limiting function of the self is not absolute. Certain impelling needs, such as the need of sexual satisfaction, if thwarted, may prove too powerful even for the self system. Fortunately children retain a capacity for change. A loving teacher may undo somewhat the effects of a destructive parent, but a hateful destructive teacher may limit or slow up the effects of the loving care of tender parents.

To the extent to which limitations and peculiarities of the self interfere with biologically necessary satisfactions and security, then to that extent a person is mentally ill.

The self-dynamism is not synonymous with momentary self-awareness. It is a more or less stable organization or configuration of interpersonal processes, past, present, and of the prospective future. The self has a before and after. Since it merges with other processes occurring outside discriminating awareness, it has "background," it shades imperceptibly into marginal processes of awareness. These marginal processes of awareness may often be noted just before one "drops off" to sleep. Because the self also manifests itself in focal awareness, it has a "foreground."

SELECTIVE INATTENTION AND DISASSOCIATION

It does not seem necessary to emphasize the fact that much of human experience and behavior occurs outside self-awareness. Freud formulated phenomena occurring outside self-awareness in terms of the "preconscious" and "unconscious." But for Freud these concepts have "topographical" and other features which are foreign to Sullivan's thought. Hence the latter usually avoids the use of such terms because they are "loaded" with meaning to which he does not subscribe.

The concepts by which he tries to formulate his thoughts on such matters are labeled "selective inattention" and "disassociation." The difference between the two is one of degree, measured by the difficulty of access to discriminating awareness.

The child gradually learns to pay close attention to behavior which is approved and disapproved. He must in order to maintain security and avoid anxiety. His attention becomes focused on these performances. This process is analogous to what goes on when, say, a music lover is present at a thrilling concert. Such a person becomes absorbed in the music, "wrapped up" in it. His attention will be entirely focused on the perform-ance and enjoyment of it. To everything else he will pay little heed. In fact, he will not be conscious of anything else, such as the people around him, the passage of time, and so on. For the child his security is at issue, which of course is vitally important, and he will pay close attention to what goes on when approval or disapproval is involved. Certain other experiences either of himself or others will not be so clearly noticed because they entail no particular approval and tenderness or disapproval. Hence, his attention and inattention become selective. To some of his experience and behavior he will be inattentive, and this will then not be carefully discriminated. It will go on outside of discriminated awareness.

SUPPLEMENTARY READINGS

Ames, L. B. The sense of self of nursery school children as manifested by their verbal behavior. *J. genet. Psychol.,* 1952, 31, 193–232.

Benedels, T. Adaptation to reality in early infancy. *Psychoanal. Quart.,* 1938, 7, 200–215.

Jersild, A. T. Emotional development. In L. Carmichael (Ed.), *Manual of child psychology.* New York: Wiley, 1954. Pp. 833–917.

Piaget, J. Principal factors determining intellectual evolution from childhood to adult life. In D. Rapaport (Ed.), *Organization and pathology of thought.* New York: Columbia Univer. Press, 1951. Pp. 176–192.

Piaget, J. *The construction of reality in the child.* New York: Basic Books, 1954.

Sullivan, H. S. *Collected works.* New York: Norton, 1965.

the need for
a "true" ego model
of psychological
functioning*

ROBERT W. WHITE

[Scientists have an apparently compelling need to reduce their descriptions of the interrelatedness of natural phenomena to the simplest possible form. This "law of parsimony" is well illustrated in the elegant simplicity of Einstein's $E = mc^2$. By following this approach, the physical scientists have been able to describe and predict extremely complex events by postulating a much smaller number of basic natural processes. Psychologists have attempted to emulate the physical scientists and have, by and large, been modestly successful in their efforts. Nevertheless, there is now some reason to believe that psychologists may have applied the principle of parsimony too mechanically and too early in their conceptualizations of human behavior. For example, it now seems improbable that the diversities of human motivation can all be traced back to basic tissue needs. It seems equally improbable that Freud's postulated instincts of Eros and Thanatos will be adequate theoretical bases for explaining the subtle complexities of ego functioning in the human personality. In the following paper, Dr. White, of Harvard University, clearly presents the reasons why many psychologists have felt it necessary to postulate independent ego energies. This report is an excellent summary of contemporary ego psychology and its relationship to the general principles of behavior and development.]

This essay can be described as an attempt to develop the psychoanalytic concept of independent ego energies in order to improve our understanding of the relation between ego and reality. It is based on the belief that recent research on animal behavior and child development provides the basis for a coherent conception of such energies and of the contribution they make

* From R. W. White. Ego and reality in psychoanalytic theory. *Psychological Issues,* 1963, 3, 182–196. (With permission.)

to ego development. This conceptualization, which emphasizes learning through action and its consequences, is held to improve our comprehension of reality testing, early ego deviations, identification as a growth process, self-esteem, and ego strength. It is held to be helpful, moreover, in resolving a number of difficulties in the psychoanalytic theory of energies.

The content of psychoanalytic ego psychology. When Freud was hardly more than on the brink of those discoveries that were to change forever our ideas about human nature, he began to construct what we would call today a psychological theory of personality. As the discoveries progressed from one triumph to another, revealing whole ranges of disguised and unsuspected motivations, the most fitting concepts appeared to be those of instinctual drive and energy, and for a time this aspect of the theory dominated all other. But soon the searching eye of psychoanalytic technique began to rest on the forces that control instinctual drives. The result was a fresh series of discoveries concerning defense mechanisms, and the beginnings of a theory of the ego as a structural system. As matters were left by Freud, the erotic and destructive instincts provided the power for all action, including that of the ego apparatus.

Since Freud's death the psychology of the ego has been the most active growing edge of psychoanalytic theory. Freud had assigned to the ego as its decisive function the maintaining of relations with reality. Hartmann presently pointed out that the performance of such a function raised the whole problem of adaptation, and required concepts of structure and of learning that were not well supplied by a theory centered upon instincts. An examination of the chief proposals for developing psychoanalytic ego psychology reveals a surprising unanimity about the needed content. Everyone is agreed that attention must be paid to the growth processes whereby man's complex repertory of adaptive behavior comes to be put together. This means that the facts of exploration, manipulation, locomotion, language, the practicing of motor skills, the growth of cognition, the development of plans and intentional actions, and the emergence of higher thought processes all become building stones for an adequate ego psychology. Such facts have long been the domain of academic child psychology, and they are by no means best observed in psychoanalytic therapy. Yet only by their inclusion is it possible to reach Freud's goal of a complete theory of personality.

Admitting this body of facts to psychoanalytic theory raises difficult theoretical problems. On the face of it, the adaptive processes just listed do not press toward erotic or destructive instinctual aims. Some theorists have thought that this discrepancy was only a matter of appearance. If one stretched the definitions of the two instincts sufficiently, and if one made generous allowance for unconscious and symbolic forms of gratification, perhaps all behavior could be brought under the twin scepters of Eros and Thanatos. Such a view was found wanting by Freud himself, who amended it by postulating a process whereby libido could be desexualized and thus made freely available for the neutral aims of the ego. This hypothesis, expanded by Hartmann and his associates to include the neutralization of both kinds of instinctual-drive energy, provides the ego with its own allowance, so to speak, but reminds us that this came from the pockets of the parent instincts. Other workers, finding the transformation of energy implausible, have preferred to postulate an independent source, a case in point being Hendrick, who proposed an instinct to master.

The position taken in this essay is located somewhere between Hartmann's and Hendrick's. It agrees with both that the energies behind adaptive activity must be neutral with respect to instinctual aims. It does not, however, require a transformation of energies originally instinctual, nor does it assume a new instinct in any ordinary sense of the word. The theory advanced here, curiously enough, fits a niche already provided in the edifice of psychoanalytic theory, but one in which no statue has ever been placed. It corresponds roughly to the idea mentioned by Freud, but never more than casually, that the ego apparatus might have intrinsic energies of its own and that there might be a natural satisfaction in the exercise of ego functions. In this essay the idea of independent ego energies is taken seriously and pursued through several of its chief developmental implications.

A way of conceiving of independent ego energies: efficacy and competence. Recent trends in animal and child psychology are decidedly helpful in forming an idea of independent ego energies. Among experimenters with animals there has been a sharp revival of interest in manipulative behavior, curiosity, and exploratory play. When all known drives are at rest, rats will examine new objects and explore new territory, kittens will find their way to toys, monkeys will manipulate whatever is at hand, and chimpanzees will subject novel objects to searching scrutiny and testing. In the absence of such opportunities animals will seek them, and they can learn maze pathways, and other habits to serve them in reaching such rewards. It seems impossible to connect all of this behavior with aims of food, sex, or avoidance of pain, and some workers have postulated additional drives to account for it.

These observations can be matched and made in much greater detail on children. Before the end of the first year the child typically spends long hours in the manipulative exploration of objects, and in the course of time there will be intensive testing of locomotion, experimenting with sounds and verbal forms, and involvement in the whole expanding realm of interests that we refer to as the child's play. Observations by Piaget show that during the second year some of this play takes on a character that deserves to be called scientific investigation: objects are explored systematically with the child's whole repertory of actions, and their potentialities are tested by putting them in different positions. Such activities are pursued with concentrated attention, with persistence, often with chuckles and other signs of satisfaction, and sometimes, when the object proves refractory, with unmistakable evidences of frustration. It is impossible not to characterize this kind of behavior as motivated, but most of it has no plausible relation to the aims of instinctual drives.

The playful exploratory and manipulative activities of children provide the basis for a theory of independent ego energies. Examining them closely, we can see that more is involved than a random overflow of activity. It is noticeable in young children—indeed even in young animals—that attention is given longest to objects upon which it is possible to have large effects. Studies of preferences show that the most interesting objects are the ones with which the most can be done. Even when an external stimulus obviously starts the transaction, the response tends to have the character of a series of varied actions producing whatever effects are possible. Noticing this interest in effects, Groos in his study of play attributed to the child a "joy in being a cause." Recent workers have begun to see the significance of these facts for learning to deal effectively with one's surroundings. It is proposed here to refer to the energy behind such behavior as *effectance,* and to the affect that attends it as *feeling of efficacy.* Effectance thus refers to the active tendency to put forth effort to influence the environment, while feeling of efficacy refers to the satisfaction that comes with producing effects.

Independent ego energies and their satisfactions are conceived to be just as basic as the instincts. They are not, however, related to particular somatic sources or to consummatory patterns of discharge. Conceivably they can be equated with the inherent energy of the nervous system. But their significance for development lies in their direct relation to the formation of psychic structure. Effectance is a prompting to explore the properties of the environment; it leads to an accumulating knowledge of what can and cannot be done with the environment; its biological significance lies in this very property of developing *competence.* Instinctual energies, of course, likewise produce action, effects, and knowledge of the environment, thus making a contribution to competence. But their contribution is necessarily narrower than that of neutral energies which stand ever ready to promote exploration for its own sake. It will be noticed that this conception of independent ego energies tends to reduce the sharp metaphorical distinction between energy and structure. If we conceive of structure as competence, we are giving it the dynamic character of patterns of readiness for future action.

Competence is the cumulative result of the history of interactions with the environment. *Sense of competence* is suggested as a suitable term for the subjective side of this, signifying one's consciously or unconsciously felt competence—one's confidence—in dealing with the various aspects of the environment. It is easier to describe these concepts in transactions with inanimate objects, but they apply equally well, and more importantly, to interactions with other human beings. Human objects present the same problem of finding out what can and cannot be done with them, a problem that is not fully covered by instinctual aims, and we can assume that great importance will always be attached to one's *sense of interpersonal competence*.

Reality and its testing. In psychoanalytic theory the ego is given the function of representing reality and of assuring that behavior is governed by realistic considerations. According to the thesis of this essay, reality testing —finding out about reality and being guided by it—comes about through attempted actions and their consequences. Reality is not passively received; it does not imprint itself on the mind. It is slowly constructed through active, varied, and persistent exploration, and what is learned about it is how to deal with it: what actions produce what effects on what objects.

This conception has by no means been overlooked in psychoanalytic theory. Freud used it explicitly to explain how one learns to distinguish between inner and outer stimuli. But the systematic application of an action theory to reality testing has been greatly impeded by attempts to work wholly with instinctual energies and to derive the entire course of events from hypothetical first situations. This tendency is shown in Freud's account of the transition from the pleasure principle to the reality principle, a change which he described entirely in terms of instinctual frustration and an unwilling reckoning with reality as the frustrator. It is shown in the idea that defense originates from a splitting of instinctual energy into cathectic and anticathectic components, with structure arising in layers from their repeated collision. These are unsuitable concepts for understanding the relation between ego and reality. They can be dressed up to plausibility only by the belated smuggling in of those ideas about action and structure which a theory of independent ego energies seeks to make explicit from the start.

According to an action theory, reality testing is not undertaken solely because of instinctual frustration. Exploration occurs in its own right, and reality can be interesting and satisfying as well as frustrating. Even in Freud's model situation it seems clear that frustration leads to action and that the pleasure principle is transcended through the discovery of some action, like crying, which influences the environment and can be used to influence it again. Tolerance of delay depends on a confidence, born of experience, that something efficacious can be done if need waxes painful.

The reality principle is thus learned by slow degrees. This applies equally to the distinction between self and not-self: it is a cumulative growth depending upon extended exploration of one's own body and its sensations as well as of sensations proceeding from external objects. This unavoidable conclusion plays havoc with much that has been written about early introjection, projection, and the externalization of libidinal and aggressive energies. Most of this speculation presupposes that self and not-self have been discriminated once and for all almost from the beginning. But many of these hypothetical events stand to gain from reconsideration.

An action theory is most particularly needed to account for the construction of a world of permanent objects having independent causal relations. If we knew the world wholly through instinctual cathexes, we would forever see objects in relation to our needs, not in impersonal relations to each other. On this point Piaget's detailed developmental studies are highly illuminating. His observations fill in the successive steps of what would otherwise be a hypothetical course of development. Growth of the concept of permanent objects is traced by means of experiments in which objects are covered and put out of sight. Before eight months, out of sight is out of mind, even if the object has been concealed only by placing a handkerchief over it. The child first looks for the hidden object when he has already begun the action of reaching for it at the moment when the cover is put down. Having learned in this way that it can be found, he can then slowly learn to transfer his action when the object is hidden under a different cover, and by the middle of the second year he can take fairly elaborate account of its successive movements. What is going on in this sequence is the disconnecting of the object from any one action and location, thus gradually constructing the idea of its independent existence. Piaget describes in like sequential fashion the growth of the concept of causality apart from one's own effort. In such fashion the child works and plays his way toward knowledge of an enduring world with impersonal causal relations.

Additional evidence for this way of thinking is provided by studies of older children's perceptions and memories of places they have visited. Werner, pointing out that the child's world long remains a world of action, reports experiments in which children of different ages brought back from places such as a canal dock or a department store entirely different descriptions depending upon what they had found to do in these locations.

The objective stable world is thus best conceived of as a construction based upon action. Knowledge about the environment is knowledge of the probable consequences of action. It is a system of readinesses for action which can properly be conceived of as patterns of facilitation and inhibition in the nervous system. This is the form in which reality leaves its record, and instinctual drives are governed by it—become bound by it—because they have to use the nervous system as their means of expression, complete with its acquired facilitations and inhibitions. There is no need to assume that cathexis plays any necessary part at all in knowledge of reality.

Early deviations in ego development. Following a suggestion of Freud's that the psychoses would shed helpful light on the ego, psychoanalytic workers in recent years have given much attention to disorders in early childhood and have conceptualized them as failures in ego development. This means in particular a deficiency in social responsiveness and object relations, a failure to achieve stable defenses, and an inadequate growth of reality testing and active mastery. The causes of these disorders were first thought to lie in the mother, who was thus assigned a position of virtual omnipotence in her child's adaptive growth. This one-sided picture was later made more interactive by allowing for constitutional deficiencies in the child and response to them by the mother.

Introduction of the concept of independent ego energies permits a closer analysis of what goes wrong in these interactions. It allows us to tighten with appropriate developmental detail the loose connections between weak ego growth and maternal coldness or deprivation. Our question comes to be phrased as follows: What happens to obstruct the infant's tendency to explore and interact with his environment, blocking the usual pathway to reality testing and structuration? In other words, what goes wrong with the expression of effectance, feelings of efficacy, and the growth of a sense of competence?

These concepts allow us, in the first place, to recast the picture of what normally goes on between mother and infant. On the mother's side, we can see that the sense of maternal competence—the ability to perform the socially vital task of bringing up children—is agreeably enhanced when the child develops well, but gravely challenged when his behavior is deviant. Children who are unusually passive, venturing little, and children who are overactive, achieving no stability, each in their own way seriously frustrate maternal competence and thus evoke some of the excessive compensations that have been described in "schizophrenogenic" mothers. On the child's side, we can see that in ordinary circumstances effectance prompts manipulative and exploratory action which is rewarded by feelings of efficacy. Such action is inherently independent, hence sometimes at odds with the mother's wishes and convenience; it does not draw its original power from maternal encouragement and reward. In normal growth the mother thus does not stand as the central motive force in ego development, though she may help or hinder it in important ways. In abnormal cases it must be shown how this development comes to be seriously obstructed.

Concepts of efficacy and competence thus allow us, in the second place, to schematize the causes of the inhibition of effectance. (1) When deprivation and anxiety are very severe, so that the infant when awake is constantly yearning for instinctual gratification and security, exploratory play, the spare-time activity between periods of crisis, may simply be swamped and crowded out. (2) There may be a specific obstruction of socially directed effectance. This is probably the situation in the autistic child whose mother, described as cold and mechanical in her ministrations, never responds to his initiative and thus permits no feelings of efficacy. (3) There may also be a specific obstruction of exploratory play with inanimate objects, though this will not usually occur alone. Such a result could be produced by circumstances that connected play with isolation, fear, or pain.

Identification as a process of development. Of late years the concept of identification has run riot through the clinical literature. The metaphor of undisciplined riot is not out of place: identification has been used in several quite different senses, applied to quite dissimilar phenomena, and never clarified with respect to implicit underlying processes.

We are obliged to lay this confusion at Freud's door. In different writings he used identification (1) as a mechanism in melancholia, where it occurred as a regression from lost object cathexes; (2) for the little boy's admiring imitation of his father, where it was conceived of as a primitive type of object relation; (3) for the internalizing of parental values during resolution of the oedipus complex; (4) for relations among siblings, where it developed as a reaction formation against rivalry; and (5) for the aim-inhibited tender tie among the members of an adult group. The most serious inconsistency in these usages is between identification as the copying of a model, based on wanting to be like the model, and identification as an emotional tie, based on loving and wanting to be close to the model. Freud clearly stated that identification meant only the first, but he frequently used it in the second sense as well.

The difficulty here is that if copying a model is taken as the central idea, then the emotional tie must be a variable, hence inessential, feature. This became clear in Anna Freud's concept of identification with an aggressor, where the imitation was of someone feared and hated. While the literature since Freud's death shows a tendency toward blurred and reckless extension of the concept, there have been attempts to restrict identification to a single clear meaning. This has been done most successfully when a firm distinction is drawn between identification and introjection. The latter then moves back chronologically to the oral stage, carrying with it the connotation of an emotional tie in some such form as a wish for union and merging with the mother. This leaves identification as an imitative process which comes to its first peak during the phallic stage and continues to influence development in the manner described by Erikson.

Thus restricted, identification signifies copying a model whose competence is admired. It is done for the sake of creating that competence in oneself. Like simpler forms of imitation, it implies that the child already has in his repertory the acts he now wants to increase and integrate. The great flowering of make-believe and dramatic play occurs only when the child is mature enough to copy fairly elaborate adult patterns. Identification must be conceived of in terms of attempted action, though this does not exclude dreaming about actions beyond the range of present possibility. Through action and its consequences the child finds out which identifications will work and which ones are doomed to fail.

It will be clear that this formulation does not require any genetic connection between introjection and identification. The two things are psychologically very different. Introjection, if it is not literally modeled on oral incorporation, at least must signify an attempted restoration of the total nursing situation with its feeling of closeness, a relatively passive state not characterized by feelings of efficacy. Identification happens actively in the interests of competence, its chief reward being an increased sense of competence. To call it a partial incorporation is to confuse two things that have no psychological resemblance.

Superego formation and the resolution of the oedipus complex, furthermore, cannot be conceived of simply in terms of identification. Several adaptive processes are at work simultaneously in a complex situation. In so far as the boy accepts prohibitions against a sexual interest in his mother he is actually abandoning part of the identification with his father and learning to act unlike him. Identification applies well to those parts of the process in which parental behavior is copied. It does not apply to the internalizing of prohibitions against behavior still allowed to the parents. But there is certainly no need to capture superego formation in a single formula.

Self-esteem, sense of competence, and ego strength. Psychoanalytic theories of self-esteem are generally cast in terms of instinctual energies and infantile fantasies. When Freud discovered narcissism he made self-regard a function of narcissistic libido, which obscured the possibility that it might have to be differentiated from self-love. In Ferenczi and Fenichel one finds the idea that self-regard is related to fantasies and feelings of omnipotence, which have their origin in the immediate gratification of all needs in the womb. From this comes the conclusion that the level of self-esteem is regulated by the inflow first of oral supplies, later of narcissistic supplies. The theme is continued in the theory that the ego ideal becomes the repository of narcissistic omnipotence. Level of self-esteem can then be conceived of as a reflection of the difference between the ideal and the actual.

Other psychoanalytic theorists, notably Silverberg, have related self-esteem to the success of one's activities directed toward the environment. In the terms used in this essay, self-esteem is correlated with sense of competence, hence ultimately with experiences of efficacy. This view of the matter rescues self-esteem from confusion with self-love by relating it primarily to independent ego energies rather than to narcissistic libido. It also suggests that Ferenczi set up the wrong image for the starting point of omnipotence when he chose a situation of instant passive gratification without a hint of efficacy. Self-esteem has its deepest root in the experience of efficacy. It is not constructed out of what others do or what the environment gratuitously provides. It springs rather from what one can make the environment do by crying, by signaling, or by coordinated acts of competence. Fantasies of omnipotence can be based upon the infant's experience of commanding the environment to serve him (the master who rings for the servants) or upon his experience of mastering it by his own efforts (Robinson Crusoe, Superman).

This account of self-esteem, which locates its inner source in efficacy and the sense of competence, is not intended to crowd out the esteem income that may or may not be provided by others. This is a very real factor, but we must remember that supplies of esteem are not bestowed whimsically; they have some relation to what the person has done. Esteem is constantly involved in a transactional process in which effort expended and encouragement received work in a complementary fashion. It is valuable to distinguish between esteem supplies (respect) and narcissistic supplies (love).

Ego strength must also be seen as clearly related to acquired competence and sense of competence. This concept, useful in clinical practice, has generally been defined negatively as the absence of crippling anxiety or of anticathectic defense processes. Such a view neglects the positive contributions of effectance, which is at work building up adaptive capacities that help in coping with dangers, and a sense of competence that opposes the development of anxiety. This work is constantly going on between times of crisis—in conflict-free situations—and its results may be highly significant when the next crisis occurs. This view of ego strength as an active, cumulative achievement is valuable in understanding the stages of development, in forming a genetic theory of psychopathology, and in explaining those not infrequent cases in which good adjustment seems to have sprung miraculously from a childhood loaded with pathological influences. A psychoanalytic case of the latter kind, presented by its author as an example of healthy growth, reveals the need to supplement psychoanalytic theory with concepts of action and efficacy. The early circumstances, impulses, fantasies, and defense mechanisms disclosed by the analysis offer no basis for predicting the relatively successful adjustment found in middle life. But the riddle can be solved if one pays careful attention to the way in which defenses adopted in crises led to actions of an efficacious sort which worked well upon the particular environment and thus became the basis for a continuing growth of competence and confidence.

Further considerations of energy: anxiety, cathexis, neutralization. Freud came to regard the instincts as the very foundation of psychoanalytic theory. He was highly partial to explanations in terms of instinctual energy, and as between the two basic instincts he was further partial to the libido, a concept to which he remained loyal throughout his life. His preferences are shown by several facts: that he never really worked out the implications of the death instinct, that he continued to use cathexis as if only libido were involved, that he gave anxiety increasing importance without letting it be an energetic rival of the instincts, and that he nipped independent ego energies in the bud by producing the hypothesis of desexualized libido. His decisions with respect to energies were not the only possible ones, and they have led to serious difficulties.

When he revised his theory of anxiety in 1926, Freud created a greater revolution than he knew. Anxiety was detached from its previous status of converted libido and assigned great power over the outflow of instinctual-drive energies. Freud did not, however, represent this power as an instinct or drive, as academic psychologists have generally done. In his conception anxiety was merely an affect giving a signal of danger, and the real power in the production of defenses lay with the pleasure-pain mechanism, to which the instincts themselves were subject. There is no way to read this account without concluding that in fact he had invoked a very strong driving force, the avoidance of anxiety, and had brought it into direct conflict with instinctual drives over the use of the pleasure-pain mechanism. One can only note with regret how much better the problems of anticathexis and defensive structure could have been solved if Freud had realized the full implications of what he had done.

Cathexis, an apt concept for describing a loving interest in objects, has come to be used in psychoanalytic theory to signify any kind of positive attitude. It is thus customary to refer to the cathexis of external objects, of the self, and even of ego functions, always the implication that these things can be of no interest unless they are cathected. Two difficulties result. One is the question of cathexis by aggressive instinctual energy. This is surely a legitimate concept in a dual instinct theory, but it implies that cathexis can be destructive, and the word is practically never used in this sense. The other is that objects must have a permanent cathexis if they are to be conceived of as having a permanent existence. This creates difficulty for the idea that instincts have a periodic character. These difficulties can be resolved by returning cathexis to its original meaning of an investment of libidinal energy, and by introducing independent ego energies to account for a "neutral" or non-libidinal interest in objects. Such interest is related to feelings of efficacy, and the permanence of objects is assured by the permanence of the acquired patterns for influencing them. The concept of the libidinal cathexis of ego functions is perhaps not an impossible one, but libido is not required to make the ego run.

Difficulties have resulted from the attempt to interpret all play and exploratory behavior as a manifestation of erotic or aggressive instinctual energies. Since erotic and aggressive aims are by no means regularly apparent, it becomes necessary to stretch the meaning of the two energies to such generalites as binding things together or pulling things apart. This analysis is fatal to an understanding of the meaning of exploratory acts. Joining and separating occur in lightning alternation in manipulative behavior, for example, but pointing out this superficial fact obscures the real meaning of the behavior, which is to find out what can be done with objects. On this point effectance and efficacy yield a more penetrating analysis than instinctual drives.

It was in part to deal with difficulties of this kind that Freud introduced the idea of desexualized libido and Hartmann expanded it to include a parallel process of neutralization of aggressive energies. The concept of neutralization contains the implicit recognition that the adaptive activities of the ego cannot be forced into the categories of instinctual aim. The assumption is made that energies originally distinguished by their aims can divest themselves of these aims and become part of a neutral reservoir available to the ego for its own purposes. There is the further proviso that during regression the energy may be reconverted to its original aims. If this idea is considered in neurological terms, it will not work. If it is accepted as a vague hydraulic analogy, it still will not work. Telling very much against it is the fact that no real progress has been made in detailing the conditions under which the remarkable transformations take place.

Even more serious for such a theory is the growing evidence that neutral energy is manifested early in life, even during the first days and weeks. If energy that is neutral in the psychoanalytic sense is conceived to be active so early, the hypothesis that it is transformed from the instincts is superfluous and the case for independent ego energies becomes virtually self-evident. But nothing is lost, because independent ego energies, adequately conceptualized, can do everything that neutralized energies could do, except to deneutralize themselves.

Freud's fundamental concepts were formed under the influence of the tremendous discoveries he made by means of the psychoanalytic method. They have the character of magnificent metaphors designed to capture these discoveries. But he also hoped to formulate a complete theory of personality, and for this it is necessary to include wide ranges of facts not readily observed by the psychoanalytic technique. His goal remains worthy, and the present essay is designed to be a step in its direction.

SUPPLEMENTARY READINGS

Fenichel, O. Ego strength and ego weakness. *Collected papers.* Vol. 2. New York: Norton, 1954. Pp. 70–80.

Ferenczi, S. Stages in the development of the sense of reality. *Sex in psychoanalysis.* New York: Brunner, 1950. Pp. 213–239.

Freud, A. *The ego and the mechanisms of defence.* New York: Int. Univer. Press, 1946.

Freud, S. Group psychology and the analysis of the ego. *Standard edition.* Vol. 14. London: Hogarth Press, 1957. Pp. 243–258.

Freud, S. Inhibitions, symptoms and anxiety. *Standard edition.* Vol. 20. London: Hogarth Press, 1959. Pp. 87–172.

Groos, K. *The play of man.* New York: Appleton, 1901.

Hartmann, H. *Ego psychology and the problem of adaptation.* New York: Int. Univer. Press, 1958.

Hendrick, I. Instinct and the ego during infancy. *Psychoanal. Quart.,* 1942, 11, 33–58.

Piaget, J. *The origins of intelligence in children.* New York: Int. Univer. Press, 1952.

Piaget, J. *The construction of reality in the child.* New York: Basic Books, 1954.

Silverberg, W. V. *Childhood experience and personal destiny.* New York: Springer, 1952.

Werner, H. *Comparative psychology of mental development.* (3rd ed.) New York: Int. Univer. Press, 1957.

patterns of
infantile attachment
to mother*

MARY D. AINSWORTH

[Animals usually prefer to mingle with members of their own species, when reared under normal environmental conditions. How are these attachments formed? Investigators of *imprinting* have shown that certain birds and mammals can be induced to seek the company of unusual companions. For example, the European naturalist Dr. Lorenz demonstrated that graylag geese prefer the company of human companions rather than members of their own species when raised by a human caretaker from the time of hatching. Dr. Hess has shown in his studies at the University of Chicago that mallard ducks, shortly after hatching, will follow almost any moving stimulus. His research has also shown that the success of early imprinting is highly correlated with the amount of energy expended by the ducks in following the stimulus. Is it possible that the findings related to imprinting in infrahuman organisms have some significance for our understanding of the formation of attachments during human infancy? The data collected by Dr. Ainsworth, of the Johns Hopkins University, suggest this possibility. She concludes that the human infant takes some measure of initiative in forming attachments to the mother figure, and that these attachments are initiated as early as the eighth week of life. Attachments to other human figures quickly follow if the infant has adequate opportunity to interact with them. It is also her impression that attachments are formed through the distance receptors as well as by close physical contact. The infant becomes attached not only to the person who feeds and comforts him, but also to others who merely play with him. Dr. Ainsworth concludes that the human infant needs something more than "sheer stimulation for the development of normal attachment behavior." He needs somebody to respond to his attachment overtures. This conclusion is consistent with Dr. Harlow's findings of the abnormal responses of rhesus monkeys reared in the presence of inanimate mother substitutes.]

* From M. D. Ainsworth. Patterns of attachment behavior shown by the infant in interaction with his mother. *Merrill-Palmer Quarterly*, 1964, 10, 51–58. (With permission.)

Since this paper is concerned with attachment, perhaps I should begin with a definition. According to the Oxford Concise Dictionary, attachment is "the act of fastening oneself to another, binding in friendship, making devoted."

The implications of this definition are as follows: (1) Attachment implies affection. (2) Attachments are specific, and imply discrimination. (3) Attachment is an act; it is behavioral and thus observable. (4) Attachment is an active process; it does not come about merely through being a passive recipient of stimulation. (5) The act of attachment affects the response of the object. Attachment is a two-way process. It implies interaction.

Let us now attempt our own definition of attachment behavior. Attachment behavior is behavior through which a discriminating, differential, affectional relationship is established with a person or object, and which tends to evoke a response from the object, and thus initiates a chain of interaction which serves to consolidate the affectional relationship.

The material that I am going to present is selected from a short-term longitudinal study of 28 babies in interaction with their mothers, visited in their own homes at intervals of approximately two weeks. The age-span best represented in the study is from two to fifteen months of age.

These babies happened to be all African—all Baganda. But for our purposes here I urge you to consider my sample as merely one of human infants and disregard the fact that they were African (for I believe the same principles of development apply to infants regardless of specific racial or cultural influences).

These African babies, however, may have been somewhat more accelerated in their development of attachment than babies in our culture. There are three reasons for this opinion. (1) They were generally accelerated in their development, according to Gesell Developmental Schedules. (2) They were breast-fed, with one exception, and this may have facilitated the development of infant-mother attachment. (3) They experienced more interaction with adult figures than many infants in our culture. The modal pattern of infant care among the Baganda was that a baby was never alone when awake. Characteristically, he is held on someone's lap, most frequently his mother's lap, but he is offered to the visitor to hold, as a courteous gesture. As soon as he can sit unsupported he may be placed on the floor, in the midst of the gathering, for everyone sits on mats on the floor. As soon as he can crawl, he is free to move about, and to initiate contacts or to withdraw from them at will.

At the beginning of my study I was interested in the strength and quality of the infant's attachment to his mother, once formed, rather than in the behavior patterns which mediated attachment. This interest led me to attempt to establish criteria of attachment. At first I looked for reactions to separation and to threat of separation—crying when the mother left, following and clinging, especially. But there were some babies, who seemed clearly attached to their mothers, who did not dependably cry, follow or cling when their mothers showed signs of leaving. What, then, gave such a clear impression that they were nevertheless strongly attached to their mothers? In an attempt to answer this question, I examined my field notes exhaustively, and the catalogue of attachment behavior shown in Table 1 is the result.

For each item, the earliest age at which the behavior pattern was observed is shown, as well as the age at which the pattern was commonly observed. Since some of these patterns were identified after the observations were completed, rather than before, and since these observations were therefore unsystematic, it may well be that the earliest and common ages indicated for these items are later than they should be. The data for those patterns are indicated in parentheses.

A CATALOGUE OF PATTERNS OF ATTACHMENT BEHAVIOR

At the outset may I say that this catalogue of thirteen patterns of attachment behavior omits behavior associated with feeding—the rooting response, sucking and, later, search for the breast—because I wanted to distinguish attachment to the mother as a person from mere attachment to the breast as a need-satisfying object. This does not imply that I consider behavior implicit in the feeding relationship to be irrelevant to attachment, particularly in the case of babies such as these who were breast-fed for most of the first year of life or longer.

The first three patterns, listed in Table 1, imply little more than discrimination of the mother from other people, and differential responsiveness to her.

Differential crying. The baby cries when held by someone other than the mother, and stops when taken by the mother. Or he cries and continues to cry when someone else attempts to comfort him, but stops crying immediately when taken by the mother. It was difficult to judge at first

Table 1—Patterns of Attachment Behavior Shown by the Infant in Interaction with His Mother

Behavior	Earliest observation	Commonly observed
Differential crying	8 weeks	12 weeks
Differential smiling	(9 weeks)	(32 weeks)
Differential vocalization	(20 weeks)	?
Visual-motor orientation	(18 weeks)	?
Crying when mother leaves	15 weeks	25 weeks
Following	17 weeks	25 weeks
"Scrambling" over mother	(10 weeks)	(30 weeks)
Burying face in mother's lap	(22 weeks)	(30 weeks)
Exploration from mother as a secure base	28 weeks	33 weeks
Clinging	25 weeks	40 weeks
Lifting arms in greeting	(17 weeks)	(22 weeks)
Clapping hands in greeting	(28 weeks)	(40 weeks)
Approach through locomotion	(26 weeks)	(30 weeks)

whether the object of attachment was the mother as a person, or a part-object—the breast—for the first act of many of these mothers after picking up a crying baby was to offer the breast.

Differential smiling. The baby smiles more readily and more frequently in interaction with his mother than in interaction with another person.

Differential vocalization. The baby vocalizes more readily and more frequently in interaction with his mother than in interaction with other people.

The next group of patterns have in common a concern on the part of the infant for the whereabouts of his mother—a concern that implies the use of distance receptors, especially vision.

Visual-motor orientation towards the mother. The baby, when apart from his mother but able to see her, keeps his eyes more or less continuously oriented towards her. He may look away for a few moments, but he repeatedly glances towards her. When held by someone else, he can be sensed to be maintaining a motor orientation towards his mother, for he is neither ready to interact with the adult holding him, nor to relax in her arms.

Crying when the mother leaves. The baby cries when the mother leaves his visual field and cannot be brought back into it through his own visual-motor adjustments. The usual occasion is when the mother leaves the room, in contrast with times when she merely moves to another part of the same room.

Following. The baby, once able to crawl, not only cries when his mother leaves the room, but attempts to follow her, by crawling after her, or, when he is older, by walking after her. By about eight or nine months, following tended to occur without crying; the baby follows, but cries only if frustrated by being held back, by a closed door, or by the mother going so fast as to outdistance him hopelessly.

Even before the baby is able to crawl and hence to follow, he can nevertheless take the initiative in making contact with his mother when on her lap or when placed on the floor beside her. There are two such patterns, scrambling over the mother, and burying the face in her lap. (I am excluding here behavior that may obviously be interpreted as a search for or a demand for the breast.)

Scrambling. This pattern differs from clinging in that there is no apparent effort to preserve a close and continuous physical contact. The baby climbs over his mother, exploring her person, and playing with her face, her hair or her clothes. On occasion, he may explore another person in this way, but since he much more frequently scrambles over his mother, this differential response is included in our catalogue.

Burying the face. The baby, whether in the course of scrambling over the mother, or having returned to her after exploring the world at some distance from her, buries his face in her lap. This behavior was observed only in relation to the mother.

As Harlow (1960) has observed with infant monkeys and Arsenian (1943) with pre-school children, the baby, once attached to his mother, can use her as a secure base from which to explore the world, or as a "haven of safety" from which he can face an external threat without panic.

Exploration from a secure base. Now that the baby is able to crawl, he does not always keep close to his mother, but rather makes little excursions away from her, exploring other objects and interacting with other people, but he returns to her from time to time. He may even go outside the room altogether if he is permitted to do so. His confidence in leaving the secure base is in remarkable contrast to his distress if the secure base gets up and moves off on *her* own initiative.

Clinging. The clinging pattern which is so conspicuous in infant monkeys was not observed in these infants until 25 weeks at the earliest. The most striking instances of clinging in the first year of life were clearly associated with fright. The only clear-cut fear-arousing stimulus which we observed was the stranger. If already in his mother's arms when faced by a stranger, the baby clings to her tightly; if apart from her, he scuttles to her as quickly as possible and then clings. From the safety of his mother's arms he can eye the stranger warily and without crying. If the mother tries to hand him to the stranger, however, the baby screams and clings desperately, resisting all efforts to disengage him. This panicky clinging in response to strangers was not observed in any child younger than 40 weeks of age. A less intense kind of clinging was seen in somewhat younger children. In one six-months-old child, for example, the cause seemed to be separation anxiety, for he wanted to be with his mother the whole time, and sometimes clung to her, but in an intermittent way and not so desperately and tightly as did the infants who were frightened by a stranger. Another child clung to his mother in the same intermittent way during a period of illness at about 32 weeks of age. Marked clinging was also manifested by some children for a period immediately following weaning.

Finally, greeting responses are classed as attachment behavior. Some infants, who had become accustomed to being put down by their mothers and left alone to sleep, showed their attachment more by the enthusiastic greeting they gave her when she returned after an absence than by a protest when she departed.

Lifting arms in greeting. The baby greets the mother after an absence by lifting his arms towards her, by smiling, and by vocalization that might be described as a "crow" or delighted shout.

Clapping hands in greeting. This response is similar to the previous one except that instead of lifting his arms, the baby, while smiling and vocalizing, claps his hands together in a gesture of obvious delight.

Approach through locomotion. After the child is able to crawl, he characteristically terminates his greeting responses by crawling to the loved person as quickly as he is able. Smiling and vocalization usually accompany this response, as they do the other greeting responses. And of course, as described earlier, the infant, if apart from his mother when frightened, crawls to her as quickly as possible and then clings.

These then, together with responses associated with feeding, constitute a catalogue of behavioral components of attachment to the mother as a special person. Let us now consider the development of attachment as a whole.

DEVELOPMENT OF ATTACHMENT

During the first year of life these infants passed through four main phases in regard to social behavior, one phase leading to another with no sharp boundary between them. First there is a phase of undiscriminating responsiveness to people. Next there is a phase of differential responsiveness to the mother, with continuing responsiveness to other people. Then there is a phase of sharply defined attachment to the mother, with striking waning of undiscriminating friendliness. This is followed quickly by, and overlaps with, a phase of attachment to one or more familiar figures other than the mother.

The second phase, in which discrimination of the mother from other people emerges, began in this sample between 8 and 12 weeks of age, with differential crying as the chief criterion. In this sample, however, it was impossible to determine how much of this earliest attachment was to the mother as a whole person and how much to the breast. During the second quarter-year of life, differential responsiveness to the mother became much more clear-cut, and included differential smiling, differential vocalization, and greeting responses. Crying when the mother left the room was common but inconsistent; infants who were used to being left with other people were more likely to cry if left alone or with a stranger than if left with a familiar figure. As soon as locomotion was attained the following response occurred, in some babies before six months of age, in others shortly afterwards. Following was not invariable or consistent at first; it was most likely to occur when the baby was judged to be hungry, tired, ill, or otherwise unhappy, and if the baby was left alone or with strangers rather than if he was left with a familiar person.

The third phase seemed to begin between six and seven months of age, but without any abrupt transition. Following the mother became more and more consistent, as though the attachment to her were becoming stronger and better consolidated. Protest at the mother's departure became more consistent too—although increasingly protest was not simultaneous with following, and tended to occur only if following was frustrated. Greeting responses became more conspicuous, and babies began to use their mothers as a secure base from which to explore the world.

The fourth phase, as I mentioned earlier, overlapped with the third. Babies who were used to care from adults other than the mother never completely lost tolerance for this care, even though they might initially protest the mother's departure. Very shortly after the baby showed a clearcut attachment to the mother he began to display attachment to other figures, often the father, chiefly through greeting responses. Sharp preferences were shown; for example, one sibling might be greeted joyously while other siblings were not. After nine months of age the baby, when left with a familiar figure, would follow it about, no longer reserving following solely for the mother. Soon after there was discrimination and attachment to figures other than the mother, fear of strangers appeared, as early as eight months with some babies.

SUMMARY AND DISCUSSION

I now wish to summarize and discuss these findings, drawing your attention to some considerations that seem important to me. I have identified thirteen patterns of behavior which seem to mediate the attachment of the infant to his mother and soon afterwards to other favorite figures. This catalogue is probably incomplete, although it goes beyond Bowlby's (1958) list, which was limited to sucking, crying, smiling, following and clinging. The behavioral components of these attachment patterns are clearly unlearned—crying, smiling, vocalization, following with the eyes, reaching for an object, locomotion, and so on. These unlearned components become tied into attachment patterns, however, only when they become differentially directed towards different figures, and in the human infant this discrimination does not seem to emerge abruptly.

Although the various patterns of attachment behavior that I have catalogued tend to become organized together with the mother as object, not all of them need be included in a particular attachment. The attachments of some infants seemed chiefly mediated by crying when mother leaves, by following, and later by clinging. This attachment of others seemed more conspicuously mediated by greeting, smiling, vocalization, and visual-motor orientation. Perhaps no one of these components is essential; for example, the behavior associated with the breast-feeding relationship is not essential to attachment in our culture.

I should like to close by emphasizing three features of attachment behavior which I believe to be clearly apparent in the findings of this study.

First, I was struck with the active part the baby himself plays in the development of attachment. All of these behavior patterns, as well as the seeking responses in feeding, show initiative. The striking part played by the infant's own activity in attachment leads me to the hypothesis that it is largely through his own activity that the child becomes attached, rather than through stimulation, or through the passive satisfaction of creature-comfort needs.

I attach a great deal of importance to the active initiative implicit in attachment behavior. I view interaction between the infant and his mother as a chain of behavioral interchange, which may be initiated either by behavior of the mother to which the infant responds, or by the infant's behavior—at first his signals and later his actual attachment overtures—which evokes a response in the mother.

Hence, as I have stated elsewhere (Ainsworth, 1962), I believe that maternal deprivation may best be defined as insufficient interaction between the infant and a mother-figure, and not as mere lack of stimulation. In deprivation the infant also lacks response of an adult to the behavior he initiates, including his attachment behavior.

Secondly, attachment behavior is not necessarily terminated by a state of close physical contact between infant and mother. Although some attachment patterns imply physical contact as an end phase, others maintain proximity and interaction without requiring actual contact—vocalization, visual-motor orientation, following, exploring from a secure base, and so on. However important actual physical contact may be to the human infant, it is clear that some of the components of attachment and much important interaction between infant and mother involve distance receptors, rather than tactual and kinaesthetic modalities. Even in infancy, attachment can be sustained through a middle distance in which seeing of expression, movement and gesture, and hearing of vocalization, may form the basis of interaction.

I will not set forth in this present discussion my reasons for believing so, but I believe that it is the anxious infant who requires close physical contact with his mother, and who is not content to maintain interaction through a middle distance at least part of the time.

Third, this study suggests strongly that attachments to other figures tend to follow attachment to the mother very quickly, provided that the infant has adequate opportunity to interact with people other than his mother. Scarcely has the infant passed the phase of undiscriminating social responsiveness and formed a specific attachment to his mother than he begins to expand his capacity for attachment to other figures—the father, other adults, or selected older siblings. At the same time that his attachment to his mother grows in depth and strength, his general capacity for attachment grows in breadth. One interesting feature of such attachments is that they can be to figures who take no part in the routine care of the infant, and who therefore do not satisfy his creature-comfort needs but merely play with him and interact with him, smiling and vocalizing.

In final summary, I have made three points. First, the baby is active and takes initiative in forming attachments. Second, attachment does not necessarily imply close physical contact, for it can be maintained through a middle distance through distance receptors. Third, the baby becomes attached not only to the mother-figure who feeds him and satisfies his creature-comfort needs, but also to others who merely play with him and interact with him.

Taken together, these three points offer support to Bowlby's (1958) challenge to the so-called secondary-drive theory of attachment which assumes that the infant becomes attached to a mother-figure solely because she is instrumental in the satisfaction of his primary visceral drives.

SUPPLEMENTARY READINGS

Ainsworth, M. D. The development of infant-mother interaction among the Ganda. In B. M. Foss (Ed.), *Determinants of infant behaviour II.* New York: Wiley, 1963. Pp. 67–112.

Ambrose, J. A. The concept of a critical period for the development of social responsiveness. In B. M. Foss (Ed.), *Determinants of infant behaviour II.* New York: Wiley, 1963. Pp. 201–225.

Caldwell, B. M. Infant interaction in monomatic and polymatic families. *Amer. J. Orthopsychiat.,* 1963, 33, 653–664.

Schaffer, H. R. Some issues for research in the study of attachment behaviour. In B. M. Foss (Ed.), *Determinants of infant behaviour II.* New York: Wiley, 1963. Pp. 179–199.

Schaffer, H. R., & Emerson, P. E. The development of social attachments in infancy. *Monogr. Soc. Res. Child Develpm.,* 1964, 29, No. 3.

Walters, R. H., & Parke, R. D. The role of the distance receptors in the development of social responsiveness. In L. P. Lipsitt & C. C. Spiker (Eds.), *Advances in child development and behavior.* Vol. 2. New York: Academic Press, 1965. Pp. 59–96.

the use

of social reinforcement

in conditioning smiling*

YVONNE BRACKBILL

[One of the great myths that has gradually been destroyed by modern psychology is the philosophical position advanced by Locke that the infant is a "blank slate on which nature writes." The more we observe and study the human infant, the more we are impressed with how effectively he "operates on" conditions in his environment to obtain satisfaction for what we infer are his psychological needs. The infant is an active participant in selecting his own experiences, and influences others in his environment as well as being influenced by them.

Smiling is a common and universal form of communication across all cultures. The "true" smile usually appears in the human infant somewhere between the fourth and eighth weeks of life—presumably on the basis of the development of an innate releasing mechanism, since congenitally blind children also display the smiling response at about the same age. What social conditions influence the growth of this response in the human personality? Why do some children smile so frequently, while others seldom smile? Why do some individuals smile under what appear to be inappropriate conditions? The findings of Dr. Brackbill, of the University of Denver, take us several steps closer to answering these questions. She has shown that the instrumental conditioning model is appropriate for understanding the social conditions under which infants begin to show wide individual differences in the frequency with which they smile. In other words, the infant learns to smile to the extent that his smiling is reinforced by positive contacts with significant others in his environment. The higher rate of smiling during extinction for the infants who were intermittently rather than regularly reinforced during conditioning may explain the more frequent smiling of infants reared by "casual" mothers as contrasted with apprehensive "good" mothers. Some incidental data of this study also suggest that crying and smiling are functionally equivalent instrumental responses that the infant may use in order to get parental attention and that the one he comes to use more often is determined by the relative frequency with which the mother reinforces each.]

* From Y. Brackbill. Extinction of the smiling response in infants as a function of reinforcement schedule. *Child Development*, 1958, 29, 114–124. (With permission.)

Scheduling of reinforcement has been investigated extensively in relation to the conditioning of non-social responses. The results of these studies indicate in general that a schedule by which reinforcement follows every response is less effective in maintaining performance of that response during extinction than is a schedule by which reinforcement follows only some of those responses (Jenkins & Stanley, 1950).

This investigation attempts to extend the study of frequency and patterning of reinforcement to the area of social learning and to cortically immature subjects. The purpose of the research is to evaluate the relative efficacy of intermittent as opposed to regular reinforcement upon frequency of smiling in infants.

METHOD

SUBJECTS

Eight normal infants between the ages of three and one-half to four and one-half months served as Ss. Six were males and two, females. All came from intact middle-class homes located within 10 miles of Stanford University.

This particular age range was selected with the consideration in mind that the subject had to be old enough to remain awake for a short time period after feeding, yet not old enough to respond differentially to "mother" vs. "others." Other requirements for selection of Ss were that the infant not cry so often, with such intensity, and for so long a time that sessions too frequently had to be terminated; that the infant show an operant rate of at least two responses per five-minute interval; and that the infant be able to maintain a supine position for intervals of five minutes without persistent struggling to regain the prone position.

EXPERIMENTAL PROCEDURE

Subjects were assigned to the regularly reinforced group or to the intermittently reinforced group in consecutive order of their acceptance as subjects. The first S was assigned to the intermittently reinforced group; the second, to the regularly reinforced group; and so on.

For both groups, the experimental procedure was divided into three periods: in the first or *operant* period E stood motionless and expressionless at a distance of approximately 15 inches above S, and observed him for eight five-minute intervals to ascertain the operant level of smiling. (Interjudge reliability concerning the decision as to whether a smile had or had not occurred was found to be 0.975, using total N of 970 such decisions in the formula: twice number of agreements/total number of judgments.) In the second or *conditioning* period, reinforcement was meted out, contingent upon S's smile. Specifically, as soon as S smiled, E smiled in return, began to speak softly to S, and picked the baby up. The child was then held, jostled, patted, and talked to for 30 seconds before being replaced in the crib. (The reinforcement procedure was recorded on 12 feet of 8mm film.) In the third or *extinction* period, the procedure was again observation without reinforcement, as in the operant period. During extinction, Ss were observed for thirteen five-minute intervals.

During all three periods, the basic interval for determining rate of responding was five minutes, and in the discussion to follow, *five-minute interval* refers to one such five-minute period of continuous experimentation. The term *rate of response* refers to number of responses per interval. Also, the terms *response* and *trial* are used interchangeably.

The two groups of Ss differed in respect to the reinforcement schedules used within the conditioning period. The regularly reinforced group was maintained on a regular reinforcement schedule during the entire conditioning period. The intermittently reinforced group was maintained on a regular reinforcement schedule until each S had responded at maximum rate(*see below*) for ten consecutive intervals. Immediately after the tenth interval at maximum rate, Ss were switched to a 2:1 randomized variable ratio reinforcement schedule for a total of 60 responses (hence, 30 reinforcements), then to a 3:1 schedule for a total of 45 responses, and finally to a 4:1 schedule for a total of 20 responses. Separate randomizations were used for each subject.

Maximum rate of response was determined as follows. Forty-five seconds were required for the administration of each reinforcement plus its accompanying events. (Five seconds were required for picking S up; thirty seconds for reinforcement; five seconds for putting S down; and five seconds for recording.) Therefore, no more than six responses could occur and be reinforced during any five-minute interval. *Maximum rate of response* was defined as no fewer than four responses per five-minute interval. That particular trial or response that marked the beginning of maximum response rate is referred to as *criterion*.

Because of intersubject variation in the total number of responses to criterion and because it was desired that the experimental results be a function only of reinforcement schedule and not a function of reinforcement schedule plus number of emitted responses, it was necessary to match the two groups for total number of trials during the conditioning period. The method of matching—like the method of group assignment mentioned earlier—was an individual one and was done in consecutive order of admission to the experiment. Specifically, S No. 2 (regularly reinforced) was matched for total number of trials with S No. 1 (intermittently reinforced); S No. 4 was matched with S No. 3, and so on.

GENERAL PROCEDURE

Each infant was placed on a schedule of social deprivation during the entire experimental period. Social deprivation was defined as minimized social and body contact between the infant and any other person in its environment except for E. In effect, this meant that the parents agreed to forego all social and body contacts that were not absolutely necessary for the infant's well being during the time their child was being used as an experimental subject.

Experimental conditions were kept as standard as possible for all sessions and for all Ss. E always wore a white laboratory coat. The subject was placed in a supine position near the open side of his crib; placement of the crib was the same for all sessions. The source and intensity of light were standardized. At the beginning of each session, the baby was freshly diapered, had just eaten to satiety, and had been awake for from 15 to 20 minutes. During the operant and extinction periods, at the end of every five-minute interval, S was placed in a prone position to rest for 3 minutes. While he was being turned over and during the rest period, E was not in his field of vision. During the experimental period, S was frequently required to work without rest for two successive intervals, but not for longer.

Typically, there were two to three sessions per day. The length of any one session ranged between 10 and 60 minutes and was a function of the length of time S remained awake. The total number of days spent in experimentation with any one S ranged from eight to sixteen. Because of the very large amount of time per day required for travel, experimentation, and maintenance of rapport with the mother, only one S was run at a time.

RESULTS AND DISCUSSION

PERFORMANCE DURING THE OPERANT PERIOD

The two groups did not differ significantly in either mean operant response rate ($t = 0.29$, 7 df) or in the total number of responses emitted ($t = 0.06$, 3 df). For this reason, scores have been combined for graphic presentation (Fig. 1).

Figure 1 also includes a cumulative plot for a ninth control S, who was run, without reinforcement, for an extended operant period of 19 intervals—or roughly three times the length of the operant period for experimental Ss. These data provide some evidence against the possible explanation that the mere presence of E—and not the reinforcement—is conducive to increased rate of response.

PERFORMANCE DURING THE CONDITIONING PERIOD

For the conditioning period, the total number of responses for each group was 927, while the mean number of responses per subject was 231.7. Mean group response rates are presented in Table 1; the most noticeable features of these data are the abrupt changes in mean response rate and in variability following criterion.

Relative stability in response rate is also reflected in Table 2, which contains the individual post-criterion response rates emitted under the regular reinforcement schedule. For the intermittently reinforced Ss, per-

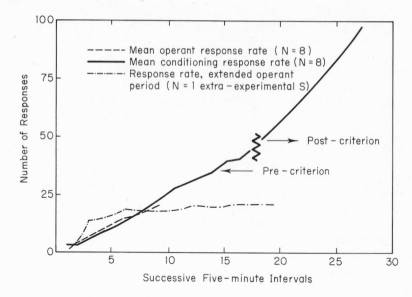

Figure 1—Cumulative curves showing rate of smiling response during operant and conditioning periods.

centages are based on the ten intervals of regular reinforcement following criterion. For regularly reinforced Ss, percentages are based on the total number of intervals following criterion. For this table it can be seen that although most Ss habitually worked at one rate of response, there were interindividual differences in the habitual or "preferred" rate.

One interesting bit of incidental data concerning performance during conditioning was provided by S No. 8, who gave a clear demonstration of the type of response that Skinner has termed "superstitious behavior" (1948). The behavioral sequence was as follows. During reinforcement, S kept his left fist doubled in his mouth. When placed in the crib, he withdrew

Table 1—Group Response Rates During Operant and Conditioning Periods

	OPERANT RESPONSE RATE		PRECEDING CRITERION		Conditioning response rate			
					FOR FIRST 10 INTERVALS FOLLOWING CRITERION		FOR 11TH–22ND INTERVALS FOLLOWING CRITERION	
Group	Mean	σ	Mean	σ	Mean	σ	Mean	σ
Regular reinforcement	2.11	.63	2.70	.47	5.15	.06	5.15	.06
Intermittent reinforcement	2.88	.36	2.43	.44	5.10	.06	6.32*	1.11*
							8.12†	.64†
							13.00‡	1.51‡
Combined groups	2.49	.64	2.56	.50	5.12	.06		

* 2:1 schedule.
† 3:1 schedule.
‡ 4:1 schedule.

Table 2—Individual Response Rates During Conditioning: Percentage of Five-minute Intervals Following Criterion During Which S Emitted Four, Five, or Six Responses Per Interval

Group	NO. OF RESPONSES PER INTERVAL		
	4	5	6
Intermittent reinforcement			
S No. 1	10%	80%	10%
S No. 3	20	70	10
S No. 5	30	10	60
S No. 7	20	40	40
Regular reinforcement			
S No. 2	4.2	58.3	37.5
S No. 4	13.3	62.2	24.4
S No. 6	80.6	19.4	0
S No. 8	0	22.7	77.3

the fist from the mouth and kept it suspended in air for the short time it took him to smile. Then, simultaneously with the beginning of the reinforcement procedure, the fist was promptly reinserted into the mouth, the head turned 90 degrees to the left and the body musculature stiffened. The onset of this stereotyped response coincided with criterion (56th trial). It disappeared for three days during a period of illness (90th through 118th trials), reappeared in full strength with recovery (119th trial), gradually diminished in intensity, and finally disappeared altogether by the 162nd trial.

PERFORMANCE DURING THE EXTINCTION PERIOD

Two statistical tests were applied to the extinction data in order to test the hypothesis that the intermittently reinforced group would be more resistant to extinction. First, McNemar's pseudo three-way analysis of variance (1955), with blocks representing the experimental variable of reinforcement schedule, was applied to the response frequencies over all thirteen extinction intervals. (Summing across thirteen intervals, the total number of responses for the intermittent reinforcement group was 331; for the regular reinforcement group, 130.) The resulting F of 17.14, with 1 and 6 df, is significant beyond the 0.01 level. Second, a mean difference was computed, using the four matched-pair differences in total number of responses during the last six extinction intervals. (In this case, total number of responses for the intermittent and regular reinforcement groups were 113 and 3, respectively.) For 3 df the resulting t of 6.77 is significant beyond the 0.005 level by a one-tailed test.

A noncumulative plot of mean response rates during extinction (Fig. 2), shows some interesting periods of sharp rise in response rate for both groups—interval No. 5 for the regularly reinforced group and intervals No. 7 and No. 8 for the intermittently reinforced group. The point of occurrence of this recovery did not appear to be a function of the length of preceding rest period. For example, in the intermittently reinforced

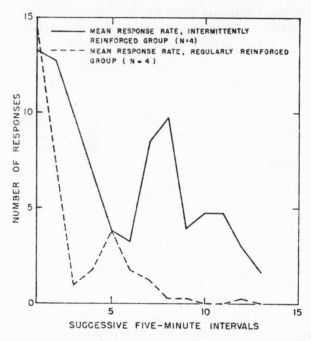

Figure 2—Noncumulative curves showing mean rates of smiling response during extinction period.

group two Ss recovered after a rest of several hours, i.e., at the beginning of a new session, while the other two Ss recovered after a rest of only three minutes, i.e., during a session.

Figure 2 also indicates that every member of the regularly reinforced group extinguished not to his previous, operant rate of response, but to a zero rate. Coincident with the beginning of zero response rate was a conspicuous behavioral change: S would no longer fixate the discriminative stimulus (E's face). Instead, the child turned his head to one side and kept it there—an occurrence, it might be pointed out, that was in distinct contrast to his persistent fixation during conditioning. When this occurred, immediately preceding the last extinction interval, E propped S's head with rolled blankets or other material, making it impossible for the infant to turn his head to the left or right, more than a few degrees. The "refusal" to fixate persisted even under these conditions; S's eyes then turned toward the ceiling. When withdrawal of reinforcement is conceptualized as frustration-producing (Adelman and Maatsch, 1955), this persistent nonfixation may be regarded as an avoidance response that is elicited by continued frustration of the original, approach response, is incompatible with the original response, and is reinforced by repeated escape from the frustrating situation.

THE RELATION OF PROTEST TO SMILING

As mentioned above, one of the criteria for subject selection was the frequency and intensity of crying. This criterion necessitated continued notations of such behavior during the operant period and first few conditioning intervals. Even after this point, however, E continued to record the incidence of crying, although at the time there seemed to be no particular reason for continuing to collect these data.

In recording crying, one of three types of notation was made, according to the intensity of response. In decreasing order of intensity, the notations were: (a) crying; (b) intense fussing: the same type of muscular and vocal involvement as in crying, but tears appeared only at the corners of eyes and did not course down the cheeks or temples; (c) fussing: considerable muscular and vocal involvement, but less than for the first two categories; no appearance of tears. In the presentation of data and discussions to follow, all three categories will be considered as one and referred to by the generic response term, *protest*.

It should be noted that interjudge reliability in discriminating protest from nonprotest was not determined. However, as indirect support for the objectivity or reproducibility of these data, the following points should be considered. First, this was a simple discrimination to make; even responses of lowest intensity represented a marked contrast to the infants' typical placid behavior. Second, the total numbers of protests for the two groups were approximately equal. Third, the orderliness of these data was not observed until the end of the experiment, when the results were actually tabulated.

The data concerning protest show that during the conditioning period, as the rate of smiling increased the rate of protest decreased—or more properly, protest extinguished with the counter-conditioning of smiling. Specifically, a perfect rank order correlation was found between the number of trials taken to extinguish the protest response and the number of trials to condition the smiling response to criterion. Similarly, during the extinction period, as the rate of smiling decreased the rate of protest increased. In this case, the rank order correlation (tau) between rates of emission of the two responses from the beginning of extinction up to the first five-minute interval at zero rate of response is -0.69, significant at the 0.02 level by a two-tailed test. (First appearance of zero response rate was chosen as the reference point for the extinction period because it was the closest counterpart of the reference point for the conditioning period, i.e., criterion or the beginning of maximum response rate.)

To express these results more generally, for all Ss combined, the ratio of protests to smiles during the conditioning period was 1:6.5 preceding criterion, and 1:276 following criterion. During the extinction period, the corresponding ratios were 1:40.5 (preceding the first interval at zero rate of response) and 1:2.7 (during and following the first interval at zero rate of response).

One might conceivably object to any interpretation of these correlations on the grounds that they merely reflect the fact that two such responses are mutually exclusive behaviors: an infant cannot protest and smile at the same time. Although this overlooks the important point that all Ss *changed* in the frequency of emission of both responses, there is a direct answer to such an objection in that the precriterion data show, for every S, both part and whole intervals during which neither protest nor smiling occurred at all.

There is a good deal of similarity between these findings and results obtained in a study by Estes (1950), in which rats were reinforced for one instrumental response while a previously reinforced, competing response was being extinguished. Estes states that, "These results seem to lend some support to the view that the 'learning' of any one response involves the concurrent extinction of others and that the amount of initial acceleration in a learning curve is determined to an important extent by the relative initial strengths of all behaviors which may occur in the experimental situation" (Estes, 1950, p. 204).

In the present case, the most important determiner of rate of acquisition of the smiling response appears to be the initial strength of the functionally equivalent, competing protest response. The main difference between procedures is that in Estes' study, the conflicting response was both reinforced and extinguished as an integral part of the experiment, while in the present study only the extinction of the competing response took place during the experiment. Its establishment had already taken place prior to the beginning of the experiment—most probably via material reinforcement. In other words, it would appear that smiling and crying are both instrumental responses that a young infant is able to use to get parental attention. However, by the time the infant is four months old, crying as an attention-getter is a much stronger response in his repertoire than is smiling, probably for two reasons. First of all, crying, unlike smiling, is both a visual and *auditory* stimulus; an infant with good lungs can reach a parent several rooms removed. Secondly, crying is a much more compelling stimulus to action than is smiling. No action *has* to be taken when the baby smiles, but when he cries, he must be attended to because he is in danger (or so thinks the mother of one or two children), or because he is making too much racket (thinks the mother of five or six children).

It is interesting to note in this connection that crying had apparently been purposely extinguished in one of the Ss prior to the experiment. This infant never once cried during operant and conditioning periods, nor was the first conditioning session over before she began to show clear indications that learning was taking place. The experimenter asked the mother if she could offer any explanation for this unusual behavior. The mother said that the child, her second, had at first had a particularly strong disposition to cry on any and all occasions. The problem was fast becoming a serious one for the family so that the mother consulted her pediatrician about it. The pediatrician advised the mother that the baby was "wrapping her around its little finger," and that from that point on, when the child began to cry, the mother was to set her kitchen timer for 10 minutes and not to go to the baby or pick her up before the end of that period. As a consequence of this procedure within a short time the crying had extinguished altogether.

SUMMARY

This investigation was concerned with the instrumental conditioning of a social response (smiling) in infants. Ss were two groups of four infants each; one group was maintained on a conditioning schedule of intermittent reinforcement and the other on a schedule of regular reinforcement. The reinforcement consisted of social and body contact between E and S. The dependent variable was relative resistance to extinction of smiling as a function of the different reinforcement schedules.

Results confirmed the expectation that intermittent reinforcement is superior in maintaining continued performance of a response during extinction. Further, a negative correlation was found between rates of emission of protest and smiling responses during both conditioning and extinction periods. It is proposed that rate of acquisition and extinction is not only a function of reinforcement schedule but also of initial discrepancy in habit strength between competing responses.

SUPPLEMENTARY READINGS

Ambrose, J. A. The concept of a critical period for the development of social responsiveness. In B. M. Foss (Ed.), *Determinants of infant behaviour II.* New York: Wiley, 1963. Pp. 201–225.

Freedman, D. G. Inheritance of behavior in infants. *Science,* 1963, 140, 196–198.

Freedman, D. G. Smiling in blind infants and the issue of innate vs. acquired. *J. child Psychol. Psychiat.,* 1964, 5, 171–184.

Gewirtz, J. L. The course of infant smiling in four child-rearing environments in Israel. In B. M. Foss (Ed.), *Determinants of infant behaviour III.* New York: Wiley, in press.

Walters, R. H., & Parke, R. D. The role of the distance receptors in the development of social responsiveness. In L. P. Lipsitt & C. C. Spiker (Eds.), *Advances in child development and behavior.* Vol. 2. New York: Academic Press, 1965. Pp. 59–96.

Wolff, P. Observations on the early development of smiling. In B. M. Foss (Ed.), *Determinants of infant behaviour II.* New York: Wiley, 1963. Pp. 113–134; discussion, pp. 160–167.

objective observations

of personality development

in early infancy*

H. RUDOLPH SCHAFFER

[The "principle of complementarity" is the physicist's concession to the need for two very different conceptual models to explain and predict different features of the same physical phenomenon. For example, a wave theory is useful for explaining and predicting certain properties of the transmission of light, whereas a quantum theory is necessary for handling the other variables of the spectrum. It now seems probable that the principle of complementarity may also apply to psychological development. Some perceptual sensitivities and behavioral skills appear to emerge in the growing infant and child as gradual, continuous functions. Others appear abruptly—from not being present at all to completely functional forms over an extremely short interval of time. Dr. Schaffer, senior clinical psychologist at the Royal Hospital for Sick Children in Glasgow, suggests in the following report that there may be a quantal shift in the infant's psychological life at about seven months of age. His conclusions are based on extensive observations of the responses of infants who have been briefly hospitalized during the first year of life. When returned to their homes, infants under seven months of age displayed a characteristic syndrome of behaviors that Dr. Schaffer has inferred are due to "perceptual deprivation." Infants over seven months of age, who have had the same experience, show clear evidence of a very different syndrome, called "maternal deprivation." Dr. Schaffer views these findings as a possible avenue from which scientists may some day be able to ". . . isolate the factors responsible for delay or impairment of development from one stage to the next."]

Genetic explanations of personality tend generally to attach a great deal of importance to the period of infancy, and mainly through the stimulus of psychoanalysis, much has been written about this stage of development.

* From H. R. Schaffer. Objective observations of personality development in early infancy. *British Journal of Medical Psychology*, 1958, 31, 174–183. (With permission.)

Direct empirical studies of infants, other than those concerned with the establishment of age norms for certain peripheral functions, are few, and our knowledge of psychological events taking place at this time is for the most part extremely scanty.

The main reason for the lack of data based on direct observation appears to arise from the difficulty of *access* to personality functioning at this age. In the present paper, however, we shall be concerned with a situation which does appear to lend itself to the isolation and study of some of the problems in this area. The observations arose in the course of a project on the effects of maternal deprivation in the first year of life as seen in a sample of hospitalized infants. Here we shall not, however, be concerned with the hospitalization issue as such, but rather with the light which it throws on the personality structure of the infants undergoing this experience. The empirical data of this project are presented in detail elsewhere (Schaffer & Callender, 1958), and only those parts of the study which are relevant to the present theme will therefore be mentioned here.

SUBJECTS AND METHODS

The subjects were 76 infants, admitted to a children's hospital for a variety of medical and surgical reasons. Their age at admission ranged from 3 to 51 weeks, and the length of hospitalization varied from 4 to 49 days, with a mean of 15.4 days. Most of the infants were in for periods between 1 and 2 weeks, and the median of the distribution is 12 days. Approximately half the children were visited daily, while of the rest only 6 were not visited at all. Developmental quotients were taken at the end of the hospitalization period with the Cattell Infant Intelligence Scale, and a range of 72 to 141 was obtained, with a mean of 100.7. All cases of possible brain injury and all premature and marasmic infants were excluded from the study.

The observations were focused on three points of the infants' experience—the period immediately following admission to hospital, the period immediately preceding discharge, and the period subsequent to return home. In order to rule out the effects of the illness factor on behaviour, only "cold" cases were studied during the initial period, i.e., infants not affected by such factors as pain or fever and who were therefore not subjectively sick. There were 25 such cases on whom observations took place for the initial period of the first 3 days. The whole sample of 76 cases was studied for the last 3 days in hospital, by which time it could be assumed that the behavioural effects of their illnesses had disappeared for all babies.

Observation in the hospital took place in the context of a fixed daily observation session, and the data, collected under a standardized procedure, were subsequently analyzed according to an Infant Behaviour Schedule. This material is described in detail elsewhere (Schaffer & Callender, 1958).

All the infants were visited at home, always within 7 days after discharge from hospital and also subsequently, until the observer considered that all overt effects of their experience had disappeared. It is the information derived from these home visits which provides us with our point of entry for the present discussion.

THE POST-HOSPITALIZATION SYNDROMES

The main findings of this study, as shown in Table 1, is the emergence

Table 1—Post-Hospitalization Syndromes

Age in weeks at discharge from hospital	Global	Overdependent	Miscellaneous	Unchanged	Total
0– 4	—	—	—	1	1
5– 8	—	—	—	1	1
9–12	2	—	—	2	4
13–16	5	—	1	—	6
17–20	5	—	1	2	8
21–24	4	—	2	1	7
25–28	4	—	1	—	5
29–32	5	4	2	1	12
33–36	1	4	3	—	8
37–40	1	2	1	—	4
41–44	—	7	1	—	8
45–48	1	3	—	1	5
49–52	—	5	—	—	5
53–56	—	2	—	—	2
Total	28	27	12	9	76

from the information obtained in the home of two distinct syndromes, each closely associated wtih a particular age range. The cutting point is at approximately 7 months, though there is some overlap. Thus one syndrome, shown by 27 cases, is not found at all below the age of 29 weeks at discharge from hospital, while only 6 of the 28 showing the other syndrome appear above that cutting point. The characteristics of the syndromes are as follows:

The global syndrome. This pattern of behaviour was mainly shown by those under 7 months. When these infants returned home they were, according to the reports of the mothers, "strange" in their behaviour. The main feature of this "strangeness" was an *extreme preoccupation with the environment.* For hours on end sometimes the infant would crane his neck, scanning his surroundings without apparently focusing on any particular feature and letting his eyes sweep over all objects without attending to any particular one. A completely blank expression was usually observed on his face, though sometimes a bewildered or frightened look was reported. In the extreme form of this syndrome the infants were quite inactive throughout, apart from the scanning behaviour, and no vocalization was heard though one or two were reported to have cried or whimpered. When confronted with a toy the infant disregarded it.

In the less extreme instances of the syndromes the preoccupation with the environment was again the central feature, but here the infant might not be completely subdued in his general activity, or there might be some vocalization, or he might momentarily show normal interest in toys before again returning to the unfocusing inspection of his surroundings. Seven of the 28 infants in this group showed such modifications.

Reactions to other people were also changed for the duration of the syndrome, and this applies equally to the familiar mother and to complete strangers. In some cases the infants were quite unheedful of all attempts on the part of the adult to make contact with them, as they appeared to be so absorbed in the scanning of their physical surroundings. In other cases the infants kept the head averted on being stimulated (almost as though deliberately avoiding the adult). In still other instances the infants gazed "through" the adult with the same blank look that was used for the rest of the environment. Finally some infants were reported to respond to stimulation with a brief sign of interest such as a smile, usually after considerable delay, before again reverting to the scanning of the surroundings.

This pattern of behaviour was sometimes first observed in the waiting room off the ward where the mothers collected and dressed their children prior to leaving hospital, at times as the infants were carried out of the hospital into the street, and sometimes not until entry into their own home. The duration of this behaviour tended not to vary a great deal for the group as a whole—in the majority of cases it continued for the rest of the first day home, but in one or two cases it lasted only 20 or 30 minutes. In some others it continued for as long as 4 days.

Accompanying this pattern a somatic upset occurred in 16 cases. In a few instances this took the form of a feeding upset such as vomiting, but mostly it constituted a sleep disturbance, in which the infant would wake in the night crying and would not settle for several hours. In 3 instances, however, the upset took the form of excessive sleeping. In these cases the infant would fall asleep some time after discharge from hospital and continue sleeping for 1 or 2 days, waking only for feedings or even having to be wakened for them.

The somatic symptoms usually outlasted the environmental preoccupation, but if the time of disappearance of the last symptom is taken as the total length of upset on discharge from hospital, a mean of 2.96 days is found for this group. It is noteworthy that neither the total duration of upset nor the duration of the environmental preoccupation was found to be in any way dependent on any of the antecedent variables such as age, amount of visiting by the mother, or even length of hospitalization. Thus an infant hospitalized for 4 weeks would show the same phenomena for the same length of time as an infant hospitalized for 4 days (the minimum hospitalization in this group).

This pattern of behaviour has been named the 'global syndrome' because, first, it appears to be related to the total environment rather than any specific aspect of it (such as the mother, as in the following syndrome). Secondly it tends to involve the total organism, and somatic as well as psychological functions. Finally because it is believed to be indicative of a global, undifferentiated, syncretic stage of development. The first two points are, as we have seen, based on the observed data, whereas the last is a hypothetical point which will be elaborated later on.

The overdependent syndrome. This pattern of behaviour, commonly found after the age of 7 months, presents a very different picture. The central feature here is overdependence on the mother after return from hospital, and it is thus of the same order as that described for older, preschool children under similar circumstances (Prugh *et al.,* 1953). The overdependence was shown in such ways as excessive crying when left alone by the mother, an almost continual clinging and a wish to be nursed by her, and a fear of strangers. Familiar figures, such as father or siblings, were sometimes regarded with suspicion. A somatic upset was found in 15 of these 27 cases, taking the form in most cases of a sleep disturbance. The mean duration of total upset is 14.69 days for this group, but there is a wide range (1–80 days).

Among the 27 cases in this group are 7 who showed a variation on this theme. These cases developed the global syndrome after discharge, and it was not till this had run its usual course that overdependence manifested itself. There are no obvious reasons for the difference between this subgroup and the other 20 cases. Their age at discharge ranged from 29 to 47 weeks, and length of hospitalization, amount of visiting, and other relevant variables are not correlated with it.

While the above two groups may be taken to represent the main syndromes of post-hospitalization behaviour as seen by us, some infants were found who did not fit into this classification. There are two subsidiary groups.

Miscellaneous. The 12 infants in this group showed only such isolated symptoms as a sleep upset, or fear of strangers, or a decrease in their general activity. There were also 2 cases, both approximately 8 months old, who were overdependent on the mother before hospitalization and where after return home the only behavioural change observed referred to a marked lessening of the overdependence.

Unchanged. Nine infants showed no reaction at all on return home, no change in their behaviour having taken place as compared with the pre-hospitalization picture. Four of these cases are the youngest of the sample, and here our observations on these infants suggested that visual awareness of the environment had not apparently sufficiently developed for them to have shown the global syndrome.

In general, apart from the 4 youngest in the "Unchanged" group, it is difficult to see why the cases falling into the last two groups do not conform to the pattern set by the first two groups. None of the obvious antecedent variables can be adduced to account for the difference, and the behaviour of these infants in hospital was in all respects comparable to that of the others. In the remainder of this paper attention is paid, in the main, to the two main syndromes, for it is hoped that through an examination of the main sample we shall eventually arrive at an understanding of the reasons why some cases fail to conform.

COGNITIVE STRUCTURE AND THE DEVELOPMENT OF OBJECT RELATIONS

The main conclusion arising from the material presented above is that the same experience of hospitalization is reacted to very differently, according to the age of the subject. After 7 months the disturbance caused thereby is in the field of object relations, with particular reference to the relationship with the mother, and is thus continuous with that found generally in the pre-school age group. Before 7 months on the other hand, the disturbance is of a very different nature and appears to be related to the total environment rather than to any one aspect of it. The reason for this difference is to be found, we can assume, in certain developmental changes taking place soon after the middle of the first year, and the possible nature of these changes deserves to be examined in relation to the two different syndromes described.

The most useful way of approaching this problem appears to be through a consideration of the type of *cognitive structure* to be found in infancy, i.e., the way in which perceptions are organized and related to each other and to their external sources by the individual. This is a function about which Piaget (1937, 1950) has written most clearly, and his theoretical propositions will therefore be examined in relation to the material presented above. In the early months, according to Piaget, there is present a state of "adualism," an undifferentiated absolute in which there is no distinction between the self and the environment. Objects at this stage do not exist in their own right but only as functional elements serving the infant's own activities, and are assimilated in terms of the present need of the individual. Moreover, once the object is out of the perceptual field the infant behaves as though it has ceased to exist. He is thus said to experience only a series of fleeting images which may be recognized but which have no continuity, permanence, or substance. There is consequently no conservation of the object, and the world is centred in the child's own activity. There is, furthermore, no appreciation of the own body as one element amongst others, and it is thus not recognized as being part of a world of distinct, stable objects.

It is only in the second half of the first year that Piaget finds a new type of cognitive structure developing. It is only then that objects become detached from action and the first fundamental step taken in attributing to them a separate, independent existence. Though the individual must yet pass through many stages to reach the adult form of cognitive organization, the most important step may be said to take place at this point, for it is now that the body of the subject becomes appreciated as distinct from the environment and relationships to external objects can therefore be established.

This formulation has definite implications for studies on separation from the mother during the first year of life. As Anthony (1956) has put it: "It is only after the child has made a permanent object that he can lose it, search for it, or form a permanent relationship with it," and from the theoretical formulations of Piaget he went on to deduce that the infant's reaction to separation from the mother must before 7 months lack the quality of separation feelings at a later stage. This is strikingly borne out by the present investigation, even in respect of the actual age stated. If we examine the initial reaction to hospitalization in the group of "cold" cases, we find a very different pattern before 7 months from that occurring after this age. In the earlier period fretting as a protest to the separation does not occur, and apart from a sharp drop in the amount of vocalization (believed to be related to the general reduction of social stimulation) the infant's responsiveness to the strangers now caring for him is maintained at normal levels. After 7 months, however, one tends to find the classical separation picture, shown in particular by fretting, strong negative responses to the strange hospital staff, and clinging to the mother during her visits. This has been detailed elsewhere (Schaffer & Callender, 1958) and supports the conclusion suggested by the home data that separation from the mother becomes an experience manifestly and immediately affecting object relations only after the middle of the first year. (This does not, of course, prove that deficient mothering before this time cannot affect the development of the child in such a way as to influence later object-relationships.)

There is, however, another point suggested by the data, namely one referring to the speed with which the new development takes place. While these conclusions are admittedly based on cross sectional material, it does seem remarkable that there is relatively little overlap between the two main syndromes, as though the new function comes into play quite suddenly around 7 months. What is more, there are indications that the intensity of the separation reaction does not increase gradually with age once this milestone has been reached, but that the upset is as great at the very beginning of the new phase of development as it is later on. There are three possible indices of the degree of upset caused by the separation.

(a) *The length of the fretting period.* Basing conclusions on the "cold" cases, a considerable range (1–22 days) was found. But as many of the infants were still fretting at discharge (including the 37 week old infant who was still fretting after 22 days), no precise statistics can be given. It is notable, however, that the very youngest in this group continued fretting for periods as long as those found at the older end of the age range. Thus of the 2 youngest, both 30 weeks at admission, 1 was still fretting when discharged on the 5th day, while the other ceased fretting only after the 6th day. One may compare such figures with those given for older children —for instance Robertson & Bowlby (1952) mention periods ranging from a few hours to 7 or 8 days in the case of children 18–24 months old, and for a group of children aged between 1 and 4 years at the time of separation, Bowlby (1953) describes the fretting period as lasting from 1 or 2 days to 17 days.

(b) *The intensity of fretting at the beginning of hospitalization.* All infants were rated on a five-point rating scale for the amount of crying observed during each daily observation session. Studying the "cold" cases again, it was found that the average rating for the first 3 days in hospital shows fretting to be as intense in the 7 and 8 months old infants as it is in those aged 11 and 12 months. Thus if the average ratings for the 7 infants aged between 29 and 40 weeks at admission are compared with those for the 8 infants aged between 41 and 52 weeks, mean figures of 3.68 and 3.55 respectively are obtained. It would appear that at the very beginning of the new developmental phase protest at separation is as vigorous as it is for the oldest subjects of our sample.

(c) *Duration of upset after return home.* Examining the group of 27 infants who were overdependent after discharge from hospital, a range of 1–80 days was found for this index. Again the very youngest infants in the group were no less affected than the oldest. Dividing the age range at 41 weeks, the mean duration of upset for those above and those below .can be compared. The outcome is, however, influenced by the fact that in the older group 3 of the longest hospitalizations are found, whereas only 1 case of similar length is present in the younger group. As length of upset after discharge has in the literature generally been found to be directly related to the length of hospitalization (except in the case of those under 7 months), we felt justified in excluding these 4 cases for the sake of uniformity and comparability of the two groups. In this way a mean of 10.18 days was obtained for the 29–40 week old group, while the mean for 41–52 week old group was 11.83 days. The difference between these means is not statistically significant.

It is implied by these figures that the intensity of separation upset is considerable at the very beginning of the new phase. Once an infant has reached the developmental stage where he becomes capable of showing a separation reaction his upset is likely to be as great then as it will be later on. The age range within which we have carried out comparisons is rather narrow, however, and the findings need therefore to be confirmed for a wider age range. Clinical impressions suggest in fact that the 7 or 8 months old infant frets at separation and clings after reunion just as intensely as the 2 or 3 year old child, and if this can be confirmed by systematic studies a *stepwise* development is thus indicated.

It seems justified to assume that the intensity of the separation reaction is an indication of the strength of the child's libidinal attachment to the mother (as a special and unique person, rather than as a "mothering agent"), and we thus have evidence that the "common sense" view of *gradual* development of the child-mother relationship in the course of the first year or so is a mistaken notion. The more likely hypothesis is that *permanent object relations (to specific persons) do not become possible until the cognitive structure of the child has developed to the point where others are seen as separate beings clearly distinguished from the self and from one another, that this occurs somewhere around 7 months, and that when this development does take place the attachment to a specific mother-*

figure is established relatively speedily and appears at once in its full intensity.

It is significant that a similar theory of two-stage development emerges from a study of dogs by Scott (1958), who found that despite the close association of the puppy with its mother during the first weeks of life, primarily social relations cannot be established until certain maturational changes have taken place. These occur after 3 weeks of age, and it is only during the critical period for the process of socialization which begins at this time that the puppy becomes able to establish permanent social relations. From another point of view Bowlby in a recent paper (1958) on the development of the child's tie to the mother, has also postulated a two-stage process of social development in infancy, according to which various instinctual components of the child's "attachment behavior" to the mother do not become integrated and focused on the one specific individual till the second half of the first year.

ANALYSIS OF THE GLOBAL SYNDROME

If we accept the view that an object relation to a specific person does not become established before approximately 7 months, it is understandable that in the earlier period hospitalization does not produce a manifest and immediate disturbance in the child-mother relationship. The problem arises, however, of why the global syndrome appeared after discharge from hospital, and what light it can shed on the processes underlying it.

In attempting to analyse this syndrome, we may take as our starting point the fact that this pattern of behaviour was elicited when the infants were moved from hospital to home. There are two possible explanations which must first be examined.

The first is that the global syndrome is the usual reaction at this age to all geographical displacement. All the mothers agreed, however, that the global pattern was quite unusual when compared with the infant's customary reaction to new surroundings, that it differed from the latter in its duration and intensity, in the inaccessibility of the infant, and in such other features as the unfocusing character of the environmental inspection and the quietness accompanying it. To check on this point the observations on the "cold" cases at the time of their admission to hospital were examined, but no trace of any pattern of behaviour resembling the global syndrome could be found.

The second possible explanation is that the global syndrome is specific to the move from hospital to home. One may wonder, for instance, whether it is related to the return to a previously familiar environment, or to renewed handling by the mother. But this explanation too can be ruled out, because it was found possible to elicit the global pattern actually within the hospital by merely moving the infant after a certain period of hospitalization from his customary place in the ward to another room. This is a development which has certain important implications to which we shall return later. In the present context, however, it indicates that the global syndrome is related to any change of environment following a period of hospitalization.

We may now ask how this effect could be brought about by hospitalization. The hypothesis suggested is that the operative factor in the infant's experience in hospital is one that can best be described as *perceptual monotony,* and that this factor is an essential precondition to the development of the global syndrome.

Close observation of the infants on whom this project is based vividly emphasized the considerable monotony of their perceptual experience. One may mention in this connexion the following four aspects in particular.

(*a*) The child's illness necessitated his confinement to bed, so that he generally remained in the same environment for the whole period of hospitalization.

(*b*) The physical nature of the environment was often of a highly constrictive kind. The smallest infants were kept in solid-sided metal cots, others were isolated in cubicles or kept in side-rooms from which they could see or hear little of what went on outside, and only those in the busy general ward had the opportunity for greater perceptual variety.

(*c*) Even those in the general ward, however, were usually prevented by the limited perceptual-motor equipment of infants in the first 12 months from making use of the greater amount of potential stimulation available. None of these infants could walk, few could stand, many could not sit up, and their sensory range tended in consequence to be limited.

(*d*) Due to factor (*c*), infants are generally very much at the mercy of others for the richness of their perceptual experience, yet in terms of human stimulation the experience of these infants was particularly deficient. Apart from the visiting hour (during which few mothers ever picked up their babies), the infants were rarely handled apart from the handling necessary for the relief of physical needs. Moreover, the feeding situation tended to be of very much shorter duration than in the home.

As a consequence of these four factors, there was considerable restriction in perceptual variation compared with the usual experience of infants cared for at home. While some variation in severity of perceptual monotony occurred from individual to individual, inspection of the data showed that the older infants (who later developed the overdependent syndrome) were also considerably affected, and that the more severe degrees of perceptual restriction occur among them as well as in the younger infants. If perceptual monotony is then to be regarded as an essential precondition for the formation of the global syndrome, it is necessary to account for the fact that it appears to play this part only within a certain age range. To do this, we must return to our discussion of the cognitive structure to be found in the first year, and advance the hypothesis, elaborated below, that *it is the interaction of perceptual monotony with the early type of cognitive structure which leads to the occurrence of the global syndrome.*

Given the early type of cognitive structure as described by Piaget (with its state of adualism, in which the self is merged with the environment in one functional whole), one may say that under normal conditions of child care the infant experiences a degree of environmental variation which will keep his perceptual field in a relatively "fluid" state, for both the external boundaries and the internal characteristics of the field will fluctuate as a result of such stimulation.

Under condition of perceptual monotony, however, the rate of change is drastically reduced, and when an infant in whom the self has not yet emerged as a differentiated unit is confronted for a lengthy period with the same relatively static surroundings, the natural tendency to merge with the environment is thereby emphasized. It is as though under these conditions the perceptual field would tend to become "set." The boundaries of the field can be thought of as remaining constant for the relevant period, and the amount of variation in internal structure will be reduced more or less in proportion to the degree of sensory restriction.

The process of "setting" which we have postulated becomes apparent when the infant is taken out of the accustomed environment and put into another. The "set" perceptual field is disrupted and disintegrates, and such disintegration may be experienced as a stress situation—hence the somatic upset found in many of the infants. A new perceptual field must now be formed, and the infant's acute awareness of new sensations is reflected in the intense concentration with which he regards his new surroundings. It is this environmental preoccupation which forms the core of the global syndrome, and the various behavioral features of the syndrome may be said to stem from the disintegration of a perceptual field in which a "setting" process has taken place and which must now be replaced by a new field.

That sensory deprivation even in adults can result in certain drastic changes of behaviour has been reported by several writers (e.g., Wexler, Mendelson, Leiderman & Solomon, 1958). Judging from the published results, however, it seems unlikely that the experimental conditions used bring about a state comparable to that described for the present sample. In the former case the self is a highly differentiated, independent unit, the dissolution of which could only be affected by the most extreme conditions. In young infants on the other hand, the global pattern can be regarded as an exaggeration of a process occurring all the time, a process of fusion of self and environment, and the complete restructuring of the perceptual field whenever the latter changes.

AN EXPERIMENTAL APPROACH

It was mentioned earlier that it was possible to elicit the global pattern by moving the infant from his accustomed place in the hospital ward to another room. A first consequence of this was that we could now observe the child's reaction rather than being forced to rely on parents' descriptions.

A second consequence was that it became possible to set up an experimental situation in which the global pattern is treated as the experimental variable and an attempt could be made to find the antecedent conditions which elicit it or produce modifications in its appearance. It should now be possible to test the operation of the perceptual monotony factor by ascertaining whether an infant who does receive sufficient stimulation after his admission to hospital will fail to manifest the global syndrome. Moreover (returning to the exceptions in Table 1 who showed miscellaneous or no reactions), it is through the use of this experimental situation that we might arrive at the reasons for the failure of some cases to develop the expected pattern of behaviour.

Although a start has only recently been made on the application of this experimental approach, and no systematic information is therefore yet available, one preliminary finding is perhaps relevant here. In some of the infants older than 7 months, and who showed the older pattern in that they fretted on admission and were overdependent after return home, the global syndrome was nevertheless elicited when this experiment was carried out during their hospitalization. In some cases fluctuations were observed in this respect, in that the pattern appeared on some days and not on others. One possible explanation of this phenomenon which may be tentatively advanced is that we are confronted here with an instance of *regression*. Just as bladder control or feeding habits regress under the stress of hospitalization in older children, so the function with which we are concerned here may well regress in the same situation. With this possibility in mind the original data summarized in Table 1 may be examined. Of the 6 infants aged above 29 weeks at reunion but showing the global syndrome, 2 fretted when first separated. There is both a statistical and a theoretical association between fretting and the overdependent syndrome, and it may be justified to regard the occurrence of the global syndrome in these 2 cases as well, as a regressive phenomenon. The same may apply to those 7 cases which showed the global syndrome and then became overdependent, though why both post-hospitalization patterns were shown by some, and only one pattern by others is not clear.

If this tentative finding can be confirmed, the possibility arises that the early type of cognitive structure may provide a reference point for regression and fixation, and may consequently be of psychopathological significance. It would then become important to attempt to isolate the factors responsible for delay or impairment of development from one stage to the next.

CONCLUSION

Two main syndromes, each associated with a particular age range, have emerged from this study of the effects of hospitalization in infancy. In this respect the findings parallel those of Spitz (1945, 1946), and they may be said to suggest the existence of two developmental stages—a *global stage* and a *differentiated stage*. The latter, centering around the differentiation of self and environment, appears to be essentially continuous with the adult form, and only when it has been attained can object relations to specific persons be established. The global stage, on the other hand, is of a very different order, and certain life experiences may thus have quite a distinct meaning according to the developmental phase of the individual. The present study, for instance, suggests that the crucial factor in hospitalization at the differentiated stage is *maternal deprivation,* whereas at the global stage it is *perceptual deprivation.*

Stages of development in personality organization during infancy have been postulated by a number of different writers, and though terminology varies the overlap in meaning is considerable. One may in this connexion mention Melanie Klein's (1952) stages of part objects and of whole objects, Hartmann's (1952) stages of the need satisfying object and of object constancy, and Hoffer's (1952) stages of the object as part of the *milieu interne* and of the psychological object. Certain similarities exist between all these formulations and the two stages outlined here, but whereas the former have arisen from reconstructive data, the present approach is based on direct empirical observations. The controversy, for instance, about the age of change-over from one phase to the next has probably been due to the indirect nature of the evidence, but while some have postulated this important milestone of development to occur as early as 3 months and others as late as 10 months, the material presented in this paper suggests 7 months as the approximate time of graduation from one stage to the next.

The hospitalization situation has thus provided us with a means of "diagnosing" the developmental phase of infants, and in the context of this situation it is possible to proceed to investigate the problems and to test the hypotheses formulated in this paper. These concern, among other things, the further characteristics of the two developmental phases, especially of the earlier one; the manner of passing from one stage to the other and the conditions, both organismic and environmental, for doing so; and the possibility of regression taking place once the later stage has been attained. Moreover, the stages may be regarded as a framework within which one can evaluate the varying effects of environmental influences on personality development and against which the growth of social relations may be assessed.

SUPPLEMENTARY READINGS

Ainsworth, M. D. Effects of maternal deprivation: A review of findings in the context of research strategy and controversy. *Public health papers, no. 14.* Geneva: World Health Organization, 1962.

Bowlby, J., Robertson, J., & Rosenbluth, D. A two-year-old goes to hospital. *Psychoanalyt. Stud. Child,* 1952, 7, 82–94.

Freedman, D. G. The infant's fear of strangers and the flight response. *J. child Psychol. Psychiat.,* 1961, 4, 242–248.

Schaffer, H. R., & Emerson, P. E. The development of social attachments in infancy. *Monogr. Soc. Res. Child Develpm.,* 1964, No. 3.

the striving for autonomy and regressive object relationships*

BENJAMIN SPOCK

[Dr. Benjamin Spock is undoubtedly the most influential pediatrician in the American culture. It has been estimated that one out of three mothers has been influenced during the last two decades, either directly or indirectly, by the down-to-earth advice on child rearing presented in *The Pocket Book of Baby and Child Care*. His book is packed with practical advice on almost every conceivable problem, both medical and psychological, related to child rearing. Because of the popularity of his book on advice to mothers, Dr. Spock's scientific contributions to a better understanding of infant behavior and development may be less well known, but as the following report shows, he is as wise a scholar as he is an effective pediatric counselor. His explanation of why the bottle fed infant rejects drinking from the cup for a longer period of time than the breast fed infant is an ingenious weaving together of many seemingly unrelated observations. The infant's strivings for autonomy without giving up all the pleasurable aspects of dependency may well be the general model for the child's relationship to his parents at all developmental levels.]

I was never able to explain why almost all breast fed babies can be weaned easily to the cup between six and nine months of age, whereas so many bottle fed babies at the same age become increasingly devoted to the bottle and suspicious of the cup.

Most breast feeding mothers will report spontaneously, when the baby is about six months old, that his interest in the breast is decreasing markedly. Instead of nursing eagerly for a quarter to a half hour, he now releases the nipple after a very few minutes, smiles and coos at his mother, has to be reminded to resume nursing several times during each feeding.

---

* From B. Spock. The striving for autonomy and regressive object relationships. *Psychoanalytic study of the child*, 1963, 18, 361–364. (With permission.)

(If the mother wishes the breast feeding to continue for a number of months longer, she can persuade the baby to keep at it.)

Some bottle fed babies at this age will show the same decreasing interest in the bottle, and will take increasing amounts of milk from the cup. Others, particularly those who are allowed to hold and drink their own bottles in bed, become more and more enamored of the bottle at seven, eight, and nine months of age, watching it all the while they are taking their solid food, reaching for it eagerly when it is offered, fondling it and murmuring to it as they drain it to the last drop. These babies, even though they were formerly willing to take sips of milk from the cup at five or six months, are now apt to turn against it with suspicion. They clamp their mouths shut when the cup is offered and knock it away. A few of them permit the mother to pour the milk into their open mouths but, grinning, let it all run onto their bibs. Yet, interestingly enough, they remain quite willing to take water and fruit juices from the cup. It is only milk-in-cup which they will not tolerate.

There are other phenomena which mothers begin to describe at the age of six or seven months, when most infants learn to sit and to handle objects deliberately. Diapering becomes increasingly difficult because a baby who has learned to sit will indignantly refuse to lie down, even for a minute. Though he formerly took his solid food cuddled in his mother's arm, he may now elbow his way out of this dependent position and demand to be fed sitting up. He may also want to take his bottle sitting up, though this involves craning his neck in a position that looks uncomfortable. Most babies now want to hold into their own bottles, and some of them will impatiently jerk the bottle sideways while drinking, to get the mother's hand off it. These all seem evidences of the baby's drive to outgrow the symbiotic enveloped relationship at this age.

A mother who responds to her infant's cues, seeing that he no longer wants her to cuddle him or hold his bottle, may form the habit of laying him in his crib, where he drinks his bottle and puts himself to sleep in one convenient process. Once this pattern has been established, it usually becomes obligatory until the child is between eighteen months and two years; he cannot possibly fall asleep unless he has his bottle.

In our current Child Rearing Study the dozen babies who were breast fed for six months all showed the usual early readiness for weaning. They were weaned easily to the cup as soon as their mothers were able to take the cue. Some of the mothers needed prompting from their counselors, however. As for the mothers who were bottle feeding, they were advised not to give the bottle in bed and they followed this advice. The only babies who remained on bottles into the second year were those whose mothers were unwilling to wean—most often for fear that not enough milk would be consumed from the cup alone.

As a result of observations of weaning behavior I came to the hypothesis many years ago that perhaps the most influential factor in readiness for weaning is not the lessening of the baby's need to suck but his urge to outgrow the totally dependent and closely cuddled relationship with his mother. That is to say, he gives up the breast—or the bottle which his mother holds—because he cannot use it apart from her. When he takes a bottle to bed, he can have his sucking pleasure and his autonomy too. This hypothesis, however, did not explain the *increasing* infatuation with the independently held bottle after six months. When our staff was discussing the attachment of a majority of the children in our study to such soft objects as a favorite blanket, diaper, woolly toy, to fondle at regressive times of day (half of the children sucked their thumbs at the same time) our attention was called to the papers of Winnicott (1953) and Stevenson (1954) on transitional objects. Winnicott used the word "transitional" to signify an object that lies, developmentally speaking, between the auto-erotically sucked thumb and the ordinary toy which has its own reality to start with and is presented as a gift. Stevenson chose not to include the nursing bottle or the pacifier (dummy) among the variety of objects she discussed, on the basis that their use is comparatively brief.

But the reading of those two articles stimulated another train of thought in my mind: The nursing bottle to which many a baby becomes increasingly attached after six months is similar in several respects to the soft transitional object. The child's greatest need for either is at bedtime, when he is both regressed and separated from his mother. His dependence on either may be almost desperate. He is suspicious of any substitution. The bottle continues to provide the oral component of the earlier symbiotic feeding situation. The soft transitional object continues to provide the tactile pleasure which the baby used to gain, between three and six months, by gently stroking his mother's skin or clothing, or the blanket in which he was wrapped, while he was being fed in her arms. (This may be a vestige of the instinct, seen for instance in puppies and kittens, to massage the mother's udders during nursing, presumably to aid the release of milk.)

This analogy suggested to me that the soft transitional object and the bottle in bed each acquires its very special cathexis because the child's developing nature is now obliging him to detach himself from his mother. Soft object or bottle allows him to have within his own control, at times of regression, an object which affords some of the autoerotic pleasure and the reassurance that he formerly secured through the symbiotic relationship, without his having to relinquish his newly won autonomy.

This concept would explain the increasing attachment to bottle and suspicion of cup after six months which causes so many weaning problems. It would substantiate my belief that weaning from bottle as well as from breast, when properly conducted, is not a deprivation imposed on babies but a step in maturation which they ask to take. It would give a rational basis for the impression I have always had that the sucking of thumb or pacifier satisfies the sucking need up to about six months of age but thereafter satisfies the need for a comforter at times of regression. (Thus the thumb sucking itself acquires a transitional as well as an autoerotic meaning.) And finally this concept suggests that the precious soft object, or the precious bottle after six months, could be called transitional in more than one sense: Its appeal is both autoerotic and as an object. It is cathected at the time of sharpest transition from symbiosis to early autonomy. It is reminiscent of pleasurable aspects of mother, it is a substitute for mother, but it is also a defense against re-envelopment by mother. It invites regression but also limits it.

Incidentally, the suspiciousnes with which a child rejects any susbtitute for the favorite soft object and rejects milk-in-cup as a substitute for milk-in-bottle is reminiscent of the specificity of the process of "imprinting": Very young animals, such as newly hatched ducklings, become exclusively attached to the mother (or whatever other creature is present at the crucial period) and fearful of strange members of the species as well as of other species (Scott, 1962). The analogy with imprinting suggests the original biological importance of the exclusivity of all such attachments. It suggests the reason why in the human infant the phenomena of stranger anxiety, separation anxiety, depression as a result of maternal deprivation, all appear in the middle of the first year.

SUPPLEMENTARY READINGS

Beller, E. K. Dependency and autonomous achievement striving related to orality and anality in early childhood. *Child Develpm.*, 1957, 28, 287–315.

Hartup, W. W. Dependence and independence. In H. W. Stevenson (Ed.), *Child psychology: The sixty-second yearbook of the national society for study of education, part I.* Chicago: Univer. Chicago Press, 1963. Pp. 333–363.

Heinstein, M. I. Behavioral correlates of breast-bottle regimes under varying parent-infant relationships. *Monogr. Soc. Res. Child Develpm.*, 1963, 28, No. 4.

Schaefer, E. S., & Bayley, N. Maternal behavior, child behavior, and their intercorrelations from infancy through adolescence. *Monogr. Soc. Res. Child Develpm.*, 1963, 28, No. 3.

Sears, R. R., Whiting, J. W. M., Nowlis, V., & Sears, P. S. Some child-rearing antecedents of aggression and dependency in young children. *Genet. Psychol. Monogr.*, 1953, 47, 135–203.

Walters, R. H., & Parke, R. D. Social motivation, dependency, and susceptibility to social influence. In L. Berkowitz (Ed.), *Advances in experimental social psychology I.* New York: Academic Press, 1964. Pp. 231–276.

references

Abraham, K. Contributions to the theory of the anal character. *Selected Papers.* London: Institute of Psychoanalysis and Hogarth Press, 1927. (a)
—————— The first pregenital stage of the libido. *Selected Papers.* London: Institute of Psychoanalysis and Hogarth Press, 1927. (b)
—————— The narcissistic evaluation of excretory processes in dream and neuroses. *Selected Papers.* London: Institute of Psychoanalysis and Hogarth Press, 1927. (c)
—————— A short study of the development of the libido. *Selected Papers.* London: Institute of Psychoanalysis and Hogarth Press, 1927. (d)
Adelman, H. M., & Maatsch, J. L. Resistance to extinction as a function of the type of response elicited by frustration. *J. exp. Psychol.,* 1955, 50, 61–65.
Ahrens, R. Z. *Exp. Angew. Psychol.,* 1954, 2, 412.
Ainsworth, Mary D. The effects of maternal deprivation: A review of findings in the context of research strategy and controversy. *Public Health Papers, No. 14.* Geneva: World Health Organization, 1962.
Ainsworth, Mary D., & Bowlby, J. Research strategy in the study of mother-child separation. *Courrier,* 1954, 4, 105–131.
Alexander, F. The influence of psychologic factors upon gastro-intestinal disturbances: A symposium. I. General principles, objectives, and preliminary results. *Psychoanalyt. Quart.,* 1934, 3, 501.
Alm, I. The long term prognosis for prematurely born children: A follow-up study of 999 premature boys born in wedlock and 1002 controls. *Acta Paediat.,* 1953, 42 (suppl. 94).
Alpert, A., Neubauer, P. B., & Weil, A. P. Unusual variations in drive endowment. *Psychoanalyt. Study Child,* 1956, 11, 125–163.
Ammons, R. B., & Ammons, H. S. *Full-range picture vocabulary test.* Missoula, Montana: Psychological Test Specialists, 1948.
Anderson, A. R. & Moore, O. K. Autotelic folk-models. *Technical Report No. 8,* New Haven: Office of Naval Research, Group Psychology Branch, 1959.
Anderson, J. E. The limitations of infant and preschool tests in the measurement of intelligence. *J. Psychol.,* 1939, 8, 351–379.
Anderson, L. D. The predictive value of infancy tests in relation to intelligence at five years. *Child Develpm.,* 1939, 10, 203–212.
Anthony, E. J. The significance of Jean Piaget for child psychiatry. *Brit. J. Med. Psychol.,* 1956, 29, 20–34.
Antrobus, Judith. Unpublished doctoral dissertation, Columbia Univer., 1962.
Arkhangel'skaia, N. A. *Tesizy i ref. dokl. XVI soveshch. po probl. vyssh. nervn. deiat. (Proceedings of the 16th Conference on Problems in Higher Nervous Activity),* USSR Academy of Sciences Press, 1949.
Arkhangel'skaia, N. A., & Poiurovskaia, E. Ia. In the collection *Opyt izucheniia reguliatsii fiziologicheskikh funktsii (Studying the regulation of physiological functions),* USSR Academy of Sciences Press, 1949.

Arsenian, J. M. Young children in an insecure situation. *J. abnorm. soc. Psychol.*, 1943, 38, 225–249.

Aserinsky, E., & Kleitman, N. Two types of ocular motility occurring in sleep. *J. appl. Physiol.*, 1955, 8, 1–10. (a)

Aserinsky, E., & Kleitman, N. A motility cycle in sleeping infants as manifested by ocular and gross body activity. *J. appl. Physiol.*, 1955, 8, 11–18. (b)

Babkin, P. S. Head turning reflexes in infants. *Zh. Nevropat. Psychiat.*, 1953, 53, 692–696.

Bach, I. *Pupillenlehre*. Berlin, 1908.

Bakwin, H. Thumbsucking and fingersucking in children. *J. Pediatr.*, 1948, 32, 99.

Bandura, A. Social learning through imitation. In M. R. Jones (Ed.), *Nebraska symposium on motivation*. Lincoln: Univer. Nebraska Press, 1962. Pp. 211–269.

Bandura, A., & Huston, Aletha C. Identification as a process of incidental learning. *J. abnorm. soc. Psychol.*, 1961, 63, 311–318.

Barnett, P. H., Hines, E. A., Jr., Schirger, A., & Gage, R. P. Blood pressure and vascular reactivity to the cold pressor test: Restudy of 207 subjects 27 years later. *J. Amer. Med. Ass.*, 1963, 183, 845–848.

Barrett, H. E., & Koch, H. L. The effect of nursery-school training upon the mental-test performance of a group of orphanage children. *J. genet. Psychol.*, 1930, 37, 102–122.

Bartel, M. *Ztschr. f. Augenheilkunde*, 1904, 12, 638.

———— Ueber welkürliche und unwelkürliche Augenbewegungen. *Klin. Monatsbl. f. Augen.*, 1914, 53, 58.

Bartoshuk, A. K. Human neonatal cardiac acceleration to sound: Habituation and dishabituation. *Percept. mot. Skills*, 1962, 15, 15–27. (a)

———— Response decrement with repeated elicitation of human neonatal cardiac acceleration to sound. *J. comp. physiol. Psychol.*, 1962, 55, 9–13. (b)

Bateman, W. G. The language status of three children at the same age. *Ped. Sem.*, 1916, 23, 211–241.

Batson, W. H. Acquisition of skill. *Psychol. Rev.*, 1916, 21.

Bayley, Nancy. Mental growth during the first three years: An experimental study of sixty-one children by repeated tests. *Genet. Psychol. Monogr.*, 1933, 14, 1–92.

———— Mental growth in young children. *Yearb. nat. Soc. Stud. Educ.*, 1940, 39, 11–47. (a)

———— Factors influencing the growth of intelligence in young children. *Yearb. nat. Soc. Stud. Educ.*, 1940, 39, 49–79. (b)

———— Consistency and variability in the growth of intelligence from birth to eighteen years. *J. genet. Psychol.*, 1949, 75, 165–196.

———— Development and maturation. In H. Nelson (Ed.), *Theoretical foundations of psychology*. New York: D. Van Nostrand, 1951. Pp. 145–149.

———— Some increasing parent-child similarities during the growth of children. *J. educ. Psychol.*, 1954, 45, 1–21.

———— On the growth of intelligence. *Amer. Psychologist*, 1955, 10, 805–818.

———— A new look at the curve of intelligence. In *Proceedings of 1956 Invitational Conference on Testing Problems*. Princeton: Educational Testing Service, 1956.

———— Data on the growth of intelligence between 16 and 21 years as measured by the Wechsler-Bellevue Scale. *J. genet. Psychol.*, 1957, 90, 3–15.

Bayley, Nancy, & Jones, H. E. Environmental correlates of mental and motor development: A cumulative study from infancy to six years. *Child Develpm.,* 1937, 4, 329–341.

Bayley, Nancy, & Oden, M. H. The maintenance of intellectual ability in gifted adults. *J. Geront.,* 1955, 10, 91–107.

Bekhterev, V. M., & Shchelovanov, N. M. *Novoe v refleksologii i fiziologii nervnoi sistemy. (Recent advances in reflexology and physiology of the nervous system.)* 1925.

Benedek, T. Dominant ideas and their relation to morbid cravings. *Int. J. Psychoanal.,* 1936, 17.

Berger, R. Tonus of extrinsic laryngeal muscles during sleep and dreaming. *Science,* 1961, 134, 840.

Bergler, E., & Eidelberg, L. Der Mammakomplex des Mannes. (The mother complex in man.) *Internationale Zeitschrift fuer Psychoanalyse,* 1933, 19.

Bergman, P., & Escalona, S. K. Unusual sensitivities in very young children. *The psychoanalytic study of the child,* 1949, 4, 333–352.

Bernard, H. M. Studies in the retina. *Quart. J. Microsc. Sci.,* Part I–V, 1900–1903, 43–46.

Bickel. Experimentelle Untersuchungen ueber die Magensaftsekretion beim Menschen. (Experimental investigation on gastric juice secretion in the human.) *Deutsche med. Wochenschrift,* 1906, 33, 1323.

Binet, A. La Perception des longueurs et des nombres chez quelques enfants. (The perception of lengths and numbers in some infants.) *Rev. Philos.,* 1890, 2, 68.

———— *Sovremennyye idei o detyakh. (Modern ideas about children.)* Moscow, 1910.

Biriukov, D. A. *Novosti Meditsiny,* 1949, 14, 27.

———— *Zh. vyssh. nerv. Deiatel.,* 1952, 2, 518.

Birns, B., Blank, M., Bridger, W. H., & Escalona, S. K. Behavioral inhibition in neonates produced by auditory stimuli. *Child Develpm.,* 1965, 36, 639–645.

Birukow, G. Purkinjesches Phaenomen and Farbensehen beim Grasfrosch (Rana temporaria L.). (Purkinje phenomenon and color vision in the grass frog [Rana temporaria L.].) *Z. vergl. Physiol.,* 1940, 27, 41.

———— Die Entwicklung des Tages-und des Daemmerungssehens im Auge des Grasfrosches. (The development and twilight vision in the eye of the grassfrog.) *Z. vergl. Physiol.,* 1949, 31, 322.

———— Zentrale und periphere Bedingungen des Farben- und Helligkeitssehens beim Grasfrosch. (Central and peripheral conditions of color and brightness vision in the grass frog.) *Verh. dtsch. Zool.,* 1948, 242.

Bishop, E. J. The strychnine spike as a physiological indicator of cortical maturity in the postnatal rabbit. *EEG clin. Neurophysiol.,* 1950, 2, 309–315.

Bjoerk, A., & Karpe, G. The electroretinogram. V. The electroretinogram in retinitis pigmentosa. *Acta Ophthalm.,* 1951, 29, 361.

Blackhurst, D. J. The value of play apparatus for developing motor control in preschool children. Iowa City: State Univer. Iowa Library, 1927. (Abstract *28th Yearb. nat. Soc. Stud. Educ.,* 1929, 472–473.)

Blanton, M. G. The behavior of the human infant during the first thirty days of life. *Psychol. Rev.,* 1917, 24, 456–483.

Blum, G. S. *The Blacky Pictures.* Psychol. Corp., 1950.

Boehm, F. Anthropophagy, its forms and motives. *Int. J. Psychoanal.,* 1935, 16.

Boldireff. Ueber die Bildung kuenstlicher Bedingungsreflexe und ihre Eigenschaften (Verwandlung von Lauten, Geruechen und Licht in kuenstliche Erreger der Speichelabsonderung). (On the formation of artificial conditioned reflexes and their characteristics [the modification of sounds, smells and light into artificial stimuli for saliva secretion].) *Arbeiten d. Gesellsch. russ. Aerzte.*, April 1905. Reviewed in the *Biophysikal. Centralbl.*, Bd. 1, 1905, 211.

——— Die Hervorrufung kuenstlich bedingter (psychischer) Reflexe und ihre Eigenschaften. Zweite Mitteilung (Verwandlung lokaler Erkaeltung der Haut in den Erreger der Speichelabsonderung). (The induction of artificially conditioned (psychic) reflexes and their characteristics. Second contribution [Modification of localized skin cooling into the stimulus for saliva secretion].) *Arbeiten d. Gesellsch. russ. Aerzte.*, January 1906. Reviewed in the *Biophysikal. Centralbl.* Bd. II, 1906, 52.

Bowlby, J. Some pathological processes set in train by early mother-child separation. *J. ment. Sci.*, 1953, 99, 265–272.

——— The nature of the child's tie to his mother. *Internat. J. Psychoanal.*, 1958, 39, 1–34.

Brackbill, Yvonne. Extinction of the smiling response in infants as a function of reinforcement schedule. *Child Develpm.*, 1958, 29, 115–124.

——— Research and clinical work with children. In R. A. Bauer (Ed.), *Some views on Soviet Psychology*. Washington, D.C.: Amer. Psychol. Ass., 1962, 99–164.

Braine, M. D. S. The ontogeny of certain logical operations: Piaget's formulation examined by nonverbal methods. *Psychol. Monogr.*, 1959, 73, (Whole No. 475).

Brazier, M. A. B. *The electrical activity of the nervous system*. New York: Macmillan, 1951.

Bridger, W. H. Sensory habituation and discrimination in the human neonate. *Amer. J. Psychiat.*, 1961, 117, 991–996.

Bronfenbrenner, U. Freudian theories of identification and their derivatives. *Child Develpm.*, 1960, 31, 15–40.

Bronshtein, A. I. *Leningradskii Med. Zh.*, 1928, 22, No. 3.

Bronshtein, A. I., Antonova, T. G., Kamenstkaya, A. G., Luppova, N. N., & Sytova, V. A. On the development of the functions of analysers in infants and some animals at the early stage of ontogenesis. In *Problemy evolyutaii fisiolgicheskikh funkisii. (Problems of evolution of physiological functions.)* Office of Technical Services Report No. 60-61066, 1960, Pp. 106–116. (Translation obtainable from the United States Department of Commerce, Office of Technical Services.) Moscow-Leningrad: Academiya Nauk USSR, 1958.

Brown, D. G. Sex-role preference in young children. *Psychol. Monogr.*, 1956, 70, No. 421.

——— Sex-role development in a changing culture. *Psychol. Bull.*, 1958, 55, 232–242.

Brown, D. G., & Caffrey, J. G. *California Auding Test*. (Rev. ed.) Redwood City: Council on Auding Research, 1952.

Bühler, Charlotte. *The first year of life,* translated by Pearl Greenberg & Rowena Ripin. New York: John Day, 1930.

Bühler, Charlotte, & Hetzer, Hildegard. *Testing children's development from birth to school age,* translated by H. Beaumont. New York: Farrar & Rinehart, 1935.

Bumke, Q. *Die Pupillenstoerungen. (Pupillary disturbances.)* Jena, 1904.

Burlingham, D. T. *Twins*. London: Imago, 1951.

Burtt, H. E. An experimental study of early childhood memory. *J. genet. Psychol.*, 1932, 40, 287–295.

———— A further study of early childhood memory. *J. genet. Psychol.*, 1937, 50, 187–192.

Butler, R. A., & Harlow, H. F. Discrimination learning and learning sets to visual exploration incentives. *J. gen. Psychol.*, 1957, 57, 257–264.

Bystroletova, G. N. Obrazovanie u novorozhdennykh detei uslovnogo refleksa na vremia v sviazi s sutochnym ritmom kormleniia. (The formation in neonates of a conditioned reflex to time in connection with daily feeding rhythm.) *Zhurnal vysshei nervnoi Deiatelnosti,* 1954, 4, 601–609.

Caffrey, J. Auding. *Rev. educ. Res.*, 1955, 25, 121–138.

Cameron, J. The development of the retina in amphibia. *J. Anat. a. Physiol.*, 1905, 35, 471.

———— Further researches on the rods and cones of vertebrate retinae. *J. Anat. a. Physiol.*, 1912, 46, 45.

Canby, H. S., Opdyke, J. B., & Gillu, Margaret. *High school English.* New York: Macmillan, 1934.

Canestrini, S. Uber das Sinnesleben des Neugeborenen (nach physiologischen Experimenten). (On the sensory life of the newborn [according to physiological experiments].) *Gesamtgebiete Neurol. Psychiat.*, 1913, 5, 1–104.

Cantor, G. N. Responses of infants and children to complex and novel stimulation. In L. P. Lipsitt & C. C. Spiker (Eds.), *Advances in child development and behavior.* New York: Academic Press, 1963. Pp. 1–30.

Carmichael, L. The development of behavior in vertebrates experimentally removed from the influence of external stimulation. *Psychol. Rev.*, 1926, 33, 51–58.

———— *Manual of child psychology.* (2nd ed.) New York: Wiley, 1954.

Carr, V. S. The social and emotional changes in a group of children of high intelligence during a program of increased educational stimulation. Unpublished master's thesis, Univer. of Iowa, 1938.

Catalano, F. L., & McCarthy, Dorothea. Infant speech as a possible predictor of later intelligence. *J. Psychol.*, 1954, 38, 203.

Cattell, Psyche. *The measurement of intelligence of infants and young children.* New York: Psychol. Corporation, 1940.

Cavanaugh, Maxine C., Cohen, I., Dunphy, D., Ringwall, E. A., & Goldberg, I. D. Prediction from the Cattell Infant Scale. *J. consult. Psychol.*, 1957, 21, 33–37.

Charles, D. C. Ability and accomplishment of persons earlier judged mentally deficient. *Genet. Psychol. Monogr.*, 1953, 47, 3–71.

Chechulin, S. I. *Arkh. biol. Nauk.*, 1923, 23, 143.

Chesnokova, A. P. Dynamism of higher nervous activity in puppies during their individual development. *Zh. vys. nerv. Deiat.*, 1951, 1, 555–565.

Chievitz, J. H. Die Area und Fovea centralis retinae beim menschlichen Foetus. (The area and fovea centralis retinae in the human fetus.) *Internat. Mschr. Anat. Physiol.*, 1887, 4, 201.

Chomsky, N. *Syntactic structures.* Mouton, 1957.

———— Explanatory models in linguistics. Mass. Inst. Tech., 1961.

Cochran, W. G., & Cox, Gertrude M. *Experimental designs.* New York: Wiley, 1950.

Coghill, G. E. *Anatomy and the problem of behavior.* Cambridge: Cambridge Univer. Press, 1929.

Conel, J. L. *The postnatal development of the human cerebral cortex.* Vol. I.

The cortex of the newborn. Cambridge, Mass.: Harvard Univer. Press, 1939.

────── *The postnatal development of the human cerebral cortex. Vol.* II. *The cortex of the one-month infant.* Cambridge, Mass.: Harvard Univer. Press, 1941.

────── *The postnatal development of the human cerebral cortex.* Vol. III. *The cortex of the three-month infant.* Cambridge, Mass.: Harvard Univer. Press, 1947.

────── *The postnatal development of the human cerebral cortex.* Vol. IV. *The cortex of the six-month infant.* Cambridge, Mass.: Harvard Univer. Press, 1951.

────── Histologic development of the cerebral cortex. In *The biology of mental health and disease.* New York: Hoeber, 1952.

Crowell, D. H., Yasaka, E. K., & Crowell, D. C. Infant stabilimeter. *Child Develpm.,* 1964, 35, 525–532.

Dann, M., Levine, S. Z., & New, E. The development of prematurely born children with birth weights or minimal postnatal weights of 100 grams or less. *Pediatrics,* 1958, 22, 1037.

Darrow, C. W., & Heath, L. L. Reaction tendencies relating to personality. In K. S. Lashley (Ed.), *Studies in the dynamics of behavior.* Chicago: Univer. Chicago Press, 1932.

Dashkovskaia, V. S. The first conditioned responses in newborns under normal and pathologic conditions. *Zh. vys. nerv. Deiat.,* 1953, 3, 247–259.

Dearborn, W. F., & Rothney, J. W. M. *Predicting the child's development.* Cambridge: Sci-Art, 1941.

Dearborn, W. F., Rothney, J. W. M., & Shuttleworth, F. K. Data on the growth of public school children from the materials of the Harvard-Growth study. *Monogr. Soc. Res. Child Develpm.,* 1938, 3 (1), 1–136.

deKleyn, A., & Schenk, V. Uber den Reflexbogen des vestibularen Augennystagmus beim Menschen. *Acta oto-laryng.,* 1931, 15, 439.

Del Castillo, J., & Vizoso, A. D. The electrical activity of embryonic nerves. *J. Physiol.,* 1953, 122, 33–34.

Dement, W. The effect of dream deprivation. *Science,* 1960, 131, 1705–1707.

────── Eye movements during sleep. *USPHS Symposium on the Oculomotor System,* April 14–15, 1961, in press.

────── Experimental dream studies. In J. Masserman (Ed.), *Science and psychoanalysis.* Vol. 7. New York: Grune & Stratton, 1964.

Dement, W., & Fisher, C. Dream deprivation and the psycho-physiology of dreaming. *Psychol. Issues Monogr.,* in preparation.

Dement, W., & Kleitman, N. Cyclic variations of EEG during sleep and their relation to eye movements, body motility, and dreaming. *EEG clin. Neurophysiol.,* 1957, 9, 673–690. (a)

────── The relation of eye movement during sleep to dream activity: An objective method for the study of dreaming. *J. exp. Psychol.,* 1957, 53, 339–346. (b)

Dement, W., & Worlpert, E. The relation of eye movement, body motility, and external stimuli to dream content. *J. exp. Psychol.,* 1958, 55, 543–553.

Denisova, M. P., & Figurin, N. L. The question of the first associated appetitional reflexes in infants. *Vopr. genet. Refleksol. Pedol. Mladen.,* 1929, 1, 81–88.

Dennett, R. H. *The healthy baby.* New York, 1912.

Dennis, W. The age at walking of children who run on all fours. *Child Develpm.*, 1934, 5, 92–93.

———— Description and classification of the responses of the newborn infants. *Psychol. Bull.*, 1954, 31, 5–22.

———— Performance of Near Eastern children on the draw-a-man test. *Child Develpm.*, 1957, 28, 427–430.

Dennis, W., & Dennis, M. G. Development under controlled environmental conditions. In W. Dennis (Ed.), *Readings in child psychology*. New York: Prentice-Hall, 1951, Pp. 104–131.

Deriabin, V. S. *Zh. vyssh. nerv. Deiatel.*, 1951, 1, 469.

Detwiler, S. R. Experimental observations upon the developing rat retina. *J. comp. Neur.*, 1932, 55, 473.

Detwiler, S. R. *Vertebrate photoreceptors*. New York: Macmillan, 1943.

Detwiler, S. R., & Laurens, H. Histogenesis of the visual cells in amblystoma. *J. comp. Neur.*, 1921, 33, 493.

Disher, D. R. The reactions of newborn infants to chemical stimuli administered nasally. In F. C. Dockeray (Ed.), *Studies of infant behavior*. Columbus: Ohio State Univer. Press, 1934. Pp. 1–52.

Dittrichová, J. Nature of sleep in young infants. *J. appl. Physiol.*, 1962, 17, 543–546.

Dittrichová, J., Janoš, O., & Papoušek, H. Characteristics of higher nervous activity in newborns. *Sb. Csl. Lekar. Kongresu* (Prague), 1962, 254–255.

Dolin, A. O. *Zh. vyssh. nerv. Diatel.*, 1951, 1, 165.

Douglas, J. W. B. Mental ability and school achievement of premature children at eight years of age. *Brit. Med. J.*, 1956, 1, 1210.

Drillien, C. M. Physical and mental handicaps in the prematurely born. *J. Obstet. Gynaec. Brit. Comm.*, 1959, 66, 721.

———— The incidence of mental and physical handicaps in school-age children of very low birth weight. *Pediatrics*, 1961, 27, 452.

Durrell, D. D., & Sullivan, Helen B. *Newsnote*. USDHEW Office of Education, Cooperative Research Program, 1958. (Reprinted from *Sch. Life*.)

Ekman, G., Goude, G., & Warren, Y. Subjective similarity in two perceptual continua. *J. exp. Psychol.*, 1961, 61, 222–227.

Ellingson, R. J. "Arousal" and evoked responses in the EEGs of newborns. *Proc. First Internat. Congr. Neurol. Sci.*, 1957, 3, 57–60.

———— Electroencephalograms of normal full-term newborns immediately after birth with observations on arousal and visual evoked responses. *EEG clin. Neurophysiol.*, 1958, 10, 31–50. (a)

———— Occipital evoked potentials in human newborns. *EEG clin. Neurophysiol.*, 1958, 10, 189. (b)

Ellingson, R. J., & Wilcott, R. C. The development of evoked responses in visual and auditory cortices of kittens. *J. Neurophysiol.*, 1960, 23, 364–375.

Engel, G. L. Homeostasis, behavioral adjustment and the concept of health and disease. In R. Grinker (Ed.), *Mid-century psychiatry*. Springfield, Ill.: Charles C. Thomas, 1953.

Engel, G. L., & Reichsman, F. Spontaneous and experimentally induced depression in an infant with a gastric fistula: A contribution to the problem of depression. *J. Amer. Psychoanal. Ass.*, 1956, 428–452.

Engen, T., & Pfaffmann, C. Absolute judgments of odor quality. *J. exp. Psychol.*, 1960, 59, 214–219.

Engen, T., Lipsitt, L. P., & Kaye, H. Olfactory responses and adaptation in the human neonate. *J. comp. physiol. Psychol.*, 1963, 56, 73–77.

Escalona, Sibylle. The use of infant tests for predictive purposes. *Bull. Menninger Clin.*, 1950, 14, 117–128.

—— *Emotional development in the first year of life, 6th conf.* New York: Macy, 1952.

Estes, W. K. Effects of competing reactions on the conditioning curve for bar pressing. *J. exp. Psychol.*, 1950, 40, 200–205.

Ezekiel, M. *Methods of correlation analysis.* New York: Wiley, 1930.

Falchi, F. Ueber die Histogenese der Retina und des Nervus opticus. (On the histogenesis of the retina and of the optical nerve.) *Graefe's Arch.*, 1888, 34, 67.

Fantz, R. L. Visual discrimination in a neonate chimpanzee. *Percept. mot. Skills*, 1958, 8, 59–66.

Fenichel, O. The dread of being eaten. *Int. J. Psychoanal.*, 1929, 10.

—— Fruehe entwicklungsstadien des ichs. (Early stages of development of the ego.) *Imago*, 1937, 23.

Ferenczi, S. Flatus as an adult prerogative. *Further contributions to the theory and technique of psychoanalysis,* London: Institute of Psychoanalysis and Hogarth Press, 1926.

Figurin, N. A., & Denisova, M. P. *Etapy razvitiia povedeniia detei v vozraste ot rozhdeniia do i goda.* (*Stages in the development of the child's behavior from birth to one year.*) Medgiz, 1949.

Fisher, C., & Dement, W. Dreaming and psychosis: Observations on the dream-sleep cycle during the course of an acute paranoid psychosis. *Bull. Phila. Assoc. Psa.*, 1961, 11, 130–132.

Fisher, Mary S. Language pattern of the preschool child. *Child Develpm. Monogr. No. 15*, 1934.

Flechsig, P. *Die Leitungsbahnen im Gehirn und Rückenmark des Menschen auf Grund Entwick ungsgeschichtlicher Untersuchungen.* Engelmass, Leipzig, 1876.

—— *Anatomie des Menschlichen Gehirns und Rückenmarks auf Myleogenetischer Grundlage.* Leipzig: Thieme, 1920.

Fleishman, E. A. A comparative study of aptitude patterns in unskilled and skilled psychomotor performances. *J. appl. Psychol.*, 1957, 41, 263–272.

Fois, A., & Low, N. *The electroencephalogram of the normal child.* Springfield, Ill.: Charles C. Thomas, 1961.

Ford, F. R. *Disease of nervous system in infancy, childhood and adolescence.* (2nd ed.) Springfield, Ill.: Charles C. Thomas, 1944.

Frank, H. Untersuchung ueber Sehgroessenkonstanz bei Kindern. (Study of size constancy in children.) *Psychol. Forsch.*, 1925, 7, No. 1-2, 137.

Fredeen, R. C. Cup feeding of newborn infants. *Pediatrics*, 1948, 2, 544.

Freeman, F. N., & Flory, C. D. Growth in intellectual ability as measured by repeated tests. *Monogr. Soc. Res. Child Develpm.*, 1937, 2, 116.

French, J. R. P., Jr., Morrison, H. W., & Levinger, G. Coercive power and forces affecting conformity. *J. abnorm. soc. Psychol.*, 1960, 61, 93–101.

French, J. R. P., Jr., & Raven, B. The bases of social power. In D. Cartwright (Ed.), *Studies in social power.* Ann Arbor, Mich.: Institute for Social Research, 1959. Pp. 150–167.

French, J. W. The description of aptitude and achievement tests in terms of rotated factors. *Psychometr. Monogr.*, 1951, No. 5.

—— The factorial invariance of pure-factor tests. *J. educ. Psychol.*, 1957, 48, 93–109.

Freud, Anna. *Infantile feeding disturbances,* Vol. II. *Psychoanalyt. Study Child,* 1946, 2, 120. (a)

———— *The ego and the mechanisms of defense*. New York: International Univ. Press, 1946. (b)

Freud, Anna, & Burlingham, Dorothy T. *Infants without families*. New York: International Univer. Press, 1944.

Freud, S. Analysis of a phobia in a five-year-old boy. *Collected Papers*. London: Institute of Psychoanalysis and Hogarth Press, 1924, 3. (a)

———— From the history of an infantile neurosis. *Collected Papers*. London: Institute of Psychoanalysis and Hogarth Press, 1924, 3 (b)

———— The passing of the Oedipus-complex. In *Collected papers*. Vol. 2. London: Hogarth Press, 1924. Pp. 269–282.

———— *Introductory lectures to psychoanalysis*. New York: Boni & Liveright, 1920.

———— *Three contributions to the theory of sex*. New York and Washington: Nervous and Mental Disease Publishing Co., 1910.

———— *The problem of anxiety*. New York: Norton, 1936. 3.

———— *Group psychology and the analysis of the ego*. London: Hogarth Press, 1948.

Fries, M. E. Psychosomatic relationships between mother and infant. *Psychosom. Med.*, 1944, 6, 159.

Fuerst, C. M. Zur Kenntnis der Histogenese und des Wachstums der Retina. (On the knowledge of the histogenesis and the growth of the retina.) *Acta Univ. Lund.*, 1904, 40, 1.

Furfey, P. H., & Muehlenbein, J. The validity of infant intelligence tests. *J. genet. Psychol.*, 1932, 40, 219–233.

Fursikov, D. S. *Russk. fiziol. Zh.*, 1921, 4, 248.

———— *Arkh. biol. Nauk.*, 1922, 22, 83.

Gallagher, J. J. Clinical judgment and the Cattell Infant Intelligence Scale. *J. consult. Psychol.*, 1953, 17, 303–305.

Garrett, H. E. A developmental theory of intelligence. *Amer. Psychologist*, 1946, 1, 372–378.

Gates, A. L., & Taylor, G. A. An experimental study of the nature of improvement resulting from practice in a mental function. *J. educ. Psychol.*, 1925, 16, 583–592.

———— An experimental study of the nature of improvement resulting from practice in a motor function. *J. educ. Psychol.*, 1926, 27, 226–236.

Geber, M. *Courrier*, 1956, 6, 17.

Geldard, F. A. *The human senses*. New York: Wiley, 1953.

Gesell, A. *The mental growth of the pre-school child*. New York: Macmillan, 1925.

———— The neonatal growth of prematurely born infants. *J. Pediatr.*, 1933, 2, 676.

———— Cinemanalysis: A method of behavior study. *J. genet. Psychol.*, 1935, 47, 3–16.

———— The ontogenesis of infant behavior. In L. Carmichael (Ed.), *Manual of child psychology*. New York: Wiley, 1954. Pp. 335–373.

———— The tonic-reflex in the human infant: Its morphogenic and clinical significance. *J. Pediatr.*, 1938, 13, 455.

———— Cinematography and the study of child development. *Amer. Nat.*, 1946, 80, 470–475.

Gesell, A., & Amatruda, Catherine S. *Developmental diagnosis*. (2nd ed.) New York: Hoeber, 1947.

Gesell, A., Castner, M., Thompson, H., & Amatruda, C. S. *Biographies of child development: The mental growth careers of eighty-four infants and children.* New York: Hoeber, 1939.

Gesell, A., & Ilg., Frances L. *Infant and child in the culture of today: The guidance of development in home and nursery school.* New York: Harper, 1943.

Gesell, A., Ilg, Frances L., & Bullis, Glenna E. *Vision, its development in infant and child.* New York: Hoeber, 1949.

Gesell, A., & Thompson, Helen. Learning and growth in identical infant twins: An experimental study by the method of co-twin control. *Genet. Psychol. Monogr.,* 1929, 6, 1–124.

Gesell, A., & Thompson, Helen. *The psychology of early growth.* New York: Macmillan, 1938.

Gesell, A., *et al. The first five years of life.* New York: Harper, 1940.

Gibson, J. J. *The perception of the visual world.* Boston: Houghton Mifflin, 1950.

Gibson, J. P. Reaction of 150 infants to cold formulas. *J. Pediatr.,* 1958, 52, 404.

Giering, H. Das Augenmass bei Schulkindern. (Eye-measure in school children.) *Ztschr. f. Psychol. u. Physiol. d. Sinnesorq.,* 1905, 39, 42.

Giesecke, M. The genesis of hand preference. *Monogr. Soc. Res. Child Develpm.,* 1936, 1, No. 5.

Glaser, K., & Eisenberg, L. Maternal deprivation. *Pediatrics,* 1956, 18, 626–642.

Goins, Jean T. Visual perceptual abilities and early reading progress. *Suppl. educ. Monogr.,* 1958, 87.

Gollin, E. S. Some research problems for developmental psychology. *Child Develpm.,* 1956, 27, 223–235.

Goodenough, Florence L. *The measurement of intelligence by drawings.* New York: World Book Co., 1926.

——— A preliminary report on the effect of nursery school training upon the intelligence test scores of young children. *27th Yearb. nat. Soc. Stud. Educ.,* 1928, 361–369.

——— *Mental testing.* New York: Rinehart, 1949. P. 609.

Goodenough, Florence L., & Brian, C. R. Certain factors underlying the acquisition of motor skill by children of preschool age. *J. exp. Psychol.,* 1929, 12, 127–155.

Gordon, H. H., Lubchenco, L. O. & Hix, I. E. Jr. Observations on the etiology of retrolental fibroplasia. *Bull. Johns Hopkins Hosp.,* 1954, 94, 34.

Gordon, M. B. The Moro embrace reflex in infancy. *Amer. J. Dis. Child,* 1929, 38, 26–34.

Graber, G. H. Die zweierlei Mechanismen der Identifizierung. (The two mechanisms of identification.) *Imago,* 1937, 23.

Grabke, H. Ueber die Groesse der Sehdinge im binokularen Sehraum bei ihrem Auftreten im Zusammenhang miteinander. (On the size of visual objects in the binocular visual space, at their occurrence in relation to each other.) *Arch. f ges Psychol.,* 1924, 47, 238.

Granit, R. *Sensory mechanisms of the retina.* Oxford, 1947.

Greene, W. A., Jr. Process in psychosomatic disorders. *Psychosom. Med.,* 1956, 18, 150.

Griffith, J. P. *The care of the baby.* Philadelphia, 1916.

Griffiths, Ruth. *The abilities of babies.* New York: McGraw-Hill, 1954.

Grossman, C. Electro-ontogenesis of cerebral activity: Forms of neonatal responses and their recurrence in epileptic discharges. *Arch. Neurol. Psychiat.,* 1955, 74, 186–202.

Guilford, J. P. *Psychometric methods.* New York: McGraw-Hill, 1936. Pp. XVI, 361–366, & 566.

———— The structure of intellect. *Psychol. Bull.,* 1956, 53, 267–293.

———— A revised structure of intellect. *Rep. psychol. Lab.,* 1957, No. 19.

———— A system of the psychomotor abilities. *Amer. J. Psychol.,* 1958, 71, 164–174.

Gundobin, N. P. *O morfologii i patologii krovi u detei.* (*Blood morphology and pathology in children.*) St. Petersburg, 1892.

Halverson, W. W. The development of prehension in infants. In R. G. Barker, J. S. Kounin, & H. F. Wright (Eds.), *Child behavior and development.* New York: McGraw-Hill, 1943. P. 40.

Hamburger, F. A. *Das Sehen in der Daemmerung.* (*Vision in twilight.*) Vienna, 1949.

Hammar, S., & Obrink, K. J. The inhibitory effect of muscular exercise on gastric secretion. *Acta. physiol. Scandinav.,* 1953, 28, 152.

Harlow, H. F. Primary affectional patterns in primates. *Amer. J. Orthopsychiat.,* 1960, 30, 676–684.

Harper, P. A., Fischer, K., & Reder, R. V. Neurological and intellectual status of prematures at three to five years of age. *J. Pediatr.,* 1959, 55, 679.

Hartmann, H. The mutual influences in the development of ego and id. *Psychoanalyt. Study Child,* 1952, 7, 9–30.

Hasama, B. I. Ob und in welcher Embryonalzeit wird die Netzhaut des Huhns fuer verschiedene Strahlen empfindlich. (Whether and at what embryonic level does the retina of the chicken become sensitive to different rays.) *Pflueger's Arch.,* 1941, 244, 337.

Hasselmeyer, E. G. Behavior patterns of premature infants. *Public Health Service No. 840.* Washington: U.S. Dept. Health, Educ., & Welf., 1961.

Hastings, H. J. The predictive value of individual items in preschool intelligence tests. Unpublished doctoral thesis, Univer. California, 1952.

Hebb, D. O. *The organization of behavior.* New York: Wiley, 1949.

———— Drives and the C. N. S. (Conceptual nervous system). *Psychol. Rev.,* 1955, 62, 243–254.

Helson, H. (Ed.) *Theoretical foundations of psychology.* New York: D. Van Nostrand, 1951. P. 170.

Hempel, W. E., Jr., & Fleishman, E. A. A factor analysis of physical proficiency and manipulative skills. *J. appl. Psychol.,* 1955, 39, 12–16.

Hernandez-Peon, R. Neurophysiological correlates of habituation and other manifestations of plastic inhibition. *EEG clin. Neurophysiol.,* 1960, Suppl. No. 13, 101–114.

Hess, J. Experiences gained in a 30-year study of prematurely born infants. *Pediatrics,* 1953, 11, 425.

Hewitt, D., & Stewart, A. The Oxford child health survey: A study of the influence of social and genetic factors on infant weight. *Hum. Biol.,* 1952, 24, 309.

Hicks, J. A. The acquisition of motor skill in young children. *Child Develpm.,* 1930, 1, 90–105. (a)

———— The acquisition of motor skill in young children: II. The influence of specific and of general practice on motor skill. *Child Develpm.,* 1930, 1, 292–297. (b)

Hildreth, Gertrude M. The effect of school environment on the Stanford-Binet tests of young children. *27th Yearb. nat. Soc. Stud. Educ.,* 1928, (1), 355–359.

Hinde, R. A. Factors governing the changes in strength of a partially inborn response. *Proc. Roy. Soc. Lond.,* 1954, 142, *Ser. B,* 306–358.

Hirsch, N. D. M. An experimental study upon three hundred school children over a six-year period. *Genet. Psychol. Monogr.,* 1930, 7, 487–548.

Hoffer, W. The mutual influences in the development of ego and id: Earliest stages. *Psychoanalyt. Study Child,* 1952, 7, 31–41.

Hofstaetter, P. R. The changing composition of "intelligence": A study in T-technique. *J. genet. Psychol.,* 1954, 85, 159–164.

Holden, W. A., and Bosse, K. K. The order of development of color perception and of color preference in the child. *Arch. Ophthalm.,* 1900, 29, 261.

Holt, L. *Diseases of infancy and childhood.* New York, 1912.

Honzik, Marjorie P. The constancy of mental test performance during the preschool period. *J. genet. Psychol.,* 1938, 52, 285–302.

—— Age changes in relationship between certain environmental variables and children's intelligence. *Yearb. nat. Soc. Stud. Educ.,* 1940, 39 (2), 185–205.

Honzik, Marjorie P., Macfarlane, Jean W., & Allen, Lucile. The stability of mental test performance between two and eighteen years. *J. exp. Educ.,* 1948, 17, 309–324.

Hooker, D. Fetal reflexes and instinctual processes. *Psychosom. Med.,* 1942, 4, 199.

Hull, C. L. Quantitative aspects of the evolution of concepts. *Psychol. Rev. Monogr.,* 1919.

Hunt, W. A. Studies of the startle pattern: I. Introduction. *J. Psychol.,* 1936, 2, 201–205. (a)

—— Studies of the startle pattern: II. Bodily behavior. *J. Psychol.,* 1936, 2, 207–213. (b)

Hunt, W. A., & Landis, C. The overt behavior pattern in startle. *J. exp. Psychol.,* 1936, 19, 309–315.

Hunt, W. E., & Goldring, S. Maturation of evoked response of the visual cortex in the postnatal rabbit. *EEG clin. Neurophysiol.,* 1951, 3, 465–471.

Hursch, J. B. Conduction velocity and diameter of nerve fibers. *Amer. J. Physiol.,* 1939, 127, 131–139. (a)

—— The properties of growing nerve fibers. *Amer. J. Physiol.,* 1939, 127, 140–153. (b)

Irwin, O. C. Effect of strong light on the body activity of newborns. *J. comp. Psychol.,* 1941, 32, 233–236.

—— Reliability of infant speech sound data. *J. speech hearing Dis.,* 1945, 10, 227–235.

—— Development of speech during infancy: Curve of phonemic frequencies. *J. exp. Psychol.,* 1947, 37, 187–193.

—— Infant speech: The effect of family occupational status and of age on sound frequency. *J. Speech Hearing Dis.,* 1948, 13, 320–323.

—— Correct status of a third set of consonants in the speech of cerebral palsy children. *Cerebr. Pal. Rev.,* 1957, 3, 17–20.

Irwin, O. C., & Chen, H. P. Development of speech during infancy: Curve of phonemic types. *J. exp. Psychol.,* 1946, 36, 431–436.

Irwin, O. C., & Weiss, A. P. A note on mass activity in newborn infants. *Ped. Sem.,* 1930, 38, 20–28.

Irwin, O. C., & Weiss, L. A. Differential variations in the activity and crying of the newborn infant under different intensities of light: A comparison of observational with polygraph findings. *Univer. Iowa Stud. Child Welf.,* 1934, 9, 139–147. (a)

———— The effect of clothing on the general and vocal activity of the newborn infant. *Univer. Iowa Stud. Child Welf.,* 1934, 9, 151–162. (b)

———— The effect of darkness on the activity of newborn infants. *Univer. Iowa Stud. Child Welf.,* 1934, 9, 165–175. (c)

Irzhanskaia, K. N., & Felberbaum, R. A. Some data on conditioned activity in premature infants. *Fiziol. Zh. SSSR,* 1954, 40, 668–672.

Ivanov-Smolenskii, A. G. *Russkii Fiziol. Zh.,* 1927, 10, 257.

———— (Ed.) *Opyt sistematichoskovo issledovaniya uslovnoreflektornoy deyatel'nosti rebenka.* (*The systematic investigation of conditoned reflex activity in the child.*) No. 1, Moscow-Leningrad 1930.

———— *Metodika issledonvaniia uslovnykh refleksov u cheloveka.* (*Methods of studying conditioned reflexes in man.*) 1933.

———— *Russkii Fiziol. Zh.,* 1935, 19, 133.

———— (Ed.) *Opyt sistematicheskovo eksperimental'novo issledovaniya ontogeneticheskovo razvitiya korkovoy dinamiki cheloveka.* (*The systematic experimental investigation of the ontogenetic development of cortical dynamics of man.*) No. 5, Moscow: All-Union Institute of Experimental Medicine, 1940.

———— Studies on the types of higher nervous activity in animals and in man. *Zh. vys. nerv. Deiat.,* 1953, 3, 36–54.

———— (Ed.) *Tr. In-ta. Vyssh. Nervn. Deiat.* (*Transactions of the Institute of Higher Nervous Activity.*) USSR Academy of Science Press, 1955.

Jack, L. M. An experimental study of ascendant behavior in preschool children. *Univer. Iowa Stud. Child Welf.,* 1934, 9, No. 3.

Jackson, R. L., & Kelly, H. G. Growth charts for use in pediatric practice. *J. Pediatr.,* 1945, 27, 214.

James, W. *Principles of psychology.* New York: Holt, 1890.

Janoš, O. *Age and individual differences in higher nervous activity in infants.* Prague: SZdN, 1965.

Janoš, O., Papoušek, H., & Dittrichová, J. The influence of age upon various aspects of higher nervous activity in the first months of life. *Activ. Nerv. Super.,* 1963, 4, 407–410.

Jekels, L. Analerotik. (Anal eroticism.) *Internationale Zeitschrift fuer Psychoanalyse,* 1913, 1.

Jenkins, W. O., & Stanley, J. C., Jr. Partial reinforcement: A review and critique. *Psychol. Bull.,* 1950, 47, 193–234.

Jensen, K. Differential reactions to taste and temperature stimuli in newborn infants. *Genet. Psychol. Monogr.,* 1932, 12, 361–479.

Jersild, A. T., & Fite, M. D. Children's social adjustment in nursery school. *J. exp. Educ.,* 1937, 6, 161–166.

Jones, H. E. A first study of parent-child resemblance in intelligence. *Yearb. nat. Soc. Stud. Educ.,* 1928, 27, 61–72.

Jones, H. E., & Bayley, Nancy. The Berkeley Growth Study. *Child Develpm.,* 1941, 12, 167–173.

Jones, H. E., & Conrad, H. S. The growth and decline of intelligence: A study of a homogeneous group between the ages of ten and sixty. *Genet. Psychol. Monogr.,* 1933, 13, 223–294.

Jones, H. E., & Seashore, R. H. The development of fine motor and mechanical abilities. *Yearb. nat. Soc. Stud. Educ.,* 1944, 43.

Jouvet, D., Valatx, J., & Jouvet, M. Etude polygraphique du sommeil du chaton. *C. R. Soc. Biol.,* 1961, 155, 1660–1664.

Jouvet, M. Telencephalic and rhombencephalic sleep in the cat. In G. Wolstenholme & M. O'Connor (Eds.), *Ciba Foundation Symposium on the Nature of Sleep.* Boston: Little, Brown, 1961. Pp. 188–206.

Jouvet, M., Dechaume, J., & Michel, F. Etude des mécanismes du sommeil physiologique. *Lyon Med.,* 1960, 38, 1–39.

Jung, R. Neuronal discharge. *EEG clin. Neurophysiol.,* 1953, Suppl. 4, 59–71.

Kagan, J. The concept of identification. *Psychol. Rev.,* 1958, 65, 296–305.

Kamiya, J. Behavioral, subjective, and physiologic aspects of drowsiness and sleep. In D. Fiske & S. Maddi (Eds.), *Functions of Varied Experience.* Homewood, Ill.: Dorsey Press, 1961. Pp. 145–174.

Kanfor, I. S., & Voronkova, A. A., cited in R. P. Ol'nianskaia.

Kantrow, R. W. Studies in infant behavior. IV. An investigation of conditioned feeding responses and concomitant adaptive behavior in young infants. *Univer. Iowa Stud. Child Welf.,* 1937, 13, No. 3, 1–64.

Kaplan, L. I. To the question of the development of individual typologic differences of higher nervous activity in infants. *Mater. 6th Scient. Conf. devel. Morphol. Physiol. Biochem.* Moscow: Izd. APN, 1963. P. 354.

Kaplan, M. Psychological implications of thumbsucking. *J. Pediatr.,* 1950, 37, 555.

Karpe, G. The basis of clinical electroretinography. *Acta Ophthalm.,* 1945, 24.

Kasatkin, N. I. *Biull. VIEM,* 1936, No. 3–4.

—————— Rannie uslovnye refleksy v ontogeneze cheloveka. (Early conditioned reflexes in human ontogenesis.) *Izd. Akad. Med. Nayk SSSR,* 1948.

—————— *Ocherk razvitiia vysshei nervnoi deiatelnosti rebenka rannego vozrasta. (The development of higher nervous activity in the young child.)* 1951.

—————— *Fruehe bedingte Reflexe beim Kinde. (Early conditioned reflexes in the child.)* Leipzig, 1953.

—————— (Ed.) *From the simple to the complex.* (Rus.) Moscow-Leningrad: *Izd. Nauka.,* 1964.

Kasatkin, N. I., & Levikova, A. M. On the development of early conditioned reflexes and differentiation of auditory stimuli in infants. *J. exp. Psychol.,* 1935, 18, 1–9.

Kasatkin, N. I., Mirzoiants, N. S., & Khokhitva, A. P. *Zh. vyssh. nerv. Deiatel.,* 1953, 3.

Katona, G. Experimente ueber die Groessenkonstanz. (Experiments on size constancy.) *Ztschr. f. Psychol.,* 1925, 97, 215.

Kaverina, K. Ye. *O razvitii rechi detei pervykh dvukh let zhizni. (On the development of speech in children in the first two years of life.)* Moscow: Medgiz, 1950.

Keeler, C. E., Sutcliffe, & Chaffee, E. L. A description of the ontogenetic development of retinal action currents in the house mouse. *Proc. Nat. Acad. Sci.,* 1928, 14, 811.

Keeney, A. H. *Chronology of ophthalmic development.* Springfield, Ill., 1951.

Klein, M. *The psychoanalysis of children.* London: Hogarth Press and Institute of Psychoanalysis, 1932.

Klein, M., & Riviere, J. *Love, hate and reparation.* London: Hogarth Press, 1938.

Keister, Mary Elizabeth. The behavior of young children in failure: An experimental attempt to discover and to modify undesirable responses of preschool children to failure. In R. Updegraff, Mary Elizabeth Keister, L. Heiliger, and others. *Studies in preschool education. Univer. Iowa Stud. Child Welf.,* 1937, 14, No. 1, 27–82.

Kelley, T. L. *Crossroads in the minds of man.* Stanford: Stanford Univer. Press, 1928.

Khamis, S. H., & Powers, L. E. Report on infant mortality survey of rural Lebanon. Mimeographed report, Amer. Univer. of Beirut, June, 1955.

Kinsey, V. E., Jacobus, J. T., & Hemphill, F. M. Retrolental fibroplasia: Co-operative study of retrolental fibroplasia and the use of oxygen. *AMA Arch. Ophthalm.*, 1956, 56, 481.

Kirk, S. A., & McCarthy, J. J. A study of the language process of preschool cerebral palsied children. *Progress Report to the United Cerebral Palsy Foundation*, 1950.

Klackenbush, G. Studies in maternal deprivation in infants' homes. *Acta Pediatr.*, 1956, 45, 1–12.

——— Thumbsucking and its etiology. *Pediatrics*, 1949, 4, 418.

Klein, Melanie. *The psycho-analysis of children.* London: Hogarth, 1949.

Klein, Melanie, Heimann, P., Isaacs, S., & Rivere, J. *Developments in psychoanalysis.* London: Hogarth, 1952.

Kleitman, N. *Sleep and wakefulness.* Chicago: Univer. Chicago Press, 1939.

Knobloch, H., & Pasamanick, B. Prematurity and development. *J. Obstet. Gynaec. Brit. Comm.*, 1959, 66, 729.

Knobloch, H., Rider, R., Harper, R., & Pasamanick, B. Neuropsychiatric sequels of prematurity. *J. Amer. Med. Ass.*, 1956, 161, 581.

Koch, J. Die Veränderung des Exzitationsprozesses nach der Nahrungseinnahme und nach dem Schlafe bei Sauglingen im Alter von 5 Monaten. *Z. arztl. Fortb.*, 1962, 55, 219–223.

Kohler, W. *Dynamics in psychology.* New York: Liveright, 1940.

Koltsova, M. M. *Trudy fiziol. Inst. im. I. P. Pavlova*, 1949, 4, 49.

——— Materialy po izucheniyu formirovaniya signal'nykh sistem daetelnosti u rebenka. (Formation of signal systems activity in the child.) Doctorate Thesis, Leningrad, 1953. (Presented at Congress of physiologists, biochemists, and pharmacologists, 1955.)

Kotliarevskii, L. I. *Zh. vyssh. nerv. Deiatel.*, 1951, 1, 479.

Koupernik, C. *Développement psycho-moteur du premier âge.* Paris, 1954.

Krasnogorskii, N. I. An experience with establishing experimental conditioned reflexes in infants. *Russkii Vrach*, 1907, 36, 1245. In *Studies in the research of higher nervous activity in man and animals.* Moscow: Medgiz, 1954.

——— Ueber die Grundmechanismen der Arbeit der Grosshirnrinde bei Kindern. (On the basic mechanisms of the activity of the cortex in children.) *Jb. Kinderheilk.*, 1913, 78, 373.

——— Razvitie ucheniia o fiziologicheskoi deiatelnosti mozga detei. (Principles of physiological function in the brain of the child.) *Izd. Inst. OZDP*, 1939.

——— *Zh. vyssh. nerv. Deiatel.*, 1951, 1, 793.

——— *Tr. po izuch. vyssh. nervn. deiat. cheloveka i zhivotnykh.* (*Papers on the investigation of higher nervous activity in man and in animals.*) Medgiz, 1954.

——— *Higher nervous activity in the child.* Leningrad: Medgiz, 1958.

Kries, J. V. Zur Theorie des Tages-und Daemmerungssehens. (On the theory of daylight and twilight vision.) In Bethe's *Handbuch der Physiologie*, Bd. XII/1, 1931, 678.

Kriuchkova, A. P., & Ostrovskaia, I. M. Developmental and individual differences of higher nervous activity in infants. *Zh. vyssh. nerv. Deiat.*, 1957, 7, 63–74.

Lacey, J. I., Bateman, Dorothy E., & Van Lehn, Ruth. Automatic response specificity: An experimental study. *Psychosom. Med.*, 1953, 15, 8–21.

Lacey, J. I., & Lacey, B. C. Verification and extension of the principles of autonomic response-stereotypy. *Amer. J. Psychol.*, 1958, 71, 50–73.

Ladd, G. T., & Woodworth, R. S. *Elements of physiological psychology*. New York, 1911.

Landis, C., & Hunt, W. A. *The startle pattern*. New York: Rinehart, 1939.

Langworthy, O. R. Development of behavior patterns and myelinization of nervous system in human fetus and infant. *Contrib. Embryol.*, 1933, 24, 1.

Lashley, K. S. The problem of cerebral organization in vision. In M. Kluver (Ed.), *Visual mechanisms. Biol. Sympos.*, 1942, 7, 301–322.

Leboucq, G. Contribution a l'etude de l'histogenese de la retine chez les mammiferes. (Contribution to the study of the histogenesis of the retina in the mammals.) *Arch. d'Anat. microsc.*, 1909, 10, 556.

Lederer, R. K. An exploratory investigation of handed status in the first two years of life. *Univer. Iowa Stud. Infant Behav.*, 1939.

Lesne, M., & Peycelon. A quel age un enfant cesse-t-il d'etre ambidextre pour devenir droiter? *Bull. Soc. Pediatr.*, Paris, 1934, 32, 436–439.

Levine, M. I., & Bell, A. I. Treatment of colic in infancy by the use of pacifier. *J. Pediatr.*, 1950, 37, 750.

Levy, D. M. Fingersucking-etiology. *Amer. J. Psychiat.*, 1928, 7, 881.

Lewin, B. D. Kotschmieren, Menses and weibliches Ueber-ich. (Feces smearing, menstruation and the female superego.) *Internationale Zeitschrift fuer Psychoanalyse*, 1930, 16.

Lewis, M. M. *How children learn to speak*. New York: Basic Books, 1959.

Lewis, S. J. Thumbsucking as a cause of malocclusion. *J. Amer. Dent. Ass.*, 1930, 17, 1060.

Lipsitt, L. P. Learning in the first year of life. In L. P. Lipsitt & C. C. Spiker (Eds.). *Advances in child development and behavior*. New York: Academic Press, 1963. Pp. 147–195.

Lipsitt, L. P., & DeLucia, C. A. An apparatus for the measurement of specific response and general activity in the human neonate. *Amer. J. Psychol.*, 1960, 73, 630–632.

Lipsitt, L. P., & Kaye, H. Conditioned sucking in the human newborn. *Psychon. Sci.*, 1964, 1, 29–30.

Lipton, E. L., Richmond, J. B., & Lustman, S. L. Autonomic function in the neonate and psychosomatic disease. *Amer. J. Dis. Child.*, 1955, 90, 491. (Abstract)

Lipton, E. L., Steinschneider, A., & Richmond, J. B. Autonomic function in the neonate. II. Physiological effects of motor restraint. *Psychosom. Med.*, 1960, 22, 57–65. (a)

—————— The maturation of autonomic nervous system function in the early months of life. *Psychosom. Med.*, 1960, 22, 325–326. (Abstract) (b)

—————— A study of the sensitivity of newborn infants to stimulation. Evaluation by means of the autonomic and somatic responses. *Amer. J. Dis. Child.*, 1961, 102, 537. (Abstract) (a)

—————— Autonomic function in the neonate. III. Methodological considerations. *Psychosom. Med.*, 1961, 33, 461–471. (b)

—————— Autonomic function in the neonate. IV. Individual differences in cardiac reactivity. *Psychosom. Med.*, 1961, 23, 472–484. (c)

—————— Auditory discrimination in the newborn infant. *Psychosom. Med.*, 1963, 23, 490. (Abstract)

—————— Autonomic function in the neonate. VIII. Cardio-pulmonary observations. *Pediatrics*, 1964, 33, 212.

—————— Autonomic function in the neonate. VII. Maturational changes in cardiac control. Unpublished manuscript.

—— Swaddling, a child care practice: Historical, cultural and experimental observations. *Pediatrics,* 1965, 35, 521–567.

Lipton, E. L., Walsh, L., Mueller, W., & Salamy, B. A respiratory alarm for infants. *J. Pediatr.,* 1964.

Lorand, S. Aggression and flatus. *Int. J. Psychoanal.,* 1931, 12.

Lossen. Ueber die idiopathische Erweiterung des Oesophagus. (On the idiopathic enlargement of the esophagus.) *Mitteilungen aus den Grenzgebieten der Medizin und Chirurgie.* Bd. XII, 1903, 33.

Lubchenco, L. O. The relationship of fetal size to later physical growth of prematurely born children. Abstract No. 33, read by title, at the meeting of the American Pediatric Society, Atlantic City, May, 1962.

McCarthy, Dorothea. *Language development of the preschool child.* Minneapolis: University of Minnesota Press, 1930.

—— Language development. In Carl Murchison (Ed.), *A handbook of child psychology.* London: Clark University Press, 1931.

—— Children's speech. In L. Carmichael (Ed.), *Manual of child psychology.* (1st. ed.) New York: Wiley, 1946.

—— Language development in children. In L. Carmichael (Ed.), *Manual of child psychology.* (2nd ed.) New York: Wiley, 1954, Pp. 492–630.

Maccoby, Eleanor E. Role-taking in childhood and its consequences for social learning. *Child Develpm.,* 1959, 30, 239–252.

McDougall, W. An investigation of the colour sense of two infants. *Brit. J. Psychol.,* 1908, 2, 338–352.

Macfarlane, Jean W. Studies in child guidance. I. Methodology of data collection and organization. *Monogr. Soc. Res. Child Develpm.,* 1938, 3, No. 6.

McGraw, Myrtle B. From reflex to muscular control in the assumption of an erect posture and ambulation in the human infant. *Child Develpm.,* 1932, 3, 291.

—— *Growth, a study of Johnny and Jimmy.* New York: D. Appleton Century, 1935.

—— Development of rotary-vestibular reactions of the human infant. *Child Develpm.,* 1941, 12, 17.

McNemar, Q. *The revision of the Stanford-Binet Scale: An analysis of the standardization data.* Boston: Houghton Mifflin, 1942.

—— *Psychological statistics.* New York: Wiley, 1955.

Magnus, R. *Körperstellung.* Berlin: Julius Springer, 1924. P. 710.

Maiorov, F. P. *Arkh. biol. Nauk,* 1929, 29, 341.

Maiorov, F. P., & Byrzhikovskii, S. P. *Trudy fiziol. Labor. Akad. I. P. Pavlova,* 1933, 5, 171.

Malinowski, B. *The sexual life of savages.* London: Routledge, 1929.

Mann, I. *The development of the human eye.* (3rd. ed.) New York: Grune & Stratton, 1964.

Margolin, S. G. The behavior of the stomach during psychoanalysis. *Psychoanalyt. Quart.,* 1951, 20, 349.

Marquis, D. P. Can conditioned responses be established in the newborn infant? *Ped. Sem.,* 1931, 39, 479–492.

Marsden, R. E. A study of the early color sense. *Psychol. Rev.,* 1903, 10, 37, 297.

Martin, I. Adaptation. *Psychol. Bull.,* 1964, 61, 35–44.

Marty, R., Contamin, F., & Scherrer, J. Cortical response to photic stimulation in a newborn cat. *EEG clin. Neurophysiol.,* 1958, 10, 761.

Maurer, Katharine M. *Intellectual status of maturity as a criterion for selecting items in preschool tests.* Minneapolis: Univer. Minnesota Press, 1946.

Mead, G. H. *Mind, self and society. From the standpoint of a social behaviorist.* Chicago: Univ. Chicago Press, 1934.

Mead, Margaret. *Contributions from the study of primitive cultures.* New York: Macy Conference (1st), 1947. P. 37.

Menyuk, Paula. A descriptive study of the syntactic structures in the language of children: Nursery school and first grade. Unpublished doctoral dissertation, Boston Univer., 1961.

Metcalf, D. R. Electroencephalographic findings in ex-premature infants with partial and complete blindness due to retrolental fibroplasia. *EEG clin. Neurophysiol.,* 1959, 11, 182. (a)

—————— The significance of 14 and 6 per second spikes in EEG's of children with disorders of impulse-control. Presented at Western Institute on Epilepsy, Sept., 1959. (b)

—————— Normal EEG development in longitudinally studied children. Unpublished data, Child Research Council, Univer. Colorado.

Miles, R. Psychological aspects of aging. In E. V. Cowdry (Ed.), *Problems of aging.* (2nd ed.) Baltimore: Williams & Wilkins, 1942. Pp. 756–784.

Miller, N. E., & Dollard, J. *Social learning and imitation.* New Haven: Yale Univer. Press, 1941.

Minkowski, H. Neurobiologische Studien an menschlichen Früchten. *Abderhalden's Handb. biolog. Arbeitsmeth.,* 1928, 5b, 511–618.

Moeller, A. Die Struktur des Auges bei Urodelen verschiedener Koerpergroesse. (The structure of the eye in the urodele of different physical size.) *Zool. Jb. (Zoological Yearbook) Abt. allg. Zool. und Physiol.,* 1950, 63, 138.

Mohr, G. J., Richmond, J. B., Garner, Ann, & Eddy, Evelyn. A program for the study of children with psychosomatic disorders. In G. Caplan (Ed.), *Emotional problems of early childhood.* New York: Basic Books, 1955.

Monnier, M. Retinal, cortical, and motor responses to photic stimulation in man: Retino-cortical time and opto-motor integration time. *J. Neurophysiol.,* 1952, 15, 469–486.

Monroe, M. *Reading aptitude tests.* Boston: Houghton Mifflin, 1935.

Moore, O. K. Orthographic symbols and the preschool child—a new approach. *Proceedings of the third Minnesota conference on gifted children.* Minneapolis: Univer. of Minnesota Press. Pp. 91–101.

Moro, E. Das erste Trimenon. *Münch. med. Wsch.,* 1918, 42, 1147.

Moroff, T. Cyto-Histogenese und Bau der Staebchen und Zapfen der Retina bei Anuren. (Cyto-histogenesis and structure of the rods and cones of the retina in anurae.) *Anat. Anz.,* 1922, 55, 316.

Mowrer, O. H. Identification: A link between learning theory and psychotherapy. In *Learning theory and personality dynamics.* New York: Ronald Press, 1950. Pp. 69–94.

—————— Hearing and speaking: An analysis of language learning. *J. speech hear. Disord.,* 1958, 23, 143–152.

Mueller, H. Bau und Wachstum der Netzhaut des Guppy Lebistes reticulatus. (Structure and growth of the retina of the guppy lebistes reticulatus.) *Zool. Jb. (Zoological Yearbook) Abt. allg. Zool. und Physiol.,* 1952, 63, 275.

Mueller-Limmroth, H. W., & Andree, G. Die ontogenetische Entwicklung des Elektroretinogramms des Frosches. (The ontogentic development of the electroretinogram of the frog.) *Z. Biol.,* 1954, 107, 25.

Munn, N. Learning in children. In L. Carmichael (Ed.), *Manual of child psychology.* New York: Wiley, 1946. Pp. 370–449.

Musiashchikova, S. S. *Fiziol. zh. SSSR,* 1951, 37, 743.

Mussen, P., & Distler, L. Masculinity, identification, and father-son relationships. *J. abnorm. soc. Psychol.*, 1959, 59, 350–356.

Myers, C. S. Some observations on the development of the colour sense. *Brit. J. Psychol.*, 1908, 2, 353.

Neilon, Patricia. Shirley's babies after fifteen years: A personality study. *J. genet. Psychol.*, 1948, 73, 175–186.

Nelson, Virginia L., & Richards, T. W. Studies in mental development: I. Performance on Gesell items at six months and its predictive value for performance on mental tests at two and three years. *J. genet. Psychol.*, 1938, 52, 303–325.

———— Studies in mental development: III. Performance of twelve months-old children on the Gesell schedule and its predictive value for mental status at two and three years. *J. genet. Psychol.*, 1939, 54, 181–191.

———— Fels mental age values for Gesell schedules. *Child Develpm.*, 1940, 11, 153–157.

Nemanova, C. P. The earliest positive and negative aversive and nutritive conditioned responses to vestibular stimuli in infant. *Vopr. Pediat.*, 1935, 7, 278.

Nice, Margaret M. Ambidexterity and delayed speech development. *Ped. Sem.*, 1918, 25, 141–162.

Northington, P. In E. P. Fowler, Jr., (Ed.), *Medicine of Ear.* Philadelphia: Williams & Wilkins, 1939. P. 433.

Nussbaum, M. Entwicklungsgeschichte des menschlichen Auges. (Developmental history of the human eye.) In GraefeSaemisch, *Handbuch der Augenheilkunde,* Bd. II/I, 1908.

Nygaard, P. H. A percentage equivalent for the coefficient of correlation. *J. educ. Psychol.*, 1926, 17, 36–92.

Olson, W. C. *Measurement of nervous habits in normal children.* Minneapolis: Univer. Minnesota Press, 1929.

Ophuijsen, J. H. W. V. The sexual aim of sadism as manifested in acts of violence. *Int. J. Psychoanal.*, 1929, 10.

Orlinsky, D. Psychodynamic and cognitive correlates of dream recall: A study of individual differences. Unpublished doctoral dissertation, Univer. Chicago, 1962.

Osgood, C. E., & Sebeok, T. A. (Eds.) Psycholinguistics: A survey of theory and research problems. *J. abnorm. soc. Psychol. Suppl.*, 1954, 49, 203.

Owens, W. A. Age and mental abilities: A longitudinal study. *Genet. Psychol. Monogr.*, 1953, 48, 3–54.

Page, M. L. The modification of ascendant behavior in preschool children. *Univer. Iowa Stud. Child Welf.*, 1936, 11, No. 3, 1–68.

Papoušek, H. A method of studying conditioned food reflexes in young children up to the age of six months. *Zh. vyssh. nerv. Deiat.*, 1959, 9, 136–140.

———— Conditioned motor alimentary reflexes in infants. I. Experimental conditioned sucking reflexes. *Cs. Pediat.*, 1960, 15, 861–872.

———— Conditioned head rotation reflexes in infants in the first months of life. *Acta Paediat.*, 1961, 50, 565–576. (a)

———— Conditioned motor nutritive reflexes in infants. *Thomayer. Sb.*, 1961, 409. (b)

Parsons, T. Family structure and the socialization of the child. In T. Parsons & R. F. Bales (Eds.), *Family, socialization, and interaction process.* Glencoe, Illinois: Free Press, 1955. Pp. 35–131.

Parten, M. B. Social participation among preschool children. *J. abnorm. soc. Psychol.*, 1932–33, 27, 243–269. (a)

———— Leadership among preschool children. *J. abnorm. soc. Psychol.*, 1932–33, 27, 430–440. (b)

Patz, A., Hoeck, L. E., & DeLaCruz, E. Studies on the effect of high oxygen administration in retrolental fibroplasia: I. Nursery Observations. *Amer. J. Ophthalm.*, 1952, 35, 1248.

Pavlov, I. P. *Lectures on conditioned reflexes.* New York: Int. Publishers, 1928.

———— *Polnoe sobranie trudov.* (*Complete works.*) 1949, 3. (a)

———— *Polnoe sobranie trudov.* (*Complete works.*) 1949, 4. (b)

———— *Sochineniya.* (*Works.*) 1951, 4.

Peiper, A. Ueber einen Augenreflex auf den Hals im fruehen Saeuglingsalter. (On an eye reflex on the neck in early infancy.) *Jb. Kinderheilk.*, 1926, 113, 87.

———— Über die Helligkeits- und Farbenempfindungen der Frühgeburten. (On light and color perception in premature infants.) *Arch. Kinderhk.*, 1927, 80, 1.

———— *Die Eigenart der kindlichen Hirntaetigkeit.* (*Characteristics of brain activity in children.*) Leipzig, 1949.

———— Unbedingte und bedingte Reflexe der Nahrungs aufnahme. *Kinderarzt. Prax.*, 1958, 26, 507–515.

Pfister, H. *Arch. f. Kinderheilkunde*, 1899, 11, 26.

Piaget, J. *The language and thought of the child.* New York: Harcourt, Brace, 1926.

———— (1937) Principal factors determining intellectual evolution from childhood to adult life. In D. Rapaport (Ed.), *Organization and Pathology of Thought.* New York: Columbia Univer. Press, 1951.

———— *The Psychology of Intelligence.* London: Routledge & Kegan Paul, 1950.

Pierce, C., Whitman, R., Maas, W., & Gay, M. Enuresis and dreaming; experimental studies. *Arch. Gen. Psychiat.*, 1961, 4, 166–170.

Pinneau S. R. Changes in performance on intelligence tests from one month to eighteen years. Paper read at Western Psychol. Ass., Seattle, 1953.

Polikanina, R. I. Origin and development of a nutritive conditioned response to sound in premature infants. *Zh. vyssh. nerv. Deiat.*, 1955, 5, 237–246.

Polikanina, R. I., & Probatova, L. J. Development of an orienting response and a conditioned motor nutritive response to color in premature infants. *Zh. vyssh. nerv. Deiat.*, 1957, 7, 673–682.

Polyak, S. L. *The retina.* Chicago, 1941.

Pratt, K. C. The neonate. In C. Murchison (Ed.). *A handbook of child psychology.* Worcester, Mass.: Clark Univ. Press, 1933.

Pratt, K. C., Nelson, A. K., & Sun, K. H. *The behavior of the newborn infant.* Columbus, Ohio: Ohio State Univer. Press, 1930.

Prechtl, H. F. R. Die Kletterbewegungen beim Saugling. *Mnschr. Kinderhk.*, 1953, 101, 519–521.

Preyer, W. *Die Seele des Kindes.* (4th ed.) Leipzig, 1859.

Prugh, D. G., Staub, E. M., Sands, H. H., Kirschbaum, R. M., & Lenihan, E. A. A study of the emotional reactions of children and families to hospitalization and illness. *Amer. J. Orthopsychiat.*, 1953, 23, 70–106.

Raehlmann, E. Ueber den Farbensinn des Kindes. (On the color sense of the child.) *Ophth. Klinik*, 1903, 7, 321.

Ramsey, W. R. *Care and feeding of infants and children.* Philadelphia, 1916.

Ray, W. S. A preliminary report on a study of fetal conditioning. *Child Develpm.*, 1932, 3, 175–177.

Rechtschaffen, A., Goodenough, D., & Shapiro, A. Patterns of sleep talking. *Arch. gen. Psychiat.*, 1962, 7, 418–426.

Rechtschaffen, A., & Maron, L. *EEG clin. Neurophysiol.*, 1964, 16, 438.

Rechtschaffen, A., Wolpert, E., Dement, W., Mitchell, S., & Fisher, C. Nocturnal sleep of narcoleptics. *EEG clin. Neurophysiol.*, 1963, 15, 599–609.

Redfield, J. E. A preliminary report of dark adaptation in young infants. *Child Develpm.*, 1937, 8, 263–269.

———— A preliminary report of dark adaptation in young infants. *Univ. of Iowa Stud. Child Welf.*, 1939, 16, No. 2, 105–145.

Reese, A. B., King, M., & Owens, W. C. A classification of retrolental fibroplasia. *Amer. J. Ophthalm.*, 1953, 36, 1333.

Reich, W. *Der Einbruch der Sexualmoral. (The inroad of sexual morality.)* Berlin: Sexpol, 1932.

Rheingold, Harriet L. The modification of social responsiveness in institutional babies. *Monogr. Soc. Res. Child Develpm.*, 1956, 21, No. 2, (Serial No. 63).

Rheingold, Harriet L., Gewirtz, J. L., & Ross, Helen W. Social conditioning of vocalizations in the infant. *J. comp. physiol. Psychol.*, 1959, 52, 68–73.

Rheingold, Harriet L., & Stanley, W. C. Developmental psychology. *Ann. Rev. Psychol.*, 1963, 14, 1–23.

Rheingold, Harriet L., Stanley, W. C., & Cooley, J. A. Method for studying exploratory behavior in infants. *Science*, 1962, 136, 1054–1055.

Ribble, Margaret. *The rights of infants.* New York: Columbia Univer. Press, 1943.

———— Infantile experience in relation to personality development. In J. McV, Hunt (Ed.), *Personality and the behavior disorders.* (Vol. 2). New York: Ronald Press, 1944. Pp. 621–651.

Richards, T. W., & Nelson, Virginia L. Studies in mental development: II. Analysis of abilities tested at the age of six months by the Gesell Schedule. *J. genet. Psychol.*, 1938, 52, 327–331.

———— Abilities of infants during the first eighteen months. *J. genet. Psychol.*, 1939, 55, 299–318.

Rickman, J. (Ed.) *On the bringing up of children.* London: Kegan Paul, 1936.

Richmond, J. B., & Lipton, E. L. Some aspects of the neurophysiology of the newborn and their implications for child development. In Lucy Jessner & Eleaner Pavenstedt (Eds.), *Psychopathology in children.* New York: Grune & Stratton, 1959.

Richmond, J. B., Lipton, E. L., & Steinschneider, A. Autonomic function in the neonate. V. Individual homeostatic capacity in cardiac response. *Psychosom. Med.*, 1962, 24, 66–74. (a)

————Observations on differences in autonomic nervous system function between and within individuals during early infancy. *J. Amer. Acad. Child Psychiat.*, 1962, 1, 83–91. (b)

Ripin, R., & Hetzer, H. Frühestes Lernen des Säuglings in der Ernährungssituation. *Z. Psychol.*, 1930, 118, 82–127.

Riviere, J. Symposium on child analysis. *Int. J. Psychoanal.*, 1927, 8.

Roberts, E. Thumbsucking in relationship to feeding in early infancy. *Amer. J. Dis. Child*, 1944, 68, 7.

Robertson, J., & Bowlby, J. Responses of young children to separation from their mothers. *Courrier*, 1952, 2, 131–142.

Roffwarg, H. P., Dement, W. C., & Fisher, C. Preliminary observations of the sleep-dream patern in neonates, infants, children and adults. *Int. Ser. Monogr. Child Psychiat.*, 1964, 2, 60–72.

Roffwarg, H. P., Dement, W. C., Muzio, J., & Fisher, C. Dream imagery and it relationship to the rapid eye movements of sleep. *Arch. Gen. Psychiat.,* 1962.

Roffwarg, H. P., Muzio, J., & Dement, W. C. Ontogenetic development of the human sleep dream cycle. *Science,* 1966, in press.

Rose, J. E., Adrian, H., & Santibanez, G. Electrical signs of maturation in the auditory system of the kitten. *Acta Neurol. Latin Amer.,* 1957, 3, 133–143.

Rosental, I. S. *Russk. fiziol. Zh.,* 1924, 7, 330.

Roudinesco, J., & Guiton, M. *Le developpement de l'enfant.* Paris, 1950.

Rozengart-Pupko, G. L. *Rech' i razvitiye vospriyatiya v rannem vozraste. (Speech and development of perception in the young child.)* Moscow: Medgiz, 1948.

Rudder, B. de Beitraege zur Sinnesphysiologie des fruehen Lebensalters: Zum Farbensinn des Saeuglings. (Contributions on the sensory physiology of the early age of life: On the color sense of the infant.) *Z. Kinderhelk.,* 1927, 43, 323.

Rust, Metta M. The effect of resistance on intelligence scores of young children. *Monogr. Soc. Res. Child Develpm.,* 1931, No. 6.

Saint-Anne Dargassies, S. Méthode d'examen neurologique du nouveau-né. (Methods of examining neurology in the newborn.) *Et. néo-natales,* 1955, 4, 71.

Salk, L. The effects of the normal heartbeat sound on the behavior of the new-born infant: Implications for mental health. *World Ment. Hlth.,* 1960, 12, 168–175.

——— The importance of the heartbeat rhythm to human nature: Theoretical, clinical, and experimental observations. *Proc. Third World Congr. Psychiat.,* Montreal: McGill Univer. Press, 1961, 1, 740–763.

——— Mothers' heartbeat as an imprinting stimulus. *Trans. New York Acad. Sci.,* 1962, 24, 753–763.

Sarason, S. B., & Gladwin, T. Psychological and cultural problems in mental subnormality: A review of research. *Genet. Psychol. Monogr.,* 1958, 57, 3–290.

Sassenrath, J. M., & Holmes, J. A. Auding and psycho-educational variables. *Calif. J. educ. Res.,* 1956, 7, 99–104.

Saxen, L. Development of visual cells and photomechanical movements in amphibia. *Ann. med. exper. biol. fenn.,* 1953, 31, 254.

——— The development of the visual cells. *Ann. Acad. Sci. fenn.,* 1954, 23.

Schaffer, H. R., & Callender, W. M. Psychological effects of hospitalization in infancy. Unpublished paper, 1958.

Schaper, G. Discussion of Kellaway's Ontogenic evolution of the electroencephalogram in humans and animals. *Proc. IVth Internat. Cong. EEG clin. Neurophysiol.,* 1957, 31–32.

Scherrer, J., & Oeconomos, D. Résponses corticales somesthesiques dur mammifere nouveau-né comparées a celles de l'animal adulte. *Et. Neonat.,* 1954, 3, 199–216.

———Responses evoquees corticales somesthesiques des mammiferes adulte and nouveau-né. In *Les Grandes Activites du Lobe Temporal.* Paris: Masson, 1955.

Scott, J. P. Critical periods in the development of social behavior in puppies. *Psychosom. Med.,* 1958, 20, 42–54.

——— Critical periods in behavioral development: A review. *Science,* 1962, 138.

Sears, R. R. Identification as a form of behavioral development. In D. B. Harris

(Ed.), *The concept of development.* Minneapolis: Univer. Minnesota Press, 1957. Pp. 149–161.

Sears, R. R., & Wise, G. W. Approaches to dynamic theory of development; Roundtable 1949; relation of cupfeeding in infancy to thumbsucking in oral drive. *Amer. J. Orthopsychiat.,* 1950, 20, 123.

Seashore, R. H. Work and motor performance. In S. S. Stevens (Ed.), *Handbook of experimental psychology.* New York: Wiley, 1951. Pp. 1341–1362.

Seefelder, R. Beitraege zur Histogenese und Histologie der Netzhaut, des Pigmentepithels und des Sehnerven. (Contributions to the histogenesis and histology of the retina, of the pigment epithels and of the visual nerve.) *Graefes Arch.,* 1910, 73, 419.

Shepard, J. E., & Breed, F. S. Maturation and use in the development of an instinct. *J. Anim. Behav.,* 1913, 3, 274–285.

Shirley, Mary M. The first two years: A study of twenty-five babies. II. Intellectual development. *Child Welf. Monogr.,* 1933, No. 7.

———— Development of immature babies during their first two years. *Child Develpm.,* 1938, 9, 347.

Shontz, F. C. Evaluation of intellectual potential in hemiplegic individuals. *J. clin. Psychol.,* 1957, 13, 267–269.

Shotwell, Anna M., Dingman, H. F., & Tarjan, G. *Pacific State Hospital Numbers Concept Test.* Sacramento: Calif. State Dept. Ment. Hygiene, 1957.

Sievers, Dorothy. Development and standardization of a test of psycholinguistic growth in preschool children. Unpublished doctoral dissertation, Univer. Illinois, 1955.

Simmons, M. W. Operant discrimination in infants. Unpublished doctoral dissertation, Brown Univer., 1962.

Simmons, M. W., & Lipsitt, L. P. An operant-discrimination apparatus for infants. *J. exp. anal. Behav.,* 1961, 4, 233–235.

Siqueland, E. R. Operant conditioning of head turning in four-month infants. *Psychon. Sci.,* 1964, 1, 223–224.

Siqueland, E. R., & Lipsitt, L. P. *J. exp. child Psychol.,* in press.

Skeels, H. M. Mental development of children in foster homes. *J. genet. Psychol.,* 1936, 49, 91–106.

———— Mental development of children in foster homes. *J. consult. Psychol.,* 1938, 2, 33–43.

Skeels, H. M., & Fillmore, E. A. The mental development of children from underprivileged homes. *J. genet. Psychol.,* 1937, 50, 427–439.

Skeels, H. M., Updegraff, Ruth, Wellman, Beth L., & Williams, H. M. A study of environmental stimulation: An orphange preschool project. *Univer. Iowa Stud. Child Welf.,* 1935, 15, No. 4.

Skinner, B. F. Superstition in the pigeon. *J. exp. Psychol.,* 1948, 38, 168–172.

Skodak, Marie. The mental development of adopted children whose true mothers are feebleminded. *Child Develpm.,* 1938, 9, 303–308.

———— Children in foster homes. *Univ. Iowa Stud. Child Welf.,* 1939, 16, 1–155.

Skodak, Marie, & Skeels, H. M. A final follow-up study of one hundred adopted children. *J. genet. Psychol.,* 1949, 75, 85–125.

Sloan, W. The Lincoln-Oseretsky Motor Development Scale. *Genet. Psychol. Monogr.,* 1955, 51, 183–252.

Smith, J. M. The relative brightness values of three hues for newborn infants. (Studies in infant behavior III). *Univer. Iowa Stud. Child Welf.,* 1936, 12, No. 1, 93.

Smith, M. E. An investigation of the development of the sentence and the extent of vocabulary of young children. *Univer. Iowa Stud. Child Welf.,* 1926, 3, No. 5, 1–92.

Sontag, L. W., & Wallace, R. F. Preliminary report on the Fels Fund: Study of fetal activity. *Amer. J. Dis. Child,* 1934, 49, 1050.

—— Changes in the rate of the human heart in response to vibratory stimuli. *Amer. J. Dis. Child,* 1936, 51, 583.

Spalding, D. A. Instinct and acquisition. *Nature,* 1875, 12, 507.

Spears, W. C. Sensation and perception. In Yvonne Brackbill (Ed.), *Research in infant behavior: A cross-indexed bibliography.* Baltimore: Williams & Wilkins, 1964. Pp. 207–217.

Spelt, D. K. Conditioned responses in the human fetus in utero. *Psychol. Bull.,* 1938, 35, 712–713.

—— The conditioning of the human fetus in utero. *J. exp. Psychol.,* 1948, 38, 375–376.

Spitz, R. A. Hospitalism. An inquiry into the genesis of psychiatric conditions in early childhood. *Psychoanalyt. Stud. Child,* 1945, 1, 53–74.

—— Hospitalism: A follow-up report. *Psychoanalyt. Stud. Child,* 1946, 2, 113–117.

—— Anaclitic depression. *Psychoanalyt. Stud. Child,* 1946 2, 313–342(b). New York: Univer. Press, 1946. Pp. 313–342. (b)

—— The psychogenic diseases in infancy: An attempt at their etiologic classification. *Psychoanalyt. Stud. Child,* 1951, 6, 255–275.

Spitz, R. A., & Wolf, Katherine M. Anaclitic depression. *Psychoanalyt. Stud. Child,* 1946, 2, 313–342.

—— Autoerotism. Some empirical findings and hypotheses on three of its manifestations in the first year of life. *Psychoanalyt. Stud. Child.,* 1949, 3–4, 85–120.

Spock, B. *Common sense book of baby and child care.* New York: Duell, Sloan, & Pearse, 1945.

Staples, R. Color vision and color preferences in infancy and childhood. *Psychol. Bull.,* 1931, 28, 297.

—— The responses of infants to color. *J. exp. Psychol.,* 1932, 15, 119.

Starch, D. *Educational psychology.* New York, 1919.

Steinschneider, A., Lipton, E. L., & Richmond, J. B. Autonomic function in the neonate. VI. Discriminability, consistency, and slope as measure of an individual's cardiac responsivity. *J. genet. Psychol.,* in press.

Stevenson, N. G. A method for analysing observational records. Unpublished Master's thesis, Stanford University, 1953.

Stevenson, H. W., & Stevenson, N. G. A method for observing children's social interaction. Unpublished manuscript, 1957.

Stevenson, O. First treasured possession. *Psychoanalytic study of the child.* 1954, 9.

Stirnimann, F. *Psychologie des neugeborenen Kindes. (Psychology of the new-born child.)* Zurich and Leipzig, 1940.

—— Ueber das Farbempfinden Neugeborener. (On the color perception of neonates.) *Ann. Paediatr.,* (Basel), 1944, 163, 1.

Stoyva, J. The effect of suggested dreams on the length of rapid eye movement periods. Unpublished doctoral dissertation, Univ. Chicago.

Strang, Ruth. *An introduction to child study.* New York: Macmillan, 1938.

Strauss, H. Das Zusammenschrecken. *J. Psychol. u. Neur.,* 1929, 39, 111–231.

Strayer, L. C. Language and growth: The relative efficacy of early and deferred vocabulary training, studied by the method of co-twin control. *Genet. Psychol. Monogr.,* 1930, 8, 209–319.

Stubbs, Esther M. The effect of the factors of duration, intensity, and pitch of sound stimuli on the responses of newborn infants. *Univer. Iowa Stud. Child Welf.*, 1934, 9, 77–135.

Studnitz, G. V. *Physiologie des Sehens.* (2 Aufl.) (*Physiology of vision.*) [2nd ed.] Leipzig, 1952.

Stutsman, R. *Mental measurement of preschool children.* New York: World Book, 1931.

Sullivan, A. W. Pathologic sucking behavior related to forced inhibition. *New York State J. Med.*, 1954, 54, 2474.

Templin, Mildred C. Certain language skills in children. *Child Welf. Monogr.*, 1957, No. 26.

Terman, L. W. An experiment in infant education. *J. appl. Psychol.*, 1918, 21, 219–228. (a)

―――― The vocabulary test as a measure of intelligence. *J. educ. Psychol.*, 1918, 9, 142–162. (b)

Terman, L. W., & Merrill, M. E. *Measuring intelligence: A guide to the administration of the new revised Stanford-Binet tests of intelligence.* Boston: Houghton Mifflin, 1937.

Thomas, A. *Equilibre et equilibration.* Paris: Masson, 1940.

Thomas, A., Chesni, Y., & Saint-Anne Dargassies, S. L'Examen neurologique du nourrisson. Paris: *La Vie Medicale*, 1955.

Thomas, A., Chess, Stella, Birch, H., & Hertzig, M. E. *Comprehen. Psychiat.*, 1960, 1, 103.

Thomas A., & de Ajuriaguerra, J. L'axe corporel, musculature et innervation. Paris: Masson, 1948.

Thomas, A., & de Ajuriaguerra, J. *Etude sémiologique du tonus musculaire.* Paris: Editions Medicales, Flammarion, 1949.

Thomas, A., & Saint-Anne Dargassies, S. *Etudes neurologiques sur le nouveau-né et le jeune nourrisson.* Paris: Masson, 1952.

Thomas, J. E., & Lambert, E. H. Conduction velocity of motor fibers of peripheral nerves in infants and children. *EEG clin. Neurophysiol.*, 1958, 10, 577.

Thomson, G. *The factorial analysis of human ability.* Boston: Houghton Mifflin, 1950.

Thompson, R. E., & Welker, W. I. Role of auditory cortex in reflex head orientation by cats to auditory stimuli. *J. comp. physiol. Psychol.*, 1963, 56, 96–1002.

Thorndike, E. L. *Educational Psychology.* New York, 1913.

―――― *The measurement of intelligence.* New York: Teachers' College, Columbia Univer., 1926.

Thorndike, R. L. Growth of intelligence during adolescence. *J. genet. Psychol.*, 1948, 72, 11–15.

Thorpe, W. H. *Learning and instinct in animals.* London: Methuen, 1956.

Thurstone, L. L. A method of scaling psychological and educational tests. *J. educ. Psychol.*, 1925, 16, 433–451.

―――― The perceptual factor. *Psychometrica*, 1938, 3, 1–17.

―――― Psychological implications of factor analysis. *Amer. Psychologist*, 1948, 3, 402–408.

Thurstone, L. L., & Thurstone, Thelma G. *SRA primary abilities, for ages 5–7.* Chicago: Science Research Associates, 1953.

Thurstone, Thelma G. Changing concepts of intelligence: Implications for test construction. *Proceedings of 1956 Invitational Conference on Testing Problems.* Princeton: Educational Testing Service, 1956, 26–37.

Tippett, L. H. C. Random sampling numbers. *Tracis for computers, No. 15.* London: Univer. London, 1927. P. 55.

Tracy, F., & Stimpfl, J. *The psychology of childhood.* Boston, 1909.

Trendelenburg, W. *Der Gesichtssinn. (The visual sense.)* Berlin, 1943.

Trillin, C. A reporter at large: A third state of existence. *The New Yorker,* Sept. 18, 1965. Pp. 58–125.

Trincker, D. Zur Ontogenese der Zapfen-und Staebchenfunktion beim Menschen. (On the ontogenesis of cone and rod function in the human.) *Naturwiss.,* 1954, 41, 310.

—— Zur Entwickung der Zapfen-und Staebchenfunktion beim menschlichen Neugeborenen. (On the development of cone and rod function in the human neonate.) *Forschan. und Fortschr.,* 1955, 29, 12. (a)

—— Zur Entwicklung des Farbensinnes. (On the development of color sense.) *Wiss. Z. Univ. Greifswald, Math. nat. Reihe,* 1955, 4, 89. (b)

Troshikhin, V. A. Some tasks in the research of higher nervous activity in ontogenesis. *Zh. vyssh. nerv. Deiat.,* 1952, 2, 561–571.

Tulloch, J. D., Brown, R. S., Jacobs, H. L., Prugh, D. G., & Greene, W. A. Normal heartbeat sound and the behavior of newborn infants—a replication. *Psychosom. Med.,* 1964, 26, 661–669.

Tur, A. F. *Fiziologiia i patologiia detei perioda novorozhdennosti. (Physiology and pathology of newborn infants.)* Leningrad: Medgiz, 1947.

Ukhtomskii, A. A. The principle of dominant center. In I. M. Sechenov, I. P. Pavlov, & N. E. Vvedenskii (Eds.), *Physiology of nervous system.* Vol. 1. (3rd ed.) Moscow: Medgiz, 1952. Pp. 262–266.

Ulett, G., Dow, R. S., & Larsell, O. The inception of conductivity in the corpus callosum and the cortico-ponto-cerebellar pathway of young rabbits, with reference to myelination. *J. comp. Neurol.,* 1944, 80, 1–10.

Usievich, M. A. *Fiziol. Zh. SSSR,* 1951, 37, 539.

Valentine, C. W. The colour perception and colour preferences of an infant during its fourth and eighth months. *Brit. J. Psychol.,* 1914, 6, 363.

Vernon, P. E. *The structure of human abilities.* New York: Wiley, 1950.

Verrier, M. L. *Les yeux et la vision. (The eyes and vision.)* Paris, 1938.

Volokhov, A. A. Typologic differences of nervous systems in infants. *Med. Rabot.,* 1953, 16, 2–3.

—— Typologic differences in higher nervous activity in infants. *Mater. 7th Congr. Soviet Pediat.,* 1959, 77–80.

von Kuenburg, G. Über die Abstraktionsfähigkeit und die Entstehung von Relationen beim vorschulpflichtigen Kinde. (On abstract thinking and formation of relations in the preschool child.) *Z. Angew. Psychol.,* 1920, 17, 270–312.

Wagner, I. F. The establishment of a criterion of depth of sleep in the newborn infant. *J. genet. Psychol.,* 1937, 51, 17–59.

Wakim, S. Child care in Mieh-Mieh. Unpublished Master's thesis, Amer. Univer. Beirut, 1956.

Wald, G. The chemical evolution of vision. *Harvey Lect. Ser.,* 1946, 41, 117–151.

Walker, H. M., & Lev, B. *Statistical Inference.* New York: Holt, 1953.

Wallace, W. M., Weil, W. B., & Taylor, A. The effect of variable protein and mineral intake upon the body composition of the growing animal. In G. E. W. Wolstenholme (Ed.), *Ciba Foundation colloquia on aging: Water and electrolyte metabolism in relation to age and sex.* Vol. 4. London: J. & A. Churchill, Ltd., 1958. P. 116.

Walls, G. L. The reptilian retina. I. A new concept of visual cell evolution. *Amer. J. Ophthalm.,* 1934, 17, 892.

——— *The vertebrate eye and its adaptive radiation.* Bloomfield Hills, Mich.: Cranbrook Inst. Sci., 1942.

Warner, F. A method and apparatus for obtaining graphic records of various kinds of movements of the hand and of its parts, and enumerating such movements and their combinations. *J. Physiol.,* 1883, 4, 160–164.

——— *The children: How to study them.* London: Hodgson, 1887.

Watson, John. *Psychology from the standpoint of the behaviorist.* Philadelphia: J. B. Lippincott, 1919.

Wechsler, D. *The measurement of adult intelligence.* Baltimore: Williams & Wilkins, 1944.

——— *Manual for the Wechsler Intelligence Scale for Children.* New York: Psychological Corp., 1949.

Wechsler, D., Mendelson, J., Leiderman, P. H., & Solomon, P. Sensory deprivation. *Arch. Neurol. Psychiat.,* 1958, 79, 225–233.

Weiss, L. A. Differential variations in the amount of activity of newborn infants under continuous light and sound stimulation. *Univer. Iowa Stud. Child Welf.,* 1934, 9, No. 4.

Wellman, Beth L. Some new bases for interpretation of the IQ. *J. genet. Psychol.,* 1932, 41, 116–126. (a)

——— The effect of preschool attendance upon the IQ. *J. exp. Educ.,* 1932, 1, 48–69. (b)

——— Growth in intelligence under differing school environments. *J. exp. Educ.,* 1934, 3, 59–83.

——— Mental growth from preschool to college. *J. exp. Educ.,* 1937, 6, 127–138.

Wenger, M. A. An investigation of conditioned responses in human infants. *Univer. Iowa Stud. Child Welf.,* 1936, 12, 9–90.

Wexler, D., Mendelson, J., Leiderman, P. H., & Solomon, P. Sensory deprivation. *Arch. Neurol. Psychiat.,* 1958, 79, 225–233.

Whiting, J. W. M. Sorcery, sin, and the superego: A cross-cultural study of some mechanisms of social control. In M. R. Jones (Ed.), *Nebraska symposium on motivation.* Lincoln: Univer. Nebraska Press, 1959. Pp. 174–195.

——— Resource mediation and learning by identification. In I. Iscoe & H. W. Stevenson (Eds.), *Personality development in children.* Austin: Univer. Texas Press, 1960. Pp. 112–126.

Willmer, E. N. Colour vision and its evolution in the vertebrates. In J. Huxley, A. C. Hardy, & E. B. Ford (Eds.), *Evolution as a process.* London: Allen & Unwin, 1954. Pp. 264–280.

——— Determining factors in the evolution of the retina in vertebrates. *Symposia Soc. f. Exper. Biol.,* 1953, 7, 377.

Winnicott, D. W. Transitional objects and transitional phenomena: A study of the first not-me possession. *Int. J. Psycho-Anal.,* 1953, 34, 89–97.

Wittenborn, J. R. A study of adoptive children: II. The predictive validity of the Yale Development Examination of Infant Behavior. *Psychol. Monogr.,* 1956, 70 (2, No. 409).

Wolf, Katherine M. Observations of individual tendencies in the first year of life. In M. J. E. Senn (Ed.), *Problem of infancy and childhood.* New York: Josiah Macy, Jr. Foundation, 1952. Pp. 97–137.

Wolf, S., & Wolff, H. G. *Human gastric function.* New York: Oxford Univer. Press, 1943.

Wolpert, E. Studies in the psychophysiology of dreams: II. An electromyographic study of dreaming. *Arch. Gen. Psychiat.*, 1960, 2, 231–241.

Woolley, H. T. Some experiments on the color perceptions of an infant and their interpretation. *Psychol. Rev.*, 1909, 16, 363.

Zavadskii, I. V. *Materialy k voprosu o tormozhenii i rastormazhivanii uslovnykh refleksov. (Evidence on the problems of inhibition and extinction of conditioned reflexes.)* Dissertation, Saint Petersburg, 1908.

Zetterström, B. The clinical electroretinogram. IV. The electroretinogram in children during the first year of life. *Act Ophthalm.*, 1951, 29, 295–304.

——— The electroretinogram in prematurely born children. *Act Ophthalm.*, 1952, 30, 405.

——— Flicker electroretinography in newborn infants. *Act Ophthalm.*, 1955, 33, 157–166.

Zevald, L. O. *Trudy fiziol. Labor. Akad. I. P. Pavlova,* 1938, 8.

Zipf, Sheila G. Resistance and conformity under reward and punishment. *J. abnorm. soc. Psychol.*, 1960, 61, 102–109.

acknowledgments

Preparation of this volume was supported in part by NIH Grant K3-MH-5925 and NSF Grant GB-4784.

Psychophysiological Dimensions of Early Development

LIPTON and STEINSCHNEIDER

The illustrations for this paper are from articles published previously by the authors (in collaboration with J. B. Richmond, M.D.), being reproduced here with proper permission. Figure 1 has appeared in the *Journal of the American Academy of Child Psychiatry* for January 1962. The others have appeared in *Psychosomatic Medicine*—Fig. 2 in the January-February, 1960 number; Figs. 3–6 in the November-December, 1961 number. The courtesy extended by the editors of those journals in this respect is much appreciated. The studies reported here were supported, in part, by grants from the Ford Foundation, the Commonwealth Fund, and USPHS research grants MHO 4065, and I-K3-HD-21, 852–01.

ELLINGSON

Supported initially by research funds of the Board of Control of the State of Nebraska, and later by a grant (B-1558) from the National Institute of Neurological Diseases and Blindness, NIH, Bethesda.

ROFFWARG,*et al.*

This investigation was supported by Research Grant MY-3267 to Drs. Fisher and Dement from the National Institute of Mental Health.

BRACKBILL, *et al.*

This investigation was supported in part by USPHS Training Grant No. 5 Tl HD-79-02 from the National Institute of Child Health and Human Development and in part by USPHS Grants MH 5994 and 1-K3-MH-5925 from the National Institute of Mental Health.

The authors are grateful for the cooperation of the staffs of Kapiolani Maternity and Gynecological Hospital, Kaiser Foundation Hospital, and the Kindergarten and Children's Aid Association, Honolulu, Hawaii. Our thanks also to Professor Sylvia Hedgewater and to Raymond Yang and Alan Grabowsky for acting as experimenters.

LUBCHENKO

This research was carried out at the Premature Infant Center, University of Colorado Medical Center. The Premature Infant Center is supported in part by a grant-in-aid from the Children's Bureau in cooperation with the

673

Colorado State Department of Public Health and the University of Colorado Medical Center.

ENGEL, *et al.*

This investigation was supported in part by research grant MH750 from the National Institute of Mental Health of the National Institutes of Health, Public Health Service, and by a grant from the Foundations Fund for Research in Psychiatry. One of us (F.R.) received a Fellowship from the Commonwealth Fund during part of the period of this study. This material was first presented at The Chicago Psychoanalytic Society, May 25, 1954, and subsequently at The Washington Psychoanalytic Society, November 13, 1954; The American Psychosomatic Society, May 5, 1955; The American Psychoanalytic Association, May 6, 1955; and the Combined Meeting of the American, Canadian and British Pediatric Societies and the Society for Pediatric Research, Quebec, June 15, 1955.

The authors are particularly indebted to Dr. William L. Bradford, Dr. Gilbert Forbes, the nursing staff, and the house staff of the Department of Pediatrics, who cared for this child during her long hospital stay and made her available for study. Miss Catherine Daly, Dr. Albert Sullivan, Dr. Frances Parsons, Dr. Charles Lobeck, Dr. Robert G. Wright, and Mr. Harry Chinchinian provided valuable behavioral observations during the baby's stay on the ward. The authors are especially grateful to Dr. Charles Sherman, of the Department of Surgery, who originally called this patient to their attention and through whose cooperation the prolonged observation was made possible. The surgical procedures were all carried out by Dr. Sherman and will be reported elsewhere.

We are grateful for advice on statistical methods to Dr. S. Lee Crump, Associate Professor of Radiation Biology and Chief of Section (Statistics), Atomic Energy Project, University of Rochester.

Motor Development and Physical Growth

BRAZELTON

The author wishes to express his appreciation to Dr. Marian C. Putnam and Dr. Ralph A. Ross for their helpful suggestions in preparing this paper.

GEBER and DEAN

We are grateful to Professor Coralie Rendle-Short, the head of the obstetrical and gynaecological departments at Mulago African Hospital and the European and Asian Hospitals, Kampala, for allowing us to visit the maternity wards and to examine the children there, and to the nurses, who accepted most willingly our disruption of their routine. We have also to thank Dr. Saint-Anne Dargassies for her assistance in the use of technique of examination, and Dr. André Thomas for his criticism of our findings. The expenses of the investigation were paid from grants made by the International Children's Centre, Paris, and the mental health section of the World Health Organization, and we thank especially Dr. Maurice Gaud, in charge of the African affairs of the Centre, and Dr. Ronald Hargreaves, formerly chief of the section.

HUNT, *et al.*

This study from the psychological laboratory of Connecticut College for Women was made possible through a National Research Council grant to one of the authors. Thanks is due Dr. Carney Landis for his interest and helpful suggestions, and to Miss Elizabeth Brownell for her assistance in all phases of the work. Particular gratitude is due Miss Elizabeth Munger, director of the Connecticut State Farm for Women at Niantic, and to Dr. Freitag and all the other members of the staff of the above institution for their cooperation during the work.

Sensory and Perceptual Development

GORMAN, et al.

This research was supported in part by a research grant from the National Society for the Prevention of Blindness.

FANTZ

This research was carried out at the Institute of Child Welfare, University of California, Berkeley, under a postdoctoral research fellowship from the National Institute of Mental Health, U.S. Public Health Service, sponsored by H. E. Jones.

ENGEN and LIPSITT

The writers are indebted to their assistants, Joyce Ching-Yi Wu and Herbert Kaye, who assisted in the collection of some data. This research was supported by Grant No. NB 04268 (National Institutes of Health) to Lewis P. Lipsitt for the study of sensory discrimination and learning in infants. We wish to thank the staff of the Providence Lying-In Hospital for their continued encouragement and cooperation.

HOLT, et al.

We should like to express our indebtedness to the nursing staff of the Bellevue Premature Unit and to the team of observers from the Division of Nursing, United States Public Health Service, who made this study possible. Statistical analysis of the data was done by the Statistics and Analysis Branch of the Division of Nursing of the United States Public Health Service.

LAWRENCE and FEIND

Supported in part by USPHS Grant 1127. This study was made during the second author's tenure on a National Research Council Fellowship in Pediatrics under a grant from the National Foundation for Infantile Paralysis. The authors wish to thank Dr. Edmund P. Fowler, Jr., for his guidance and sponsorship of this project.

Conditioning and Learning

KOLTSOVA

Doctoral thesis, Congress of Physiologists, biochemists, and pharmacologists, 1955.

WEISBERG

This paper is based upon a dissertation submitted to the Department of Psychology, University of Maryland, in partial fulfillment of the requirement for the degree of Doctor of Philosophy. The writer is grateful to Drs. William S. Verplanck and Harriet L. Rheingold for their valuable suggestions and help throughout all phases of the study. Appreciation is extended to Sisters Mary Patricia and Thecla and to the personnel of St. Ann's Infant Asylum, Washington, D. C., where the experiment was carried out.

HILGARD

The author is indebted to Dr. Rachel Stutsman of the staff of the Merrill-Palmer School for direction in the organization of this study and in the preparation of the report, which is based on an essay submitted to the faculty of the Graduate School of Yale University in partial fulfillment of the requirements for the degree of Master of Arts in psychology, 1930. Acknowledgment is also due Professor Edward S. Robinson of Yale University for numerous suggestions.

From Vocalization to Functional Language

IRWIN

This research was carried out while the author was Professor of Psychology, Iowa Child Welfare Research Station, University of Iowa.

MOORE

I am indebted to Alan Ross Anderson and Edith S. Lisansky (also see below) for helpful criticisms of earlier drafts of this paper.

The work reported here has received the generous support of the following organizations: The Carnegie Corporation of New York; The Cooperative Research Program of the Office of Education; The McGraw Foundation; The Murray Foundation; The Office of Naval Research, Group Psychology Branch, Contract No. SAR/Nonr-609 (16); The Responsive Environments Foundation; The Higgins Fund of Yale University.

The Thomas A. Edison Research Laboratory of West Orange, New Jersey, a division of the McGraw-Edison Company, bore the entire cost of developing the automated equipment described here. I wish to thank particularly Richard Kobler, an electronic engineer at the Edison Laboratory, for his valuable contributions.

Special thanks are due to Dr. Burton Blatt, Head, Department of Special Education, Boston University; Dr. John Martin, Superintendent of Schools, Freeport, Long Island; and Edward I. McDowell, Jr., Headmaster, Hamden Hall Country Day School, for their initiative and administrative skill in establishing responsive environments laboratories.

Recognition should be given to the many essential contributions of the Project's supervisory staff at the various laboratories: Caroline Colby, Mary Coogan, Ann Ferguson, Dorothy Johnson, Ruth Moore and Ruth Wong. Also to Blanche Pierpont Blanchard, supervisor of the laboratory-connected classrooms at Hamden Hall Country Day School.

Last, but just as important, I wish to thank the following persons for their professional services: Dr. Edith Lisansky, who is in charge of the Project's work in clinical psychology; Dr. Robert F. Newton, for general physical examinations; Dr. Robert F. Nagel, Clinical Instructor of Otolaryngology, Yale University for speech and hearing evaluations; Dr. Meyer Samson for eye examinations.

MENYUK

The investigation reported here was done in partial fulfillment of the requirements for the Ed.D. degree, Boston University, and was supported by a fellowship MF-8768 from the National Institute of Mental Health, Public Health Service.

The author is indebted to Professor W. Pronovost of Boston University and Professor M. Halle of Massachusetts Institute of Technology for their critical assistance.

Grateful acknowledgment is given to the children and teachers of the Young Israel and Beacon Nursery Schools and the first grade of the Edith C. Baker School in Brookline, Massachusetts.

WILLIAMS and MATTSON

The study was made in partial fulfillment for the requirements of a Master's degree at Purdue University, Lafayette, Indiana. The work was directed by Dr. Mattson.

Intellectual Growth

DENNIS and NAJARIAN

This research was conducted at the American University of Beirut. The cost of the investigation was defrayed by a grant from the Rockefeller Brothers' Fund to the American University of Beirut. The writers wish to express their deep appreciation for the complete cooperation and assistance given by the staff of the Creche and by the Outpatient Department of the A. U. B. Hospital. Miss Leila Biksmati served as research assistant.

FREEDMAN and KELLER

Supported by the Department of Mental Hygiene, State of California (Project R60-1-17.4); serological work was performed at Irwin Memorial Blood Bank, San Francisco.

HONZIK

Acknowledgment is due Harold E. Jones and John P. McKee for their helpful suggestions and to the U.S. Public Health Service for clerical and statistical assistance.

ANDERSON

Assistance in the preparation of these materials was furnished by the personnel of Works Progress Administration Official Project No. 665-71-3-69.

MEYERS and DINGMAN

Supported in part by the National Institute of Mental Health Grant 3M-9130.

Socialization and the Development of Social Behavior

RHEINGOLD and BAYLEY

We are grateful to Father Bernard Brogan, Director of the Catholic Home Bureau of Chicago, for his generous cooperation.

BANDURA, *et al.*

This investigation was supported by Research Grant M-5162 from the National Institutes of Health, U.S. Public Health Service.

The authors are indebted to Beverly Busching, Malka Yaari, Nancy Wiggins, and John Steinbruner, who assisted in collecting the data.

This research was carried out while the junior author was the recipient of an American Association of University Women International Fellowship for postdoctoral research.

The assistance of Eleanor Willemsen with the statistical computations is gratefully acknowledged.

THOMPSON

The writer is indebted to Dr. Beth L. Wellman for her helpful supervision and criticism of this research. The writer would also like to express his appreciation of the help given by Mrs. Eleanor Lack White, Dr. Boyd R. McCandless, and Dr. Ruth Updegraff in the planning and the carrying-out of the research project.

STEVENSON and STEVENSON

The conduct of this study was supported by a grant from the Hogg Foundation for Mental Hygiene of the University of Texas, and the analysis of the data was supported in part by a grant from the U.S. Public Health Service (Grant M-1465). We are appreciative of the interest in this undertaking of Drs. Wayne Holtzman and Robert L. Sutherland of the Hogg Foundation. Our discussions with Dr. Lois Meek Stolz, Professor of Psychology at Stanford University, were of great help in planning the study. The study could not have been done without the close and thoughtful cooperation of the parents and members of the board of directors of the All-Austin Nursery School of Austin, Texas. We are especially appreciative of their consideration in meeting our needs in forming the group of children which we observed and in participating in parent interviews. We are grateful to Miss Leila Snyder, the nursery school teacher, for her assistance in preparing daily reports, conducting the parents interviews, and testing the children. We wish to thank Mr. John Kregarman, Mr. Gary Martin, and Miss Mary Bess Whidden for their careful tabulation of the results, and Mrs. Ben Smith for typing the observations.

Emotional Responses and the Developing Personality

BRACKBILL

This report is based upon a dissertation submitted to the Department of Psychology, Stanford University, in partial fulfillment of the requirements for the degree of Doctor of Philosophy. The writer wishes to thank Professors Albert Bandura, Quinn McNemar, Frances Orr Nitzberg, Robert Sears, William Verplanck, and C. L. Winder for their suggestions and help. The author is greatly indebted to Drs. John Anderson and Bruce Jessup for their cooperation in referring subjects.

Indexes

name index

Page references to entire chapters by authors are in *italics*.

681

subject index